Balance of Payments, Exchange Rates, and Competitiveness in Transition Economies

Balance of Payments, Exchange Rates, and Competitiveness in Transition Economies

edited by
Mario I. Blejer
Marko Škreb

Springer Science+Business Media, LLC

Library of Congress Cataloging-in-Publication Data
Balance of payments, exchange rates, and competitiveness in transition economies / Mario I. Blejer and Marko Skreb (Eds.).
p. cm.
Includes bibliographical references (p.) and index.
ISBN 978-1-4757-7199-2 ISBN 978-0-585-31346-7 (eBook)
DOI 10.1007/978-0-585-31346-7
1. Monetary policy—Europe, Eastern. 2. Economic stabilization—Europe, Eastern. 3. Balance of payments—Europe, Eastern.
4. Foreign exchange rates—Government policy—Europe, Eastern.
5. Competition, International. I. Blejer, Mario I. II. Skreb, Marko, 1957–
HG930.7 .B35 1999
332.4'94—dc21 99-26147
CIP

Originally published by Kluwer Academic Publishers in 1999
Softcover reprint of the hardcover 1st edition 1999

Printed on acid-free paper.

Contents

Balance of Payments, Exchange Rates, and Competitiveness in Transition Economies

1 TRANSITION AND THE OPEN ECONOMY: AN OVERVIEW

Mario I. Blejer and Marko Škreb

Markets are like parachutes: they function only when open.[1]

1.1. Introduction

The papers collected in this book[2] focus on the external-sector developments and on the process of external liberalization in transition economies, concentrating on issues related to balance-of-payments conditions, exchange-rate policies and regimes, international competitiveness, international financial flows, foreign trade, and other aspects related to the integration of the postsocialist countries into the world economy.

While external-sector issues are indeed relevant for all countries and have become more so in light of the recent currency and financial crises in Asia and Russia, they are particularly critical for the transition economies. As shown through the chapters of this book, most of the postsocialist countries are relatively small economies that have misdeveloped, in large part due to the distortions arising from widespread interventions and controls on their foreign sector. Therefore, reforming and turning to the market go hand in hand with opening up and liberalizing the external sector, while striving to maintain external equilibrium and competitiveness during the most crucial phases of the transition. The transition economies face, therefore, a myriad of questions in regard to their external-sector conditions and policies. To analyze systematically these questions, two types of central issues need elaboration. In the first place, it is important to identify the main external-sector questions that demand most attention in transition economies, as they impinge most critically on the reform process. Second, in light of the recent upheaval in the global capital markets, it is necessary to inquire about the nature of the rapid changes in the world of international finance, the world into which transition economies are becoming more and more integrated. After delving briefly into these issues we provide an overview of the papers included in this collection.

1.2. The External Sector in Transition Economies: What are the Issues?

Since the beginning of the transition process, the countries of central and eastern Europe and those of the former Soviet Union have experienced enormous changes in their external economic relations and in reorienting their trade and reintegrating their economies into the world system (see, for example, IMF, 1997). In this context and to understand the transition economies' present position and the profound need for dynamic changes, it is useful to look at the history of these countries' external relations. Prior to 1990, most of these economies belonged to the so-called Council of Mutual Economic Assistance (CMEA), a trade organization centered in Moscow and formed by most of the Soviet bloc countries. The organization promoted trade within its members and discouraged trade with the rest of the world, with the intention of creating a self-sufficient trading bloc. The trade among the members (referred as *regional trade*) was not conducted at world market prices or following world trade practices but rather was based on arbitrary prices, arbitrary conditions, and a centrally planned division of labor. Therefore, serious misallocation of resources followed. A classical example of this type of misallocation was the wide availability of subsidized oil imports from the Soviet Union that resulted in the overuse of energy across the region. Since the very idea of the CMEA was to promote some rather arbitrarily conceived and preplanned "international division of labor" and not to generate genuine trade-induced welfare gains, former communist countries had to trade with each other not because of their economic interest but primarily for political reasons. Payments and settlements among them did not follow world practices but, due to the weaknesses of their currencies and the permanent shortage of hard currencies across the region, were based on a special variety of barter that relied on a specially developed net clearing system.

Given these conditions, it was therefore inevitable that as soon as external political pressure dissipated with the collapse of communism, such a trading system would collapse as well. But its legacy was to be painfully felt in the transition economies that were left without an adequate trade-financing system and with sharply distorted trade patterns. In practice, trade among the transition economies almost disappeared in the early 1990s, and, in addition to price liberalization, macroeconomic stabilization, privatization, and the other structural tasks of transition, former communist economies had to face an additional challenge: the need to open up their external sectors and to integrate into the world economy. While some of the countries could compete, at least in some sectors, quite efficiently in world markets, transition economies were definitely not prepared to be involved, immediately, in international payment practices.

This process of reorientation was therefore a difficult one. Transition economies could not afford the luxury of liberalizing their trade gradually, as was the case for many of the GATT member states since the end of World War II. Transition economies had to adapt fast to the new circumstances and, even more difficult, to the ever-changing world trade patterns. Indeed, from the establishment of GATT in 1948 to the creation of the World Trade Organization in 1995 vast changes did take place in the volume, pattern, and modalities of world trade. And the transition economies, once liberated from the political limitations of the CMEA (and of communism), had no alternative but to adapt fast and to develop from scratch the necessary instruments for dealing with these new conditions.

In addition to the expansion and liberalization of world trade, the last twenty years have witnessed significant growth in the importance of international capital mobility. Today the estimates are that daily cross-border flows amount to more than U.S. $1.5 trillion. Moreover, international sources of finance have doubled in the last five years (BIS, 1997). This expansion in the volume of capital flows has been accompanied by a widespread liberalization of international capital movements and by the enhanced ability of many more countries to access foreign capital markets. The internationalization of financial markets have been, therefore, a further factor that conditioned the design of the reform strategies of the transition countries and compelled them to increasingly confront external-sector issues and to devise appropriate policies to deal with this new international environment.

Within this new and evolving world scenario, one can ask, What are the main characteristics of the external sector of the transition economies, what are the major challenges faced by their policymakers, and what is different in transition? Probably the principal topics around which many of these issues revolve include the current-account position, capital flows, the choice of exchange-rate regime, balance-of-payments convertibility, and trade and commercial policies.

One of the main characteristics of the external position of almost all transition economies is their growing current-account deficits. This, of course, immediately raises questions regarding the sustainability of their balance of payments and their external stability. According to the recent EBRD's Transition Report (EBRD, 1997), almost half of the twenty-six countries covered in their study had, in 1996, a current-account deficit in excess of 7 percent of GDP. Moreover, this deficit has been growing steadily since the early 1990s. Obviously, in these circumstances, the question is, How large can a current-account deficit be, and how long can it be sustained without triggering a crisis? Are the transition economies heading toward a major balance-of-payments emergency? There are no simple answers to these questions, and in fact recent developments in Asia may have changed the perception regarding the sustainability of current-account deficits. It is quite clear, however, that answers are very country specific and the ability to manage external imbalances depends largely on a number of factors such as the initial conditions, the level of the outstanding external debt (and in particular the debt-servicing ratio), the level of international reserves, the degree and the terms of access to world financial markets, and the modes of external deficit financing (short- versus long-term debt financing, foreign direct investments, and so on). While these conditions differ across countries, and while growing current-account deficits were expected in the transition economies due to the collapse of interregional trade in the early 1990s, it is not reasonable to expect that these trends can be continued in the long-run. Therefore, it is of interest to determine the roots of these continuously rising deficits. As a whole, current-account deficits mainly follow the patterns of the trade deficits, which, in turn, seem to be driven by a booming domestic demand. But a booming domestic demand is not the only reason for the rising current-account deficits. Strong capital inflows provide an additional element of the explanation.

As mentioned above, increasing capital flows are one of the main characteristics of the recent developments in world financial markets. But, for transition economies, these inflows were especially strong. In 1997 total net foreign capital flows to the countries of the region are estimated to have reached nearly U.S. $60 billion (EBRD, 1997). These volumes of capital inflows present a serious challenge to economic policymakers. Clearly, not all capital inflows could be regarded as similar. At the fundamental level, one should distinguish among short-term capital flows, long-term loans, and foreign direct investment. The main distinction should be their sustainability over time. Conventional wisdom is that short-term flows tend to be speculative in nature and should, if at all possible, be avoided, while foreign direct investment (FDI) should be promoted. Foreign borrowing falls in-between since it could be a sustainable way of financing the current-account deficit in normal conditions but in case of a crisis may be more volatile than FDI.

There seems to be a widespread consensus that FDI can potentially play a key role in the overall transformation process. FDI brings with it not only capital but also sophisticated management, advanced technology, and very often access to export markets. But can too much of a good thing be harmful? FDI may give rise to some negative side effects, particularly in transition economies. For example, FDI has sometime prevented the development of mechanisms that encourage and mobilize domestic savings and in some occasions have hindered the expansion of competitive practices. Moreover, regardless of their nature, strong capital inflows complicate monetary and exchange-rate policies and may lead to inflation and overvaluation. Therefore, it is legitimate, when analyzing external-sector issues, to focus not only on the benefits but also on the costs of FDI. Whatever these costs, however, the strong performance of FDI in the transition economies can be seen as an evidence of their increasing creditworthiness. An additional proof of this rise in confidence is the changing structure of capital inflows, which has steadily evolved from official to private sources (see IMF, 1997).

As they converge into this new and changing international environment, policymakers in the transition economies face one of the longest-running controversies in economics: the choice of the exchange-rate regime. The question of fixed versus flexible exchange rates (and all the varieties in between these two extremes) cannot be avoided. On the one had, it seems that the arguments for adopting a fixed rate are very strong, especially during the stabilization phases (see Blejer and Skreb, 1997). Five of the twenty-six transition economies that are members of the EBRD have formally pegged exchange rates, while none has a freely floating exchange-rate regime. Countries that, for a variety reasons, have not achieved macroeconomic stability in the early phases of transition are later adopting pegged rate regimes in order to stabilize their economies (most recently Bulgaria and Bosnia and Herzegovina). But as has been observed time and again, pegged exchange rates, in the context of slower-than-expected structural reforms and strong capital inflows, result in significant overvaluation of the currency and can be a recipe for a serious balance of payments crisis. The mid-1997 events in the Czech Republic are a good example of this type of danger, and the Asian crisis will certainly force many countries to reconsider their policies of maintaining a fixed rate that leads to the overvaluation of their currencies. It seems that the Asian events speak for a more flexible exchange-rate regime, although it may still be early to reach extensive conclusions from this episode. As a whole, however, it is certainly clear that the choice of a sustainable, credible exchange-rate regime is far from trivial in transition economies. They need to combine the benefits of "imported credibility," arising from fixing the exchange rate, with the adjustment mechanism that is provided by a flexible exchange-rate regime (to allow, among others, for differential productivity growth and for external shocks). But it might be appropriate to point out that no exchange-rate policy can be a substitute for sound macroeconomic policies. Indeed, what really counts for establishing a credible exchange-rate regime is the state of the fundamentals of each economy. However, the recent crisis in Southeast Asia is indicating that even an apparently healthy macroeconomic position may not be a sufficient condition to ensure stability in a world of globalized financial markets. Domestic financial and banking soundness are also indispensable ingredients for sustained growth. Clearly, the Asian crisis has stressed that it could be pointless to analyze external-sector developments without reference to the fitness of the financial and particularly the banking sectors.[3]

These questions are naturally intertwined with the policy issue of balance-of-payments convertibility. Today, practically all advanced transition countries have established full current-account convertibility, but certainly there are serious questions regarding capital-account convertibility. In transition economies the question in this respect does not refer, as in the past, to the need for capital controls to avoid capital flight. It is rather related to the issue of massive capital inflows and the exposure to a sudden reversal. Among transition economies there is a clear trend toward the liberalization of the capital account. Slovakia liberalized its account significantly, and so has the Czech Republic. Hungary and Poland are making substantial progress, especially after joining the OECD, and the Baltic countries (Estonia, Lithuania, and Latvia) have full and effective capital-account convertibility. However, the dilemma of the optimal degree and the speed of liberalization of the capital account is certain to remain present for some time in the agenda of the policymakers of transition economies.

The final issue that we want to address refers to the trade policies necessary for promoting the integration of transition countries into the world economy. Membership and complicance with the regulation of WTO is something that most transition economies, if they have not already achieved, want to accomplish as soon as possible. By the end of 1997 seven transition countries were members of the WTO, while another sixteen were granted the status of observers. WTO membership remains, indeed, a central goal of every transition economy. However, in addition, questions of regional integration have arisen. In particular, the question is whether the formation of regional free-trade areas such as CEFTA (Central European Free Trade Area), BFTA (Baltic Free Trade Area), or the CIS (Council of Independent States) is only an interim step toward the ultimate goal of full integration into the European Union (EU) or a more lasting solution. In the last six years the EU has signed ten agreements with transition economies. By the end of 1997, five countries (Hungary, the Czech Republic, Estonia, Poland, and Slovenia) were selected by the EU as immediate candidates for joining the Union, and five more are being mentioned as candidates for the second wave (Bulgaria, Latvia, Lithuania, Romania, and Slovakia). Uncertainties remain, however, regarding the actual accession to the EU of these and of the other transition economies. One source of uncertainty relates to the prospects of the Economic and Monetary Union and of the common European currency—the euro. It is still early to predict with a degree of certainty what could be the effects for transition economies of the introduction of the single currency in most of the EU.

An additional important issue that arises in connection with the analysis of the external position of transition economies is the question of the quality of statistical data, more specifically of balance-of-payments data, and their comparability with international standards. Unfortunately, reliable balance-of-payments statistics are not always available in transition economies. Numerous examples abound regarding the issues of statistical data quality. An interesting case has been Croatia's balance-of-payments statistics. Before extensive revisions were carried out, net errors and omissions were, in 1995, equal to U.S. $1.3 billion—or about 7 percent of GDP. After the statistical revisions, the amount of net errors and omissions fell to U.S. $500 (or 2.5 percent of GDP). The current-account deficit has been decreased by the statistical revision from U.S. $1.7 billion to U.S. $1.3 billion, equivalent to a decrease of about two percentage points of GDP. Obviously, these statistical issues have direct consequences for the cost of borrowing abroad, and, therefore, it seems important to point out, though it might look like a technical question, that without reliable statistics, balance-of-payments discussions might be highly misguided and policy decisions may be inadequate.

1.3. The Changing International Financial Environment

As their degree of integration increases, transition economies need to become extremely attentive to world developments and learn to adjust rapidly to changing circumstances. Given the importance of world financial markets for transition economies, we review here, in brief, the main characteristics of world markets that have a special bearing on the performance of the external sector of these economies:

- *The liberalization and deregulation of financial flows* All over the world there is a strong trend toward more reliance on market forces and less government intervention in financial markets. It might be appropriate to distinguish between two aspects of these process of liberalization. The first is the continuous lifting of constraints on the scope and depth of activities of financial institutions. This has increased the efficiency of financial intermediation and has created a variety of new financial products and new financial institutions. In addition, the deregulation process has blurred the differences between various financial intermediaries (banks, insurance companies, and so on), creating financial supermarkets. The second aspect of the worldwide liberalization process is the lifting of restrictions on cross-border capital movements and the improved access of emerging countries to foreign capital markets. The rapid growth of cross-border operations have added to the size of financial institutions and to their complexity. Financial institutions with assets of more than U.S. $500 billion are not rare. The late 1990s will probably be remembered as the era of intense mergers and acquisitions among financial institutions. Transition economies have to identify carefully those trends, adapt their regulations, and be prepared for such an environment.
- *The deepening of financial markets* There has been a very strong increase in the volume of financial transactions, both measured by their number and average value. For example, the volume of transactions that pass through the payment systems has been increasing much faster than the GDP. The total volume of transactions in the payments system in Italy, for example, is about thirty times larger than the volume of its GDP, and in Japan this multiple is about 100. Needless to say, such an increase in payment-system flows has increased payment system risks as well.
- *Financial engineering* Innovations in financial transactions have taken two basic forms. First, the appearance of new instruments and

> of new products (such as derivatives, e-money, and cybercash) makes it is possible to measure, standardize, price, and trade risks as never before. Second, the technology at the service of the financial sector enables completely different and much more efficient ways to conduct financial transactions (computers, telecommunications, RTGS systems, and so on). They permit a tremendous increase in the velocity of information transfer and have tremendously decreased the cost of information, making it available to a much larger audience. These two features pose new challenges both for regulators and supervisors of domestic markets and for all those that are involved in these transactions. They also make it more difficult and costly to insulate domestic markets and therefore tend to increase the speed of integration.

Clearly, the globalization of world financial trends is a fact of life for almost all countries in the world. International transactions are increasing ten to twenty times faster than domestic ones. For transition economies, globalization and integration in the world carry many positive implications. But there are some dangers in globalization as well. As globalization spreads, policymakers face a larger number of exogenous variables, and their degrees of freedom shrink. With increasing dependency on world markets, policymakers must be aware that each mistake (including a clumsy public statement) can be very costly. The recent crises in Asian are a reminder of the problems of fast contagion, and transition economies, when integrating into the world economy, should be fully aware of these globalization risks.

1.4. The Content of the Book

Many of the subjects discussed above are covered in a systematic manner in the various chapters of this book. The volume contains fifteen contributions, divided into three sections. Part I includes seven chapters dealing with current-account developments, capital flows, and exchange-rate policies in transition economies; Part II deals with specific international trade issues affecting these countries; and Part III consists of six selected country experiences.

Chapter 2, Current Account Sustainability in Transition Economies by Nouriel Roubini and Paul Wachtel, is an analytical overview of recent trends and developments in the current-account performance of transition economies. The central question is whether the prevailing trends would ultimately lead to currency crises. The authors' conclusion is that there are causes for concern regarding the external imbalances of transition economies because of the size and the rapid growth of the deficits in relation to GDP and because these deficits are a result of low national savings and increasing consumption. Moreover, the real appreciation of the currency indicates a loss of competitiveness, and problems in the domestic banking systems make it more difficult to deal with large capital flows. After examining ten transition countries, Roubini and Wachtel assert that it is important to distinguish between structural adjustments, on the one hand, and exchange-rate misalignment, on the other, as the cause of the current-account deficit. In the former case there should be less concern, but misalignments make it much more difficult to deal with the imbalances.

In Chapter 3, Robert A. Mundell opens the discussion on exchange-rate issues in transition economies. The chapter focus on the alternative exchange-rate arrangements available to transition economies and aims at evaluating the use of exchange-rate policies as a mechanism for stabilization and as a system of monetary control. The chapter deals concisely with the history of exchange-rate controversies, from David Hume until the present, developing a taxonomy of sixteen approaches to the balance of payments in the context of competing targets for monetary stabilization. Mundell then discusses three stages of stabilization (stage one is high inflation, stage two assumes control over budget deficits and inflation, and stage three is the fine-tuning of expectations and the management of stability). Within this framework, Mundell presents a summary analysis of twenty-four transition economies over a five-year period and discusses the advantages and disadvantages of fixing the exchange rate. Three distinctive groups of countries emerge from the analysis. The first one needs to reduce the rate of monetary expansion before fixing, the second should implement some type of inflation targeting rather than monetary targeting, while the third group, the most advanced transition countries, should proceed now to fix their currencies in light of the implementation of the third stage of European Monetary Union and of the recent introduction of the euro.

Ronald I. McKinnon's Chapter 4 deals in more detail with the issue of European Monetary Union (EMU) and its implications for transition economies. The main concern of the study is the analysis of the optimal exchange-rate rules for the European countries that remain outside of the EMU, a question of particular relevance for the transition economies in the present conjuncture. McKinnon proposes exchange-rate rules that are consistent with "virtual" exchange-rate stability in Europe. In his opinion, virtual stability in exchange rates would have positive effects by leading to rapid noninflationary export growth in economies in transition.

While Mundell and McKinnon deal with the exchange-rate issue from an applied-policy perspective, Clemens Grafe and Charles Wyplosz present in Chapter 5 an elaborated formal model for the determination of the real exchange rate during the transition process. According to Grafe and Wyplosz, two features characterize transition economies: the first is the absence of correlation between nominal and real exchange rates, and the second is a trend toward real appreciation. They explain the second trend partly by the Balassa-Samuelson effect regarding differential productivity growth in the traded and nontraded sectors and utilize their model to elucidate the first issue. The model stresses the link between productivity, capital accumulation, real wages, and relative prices. These elements are examined in the context of a shift from an old, state-owned sector toward a growing modern sector. The model yields knife-edge properties for the real exchange rate, which are enhanced by friction in the labor market and subsidies to the state sector. These properties can explain the lack of correlation between nominal and exchange rates.

Chapter 6, by John Odling-Smee and Basil Zavoico, shifts the focus toward the issue of balance-of-payment financing in the Baltic and in other former Soviet Union republics (BFSU). The authors' starting observation is that the external debt of most of the BFSU countries has been growing rapidly. Although the debt has not reached exceedingly high levels by international standards, this fact has to be considered in the context of initial conditions where, with the notable exception of Russia, the starting level of the debt was zero. After examining the main developments in the external accounts of the BFSU countries, the chapter analyzes the pros and cons of external borrowing. As transition is indeed a very costly and difficult exercise, it makes sense to borrow abroad to help finance it. This is particularly true in light of the willingness of international capital markets to lend to these countries under constantly improving terms. On the other hand, it is imperative to be cautious about borrowing to finance wasteful expenditures. The authors distinguish among foreign direct investment (which does not raise so much concern) and debt-creating capital inflows. They analyze the sustainability of increasing external debt and stress the need for speeding up structural reforms.

In the last chapter of this section, André Icard discusses the links between capital flows and the stability of financial systems in emerging countries. He argues that the trend toward increasing openness of international capital markets is one of the most momentous reforms in the developing world in the last two decades. It obviously has many positive consequences for emerging countries but involves risks as well. Icard stresses the strong connections between financial-sector and macroeconomic stability, a connection that is enhanced by the opening up of financial markets. He points out that the soundness of the financial system is without any doubt one of the most important factors to preserve stability in a globalized world and a factor that should receive particular attention in transition economies.

Part II of the book contains three papers dealing with the development of international trade and with the implementation of commercial policies in transition countries. Chapter 8, by Oleh Havrylyshyn and Hassan Al-Atrash, focuses on the increase in trade openness and on the growing geographic diversification of exports since 1990. After examining data on trade flows, the authors conclude that trade patterns have changed significantly and today many transition economies have trade to GDP ratios similar to those of market economies of comparable size and level of development. In addition, transition economies have diversified significantly their trade configuration, away from the former CMEA and toward Western Europe and the rest of the world. The more advanced a country is in the transition process, the more geographically diversified is its foreign trade. Finally, estimations based on the so-called gravity trade models indicate that many countries are still far from a trade pattern that could be expected from a fully functioning market economy. The authors also draw some policy implications, the most important being the observation that trade liberalization seems to play a specially important role in transition economies because it contribute substantially to the success in restructuring the economy and to the improvement in the allocation of resources.

Chapter 9, by Vito Tanzi, Adrienne Cheasty, and Kristina Kostial, deals with the fiscal implications of lowering trade taxes. The authors argue that although trade liberalization is essential for successful development, the optimal speed of liberalization is something to be discussed. Their concern is that rapid liberalization may have negative macroeconomic consequences because of the ensuing loss in tax revenues. Therefore, they argue for a fiscal cushion, in the form of a more modest, gradual trade liberalization. Clearly, if a country has reached a stage in which it can rely on domestic revenue sources, such as sales or income taxes, to cover its fiscal needs, it should not unduly delay trade liberalization. But in their view, if liberalization may result in an unnecessary deterioration of fiscal positions, as it is likely to be the case in many transition economies, import duties and other trade taxes should not be hastily discarded.

The issue of optimal trade policies in transition countries is discussed, within a political-economy framework, by Arye L. Hillman and Heinrich

Ursprung. In Chapter 10, "What Is Special About Endogenous International Trade Policy in Transition Economies?" they build a game-theoretic model to study the interlinkages between trade policy, privatization, and foreign investment. Their model suggests that one of the main advantages of economic integration as a trade strategy is the gain in government credibility regarding its intentions to liberalize trade. Privatization and foreign investments are a function of such credibility, and, therefore, the signaling effects arising from a commitment to free trade play an important role in facilitating privatization and in attracting foreign investments, accelerating, in this manner, the successful completion of the transition process.

Part III of the book consists of five country studies. Chapter 11, the first of these studies, by Boris Vujčić and Tomislav Presečan, looks at the Croatian experience. After briefly examining Croatia's legacy from the past and outlining its 1993 stabilization program, the authors concentrate on the external accounts. Their main concern is the widening current-account deficit. To examine the evolution of competitiveness they look at unit labor costs, costs of capital, diversification of trade, and a number of other indicators. They conclude that, in the short run, macroeconomic tightening (fiscal, incomes, and credit tightening policies) might be appropriate for reversing the trend of growing current-account deficits but that Croatia needs more than macroeconomic policies to increase its competitive position. To strengthen Croatia's external position, structural reforms must be speeded up, foreign direct investment should be promoted, and the country should strive to join the various schemes of European integration.

In the second country study, Chapter 12, Fabrizio Coricelli examines the Czech external position and focuses on the country's exchange-rate policy. Coricelli attempts to find out the causes of the May 1997 currency crisis in the Czech Republic, a country that, until that episode, was widely considered to be the most advanced transition economy. It seems that the crisis was not caused by macroeconomic imbalances (such as weak fiscal stance) but rather by slow structural reforms that were reflected in a weak banking system and in an inadequate control over firms, arising from a "fuzzy structure of property rights." In his concluding observations Coricelli argues for a more flexible exchange-rate policy and suggests that the Czech authorities should base their macroeconomic policies on the implementation of inflation targets (and not on the fixing of the exchange rate) and should somewhat slow the liberalization of capital movements. According to Coricelli's views this combination of policies would allow a deeper and faster restructuring of the Czech economy.

Gur Ofer and Vladimir Drebentsov analyze in Chapter 13 the experience of the Russian Federation regarding trade and exchange-rate policies, an experience that has become of particular concern and relevance following the August 1998 financial crisis in Russia. They examine the opening up of the Russian economy and its interaction with the transition process itself. The authors first discuss, on a theoretical level, the tensions that arise between the potential benefits from rapid liberalization and the need to make proper preparations for the restructuring of the economy. In the case of Russia, however, specific tensions arise between the country's ability to immediately export vast amounts of natural resources and the problems such a policy may create for the inefficient manufacturing sector. Russia's natural-resources richness, which allows it to cover all its import needs, is obviously a blessing but, as the authors conclude, may hamper its capability to restructure its inefficient manufacturing sector. Using updated information, they also consider the implications of the current slump in commodity prices.

In an exercise on comparative economics, Chapter 14, by Jacob A. Frenkel, analyzes the experience of Israel and derives some lessons and conclusions about the possibility of introducing external-sector reforms in the midst of a major stabilization effort. His major conclusion is that it is important not to delay the process of liberalization and reform and not to be distracted by other objectives, as important as they may actually be. It is important for policymakers to create opportunities rather than just seize them and establish irreversible changes in the right direction. Frenkel also draws some conclusions about the right response of an economy in transition to global financial turmoil of the sort that is being now experienced. In his view, the Israeli experience indicates that it is extremely important to reduce vulnerabilities by improving fundamentals—mainly through adamant and consistent implementation of a long-run market-oriented strategy of economic reforms. This will result in gains in the international competition for extra international savings for domestic investment.

The case of Hungary is analyzed in Chapter 15 by Laszló Halpern and Judit Neményi. The thrust of their chapter is their quest for a new exchange-rate regime in Hungary, leaning toward more flexibility in comparison with the current system. Until recently, the authors argue, the exchange rate has been used to boost credibility, but it is now, before a crisis erupts, that it is necessary to determine a new exchange-rate regime. They close with the somewhat surprising conclusion that in Hungary, "the equilibrium real appreciation can be achieved easier by higher inflation than by nominal appreciation."

Finally, Chapter 16, by Velimir Bole, deals with Slovenia, a small, highly developed transition economy with an unusual feature—a current-account surplus. But the title of the chapter is indeed revealing: "Current-Account Surplus and Falling Competitiveness in Slovenia." The author stresses that

Slovenia, with its current-account surplus, does not seems to fit the stylized facts that are prevalent among other chapters of this book—namely, that external deficits are a characteristic of transition (and especially of the later phases of transition). The chapter intends to answer two main questions: first, how sustainable is the present current-account performance of Slovenia, and, second, what is the state of Slovenian external competitiveness? From the analysis, an interesting feature arises: in fact, there has been an increase in the global trade deficit, but it has been more than offset by surpluses in shuttle and border trade. As a whole, several indicators show a loss of competitiveness in the Slovenian economy. The author identifies rising wages (and increasing unit labor costs) as the main causes for the loss of competitiveness, and he expresses his worries regarding the sustainability of the Slovenian balance-of-payments position.

It is worth pointing out again that the process of integration of the transition economies into the world trade and the world capital markets is a long-term, multifaceted exercise. Winston Churchill once said: "There are two kinds of success: initial and ultimate." It seems clear that transition economies have achieved initial success in the liberalization of their external economic relations. There is also little doubt that ultimate success, in the form of full integration into the world economy, would be achieved and will be reflected in a marked increased in the living standards of the population. However, to move from initial to ultimate success one has to cross the short run, where the policies of opening up could have some serious costs. The recent financial crises have shown that globalization and integration do not have only positive effects on the economy and that a crucial element to cope with these negative consequences is to ensure the soundness of the financial systems. But building up a sound financial system is not easy and cannot be done rapidly, and the type of hardships that could be a necessary component of the process may become fertile ground for populism, protectionism, and isolationism. Therefore, the adoption and implementation of transition strategies based on liberalization and opening up cannot be taken for granted but rather as the most promising alternative in the permanent struggle for a successful transformation.

Notes

1. Hillmar Koppel, former CEO of Deutsche Bank.
2. The volume collects a selection of the papers presented in the Third Dubrovnik Conference on Transition Economies.
3. The soundness of the financial sectors of transition economies is studied in Blejer and Škreb (1997).

References

Bank for International Settlements. (1997). *Annual Report*. Basle: BIS.

Blejer, Mario I., and Marko Skreb (eds.). (1997). *Macroeconomic Stabilization in Transition Economies*. Cambridge: Cambridge University Press.

Blejer, Mario I., and Marko Skreb (eds.). (1999). *Financial-Sector Transformation: Lessons from the Transition Economies*. Cambridge: Cambridge University Press.

European Bank for Reconstruction and Development. (1997). *Transition Report*. London: EBRD.

International Monetary Fund. (1997). *World Economic Outlook*. Washington, DC: IMF.

I EXCHANGE-RATE POLICIES AND THE BALANCE OF PAYMENTS

2 CURRENT-ACCOUNT SUSTAINABILITY IN TRANSITION ECONOMIES

Nouriel Roubini

Stern School of Business, New York University

Paul Wachtel

Stern School of Business, New York University, and Institute for EastWest Studies

2.1. Introduction

Recent episodes of currency crisis have been associated with large, growing, and eventually unsustainable current-account imbalances. The Mexican peso crisis of 1994 and the 1997 currency turmoil in a number of Asian countries (in particular Thailand, Malaysia, and the Philippines) appear to have been partly triggered by unsustainable current-account imbalances. Following the Mexican peso crisis of 1994, the IMF devised a warning mechanism aimed at an early recognition of potentially unsustainable current-account imbalances. In this regard, a large number of Eastern and Central European countries in transition were experiencing large and growing current-account imbalances in the 1996 to 1997 period. Deficits in excess of 5 percent of GDP (an in many cases closer to 10 percent of GDP) were observed in Croatia, the Czech Republic, the Slovak Republic, Poland, Estonia, Latvia, Lithuania, and Moldova. Moreover, similar to the crisis episodes in Mexico and East Asia, a number of Central and Eastern European countries had weak financial systems, had adopted in the 1990s semifixed exchange-rate regimes aimed at controlling inflation and were experiencing significant real appreciation of their currencies. As a combination of fixed-rate regimes, real appreciation, current-account worsening, short-term foreign debt accumulation, and weak financial systems had contributed to the earlier currency crises in Mexico and Southeast Asia, it is important to study whether the current-account imbalances in Central and Eastern Europe would be sustainable or whether there are significant risks that currency crises would also occur in the transition economies. In this respect, the currency crisis in the Czech Republic in the spring of 1997 was an early warning sign that the current-account sustainability in transition economies cannot be taken for granted. This chapter therefore systematically analyzes the sustainability of the current-account imbalances in a group of transition economies.

The current-account balance is an important and intriguing measure of macroeconomic performance for economies in transition. On the one hand, a current-account deficit is a reflection of the strength of a developing economy, insofar as it measures resources coming into the country to finance investment demand in excess of national savings. On the other hand, a current-account deficit can reflect a dangerous and unsustainable imbalance between national savings and domestic investment and the accumulation of debts that cannot be serviced. The intriguing aspect of this dichotomy is that it is often difficult to distinguish between current-account deficits that are the consequence of growth-inducing capital inflows and current-account deficits that result in debt accumulation that cannot be sustained. In the first view, the deficits reflect the success of the structural changes that have led to an inflow of capital, investment, and prospects of rapid economic growth. The other view is that these current-account imbalances are a reflection of a transition process that has not always been well managed—that the imbalances are not sustainable and balance-of-payments or exchange-rate crises might well become common in the region. Making the distinction between the two views is all the more difficult in transition economies that are subject to large and, sometimes, unpredictable shocks that can lead to temporarily very large current-account flows as well undergoing major structural changes that may require long-term current-account imbalances. Moreover, the poor quality of data available for the transition economies makes it difficult to interpret events.

The current-account balance is also the focal point for measurement of economic performance in any open economy. The reason for this is twofold. First, the current-account balance is closely related to the other components of national investment and saving—the fiscal balance and private savings. Thus, it has important implications for overall growth. Second, the current-account balance will often have implications for the exchange rate and competitiveness. An understanding of the current account sheds light on the overall prospects for an economy in transition. Thus, a study of exchange rates, competitiveness, and the balance of payments ought to begin with an examination of current-account imbalances and the extent to which they may or may not be sustainable.

Most of the transition economies experienced large current-account deficits in the aftermath of the end of the Soviet planning system. These temporary deficits were the results of the decline in output and were financed by official international assistance and borrowing. With macroeconomic stabilization, the deficits declined temporarily and in some instances turned into a surplus. Current-account deficits in this period (up to 1995) were associated with structural changes in the transition economies, and many observers accepted even relatively large current-account deficits without concern. However, in the later stages of transition, while positive economic growth has returned in most transition economies, large and increasing current-account deficits have become quite common, and the question of sustainability is important.

In this chapter we evaluate recent trends and developments in the current-account deficits of the transition economies of Central and Eastern Europe. We conclude that there are four significant issues that cause us to be concerned about the current-account imbalances in the transition economies:

- The deficits are large relative to GDP, and they are increasing.
- Income accounting data on investment and savings rates suggest that the deficits are often a consequence of consumption booms and low national savings.
- Significant real appreciation has led to a loss of competitiveness. Interestingly, countries with a more strongly pegged exchange-rate regime have experienced more real appreciation and a more severe worsening of the external balance. Thus, real exchange-rate targeting (as an intentional or unintentional policy) leads to less concern about sustainability.
- Weak banking and financial systems are often unable to cope with large capital flows.

There are, of course, some offsetting factors:

- Short-term portfolio flows ("hot money") are still relatively small.
- Large foreign-exchange reserves have been accumulated.

The chapter begins with a discussion of criteria for assessing current-account sustainability. The next section reviews balance-of-payments trends in the transition economies taken as a group. Since there are major differences between countries in advanced stages of transition (such as the Czech Republic) and countries that have barely embarked on programs of stabilization and reform (such as Bulgaria), we continue the discussion with an examination of the current accounts in a subset of ten transition countries—Bulgaria, Croatia, the Czech Republic, Estonia, Hungary, Lithuania, Poland, Romania, Slovakia, and Ukraine. The countries are chosen to reflect a variety of transition experiences but exclude some very small countries, countries of the former Soviet Union that have not yet embarked on a transition process, and countries where the data are deemed to be particularly unreliable or unavailable. We also summarize the current account trends and developments in each of the ten countries (with a fuller examination in the appendix). We then examine exchange-rate policies and movements in real exchange rates in our various criteria sample of ten transition countries and discuss the capital account and the forms of financing of current-account deficits. Finally, we examine the relationship between the banking and financial sector and current-account sustainability and discuss a broad range of additional indicators of sustainability.

2.2. Criteria for Assessing the Sustainability of Current-Account Imbalances

There is no simple rule that can help us determine when a current-account deficit is sustainable or not. If there were, foreign-exchange crises would not be so surprising when they occur. Nevertheless, there are a number of criteria that ought to be used in assessing the sustainability of current-account imbalances. Experience indicates that balance-of-payments crises can be related to one or more of these root causes even if a careful examination of the issues does not provide a reliable predictive model for crises. In this section we discuss various indicators that can be associated with persistent current-account deficits that might be sustainable or not.[1]

A theoretical criterion for current-account sustainability is not particularly stringent because the intertemporal budget constraint of a country imposes only very mild restrictions on the evolution of a country's current account and foreign debt. As long as the discounted value of the country foreign debt is nonzero in the infinite limit, the country is solvent; this means only that the country cannot increase its foreign debt faster than the real interest rate on this debt. Subject to this constraint, any path of the current account such that the infinite sum of all current accounts is equal to the initial foreign debt of the country is consistent with solvency. A country could run very large current-account deficits for a long time and remain solvent as long as there are surpluses at some time in the future. The solvency constraint also implies that the stock of foreign debt of the country can increase without limit as long as it does not increase faster than the real interest rate. If the real interest rate is greater than the rate of growth of an economy, solvency is consistent even with a foreign debt to GDP ratio that grows continuously over time.

Given the looseness of the theoretical criteria for solvency and sustainability, it is more reasonable to recur to more practical criteria for sustainability. In fact, a dynamics of the current account that leads to an increase without bounds of the foreign debt to GDP ratio can be seen as being effectively unsustainable: the financial markets will eventually get concerned about the country's ability and willingness to repay its debt and will limit its borrowing leading to a foreign-debt crisis. Therefore, *a nonincreasing foreign debt to GDP ratio* is seen as a practical sufficient condition for sustainability: a country is likely to remain solvent as long as the ratio is not growing.[2]

Along similar practical lines, Milesi-Ferretti and Razin (1996a, 1996b, 1996c) stress that sustainability depends also on the country's willingness to pay and the creditors' willingness to lend. Willingness to pay may become an issue when a country is solvent (given its expected path of trade balances), but "it is not politically feasible to divert output form domestic to external use to service the debt" (Milesi-Ferretti and Razin (1996c, p. 1). Furthermore, the traditional solvency criterion is based on the assumption that creditors will be willing to lend to the country on current terms. This may not be realistic if foreign creditors are not sure about the country's willingness to be current on its foreign debt liabilities or its ability to do that in case an external shock hits the country.

To specify an operational definition of sustainability, consider a situation where current macroeconomic conditions continue (there are no exogenous shocks) and there are no changes in macroeconomic policy. In this instance the current-account deficit can be argued to be sustainable as long as no external-sector crisis occurs. An external-sector crisis could come in the form of an exchange-rate crisis or a foreign-debt crisis. An exchange-rate crisis could be a panic that leads to the rapid depreciation of the currency or a run on the central bank's foreign-exchange reserves. A debt crisis could be the inability to obtain further international financing or to meet repayments or an actual default on debt obligations. A sustainable current-account deficit is one that can be maintained without any of these crises occurring. Of course, sustainability can be judged only after the fact, but we will be examining the characteristics of the economy that are indicative of crises occurring.

Most episodes of unsustainable current-account imbalances that have led to a crisis have occurred when the current-account deficit was large relative to GDP. Lawrence Summers, the U.S. Deputy Treasury Secretary, wrote in *The Economist* on the anniversary of the Mexican financial crisis (Dec. 23, 1995–Jan. 5, 1996, pp. 46–48) "that close attention should be paid to any current-account deficit in excess of 5% of GDP, particularly if it is financed in a way that could lead to rapid reversals." By this standard, many of the transition economies provide ample source for concern. However, large and persistent current-account imbalances do not imply unsustainability, regardless of other factors. Milesi-Ferretti and Razin (1996b, 1996c) suggest three core issues that relate to sustainability. They argue that both the theoretical and empirical evidence suggests that, *ceteris paribus*, a current-account imbalance is likely to be less sustainable if (1) the imbalance is large relative to GDP, (2) the imbalance is due to a reduction in national saving rates rather than an increase in national investment rates, and (3) national savings rates are low.

We consider next in more detail a number of criteria that are helpful in assessing the sustainability a path of current-account imbalances.

2.2.1. Sources of Current-Account Deficit

We begin with the underlying real sector sources of a current-account deficit. Since the current account is equal to the difference between national savings and national investment, a current-account deficit can emerge from either a fall in savings or an increase investment. The sustainability of a given deficit will be affected by its source—an investment increase or a saving fall—and by additional characteristics of the change in savings or investment.

Running a current-account deficit involves borrowing from abroad, which is less dangerous if it is financing new investment rather than consumption (lower savings). High investment rates lead to increased productive capacity and potentially higher future export receipts that will be available to service the foreign debt. Generally, a current-account deficit that is accompanied by a fall in savings rates will be more problematic than a deficit accompanied by rising investment rates. Moreover, certain types of investment are more likely to be associated with sustainable deficits than others. Private-sector investments in productive capital, particularly in traded goods industries, will make a current-account deficits more sustainable, as opposed, for example, to borrowing from abroad to make real estate investments.

A related issue is the relationship between the rate of economic growth and the current account. Large current-account deficits may be more sustainable if economic growth is higher. High GDP growth tends to lead to higher investment rates as expected profitability increases. At the same time, high growth might lead to higher expected future income and (as noted above) transitory declines in private savings rates. Generally, higher growth rates are related to more sustainability of the current-account deficit because, everything else equal, higher growth will lead to a smaller increase in the foreign debt to GDP ratio and make the country more able to service its external debt.

A current-account imbalance caused by a fall in the national savings rates can be due to either a fall in private savings or in public savings (higher budget deficits). A fall in national savings caused by lower public savings (higher budget deficit) is potentially more dangerous than a fall in private savings.[3] The reason for this is that a fall in private savings is more likely to be a transitory phenomenon while structural public-sector deficits are often hard to get rid of. A transitory fall in private savings rates may occur when expectations that high future GDP growth will lead to higher permanent income results in an increase in current consumption. The savings rate will recover when future income increases occur. On the other hand, large and persistent structural budget deficits may result in an unsustainable build-up of foreign debt.

Needless to say, many episodes of unsustainable current-account deficits do not fit the patterns described. In particular, the examples of Chile in 1979 to 1981 and Mexico in 1977 to 1981 come to mind. In both these instances the average real GDP growth rate in the years preceding the crisis was above 7 percent. Moreover, the deterioration of the current-account balance in the years preceding the 1994 Mexican peso crisis was largely due to a fall in private savings. In the Mexican episode, the boom in private consumption and the sharp fall in private savings rates was fueled by the combined forces of overly optimistic expectations about future growth and permanent income increase together with the loosening of liquidity constraints on consumption deriving from the liberalization of domestic capital markets. Under such conditions, the fall in private savings rates led to a rapid and eventually unsustainable current-account deterioration. Finally, in both the Chilean episode and the more recent, 1990 to 1994, Mexican episode, the crises occurred in spite of the fact that the fiscal balance was in surplus. This suggests that current-account deficits that are driven by structurally low and falling private-sector savings may be a matter of concern even if they are the results of the "optimal" consumption and savings decisions of private agents.

2.2.2. Composition of the Current Account

The composition of the current-account balance that is approximately equal to the sum of the trade balance and the net factor income from abroad will affect the sustainability of any given imbalance. A current-account imbalance may be less sustainable if it is derived from a large trade deficit rather than a large negative net factor income from abroad component. For a given current-account deficit, large and persistent trade deficits may indicate structural competitiveness problems, while large and negative net foreign factor incomes may be the historical remnant of foreign debt incurred in the past. Moreover, since a country's ability to service its external debt in the future depends on its ability to generate foreign-currency receipts, the size of its exports as a share of GDP (the country's openness) is another important indicator of sustainability.

2.2.3. Composition and Size of the Capital Inflows

The composition of the capital inflows necessary to finance a given current-account deficit is an important determinant of sustainability. Short-term capital inflows are more dangerous than long-term flows, and equity inflows are more stable than debt-creating inflows. In this regard, a current-account deficit that is financed by large foreign direct investment (FDI) is more sustainable than a deficit financed by short-term "hot money" flows that may reverse if market conditions and sentiments change. Among the debt-creating inflows, those from official creditors are more stable and less reversible in the short-run than those coming from private creditors; those taking the form of loans from foreign banks are less volatile than portfolio inflows (bonds and non-FDI equity investments). Finally, the currency composition of the foreign liabilities of the country matters as well. While foreign-currency debt may lead to greater capital inflows at a lower interest rate than borrowing in domestic currency (as risk-averse investors concerned about inflation and exchange-rate risk will prefer foreign-currency-denominated assets), foreign-currency debt may end up exacerbating an exchange-rate crisis as a real depreciation leads to an increase in the real burden of foreign debt.[4]

It is not unusual to observe very large capital inflows that are even larger than the current-account deficit. While in the short-run such inflows enhance sustainability as they finance the current-account imbalance, over time they may contribute to unsustainability for two reasons. First, such large inflows are likely to be associated with the accumulation of reversible portfolio investments ("hot money"). Second, capital inflows in excess of the current-account deficit may lead to a nominal currency appreciation that could erode the competitiveness of the country's exports and thus its ability to stem increases in the current-account deficit. If the central bank tries to avoid such appreciation, it will intervene in the forex market and buy foreign currency. In such case, foreign-currency reserves increase, which makes a current-account imbalance more sustainable.

However, if the large capital inflows that increase foreign reserves are not sterilized, they lead to excessive monetary growth that causes higher inflation and leads to greater real appreciation. If they are sterilized, domestic interest rates remain high, and the original source of nominal exchange-rate appreciation is not eliminated so that capital inflows continue and prevent any nominal depreciation that might be necessary to restore the external competitiveness of the country in face of large and growing current-account imbalances.

2.2.4. *Real Exchange-Rate Appreciation*

A real exchange-rate appreciation (from large capital inflows or any other reason) may cause a loss of competitiveness and structural worsening of the trade balance, which makes the current-account deficit less sustainable. Although the investment-saving imbalance, rather than a real appreciation, is the proximate source of a current-account deficit, the current-account deficit may be less sustainable when accompanied by a real exchange-rate appreciation that leads to a misaligned currency value. Specifically, a real appreciation may lead to an increase in consumption (of imported goods) and increase imports of capital goods for investment that result in a worsening of the current account.

However, there are often fundamental factors at work in a transition economy that warrant a real exchange-rate appreciation. Thus, not every real appreciation will be creating current-account sustainability problems for at least two reasons. First, in many transition economies, sharp nominal depreciation in the early years of the transition to a market economy led to strong real depreciation of the exchange rate. In this regard, the real appreciation observed over time may be partly a return to the long-run equilibrium real exchange rate after the initial overshooting. Second, a persistent appreciation of the real exchange rate may not be due to misalignments but rather be caused by changes in fundamentals. For example, it has been argued that high rates of productivity in the tradable sector have led to a real appreciation along the lines of a Balassa-Samuelson effect.

2.2.5. Foreign-Exchange Reserves and the Debt Burden

The current-account deficit is an imbalance between national saving and investment out of current income that needs to be financed by a capital inflow or accumulation of debt. The ability to sustain deficits will be affected by the country's stock of international assets. An existing large burden of international debt will make it more difficult to finance a current-account imbalance. Moreover, a large debt-servicing burden can easily exhaust export revenues and preclude imports of investment goods that are needed for growth. In such a case, the debt burden can create a trap that inhibits any growth policies. For this reason, many transition and developing countries are eager to reschedule sovereign debt obligations. Similarly, the existence of large foreign-exchange reserves will facilitate the financing of the current-account deficit especially when the country is pegging its exchange rate and needs foreign reserves to credibly fix its exchange rate. Foreign-exchange reserves and a small external debt burden reduce the risk of unsustainability and enable a country to finance a current-account deficit at lower cost. The real rate paid (in hard currency terms) on the country's debt is an indication of the market's evaluation of the country risk premium or its ability to sustain a current-account deficit.

2.2.6. Fragility of Financial System

The soundness of the domestic financial system, particularly the banks, has bearing on a country's ability to sustain a current-account deficit. Capital inflows and foreign direct investment will both require foreign participation in the domestic financial system and, at the very least, a willingness to hold deposits in the domestic banking system. A lack of confidence in the banking system will inhibit the willingness of foreigners to finance the current-account deficit by participating in the domestic economy. In such a case, the entire burden of current-account financing would fall on the accumulation of external debt.

Domestic banking crises are common in developing and transition economies. More often than not they are the direct result of bad lending practices, often due to political influences on bank lending or the requirement that banks (which are often state owned) allocate credit to sustain state-owned enterprises. The problem is exacerbated when the banks source of funds is borrowing from abroad in hard currencies. A collapse of the banking system has several immediate consequences. First, it leads to a fall of savings immediately or to a contraction of economic activity, which in turn causes a fall in saving. Second, uncertainty and instability concerning the payments system will quickly stem the inflow of foreign capital. Thus, banking-sector fragility can easily be the proximate cause of an unsustainable current-account deficit.

2.2.7. Political Instability and Uncertainty About the Economic Environment

Political instability or mere uncertainty about the course of economic policy will have much the same consequences as banking-sector instability. The threat of a change in regime or of a regime that is not committed to sound macroeconomics policies can reduce the willingness of the international financial community to provide financing for a current-account deficit. Thus, a deterioration in expectations about the political and financial environment can contribute to a balance-of-payments and exchange-rate crisis, especially when economic fundamentals are not very sound. Such shifts in expectations can occur quickly and sometimes without much warning. Moreover, political instability may lead to larger budget deficits that, in an open economy, will lead to larger current account deficits.[5]

In summary, the large number and wide variety of factors associated with current-account sustainability suggest that assessing sustainability or predicting balance-of-payments or exchange-rate crises is not a simple matter. However, the criteria discussed do provide a framework for analyzing the situations in transition economies and making distinctions among them.

2.3. Balance-of-Payments Trends and Developments

2.3.1. All Transition Economies

The overall current account of the group of all transition countries (see Table 2.1) shows a lot of variability over time. In 1988, the group showed a surplus of $1.5 billion, but this turned into a deficit of $7.3 billion in 1989 and widened to $21.9 billion in 1990, the first year of the transition from a

Table 2.1. Current account (in billions of U.S. dollars)

	Total for Transition Countries	*Central and Eastern Europe*	*Russia*	*Transcaucasus and Central Asia*
1988	1.5	—	—	—
1989	-7.3	—	—	—
1990	-21.9	—	—	—
1991	2.8	-6.7	4.1	5.3
1992	-2.1	0.5	-1.2	-1.5
1993	-6.6	-8.4	2.6	-0.8
1994	5.1	-4.3	10.4	-1.1
1995	-3.1	-5.9	4.8	-1.9
1996	-18.4	-17.2	2.8	-3.9
1997[a]	-24.1	-22.3	2.8	-4.6
1998[a]	-33.6	-22.6	-5.5	-5.5

Source: IMF *World Economic Outlook*, May 1997, October 1997.
a. Forecast.

socialist economic regime to a market economy in a number of these countries. In the early 1990s, there were moderate current-account deficits in the transition countries; the total was in the $2 to 6 billion range in the 1992 to 1995 period and fell to a modest $3.1 billion deficit in 1995. However, the overall deficit rose sharply to $18.4 billion in 1996, and IMF forecasts deficits are even larger in 1997 and 1998.

While the aggregate data suggest that the current-account imbalances have been modest in the 1991 to 1995 period, a disaggregation by subregions of transition economies presents a somewhat different picture. If we distinguish between three separate regions (Central and Eastern Europe, Russia, and Transcaucasus and Central Asia), we see that small overall imbalances are in large part driven by the very large current-account surpluses (in the range of $3 to 10 billion for most of the period) of Russia. The other two subgroups had large current-account imbalances, which worsened in the mid-1990s. For example, the Central and Eastern Europe group has imbalances averaging $5 billion per year in the 1991 to 1995 period; in 1996 this imbalance grew to $17.2 billion and is expected to be larger in 1997 and 1998. The Transcaucasus and Central Asia group has a surplus in 1991, but deficits emerged in subsequent years, reaching $1.9 billion in 1995 and about $5 billion per year in 1996 to 1998.

Even this subgroup data are excessively aggregated as in each subgroup we observe large current-account imbalances in some countries and surpluses in others. For example, taking the 1995 and 1996 data shown in Table

2.2, we observe that in the Central and Eastern Europe group, almost all countries had current-account deficits above 4 percent of GDP in 1995 or 1996—twelve of the fifteen countries for which data are shown.[6] In the Transcaucasus and Central Asia group, all but one of the countries for which we have had current account deficits of at least 4 percent of GDP in 1995.

Table 2.2. Current account (as a percent of GDP)

	IMF		*EBRD*	
	1995	*1996*	*1995*	*1996*
Central and Eastern Europe				
Albania	–6		–7.6	–4.7
Belarus	–2		–2.4	–6.7
Bulgaria	–0.1	–2	–0.5	1.3
Croatia	–9.5	–7.3	–9.4	–7.6
Czech Republic	–3	–7.9	–2.8	–8.1
Estonia	–5.2	–6.8	–4.7	–10.3
Hungary	–6	–4	–5.7	–3.8
Latvia	–4		–3.7	–7.2
Lithuania	–7.5	–10	–4.4	–4.4
Macedonia	–8		–6.1	–7.8
Moldova	–7		–8.6	–13.1
Poland	0	–3.5	4.7	–1
Romania	–4.2	–3.4	–4.9	–5.9
Slovak Republic	2.7	–10	–2.2	–10.2
Slovenia			–0.2	0.3
Ukraine	–4	5	–4.2	–2.7
Russia, Transcaucasus and Central Asia				
Armenia	–8		–37.5	–26.6
Azerbaijan	–13		–11.5	–23.6
Georgia	–8		–8.3	–4.9
Kazakstan	–4		–4	–3.4
Russia	1		1.3	2.3
Kygyz Republic	–15		–19.3	–23.7
Mongolia	–7			
Tajikistan			0.2	–10.9
Turkmenistan			–0.3	1.7
Uzbekistan	–1		–0.5	–7.9

Source: IMF *World Economic Outlook*, October 1996; IMF Country Reports and IMF International Financial Statistics; EBRD *Transition Report, 1997*.

The examination of the data suggests the following classification of large current-account deficit episodes:

- *Countries experiencing a collapse of output* The collapse of production in the early stages of transition are often quite large. In 1991 and 1992, real GDP growth in all of the transition countries was –7.7 and –10.9 percent, respectively. Positive real growth did not return to Central and Eastern Europe (excluding Belarus and the Ukraine) until 1993 and to the Former Soviet Union until 1997 (see IMF, *World Economic Outlook*, October 1997). As output collapses, national saving may fall a lot (more than national investment) as private savings sharply fall, and the government deficit is large. In such instances, the current-account deficit is a source of resources for both private and public consumption and is unsustainable if protracted for a prolonged period of time.
- *Countries experiencing capital inflows* Once a macroeconomic stabilization has been completed and positive GDP growth resumed, large capital inflows are fairly common. Such inflows come from portfolio investments, deposit inflows, and foreign direct investments and finance both investment and consumption. Whether such current-account deficits are unsustainable depends on the characteristics discussed in Section 2.2.

Distinguished among different types of current-account imbalances and determining whether the capital inflows are sustainable or are likely to derail the stabilization process will be a critical issue in the late 1990s. Medium-term forecasts for the transition economies suggest that rising growth rates will be accompanied by increasing current-account deficits. For the transition economies as a whole, the IMF projections (from *World Economic Outlook*, October 1997) indicate that real GDP growth will reach 4.0 percent in 1998, while the total current-account deficit will be $34 billion, ten times larger than in 1995.

A useful way to begin to understand the nature of the current-account balance is to consider that it can be disaggregated in two ways. On one side, the current account is the sum of three components: the resource balance (or net exports of goods and services), current (unilateral) transfers, and the factor income balance. On the other side, the current account is the difference between national savings and investment. The disaggregated current account is shown in Table 2.3 for the transition countries as a whole as a percent of GDP. The overall current-account imbalances (as a share of GDP) have been relatively small in the early 1990s, less than 1.4 percent of

Table 2.3. Savings, investment, current account, and its financing (as a percent of GDP)

	Savings	+	*Investment*	=	*Current Account*	=	*Resource Balance (Net exports)*	+	*Factor Income*	+	*Current Transfers*	*Capital Inflows*	*Change in Foreign-Exchange Reserves*
1990	27.7		29		−1.3		−1.2		−0.6		0.5	1.1	−0.2
1991	29.7		31.1		−1.4		0.9		−3.1		0.8	0.8	−0.6
1992	26.2		28.8		−2.5		−2.1		−2.6		2.1	4	1.5
1993	21.3		24.7		−3.4		−3.5		−1.4		1.4	6.3	2.9
1994	22.2		22.2		−0.1		−0.1		−0.9		0.9	1.9	1.8
1995	20.5		21.3		−0.8		−0.3		−1.1		0.6	4.8	4
1996	19		21.1		−2.1		−2.3		−0.5		0.6	1.9	−0.2
1997[a]	18.6		22.1		−3.5		−2.8		−1.4		0.7	4.2	0.7
1998[a]	19.9		23.9		−4		−3.2		−1.4		0.6	4.7	0.7

Source: IMF *Word Economic Outlook*, May 1997, October 1997.

a. Forecast.

GDP in every year except 1992 and 1993 (when the GDP declines were the largest). However, the imbalances grew quickly from 1.2 percent of GDP in 1995 to 2.1 percent of GDP in 1996 and were expected to worsen further in 1997 and 1998 to 3.5 and 4.0 percent, respectively.

The decomposition of the imbalance between savings and investment shows why the overall imbalances remained low (as a share of GDP). In the 1990s there has been a significant drop in the national savings rates of the transition economies, from the average of 29.7 percent in 1991 to less than 20 percent. This fall in national saving rates has been the result of persistently negative growth of output in the transition process that have depressed private savings and caused large negative public savings (large budget deficits). While the collapse in output at the outset of the transition process significantly depressed national savings, it has also drastically reduced investment rates: the investment to GDP ratio fell from 31.1 percent in 1991 to 21.7 percent in 1995. The fall in the savings rate was larger than that of the investment rate between 1990 and 1993 so that large current-account imbalance emerged in that period. Between 1993 and 1995, investment rates fell faster than savings rate so that the current-account imbalance tended to shrink. However, the data for 1996 and forecasts for the rest of the decade indicate that the current-account imbalance will significantly widen as the investment rate begins to increase while the savings rate remains stagnant below the 1995 level.

Further insights into the current-account balances can be seen from the decomposition into a resource balance, current transfers, and factor income. Swings over the 1990s in the size of unilateral transfers have a particularly important role. Unilateral current transfers were very large in the 1992 to 1994 period as the transition countries received a significant amount in official grants during the difficult early years of the transition process. Since these transfers were as large as the overall current account in those years, the current-account deficits would have been twice as large as the actual ones in the absence of such transfers: for example, in 1992 and 1993 the current-account imbalance (excluding current transfers) would have been 4.6 and 4.8 percent of GDP, respectively, rather than 2.5 and 3.4 percent. However, current transfers have significantly fallen in 1995 (to 0.6 percent of GDP) and are expected to remain fairly small.

Regarding the other two components of the current account, we observe the following features. First, the factor income balance is structurally in deficit and makes a major contribution to the overall current-account imbalance. The transition countries are all net foreign debtor countries, and the interest burden on the foreign debt is the most important cause of the large factor income imbalance. The interest burden on such foreign debt has fluctuated over time (for example, falling from over 2.6 percent of GDP in 1992 to an average of 1.2 percent in 1993 to 1994 as a number of transition countries have rescheduled their foreign debt) but is expected to constitute about one-third of the overall current account deficit for the foreseeable future (see Table 2.3).

Second, the resource balance (net exports of goods and nonfactor services) is in a structural deficit. Although such imbalances (as a share of GDP) fell from 1993 to 1995 (from 3.5 percent of GDP to 0.3 percent), trade deficits increased a lot in 1996, are expected to continue to grow significantly, and average around 3.0 percent of GDP in the next five years.

Apart from the historical trends in current-account imbalances, there is a lot of uncertainty about the future. The transition economies that implemented stabilization and structural reform policies early on have returned to positive real growth rates (see Begg, 1996). However, the return to growth has been (and will be) associated with a likely worsening of the current-account imbalances. The reason for this is that the return to growth will lead to a recovery of national investment rates that would worsen the current account. The return to growth will be likely to increase national savings rates as well but not as much as investment rates. The increase in national savings rates will be due to an increase in public savings, as budget deficits are reduced as part of the stabilization efforts. However, private savings rates might not grow a lot and might actually fall: in fact, the experience of many developing countries suggests that high expected income growth often leads to life-cycle motivated increase in consumption rates that tend to depress private savings rates. Such a boom in private consumption driven by anticipated increases in future permanent incomes is likely to be even larger when the financial sector is liberalized and household have access to credit markets for consumption purposes.

IMF medium-term forecasts (from the October 1997 *World Economic Outlook*) are consistent with this scenario of worsening current-account deficits. The overall current-account deficit for the transition economies will be 3.9 percent of GDP over the period 1998 to 2002. Such a worsening of the current account is expected to be driven by an increase in national investment rates greater than the increase in savings rates. Although savings rates are forecast to increase, national investment rates in 1999 to 2002 are expected to be greater than the 1996 investment rate by 4.5 percentage points.[7]

Another important dimension of the external accounts of the transition economies concerns the financing of the current-account deficits and the capital flows to the transition economies. Table 2.3 also shows the change in official reserves as a share of GDP and present an estimate of total capital inflows inferred from the identity:

Current account + Capital inflow = Change in official reserves.

In the early 1990s the former Soviet economies used their foreign reserves to sustain the old economic system; the formerly planned economies did not share in the large capital flows into developing economies that was having a large impact in Asia and Latin America at that time (see Calvo, Sahay, and Vegh, 1995). In 1990 and 1991, the capital inflows were actually less than the current-account deficits: therefore, the economies embarking on transition experienced declines in their international reserves. However, in 1992 a number of transition economies started to implement macro stabilization and structural reforms that led to a dramatic turnaround in the international capital positions. For the transition economies as a group, capital inflows exceed the current-account deficits since 1992. From 1993 to 1995 foreign reserves increased substantially as the current-account deficits were still modest and the capital inflows were significantly larger. The increase in foreign reserves slowed to a trickle in 1996 as the capital inflows slowed down in the year; the IMF forecasts indicate that the inflows will moderate (as a fraction of GDP) in the remainder of the 1990s but will continue to exceed the current account.

The size of capital inflows has been impressive and the ensuing increase in foreign reserves has vastly complicated in central-bank objective of reducing the rate of growth of monetary aggregates; the attempt to sterilize the effects of the increase of reserves on the money supply has proven to be a difficult policy task.[8]

Additional evidence on the composition of capital flows can be obtained directly from the capital account of the balance of payments. Table 2.4 relates capital-account transactions to the current account; the data are aggregated data for the countries in transition in billions of U.S. dollars. The first four columns are the components of total net external financing:

- Foreign direct investment,
- Net loans and credits form the IMF,
- Net external borrowing (both long- and short-term credits from official creditors, except monetary authorities) and private creditors (both banks and capital-market issues),
- Capital transfers, primarily debt forgiveness.

The capital-account balance is the sum of total net external financing, other asset transactions (mostly net portfolio investments and export credits), and

Table 2.4. Components of the capital account for transition countries (in billions of U.S. dollars)

	Foreign Direct Investment	*Net loans and Credits from IMF*	*Net External Borrowing*	*Capital Transfers*	*Asset Transactions*[a]	*Capital Account*[a]	*Change in Foreign Reserves*[b]	*Current Account*	*Capital Account*[c]
1988	0.5	–0.5	11.5	0	–7.4	4.1	5.6	1.5	2.6
1989	0.2	–0.3	12.2	0.4	1.2	13.7	6.4	–7.3	9.3
1990	0	0.3	15.8	0	–1.1	15.1	–6.8	–21.9	10.8
1991	2.3	2.4	–6.5	0.9	–2.2	–3.2	–0.4	2.8	–0.1
1992	4.1	1.6	1.5	2.5	–1.3	8.4	6.3	–2.1	7.1
1993	5.7	3.7	–3.8	2.7	11.2	19.5	12.9	–6.6	14.1
1994	5.1	2.4	–3.8	0.3	–0.8	3.2	8.3	5.1	5.1
1995	12.9	4.7	19.6	0.5	–1.1	36.7	33.6	–3.1	37.9
1996	12.4	2.2	1.6	0.2	–1.1	15.5	–2.9	–18.4	17.3
1997[d]	14.2	NA	20	0.3	0.5	29.5	5.4	–24.1	30.5
1998[d]	17.9	NA	20.7	–0.1	–0.2	40.3	6.7	–33.6	41.6

Source: IMF *World Economic Outlook*, October 1996, May 1997, October 1997.

a. Including errors and omissions.

b. += increase.

c. Excluding errors and omissions.

d. Forecast.

errors and omissions. The capital account is shown inclusive of errors and omissions under the assumption that the bulk of the residual between the measured capital and current-account balances is due to unrecorded private external-asset transactions. However, many transition countries have large amounts of hidden exports that would suggest that the errors and omissions be included in the current account. Under this assumption, the capital-account balance (excluding errors and omissions) would be as shown in the last column of the table.

The overall picture provided by the balance between capital and current accounts is consistent with the GDP shares data discussed earlier. At the start of the transition period, in 1990, the current-account deficit ($21.9 billion) was larger than the capital account balance, which showed an inflow equal to $10.8 billion ($15.1 billion including the errors and omissions). Therefore, the official reserves of the transition countries fell by $6.8 billion. In 1991, there was actually a *net capital outflow* (including errors and omissions) of $3.2 billion; since the overall current account had a surplus of $2.8 billion that year,[9] there was again a net loss of official reserves of $0.4 billion.[10]

There were dramatic changes in capital flows to the transition countries starting in 1992 when the net capital inflows were $8.4 billion (including errors and omissions) while the current-account deficit was $2.1 billion. Official reserves began to increase and the increases in foreign reserves accelerated in the following three years (1993 to 1995), as the net capital inflows have been significantly larger than the current-account deficits. In four years (1992 to 1995) official reserves increased by a total of $61.1 billion.

Taking the transition countries as a whole, there are several distinct stages to the capital flows. Prior to the transition, in 1988 to 1989, the capital inflows consisted mostly of bank and private-sector capital-market borrowing. However, these sources disappeared early in the transition period, and there were net outflows (either reduced borrowing or portfolio outflows shown as other asset transactions) in the early 1990s. This situation was dramatically reversed in 1993 to 1995 when there were significant net inflows from foreign direct investment and loans from the IMF and other official creditors.

Net loans form the IMF have been a significant but falling fraction of total net capital inflows (ranging $2 billion to $4 billion in the 1991 to 1995 period or about 20 percent of total capital inflows). Foreign direct investment that was close to zero before 1990, started to pick up in 1991 ($2.3 billion) and has steadily grown since then to reach $12.9 billion in 1995 (about 36 percent of total capital inflows in that year); however, such FDI flows have been concentrated only in a few countries that are at an advanced stage of transition (Hungary, Czech Republic, and Poland).

Capital transfers (essentially debt forgiveness) has been important only early in the transition process (1992 and 1993) and has been insignificant since 1994. The breakdown of net external borrowing (not shown in Table 2.4) indicates that this has been an important source of capital inflow when borrowing from official creditors has been large (1990 to 1992, 1995, and the forecasted data for 1996 to 1997). The private-sector components were actually negative from 1990 to 1995.

2.3.2. Current-Account Balances in Ten Transition Economies

We examine next the evolution of the current account in the ten countries under study. Here we present some general trends while the Appendix discusses in more detail the situation in each country. Table 2.5 provides a summary of the national income accounts for all ten countries. Our best estimates of national investment, savings, and current account as a fraction of GDP are shown.[11] Growth rates and inflation rates for the countries since the start of the transition are shown in Table 2.6.

All of the countries under consideration have experienced large current-account imbalances in the last two years (1995 to 1996). If we use the implicit IMF criterion that an imbalance above 5 percent of GDP should be monitored for their sustainability, we have six countries whose current-account deficits have averaged more than 5 percent per year in the 1995 to 1996 period. These are Hungary, the Czech Republic, Estonia, Croatia, Lithuania, and the Slovak Republic, and the Ukraine is very close behind. Of these, only Hungary and Ukraine were expected to show an improvement in 1997, while the others were expected to experience further significant deteriorations (or persistent imbalances) in 1997. Of the remaining countries, Bulgaria was in the midst of a serious economic crisis in 1996 to 1997 in spite of the small current-account imbalance. Poland has relatively smaller imbalances if we correct the official current-account data for unrecorded exports. However, even the corrected data show a significant imbalance for 1996 that is expected to increase in 1997 and beyond. Finally, Romania has smaller imbalances (averaging 3.8 percent of GDP in 1995 to 1996) but has shown persistent and structural deficits since 1990 and had experienced an economic crisis similar to that of Bulgaria in 1996 and 1997. However, in both Bulgaria and Romania new governments committed to market reforms were formed in 1997.

In terms of the causes of the observed imbalances, there is a wide dispersion of experiences. All of the countries had at least several years of falling real GDP at the outset of the transition. The largest declines in

Table 2.5. Current account, savings, and investment as a percent of GDP

	1989	*1990*	*1991*	*1992*	*1993*	*1994*	*1995*	*1996*	*1997*[a]
Bulgaria									
Current account		–11	0.5	–5	–10	0.1	–0.1	–2	
Savings		17.2	24.7	12.5	10.2	9.4	9.5	7	
Investment		28.2	24.2	17.5	20.2	9.3	9.6	9	
Croatia									
Current account		8	–5	8	0.9	0.9	–9.5	–7.3	–6
Savings		33.6	22.9	30.3	19.8	21.2			
Investment		25.6	27.9	22.3	18.9	20.3			
Czech Republic									
Current account	0.5	–2	0.5	–0.5	2.1	–0.1	–3	–7.9	–9.8
Savings			30.4	26.5	20.1	20.4	25.8	25.1	
Investment			29.9	27	18	20.5	28.8	33	
Estonia									
Current account				3.4	1.4	–7.4	–5.2	–6.8	–13.7
Savings				30.1	27.9	21.5	21	19.3	
Investment				26.7	26.5	28.9	26.2	26.2	
Hungary									
Current account		1.9	–2.4	–0.8	–9.4	–7.8	–6	–4	–4.2
Savings		27.3	18.1	15.3	10.6	14.4	15.2	18	
Investment		25.4	20.5	16.1	20	22.2	21.2	22	
Public savings		5.1	1.8	0.5	1.1	–1.3	–1.2		
Lithuania									
Current account		–6.1	10.2	12	–4	–3	–7.5	–10	–9
Savings		27.5	32.6	23.9	18.7	16	10.5	9.5	
Investment		33.6	22.4	11.9	22.7	19	18	19.5	

Poland									
Current account (corrected)						2	0	−3.5	−3.5
Current account (official)		5.5	−2.7	−2.4	−5.1	−2	−3	−7	−7
Savings		31.2	15.1	12.3	13.7	16.3	17.1	15.9	
Investment		25.7	17.8	15.7	18.8	18.3	20.1	22.9	
Romania									
Current account	3.3	−8.5	−5.7	−8.3	−5.1	−2.3	−4.2	−3.4	
Savings	30	21.7	22.4	22.9	23.9	24.9	25.8	25.8	
Investment	26.7	30.2	28.1	31.2	29	27.2	30	29.2	
Public savings			3.9	0.5	4.4	4.7	5		
Slovak Republic									
Current account				−0.1	−5.4	5.7	2.7	−10	−10.4
Savings				25.6	15.3	21.6	20.7	10.1	
Investment				25.7	20.7	15.9	18	21.1	
Ukraine									
Current account				−3.1	−2.5	−5.7	−4.7	−5	−3.3
Savings				30.5	31.1	19.4	14.2	15.2	
Investment				33.6	33.6	25.1	18.9	20.2	

Source: IMF country reports, IMF *International Financial Statistics*, Economist Intelligence Unit Country Reports.

a. Forecast.

Table 2.6 Fiscal balance as a percent of GDP, GDP growth rate, and inflation rate in percent

	1989	*1990*	*1991*	*1992*	*1993*	*1994*	*1995*	*1996*[a]	*1997*[b]
Bulgaria									
General government balance	–1.4	–12.8	–14.7	–13	–10.9	–5.8	–6.4	–13.4	–6.3
GDP growth	0.5	–9.1	–11.7	–7.3	–2.4	1.8	2.1	–10.9	–7
Inflation rate	na	72.5	338.9	79.4	63.9	121.9	32.9	311	591.5
Croatia									
General government balance	na	na	–5	–4	–0.8	1.7	–0.9	–0.5	–2.7
GDP growth	na	–6.9	–2	–11	–0.8	0.6	1.7	4.2	5
Inflation rate	na	136	249	937	1150	–3	3.8	3.4	4
Czech Republic									
General government balance	–2.8	0.1	–2	–3.3	2.7	0.8	0.4	–0.2	–1
GDP growth	1.4	–0.4	–14	–6	0.6	2.7	5.9	4.1	1
Inflation rate	1.5	18.4	52	12.5	18.2	9.7	7.9	8.6	9
Estonia									
General government balance	2.8	2.9	5.2	–0.3	–0.7	1.3	–1.2	–1.5	na
GDP growth	–1.1	–8	–7.9	–14.2	–8.5	–1.8	4.3	4	7
Inflation rate	6.1	23.1	304	954	36	42	29	15	12
Hungary									
General government balance	–1.4	0.4	–2.2	–5.5	–6.8	–8.2	–6.5	–3.5	–5
GDP growth	0.7	–3.5	–11.9	–3.1	–0.6	2.9	1.5	1	3
Inflation rate	18.9	33.4	32.2	21.6	21.1	21.2	28.3	19.8	17
Lithuania									
General government balance	–3.8	–5.4	2.7	0.8	–3.1	–4.2	–3.3	–3.6	–2.8
GDP growth	1.5	–5	–13.4	–37.7	–24.2	1	3	3.6	4.5
Inflation rate	na	na	345	1161	188.8	45	35.5	13.1	10

Poland									
General government balance	−4.7	3.1	−6.5	−6.6	−3.4	−2.8	−3.6	−3.1	−4
GDP growth	0.2	−11.6	−7	2.6	3.8	5.2	7	6	5.5
Inflation rate	639	249	60.4	44.3	37.6	29.4	21.6	18	15
Romania									
General government balance	8.4	1.2	0.6	−4.6	−0.4	−1.9	−2.6	−3.9	−4.5
GDP growth	−5.8	−5.6	−12.9	−8.7	1.5	3.9	7.1	4.1	−1.5
Inflation rate	0.6	37.7	223	199	296	62	28	57	116
Slovak R.									
General government balance	−2.8	0.1	−2	−11.9	−7	−1.3	0.1	−1.2	−3.5
GDP growth	1.4	−2.5	−14.6	−6.5	−3.7	4.9	6.8	6.9	4.5
Inflation rate	1.5	18.4	58.3	9.1	25.1	11.7	7.2	5.4	7
Ukraine									
General government balance	na	na	−13.6	−25.4	−16.2	−7.8	−4.9	−3.2	na
GDP growth	4	−3.4	−11.6	−13.7	14.2	−23	−11.8	−10.1	−3
Inflation rate	2.2	4.2	161	2730	10155	401	182	400	15

Source: Begg (1996) for 1989 data, EBRD *Transition Report 1997*.

a. Estimate.

b. Forecast.

output, all more than 10 percent of GDP, were in 1991 and 1992 per year (except Poland in 1990, Ukraine in 1994, and Bulgaria in 1996). In most countries (Romania, Poland, Bulgaria, Czech Republic, and Hungary, in particular), the collapse of output in the early 1990s led to significant current-account deficits as national savings rates dropped more drastically than investment rates. The collapse of GDP was exacerbated by the serious external shocks that hit the transition economies: a worsening of their terms of trade as they moved to world prices and the collapse of trade within the CEMA region. Such external shocks lead to a sharp reduction of exports and a deterioration of the current account.

GDP growth resumed in 1992 in Poland, in 1993 in Romania, in 1994 for six countries (Hungary, the Czech Republic, Croatia, Lithuania, the Slovak Republic, and Bulgaria)[12] and in 1995 in Estonia. Ukraine was the only country that had not seen a return to positive growth by 1997. The return to positive growth has been generally associated with a significant worsening of the current account over the following two years. This has been the experience of Hungary, the Czech Republic, Estonia, Croatia, Lithuania, and the Slovak Republic even if the timing and size of the worsening has differed across countries. The evidence suggests that the worsening of the trade balance and the current account in 1995 to 1996 was larger in the countries in which growth was high in the period (for example Croatia, the Czech Republic, the Slovak Republic, and Estonia). In the countries where the growth rate slowed down or was lower (such as Hungary and Bulgaria), the external balance tended to worsen less or improve.

In general, the worsening of the current account in our sample of countries in the 1994 to 1996 period has been caused by a sharp recovery of national investment rates driven by the return to positive growth. National savings rates have generally grown but more slowly than national investment rates (in Hungary, the Czech Republic), or they have remained stagnant (in Estonia, Croatia, Lithuania).[13]

An optimistic interpretation of the above trends would suggest that the return to positive growth should be associated with large current-account imbalances. As the reforms have led to increases in the profitability of capital and new investment opportunities, investment rates have soared in a number of countries. At the same time, savings rates have lagged behind investment rates as the resumption of growth has led to an increase in consumption rates. National savings rates include both private and public saving so a decline in savings rate can also be due to less government. Data on the government deficits are also in Table 2.6.[14]

National savings rates have been persistently less than 20 percent Hungary, Poland, Lithuania, and Bulgaria (Ukraine, Croatia, and Slovakia would probably be added to the list if reliable data were available). To some extent the low savings rates are due to government deficits, which are large in all of the countries except Estonia and the Czech Republic.

In some countries (Hungary, Slovakia) increased government deficits up to 1993 to 1994 seem to coincide with widening current-account imbalances. In several other countries (Ukraine, Romania, and Bulgaria) the data on savings rates are too sketchy to compare to the fiscal deficit data, and/or the data on government deficits are hard to interpret because of the large changes in the inflation rate. Finally, in Poland and Hungary improvements in the government fiscal balance since 1993 had a noticeable impact on the overall savings investment balance and the current account.

While a reduction in savings rates may be the optimal response of the private sector to changes in the expected growth rates, low savings rates are also due to changes in the fiscal balance. Whatever, the source of low savings rate, they can become a problem over time since they result in persistent current-account deficits. The above discussion suggests that the large current-account imbalances in the 1995 to 1997 period appear to be often structural, and, in many countries, the result of low and falling savings rates in the face of growing investment rates. International comparisons (see Milesi-Ferretti and Razin, 1996a, 1996b, 1996c) suggest that low and falling savings rates make a given current-account imbalance less sustainable; by that criterion, several of the countries in our sample appear to be in a potentially fragile condition.

In the appendix to this chapter, we analyze in more detail the experience of each individual country, study the causes of the worsening of their current account, and analyze the evolution of their current account in terms of the savings-investment imbalance. Our analysis suggests a subjective ranking of the countries where sustainability of the current account is of greatest concern. High on the list are the countries already in crisis in 1997: Bulgaria and the Czech Republic. Next are countries where policy responses to the current-account deficit are probably overdue: Croatia, Estonia, Lithuania, Slovakia, and Ukraine. Sustainability seems to be of less current concern in Hungary and Poland, even if the latter experienced a surge in the current-account imbalance in 1997. Finally, Romania had relatively small current-account imbalances but faced serious structural problems.

2.4. Exchange-Rate Policy and Real Exchange-Rate Appreciation

Our focus in Section 2.3 was on the investment/savings balance that determines the current-account balance. In this view, changes in the real exchange rate are a consequence of real sector fundamentals: the investment/savings balance. Although, that might well be true in the medium or long-run, over the short-run the interactions are more complex. Private-sector capital flows can, at times, differ significantly from the flows necessary to finance the current-account balance (evidence on this is discussed in Section 2.5). That is, capital flows are hardly a passive financing response to a current-account balance. Thus, there are other influences on the exchange rate that can in turn influence the current-account balance—that is, causation runs in both directions.

Specifically, the large and growing current-account imbalances in many transition economies leads to the question of whether such imbalances may be partly due to a loss of competitiveness associated with a real appreciation of the exchange rate. Various measures suggest that many of the countries studies here have experienced significant appreciation of their real exchange rates in the 1993 to 1996 period. While the evidence of a real appreciation is not debated, there is currently a wide debate on the causes and effects of this real appreciation (see Table 2.7 for CPI-based measures of the real exchange rate).

In one view (the *misalignment view*), the real exchange-rate appreciation has caused a loss of competitiveness that worsens the current-account balance. In the other view (the *fundamentals view*), it represents changing real-sector fundamentals that alter the balance of savings and investment. In this case any real appreciation is an appreciation of, or return to, the long-run equilibrium exchange rate.

Table 2.7. Real exchange rates[a]

	1990	*1991*	*1992*	*1993*	*1994*	*1995*	*1996*
Bulgaria		61.6	100	133.6	133.2	148.1	
Croatia		94.8	100	139.2	134.7	141.3	145.4
Czech Republic	92.9	87.7	100	105.2	121	138.6	140.3
Estonia			100	133	191.1	241.9	293.5
Hungary	100	116	100	109.2	108.4	104.8	102.6
Lithuania			100	165	229	244	263
Poland	60.2	93.8	100	107.6	108.5	116.4	122.8
Romania	180.1	160.9	100	138.7	150.2	127	
Slovak Republic	100	121	100	105.3	114.6	123.8	

Source: Authors' calculations based on the following: IMF *International Financial Statistics*; IMF country reports; IMF *World Economic Outlook*, 1996, 1997; EBRD *Transition Report* 1996, 1997.

a. End-of-year data, based on consumer price indexes, 1992 base year = 100. Blank indicates data were not available; no data were available for the Ukraine.

2.4.1. Misalignment View

According to this view, the real appreciation is the consequence of the choice of the exchange-rate regime and the ensuing capital inflows; therefore, it represents a loss of real competitiveness. If this view is correct, the large and growing current-account imbalances would be caused in part by the real appreciation of the currency. This would also imply that the growing current-account imbalances are not sustainable and might be reversed only through a process of nominal and real deprecation of the currency.

The arguments for this view are based on the following reasoning. A real appreciation of the currency is very likely to occur when the exchange rate is pegged and used as a nominal anchor for monetary policy (as it has been in the Czech Republic, the Slovak Republic, Estonia, and Lithuania). In fact, while fixing the exchange rate is a fast way to disinflate an economy starting with high inflation, pegging the exchange rate will not reduce the inflation rate instantaneously to the world level. The reasons that inflation will not fall right away to the world level are many:

- PPP does not hold exactly in the short run since domestic and foreign goods are not perfectly substitutable. So domestic firms will reduce the inflation rate when the exchange rate is pegged but may not push it immediately down to the world level.
- Nontradable goods prices do not feel the same competitive pressures as tradable goods prices; thus inflation in the nontraded sector will fall only slowly.
- Since there is significant inertia in nominal wage growth, wage inflation might not fall right away to the world level. Many wage contracts are backward looking, and the adjustment of wages will occur slowly. Also, in countries where there is formal indexation of nominal wages, wage inflation is based on past (higher) inflation rather than current (lower) inflation; so this inertia in the wage setting in the economy means that wage inflation will remain above the world rate.

If domestic inflation does not converge immediately to the world level when the exchange-rate parity is fixed, a real appreciation will occur over time. This appreciation of the real exchange rate implies a loss of competitiveness of the domestic economy: exports become more expensive relative to imported goods; this worsens the trade balance and the current account over time. Even small differentials between domestic and foreign inflation rates can compound rapidly into a substantial real appreciation.[15]

Therefore, the problem of anti-inflation stabilization policies that use the fixed exchange rate as the policy tool to fight inflation is that fixed rates lead to a real exchange-rate appreciation and to a significant worsening of the current account.

While a real appreciation is more likely to occur (and persist) when the currency is pegged to a fixed exchange rate, misalignments of the real exchange rate may also occur under a regime of managed floating exchange rates unless the central bank follows a crawling peg policy of targeting the real exchange rate. Nominal and/or real appreciation under a managed float may occur as a result of large capital inflows. Such inflows may have diverse causes:

- Optimism about a transition economy that has successfully started to stabilize and structurally reform its economy,
- Short-term speculative capital flowing to transition countries with high real interest rates.

In both instances, speculative capital inflows may prevent the nominal depreciation of the currency necessary to maintain a stable real exchange rate in the presence of persistent differentials between domestic and foreign inflation. Attempts to prevent a nominal appreciation through foreign-exchange intervention (in the absence of capital controls) may not be able to prevent the real appreciation. If the interventions are not sterilized, monetary growth will increase and lead to higher domestic inflation that in turn causes a real appreciation; if they are sterilized, domestic interest rates remain high, capital inflows continue, and the pressures toward a nominal appreciation persist. This is why controls on capital inflows have been suggested (and implemented in Slovenia and the Czech Republic) as a way to stem inward inflows causing the real appreciation of the domestic currency.

4.2. Fundamentals View

According to this view, the appreciation of the real exchange rate is not a signal of exchange-rate misalignment and competitiveness loss; instead, it represents an appreciation of the long-run equilibrium or fundamental real exchange rate. Thus, the worsening of the current account has not been caused by the real appreciation; it is instead the optimal response to the underlying structural and fundamental changes in the economy. If no real misalignment has occurred, the current-account imbalance can be interpreted as the optimal response of the economy to the changes in desired national savings and investment rates. Over time, the imbalances would reverse themselves as the investment and savings fundamentals shift and there would be no need for currency corrections.

A fundamental real exchange-rate appreciation can occur for either of two reasons:

- The observed real appreciations represent a correction of earlier depreciations and a return to equilibrium;
- There are shifts in the macroeconomic fundamentals (such as productivity or technology) that lead to an appreciation of the equilibrium real exchange rate.

The recent real appreciation of exchange rates is viewed by some authors as a correction of the depreciation overshooting that occurred in the first stages of the transition process (see Halpern and Wyplosz, 1996). The economic instability associated with the collapse of the planned economies around 1989 to 1990 led to large nominal currency depreciations that were well in excess of even very high inflation rates. Therefore, in this early stage there were real depreciations that overshot the equilibrium real exchange rate. Thus, part of the real appreciation in the mid-1990s is just a return of the real exchange rate to equilibrium after the overshooting or excessive real depreciations of the early transition period.

While the evidence for some countries (for example the Czech Republic, Bulgaria, and Croatia) is consistent with this overshooting view, there are a few facts that are not fully consistent with it. First, in some countries such as Poland and Hungary, CPI-based measures of the real exchange rate (see Table 2.7) show a persistent and uninterrupted appreciation of the real exchange rate since 1989 without an initial real depreciations. Second, in most of the transition countries (namely, the Czech Republic, Poland, Croatia, the Slovak Republic, and Hungary), the real exchange rate was appreciated in 1996 relative to its level in the 1989 to 1990 period. Therefore, the initial overshooting had been more than compensated for by the subsequent appreciation. This is, the real exchange rates had not merely returned to their 1989 to 1990 levels after the initial large real depreciation; they had instead significantly appreciated relative to their parity before the transition started.

Given the above evidence on "reverse overshooting," to take the fundamentals viewpoint that the real appreciation does not represent a loss of competitiveness, one needs to show that the long-run equilibrium real exchange rate has appreciated. In this regard, it has been argued that the structural reforms implemented in some of the transition economies have led to just such a change for several reasons:

- First, the significant increases in productivity growth observed in the transition process may imply that unit labor costs have not significantly increased in spite of the real appreciation of the currency. So while "dollar wages" have sharply increased in the transition economies both in absolute terms and relative to OECD competitors (see IMF *World Economic Outlook*, May 1997 and Halpern and Wyplosz, 1996, for evidence on this), this appreciation of the real exchange rate based on relative wages may not imply an appreciation of the real exchange rate based on unit labor costs.
- Second, the Balassa-Samuelson model implies that productivity growth in the traded goods sector in excess of that of the nontraded goods sector will lead to a real appreciation of the CPI-based real exchange rate. The real appreciation is then caused not by a loss of competitiveness (an increase in the price of domestic traded exports relative to importable goods) but rather because of the increase in the relative price of nontraded to traded goods caused by the differential productivity growth in the two sectors.
- Third, the structural reforms in the economies have led to capital inflows that have financed both investment demand for nontradable factors (such as land, real estate, and the service-sector labor force) and nontradable goods and services. The ensuing increase in the relative price of nontraded to traded goods shows up as an appreciation of the CPI-based real exchange rate.

In the absence of good measures of the equilibrium real exchange rate, it is hard to assess how much of the observed real appreciation are due to misalignments and how much is due to an equilibrium appreciation.[16] However, we will argue that while some equilibrium real appreciation might have taken place, some of the real exchange-rate movements (especially in the countries that have aggressively pursued exchange-rate pegs as a nominal anchor for monetary policy) suggest a significant loss of competitiveness that has exacerbated the current-account imbalances. Since it is impossible to derive a good measure of the equilibrium real exchange rate, our case in favor of the misalignment view will be circumstantial.[17]

4.3. Exchange-Rate Movements in Ten Transition Economies

We will interpret the exchange-rate movements by looking at the exchange-rate regimes chosen by the countries in our sample. Most of the transition countries' governments tried at some point in the 1990s to use a fixed exchange-rate peg as the nominal anchor for an anti-inflationary strategy. Some countries have more credibly and successfully pursued such exchange-rate pegs, while some others adopted a currency-board arrangement to maintain a peg. The exceptions are countries that were unable to maintain a fixed rate because of high inflation and very small reserves that precluded a move to a nominal anchor provided by a fixed exchange rate.

After a series of devaluations in 1990 that halved the value of the Czechoslovak koruna, the currency was successfully pegged at the end of 1991 for almost six years (until May 1997). The market basket used for the peg was revised (particularly after the breakup of Czechoslovakia), and the exchange-rate band was widened in early 1996. The Slovak currency was devalued by 10 percent after the breakup but then remained on a fixed peg. Three countries in our sample have taken the exchange-rate peg idea to its extreme by forming a formal currency board. These are Estonia, whose currency has been tied to a fixed parity with the DM since 1992, and Lithuania, which introduced a currency board in 1994. More recently, Bulgaria, whose currency had been in a free fall (a 627 percent depreciation in 1996), adopted a currency board as well. From 1991 to 1997, Bulgaria had a floating exchange-rate regime as small and depleted foreign reserves did not allow the central bank to stabilize the exchange rate. Poland tried to use an exchange-rate peg early in the transition process (in 1990 and again in 1991), but the inertial high inflation led to a real appreciation that forced it first to have depreciation and then to move to a managed float or a crawling peg. Other countries such as Hungary and Croatia followed a managed float policy or some variant of a crawling peg from the outset. Finally, the Ukraine, Romania, and Bulgaria (until 1997) have been effectively on a free float. The Ukraine currency introduced at the end of 1992 after it was forced to exit the rouble zone has been persistently depreciating given the country's very high inflation. The depreciation rate was particularly sharp in 1993 and 1994 when domestic inflation surged but subsided to only 31 percent in 1995; during 1996 to 1997, the currency remained quite stable. Romania introduced a unified exchange rate at the end of 1991 and the official parity pegged to the dollar. However, high inflation and low foreign reserves led to a drastic fall in the value of the currency in 1992 and 1993. A successful economic stabilization program in 1994 led to some stabilization of the currency value. However, the persistent current-account imbalances since 1995 and the low level of foreign reserves have led to a persistent fall in the value of the currency in 1995 and 1996.

Recent experience suggests that more real appreciation occurs with a (semi) fixed exchange rate that is being used as the nominal anchor for a anti-inflationary policy than under a free or managed float. Thus, the real appreciation is more likely to signal a misaligned currency when the exchange-rate regime is fixed. One caveat is that a real appreciation might occur even under a managed float when large capital inflows lead to nominal appreciation or prevent a depreciation from occurring in spite of the positive differential between domestic and foreign inflation.

To examine the evidence on the two alternative views of the real appreciation, we will first consider three countries whose experiences are quite representative: the Czech Republic, Poland, and Hungary. The Czech Republic maintained a fixed peg from 1991 to 1997, while Poland and Hungary have been on a managed float or crawling peg. However, there are important differences in the approach to the managed float in these two countries. Poland has had infrequent devaluations and has tried to limit over time the rate of crawl of its currency. Therefore, while not being on a strict fixed peg, Poland has tried to benefit from the constraints of nominal anchor. Hungary, instead, has been explicitly more concerned with preventing a real currency appreciation and has had very frequent and repeated devaluations since 1991. Throughout the period these large devaluations have been justified as a way to maintain the competitiveness of the currency.

One would expect that these different degrees of commitment to an exchange-rate peg (the strongest for the Czech Republic, the lowest for Hungary, and medium for Poland) have implied very different inflationary experiences. In fact, the inflation rate (see Table 2.6) has been the lowest in the Czech Republic in 1995 to 1996 (10 and 9 percent in those two years), higher in Poland (23 and 20 percent), and even higher in Hungary (28 and 24 percent).

While the commitment to a stronger peg has led to a more rapid disinflation, it has also implied a greater amount of real exchange-rate appreciation. In the Czech Republic the real exchange rate strongly depreciated in the unstable period preceding the move to a pegged parity (1989 to 1991). However, the real exchange rate has persistently appreciated since the move to a fixed exchange rate late in 1991. The real appreciation between the end of 1991 and the end of 1996 has been equal to 60 percent (see Table 2.7). At the other extreme Hungary has followed an active crawling-peg policy of real exchange-rate targeting since 1992. Before the move to a more active real exchange-rate targeting, the Hungarian currency experienced a large appreciation (about 20 percent in the 1990 to 1992 period). Since the end of 1992, however, the real appreciation has been very modest; between the end of 1992 and the end of 1996, the real appreciation has been minimal, only 3 percent. An intermediate case is the one of Poland where the commitment to an exchange-rate nominal anchor has not been as tight as in the Czech Republic and not as loose as in Hungary. The real exchange rate appreciated sharply (by over 50 percent in 1990 and 1991 when Poland followed a fixed peg. Between 1992 and the end of 1996, instead, the real appreciation has been more limited (about 23 percent), in between the levels of the fixed-rate pegger, the Czech Republic, and the real exchange-rate targeter, Hungary.

While the above discussion suggest that the real exchange-rate appreciation is related to the choice of the exchange-rate regime, these differential movements of real exchange rates have also affected the real competitiveness of these countries and their current account developments. The country with the stronger commitment to fixed rates and the largest appreciation of the real exchange rate—the Czech Republic—has also had the most significant worsening of its external balance: the current account was in a surplus of 2.1 percent of GDP in 1993, but this surplus turned into a large deficit of 7.9 percent of GDP by 1996. The opposite case is the one of Hungary that followed since 1993 an explicit policy of targeting of the real exchange rate and was successful in preventing a real appreciation in the 1993 to 1996 period. This exchange-rate policy has positively affected Hungary's external balance: while the current-account deficit was equal to 9.4 percent of GDP in 1993, the imbalance has gotten progressively smaller and was down to 4 percent of GDP in 1996 and was likely to remain at that level in 1997. An intermediate case is the one of Poland. While analysis of the external balance of Poland is complicated by the existence of large unrecorded exports, both the official and the corrected current-account figures show a worsening of the current account between 1994 and 1996. According to the official numbers, the deficit increased from 2 percent of GDP to 7 percent of GDP; according to the probably more accurate figures that correct for unrecorded exports, as 2 percent of GDP surplus in 1994 turned into a 3.5 percent of GDP deficit in 1996 and 1997.

The above discussion suggests that the observed real appreciation may be partly due to a misalignment caused by the choice of the exchange-rate regime. The country with the strongest commitment to fixed rates (the Czech Republic) had the largest real appreciation (since the start of the peg) and the largest worsening of its current account. Conversely, the country (Hungary) with the strongest commitment to a real exchange-rate target had the smallest real appreciation (since the start of the crawling-peg policy) and the largest improvement in its current-account imbalance. The country (Poland) with an exchange-rate policy in between that of the Czech Republic and Hungary experienced real exchange-rate movements and changes in the current account that lie in between the two extreme cases.

The experiences of these three countries are quite representative of other country experiences. For example, in addition to the Czech Republic, three other countries have followed an exchange-rate policy that is close to a tight exchange-rate peg: the Slovak Republic (apart from a 1993 devaluation of its peg), Estonia (which has had a currency board since 1992), and Lithuania (which chose a currency board in 1994). In all three countries, the move to a peg has been associated with a large real appreciation of their currency. In Estonia and Lithuania, the slowdown in inflation has not been as large as hoped for; in spite of the fixed exchange-rate parity it was in the midteens in both countries in 1996. In Estonia, the real appreciation of the currency since the adoption of the currency board in 1992 has been equal to over 70 percent. In Lithuania, the real appreciation has been 59 percent since the adoption of the currency board in 1994. Lithuania entered the currency board in 1994 with an exchange rate that was undervalued in real terms so that some real appreciation was expected to occur.[18] However, even considering the initial undervaluation, there has been a significant real appreciation since 1994.[19] These real appreciations have had dramatic effects on the competitiveness of exports of these countries and have been confirmed by recent current-account data. Firms in Estonia and Lithuania complain that they are unable to compete in international markets. In 1992, Estonia ran a current-account surplus equal to 3.4 percent of GDP; this had turned into a current-account deficit of 6.8 percent of GDP in 1996 and was expected to be almost 14 percent of GDP in 1997. In Lithuania, a current-account deficit of 3 percent of GDP in 1994 has turned into a current-account deficit of about 10 percent of GDP in 1996 and 1997. Given the poor performance of the currency board and the serious misalignment of the real exchange rate, the monetary authorities in Lithuania have been considering the idea of phasing out the currency board in 1998 (Bank of Lithuania, 1997). While they argue that a fixed parity would be maintained even without a currency board, it is now likely that a currency devaluation will be required to reverse some of the loss of competitiveness suffered since 1994.

In the Slovak Republic, the move to a peg associated with a much more rapid disinflation than in Estonia or Lithuania; the inflation rate in 1996 was less than 6 percent. As a consequence of this more rapid disinflation, the real appreciation of the exchange rate in Slovakia has been more modest than in the two Baltic countries and equal to about 24 percent since the beginning of 1993. The current-account implications of this real appreciation are more complex in Slovakia since the current-account deficits of 1992 to 1993 turned into surpluses by 1994 to 1995, partly the result of the 10 percent devaluation of the peg late in 1993 after the breakup of the CSFR.

However, in 1996 to 1997 the current account turned into a large deficit of about 10 percent of GDP, suggesting that the real appreciation that has occurred since 1993 is affecting the country's competitiveness.

As noted earlier, Romania, Bulgaria, and the Ukraine have had exchange-rate regimes close to a float throughout the early and mid-1990s as structural weaknesses have not allowed them to stabilize the value of their currency. This lack of commitment to stable currency values is reflected in the significantly higher levels of inflation experienced by these countries than elsewhere. Although Bulgaria and Romania have not experienced significant real appreciation of their currencies, these economies were in sever crisis in 1996 as reform programs have not been effective. In Romania, one observes very sharp swings in the real exchange rate since 1990 with a sharp real depreciation followed by a stabilization program and a real appreciation. The real appreciation of 1993 to 1994 was undone in 1995 and 1996 when the currency started to depreciate sharply in excess of the inflation rate. In Bulgaria, the real exchange rate appreciated by 11 percent between 1993 and 1995. However, in 1996 the fall in the currency has been well above the inflation rate for the year; therefore, a sharp real depreciation occurred during the year. The large nominal depreciations in 1996 led to a very serious resurgence of inflation in these two countries, but they have also led to a significant real depreciation that has affected the external balance. The current-account imbalances in 1996 were smaller (–3.4 percent of GDP for Romania and –2 percent of GDP for Bulgaria) than in the transition economies with pegged exchange rates.

For the Ukraine, it is difficult to derive meaningful measures of the real exchange rate given its history of high and volatile inflation (reaching hyperinflation level in 1992 and 1993) and its system of multiple exchange rates until the end of 1994. If we use an effective market real exchange rate,[20] there were large swings in the 1992 to 1996 period. There were several episodes of sharp real appreciation and depreciation, culminating in a real appreciation of about 100 percent between mid-1993 and the end of 1995. Consistent with an overall trend of real appreciation, the current-account imbalance remained high (deficit of almost 5 percent of GDP) in the 1995 to 1996 period and significantly worse than the average imbalance in earlier years; it was, however, expected to improve in 1997. Finally, Croatia is another interesting case study as its currency appreciated in nominal terms in 1995 and 1996 as a consequence of large capital inflows. Inflation was very high, and the real exchange was quite volatile between 1992 and October 1993, when a stabilization program was announced; the overall real exchange rate appreciated only by 14 percent between January 1992 and June 1993 but appreciated by another 28 percent between June and

November 1993, when the stabilization program led to a sharp fall of inflation. The real exchange rate then remained stable until the end of 1994 but has been appreciating gradually since then with the nominal appreciation of the Kuna. The trade deficit tripled in 1995 to $2.9 billion (from $0.96 billion in 1994) with import growth vastly above export growth; in 1996 the trade balance worsened further to a $3.3 billion deficit as exports actually declined, while imports rose. The current account turned from a small surplus in 1994 (0.9 percent of GDP) to very large deficit in 1995 and 1996 (–9.5 and –7.3 percent, respectively).

Our overall analysis of exchange-rate movements in the transition economies differs from the views of others on the causes and effects of the real exchange-rate appreciation. The standard or *fundamentals* view attributes the appreciation to a change in the equilibrium real exchange rates (see Halpern and Wyplosz, 1996; EBRD *Transition Report 1996 and Update*). The worsening of current-account balance throughout the region in the 1995 to 1996 period was not due to a loss of competitiveness but rather to booming investment and private consumption that followed the implementation of structural reforms. According to this view, the increase in dollar wages observed in the 1990s (and the real appreciation of the wage-based real exchange rate) was mostly due to two factors: first, a return to equilibrium following the real depreciation and real wage squeeze observed in the early transition period; second, a equilibrium real appreciation and real wage increase due to the labor productivity effects of restructuring, structural reform and capital deepening (see Halpern and Wyplosz, 1996; EBRD *Transition Report 1996 and Update*; IMF *World Economic Outlook*, May 1997). In this view, the real appreciation of the CPI-based real exchange rate was the consequence of two factors: (1) the differential growth rate of productivity in the traded sector relative to nontraded sectors (the Balassa-Samuelson effect) and (2) the increased investment and consumption demand for nontraded goods and factors financed by the reform-induced capital inflows. The policy implication of these arguments was that since the real appreciation was an equilibrium phenomenon, it could not (and should not) be prevented through the choice of the exchange-rate regime, a different monetary policy, or the use of capital controls on inflows.[21]

We instead believe that a significant component of the deterioration of the current-account balances in the 1995 to 1996 period can be associated with a real appreciation of currencies and a loss of competitiveness, especially in the countries with a more pegged exchange-rate regime. While part of the real appreciation observed in the last few years may be related to an appreciation of the equilibrium real exchange rate following the structural reforms in the economy, it also appears that part of the real appreciation signals a misalignment of the currency and a true loss of competitiveness. This is confirmed by the fact that the real appreciation (and current-account worsening) has been more significant in countries that have more closely followed a pegged exchange-rate policy. Moreover, the significant capital inflows of the 1993 to 1995 period are also partly the source of the real appreciation observed in the data. While countries committed to an exchange-rate peg have been generally more successful in reducing their inflation rates to low levels, they have also paid a significant price in terms of real appreciation, loss of competitiveness, and larger current-account imbalances. The analysis also suggests that, since part of the growing current-account imbalances may be associated with this loss of competitiveness, such imbalances may not be sustainable and will require a significant nominal and real depreciation to be reversed.

Moreover, there is other evidence challenging the "fundamentals" interpretation of the real appreciation. First, the increase in dollar wages in the 1990s has not been fully matched by an increase in labor productivity. Table 2.8 shows the growth rate of unit labor costs in manufacturing in U.S. dollars in six of the countries in our sample as well as in Germany, United Kingdom, and the United States. There were some very large increase in unit labor costs especially in the 1993 to 1995 period[22] that are significantly larger than those observed in Germany, United Kingdom, and the United States. In most countries such increases followed the sharp reductions observed in the early stages of transition: this is evidence in favor of the view of a return to equilibrium of real wages after the initial overshooting caused by excessive depreciation. However, even after accounting for the initial reduction in unit labor costs, the cumulative effect has lead to an increase in the unit labor cost-based real exchange rate.

Second, in the poststabilization period (1992 to 1996) there are wide differences in the movements of the real exchange rate (based on unit labor costs) between countries that followed a policy of pegged exchange rates (specifically Czech Republic and Slovak Republic) and that of countries that had a more flexible exchange rate aimed at avoiding sharp deviation from PPP (Hungary, Romania, and Poland) (see Table 2.8). While the (unit labor-cost based) real exchange rate of the Czech Republic and the Slovak Republic appreciated significantly between 1992 and 1996, the real exchange rate of Hungary, Poland, and Romania appreciated by a much more modest amount in the same period.

Third, it is not obvious that the productivity growth in the service sectors has lagged behind the growth of productivity in the traded sector. As suggested by *EBRD Transition Report 1996 Update*, since nontradables were

Table 2.8. Annual percentage change in unit labor costs in dollars

	1990	*1991*	*1992*	*1992*	*1994*	*1995*	*1996*[a]
Bulgaria	–37.8	–35.1	85.4	21.5	–31.4	17.3	–15.2
Czech Republic	–17.3	–14.8	32.8	25.8	13.2	6.9	3.9
Hungary	14.4	29.4	7.6	–9.6	–1	–8.7	–7.8
Poland	–9.8	66.5	–8.7	–8.8	–7.3	15.1	–7.8
Romania	3.5	–18.9	–22.6	13.1	–4.7	5	–6.3
Slovak Republic			13	12.4	5.9	19.3	11
Germany	19	11.6	12.2	–2.1	–4.1	13	5.1
United Kingdom	14.4	6.1	1.8	–14.6	2	6.7	2.2
United States	4.5	2.9	2	1	0.5	2.3	1.2

Source: EBRD *Transition Report Update, April 1997*; U.S. Bureau of Labor Statistics for 1996 US data.
a. 1996 data are for Q1–Q3.

given low priority under central planning, their relative productivity was very low before the transition to a market economy, and they might have been undersupplied. Then an increase in the resources and factors going to the service sector during the transition to a market economy would lead to a fall in the relative price of these goods, not an increase—that is, productivity growth may be very large in the previously very inefficient service sector. Since systematic country data and studies are not available yet regarding the relative growth of productivity in traded and nontraded sectors, we cannot be sure that the real appreciation was in large part due to the Balassa-Samuelson effect.

Our view about the current-account deficits being partly caused by currency misalignments is confirmed by developments in the Czech Republic in 1997. The large, persistent, and growing current-account imbalances caused by the real appreciation led to an attack on the koruna. After losing over $3 billion of foreign reserves in efforts to defend the exchange-rate bank, the central bank was forced on May 27 to let the currency float; the koruna rapidly depreciated by over 10 percent. It is interesting to note that the depreciation has been rather modest given the extent of the real appreciation that occurred under the exchange-rate regime. This suggests that some appreciation of the long-run equilibrium exchange rate had also occurred. Even the Czech prime minister Vaclav Klaus, who had been the strongest defender of view that the country should maintain a fixed exchange rate, admitted in a recent postmortem of the Czech crisis that the prime lesson from the crisis was that a "fixed exchange-rate regime should not last too long" (Klaus, 1997, p. 3).

It is likely that the current-account imbalance of several other countries is also not sustainable and will require a real depreciation. The clearest case is the one of Lithuania, which is already planning to phase out its currency board. While Estonia is more strongly committed to its currency board, the current-account imbalances in that country since 1994 appear to be structural and might eventually require a real depreciation as well. The Slovak koruna came under pressure in the months after the Czech crisis. Such pressure was not simply a contagion effect; the current-account imbalance in the Slovak Republic has been larger (as a share of GDP) than that in the Czech Republic since 1995, and the real appreciation of the currency almost as large as that of the Czech koruna. A real exchange-rate adjustment might be necessary to reduce the external imbalance unless there is a strong reduction in domestic consumption and investment demand.

Our analysis also suggests some skepticism about the adoption of currency-board plans in Bulgaria and perhaps elsewhere. While the loss of fiscal and inflation credibility of Bulgaria in recent years may be a strong argument in favor of the binding constraints of a currency board, there are at least two problems with such a step. First, a real appreciation might occur over time and lead to a destabilizing loss of competitiveness over the medium term. Second, there is a serious question that the exchange-rate parity when Bulgaria adopted the currency board may not be correct. The leva depreciated dramatically in 1996 (by more than 600 percent) to over 1,600 leva per DM. However, there were large inflows of capital after the 1997 election, and the currency appreciated to 1,000 leva per DM, the rate at which the leva entered into a currency board in July 1997. While a rate of 1,600 represented a significant real undervalution of the leva, a rate of 1,000 implied a significant real overvaluation (relative to the 1995 values) given that the past depreciations had fed into the price system in 1997. Entering in a currency board at the wrong parity, as it is likely that Bulgaria did, can have serious competitiveness consequences in the medium run. But it appears that the currency board was introduced at the then existing exchange rate without serious consideration of its relationship to equilibrium and the long-term competitiveness consequences of such a parity.

2.5. Capital Inflows and Financing of the Current Account

While a current-account deficit is financed by capital-account transactions, the magnitude and sources of the capital flows are extremely important in determining sustainability. In this section, we examine the too often sketchy data on capital inflows into the transition economies.

Basic data on the capital account for each of the ten countries studied is found in Table 2.9. The capital-account balance includes errors and omissions under the assumption that this item includes unrecorded capital flows. The overall balance is equal to the sum of the current and capital accounts. The overall balance is also equal to the change in foreign-exchange reserves plus the use of IMF financing and other extraordinary financing.[23] Data on the composition of the capital account are rarely complete or reliable; the only item shown is Foreign Direct Investment. All the data are obtained from various IMF sources.

Although the early 1990s were a period of large capital inflows to many developing economies, the transition economies initially did not benefit significantly from this trend. In 1990 to 1991, there were actually net capital outflows and a net loss of official reserves in the transition economies (see Table 2.4). This poor performance of the capital account was a reflection of the serious domestic and external macroeconomic problems faced by the transition economies. Expectations concerning the success of the transition were not very optimistic, and capital flight ensued. Such capital outflows were particularly large for a subgroup of transition countries including Bulgaria, the Czech Republic, Hungary, Poland, Romania, and the Slovak Republic. For this subgroup, the capital-account deficit (including errors and omissions) was $4.7 billion in 1990 and $ 8.0 billion in 1991, and the loss of foreign reserves amounted to $8.0 billion in 1990 and $10.9 billion in 1991 (see Calvo, Sahay, and Vegh, 1995).

However, in 1992 a number of transition economies (the Czech Republic, Hungary, Poland, the Slovak Republic) started to implement macro stabilization and structural reforms that led to a modest turnaround in the international capital flows. The capital inflows were however quite limited in 1992. In Hungary, Estonia, and Lithuania, the modest increase in foreign reserves was the outcome of current-account surpluses and capital inflows. In countries such as Poland, Romania, and Bulgaria, foreign reserves increased in spite of large current-account and overall balance-of-payments (BP) deficits only because of IMF loans and other "exceptional financing" flows.[24] In other countries such as the Czech Republic, the Slovak Republic, and Ukraine, the overall BP had a deficit leading to further reserves losses.

Thus, the first few years of transition are characterized by a mix of experiences. In some countries there were modest capital inflows, and in others capital outflows continued and official financing played an important role. In some countries, the capital inflows reflected the renewed optimism about the

Table 2.9. Balance-of-payments data (in billions of U.S. dollars)

	1989	*1990*	*1991*	*1992*	*1993*	*1994*	*1995*	*1996*
Bulgaria								
Current account		−0.97	−0.4	−0.8	−1.38	−0.02	−0.04	−0.21
Capital account		−2.53	−1.85	−0.32	−0.24	−0.35		
Balance of payments		−3.5	−2.25	−1.12	−1.62	−0.37		
Change in foreign reserves		−0.88	0.35	0.6	−0.27	0.34		
Foreign reserves, end-of-year stock		0.3	0.63	1.24	0.96	1.31	1.2	0.54
Foreign direct investment			0.06	0.04	0.04	0.1	0.17	0.18
Croatia								
Current account				0.82	0.1	0.1	−1.71	−1.45
Capital account				−0.43	0.08	0.33	1.8	1.79
Balance of payments				0.39	0.18	0.43	0.09	0.34
Change in foreign reserves				0.39	0.45	0.79	0.49	0.42
Foreign reserves, end-of-year stock				0.17	0.62	1.41	2.03	2.44
Foreign direct investment				0.01	0.07	0.1	0.08	0.35
Czech Republic								
Current account				−0.46	0.68	−0.08	−1.37	−4.48
Capital account				−0.05	2.38	3.56	8.82	3.66
Balance of payments				−0.51	3.06	3.48	7.45	−0.82
Change in foreign reserves				−0.51	3.06	2.36	7.45	−1.49
Foreign reserves, end-of-year stock					3.79	6.14	13.84	12.35
Foreign direct investment				0.98	0.56	0.76	2.53	1.39

Table 2.9. (continued)

	1989	1990	1991	1992	1993	1994	1995	1996
Estonia								
Current account				0.04	0.02	−0.16	−0.17	−0.45
Capital account				0.02	0.14	0.18	0.25	0.56
Balance of payments				0.06	0.16	0.02	0.08	0.11
Change in foreign reserves				0.07	0.21	0.02	0.11	
Foreign reserves, end-of-year stock				0.17	0.39	0.44	0.58	0.64
Foreign direct investment				0.08	0.16	0.21	0.2	0.11
Hungary								
Current account		0.38	0.4	0.35	−4.26	−4.05	−2.53	−1.69
Capital account		−0.79	1.39	0.42	6.8	3.58	7.93	0.45
Balance of payments		−0.41	1.79	0.77	2.54	−0.47	5.4	−1.24
Change in foreign reserves		−0.55	2.7	0.76	2.57	−0.64	4.61	
Foreign reserves, end-of-year stock		1.07	3.93	4.42	6.77	6.81	12.05	9.79
Foreign direct investment			1.46	1.48	2.34	1.1	4.48	1.99
Lithuania								
Current account				0.02	−0.09	−0.09	−0.61	−0.72
Capital account				0.01	0.3	0.07	0.48	0.32
Balance of payments				0.03	0.21	−0.02	−0.13	−0.4
Change in foreign reserves				0.03	0.3	0.18	0.23	
Foreign reserves, end-of-year stock				0.05	0.35	0.53	0.76	0.77
Foreign direct investment				0.01	0.03	0.03	0.07	0.15

Poland								
Current account	−1.4	3.07	−2.15	−3.1	−5.79	−2.59	−4.25	
Capital account	−1.9	−8.57	−4.92	−1.23	2.56	2.03	14	
Balance of payments	−3.3	−5.5	−7.07	−4.33	−3.23	−0.56	9.75	
Change in foreign reserves	0.3	2.4	−0.8	0.6	0.1	1.5	8.4	
Foreign reserves, end-of-year stock	2.31	4.49	3.63	4.09	4.09	5.84	14.77	17.84
Foreign direct investment		0.09	0.28	0.67	1.7	1.85	3.62	2.21
Romania								
Current account	2.51	−3.25	−1.01	−1.51	−1.23	−0.45	−1.78	−2.58
Capital account	−0.99	1.76	0.34	1.38	0.8	0.28	1.3	2
Balance of payments	1.52	−1.49	−0.67	−0.13	−0.43	−0.17	−0.48	−0.58
Change in foreign reserves	1.11	−1.49	0.1	0.1	−0.05	0.61	−0.26	
Foreign reserves, end-of-year stock	1.85	0.52	0.69	0.82	0.99	2.08	1.58	2.1
Foreign direct investment			0.04	0.07	0.1	0.35	−0.42	0.26
Slovak Republic								
Current account				0.05	−0.58	0.72	0.39	−2.09
Capital account				−0.09	0.59	0.49	1.4	2.48
Balance of payments				−0.04	0.01	1.21	1.79	0.37
Change in foreign reserves				−0.04	0.1	1.25	1.59	
Foreign reserves, end-of-year stock					0.41	1.69	3.36	3.41
Foreign direct investment				0.05	0.13	0.19	0.17	0.23
Ukraine								
Current account						−1.16	−1.15	
Capital account						−0.04	−0.47	
Balance of payments						−1.2	−1.62	

economic prospects (the Czech Republic, Hungary, the Slovak Republic, Estonia, and Poland). However, in a number of experiences (Poland, Croatia, Romania, Lithuania, and Ukraine) the increase in reserves exceeded the overall BP balance (that was at times in deficit) because of IMF and other "exceptional" official financing.[25] Therefore, in some cases the buildup in reserve was significantly aided by nonprivate forms of capital inflows.

The situation changed dramatically in 1993 to 1995 when most of the countries examined experienced large capital inflows that frequently exceeded their current account deficits. Between 1992 and 1995, official reserves more than doubled in every country except Bulgaria and Romania. More recently, as current-account deficits widened, the increases in reserves diminished and in some cases disappeared.

The composition of the large capital inflows of the 1993 to 1995 period are summarized in Table 2.10.[26] Cumulative flows are shown for the three-year period for several reasons:

- For most countries earlier data are not available.
- The data are so frequently revised that it is difficult to sue annual capital flows to describe how the current account is financed.

Table 2.10. Cumulative flows of capital, 1993 to 1995 (billions of U.S. dollars)

	Foreign Reserves	*Foreign Direct Investment*	*Portfolio Investment*	*Errors and Omissions*	*Other Investment*
Bulgaria		0.32			
Croatia	1.73	0.27		1.44	0.5
Czech Republic	12.87	3.53	3.57	−0.44	8.33
Estonia	1.4	0.56	0.02	−0.01	0.06
Hungary	6.54	7.84	8.6	2.23	−0.47
Poland	10	7.16[a]	1.3	−0.35	11.23
Slovak Republic	3	0.5[b]	0.82[c]	0.78	0.33
Ukraine	1.9	0.56	0.02	0.47	−1.5
Lithuania	1.6	0.14	0.03	0.17	
Romania	0.3	0.87	0	0.06	1.34

Source: IMF *Intemational Financial Statistics, April 1997* and IMF *World Economic Outlook* May 1997.

May 1997 *World Economic Outlook* provides different figures:

a. 2.3.

b. 0.37.

c. 0.18.

- The form of the stock of capital investments is an important determinant of current-account sustainability. The stock is not readily measured, but the cumulated flows provide reasonable measures of, for example, the stock of short-term debt as compared to the stock of foreign direct investment.

The composition of the capital account is important because short-term capital inflows are more easily reversed than long-term flows and equity inflows are more stable than debt-creating inflows. Foreign direct investment (as long as it is sustained) provides the least threat of reversibility. A current-account deficit that is financed by extensive foreign direct investments (FDI) is more sustainable than a deficit financed by short-term portfolio investments ("hot money") that may be easily liquidated if market conditions or sentiment change. Moreover, FDI tends to finance long-term investment projects that increase the capital stock of the country and tend to generate revenues required to repay the foreign debt in the future. Conversely, short-term hot money tends to finance consumption booms.

While FDI capital inflows represent long-term investment, debt-creating inflows may be short-term or medium-on long-term investments. It is hard to measure precisely the short-term component of capital inflows. One capital account item that is likely to be short-term is portfolio investment. Another item may be errors and omissions that often represent unrecorded capital inflows.

If portfolio investments and errors and omissions represent "hot money" or short-term "speculative inflows," these are volatile capital flows in several countries. Portfolio investment inflows have been very large in Hungary ($8.6 billion), the Czech Republic ($3.6 billion), Poland ($1.3 billion), and the Slovak Republic ($0.8 billion). If we consider errors and omissions as unrecorded short-term inflows, we obtain large figures for Hungary ($2.2 billion), Croatia ($1.4 billion), and the Slovak Republic ($0.8 billion). Relative to the increase in foreign reserves over the same period, cumulative portfolio investment inflows plus errors and omissions appear to be large in Hungary, Croatia, and the Slovak Republic.

There is an important caveat to be mentioned before we express additional concern about short-term portfolio flows. Countries with developed capital-market structures that are able to allocate capital efficiently are going to attract more capital. Capital markets increase allocative efficiency and provide liquidity. For both reasons they are an essential element in creating an environment that is favorable to foreign capital. However, capital-market instruments are likely to facilitate short-term portfolio flows that can be destabilizing. Thus, capital-market development is a two-edged sword. On the one hand, it increases capital inflows, and on the other hand, it facilitates potential outflows. The countries with the highest amount of portfolio investment—Hungary and the Czech Republic—also tend to have the largest total capital inflows.

Of course, there are other forms of capital inflow as well in many countries, including those without well-developed financial markets (Romania, Croatia). These other capital inflows will increase the liquidity of the domestic banking system—sometimes in terms of foreign-exchange-denominated liabilities and sometimes in the form of the domestic currency if the central bank buys the foreign exchange to avoid an appreciation of the exchange rate. In either case, the domestic banks can have severe liquidity problems in the event of a capital outflow, particularly if their assets are in domestic currency and illiquid. Thus, the capital inflows can increase the riskiness of the banks. A capital outflow then can have severe macroeconomic consequences if it creates a domestic banking liquidity crisis that the central bank is unable to manage.

A final form of financing that is not listed here is financing from official sources. Of course, financing from the IMF may be less unstable than financing from hot money. However, official financing does not make a current-account deficit more sustainable; rather, large IMF loans are a usually a signal that unsustainable current-account imbalances led to a crisis that resulted in official intervention.

It must also be observed that while in 1990 to 1991, the largest fraction of capital flows to the transition countries came in the form of official flows (grants and bilateral, multilateral, and IMF loans), the share of private flow has become dominant in recent years. For example, in 1991 only 29 percent of the net medium- to long-term financial flows to central and Eastern European countries (including the Baltic ones) were private; this share went up to 92 percent in 1995 (see IMF *World Economic Outlook*, October 1996). The greater reliance on private creditors and lower flows from official creditors signals the increasing creditworthiness of the transition economies who are now able to rely on private international financial channels for their financing needs. Similarly, the improved macroeconomic environments in some of the transition economies has led to the rapid development of capital markets (including equity markets with significant foreign participation) and international bank loans. But increased reliance on private rather than official financing and portfolio investment also means that such flows may dry up and/or reverse if poor domestic and external economic performance leads to increased country riskiness.

The large capital inflows of the 1993 to 1995 period also led to serious problems for monetary policy and exchange-rate management. In fact, capital inflows in excess of the current-account deficit would have led to nominal appreciations of the domestic currency that would worsen the country's competitiveness. Several central banks of the region tried to avoid such appreciation and intervened in the foreign-exchange market by buying foreign currency in large amounts. Therefore, capital inflows in excess of current-account deficits led to increases in foreign official reserves. While the increases in foreign reserves made the current-account imbalances of the period more sustainable, such large capital inflows also exacerbated the real appreciation of the currency observed in many countries. In fact, when such interventions were not sterilized, they led to excessive monetary growth, causing higher inflation that in turn led to further real appreciation of the exchange rate. When they are sterilized, domestic interest rates remained high; therefore, the original cause of nominal exchange-rate appreciation was not eliminated.[27] Therefore, capital inflows continued and prevented larger nominal depreciations that were necessary to restore external competitiveness in face of large and growing current-account imbalances.[28]

Note that similar phenomena occurred in Mexico in the 1991 to 1993 period, in Thailand in the 1990 to 1996, period and in the Czech republic in 1995 to 1995, when large current-account deficits were associated with large increases in foreign-exchange reserves as capital inflows were larger than the current-account deficits. Such inflows maintained the strength of the Mexican peso and the Thai baht in spite of the loss of competitiveness and sharp worsening of the trade balance. In this sense large capital inflows and rising foreign reserves may at times give the wrong signal about the long-run sustainability of a persistent current-account imbalance. While in the short-run they enhance sustainability, they might also prevent the necessary exchange-rate adjustment required to reduce in the medium term the loss of competitiveness caused by a real appreciation. Once investors realize that such imbalance are not sustainable, a sudden reversal of capital flows may lead to a sharp reduction of exchange-rate reserves and eventually cause an exchange-rate crisis as happened in Mexico in December 1994, in the Czech republic in May 1997, and in Thailand in July 1997.

Consistent with the above analysis, it must be observed the year 1996 has signaled a new stage of the capital flows trend to transition economies that can be described as one of "capital inflow fatigue." In fact, in 1996, as current-account deficits increased, we start to observe significantly reduced capital inflows. The inflows are often below current-account financing needs and therefore the stock of foreign reserves has stagnated or even fallen. The fall in reserves has been quite sharp in Hungary, the Czech Republic, and Bulgaria as capital inflows have been sharply below widening current-account imbalances. In other cases, foreign-reserve stocks have substantially stagnated (relative to 1995) as capital inflows have been just enough to finance the larger current-account imbalances; these cases include Estonia, the Slovak Republic, and Lithuania. Further increases in foreign reserves in spite of large current-account imbalances have occurred only in Croatia, Poland, and Romania. In the case of the Ukraine, an increase in reserves occurred, but it was only the consequence of increased IMF support in 1996.

Since current-account imbalances are likely to remain large, this capital inflow fatigue—if continued—may become a matter of concern as it would lead to further losses of foreign reserves. The problem for the transition economies would be exacerbated by a higher interest rates in the developed countries. Sustained growth in the United States and economic recovery in Japan and the European Union could well result in tighter monetary policy. Even if the increase in world interest rates in the late 1990s would not turn out to be large as in 1994, when it severely slowed capital flows to developing countries,[29] higher world interest rates would hurt the transition economies in two ways. First, countries with large amounts of foreign debt would experience an increase in their debt-servicing payment that would directly further worsen their current-account balances. Second, higher world interest rates may further reduce the capital inflows to the transition group and, for given unchanged current-account balances, lead to further losses of foreign-exchange reserves.

2.6. Banking and Financial System Weakness

The health of the financial sector is linked to current-account sustainability because financial-sector crisis will affect a country's ability to finance the current-account deficit. First, a financial crisis will quickly reduce the willingness of foreign investors to hold portfolio or fixed assets in the country or their willingness to extend credit to a country. A weak banking system will lead to capital flight by domestic savers, which increases the difficulty of financing a current-account deficit. Second, banks facilitate international payments and foreign-exchange transactions. A weak banking system that cannot provide such services will inhibit trade. Third, the overall quality of the financial system and the efficiency of financial intermediation are important indicators of political and economic stability, the ability to withstand shocks, and the ability to develop a market economy.[30] Finally, a financial crisis that leads to a decline in output will worsen the current-account balance because the fall in national savings usually exceeds the decline in investment (see Section 2.2).

All of the transition economies have experienced banking-sector crises since the start of the transition process.[31] Typically, the crisis dates to the establishment of the commercial banking system at the start of the transition process. In most transition economies the monobanks were transformed into central banks and several state-owned commercial banks between 1989 and 1992. Banks established from the Soviet era monobank were often poorly capitalized and often lacked the managerial incentives to avoid accumulating large portfolios of nonperforming loans. The banks, either under instructions from the government or by force of habit, provided credit to state-owned enterprises without applying the standards that should be applied to commercial lending.

As a result, the state-owned banks quickly became insolvent in the early part of the transition process. Various methods of recapitalization or restructuring the banks were undertaken, mostly between 1992 and 1994 and frequently more than once. Typically, restructuring involved the provision of government debt to the banks, direct government support, the transfer of bad loans to a separate institution, a so-called hospital bank, a loan workout program, or a combination of approaches. In addition, entry into the banking business was liberalized in the early transition period leading to a large number of private banks with small capitalization, limited banking skills, and, most important, little regulatory oversight. Thus, irregular banking practices and banking-sector crises were a common feature of all the transition economies.

Only in the mid-1990s did major changes in the banking sectors of transition economies become widespread. Privatization efforts started with the Czech voucher scheme in 1992 and picked up steam in Poland from 1993 on and in Hungary from 1994 on. Several approaches to privatization have been employed including voucher privatization, initial public offerings, and participation of a (usually foreign) strategic investor or a combination of several techniques. Privatization began with the Czech voucher privatization programs in 1992 and picked up steam in Poland from 1993 on and in Hungary from 1994 on. Privatization does not guarantee a change in the management and behavior of the banks. In many instances, the state retains a large share of privatized banks and/or mass privatization has enabled existing management structures to become entrenched. By 1997, large parts of the banking system in Hungary and to a somewhat lesser extent in Poland were privately owned. In the other transition economies, privatization of state-owned banks has not yet occurred, although in some instances new private banks have attained significant market shares. Other countries, including the Czech Republic, have made less progress in privatizing ownership or even restructuring financial institutions.

The existence of a current-account deficit can have implications for the stability of the domestic financial system in two ways. First, monetary policy enacted to enable a country to finance a current-account deficit can be destabilizing for the macroeconomy and can lead to a banking-sector crisis. Sharp increases in domestic interest rates, which were introduced to attract and retain capital when capital inflows slow in the face of stubborn and large current-account imbalances, can lead to financial-sector insolvency. Firms are unable to pay high rates and will default on existing bank debt or be given additional credits by the banks. Over time, efforts to finance the current account result in a banking sector with large portfolios of nonperforming loans. The banks may in fact be insolvent if loan portfolios are marked to market. Thus, the efforts to finance the current account can be extremely disruptive to the financial system.

Second, the efforts of the banks to finance their activities can precipitate a foreign-exchange crisis. With a current-account deficit, the domestic banks can borrow abroad to provide financing.[32] Easy access to foreign sources of funds can lead to poor lending and to severe difficulties when the domestic currency depreciates. Furthermore, a foreign-exchange crisis can be the result of poor lending practices by banks that use foreign funding sources.

There are additional relationships between the current-account and banking-sector conditions. For example, countries with relatively sound banking systems and somewhat developed financial and securities markets may well attract portfolio investments. But financial-sector development can be a mixed blessing; if it encourages short-run portfolio investments ("hot money"), the investments can be easily reversed and lead to sustainability problems. The converse to this problem is that a weak banking sector leads to capital flight that can lead to an unsustainable and undesirable current-account surplus.

An examination of the ten transition countries studied here suggests that external-sector developments in the early transition era were not closely related to the banking sector. The relationship between banking-sector crisis and the current account was strongest in the initial stages of transition. The banking-sector crises were an important factor in the collapse in output in the initial stages of transition that often led to deterioration of the current account. However, it would be difficult to demonstrate causality in these experiences. For example, the precarious situation of the banks in Poland and Hungary in 1991 to 1993 and the current-account deficits were both related to the underlying macroeconomic situation rather than one causing the other.

The current-account deficits observed in the later transition years, 1995 to 1997, are severe in countries with widely improved banking systems (such as Poland) as well as those which still have severe banking-sector problems (such as the Slovak Republic and Bulgaria). Nevertheless, there is an important link between the banking sector and the current account. A modern banking sector will enable a country to finance a current-account deficit and withstand a balance-of-payments crisis. That is, a functioning banking sector provides a signal of stability to the international community and will therefore make, *ceteris paribus*, financing a current-account deficit easier than it would be otherwise. There is an additional observation that links banking-sector crises to the balance of payments; banking crises are often a precursor of balance-of-payments crises in developing countries.[33] A banking-sector crisis can lead to a rapid deterioration of confidence in the economy and the ease of financing a current-account deficit can quickly erode.

We can apply these generalities to some of the recent experience in the transition economies. In Hungary (since 1994) and in Poland (since 1993), there is a general perception that the quality of banks loan portfolios has improved. In both countries, the bank privatization process has picked up steam in both a formal and effective sense. State ownership is declining, and, in addition, foreign strategic investors in both countries are making managerial control a condition for their investments. These conditions mitigate against difficulties in sustaining the current-account deficits and stand in stark contrast to the situation in the Czech Republic. Although Czech voucher privatization started in 1992 well before any bank privatization in other Visegrad countries, the banks have not adequately restructured their activities. The Consolidation Bank successfully cleaned up bank portfolios in the early 1990s, but the quality of loan portfolios deteriorated in 1993 to 1995, the banks are undercapitalized, and irregularities in bank management behavior have recently surfaced. As noted by Velimir Đonje, the Czech banks increased their net borrowing from abroad dramatically in this period. He maintains that the increase in borrowing was an indication of bank insolvency and may well have been the distinctive feature of the Czech crisis in 1997. That is, the current-account deficit may have been sustainable except for the banking crisis caused by foreign borrowing. Other countries, including Poland and Slovakia, sustained large current-account deficits because their domestic banking sectors were not overextended.

Banking-sector reform has been slower in the other transition economies in our sample. There are differences in progress toward establishing a modern banking sector among the countries. Slovakia recapitalized the banks in 1992 to 1993, but the state-owned banks continued to accumulate classified assets. In 1995, a broad program for the restructuring of the banks and the reclassification of loans. If successful, the program will be an important step toward establishment of a modern banking environment. The slow development of the financial sector in Slovakia makes it more difficult to finance and sustain a current-account deficit than would be the case in the other Visegrad countries.

Ukraine established its two-tier banking system only in 1991. The formation of a modern banking system is inhibited by the mass privatization of banks in 1993 that entrenched management control and the large number of private wildcat banks that emerged in 1992 to 1994. Uncertainty about the stability of the banking system is a major concern. As in Slovakia, the low level of financial-sector development mitigates against sustainability.

Bulgaria recapitalized its banks several times since 1994 but was never able to stem the tide of bad loans or to attract significant foreign entry into banking. The very bad condition of the banks in 1995 to 1996 was clearly a precursor to the exchange-rate crisis that started in mid-1996. This experience matches the profile found in other developing countries (Mexico and Israel, among others) where banking crises precipitated foreign-exchange crises.

Croatia has recapitalized its banks, and there is an understanding that loan quality is improving. However, it is not clear that the financial sector has developed to the point where institutions and markets will help finance the current-account deficit and efficiently make use of the large capital inflows. This might change in 1997 as foreign bank activity in Croatia is increasing.

The Lithuanian banking system is small and undercapitalized. There was a major banking crisis in 1995 and a restructuring of the banks is underway. The current-account deficit widened considerably in 1995 and 1996 as a result of a sharp fall in savings rates (see Section 2.4). It would surely not be unfair to relate this to the collapse of the banking sector. If the current-account deficit turns out in 1997 or 1998 to be unsustainable, this would fit the pattern suggested by Kaminsky and Reinhart (1996) very closely.

The banking system in Estonia has been largely privatized although steps toward modernization have been slow and there have been several banking problems. Capital markets are relatively undeveloped in the Baltics; the countries may be too small to develop much market depth. The currency-board exchange-rate regime makes the state of the banking system less of an issue in Estonia. However, banking-sector problems (as in Lithuania) could easily create a current-account deficit that threatens the ability to maintain the exchange-rate peg.

Banking-sector reform—improved supervision, reduced bad loan portfolios, and privatization—did not start in Romania until 1995. Since these efforts were undertaken without any widespread banking crisis, they may make it easier for Romania to sustain its current-account deficit. Improvements in financial-sector efficiency and the continued absence of financial crisis are likely to be of great benefit.

For the most part, the trends in current-account balances in the transition economies in the last ten years are more closely related to macroeconomic fundamentals than to the incidence of banking crises. Nevertheless, the well being of the banking and financial sector will be of increasing importance to the transition economies in the future as it is in other developing economies. Banking crises are a strong indication of the severity of the fundamental problems and also a cause of loss of international confidence in the economy. In the face of that combination of problems it may be very difficult to avoid an external crisis in the future when there is a banking-sector crisis.

2.7 Additional Indicators of Current-Account Sustainability

We finally consider a number of other financial criteria or indicators of sustainability, including foreign reserves, openness, foreign debt burden, country risk, and the composition of capital inflows and political instability.[34] An exhaustive survey of literature that relates a wide variety of indicators to exchange-rate crises is found in Kaminsky, Lizondo, and Reinhart (1997).

2.7.1. Foreign-Exchange Reserves

A traditional measure of the adequacy of foreign-exchange reserves is the stock of reserves in months of imports (of goods and services). Table 2.11 reports data for 1994 and 1995 from the IMF *World Economic Outlook*, May 1997. In 1995, only four countries had foreign reserves in excess of four months of imports; these were the Czech Republic, Hungary, Poland, and the Slovak Republic. Other countries had relatively few reserves (two months or less of imports): Croatia, Estonia, Romania, and Ukraine. Full data are not available for 1996, but the share of reserves to imports appears to have fallen in all countries but Poland and the Ukraine. In several countries (Czech Republic, Hungary, and Bulgaria) the fall in the ratio in 1996 has been driven by an absolute fall in the stock of reserves on top of sharp increases in imports.

The ratio of money assets to foreign reserves is an additional indicator

Table 2.11. Adequacy of foreign-exchange reserves and oppenness

	Stock of Foreign Reserves (in months of imports)		*Ratio of Money to Foreign Reserves*		*Openness, 1996*
	1994	*1995*	*M0/FX*	*M2/FX*	*(X + M)/GDP*
Bulgaria	2	3	NA	NA	32
Croatia	2	2	0.65	2.70	49
Czech Republic	4	7	1.10	3.38	60
Estonia	3	2	0.78	1.79	80
Hungary	7	9	1.03	1.84	33
Lithuania	5	3	0.81	1.81	30
Poland	3	6	0.81	3.18	26
Romania	2	2	1.06	1.27	30
Slovak Republic	2	4	0.76	3.76	63
Ukraine	1	1	1.44	2.70	44

Source: IMF *International Financial Statistics*; IMF *World Economic Outlook* (May 1996, May 1997).

of reserves adequacy because, in the event of an exchange-rate crisis or panic, liquid money assets can be converted into foreign exchange. Calvo (1995) suggests the use of the ratio of a broad measure of liquid monetary assets to foreign reserves and Sachs, Tornell, and Velasco (1996) use the ratio of M2 to foreign reserves.[35] An alternative view suggests looking at the ratio of the monetary base (M0) to foreign reserves; Table 2.11 shows both measures. At the end 1996, the M2 to reserve ratio was above 3 in the Czech Republic, Poland, the Slovak Republic, and Bulgaria. The ratio was also relatively high (between 2 and 3) in Croatia and Hungary and relatively lower (less than 2) in Estonia, Lithuania, Hungary, and Romania. The ratio of M0 to gross foreign reserves was slightly above unity in Bulgaria, Czech Republic, Hungary, Romania, and Ukraine and below unity in the other countries. In general reserves do not look small if compared to monetary base but may not be as adequate relative to total liquid assets in the Czech Republic, Poland, Slovak Republic, and Bulgaria. Note in this regard that Brazil and Argentina, the two countries that were most affected by the Mexican peso "tequila effect," had a ratio of M2 to reserves of 3.6 in November 1994.

2.7.2. Openness

An economy more open to trade may be less fragile to external imbalances than a more closed economy because a country's ability to service its external debt in the future depends on its ability to generate foreign-currency receipts. The size of exports (relative to GDP) is another important indicator of sustainability. Table 2.11 presents a measure of the openness of the countries under study. Openness is measured by the ratio of the average of exports and imports to GDP. There is a wide dispersion in the openness measure; the more open countries are Estonia (80 percent), the Czech Republic (60 percent), and the Slovak Republic (63 percent). The more closed economies are Bulgaria (32 percent), Hungary (33 percent), Lithuania (30 percent), Poland (26 percent), and Romania (30 percent).

2.7.3. Foreign Debt

Additional indicators of sustainability are the foreign debt to exports ratio and the debt service to exports ratio. According to the World Bank classification, a country is heavily indebted when the debt to export ratio is above 220 percent and moderately indebted when the ratio is above 132 percent. At Table 2.12 shows, in 1991 Bulgaria, Hungary, and Poland were severely indebted. However, between 1991 and 1996, the debt-to-exports

Table 2.12 Foreign-debt and debt-service ratios (in percent)

	Debt to Exports			Debt Service to Exports	
	1991	1994	1996	1994	1995
Bulgaria	387	208	160	8	11
Croatia	34	53	70	11	8
Czech Republic	71	65	60	14	10
Estonia	0	6	11		
Hungary	219	320	201	53	52
Lithuania	2	20	32	2	3
Poland	308	184	112	12	5
Romania	51	77	98	7	6
Slovak Republic	81	44	49	9	14
Ukraine	0	49	43	7	9

Source: IMF *World Econimic Outlook*, May 1997.

ratio has significantly fallen in all these highly indebted countries. In 1996, the ratio was above 100 percent only in Bulgaria, Hungary, and Poland. The high debt to exports ratios in 1991 were the result of large current-account deficits in the 1980s that lead to a surge of the foreign debt of several countries. The observed reduction in the ratio of the highly indebted group in the 1990s was mostly the result of a process of debt restructuring and debt rescheduling conducted in the framework of the Paris Club and London Club negotiations.

Note also that, while debt-to-export ratios remain low in the remaining countries, they have significantly increased between 1991 and 1996 in several countries—namely, Croatia, Lithuania, Romania, and Ukraine. Debt service to exports ratios (also in Table 2.12) tend to be relatively low (usually below 10 percent), with two exceptions. The ratio is 52 percent in Hungary, which has not rescheduled its foreign debt and has a relatively high share of shorter-term foreign liabilities. Bulgaria faced a liquidity crisis in early 1997 as debt-service payments for 1997 were expected to be very large (close to 20 percent of its exports and above 200 percent of its 1996 stock of foreign-exchange reserves).

2.7.4. Country Risk

We considered next two measures of country risk. The first is the country-risk ranking published by *Euromoney* magazine. The second is an average measure of sovereign ratings from rating agencies. Table 2.13 presents the *Euromoney* country-risk rankings. Such rankings significantly improved for all of our transition economies between 1993 and 1996, even if the 1996 rankings remain very low for a few countries (Ukraine and Bulgaria, in particular). The rankings published in March 1997 show some significant slippage in several economies between 1996 and 1997. This is particularly the case for Bulgaria and Romania, which suffered a major economic crisis and surge in inflation in 1996. Rankings have also worsened in the Czech Republic, Hungary, Lithuania, Poland, the Slovak Republic, and Ukraine.[36]

The second measure represents the average measure of sovereign ratings from Moody's, Standard & Poor's, and IBCA (with 10 representing the highest rating). According to this measure, the Czech Republic has the highest rating (among this group of transition economies). Croatia, Hungary, Poland, and the Slovak Republic have also relatively high rankings. Bulgaria and Romania are at the bottom with very weak credit ratings. Historical time series are not widely available, but evidence suggests that the credit rating of successful transition economies has significantly

Table 2.13. Country-risk indicators

	Euromoney 1993	*Country-Risk 1996*	*Rankings 1997*	*1997 Credit Ratings (Max:10)*
Bulgaria		92	111	0.63
Croatia		74	61	4.38
Czech Republic	43	35	37	6.25
Estonia	122	71	69	
Hungary	46	44	46	4.38
Lithuania	130	59	72	3.44
Poland	72	55	62	4.58
Romania	75	61	75	2.5
Slovak Republic	63	49	53	4.38
Ukraine		135	136	

Source: *Euromoney*.

improved in recent years. Croatia, the Czech Republic, Hungary, Poland, and the Slovak Republic have now investment-grade ratings while Bulgaria, Lithuania, and Romania still receive subinvestment grades from the rating agencies (Standard & Poor's and Moody's).

2.7.5. Foreign Direct Investment

Of all the different forms of capital inflow, foreign direct investment (FDI) is the most stable and the least likely to be reversed (see Section 2.5). Thus, the extent to which FDI as opposed to short-term capital inflows ("hot money") or even long-term portfolio investments finance the current-account deficit is an indicator of sustainability. In addition, FDI is almost always linked to the expansion of the capital stock while other capital inflows may be financing consumption.

In Table 2.14 we compute two measures: the absolute cumulative amount of net FDI inflows in our sample countries in the 1992 to 1996 period and the fraction of cumulative current-account deficits in 1992 to 1996 that have been financed by FDI. While net FDI inflows were very small in the early stage of transition (1990 to 1992), they have significantly increase in 1993 to 1996.[37] FDI inflows have been mostly concentrated in a small group of countries (Hungary with net cumulative inflows of $11.4 billion in 1992 to 1996, Poland with $10.1 billion, and the Czech Republic with $6.2 billion). These three countries account for 84 percent of the total FDI inflows for

Table 2.14. Cumulative foreign direct investment, 1992 to 1996

	In billions of U.S. dollars	*Ratio to Current Account in Percent*
Bulgaria	0.53	22
Croatia	0.61	29
Czech Republic	6.22	109
Estonia	0.76	106
Hungary	11.39	94
Lithuania	0.29	19
Poland	10.05	42
Romania	1.18	16
Slovak Republic	0.77	51
Ukraine	1.22	18

Source: IMF *International Financial Statistics* and Table 2.9.

our sample in the 1992 to 1996 period. A large fraction of the 1992 to 1996 current-account deficits in these countries has been financed by long-term FDI capital inflows (109 percent in the Czech Republic, 94 percent in Hungary, and 42 percent in Poland). In other countries, absolute FDI flows are still small, but they represent a large fraction of the financing of the current-account deficit; particularly in Estonia and the Slovak Republic, 106 and 51 percent, respectively, of the current-account deficit has been financed by FDI. FDI inflows have accounted for a much smaller share of the financing of the current account in Bulgaria, Croatia, Lithuania, Romania, and Ukraine.

2.7.6. Political Instability

Many of the countries in our sample are experiencing difficult political environments and varying degrees of political instability caused by a combination of domestic and external political problems.

The economic and currency crisis in the Czech Republic in May 1997 was associated with a political crisis that threatened the survival of the strongly market-oriented coalition. The neighboring Slovak Republic also suffered from serious domestic and external political problems. An early NATO and EU membership may be unlikely given the recent criticism of the authoritarian trends in the government and lack of democratic reforms; in addition, there were severe tensions between the president and the opposition.

In Bulgaria and Romania, the economic crisis of 1996 led to the election (in November 1996 and April 1997, respectively) of new governments formally committed to strong market reforms. Such commitment will however be tested; for example, members of the 1997 Bulgarian coalition were already in power in the early 1990s, and their macroeconomic performance then was quite disappointing. Croatia has a stable government, but authoritarian trends in its domestic politics have been subject to external (U.S.) criticism and may jeopardize needed lending from international financial institutions (IMF and World Bank). Future developments of the Bosnian conflict may also negatively affect the country risk. Parliamentary elections in Poland in 1997 resulted in a delicately balanced coalition government where the economic ministries remain in the hands of the reform-oriented.

Estonian and Lithuanian country risk may suffer from the Russian opposition to these countries' stated goal to join NATO. Similar issues will affect Ukraine whose political developments will also be affected by the its macroeconomic developments (as GDP has not yet returned to positive growth after six years of contraction), the pace of economic reform, and its foreign-policy developments. The socialist-led government in Hungary appears to be stable and committed to continued market reforms, even if at a slower pace; early membership of NATO and the EU (among other transition countries) may enhance the political stability of the country.

2.8. Conclusion

The current-account imbalances in the transition economies are not an easy subject to investigate for several reasons. To begin, the data are often inadequate because many of the countries are just beginning to collect data consistent with international standards. Some countries have only begun to build national income accounts that can show savings and investment balances reliably. In addition, data on capital flows, which are often notoriously inaccurate, are also less reliable with transition economies without systems of financial recording. Also, judgments about the current account often require an understanding of real exchange rates, which are particularly hard to define in transition economies. Finally, the available data are hard to interpret because the macroeconomic situations in these countries are evolving very rapidly.

Although difficult, assessing the current-account imbalances in transition economies is of great importance. Recent events in the Czech Republic and elsewhere underscore the importance of these issues. The distinction between structural adjustments and exchange-rate misalignment must be continuously monitored as the economies develop. Improved income-account data, more detailed information on the composition of capital flows, and better measurement of real exchange rates require additional research that would be well worth the effort.

Appendix. The Current Account in Ten Transition Economies

In this appendix we analyze in more detail the experience of each individual country, study the causes of the worsening of their current account, and analyze the evolution of their current account in terms of the savings-investment imbalance. The underlying data for the analysis are presented in Tables 2.5 and 2.6 and additional information from country sources (Economist Intelligence Unit reports, IMF country studies, OECD country surveys).

Hungary

The transition to a market economy in Hungary was been characterized by very large current-account deficits, both in absolute number and as a share of GDP. We computed two series for the current-account balance, one based on national income accounts (NIA) and the other based on balance-of-payments (BOP) data. While the year-by-year numbers do not match, over time both series give the same picture. Between 1990 and 1992, Hungary had a small current-account surplus (according to the BOP data) or a small current-account deficit (according to NIA): the surplus was 0.7 percent of GDP on average in 1990 to 1992 or a 0.4 percent deficit in 1990 to 1992. The current-account imbalance significantly deteriorated in 1993 to 1995: in 1993 the deficit rose to 9.0 percent (9.4 percent according to NIA), worsened to 9.5 percent in 1994 (7.8 percent according to NIA), and improved to 5.6 percent in 1995 (6 percent according to NIA). Preliminary estimates for 1996 suggest that the deficit has fallen to about 4.0 percent of GDP, and forecasts for 1997 predict no improvement.

What were the causes of the serious deterioration in the current account in the 1993 to 1995 period relative to 1990 to 1992? In 1990 to 1992 the fall in output associated with the transition to a market economy led to a sharp fall in national savings, from 27.3 percent in 1990 to 15.3 percent in 1992. This fall in savings was driven by a fall in private savings (from 22.2 percent to 14.8 percent) and a fall in public savings (from 5.1 percent to 0.5 percent). This major drop in national savings did not affect very much the current account because there was a matching fall in national investment rates from 25.4 to 16.1 percent. With the resumption of output growth in 1993, investment rates started to increase from 16.1 percent in 1992 to 22.2 percent in 1994; savings rates instead dropped further in 1993 (to 10.6 percent) and started to increase only in 1994 (to 14.4 percent). The serious worsening of the current account in 1993 to 1994 was therefore a combination of a major investment boom and moderate fall in national saving rates.

Monetary and fiscal authorities took a series of policy actions starting in mid-1994 designed to bring down the current account deficit. These actions were not always successful until the austerity program was introduced in 1995.[38] The improvement in the current account in 1995 and 1996 (to 6 percent and down to 4 percent) was mostly driven by an improvement in the savings rate that rose three percentage points to 18.0 percent while the investment rate remained stable at 22.0 percent. While it is predicted that there is not going to be any further improvement in the current account in 1997, it is likely that the external balance will not worsen. The large deficits of the 1993 to 1994 period seem more the results of an investment boom led by the return to growth that was not accompanied right away by an increase in national savings. The significant increase in the savings rate since 1994 in face of a stable investment rate suggests that the current-account imbalance may be sustainable. In addition, the effects of the austerity program are still being felt, and there may be an expectation that policymakers will act decisively again (although the Finance Minister responsible for the measures, L. Bokros, is no longer in office). Also important to this conclusion is that the government deficit does not widen; sustainability probably requires that it continue to diminish.

The Czech Republic

The current-account developments in the Czech Republic are partly similar to those in Hungary. In the early years of the transition (1990 to 1993) we observe alternating current-account deficits and surpluses. The turn to negative growth in 1990 was first associated with a current-account worsening. As in Hungary, the negative growth rate of output in the 1991 to 1993 led both to a major fall in the investment rate (from 29.9 percent in 1991 to 18 percent in 1993) and a comparable fall in the savings rate that was equal to 20.1 percent in 1993. Since the fall in investment was larger than that of savings, the Czech Republic had actually a current-account surplus of 2.1 percent of GDP in 1993. The resumption of GDP growth in 1994 after four years of negative growth led to rapid recovery of investment and savings rates. The increase in the investment rate was much larger (from 18 percent in 1993 to 28.8 percent in 1995) than the rise in the savings rate (from 20.1 percent in 1993 to 25.8 percent in 1995); therefore, the current account turned from a 2.1 percent surplus in 1993 to a 3 percent deficit in 1995. In 1996, there was a further significant worsening in the current-account balance as the deficit rose to 7.9 percent of GDP. Such a significant worsening is almost completely explained by an increase in the investment rate that rose by 4 percent of GDP to a level of 33 percent; savings rates, instead, declined a little in 1996 at 25.1 percent of GDP. For 1997, it appears that the current-account deficit worsened and was predicted to approach 10 percent of GDP.

The large current-account imbalance was already a matter of concern in 1997; the Czech crown had been under a pressure, and in late May the central bank abandoned its exchange-rate peg. This has occurred even though the imbalance was driven by a sharp increase in investment rates in the space of two years that vastly outstripped the increase in savings rates. Although the overall development of savings and investment in Hungary and the Czech Republic are similar, the Czech imbalance has proven to be less sustainable. Four reasons for this can be cited:

- The projected imbalance is very large.
- The imbalance is driven by an investment boom that is probably not sustainable without generating inflationary pressures. Unemployment in the Czech Republic is lower than it is in any other transition economy, while the 1994 to 1995 austerity program led to a slowdown in Hungary.
- Significant increases in the saving rate are unlikely because (1) the government fiscal position is in balance (while in Hungary the government fiscal balance has been improving) and (2) increasing real income has generated a consumption boom.
- The economic and exchange rate crisis during 1997 is forecasted to bring a virtual halt to real growth. The fall in growth and the fiscal austerity package in 1997 should reduce the current account balance from the unsustainable levels of 1995 to 1996.

Estonia

The current-account developments in Estonia is another example of a current-account surplus in the early stage of the transition that turns into a very large current-account deficit as the transition leads to a resumption of growth. However, differently from Hungary and the Czech Republic, the imbalance in Estonia appears to be driven mostly by a fall in savings rates rather than an increase in investment rates. In 1992 and 1993, the current account was in a shrinking surplus (3.4 and 1.4 percent of GDP, respectively) as falling savings rates (falling from 30.1 percent in 1992 to 27.9 percent of GDP in 1993) remained above stable investment rates (equal to 26.7 and 26.5 percent of GDP in those two years). The situation changed radically in 1994 when the growth rate of GDP became positive (+6 percent) for the first time in four years and reversed the negative growth of –7.0 percent of 1993.[39] At the same time the inflation rate that had dramatically fallen in 1993 to 36 percent from the 954 percent of 1992 stabilized at the 42 percent level in 1994; the move to a currency board in 1992 was an important element of the Estonian disinflation process. The resumption of growth led only to a very modest increase in the investment rate: the rate rose to 28.9 percent in 1994 but then fell back to a level of 26.2 percent in the 1995 to 1996 period, slightly below the 1992 to 1993 level. Conversely, the savings rate has been continuously falling since 1993: it first dropped sharply in 1994 to 21.5 percent from the 27.9 percent of 1993; it fell further in the next two years and reached a low of 19.3 percent in 1996. Consequently, the current account turned from a surplus of 1.4 percent of GDP in 1993 to a deficit of 7.4 percent in 1994. Such a deficit dropped only marginally in the next two years and remained at the very high 6.8 percent of GDP in 1996. These developments clearly show that, unlike Hungary and the Czech Republic, the worsening of the current account in Estonia has been mostly driven by a sharp fall in national savings rates as the investment rate has remained stable during the last five years.

Furthermore, the trade balance was expected to widen substantially in dollar terms in 1997 as imports increased rapidly due to a currency overvaluation. Forecasts for the current-account balance for 1997 placed it at 13.7 percent of GDP. This is clearly unsustainable and brings into question the continued viability of the currency-board arrangement.

Romania

The current-account developments in Romania differ somewhat from those in other transition countries. Until 1989, Romania was running a substantial current-account surplus (of about 3.3 percent of GDP in 1989). The transition to a market economy in 1990 was associated with a rapid deterioration of the current account: exports collapsed that year (down by 45 percent that year), while imports surged. The current account turned into a deficit of 8.5 percent of GDP in 1990 and very large in the following two years (5.7 percent in 1991 and 8.3 percent in 1992). The data suggests that a very sharp drop in the national savings rate caused the dramatic deterioration of the current account (from 30.0 percent in 1989 to 22.9 percent in 1992). Measured investment rates actually show an increase; the investment to GDP ratio increased from 26.7 percent to 31.2 percent between 1989 and 1992. This increase is surprising given the sharp drop in economic activity in the 1990 to 1992 period. However, disaggregation of the data shows that a large fraction of the measured increase in the investment rate was due to the sharp accumulation of inventories during the 1990 to 1992 period of output contraction.

Romania's experience is also different from the previous countries because the resumption of positive GDP growth in 1993 was associated with an improvement in the current-account imbalance rather than a worsening. While current-account deficits have remained large (averaging 3.8 percent of GDP) in the 1993 to 1996 period, they are significantly lower than the average 7.5 percent in the 1990 to 1992 period. The data suggest that most of the improvement in the current-account balance in the 1993 to 1996 period is due to an increase in the national savings rate. While private savings as a share of GDP have remained stable since 1992, there has been a marked improvement in public savings. The rapid depreciation of the currency in 1996 was associated with a significant increase in the inflation rate and a serious economic and political crisis. A government committed to more radical market reforms was elected after the November 1996 elections.

Ukraine

Ukraine differs from the previous transition economies in an important characteristic. While in most transition economies, the early drop in GDP associated with the transition has by now turned into positive rates of growth of GDP, in Ukraine the turnaround in GDP growth has not occurred yet as measured GDP was still falling in 1996. It is true that since 1995 the sharp contraction in output observed in the 1991 to 1994 period (on average −16 percent per year) has somewhat slowed; however, the measured growth rate of GDP was still negative in 1995 and 1996 (averaging −4.0 percent per year).

For what concerns the current account, we observe a structural deficit that has actually worsened over the years. In 1992 and 1993, the current account deficit was 3.1 and 2.5 percent of GDP, respectively. However, the imbalance deteriorated significantly in 1994 (to 5.7 percent of GDP) and has remained at those high levels in 1995 and 1996 (4.7 and 5.0 percent, respectively). Data on savings and investment rates in Ukraine are not very good or reliable. However, a first analysis suggests that both investment and savings rates have been falling in the 1994 to 1996 period; the deterioration of the current account in that period derives from a fall of savings at a faster rate than the fall in investment.

Croatia

The current account of Croatia in the early 1990s has been characterized by high volatility and large swings in sign, which is not surprising given the sharp political and military conflict in the ex-Yugoslav Republic region and the ensuing economic instability and large declines in GDP. From 1990 to 1992 the current-account balance went from a large surplus to a large deficit and back again. The current-account surplus shrank significantly in 1993 and 1994 showing a modest surplus. The return to positive growth since 1994 is associated with an increase in the investment rate (that had been sharply falling in 1991 to 1993). The 1995 to 1996 period represents a new phase in the external balance of Croatia. In 1995, a surge of imports led to a major worsening of the current account that showed a deficit of 9.5 percent of GDP for the year. In 1996, the external imbalance was only slightly smaller, 7.3 percent of GDP (based on National Bank of Croatia data). Forecasts for 1997 indicate that the imbalance will be smaller, but deficits in the 5 to 6 percent of GDP range are expected to persist for the next few years.

These large imbalances for 1995 to 1997 appear to be structural rather than temporary. However, national income accounts for the period are not available yet, so that it is hard to assess how much of the worsening has been due to a change to investment rather than a change in savings.

Poland

Analyzing the current-account developments in Poland is difficult because of the existence of a large number of unrecorded export and imports.[40] While the official statistics show large and growing current-account deficits, the OECD estimates unrecorded net exports at $4 billion to $5 billion in 1995. Although such estimates are imprecise, it appears that the hidden exports throughout the transition era have been large enough to make the measured trade balances surpluses rather than deficits.

Using the official data, Poland started the decade with a 5.5 percent current-account surplus in 1990. The subsequent sharp drop in economic activity led to large fall in investment and savings rates with the fall in the savings rate much wider than that of investment, the current account turned into a deficit in 1991 (2.7 percent of GDP). Such official current-account deficit persisted in the following years worsening in 1993 and 1995 (–5.1 and –3.0 percent of GDP) and improving in 1992 and 1994 (–2.4 and –2.0 percent of GDP). After 1992, both investment and savings rate recovered relative to their sharp drop in 1991 to 1992; they both went up by about five percentage points of GDP between their low in 1992 and 1995.

As suggested above, the official statistics should be taken with caution, as there is a large amount of unrecorded net exports, especially after 1994. For 1995, such unrecorded exports have been estimated to be in the $3 billion to $5 billion range (the outcome of about $4 billion to $6 billion of unrecorded export and about $1 billion of unrecorded imports). Since the official current account deficit for 1995 was $4.2 billion, the corrected number suggest that the true current account balance for Poland in 1995 was either a $1 billion surplus or a $1 billion deficit. While the current account in 1995 might have been much better than official estimates, early results for 1996 suggest a significant worsening. The official numbers for 1996 show a $8 billion deficit (or about 7 percent of GDP). Even considering the fact that there are large net unreported exports, the 1996 current account would be in deficit ranging between $4 billion (or 3.5 percent of GDP) and $2 billion (or 1.8 percent of GDP). Moreover, early forecasts suggest that the official current account imbalance will be as large in 1997 as it was in 1996.

This implies that, while until 1995 Poland was running a "corrected" current-account surplus, since 1996 we observe "corrected" deficits. The national income account suggests that two forces have driven this significant worsening in the current account since between 1995 and 1996 to 1997: an increase in the investment rate in 1996 to 1997 and a fall in the national savings rates. Thus, the situation in Poland bears comparison to that in the Czech Republic. The investment boom in Poland has not been as pronounced as in the Czech Republic, and there is still slack in the economy. The fiscal balance in Poland improved dramatically after 1992. While the (corrected) current-account imbalance in Poland is not as large as in some other advanced transition economies, its rapid deterioration over the last years and the overall low level of national savings may become a matter of concern in the future.

Lithuania

Current-account developments in Lithuania in the early 1990s were significantly affected by the very sharp reductions in output in the 1990 to 1993 period that reached a peak of –38 percent in 1992. While Lithuania has started the decade with a large current-account deficit (–6.1 percent in 1990), the very sharp reduction in the investment rate between 1990 and 1992 (from 33.6 to 11.9 percent) was much larger than the reductions in savings rates (from 27.5 to 23.9 percent). Therefore, in 1991 and 1992 the current account turned into a very large surplus (+10.2 percent in 1991 and +12 percent in 1992). The sharp recovery of investment in 1993 (to 22.7 percent of GDP) together with a reduction in the savings rate turned the large current-account surplus of 1992 into a large deficit in 1993 (–4.0 percent of GDP). In April 1994, Lithuania moved a currency board that fixed the value of its currency against the U.S. dollar; in the same year output growth become positive for the first time in the 1990s. The current-account deficit improved marginally in 1994 to 3.0 percent of GDP. The real appreciation of the currency following the move to a currency board led to a significant deterioration of the current account in 1995 to 1996: the deficit widened to 7.5 percent of GDP in 1995 and over 10 percent of GDP in 1996. Equally large current-account imbalances are expected to persist in 1997 to 1998. It appears that both investment and savings rates sharply dropped in the 1991 to 1994 period; instead, in the 1995 to 1996 period of growth recovery, the investment rate stabilized around 19 percent of GDP while savings rates kept on falling; hence, the emergence of very large current-account deficits in those years.

There are several other concerns that bring into question the sustainability of the current-account deficit. First, the real appreciation caused by the move to a currency board has hurt the competitiveness of the domestic exports. Second, government deficits are still large. Third, it is unclear whether the 1996 restructuring of the banking system following a crisis in 1995 will succeed in stabilizing the financial system.

Bulgaria

Bulgaria's external balance developments are important for two reasons. First, the country had very large swings in its external balance in the 1990s. Second, while the size of the current-account imbalance in 1996 and 1997 is modest as a share of GDP, Bulgaria was in the midst of a very serious economic and financial crisis that threatened the external solvency of the country in early 1997. With GDP collapsing in 1996, the risk of a hyperinflation looming over the country and the gross foreign reserves of the country below $500 million at the end of 1996, the country risked a foreign-debt crisis at the beginning of 1997. In fact, the foreign debt of the country was above $10 billion, and debt-service payments totaled over $1.3 billion for 1997.

Bulgaria ran very large current-account deficits in the 1986 to 1990 period, and its external debt rose from $2.3 billion at the end of 1984 to $11 billion at the end of 1990. The current-account deficit in 1990 was about $860 million or about 11 percent of GDP. In that year, Bulgaria was faced with serious debt-servicing problems and suspended repayments of principal and interest on its hard-currency debt. The current account improved to a small surplus of $33 million (or 0.5 percent of GDP) in 1991, the year when output fell by 15 percent. The adjustment of the current account in 1991 was driven by the sharp fall in the investment rate (from 28.2 percent in 1990 to 24.2 percent in 1991). The current account worsened in 1992 and sharply deteriorated in 1993 reaching a deficit of $1.09 billion in 1993 (or 10 percent of GDP). A strong depreciation of the leva in 1994 (that had been excessively overvalued in real terms in 1991 to 1993) led to the restoration of a current-account balance in 1994 ($16.9 million or 0.1 percent of GDP) and the return to positive GDP growth for the first time since 1990. Between 1990 and 1994, both investment and savings rate fell as a share of GDP with the drop in the investment rate being much larger than that of the savings rate: therefore, between 1990 and 1994 the share of total consumption in GDP has grown significantly, while the share of capital formation sharply dropped. The current account remained near balance in 1995 while it worsened to a $214 million deficit in 1996. While the size of the current-account imbalance in 1996 is not very large (about 2 percent of GDP), the collapse of GDP growth in 1996 (–11 percent after two years of positive growth), the resurgence of very high inflation and the collapse of the currency in 1996 led to a serious economic and financial crisis.

In mid-1997 a new government that is more committed to structural reform took office and, among other things, introduced a currency-board arrangement and secured a financial-support program by the IMF in exchange for a serious fiscal stabilization program. The results of these policies will not be evident until 1998 and beyond.

Slovak Republic

The Czechoslovak federation split into two independent nations at the end of 1992. The newly formed Slovak Republic had a loss of a third of its trade with the Czech Republic after the split in 1993 and suffered from low demand in Europe caused by recessionary conditions. Therefore, the current account that had been in near balance in 1992 turned into a large deficit in 1993 ($580 million or 5.4 percent of GDP). In 1994, the recovery of output in Europe led to a strong revival of Slovak exports, positive GDP growth for the first time since 1990 and a strong improvement of Slovak current account that showed a $719 million surplus (or +5.7 percent of GDP). The turnaround in the current-account balance between 1993 and 1994 was the combined result of an increase in the national savings rate and a fall in the investment rate. The current-account surplus shrank in 1995 to $390 million (or +2.7 percent of GDP) and has turned into a very large deficit in 1996 estimated to be equal to $1.3 billion (or about 10.0 percent of GDP). For 1997, the current account is expected to remain as large as in 1996, both in dollar terms and as a share of GDP. The available income-account data suggest that the very large current-account deficits emerged from a sharp falloff of national savings. Although the government steadily reduced the size of the government deficit after 1993, it worsened in 1996 and 1997. Another factor relevant to current account sustainability is the stability of the financial sector. The Slovak banking sector is still largely state-owned and severely undercapitalized.

Notes

1. There are a number of recent taxonomies of balance-of-payments crises that provide additional discussions of many of the points in this section and systematic analyses of other experiences. See Milesi-Ferretti and Razin (1996a, 1996b, 1996c), Dornbusch, Goldfajn, and Valdes (1995) and Sachs, Tornell, and Velasco (1996). For a recent systematic analysis of the ERM crisis, see Buiter, Corsetti, and Pesenti (1997).

2. This criteria is related to the "resource balance gap." In a country where the debt to GDP ratio is growing, the gap is the difference between the current trade balance and the trade surplus required to stabilize the debt to GDP ratio. Such a required trade surplus will be larger the bigger are the debt to GDP ratio and the differential between the real interest rate and the growth rate of the economy.

3. Note that one does not have to be non-Ricardian to believe that budget deficits cause current-account deficit. In fact, even in a Ricardian world, a transitory increase in government spending will lead to a budget deficit and a current-account deficit as well. Moreover, if the government follows a tax-smoothing rule in its budget-deficit policy, transitory negative output shocks will optimally cause both a budget deficit and a current-account deficit.

4. As the Mexican experience of 1995 suggests, large short-term dollar-denominated Tesobonos threatened to turn a liquidity crisis into a default situation.

5. For a formal model of how political instability may exacerbate a fiscal and current-account deficit, see Corsetti and Roubini (1997).

6. Table 2.2 presents two sets of current-account data, one from the IMF and the other from the EBRD. In the text, we follow the IMF series.

7. It should also be noted that such forecasts are subject a large degree of uncertainty; for example, in the May 1995 *World Economic Outlook*, the IMF was forecasting that the current-account deficit of the transition economies would be 4.9 percent of GDP in 1995 and grow to 6.0 percent of GDP in 1996. The outcome reported in the May 1997 *World Economic Outlook* was a current-account deficit of 0.8 percent of GDP in 1995 and 2.1 percent in 1996.

8. On the sterilization problems imposed by the increase in foreign reserves, see Begg (1996) and Siklos (1996).

9. The data for the current account in Table 2.4 for 1991 is positive while the GDP shares data in Table 2.3 is negative because the shares data is an average weighted by GDP while the data here is a simple aggregate amount.

10. Such capital outflows were even larger for a subgroup of transition countries including Bulgaria, the Czech Republic, Hungary, Poland, Romania, and the Slovak Republic. For this subgroup, the capital-account deficit (including errors and omissions was $4.7 billion in 1990 and $8.0 billion in 1991, and the loss of foreign reserves amounted to $8.0 billion in 1990 and $10.9 billion in 1991 (see Calvo, Sahay, and Vegh, 1995).

11. The quality of the data is not always ideal. While the current account data are similar across the different sources we have used (IMF *International Financial Statistics*, IMF *World Economic Outlook*, IMF country reports, and EBRD *Transition Report*), deriving good estimates of national savings and national investment rates has been quite difficult as different sources give very different estimates of savings, investment, and real GDP. We tried to derive savings and investment data that are consistent with the current-account data. Current account data from the savings-investment imbalance do not always match those derived from balance-of-payments data. Since we were more confident about the current-account data deriving from the balance-of-payments accounts, we adjusted the various estimates of savings and investment to get consistency with the identity that the current account should be equal to the difference between national savings and investment. The estimates of national savings and investment rates are quite volatile over time even within the same source; this is a reflection of: (1) the actual sharp changes in output, consumption, and investment in the transition period and (2) measurement error due to serious problems of correctly measuring national income during the transition.

12. Bulgaria and Romania have had reversals in their return to a positive GDP growth path. GDP in Bulgaria fell by 10 percent in 1996, and the EBRD forecasts a decline in GDP in Romania for 1997.

13. For several countries the national income account data on savings and investment are incomplete or not available, especially for the most recent 1995 to 1996 period.

14. The deficit measure is the general government balance (as a share of GDP) from the EBRD *Transition Report 1997*. The deficit ratios are calculated in nominal terms; therefore, very high nominal deficits to GDP are found in high inflation periods when nominal interest payments by the government are very high. See Buiter (1997) for a more detailed analysis of the fiscal imbalances of the transition economies and estimates of the real fiscal deficits.

15. As an example, Mexico had a semifixed exchange rate relative to the dollar between 1990 and 1994. Since inflation in Mexico was on average 5 percent above the U.S. one during this period, over those five years this implied a real appreciation of the Mexican peso of over 30 percent relative to the parity of 1990. Partly as a consequence of this real appreciation, the current account that was close to balance in 1989 went to a $28 billion deficit by the end of 1994.

16. See Halpern and Wyplosz (1996) and Krajnyak and Zettelmeyer (1997) for two recent attempts to estimate empirically the changes in the equilibrium real exchange rate.

17. The case of the Czech Republic illustrates the difficulty in interpreting exchange-rate

movements. Using price indexes, the real exchange rate appreciated by about one-third from 1990 to 1995. However, PPP calculations in 1995 suggested that the nominal exchange rate was undervalued by about the same amount. The latter evidence led the central bank (and others) to be unconcerned with the widening current-account deficit. See the *1996 OECD Survey* on the Czech Republic.

18. See the 1996 IMF country report on Lithuania for a more detailed discussion of the real exchange trends in Lithuania.

19. The real appreciation in Estonia and Lithuania is also evident from the data on U.S. dollar wages that have grown faster in these two countries than in any other country in our sample. Dollar wages went from $46 to $255 per month between 1992 and 1996 in Estonia and from $20 to $170 per month in Lithuania during the same period (see IMF *World Economic Outlook*, May 1997).

20. As published in the 1996 IMF country report on Ukraine.

21. As argued by Halpern and Wyplosz (1996, p. 31): "Resisting a real appreciation is not only hopeless. It also leads to potentially speculative capital inflows and interventions, which, if not sterilized, lead to faster monetary growth and eventually inflation. If sterilized, they can be a build-up of reserves fueling further inflows in an unending spiral. Even more destabilizing would be a policy of nominal depreciation, e.g., based on a PPP rule, which will lead to a dangerous cycle of inflation and depreciations."

22. The increase in dollar wages in 1996 were moderated by the appreciation of the U.S. dollar against the DM and other European currencies. As suggested in the IMF *World Economic Outlook* (May 1997), p. 100: "When measured in deutsche mark rather than dollars, wages in most transition economies continued to grow substantially in 1996, pushing up unit labor costs in deutsche mark terms and substantiating concerns about competitiveness."

23. While in principle, the change in reserves obtained from balance of payments (BP) data should be equal to the change in the stock of foreign reserves of the central banks derived from the central-bank balance sheet, a number of accounting difference lead to small discrepancies between the two data sources.

24. The difference in Table 2.9 between the BP row (that represents the overall BP balance) and the change in foreign reserves is exactly due to IMF loans/credits and other exceptional financing to the monetary authorities.

25. In some cases such as the Ukraine, the increase in reserves occurred in spite of an overall large BP deficit as IMF, and other exceptional financing was very substantial.

26. Differences between data in Tables 2.9 and 2.10 are due to revisions. Table 2.9 uses the IMF IFS for October 1997, while Table 2.10 uses IFS for April 1997.

27. Begg (1996) and Siklos (1996) discuss in detail the sterilization problems created by the large capital inflows.

28. See Section 2.4 on exchange-rate developments for more detail on the effects of capital inflows on the countries' competitiveness.

29. The increase in interest rates at that time was an important factor precipitating the Mexican crisis at year's end.

30. The connection between banking and financial-sector crises and current-account crises in developing economies is discussed by Kaminsky and Reinhart (1996), Lindgren, Garcia, and Saal (1996), and Milesi-Ferretti and Razin (1996a, 1996b, 1996c).

31. For further discussion of banking crises in the Visegrad countries in particular, see Bonin and Wachtel (1996) and Bonin, Mizsei, Szekely, and Wachtel (1997).

32 The importance of bank borrowing abroad and its role in currency crises was pointed out to us by Velimir Šonje in his discussion of this paper at the Dubrovnik conference.

33. This is the conclusion reached, albeit cautiously, by Kaminsky and Reinhart (1996) in

their analysis of banking and balance-of-payments crises in developing economies. They find no evidence of causality from balance-of-payments crises to banking crises.

34. This discussion supplements the earlier sections of the chapter. For example, a list of sustainability indicators would surely include a measure of currency overvaluation, but that topic was examined extensively in Section 2.4 and is not repeated here.

35 These ratios may be hard to interpret because the ratio of M2 to GDP varies a great deal across countries depending on the development of the banking system and the amount of financial intermediation that occurs. Thus, the M2 to reserves ratio may high because banking intermediaries are relatively more developed.

36. In the words of *Euromoney* (1997): "The rise of central and eastern European countries has faltered: the Czech Republic falls to 37 following last autumn's crisis in the banking sector and Slovenia falls to 38 as structural and economic concerns impinge on export performance. Lithuania, which rose 26 places last September, drops back to 72 as worries persist about economic policy and the exchange rate. Economists expect a difficult year for Romania, which falls to 75, as the new reformist government struggles to revive the economy. Bulgaria's recent poor performance and political unrest have cost it 19 places. More upbeat in emerging Europe is Croatia, which moves up thanks to its political risk score—11.25, up from 7.67 last September. Analysts are optimistic as the country rebuilds infrastructure, tourism develops, and the economy improves."

37. Year-by-year FDI flows are shown in Table 2.9.

38. See OECD *Economic Survey: Hungary, 1995.*

39. The EBRD estimates of GDP growth in Table 2.6 show a more gradual turnaround: 1993: –9 percent, 1994: –2 percent, and 1995: +4 percent.

40. See the OECD *Economic Survey: Poland*, 1997 for a discussion of border trade.

References

Bank of Lithuania. (1997). *Monetary Policy Programme of the Bank of Lithuania for 1997–1999.*

Begg, D. (1996). "Monetary Policy in Central and Eastern Europe: Lessons After Half a Decade of Transition." IMF Working Paper 96-108, September.

Bonin, J., K. Mizsei, I. Szekely, and P. Wachtel. (1997). *Creating Market-Oriented Banking Sectors for Transition Economies*. Elgar.

Bonin, J., and P. Wachtel. (1996). "Towards Market-Oriented Banking in the Economies of Transition." In M. Blejer and M. Skreb (eds.), *Financial-Sector Transformation: Lessons for the Economies in Transition*. Cambridge: Cambridge University Press.

Buiter, W. (1997). "Aspects of Fiscal Performance in Some Transition Economies Under Found-Supported Programs." IMF Working Paper 97-31.

Buiter, W., G. Corsetti, and P. Pesenti. (1997). *Financial Markets and European Monetary Cooperation: The Lesson from the 1992–93 ERM Crisis*. Cambridge: Cambridge University Press.

Calvo, G. (1995). "Varieties of Capital Market Crises." Paper, University of Maryland, April.

Calvo, G., R. Sahay, and C. Vegh. (1995). "Capital Flows in Central and Eastern

Europe: Evidence and Policy Options." In G. Calvo, M. Goldstein, and E. Hochreiter (eds.), *Private Capital Flows to Emerging Markets After the Mexican Crisis*. Washington, DC: Institute for International Economics.

Corsetti, G., and N. Roubini. (1997). "Politically Motivated Fiscal Deficits: Policy Issues in Closed and Open Economies." *Economics and Politics*, 9(1) (March): 27–54.

Dornbusch, R., I. Goldfajn, and R.O. Valdes. (1995). "Currency Crises and Collapses." Brookings Papers on Economic Activity No. 1, 219–270.

Halpern, L., and C. Wyplosz. (1996). "Equilibrium Exchange Rates in Transition Economies." IMF Working Paper 96-125, November.

Kaminsky, G., S. Lizondo, and C. Reinhart. (1997). "Leading Indicators of Currency Crises." IMF Working Paper 97-79, July.

Kaminsky, G., and C. Reinhart. (1996). "The Twin Crises: The Causes of Banking and Balance-of-Payments Problems." International Finance Discussion Paper 544, Board of Governors of the Federal Reserve System.

Klaus, Vaclav. (1997). "Promoting Financial Stability in the Transition Economies of Central and Eastern Europe." Paper presented at the conference on Maintaining Financial Stability in a Global Economy organized by the Federal Reserve Bank of Kansas, August.

Krajnyak, K., and J. Zettelmeyer. (1997). "Competitiveness in Transition Economies: What Scope for Real Appreciation?" IMF Working Paper.

Lindgren, Carl-Johan, Gillian Garcia, and Matthew I. Saal. (1996). *Bank Soundness and Macroeconomic Policy*. International Monetary Fund.

Milesi-Ferretti, G.M., and A. Razin. (1996a). "Current Account Sustainability." Princeton Studies in International Finance, No. 81, October.

Milesi-Ferretti, G.M., and A. Razin. (1996b). "Current Account Sustainability: Selected East Asian and Latin American Experiences." NBER Working Paper 5791, October.

Milesi-Ferretti, G.M., and A. Razin. (1996c). "Sustainability of Current Account Deficits." NBER Working Paper 5467, February.

Sachs, J., A. Velasco, and A. Tornell. (1996). "Financial Crises in Emerging Markets: The Lessons from 1995." Brookings Papers on Economic Activity, No. 1, 147–215.

Siklos, P. (1996). "Capital Flows in a Transitional Economy and the Sterilization Dilemma: The Hungarian Case." IMF Working Paper 96-86, August.

3 EXCHANGE-RATE ARRANGEMENTS IN THE TRANSITION ECONOMIES

Robert A. Mundell

Columbia University

3.1. Introduction

This chapter is concerned with the exchange-rate arrangements in the transition countries. Its major purpose is to assess the prospects for the use of exchange-rate policies as a vehicle for stabilization and as a permanent system of monetary control. It will take the opportunity to clarify some ideas about the international adjustment process that remain a source of controversy.

In one sense the transition countries have been a victim of bad timing. Had communism collapsed in the 1950s or 1960s, they would have had a stable international monetary system to join. That system, in which other currencies were fixed to the U.S. dollar and the dollar fixed to gold, would have provided an anchor for the new currencies, and there would have been a coherent philosophy of stabilization offered under the guidance of the international institutions. As it turned out, the international monetary system broke down, and the Articles of Agreement of the International Monetary Fund were amended to enact a system of managed flexible exchange rates. As a result, the institutions lost their sense of policy coherence, and countries gravitated to the least common denominator of discipline. This bad luck of the system must certainly bear a substantial part of the blame for the poor performances of the transition countries, nearly all of which have suffered from plummeting output, rampant inflation, fiscal deficits, and depreciating currencies on a scale never before seen in the world economy.

In principle, the movement of over 180 countries to flexible exchange rates could have led to chaos. In reality, however, chaos did not arise. Coherence in the world economy was maintained by the monetary oligopoly and especially its leading spirit, the dollar. Dollarization of the world economy and the formation of an important currency area in Europe in effect recreated an international monetary system on informal lines that is developing its own rules of the game. The situation for the transition countries is not, therefore, so hopely, and should they choose to adopt an exchange-rate anchor, they will be able to choose one among the dollar, the euro (if and when it comes into existence), the yen, or a compromise currency basket.

3.2. The Great Exchange-Rate Controversy

The appropriate role of exchange rates in economic policy is one of the most complicated issues in international economics and public policy. The difficulty stems from the fact that the exchange rate is a ratio of two monetary quantities and most targets of economic policy are real quantities. Solution of the problem requires specification of how nominal variables affect real variables. The same difficulty arises in relating nominal to real variables in closed-economy macroeconomic theory.

Much of the controversy in the literature has turned on differences relating to (1) the mechanism for changing exchange rates in a flexible exchange-rate system, (2) the effect of devaluation on absolute and relative prices, (3) the relation between the exchange rate and the trade balance, (4) the relation between changes in the trade balance and relative prices, (5) the role of exchange rates in general equilibrium theory, (6) the link between the international monetary system and exchange-rate changes, and (7) the relation of national currencies to the international standard (if any).

The classical economists made a clear dichotomy between real and monetary variables. Currency supplies, wages, prices, and exchange rates were monetary variables; employment, output, interest rates, and trade balances were real variables. In the classical, long-run view, monetary variables did not affect real variables. An implication of this dichotomy, as expressed in one application of the principle of effective market classification,[1] is that monetary instruments should be assigned to monetary targets—real instruments to real targets.

The neo-Keynesian view, which has been very influential in postwar years but which is essentially short-run, is that monetary variables have real effects. Monetary policy, for example, can be used to increase employment, and exchanges-rate policy can be used to change the balance of trade. Time has not dealt kindly with this view, not because monetary events cannot have short-run real effects but because, when full account is taken of expectations, the effects are smaller than expected and are likely to be reversed in the future.

It would be a mistake, however, to adopt the position that all of the controversy centers on the real-monetary dichotomy or even on the difference between classical and Keynesian economics. There are purely intellectual differences based on different conceptions of the adjustment mechanism. Before discussing exchange-rate policies in the transition countries it seems to be necessary to clear the deck, so to speak, of some issues surrounding the international adjustment mechanism.

The roots of the adjustment controversy go back to the very origins of the international adjustment mechanism in the eighteenth century, where two views crystalized. One view argued that relative price changes were needed to correct balance-of-payments disequilibrium; the other, that relative price changes were not fundamental to the adjustment mechanism. These competing positions to some extent came to coincide respectively with the positions of flexible and fixed exchange rates.

David Hume is generally credited with the self-adjusting mechanism of the balance of payments. Hume was concerned to refute the mercantilist view that tariffs or exchange-rate changes were required to maintain the "appropriate" quantity of money at home. He showed that the balance of payments, if left to itself, would automatically correct itself. There is in every country an equilibrium quantity of money that would automatically become established by the free flow of the precious metals. Countries would get the quantity of specie they demanded.

Hume's work, published in 1752, marked a great advance in the development of economic theory. It also, however, contained within itself two versions of the adjustment mechanism. Hume's problem was to reconcile the operation of the quantity theory of money with the automatic adjustment of the balance of payments under a common currency or specie standard. Prior to 1752, in a letter to the French economist and philosopher Montesquieu, Hume had argued that a balance-of-payments disequilibrium would increase money and prices in the surplus country and decrease money and prices in the deficit country, shifting expenditure from the surplus country to the deficit country and restoring equilibrium. It is this version of the adjustment mechanism that influenced a whole school of economists, including John

Stuart Mill, Alfred Marshall, Frank Taussig, Jacob Viner, John Maynard Keynes, James Meade, and a host of modern writers.

Hume's work, however, did not end there. He sent the first draft of his essay (which, unfortunately, has not survived) based on the Montesquieu letter, to his friend, the economist, James Oswald, who wrote a long letter in reply in which he sent his criticisms. One of these criticisms was based on the law of one price: although he recognized that, for example, prices of purely domestic commodities might rise or fall with a change in the quantity of money, he did not see how it could apply to commodities that were traded internationally. Hume promised to revise his draft to take account of the criticisms.

In the published draft of his essay, Hume (1752) makes it clear that money, like water, wherever it communicates, "remains always at a level." Thus the difference in prices is only incipient: "the same causes which would correct these exorbitant inequalities, were they to happen miraculously, must prevent their happening in the common course of nature, and must forever, in all neighbouring nations, preserve money nearly proportionable to the art and industry of every nation." It is not price changes that correct the balance of trade because they are prevented from doing so by the law of one price.

Now, however, there is a problem. If Hume rejects the price-specie-flow mechanism, what is it that brings about international adjustment? On this Hume is a blank. He leaves it to the reader to guess. It is tempting to think that Hume implicitly understood that changes in the quantity of money would alter expenditure through wealth effects. This would indeed be the additional idea needed to complete Hume's exposition. But to attribute that idea to Hume would mean attributing also a notion of the balance of trade as the discrepancy between income and expenditure. Such ideas did exist in the earlier literature (e.g., Gervaise and Cantillon), but there is no indication that Hume utilized that concept or even was aware of its significance for the adjustment mechanism.

It is a mystery how the price-specie-flow mechanism, credited to but rejected by Hume, should have passed muster as the prevailing theory of international adjustment for the next two centuries. The much-quoted Cunliffe Report repeats the theory, and so do most of the leading textbooks in economics or international economics in the rest of the century. Taussig (1919, p. 458), for example, in his textbook depicts the adjustment mechanism in the following way:

> Suppose, now, that the total exports do not suffice to pay for the total imports. Then they must be paid for in specie. Will that specie flow out for an indefinite

> time? and what likelihood is there that a balance will permanently remain to be paid in this way?
>
> The accepted answer to these questions, *and in essentials the accurate one* [my italics], is that the flow of specie sets in motion forces which sooner or later stop the flow. When specie leaves a country, prices tend to fall. Hence that country becomes one in which it is advantageous to buy. Lower prices stimulate exports. Conversely, the country to which specie flows tends to have rising prices. It becomes one in which it is advantageous to sell. Higher prices stimulate imports. Hence the flow of specie has an automatic limitation. The greater it is, the more certain is it likely to cease; the longer it has gone on, the sooner is it likely to cease. Merchandise exports and imports on the whole and in the long-run balance, in consequence of the effect of the quantity of money on prices.

There was, however, no evidence whatsoever that relative price changes were important aspects of the international adjustment mechanism any more than that they were important aspects of adjustment between regions in one country. No wonder *haute finance* brushed aside the mutterings of international trade economists in this period. Taussig (1919, p. 462) himself notes the resistance to the theory:

> So insignificant are the ordinary currents of gold from one country to another, so likely to be designed by eddies and cross currents due to the complexity of international dealings, that some writers have pooh-poohed the whole theory of the equalization of imports and exports by changes in international prices. Yet without this theory it is impossible to explain the facts, and especially the adjustment of the money value of exports and imports.

Even two centuries after Hume's work, economists had not solve the Hume puzzle: how adjustment could take place without price adjustments. Even today there is not in the literature an explicit account of the adjustment mechanism in which relative price changes are ruled out by the law of one price.

A related strand in the literature concerned the transfer problem. If one country had to make a recurrent payment—let us say a tribute or reparations—the financial transfer must ultimately be effected in real terms, which means that the transferring country had to generate a balance-of-trade surplus and the receiving country, of course, a trade deficit. How was this to be accomplished? Again two strands in the literature developed: one insisted, that prices must fall in the paying country relative to the receiving country; the other that price changes were not a fundamental part of the adjustment process and that relative prices in the paying country may actually go in the opposite direction to that supposed by the relative price school. In the history of the transfer problem, Thornton, Mill, Marshall, Taussig, and Keynes took the relative price position, while Wheatley,

Ricardo, Bastable, Wicksell, and Ohlin argued that relative price changes were not necessarily required.

The controversy has not died in modern economics.[2] It crops up in modern economic policy discussions in the debate over fixed and flexible exchange rates. Policy advice, reflecting the pluralism that characterizes the current economic system, has become eclectic. Whereas countries were once urged by the international institutions to anchor their currencies to the world system, they are now asked, within the framework of the IMF system of managed flexible rates, to choose among competing targets of macroeconomic policy. Before turning to that policy issue, it will be necessary to describe the general equilibrium approach to the balance of payments and present a model of the adjustment process.

3.3. The Sixteen Approaches to the Balance of Payments

There is no single correct way of analyzing the balance of payments of a country. Because spending decisions are connected to financing decision, one country's imports are the rest of the world's exports, and debts have to be repaid, there is an interlocking of international and intertemporal deficits that present alternative approaches to the balance of payments. In the literature of the 1950s and 1960s and in many textbooks, it became conventional to enumerate three approaches to the balance of payments, usually identified as the *elasticity* approach, the *absorption* approach and the *monetary* approach. However, when account is taken of all the information contained in the global general equilibrium system, there are many more than three approaches.

To be precise, there are exactly sixteen ways of looking at the balance of trade (or balance of payments).[3] Eight of the approaches can be deduced directly from the applications of Walras's law[4] and Cournot's law[5] in the international economy; the other eight approaches derive from the application of Fisherian intertemporal budget constraints.

General equilibrium requires analysis of the conditions of equilibrium in three broad aggregates: goods, securities, and money. Each sector, of course, could be disaggregated into domestic and foreign components and subdivided further into the innumerable categories relevant in the real world. To illustrate the sixteen approaches to the balance of trade or payments, however, is sufficient to maintain the degree of aggregation implied by the threefold classification. For the sake of simplicity, I shall also bypass the difference between GDP and GNP, and the corresponding difference between the trade balance and the current account. But a big warning is in order: this difference cannot be ignored when we deal with the eight intertemporal approaches to the balance of payments.

The first equation we write down is the identity utilized by practitioners of the elasticity approach—namely, that the balance of trade is equal to exports minus imports, $B = X - M$. By specifying the arguments of the functions relations determining supplies of exports and demands for imports, we arrive at approach 1 to the balance of payments. Approach 2 is in the same family; it results from specifying the functions determining the supply of exports and the demand for imports in the foreign country. From Cournot's law, the trade surplus of one country is the trade deficit of the rest of the world, due allowance being made for asymmetries in the treatment of reserve suppliers and gold producers.

Analysis of these factors owe much, as we have seen, to Edgeworth and Bickerdike, subsequently elaborated by Robinson, Lerner, Haberler, Meade, Machlup, and Metzler. A more sophisticated development of this approach would incorporate into the demand functions for exports and imports not just exchange rates, prices, and output, but domestic expenditure, capital movements, and wealth; it should then not be called the elasticity approach (why not income propensities approach?) but rather the *direct* approach because it examines directly the forces determining exports and imports. The lesson from the direct approach is that no policy variable, including the exchange rate, can improve the balance of trade without increasing exports relative to imports. The direct approach is no more and no less valid than the other seven pairs.

The next pair of approaches makes use of the absorption relations: $B = Y - E$ where Y is income and E is expenditure (absorption). This relationship can be subdivided into separate sectors to yield the equation $S - I + T - G = B$, where S, I, T, and G, refer, respectively, to savings, investment, tax revenues, and government spending. There are two equations of this type, of course—one for the country under analysis and the other for aggregate of economies in the rest of the world. These approaches owe much to Gervaise, Metzler, Machlup, Chipman, Meade, Alexander (especially), and Harry Johnson. Alexander called "absorption" what Meade had called "domestic expenditure," and this inspired the name usually given to the approach. The lesson from this approach is that no policy variable, including the exchange rate, can alter the equilibrium balance of trade (current account balance) unless it increases output (income) more than expenditure.

The next pair of approaches relies on the balance-of-payments identity. The accounting balance of payments is the external counterpart to Walras's law. The current-account surplus is equal to net capital exports plus the balance-of-payments deficit. Put another way, the current-account surplus finances an import of securities (which is a capital export) or an inflow of money (balance-of-payments surplus). We can write $B = K + P$, where K is the net capital outward flow and P is the balance-of-payments surplus. Similarly, any current-account surplus of the rest of the world must be matched by net capital exports of the rest of the world or an increase in its net reserve assets. The lesson from this approach is that no policy variable can improve the balance of trade without generating a greater net capital outflow and/or increase in international reserve assets that is acceptable in the rest of the world.

It is worth noting here a long-standing dispute about the direction of causation in the balance-of-payments identity. There are those who argue that trade balance has an independent existence requiring external finance; on the other hand, there are those who argue that capital exports and other transfers induce changes in the balance of trade through the mechanism of financing changes in expenditures. It should be emphasized, however, that the identity itself says nothing about causation; there are merely two sides to the same coin. It cannot be inferred from the balance-of-payments identity whether the financial transfer determines the trade balance or the trade balance determines the financial transfer.

The classical school, up until Mill, put the capital flow in the driver's seat. It emphasized the fact that the mere act of making a financial transfer automatically implies the additional saving to finance it, so that the mere existence of an outward capital flow implies an excess of income over expenditure. But the Mill-Taussig-Keynes omission of expenditure effects in the adjustment mechanism opened the way for Keynes's idiosyncratic view of the trade balance as a given entity independent of financial transfers. Although this involves a false dichotomy—independence of spending from finance—Keynes's view has strongly influenced the modern literature (in my opinion to its detriment). It is easy to see why economists who write down equations specifying exports as a function of output and prices fall prey to the single-entry bookkeeping approach that ignores the mechanism though which capital inflows or transfers stimulate an increase in expenditures.

Causation can in principle go in either direction. But it is unlikely that enduring changes in the balance of trade can be motivated other than by basic financial transfers. It is true that a shift of domestic expenditure from home to foreign goods will worsen the balance of trade and immediately force accommodating finance, a loss of reserves, or a change in the exchange rate. But accommodating finance is purely temporary and short-run. Major trade deficits and surpluses are nearly always not only accompanied by but induced by voluntary financial transfers of one kind or another.

Because there are two balance-of-payments equations—one for the home country and one for the rest of the world—we now have six approaches to the balance of trade; there are only ten remaining.

Approaches 7 and 8 make use of Walras's law directly. The sum of all excess demands is zero, so that any excess supply of commodities must be matched by an equivalent excess demand for securities and money. Because the trade balance is equal to the excess supply of goods, it must also be equal to the excess demand for securities and money. Formulated in a different way, the excess supply of goods is equal to the sum of the budget surplus and the excess of saving overinvestment. Any budget surplus must be expended on money or securities; it implies an excess demand for money or government bonds on the part of the government. Similarly, an excess of saving overinvestment equals an excess demand for securities and/or money. We can therefore deduce the current account deficit solely by examining the markets for securities and money. This approach applies to both countries so that we now have eight approaches to analysis of the balance of trade.

It will be convenient at this point to pause to summarize the eight approaches in the form of a system of equations. These equations can be looked on as identities after the fact or as equilibrium conditions when they are defined in terms of intentions and plans.

$$Y - E = B = -B^* = E^* - Y^* \text{ (Goods)} \tag{3.1}$$

$$A - Z = -K = K^* = Z^* - A^* \text{ (Securities)} \tag{3.2}$$

$$G - H = -P = P^* = H^* - G^* \text{ (Money).} \tag{3.3}$$

All the variables in the above equations are flows. A and Z refer to the supply and demand for securities, respectively, and G and H refer to money creation and hoarding, respectively, and P is the balance-of-payments surplus. The plus signs between the lines are inserted to indicate that the rows can be added vertically to equal zero.

Now for the intertemporal dimension, the other eight approaches. Intertemporal conditions are implied when we say that a deficit is "unsustainable." If a deficit is unsustainable, the worry is not that it will endure but that it will disappear in an unpleasant way. The above equations do not reflect this fact because they have not as yet taken into account the intertemporal version of Walras's law. Trade deficits integrated over time yield net debt, and debt has to be paid back. We owe to David Hume—the theorem that Charles Kindleberger called Hume's law—that exports equal imports. Hume meant that the balance-of-payments adjustment mechanism would eventually bring imports into equality with exports. This is emphatically not true in the short run; the United States has had a trade deficit for nearly a generation, as it had a surplus for two prior generations. But there is a sense in which Hume is right after all. Exports equal imports over long periods of time.

A country's net indebtedness is limited by its perceived export capacity. The United States can sustain a trade deficit because it has the productive power to service and ultimately repay its debts. If, on the contrary, it were perceived that the United States could not generate the future trade surpluses to service a growing debt, external finance would dry up, and expenditure would be brought back in line with income, eliminating the deficit. No country, of course, can pile up debts indefinitely unless they are at the same time generating increased means for repaying them. A country borrowing to expand its capital plants and productive power has more credibility than a country borrowing to finance pure consumption spending. It is sometimes relevant to note which sectors are doing the borrowing or lending. If the private sectors do the borrowing, the responsibility for making repayments rest with the individuals; households or firms might legitimately borrow to achieve a better intertemporal pattern of consumption along life-cycle lines.[6] Budget deficits, however, raise other questions, creating the potential for mistaken shifts in the intergeneration distribution of income.

At some point diminishing returns will set in, and a country will reach its debt limit—the limit beyond which it can no longer finance current-account deficits. Higher debts require larger interest payments, which at some stage would require unattainable trade surpluses to maintain debt service. At this stage risk of default soars. An example is afforded by many of the less developed countries. The LDC's borrowed excessively in the negative real interest days of the late 1970s and early 1980s. When real interest rates rose and their future export capacity seemed insufficient to service their debts, the flow of capital dried up, and they were left with a painful adjustment process that has abated only moderately.

And so we come, finally to the additional eight approaches to the balance of trade, that each one of the above-mentioned eight approaches has its reverse counterpart in the intertemporal dimension when surpluses and deficits have to be reversed. In the long run, therefore, we need to pay special attention to the difference between the GDP and GNP and to the equivalent difference between the trade balance and the current account balance. Expected future net outpayments to service the debt, or inpayments of debt service, like repayments, to lower or raise disposable income and domestic expenditure. The larger the debt, the larger the gap between GDP and GNP and between the trade balance and the current account.

We must also pay attention to the pall that heavy indebtedness casts over expectations about the exchange rate and bond prices signaling decreased creditworthiness. In the long run debts involve a subtraction from wealth that should affect our current propensities to save. Individuals pay attention to those negative factors pertaining to personal debts, but only super-rational individuals correctly subtract from personal wealth the share of the national debt that implies future tax obligations.

3.4. Competing Targets for Monetary Stabilization

The case for flexible exchange rates is sometimes presented as a way of achieving an extra degree of freedom for economic policy. This, however, is a false way of posing the issue. In a general equilibrium system, there is one degree of freedom. How this extra degree of freedom is used characterizes the system. There are, in the abstract, several alternatives for monetary targeting: the price level, the money supply, the exchange rate, the price of gold, and the wage rate are popular alternatives that have often been suggested. The variable that is targeted characterizes the "standard." Thus, a country can have a commodity standard by targeting the price level, a monetary standard by targeting (one of the definitions of) the money supply, a foreign-currency standard by targeting a particular foreign currency, a gold standard by targeting the price of gold, or a wage standard by targeting the wage rate.

In the international monetary system of the 1960s, the price of gold was "targeted" by the United States and the dollar was targeted by foreign countries. Moving toward flexible exchange rates (and a flexible price of gold for the United States) shifts the burden of stabilization policy onto a monetary standard (a lá Friedman) or a commodity standard (a lá Thomas Attwood or Irving Fisher or Frank Graham) or a wage standard (a lá neo-Keynesians). In practice, a wage standard has to be ruled out in countries with strong trade unions because it would lead to, as Keynes (1996, p. 261) put it, "monetary management by the Trade Unions instead of by the banking system." Four other possibilities are given in Table 3.1.

When the issue is posed in this way, one variable is fixed and three are flexible; there is no extra degree of freedom in a framework of a stable system. Of course, it is possible for the authorities not to fix any single variable but instead a weighted average of the price level, the money supply,

Table 3.1. Standards: targets and variables

Standard	*Fixed Target*	*Variable*	*Variable*	*Variable*
Commodity	Price level	Exchange rate	Money supply	Gold price
Monetary	Money supply	Exchange rate	Price level	Gold price
Foreign currency	Exchange rate	Money supply	Price level	Gold price
Gold	Gold price	Money supply	Exchange rate	Price level

the exchange rate, and the price of gold. Even in this case, however, there is no extra degree of freedom. In the present international monetary system, gold remains an important component of international reserves. Because no major country currently fixes the price of gold, however, it would not be a useful target for the monetary policies of the transition countries. We shall therefore confine our discussion to three alternatives: the monetary standard, the commodity standard, and the foreign exchange standard. The three main alternatives are therefore the following:

- *Target the money supply* Stabilize one of the definitions of the money supply (e.g., M_0, M_1, M_2, M_3) and fix its rate of growth equal to the long-run rate of growth of output; this means letting the price level, interest rates, and exchange rates float in accordance with market forces. The case for quantity fixing rests on five assumptions: (1) there is a close relationship between reserve money and the money supply; (2) there is a stable demand for money; (3) the demand-for-money equation and the long-run growth rate can be estimated by econometric studies and used by the central bank; (4) there is a close correlation between the money supply and money income; and (5) the price level will be stable if the money supply grows at the same rate as output. Decision to implement the monetarist solution requires the following decisions: (1) select the concept of money the rate of growth of which is going to be stabilized; (2) determine the rate of monetary expansion that is most likely to yield long-run stability; and (3) determine the functional relationship between central bank money and the definition of the money supply chosen.
- *Target the price level* Stabilize one of the definitions of the price level (such as the consumer price index, the wholesale price index, a wage index, and an index of commodity prices or a particular com-

modity, such as the price of gold), and dedicate monetary policy to stabilizing the rate of change of that index at the targeted rate of inflation (possibly zero). The case for stabilizing a price index rests on a simple version of the quantity theory of money—that the money supply is proportionate to some price level and that changes in the money supply are proportionate to change in the price level without disturbing lags that upset expectations. Decision to stabilize the price level requires the following decisions: (1) choose the price index; (2) determine the inflation target; and (3) establish the differential equation that relates changes in central bank operations to changes in the price level.

- *Target the exchange rate* Stabilize "the" exchange rate (or its rate of change); this means allowing the money supply to change in accordance with the demand for money and the balance of payments. The case for stabilizing an exchange rate is that it fixes the price of international goods and allows a country to import the foreign country's monetary stability (whatever it is). Stabilization of an exchange rate requires the following procedures: (1) build up a stock of foreign exchange to use as working balances and as a reserve to build up confidence; (2) designate the foreign currency (or basket of currencies) to which the currency is to fixed; (3) commit the central bank to buying and selling the designated currency at a fixed price (or within small margins between upper and lower limits); (4) ensure that the automatic effect of central bank intervention on bank reserves is not sterilized by offsetting central bank operations; (5) establish a commitment mechanism to prevent the government from forcing the central bank to finance future budget deficits; (6) remove most or all exchange controls; and (7) solicit the participation and assistance of the partner country and/or IMF to assist in building confidence in the currency in the early stages of the reform.

These three mechanisms have very different consequences, as we show below. It should be emphasized, however, that the differences between the three mechanisms is much smaller than the difference between any one of the three mechanisms in comparison to the nonmechanisms that prevail in many of the transition countries. If a country is suffering from rapid inflation, it is almost certainly also suffering from a rate of monetary expansion that is incompatible with price stability. In such a situation, slowing the rate of monetary expansion, reducing the rate of inflation, and slowing the rate at which the currency is depreciating are all viable policies.

The differences among the three approaches to monetary stabilization are relatively unimportant in the early phases of stabilization when the inflation rate is high. They become much more important, however, in the final stage of stabilization when the country has not only achieved fiscal balance but also reduced the rate of inflation to single-digit levels and preferably below 5 percent.

3.5. Phases of Stabilization

Let us envisage a stabilization process as taking place in three phases:

Stage I. In the first phase, the rate of inflation is high, and central-bank policy is dominated by the requirement to finance the budget deficit that still remains high. At this stage, monetary targeting and correction of the budget deficit seem to come to much the same thing. They are nevertheless different. It would be a mistake to think that balancing the budget would *ipso facto* reduce the rate of monetary expansion. The central bank, freed from the need to finance government operations, could continue to create inflation by excessive finance of commercial operations. The budget deficit has to be brought under control *and* monetary policy must be targeted.

Stage II. In the second phase, it can be assumed that the budget deficit has been brought under control so the inflation tax is no longer needed. The rate of inflation has been brought to single-digit levels and money-supply growth is approximately equal to the sum of the growth rate of nominal GDP and the rate of increase in the demand for money due to increasing confidence. In this situation, it becomes important to shift from targeting the money supply to targeting the inflation rate. In this stage velocity is shifting rapidly and to a considerable extent unpredictably because the public will not be sure how far the stabilization plan will proceed or how long it will last—taking into account political uncertainties. Inflation targeting is much superior at this second stage than monetary targeting, and exchange-rate targeting is premature. The history of stabilization policies suggests that premature fixing of the exchange rate can help to brake inflation and adjust expectations but that the price level will overshoot the real exchange-rate equilibrium leaving the country with an overvalued exchange rate and need to compensate by deflationary policies or else breaking the commitment to the fixed parity by devaluation.

There are those who argue that exchange-rate targeting is useful at this stage, using a crawling peg system, much like the *tablita* system used by Portugal and several Latin American countries in the late 1970s and early

1980s. These arrangements, however, proved to be a mistake. They inculcated in policymakers the notion that exchange-rate "pegs" are useful as an anti-inflationary device without a direct commitment of monetary policy to that exchange rate. Not only did the arrangements fail in the countries where they were tried, but they created a false view of fixed exchange rates.

Stage III. In the third phase of the stabilization process, the emphasis must be on fine tuning, expectations, and permanence. This phase can be characterized by budget balance and a rate of inflation that has been reduced to 5 percent or lower. In this phase, monetary targeting is too imprecise to be useful, and reliance will have been placed on inflation targeting. It is here that fixing the exchange rate emerges as a feasible tool of stabilization.

At this point it is important to emphasize the difference between a *fixed* exchange rate and a *pegged* exchange rate. The fixed system, as I have always used the term, presupposes that the rate is permanently fixed and that the money supply is allowed to increase and decrease with balance-of-payments surpluses or deficits; the adjustment system proceeds automatically if the central bank resists the temptation to sterilize the monetary impact of purchases and sales of foreign exchange. Temporarily fixed or pegged rates, however, in which intervention in the foreign-exchange market is offset by sterilization operations, and the money supply is directed at other objectives, inevitably collapses because the "system" contains no adjustment mechanism. Nothing short of an infinite level of reserves would preserve the fix!

The pegged-rate system deserves to be discredited as the worst of all systems, whereas the former will be, for many countries, the best of all systems. In the literature, however, much confusion arises because of the failure to distinguish between the two arrangements. Several of the countries in Latin America created new currencies in the 1980s and fixed exchange rates in an attempt at stabilization, only to fail miserably because they did not realize that fixed rates can last only if they are allowed to be a system of monetary control.

It cannot be emphasized too strongly that fixed exchange rates should not be attempted until the government has brought its budget into balance and has a good prospect of keeping it in balance in the future. Only in this way can the money supply fulfill its proper role under fixed exchange rates as an equilibrator of the balance of payments. If confidence in the present and future exchange rate is preserved, financial arbitrage will ensure that interest rates converge to the international level,[7] and commodity arbitrage will ensure that the price level changes at the same rate that it is changing internationally.

In this way the country imports both the price-stability and the capital-market attributes of the money market of the foreign country to which it fixes its currency. Let me underline, however, how important it is to follow the seven steps listed above that are required for stabilization. Failure to follow any single one of the steps would put the entire stabilization process in jeopardy. It is for that reason that monetary leadership is needed to put an effective stabilization plan based on a fixed exchange-rate parity in place. If that leadership is lacking, a country would be better advised to continue, as a second-best policy, inflation targeting or adopt the simpler regime of a currency board. A currency-board system has virtually nothing in common with a pegged exchange rate, but it can be looked on as an extreme case of a fixed exchange-rate system. Under a currency-board system, the central bank buys and sells only foreign exchange, maintaining its reserves entirely in foreign exchange or liquid foreign-exchange earning assets. It may maintain 100 percent reserves or even a higher proportion if it sees fit to establish a supplementary fund to fulfill a role as lender of last resort to the commercial banks. The key element in a currency-board system is that the exchange rate is kept fixed within narrow or zero margins and that the peg can be changed only by parliamentary or constitutional changes that can only be negotiated with considerable difficulty, thus generating confidence in the continuation of the system. I am very glad to see that the IMF is now supporting the idea of currency boards for some countries.

The most important element in any sound monetary system is that monetary policy be predictable. In a firmly fixed exchange-rate system, the key element is that there is little if any expectation of a change in the exchange rate because the monetary policy of the country is automatically geared to making that exchange rate an equilibrium rate. A sufficient directive to central banks would be that the central bank deal only in foreign assets within the required margins of the par value. If applied strictly, the reserve base of the money supply could increase only as a result of a balance-of-payments surplus. (In a large and growing country, with sufficient reserves, some allowance could be made for fiduciary monetary expansion after the confidence of the public in the system has been earned.)

3.6. The Situation in the Transition Countries

Let us now apply these principles to the actual situation prevailing in the transition countries. The quickest summary of the situation would say that on average, the transition countries have been plagued with negative growth, rampant inflation, large budget deficits, and depreciating currencies. Before discussing policies, let us look first at the actual situation prevailing in the countries and then proceed to put them in the relevant stage of stabilization. Table 3.2 shows the results for the years 1993 to 1997.

Most of the transition countries are far away from a position to stabilize. Table 3.3 divides the transition countries into three categories based on their performance in achieving growth, slowing inflation, and curbing budget deficits. In this table only five countries are presented as ready for exchange-rate stabilization. They are each, of course, in different positions. Slovakia needs to work in reducing its budget deficit. China and Slovenia both need to continue reducing their inflation rates. It is now necessary, however, to turn to some of the issues and problems associated with practical stabilization decisions.

There are many different types of exchange-rate regimes that can be presented in a spectrum of alternatives. There range from a clean float (no official intervention in the foreign-exchange markets) to currency boards and monetary unions. Table 3.4 presents the main alternatives on the spectrum relevant for the transition countries.

Once fiscal balance has been achieved, and an apparatus for fiscal discipline in the future is set up, the rate of monetary expansion can be brought down to the level that will achieve the inflation target. At this stage it becomes possible to organize a stabilization program involving fixed exchange rates. After that step is taken the fixed exchange-rate policy becomes the axis around which all other macroeconomic policies must move. Before that step is taken, there are some general considerations that should be discussed concerning fixed exchange-rate anchors.

3.7. Cases Against and for a Fixed Exchange-Rate Anchor

There are arguments both for and against fixed exchange rates in the present world. Because there is no generalized system of fixed exchange rates, a country's decision to fix must take into account that fact that fixing to one country will mean *ipso facto* flexing with one or more other countries. Countries will have to choose which currency area to become a part of. Before turning to that issue, it will be useful to list situations in which a country might or should decide *against* fixing the exchange rate or joining a currency union.[8]

Table 3.2. GDP growth, inflation, budget deficits, and exchange rates in transition countries, 1993 to 1997

	1993	*1994*	*1995*	*1996*	*1997*[a]
Armenia					
GDP	–8.6	5.5	6.9	5.3	5.0
Prices	10,877.9	4,962.0	32.2	5.7	10.0
Deficit/GDP %	1.2	10.1	9.0		
Exchange rate (Dram/$)	75	406	402	442	510
Azerbaijan					
GDP	–23.1	–21.9	–17.2	1.6	3.0
Prices	1,113.0	1,609.7	84.6	6.7	10.0
Deficit/GDP 5	7.1	10.7	0.9		
Exchange rate (Manat/$)	118	4,182	4,440	4,120	3,800
Belarus					
GDP	–10.6	–12.6	–10.0	2.6	5.0
Prices	1,995.5	1,959.9	244.0	39.3	50.0
Deficit/GDP	5.6	3.4	4.0	2.3	
Exchange rate B = ruble/$	6,990	10,600	11,500	15,500	32,000
Bulgaria					
GDP	–2.4	1.4	2.5	–10.9	–9.0
Prices	63.9	121.9	32.9	310.8	730.0
Deficit/GDP	10.9	6.6	6.8	16.7	
Exchange rate lev/$	32.7	66.0	70.7	495.7	2,100
China					
GDP	13.5	12.7	10.5	9.7	10.0
Prices	14.7	24.1	17.1	8.4	7.6
Exchange rate yuan/$	5.76	8.62	8.35	8.31	8.45
Croatia					
GDP	–3.7	0.8			
Prices	1,149.3	–3.0	3.7		
Exchange rate kuna/$	3.58	6.0	5.2		
Czech Republic					
GDP	–0.7	2.6	4.8	4.4	2.8
Prices	18.2	10.2	7.9	8.6	8.0
Deficit/GDP %	–1.3	–0.9	–0.7	0.1	
Exchange rate crown/$	30.0	28.0	26.6	27.3	29
Estonia					
GDP	–8.6	–3.2	2.9	3.0	5.0
Prices	35.0	41.7	28.9	14.8	10.0
Deficit/GDP %	–1.4	0.0	–1.0	1.5	
Exchange rate kroon/$	13.88	12.48	11.52	12.44	12.5

Table 3.2. (continued)

	1993	*1994*	*1995*	*1996*	*1997*[a]
Georgia					
GDP	–39.4	–30.0	2.4	11.0	7.0
Prices	5,000.0	7,380.0	57.4	13.5	12.0
Deficit/GDP %	16.8	16.5	6.0	4.4	
Exchange rate lari/$	102,300	1,330,000	1.245	1.280	1.35
Hungary					
GDP	–0.6	2.9	1.5	1.0	2.7
Prices	22.5	18.8	28.3	23.6	20.0
Deficit/GDP	6.0	7.5	2.4	–1.5	
Exchange rate forint/$	100.7	110.7	139.6	164.7	190
Kazakhstan					
GDP	–15.6	–18.8	–8.9	1.1	2.0
Prices	2,165.0	1,159.1	60.3	28.7	20.0
Deficit/GDP %	–3.3	7.0	4.0	2.8	
Exchange rate tenge/$	6.31	54.26	63.95	73.15	85
Kyrghizstan					
GDP	–15.5	–20.1	–6.2	5.6	6.0
Prices	1,366.0	87.2	31.2	35.0	20.0
Deficit/GDP %	6.2	9.0	11.2	5.8	
Exchange rate	8.0	10.6	11.4	16.95	20.0
Latvia					
GDP	–14.9	0.6	–1.6	2.8	3.5
Prices	109.0	35.9	24.2	13.1	10.0
Deficit/GDP %	0.6	2.0	1.6		
Exchange rate lat/$	0.59	0.55	0.54	0.56	0.55
Lithuania					
GDP	–30.4	6.0	3.0	3.0	4.0
Prices	188.7	45.1	35.7	13.1	12.0
Deficit/GDP %	–0.8	1.8	1.0		
Exchange rate litas/$	3.9	4.0	4.0	4.0	4.0
Moldova					
GDP	–1.2	–31.2	–3.0	–8.0	–3.0
Prices	1,194.0	104.5	23.8	15.1	10.0
Deficit/GDP %	6.2	4.7	4.9	5.3	
Exchange rate lei/$	3.64	4.27	4.47	4.664	4.70
Poland					
GDP	3.5	5.1	7.0	6.0	5.5
Prices	33.9	32.1	21.6	18.5	16.0
Deficit/GDP %	2.8	2.8	2.8	2.6	
Exchange rate zloty/$	2.11	2.43	2.47	2.87	3.4

Table 3.2. (continued)

	1993	*1994*	*1995*	*1996*	*1997*[a]
Romania					
GDP	1.3	3.4	7.1	4.1	–3.0
Prices	295.5	61.7	27.8	56.9	120.0
Deficit/GDP %	1.7	4.3	4.1	5.8	
Exchange rate lei/$	1,276	1,767	2,578	4,035	10,600
Russia					
GDP	–8.7	–12.6	–4.4	–6.0	1.0
Prices	844.2	214.7	131.9	21.8	18.0
Deficit/GDP %	9.6	10.3	3.7	3.3	
Exchange rate rubles/$	1,247	3,550	4,640	5,556	6,200
Slovakia					
GDP	–3.7	4.9	6.8	6.9	6.4
Prices	23.2	13.4	9.9	5.8	7.3
Deficit/GDP %	6.3	2.8	1.6	4.4	
Exchange rate crown/$	32.8	31.5	29.7	31.7	33
Slovenia					
GDP	1.3	5.3	3.9	3.1	4.0
Prices	22.9	18.3	8.6	8.8	9.0
Deficit/GDP %	–0.3	0.10	0.03	0.1	
Exchange rate tolar/$	131.8	126.5	129.9	141.3	168
Tajikistan					
GDP	17.3	–12.7	–12.4	–16.7	2.0
Prices	1,194.0	278.0	1,200.0	40.6	50.0
Deficit/GDP %	24.8	10.1	6.4		
Exchange rate Taj. rub/$			284	298	375
Turkmenistan					
GDP	10.0	–24.0	–7.5	–4.0	–3.0
Prices	10,825.9	1,328.0	2,400.0	100.1	75.0
Deficit/GDP %	3.6		1.1		
Exchange rate manat/$	2	220	200	4,065	7,115
Ukraine					
GDP	–14.2	–23.0	–11.8	–10.1	–5.0
Prices	10,156.0	410.0	181.7	39.9	20.0
Deficit/GDP %	1.2	10.1	9.0		
Exchange rate hryvna/$	12,610	104,200	179,400	1.886	1.90
Uzbekistan					
GDP	–2.3	–4.2	–1.2	1.6	5.0
Prices	1,232.0	1,550.0	76.8	64.0	40.0
Deficit/GDP %	3.0	4.2	2.8	3.5	
Exchange rate sum/$	1,247.0	25.0	35.5	54.5	100.0

Source: Adapted from WEFA Group, *Eurasia Economic Outlook*, May 1997.
a. Forecast.

Table 3.3. Performance stages of the transition countries base on 1996 data

Country	*Growth*	*Inflation*	*Deficit percent of GDP*
Stage I countries (monetary targeting required)			
Belarus	2.6	39.3	2.3
Bulgaria	−10.9	310.8	16.7
Kazakhstan	1.1	28.7	2.8
Kyrghizstan	5.6	35.0	5.8
Moldova	−8.0	15.1	5.3
Romania	4.1	56.9	5.8
Russia	−6.0	21.8	3.3
Tajikstan	−16.7	40.6	6.4 (1995)
Turkmenistan	−4.0	100.1	1.1 (1995)
Ukraine	−10.1	39.9	9.0 (1995)
Stage II countries (inflation targeting required)			
Armenia	5.3	5.7	9.0 (1995)
Azerbaijan	1.6	6.7	0.9 (1995)
Estonia	3.0	14.8	1.5
Georgia	11.0	13.5	4.4
Hungary	1.0	23.6	−1.5
Latvia	2.8	13.1	1.6 (1995)
Lithuania	3.0	13.1	1.0 (1995)
Poland	6.0	18.5	2.6
Stage III countries (ready for exchange-rate stabilization)			
Czech Republic	4.4	8.6	0.1
Croatia			
Slovakia	6.9	5.8	4.4
Slovenia	3.1	8.8	0.1
China (?)	9.7	8.4	

Disadvantages of Fixing

1. The country wants a rate of inflation different from the currency area inflation rate;
2. The country wants to use the exchange rate as an instrument of employment policy to lower or raise wages;
3. The country wants to use the exchange rate as a beggar-thy-neighbor instrument to capture employment from other countries;
4. As a large country, the country does not want an unfriendly country to benefit from the economies-of-size advantages of the large

Table 3.4. Spectrum of exchange-rate arrangements

System	*Monetary Policy*	*Par Value*	*Margins*
Variable rates			
Clean float	Independent	None	None
Dirty float	Independent	None	None
Sliding-gliding parity or tablita	Independent	Variable	Optional
Ad hoc rates			
Pegged rates	Independent	Short-term	Optional
Fixed rates			
Fixed exchange rates	Adaptive or automatic	Long-term	Narrow
Currency board	Adaptive or automatic	Long-term	Tiny or zero
Monetary union	Automatic	Forever	None

currency area, or else it fears that the addition of another currency will make national macroeconomic policy more difficult;

5. The country wants to use the money expansion or the "inflation tax" to finance government spending, and it would be prevented from doing so to the extent desired by the discipline of fixed exchange rates;
6. The country does not want to sacrifice seigniorage from the use of its money as an international means of payment; this applies especially to a large country;
7. The government of the country wants to use seigniorage as a source of hidden or off-budget funding for personal use by members of a corrupt dictatorship or naive democratic government;
8. A regime of fixed exchange rates could conflict with the required policies of a central bank that had a constitutional mandate to preserve price stability;
9. Monetary integration with one or more other countries would remove a dimension of national sovereignty that is a vital symbol of national independence;
10. The country wants to optimize the currency denominations appropriate to its per capita incomes (this would be relevant only in the case of currency unions, not fixed exchange rates);
11. The country wants to maintain its monetary independence in order to use the money expansion or inflation tax in the event of a war;

12. The country wants to protect the secrecy of its statistics, as in the case when the Soviet Union opted out of the IMF and forced its Eastern European satellites to leave the Fund;
13. There is no domestic political and economic leadership capable of maintaining a fixed exchange-rate system in equilibrium;
14. The political authorities cannot achieve budget balance and/or establish confidence in the permanence of budgetary equilibrium or the viability of fixed exchange rates;
15. The partners in the prospective currency area are politically unstable or prone to invasion by aggressor countries;
16. The partner countries are poorer and will expect aid, "equalization payments," or an unduly large proportion of the OCA's expenditures;
17. The country does not want to accept the degree of integration implied by the OCA agreement, such as common standards or immigration, labor, or tax legislation.

Advantages of Fixing

On the other hand, there are a large number of advantages to joining a fixed exchange-rate zone or currency area.

1. To gain the inflation rate of the currency area;
2. To reduce transactions costs in its trade with a major partner;
3. To eliminate the cost of printing and maintaining a separate national currency;
4. To participate in a purchasing power parity area, which would be fostered by fixed exchange rates and even more by monetary union;
5. To establish an anchor for policy, a fixed point around which expectations can be formulated and policies can revolve;
6. To remove discretion from monetary and fiscal policy authorities;
7. To keep the exchange rate from being kicked around as a political football by vested interests that want depreciation to increase profits, or to bail out debtors;
8. To establish an automatic mechanism that will enforce monetary and fiscal discipline;
9. To have a multinational cushion against shocks;
10. To participate more fully and on more equal terms in the financial center and capital market of the union;
11. To provide a catalyst for political alliance or integration;

12. To establish a power bloc as a countervailing influence against domination of neighboring powers;
13. To share in the political decision of determining the OCA's inflation rate;
14. To establish a competing international currency as a rival to the dollar and earn, instead of pay, seigniorage;
15. To reinforce or establish an economic power bloc that will have more clout in international economic discussions and have a greater power to improve, by its trade policy, its terms of trade;
16. To delegate to a mechanism outside the domestic political process the enforcement of monetary and fiscal discipline;
17. To participate in a restoration of a reformed international monetary system.

3.8. Choice of Exchange-Rate System

There remain two questions of great importance to the stabilization process. One concerns the rate at which the exchange rate should be stabilized and the mechanism of adjustment; the other concerns the choice of foreign partner or, the "optimum currency area" problem. We must consider these two issues in turn.

The Exchange-Rate Mechanism

A decision to administer the exchange rate (as opposed to the money supply or the price level) does not solve the problem of choice. For purposes of this discussion, we abstract from the optimum currency area problem, discussed in the following section, of which currency should be selected as the partner currency so that for all practical purposes in this section we assume there is a unified currency in the rest of the world. What point on the flexibility spectrum, starting from completely flexible and ranging to the completely fixed rates implied by a monetary union, is the appropriate choice for an Eastern European country?

The alternatives can be ranked according to the degree of monetary integration as follows:

A. Clean float (no intervention)
B. Dirty float (flexible rates with sporadic intervention)
C. Flexible rates with systematic intervention (e.g., to smooth trends)

D. Crawling peg (frequent minidevaluations), no adjustment mechanism
E. Adjustable peg[19] (infrequent devaluation), no adjustment mechanism
F. Tablita system (a) (crawling peg with partial adjustment)
G. Tablita system (b) (crawling peg with automatic adjustment mechanism)
H. Fixed spot rates with semiautomatic adjustment mechanism (flexible forward rates)
   a. Wide margins
   b. Narrow margins
   c. Zero margins
I. Fixed spot exchange rates, automatic adjustment, irrevocable parity (fixed forward rates)
   a. Wide margins
   b. Narrow margins
   c. No margins
J. Fixed rates, automatic adjustment, fixed relationship between foreign-exchange reserves and central-bank money
K. Currency board system (100 percent reserves backing central-bank money)
L. Monetary union (common central bank)
M. Common currency (monetary union plus a common currency)

The dividing line between fixed and flexible systems is a matter of degree.[10] The tablita systems, F or G, with partial or complete adjustment mechanism may be a useful preparatory step in the second phase of stabilization. But because the exchange rate is changing at an announced rate, it always risks the danger that the rate of depreciation will be speeded up. As a provisional measure in the second phase, it may be useful; as a final resting point it lacks credibility.

System H(a) was the fixed exchange-rate system based on the Bretton Woods arrangements. Exchange margins were narrow (3/4 of 1 percent of parity), and countries were in practice forced to use their monetary policy to protect their balance of payments. The function of the band was to allow the interplay of some uncertainty within the narrow margins about future exchange rates and to all differentials to appear in interest rates, creating a modest degree of central-bank discretion.

The main difference between H and I is that devaluation remains possible under the former and is ruled out in the latter. In the real world, of course, these must be reflected in degrees of confidence in the future rate.

There is no such thing as absolute certainty about exchange rates. The parity might be written into the constitution, but even a constitution can be changed; it might even be overthrown by a military coup. The idea of fixing the exchange rate (of course, to an anchor currency of the desired stability) for the foreseeable future, making it independent of the government or even of a change of government, would go far to building confidence in the currency and establishing a stable monetary framework for economic efficiency and growth.

J and K establish a commitment to a fixed parity and at the same time ensure that the money supplies adapt to make the fixed parity an equilibrium. The main difference between J and K is that the latter requires 100 percent reserves backing the money supply, whereas the former (similar to the Argentine case of 1991 to 1994, and Britain after the Bank Act of 1944) allows for a fiduciary issue of national currency backed by domestic assets. K might be most appropriate for a minicountry, but J would be more appropriate—because it economizes on reserves—for a midicountry. In the case of J the ratio of foreign-exchange reserves to central-bank money should err on the high side until confidence in the longevity of the system has been achieved. (At the introduction of any such system, an "overkill" ratio is desirable and may be provided by the partner country or by the IMF or by a combination of the leading financial powers.)

With three exceptions, the establishment of monetary or currency union is not at the present time an option for the East European countries, although that may change in the future. The main exception is East Germany, which has already exercised its option; no one now doubts the monetary stability of East Germany or its currency. The other possibility of monetary union now would be for one or more of the FSU countries—such as Belarus or Georgia—to join the ruble area, closing their central banks and accepting a monetary policy made in Russia or by new authorities set up to run the monetary union. Once Russia itself has restored monetary stability, the formation of a wider ruble zone would become a distinct possibility.

The third exception is the prospect for joining the European Community and, in particular, the EMS, ERM, and eventually, when and if it comes about, EMU. The attractiveness of this possibility is so great—given the large differences between standards of living in Eastern and Western Europe—that no country in Eastern Europe would be likely to reject it. Poland, Hungary, the Czech Republic, and Slovakia (and perhaps Slovenia) are early candidates for admission (with the Czech Republic closest to the monetary stability needed for *de facto* entry into the ERM or the DM area).

The attractiveness of this option is so great that monetary stability should be given a high priority in the transition countries.

3.9. Choice of Exchange Rate

The choice of exchange rate is an important one. If the home currency is overvalued, the balance of payments would be in deficit, money would be reduced, and deflation would be imposed, bringing in its wake unemployment. On the other hand, if a currency is undervalued, balance-of-payments surpluses would produce inflationary pressure that could change expectations and set in motion a wage explosion that might overshoot the equilibrium. Governments therefore have to find the exchange rate that steers between the Charybdis of overvaluation and unemployment, and the Scylla of undervaluation and inflation.

The problem of choosing an exchange rate is an old problem that has existed since coins and currencies were first introduced. The difficulty lies in choosing from among different criteria, each of which have relevance to policy. For example, the exchange rate that would bring about equilibrium in the money market may not be the same as the one that would render unecessary any change in wage rates of prices.

After major wars, in which inflation has been allowed to develop, a country has the choice of bringing prices back down to the old exchange-rate parity, or adjusting the exchange rate to make it consistent with the new price level. Thus, after the Napoleonic Wars, Britain went back to the old parity and suffered[11] deflation; similarly, after the Civil War, the United States went back to the old parity and suffered deflation. After World War I, Britain again went back to the old parity, but many other countries, like France, adapted the exchange rate to the new price level. After World War II, most countries after the Great Depression more worried about unemployment than inflation, adapted the exchange rate to the new price level. In most postwar cases, the Ricardo-Cassel purchasing-power-parity criterion was used to determine the "necessary" change in the exchange rate.

An important provision is to make sure that the exchange rate chosen will not require a deflation of money wages. It is always desirable to have concurrence of labor to the stabilization process and its agreement, where possible, on wage projections in the future within the scope of advances of productivity. Of the two evils of overvaluation and undervaluation, it is better to err, but only slightly, on the side of undervaluation.

3.10. Choice of Currency Area

The choice of currency (or basket) to fix, if any, is another important issue. It would be a great convenience to the Eurasian countries if they faced a unified system of fixed exchange rates in the rest of the world such as the one that prevailed in the nineteenth century and between the end of World War II and 1971. If there were a worldwide fixed exchange-rate system or, even better, a world currency, the transition countries would not have to choose between the major currencies. As the world is, and as it is likely to remain over the next decade, the transition countries have to cope with the problem of determining to which currency area they should belong.

The three most important currencies in the world today are of course the U.S. dollar, the Japanese yen, and the German mark; these countries would automatically be candidates for being a currency anchor. Other currencies that could be considered are the French franc, the pound sterling, the Swiss franc, and the Italian lira. All these currencies except the lira make up the IMF basket currency, the SDR.

Because fixing the exchange rate ultimately leads to importing the inflation rate of the country to whose currency the home currency is attached, recent records of inflation become relevant. The dollar has had an unbroken history in the sense that, since 1972, the United States has never repudiated its currency or had any kind of currency reform, but its performance in the past two decades has been somewhat more inflationary than the performances of Japan and Germany. It is true that the dollar is no longer defined in terms of gold and silver, but then no other country's currency is either. From the standpoint of inflation history over the past two centuries, the U.S. currency is clearly the best.

The Japanese yen had a 10 for 1 currency reform in 1948, but since that time, the yen has been more stable than the dollar. Germany had a trillion for one currency reform in 1923, and a 10 for 1 currency reform in 1948; despite—and partly because of—this war-related instability, the German mark has been one of the most stable currencies in the postwar period. The end of the Cold War, by drastically reducing the threat of invasion from the Soviet Union, coupled with the unification of Germany, which increased Germany's size, have greatly increased the mark's potential as an international currency.[12]

Recently Japan, with a currency that is overvalued on a purchasing-power-parity basis, has had the lowest rate of inflation, averaging around 2 percent. The dollar inflation rate has been around 3 percent, and the mark inflation rate, coping with the hurdles of unification, was initially around 4 percent but has since come down to 3 percent. From the standpoint of inflation rates there is not much to choose between the three currencies.

There are, however, other issues that are of great importance. One is size. This is relevant because the size of the basket of goods over which a currency has purchasing power is relevant to the choice of currency area. The Swiss franc, for example, has had a track record of stability equal to the mark. But because Switzerland's GDP is a small fraction of world GDP (it is about 1.25 percent of OECD output) and less than 1 percent of world output, stabilizing a currency of any substantial transactions area to the Swiss franc could have the effect of making it unstable.

The larger an economy, the less susceptible it is to external shocks and the more stable it is as a currency anchor. In 1996, the internal dollar area, as measured by GDP, was 25 percent of the world economy; its total transactions area, counting the groups of currencies tied to it, makes this size much larger. By contrast, Japan's GDP was 15 percent of the world economy and Germany's 7.8 percent. The sizes of other countries relevant to the Eurasian countries is noted in Table 3.5. It is clear that, measured by size alone, the dollar makes the best anchor. The dollar provides the advantage also that it is the currency in which most of international reserves are held, it is the most marketable and acceptable worldwide, it is the most widely used unit of account for deferred payments in the capital markets, and it has had recently an average inflation rate that is only slightly higher than Japan or Germany.

Let me hasten to add that there are two factors that mitigate the apparent disadvantage of the mark, from the standpoint of its position as an anchor. One, of course, is geography. Other things equal, it is a great

Table 3.5. Potential anchors, 1996 data

Country	*Currency*	*IMF Quota (billions of dollar)*	*GDP*	*Percent of World GDP*
United States	Dollar	$26.5	$7,576.2	25.4%
Japan	Yen	8.2	4,602.2	15.4
Germany	Mark	8.2	2,352.8	7.8
France	Franc	7.4	1,544.3	5.2
Italy	lira	4.6	1,193.8	4.0
United Kingdom	Pound sterling	7.4	1,151.1	3.9
European Union	Euro	42.7	8,557.7	28.7
World	None	145.3	29,843.5	100.0

Source: *International Financial Statistics and WEFA Economic Outlook*, May 1997.

convenience to be situated near the country that is the anchor currency—assuming that country is a friend. Geography plays a role in factors that reinforce frequency of contact, familiarity, channels of communication, and the commercial habit. Transport costs are lower, and neighbors lean on each other.

The second factor is that the DM area is larger than Germany itself. The Dutch guilder, the Belgian (and Luxembourg) franc, and the Austrian schilling are rigidly fixed to the DM and those four countries for all practical purposes share in the German capital market. If we add the 1996 GDPs of these three countries to Germany's GDP, we get $3.2 trillion or 11 percent of world output. If in addition we add France's $1.5 trillion GDP, we get 16 percent of world output, larger than Japan. The more countries join EMU, the larger the DM-euro bloc, and the better suited it will be to act as an anchor for the Eurasian countries.

If EMU gets started in 1999, it is likely that it will expand rapidly as the other members see its benefits to stability and productivity. It is likely therefore that there will be a formidable bloc of countries committed to anti-inflationary policies. The case for the European anchor is further enhanced by the prospects that other countries on the waiting list to join the EU will see an attachment to the euro as a factor accelerating their entry. Taking these factors into account, the euro-bloc anchor is only slightly less attractive on purely economic grounds to the dollar, and Pan-Europa sentiment may be enough to tilt the balance in favor of a fix to the euro. The euro would be especially attractive if the United Kingdom, the home of what is likely to remain for some time the Continent's leading financial center, were to join the EMU.

It is important to emphasize that the "optimum currency area" problem would not arise for Eurasian countries if the DM-euro and the dollar were to be closely linked. It would be an additional—but less necessary—benefit if the yen were also tied with the other two. Such an arrangement of quasi-fixed parities could indeed come about in the not-too-distant future. If any four of the five currencies that currently make up the SDR[13] pegged their own currencies to it, the mainstream of the world economy would have returned to fixed exchange rates. It is precisely because of the difficulty for the non-German European countries created by dollar-mark (euro) variations that such a possibility is not completely remote.[14]

In all cases, economic choices will be strongly influenced by political considerations. For those countries like Poland, Hungary, the Czech Republic, Slovakia, and Slovenia, with the possibility of (comparatively) early entry into the European Union, the DM-euro would be the natural alignment (bearing in mind, however, difficulties of adjustment already mentioned when the dollar-DM rate changes significantly). It is probable that the Baltic states will also fit into this category, although the expansion of the EU to include non-NATO countries would pose some difficult problems for which there is no easy solution. For the other countries the dollar remains the best single option.

One way of avoiding a choice between using the dollar or the mark is to stabilize the exchange rate in terms of a basket. Two established baskets are the SDR of the IMF and the ECU—to become the euro—of the Economic Union. The SDR has never become important in capital market transactions, and a country would not thereby achieve many of the benefits of a wider monetary area. The SDR nevertheless has the advantage that it includes the dollar and yen in addition to the three most important European currencies. The SDR depreciates against commodities at a rate equal to the average of the five country's inflation rates.

Until recent years, the ECU was not much better, from the standpoint of capital transactions, than the SDR. But in recent years, because of the drive to European Monetary Union after the signing of the Maastricht Treaty in 1991, the ECU has become more important. At an important meeting of the EU summit in Madrid in 1996, it was decided that the euro would be equivalent to the ECU when it replaces the latter at the end of 1998.

For the Eastern European countries, the most difficult problem is that of changes in the dollar-mark rate. A basket composed of only two currencies, the dollar and the mark, might be attractive to East European countries as an interim solution pending developments toward EMU in Western Europe. Each country could choose its own weight for the two currencies based on considerations of optimum currency-area theory. To the extent that it is useful to encourage trade within Eastern Europe, an argument could be made for a common basket. Simplicity is a great convenience in agreeing on a common basket, and a basket equal to 1 dollar + 1 DM would have the great attractions of simplicity, in effect giving a weight—given current exchange rates—of two-thirds to the dollar and one-third to the DM.

3.11. Conclusion

Based on the preceding arguments, we have arrived at the following conclusions:

1. Belarus, Bulgaria, Kazakhstan, Kyrghizstan, Moldova, Russia, Tajikstan, Turkmenistan, and the Ukraine need to reduce the rate of

monetary expansion. In most cases, a prior condition requires the achievement of fiscal balance, but in a few cases, the culprit is not the budget deficit but excessive credit to the semiprivate sector (which typically involves state-owned enterprises).

2. Armenia, Azerbaijan, Georgia, Hungary, Lithuania, and Poland have reached the stage where inflation targeting is preferable to monetary targeting, and inflation should be reduced below 5 percent, at which time, these countries could consider moving toward stage 1. The Caucasian Republics should prepare themselves to fix their currencies to the dollar, possibly using currency-board arrangements. When their inflation rates have been sufficiently reduced, Hungary, Lithuania, and Poland should prepare to fix their currencies to the mark.

3. The Czech Republic, Croatia, Slovakia, and Slovenia have reached the stage where they can and should fix their currencies to the mark, in preparation for the monetary policies that would be automatic should they join EMU. In every case, however, it would be necessary to adopt the currency-board framework to control expectations and eliminate the one-way speculative option that often accompanies fixed exchange rates without allocation of monetary policy to protect the balance of payments.

4. China is a special case. The sharp devaluation of the renminbi at the beginning of 1994 produced an inflation spike in that year and 1995 that has by now been gradually corrected. Once complete convertibility is achieved, it would be desirable to fix the exchange rate to the U.S. dollar around current levels or somewhat lower to allow for what may turn out to be an excessive appreciation of the real exchange rate.

Notes

1. The principle of effective market classification (POMC) was introduced in my paper Mundell (1960). It asserts that policy instruments should be assigned to policy targets that they have a comparative advantage in affecting.

2. In the 1980s there was still a substantial body of opinion that has argued that the remedy for the U.S. trade deficit is a depreciation of the U.S. dollar, a view that found substantial support in policy circles in the 1980s and 1990s. Despite the sharp depreciation of the dollar in the late 1980s and early 1990s, the U.S. trade deficit remained close to an all-time high. The opposing school, of which I formed a part, argued that the U.S. deficits would have persisted even if exchange rates had remained completely fixed because the trade deficit was driven by net capital imports arising from the excess of savings (and the budget surplus) over investment in countries like Japan and (before unification) Germany, and a corresponding excess of investment (plus the budget deficit) over savings in the United Sates. See Bergsten (1991) for the proceedings of a conference devoted to the subject, and my paper in that volume (Mundell, 1991) for a discussion of the exchange rate controversy from a general equilibrium theorist's point of view.

3. The next few paragraphs draw on and summarize the analysis of a paper delivered first at the Caracas Conference on Financial Markets in January 1979 and published in Spanish in the Conference volume. See also Mundell (1989, 1990).

4. Walras's law asserts that the sum of all excess demands in a general equilibrium system is identically zero.

5. Cournot's law asserts that the sum of all trade balances is zero; see Mundell (1960).

6. Even where the intertemporal borrowing is legitimate, however, there might be externalities associated with changes in the terms of trade that may create a divergence between private and social benefits from external borrowing.

7. Interest rates converge exactly only if tax rates are the same. Permanent differentials will reflect differential tax rates.

8. This section, borrows from my paper presented at the Optimum Currency Area Conference at the University of Tel Aviv, December 5–6, 1996.

9. The Bretton Woods arrangements were sometimes characterized as an "adjustable peg" system, a term invented by Professor (now Sir) James Meade to emphasize the right of each country to devalue; the IMF rules provided for exchange-rate changes in the event of a "fundamental disequilibrium." The system did not work out that way, much to the consternation of advocates of flexible exchange rates. The short-run rigidities quickly turned into medium- and then long-run rigidities as countries realized the importance of confidence in the parity, and the cost—quickly reflected in interest rates—of doubts about the continuation of a parity. Apart from the whopping devaluation of the sterling area in 1949—arguably a mistake forced on the reluctant British by American bureaucrats—a couple of French devaluations, and the foolish but almost irrelevant 5 percent appreciations of the mark and guilder in 1961, there were very few exchange-rate changes among the major countries until the British and French devaluations and the German appreciation in the late 1960s.

10. One of the reasons for the success of the international gold standard that ensured fixed exchange rates and substantial stability of the price level was that there was confidence that the mechanism would be retained without devaluation (except perhaps in wartime); and confidence (sometimes unfounded) that the mechanism would be restored after the war gave countries the ability to finance wars at lower interest rates than would otherwise have been possible; a recent paper, "Gold as a Commitment Mechanism: Past, Present and Future," by Michael D. Bordo, prepared for the World Gold Council Central Bank Advisory Group (July 1944) has further developed this theme. The parity system that operated under the Bretton Woods arrangements before 1971 also involved a commitment requiring, theoretically, approval for exchange-rate changes from the IMF. In the post-1971 era, the IMF has been of little use from the standpoint of establishing an exchange-rate commitment mechanism, and countries have had to invent them for themselves. Argentine, Brazil, and Israel have all tried, unsuccessfully, to establish a fixed rate, but their earlier experiments failed because they never acquired control of the budget deficit and thus had to have continued recourse to inflationary finance. Recently, however, Argentine has embarked on a closely watched experiment with its new *peso argentino*, rigidly fixed to the dollar and requiring, through its convertibility law, $1 worth of foreign-exchange backing every new peso issued, with no (or very limited) possibility of credit extension to the government. This arrangement is similar but not identical to currency-board arrangements that have worked in several former colonies of the European empires in the past and are being experimented with in the Baltic states.

11. Ricardo advocated resumption of payments at par, but in a speech before Parliament in 1820, he stated that if the premium on gold had not fallen to 5 percent while the 1819 Committees were sitting, he would have favored an alternation of the standard in preference to a return to cash payments at the old standard. On this see Viner (1937, p. 204).

12. The end of the Cold War greatly increased the potential for Germany to lengthen the maturity of its long-term bonds, which hitherto had been impeded by the possibility, however, remote, of war.

13. When first created by the Board of Governors of the IMF, the SDR was a gold-weight guaranteed reserve asset (currency?) equal to one U.S. dollar "of the weight and fineness" in 1944 (when the Articles of the IMF were drawn up)—1/35 ounce of gold. Beginning in July 1944, the gold guarantee was stripped away from the SDR, and it was transformed into a basket of initially sixteen inflating currencies. A third version was created later in the 1970s when the basket was reduced to the five currencies of the "G-5" countries. Since January 1, 1991, the SDR has consisted of the currencies of the five members having the largest exports of goods and services during the period 1985 to 1998, with the following weights: U.S. dollar, 40 percent; DM, 21 percent; yen, 17 percent; and French franc and pound sterling, 11 percent each. In calculating the value of the SDR, the U.S. dollar equivalent of each of the currencies are summed to yield the rate for the SDR in terms of the U.S. dollar, and the rates for the SDR in terms of other currencies are in turn derived from the market exchange rates of those currencies for the U.S. dollar and the U.S. dollar rate for the SDR.

14. It could be argued that Europe was more closely integrated together financially under the fixed exchange-rate system based on the dollar in the era of the Bretton Woods agreement when for two decades most currencies were fixed to the dollar with margins of 3/4 of 1 percent on either side of parity. The arrangements broke down not because there were any defects with the fixed exchange-rate mechanism—adjustment between countries with different currencies need not have been any different than any adjustment between regions of a single currency area—but because postwar and subsequent inflation had undervalued gold and made it scarce. (For political reasons, the price of gold could not be doubled—the proposal made by the French—because it would help South Africa and the Soviet Union, the two largest gold producers and for different reasons not candidates for foreign aid from the United States. As it turned out, the laws of economics triumphed over politics and the price of gold soared!) The basic problem with a return to the fixed-rate system is to find a politically acceptable method of delegating responsibility for the fixing.

References

Bergsten, C.F. (ed.). (1991). *International Adjustment and Finance: The Lessons of 1985–90*. Washington, DC: Institute for International Economics.

Hume, David. (1752). "On the Balance of Trade." Gssay 27 in *Hume's Essays: Literary, Moral and Political*. London: Ward, Lock.

Keynes, John Maynard. (1936). *The General Theory of Employment, Interest, and Money*. London: Macmillan.

Mundell, Robert A. (1960a). "The Monetary Dynamics of International Adjustment Under Fixed and Flexible Exchange Rates." *Quarterly Journal of Economics* 84(2) (May): 227–257. Reprinted in Mundell (1968).

Mundell, Robert A. (1960b). "The Pure Theory of International Trade." *American Economic Review* 50 (March): 67–110.

Mundell, Robert A. (1961a). "Flexible Exchange Rates and Employment Policy."

Canadian ***Journal*** *of Economics and Political Science* 27(4) (November): 509–517. Reprinted in Mundell (1968).

Mundell, Robert A. (1961b). "The International Disequilibrium System." *Kyklos* 14(2): 154–172. Reprinted in Mundell (1968).

Mundell, Robert A. (1961c). "A Theory of Optimum Currency Areas." *American Economic Review*, 51(4) (November): 509–517. Reprinted in Mundell (1968).

Mundell, Robert A. (1963). "The Gold Herring," U.S. Congress, Joint Economic Committee, Hearings on the U.S. Balance of Payments. Washington, DC, November.

Mundell, Robert A. (1964). "Capital Mobility and Size." *Canadian Journal of Economics and Political Science*, 30(3) (August): 421–431. Reprinted in Mundell (1968).

Mundell, Robert A. (1965a). *The International Monetary System: Conflict and Reform*. Montreal: Private Planning Association of Canada.

Mundell, Robert A. (1965b). "The Proper Division of the Burden of the International Adjustment." *National Banking Review*, 3(1) (September): 81–87.

Mundell, Robert A. (1968a). "Gold and the Gulliver Problem." Lecture presented at the University of Chicago, February 8.

Mundell, Robert A. (1968b). "A Plan for a World Currency." U.S. Congress, Joint Economic Committee, Hearings Before [Reuss] Subcommittee on International Exchange and Payments, Washington, DC, September 9.

Mundell, Robert A. (1969). "The Case for a European Currency." Paper presented at a meeting of the American Management Association in New York, December.

Mundell, Robert A. (1973). "A Plan for a European Currency." Paper presented at the Optimum Currency Areas Conference in Madrid, March 1970. Reprinted in H. Johnson and A. Swoboda (eds.), *The Economics of Common Currencies* (pp. 143–173). London: George Allen & Unwin.

Mundell, Robert A. (1970). "African Trade, Politics and Money." In R. Tremblay (ed.), *Africa and Monetary Integration* (pp. 11–67). Montreal: Les Editions HRW. Paper originally prepared for the United Nations Economic Commission for Africa (August).

Mundell, Robert A. (1971). "The Optimum Balance of Payments Deficit and the Theory of Empires." In P. Salin and E. Claassen (eds.), *Stabilization Policies in Interdependent Economies* (pp. 69–86). Amsterdam: North Holland Press.

Mundell, Robert A. (1972). "The Choice of Monetary Systems: African Currency Problems." In R. Tremblay (ed.), *Africa and Monetary Integration* (pp. 363–368). Montreal: Les Editions HRW.

Mundell, Robert A. (1976). "The Geography of Inflation and the Reform of the Gold Standard." In *Geographical Aspects of Inflation Processes*. New York: American Geographical Society.

Mundell, Robert A. (1991). "The Great Exchange Rate Controversy: Trade Balances and the International Monetary System." In Bergsten (1991, pp. 187–238).

Mundell, R.A., and Arrigo Sadun. (1996a). "*Piano di paritB lira-marco:* entrare in

Europa passando per Francoforte." *Rivista di Politica Economica* Anno 86-Serie III Fasciocolo VII–VIII (Luglio-Agosto) 1996: 121–141.

Mundell, R.A., and Arrigo Sadun. (1996b). "The Lira-Mark Parity Plan" (with Arrigo Sadun) *Rivista di Politica Economica* (September–October 1996). English version of the above.

Taussig, Frank W. (1919), *Principles of Economics*. New York: Macmillan.

Viner, Jacob. (1937). *Studies in the Theory of International Trade.* London: George Allen & Unwin.

4 TOWARD VIRTUAL EXCHANGE-RATE STABILITY IN WESTERN AND EASTERN EUROPE WITH THE ADVENT OF EMU

Ronald I. McKinnon

4.1. Introduction

With European monetary integration having started as scheduled on January 1, 1999, what should be the exchange-rate rules governing other European countries that want free access to the European common market but that would not, at least at the outset, be part of the common monetary regime? Some Central and Eastern European counties (CEECs) have already applied for membership in the European Union (EU)—the so-called Visegrad-5 consisting of the Czech Republic, Hungary, the Slovak Republic, Slovenia, and Poland. Other CEECs could be considered for EU membership in the not-too-distant future—the Balkan-2 (Bulgaria and Romania), the Baltic-3 (Estonia, Latvia, and Lithuania), and counties like Croatia and other parts of the former Yugoslavia or the former Soviet Union.

In their comprehensive study "The Costs and Benefits of Eastern Enlargement: The Impact of on the EU and Eastern Europe," Richard Baldwin, Joseph Francois, and Richard Portes (1997) estimate that the net benefits of EU enlargement greatly exceed the costs. While still being positive—albeit modest—in Western Europe, these benefits would be greatest in the CEECs themselves. But implicit in the three authors' "real-side" analysis is that trade takes place over an exchange-rate regime that is mutually acceptable between East and West.

In this chapter, I propose exchange-rate rules that are consistent with *virtual exchange-rate stability* within Europe. Virtual stability in exchange rates would allow for rapid, noninflationary export growth in the transitional CEECs. But fears of beggar-thy-neighbor undervaluations or unfair trading practices, which Western Europeans might have about CEEC policies, would be allayed. As far as possible, any lapses from traditional exchange parities would be only temporary.

To organize ideas, I assume that EMU succeeds for an inner group of European countries in the sense that the new European Central Bank (ECB) stabilizes the common price level in tradable goods. For the remaining "out" countries whose national currencies continue to circulate separately, the new euro now becomes the focal point of their exchange-rate policies. A cooperative monetary regime—like the old exchange-rate mechanism (ERM)—for establishing bands of exchange-rate variation against the euro will still be necessary. This new "ERM II" would apply to all Western European countries that defer their date for joining EMU—such as seems likely for Britain, Sweden, Denmark, and Greece—and to those CEECs who are in the process of applying for EU membership.

4.2. ERM II: Exchange-Rate Rules for European Countries Outside the Monetary Union

Suppose an inner group of European countries succeeds in forming EMU. Euros with reasonably stable purchasing power begin to circulate. For those EU countries not (yet) in the monetary union, the natural monetary anchor would be its exchange rate with the euro.

This clarity of purpose would make ERM II much easier to manage than the old ERM, where the ecu was a rather weak and seldom-used monetary indicator, and where the old bilateral parity grid was overly cumbersome because each national central bank had become responsible for maintaining too many cross rates of exchange. Instead of a bilateral parity grid, each "out" (a European country not in EMU), would peg its exchange rate unambiguously to the euro within, say, ±2 percent. Then the whole constellation of exchange rates with other outs would be determined by triangular arbitrage in private markets. The range of exchange-rate variation between any pair of outs would be twice as wide—that is, ±4 percent. No further official interventions to establish cross rates of exchange would be necessary. Like the "classical" fixed-rate dollar standard of the 1950s and

1960s, where every country other than the United States declared a fixed dollar parity within ±1 percent, variation between any pair of nondollar currencies was confined to ±2 percent by triangular arbitrage. Indeed, if experience with ERM II proved successful, its band widths could later be narrowed to become like those of its Bretton Woods predecessor.

Also like the classical dollar standard, the conduct of monetary policies under ERM II would be more purely asymmetrical across "in" and "out" countries. The European Central Bank (ECB) would formulate its monetary policy independently of the foreign-exchange problems of any individual out country. (But the ECB might still take the euro's strength or weakness against major international currencies, such as the U.S. dollar, into account.) Ideally, the ECB should target the level (rather than the rate of change) of a producer price index (PPI) weighted across all the "ins"—that is, those countries in EMU (McKinnon, 1996b). In effect, the value of the euro would then be stabilized in terms of the broadest possible basket of tradable goods. But the ECB would typically not enter the foreign-exchange markets to support the interventions of the out countries.

Each "out" central bank would have the primary responsibility of bending its monetary policy toward maintaining its exchange rate, by unsterilized intervention if necessary, with the euro. And to honor its obligation to maintain a fixed exchange parity with the euro in the long run, the out country's domestic credit expansion would be subordinated to stabilizing the level of its producer price index. If necessary, each out central bank would alone intervene directly in the foreign exchanges to maintain its exchange rate within its agreed-on band against the euro.

This does not rule out the possibility that an "out" country with chronic, but moderately higher, inflation would opt for a downward crawling peg against the euro. Again, the objective would be to maintain approximate purchasing power parity with the EU countries as measured by a broad basket of tradable goods—that is, producer or wholsale price indices. Israel, Chile, and Indonesia (before the Asian crash) have had long experience with crawling or sliding bands.

One great advantage of this fundamental asymmetry in the conduct of monetary policies—where the ECB (representing the "in" countries collectively) practices monetary autonomy and each "out" country gears national monetary policy toward stabilizing its exchange rate with the euro—is that ERM II can easily accommodate new members. The accession, first to the EU and then to ERM II, of the CEEC countries (and other transitional economies) is made easier. Each new member is assigned monetary responsibility for maintaining just one exchange rate: its currency versus the euro. Unlike the bilateral parity grid of the old ERM, a new member in ERM II would have no additional responsibilities for direct stabilizing cross rates of exchange with all other members. Nor would existing members find that their life was more complicated—more cross rates of exchange to manage—with the accession of new members. In this respect, such a regime would again be much like the worldwide fixed-rate dollar standard of the 1950s and 1960s, which could, and did, easily accommodate new members—each responsible for maintaining its own dollar parity.

But the new ERM II would also differ in some significant respects from the classical dollar standard, where most countries other than the United States itself retained exchange controls on capital account.

First, because of the single European act of 1986, the outs in Western Europe—including Sweden and Britain—would start without exchange controls on capital account. Thus they would be more vulnerable to self-fulfilling speculative attacks, as per the "new crisis" literature (Obstfeld, 1994; Krugman, 1997). Less highly developed outs with a proclivity to inflate, such as some in central and eastern Europe including Greece, would be even more vulnerable to a speculative attacks in the absence of controls on financial capital flows—as we discuss below.

Second, many (although not all) of the outs would differ from the participants in the classical dollar standard insofar as they were aiming to converge to a common currency regime. Those outs, which did not intend to inflate at a higher rate than the EMU core countries, would not want to avail themselves of the Bretton Woods option of occasional controlled devaluations. Expectations effects would be too adverse.

When their underlying monetary policy was sound, how should out countries manage attacks on their exchange rates? Can the rules of the game be such that speculative attacks, even when successful, are unlikely to fatally undermine the ERM II agreement itself—while leaving the door open for the out country in question to join EMU in the future?

4.3. Temporary Suspensions of Exchange Parities: The Restoration Rule

The behavior of countries operating under the international gold standard before 1914 is instructive. In the face of a liquidity crises, a country would sometimes resort to gold devices: it would raise the buying price for gold or interfere with its exportation. This amounted to a minor, albeit temporary, suspension of its traditional gold parity. In more major crises including wars, a few outright suspensions for some months or years occurred. In the long run, however, the gold standard was very successful in having countries adhere to their traditional exchange parities while anchoring the common price level. In early 1914, exchange rates and wholesale prices were virtually the same as they had been in the late 1870s.

What gave the pre-1914 gold standard its long-run resilience? After any short-run crisis that forced the partial or complete suspension of a gold parity, the country in question was obliged to return to its traditional parity as soon as practicable (Bordo and Kydland, 1995). I have dubbed this unwritten obligation of the classical gold standard "the restoration rule" (McKinnon, 1996b, ch. 2). Even when a currency crisis undermined the government's ability to sustain convertibility in the near term, longer-term exchange-rate expectations remained regressive with respect to the country's traditional gold parity because of the restoration rule. Correspondingly, long-term interest rates showed little volatility by modern standards (McKinnon and Ohno, 1997, ch. 8); and, without significant financial risk, their levels also remained low: about 3 percent in the United Kingdom and 4 percent in the United States.

The parallel for the case of the euro-based ERM II is quite clear. Each out country sets its long-run monetary policy to be consistent with maintaining a "traditional" exchange rate against the euro within a narrow band, which amounts to having the same long-run rate of price inflation (optimally zero) in its producer price index as those in EMU. The out country's central bank also announces that it will adjust short-run monetary policy and intervene to keep its exchange rate within, say, ±2 percent. (The central rate is calculated to be align to the two PPIs—a version of purchasing power parity.) But faced with a massive speculative attack like Sweden faced in September 1992, convertibility of its currency into euros at a fixed rate of exchange would be temporarily suspended. In the face of an unexpected macroeconomic shock such as a cyclical downturn not of its own making, the government would otherwise have to increase short-run interest rates exorbitantly to defend the currency.

However, this is not the end of the story. Any suspension of convertibility into the euro at the traditional exchange rate would be only temporary. As soon as practicable after the speculative attack, the out country's central bank would begin nudging its exchange rate back up toward its traditional euro parity. France provides the best modern example of a country following the restoration rule *de facto*. The massive speculative attack against the franc in September 1993 forced a virtual suspension of the ERM bilateral parity grid: official exchange-rate margins were widened from 2.25 percent to a ridiculous ±15 percent. Yet, subsequently, the franc-mark exchange rate quickly returned close to its traditional level (Figure 4.1); and, compared to the 1980s, French short- and long-term interest rates closely tracked

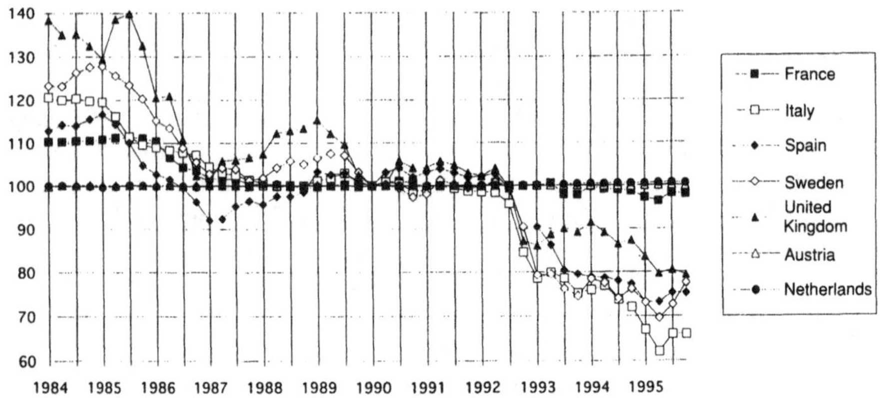

Figure 4.1. Nominal Exchange Rates Verses German Mark (1990 Q1 = 1000) (quarterly observations)
Source: IMF International Financial Statistics CD ROM, March 1996, line rf.

German ones in the 1990s (Figures 4.2 and 4.3). Because the French monetary and fiscal "fundamentals" were not out of alignment with Germany's, restoration was easy—even though defending against the initial massive attack was impossible.

Allowing for temporary crisis-based suspensions of convertibility, followed by (gradual) restoration of the traditional parity, poses problems for speculators. They don't have any clear point at which to get out of their contract (short in the out-country's currency) to realize speculative profits. In contrast, a more or less discrete devaluation in response to a speculative attack, with no attempt at restoration, makes it easy for speculators to get out safely. Paradoxically, even though speculators know that temporary suspensions of convertibility are possible, speculative attacks may well be less likely if they also know in advance that the restoration rule is in place.

In summary, suppose that the long-run monetary and price-level, fundamentals of the country itself are not in question. But nevertheless, the national currency is subject to a massive speculative attack—possibly aggravated by contagion from neighboring countries as occurred in the Asian currency crisis of 1997. Then temporary parity suspension with some depreciation, coupled with the promise of eventually restoring the initial par value of the currency (our restoration rule) would have substantial advantages:

In the *short run*, any single "out" government isn't forced to increase near-term interest rates so sharply in a cyclical downturn—or when its banks are particularly weak from maturity mismatches. The expectation of eventual exchange-rate appreciation minimizes (but need not eliminate)

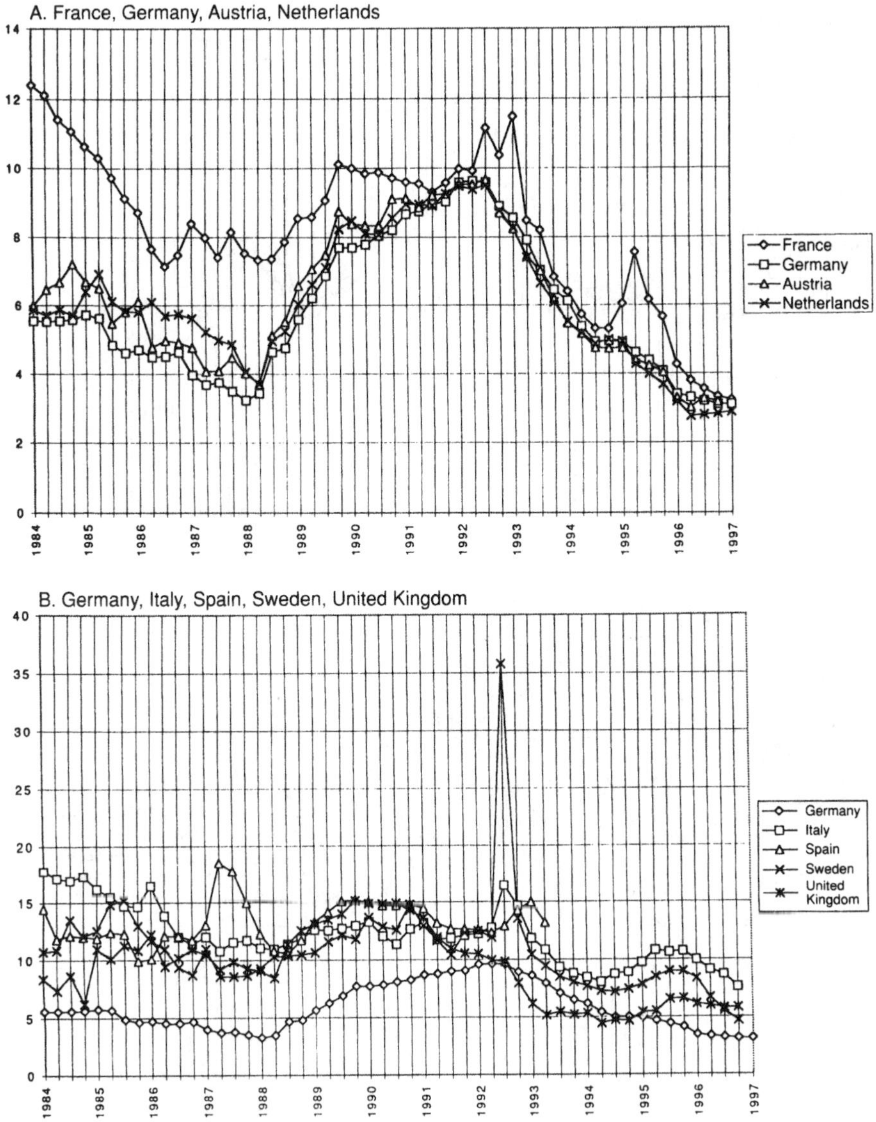

Figure 4.2. Short-Term Interest Rates (quarterly observations)
Source: IMF International Financial Statistics, line 60b, money-market rate.

the need to increase interest rates currently to assure the markets that restoration is in prospect.

In the *medium run* when the errant exchange rate is nudged back up, the problem of "accidental" competitive devaluation is mitigated. Despite a

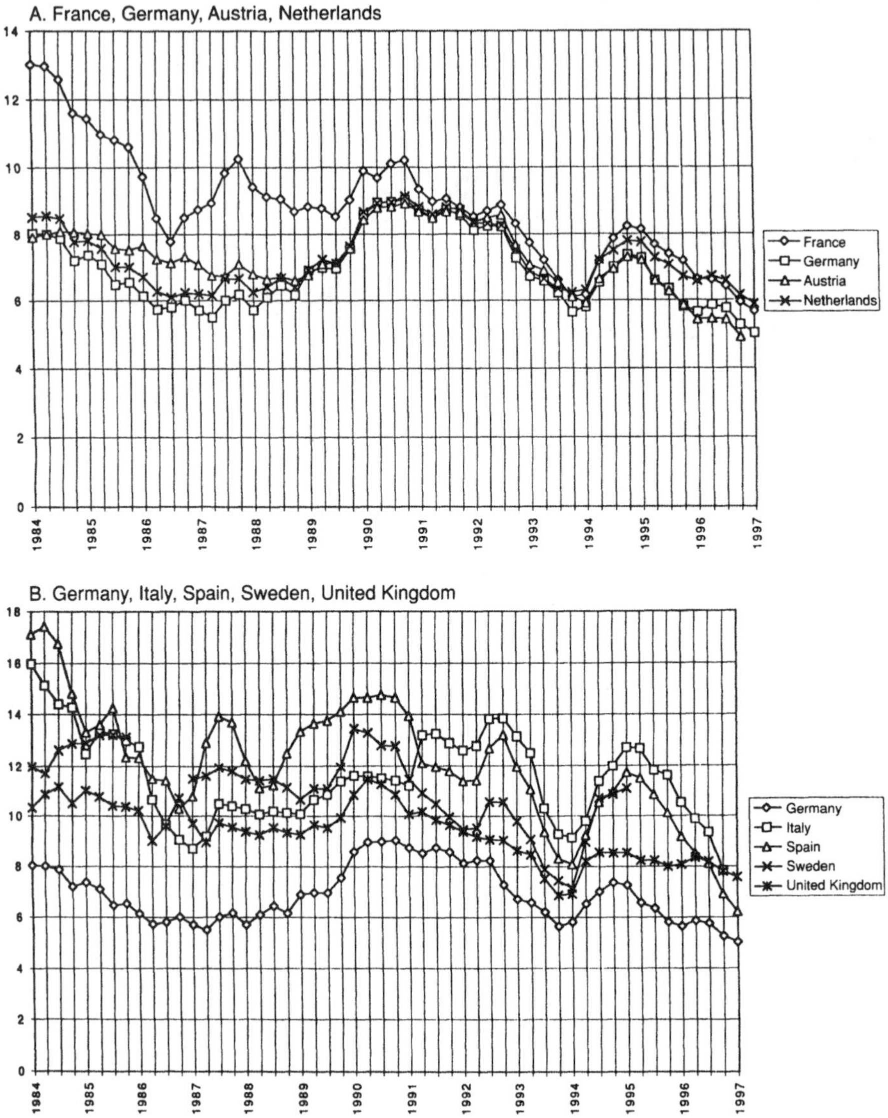

Figure 4.3. Long-Term Interest Rates (quarterly observations)
Source: *IMF International Financial Statistics*, line 61, government bond yield.

temporary devaluation at the outset of the attack, the core countries within EMU need not worry about persistent beggar-thy-neighbor policies by the out countries—nor need the out countries worry about each other.

In the *long run*, the out country's central bank can keep the domestic price level consistent with eventually joining EMU at its "traditional" euro exchange parity. Ideally, its long-term interest rates would remain fairly stable at levels close to those of the core European countries—even during a foreign-exchange crisis.

This scheme differs from other suggestions for target zones for exchange rates with "soft buffers." To stabilize the real exchange rate at some preassigned level, John Williamson (1985, 1994) proposed target zones for nominal exchange rates. But targeting the *real* exchange rate requires the *nominal* central parity of the target zone to continually adjust. For example, if domestic inflation happens to be higher than that of trading partners, the nominal central parity must continually depreciate. In the extreme if the authorities mistakenly aimed to keep the real exchange rate undervalued, a monetary explosion—with inflation and unending nominal depreciation—could result. Williamson's target zone for the real exchange rate is not a suitable commitment device for stabilizing the domestic price level in the longer run. Nor would it generate the expectation that an errant exchange rate will return to its traditional *nominal* exchange parity. Thus, long-term interest rates could remain quite volatile.

Recently, Bartolini and Prati (1997) proposed keeping a moving average of nominal exchange rates, which are subject to random shocks, within a prespecified exchange-rate band. So on any one trading day, the authorities might allow the spot exchange rate outside of its band as long as the (backward-looking) average rate was still within the band. But under their averaging rule, the longer the market rate was outside the band, the more pressure there would be to drive it back. So some welcome regressive expectations would be built in to their system. The authors show that this regime of continually soft buffers would be less prone to successful speculative attack than would a hard band of comparable width.

But the formal Bartolini-Prati averaging rule holds only as long as the authorities don't run out of exchange reserves. It is silent about what the government's obligations might be *after* a successful speculative attack. Before any such attack, it provides some automatic flexibility for the exchange rate—the soft buffer on the edge of the band. Yet in the absence of a speculative attack, this day-to-day flexibility under the Bartolini-Prati rule to go outside the band is unnecessary and lacks transparency. It might even weaken the government's commitment to a noninflationary policy consistent with long-run exchange-rate stability.

Better to keep a rather vigorously enforced hard exchange-rate band as long as possible. As under the gold standard, only in extreme situations would the band be temporarily abandoned after a successful speculative attack. But then the promise to restore the traditional exchange parity, as advocated above, becomes all important for maintaining regressive expectations in exchange rates and corresponding stability in long-term interest rates (McKinnon, 1996b).

4.4. Lessons from the East Asian Currency Crises

The behavior of the East Asian dollar standard both before and after the contagious currency attacks of 1997 illustrates the case for virtual exchange-rate stability rather well. For more than a decade before 1997, what are now the Asian crisis economies—Indonesia, Korea, Malaysia, Philippines, and Thailand—had all pegged to the dollar and had converged to WPI inflation (adjusted for a downward crawl in Indonesia's case) similar to the United States (McKinnon, 1999). Fiscal deficits were negligible so that, precrisis, their nominal (and real) exchange rates looked sustainable. Indeed, together with the noncrisis creditor economies—Hong Kong, Singapore, and Taiwan—these individual dollar pegs secured their domestic price levels. They also provided collective exchange-rate security by protecting against (accidental) competitive devaluations by neighboring countries. In the 1980s through to 1997, this Asian dollar standard was the collective monetary anchor during a remarkable period of rapid economic growth and transformation—what the World Bank (1993) prematurely called the "East Asian Miracle."

What then went wrong with this fixed exchange-rate regime? First, the largest East Asian economy, Japan, was not part of it. The "loose cannon" in the pre-1997 East Asian exchange-rate regime was the yen/dollar exchange rate (McKinnon and Ohno, 1997). Cyclical variations in the real yen/dollar rate upset the competitive positions of the dollar-bloc countries and destabilized flows of direct investment from Japan to the others. The expected upward drift in the nominal dollar value of the yen drove nominal interest rates on yen assets far below those prevailing elsewhere in Asia. Banks in other Asian economies were tempted to accept cheap yen deposits without covering the foreign-exchange risk.

So the second big problem in East Asia was the failure to regulate properly banks and other financial institutions. Banking crises in the East Asian Five preceded the attacks on their currencies that began in July 1997. For many years, diverse financial institutions in each of the five countries had struggled with festering bad loan problems from overinvestment in real estate, lending to profitless heavy industry, government-sponsored megaprojects, subsidized rural lending, and so on. The Asian tradition of governments leaning on financial institutions to direct credit to favored sectors led to inflated property markets in Thailand, allowed Korean very large chaebol (conglomerates) to grow at the expense of the rest of the economy, propped up state-owned or politically connected enterprises everywhere, and undermined the capital position of the banks.

Although partially covered up, these bad loans were more or less known to the public. But nobody much cared. Each person felt that his deposits in his country's financial institutions would be guaranteed by his national government. Banks and a variety of other financial institutions could take excessive risks—including massive foreign-exchange exposure (currency risk)—without frightening their depositors or overseas (dollar) creditors. Borrowing uncovered in dollars at 6 percent or in yen at 2 percent looks excessively cheap if a Thai bank can on-lend in baht at 12 percent. If the gambles pays off in a short time frame, the owners of the banks or their designees became wealthy. If they fail collectively as in the case of a major devaluation, then they can "put" the bailout costs to the national government and ultimately to the nation's taxpayers (McKinnon and Pill, 1998).

This moral hazard in banks, and to some extent nonfinancial corporations, in the East Asian Five was exacerbated by the absence of capital controls in the balance of payments. (In the case of Korea, it was the premature removal of the controls as a condition for Korea joining the OECD three years before!) If prudential regulations requiring banks and corporations to cover their foreign-currency and term-structure risks are ineffective, then capital controls can brake the build up of short-term indebtedness in foreign currencies. Indeed, it had been virtually textbook wisdom that, in the optimum order of economic liberalization, capital controls should be removed only after everything else in the domestic economy had been got "right" (McKinnon, 1993).

But give credit where credit is due. Before the 1997 crisis, the macroeconomic policies of the East Asian Five looked good. Their dollar exchange rates had been fairly stable for more than a decade and, by the purchasing-power-parity criterion, were more or less correctly aligned with each other and with the American price level. Rather than the misalignment of exchange rates, the problem was the massive build up of short-term foreign-currency indebtedness which, when revealed, made the otherwise successful exchange-rate mechnism impossible to defend.

In the spring of 1997, the crash was triggered by doubts over the solvency of Thai banks and finance companies leading to massive withdrawals of *foreign*-currency deposits. This created domino beggar-thy-neighbor bank runs and devaluations in the other debtor economies. Beginning in July 1997 in Thailand, the depreciations had cumulated through successive rounds in all five countries to a loss of 40 to 50 percent of their nominal dollar values (or, equivalently, a doubling of the number of domestic currency units necessary to buy one dollar) by February 1998. But instead of being therapeutic, these discrete depreciations of the East Asian Five in 1997 destroyed their macroeconomic equilibrium as inflationary pressure became intense. They also caused widespread bankruptcy as the domestic-currency cost of servicing foreign-currency debt soared.

So according to our principle of "virtual" exchange-rate stability, what should have been the Asian governments' responses once the extent of their of short-term foreign-currency indebtedness was suddenly revealed? Because these countries had run out of official exchange reserves, they certainly had to suspend official market interventions to maintain their dollar pegs—as they did in practice. Some temporary devaluation could hardly be avoided. But to stem the complete loss of confidence in, and deep devaluations of, their currencies, each national government could have announced their intention to restore their traditional dollar parties as soon the dust settled. To be sure, renegotiating the external debt to greatly lengthen its term structure while improving the prudential regulation of the banks would be an important part of the necessary reforms. However, immediately announcing that the government intended to restore its traditional dollar parity within one or two years (wherever it became able to do so) would have provided an important signal to the market of future intent.

By late 1998, Korea and Thailand have already made substantial progess in nudging their exchange rates back up and have been rewarded by interest rates coming back down to single-digit levels. But by delaying the implementation of this "restoration rule," their currencies were left undervalued for too long—leading to sufficient domestic price inflation so that the original exchange-rate "parities" may now be too difficult to retrieve. (Contrast this with the the French devaluation of 1993. The original mark/franc exchange rate was restored so quickly that it had a negligible effect on the French price level.)

However, after the East Asian Five's exchange rates are nudged upward enough to again approximate purchasing-power parity against the dollar, returning to a policy of jointly stabilizing dollar exchange rates in East Asia more generally could again be right. Unlike what is sometimes alleged, *the previous system of dollar pegging for more than a decade was not one of the mistakes responsible for the 1997 attacks.* But a successful return to exchange-rate stability in the East Asian Five depends on (1) much improved prudential regulations over banks and other financial institutions and (2) stabilizing the yen/dollar exchange rate.

4.5. Reinterpreting the 1992 to 1993 Turmoil in the EMS

Might the different kind of turmoil that roiled the old ERM when Britain and Italy—and then then Spain and Sweden—were forced to suspend their parity obligations in 1992 (Figure 4.1), followed in August 1993 by a speculative attack on France and other inner core EMS countries that forced a dramatic widening of the ERM bands, recur under ERM II? Before the 1997 Asian crisis, academic wisdom on self-fulfilling speculative attacks arose out of the 1992 to 1993 upheavals in the EMS associated more with concern over mounting unemployment—rather than the Asian problem of unsustainable short-term foreign borrowing. However, this received view of the empirical importance of self-fulfilling speculative attacks from asymmetric business cycles is too pessimistic about the prospects for stabilizing exchange rates among national monies in separate circulation. I argue that writers in this "new" crisis literature—such as Eichengreen, Rose, and Wypolsz (1995) or Obstfeld and Rogoff (1995)—are overreacting to the European exchange-rate mayhem of the early 1990s, mayhem that was far more idiosyncratic than the formal academic analysis would suggest.

Instead, the exchange-rate mayhem in 1992 to 1993 resulted from the unlucky juxtaposition of two parallel sequences of financial events: (1) a boom-and-bust cycle generated simultaneously in Britain, France, Italy, Spain, and Sweden (with echo effects in other European countries) because of their attempts to disinflate using their peg to the deutsch mark as a nominal anchor in the absence of controls on inflows of financial capital and (2) fiscal upheaval in Germany associated with costs of reunification after 1990. Let us discuss each in turn.

First, the boom-and-bust cycles in Britain, Spain, and Sweden (a shadow ERM member)—and to a lesser extent Italy and France—from the mid-1980s to the early 1990s resulted from attempting to disinflate by using the exchange rate as the nominal anchor. While still facing some residual inflation by the mid-1980s, Britain, France, Italy, and Spain opted to peg their currencies to the mark (imperfectly by means of the bilateral parity grid) as a nominal anchor for lending credibility to their anti-inflationary policies. Sweden was not part of the bilateral parity grid, but it did use a basket peg dominated by the DM.

Because they had experienced higher inflation than in Germany with occasional devaluations against the mark in the 1980s (Figures 4.4 and 4.1), all had nominal interest rates that were substantially higher than those in Germany (Figure 4.2 and 4.3). However, by 1987, new commitments to peg their exchange rates had become firm, at least in the short and medium terms, even though interest rates remained misaligned. (Not even minor

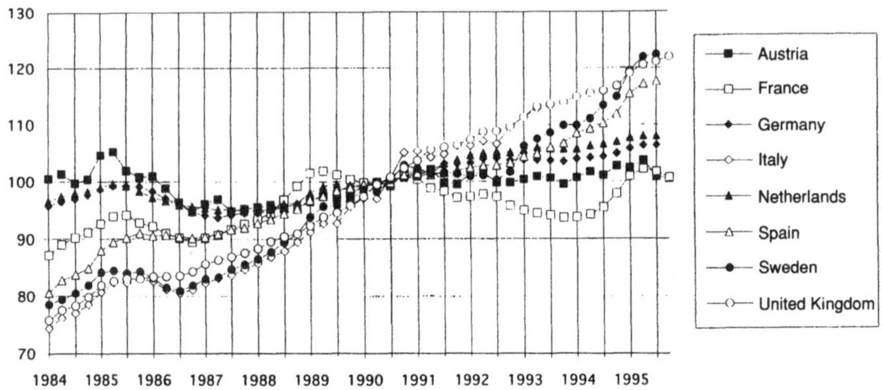

Figure 4.4. Producer Prices (1990 = 100) (quarterly observations)
Source: *IMF International Financial Statistics* CD ROM, March 1996, line 63.

exchange-rate adjustments occurred between 1987 and the September crisis of 1992.) With little or no possibility of devaluation in the short run, speculators found the higher nominal interest rates in all five countries very attractive because capital controls had been abolished in the Single European Act of 1986. Inflows of international financial capital became substantial: what I call the *capital inflow* effect.

To prevent their currencies from appreciating in the face of actual or incipient capital inflows in the late 1980s, the five monetary authorities had to be more expansionary than they would have liked. Thus, both internal and external credit constraints were relaxed, with inflationary consequences.[1] Figure 4.4 shows that the rates of inflation in the PPIs of all five countries continued to be higher than that of Germany's from 1984 through 1991, leading to some cumulative real overvaluation of their currencies (Figure 4.5a).

Depending on the degree of credibility about their exchange-rate pegs, the five countries' interest differentials with Germany narrowed after pegging but still remained significant as late as 1992 (Figure 4.3b). Was this apparent lack of credibility in the (long-run) prospects for their exchange-rate pegs itself responsible for the inflationary booms?

Surprisingly, no. Suppose that among our five countries, country A's nominal interest rates had falled rapidly to the German level because of full credibility of its exchange-rate peg after 1986. A's problem of an excessively stimulative macroeconomic policy would still remain. Although A's nominal interest rates were now the same as Germany's, its ongoing residual inflation, as aggravated by (temporary) capital inflows, would imply that its real rate of interest would fall well below that prevailing in Germany. This *real interest rate* effect led to the famous Walters' critique of

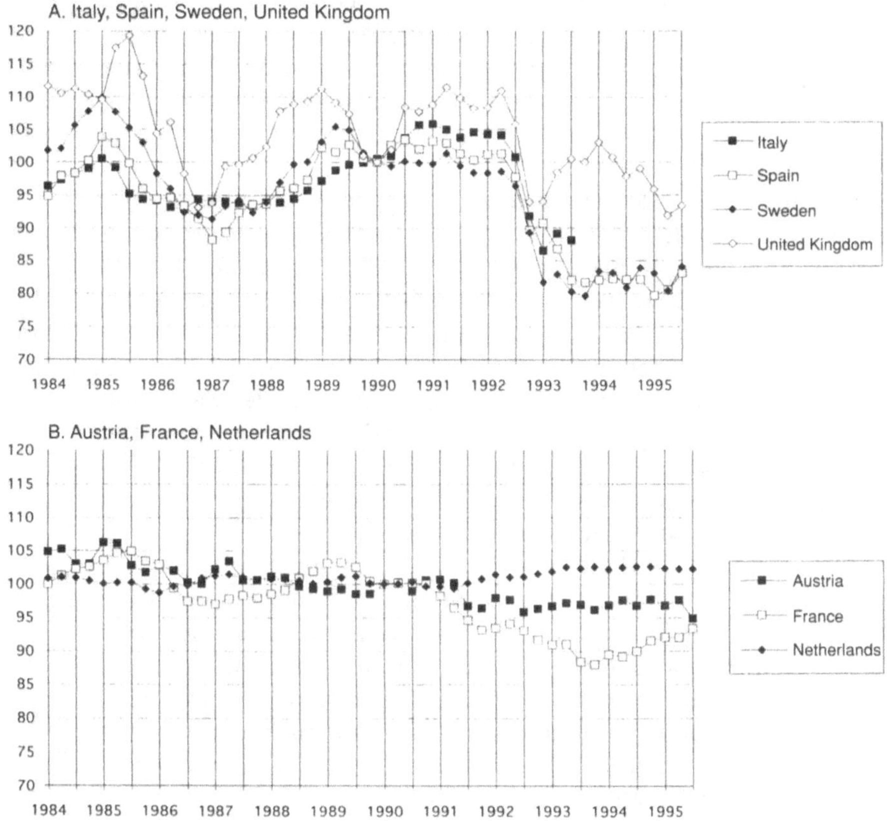

Figure 4.5. Real Exchange Rates Verses German Mark (1990 Q1 = 100) (quarterly observations)
Source: *IMF International Financial Statistics* CD ROM, March 1996, lines rf, 63.
Note: Bilateral nominal exchange rates deflated by producer-price indices.

disinflating with an exchange-rate anchor and no capital controls. Alan Walters (1986, 1990) criticized Chancellor Nigel Lawson for his policy of shadowing the mark beginning in 1986 on just these grounds. Walters focused on the real interest-rate effect (for a more formal analysis of the Walters critique, see Miller and Sutherland, 1991) and did not recognize the inflationary impact of the capital flows themselves (Pill, 1995a).

Contrary to what is commonly thought, the credibility of the exchange rate pegs to the mark wasn't the key issue in generating continued inflationary pressure. True, if interest rates didn't converge quickly, then the capital-inflow effect would undermine domestic monetary policy in the short run.

But if interest rates converged immediately because of the peg's high credibility, then the real interest-rate effect (the Walters critique) could still lead to an inflationary boom. In the late 1980s, some combination of the capital-inflow effect and the real-interest-rate effects was operative in all five countries. This prevented inflation in their PPIs from converging to the German level, as Figure 4.4 shows.

Because their exchange rates were pegged in the face of this ongoing inflation, the profitability of investing in tradable goods production began to look increasingly unattractive after 1987. Thus, in the late 1980s, the expanded credit flows went into nontradables such as residential and commercial real estate—and, in some cases such as Britain's, fueled a substantial increase in expenditures for personal consumption. The subsequent collapse in real estate prices (the bust part of the cycle) was aggravated by threatened bank insolvencies in 1990 to 1993 in Sweden, Spain, and France. Also on the bust part of this cycle, the burgeoning unemployment and fiscal deficits in these countries sparked the speculative attacks on all their currencies, as per the new crisis literature.

Courtesy of the OECD, the output gaps (deviations from trend GNP growth) plotted in Figure 4.6a shows rather dramatically this boom-and-bust cycle for all five of our peripheral countries, peaking about 1989 to 1990, with the nadir of the bust in real output in 1993. In contrast, the monetarily integrated inner core—Austria, Germany, and the Netherlands, where disinflation was not necessary—showed much less cyclical variation over this period (Figure 4.6b). The different cyclical variation in the unemployment rates of these two groups, from the late 1980s to the early 1990s, tells the same story.

What have we learned? In the absence of controls on capital inflows, the dangers of disinflating by relying on the exchange rate as an nominal anchor are now well understood. Only when domestic rates of inflation and nominal interest rates are more or less aligned with those prevailing in the putative anchor country or group, is it safe to enter into a fairly tight exchange-rate agreement without protection from international financial flows on capital account. (And this is precisely the success of the inflation and interest convergence leading to sustained exchange-rate stability achieved by the eleven charter members of EMU as of January 1, 1999.)

Conversely, if a country chooses to disinflate with the help of an exchange-rate anchor, it should also maintain controls on flows of liquid financial capital. Under the first Mitterand government, in 1981 to 1984, France leaned heavily on its peg to the mark and controls on capital account to disinflate and successfully discipline a potentially high-spending government into fiscal and monetary moderation. But France experienced

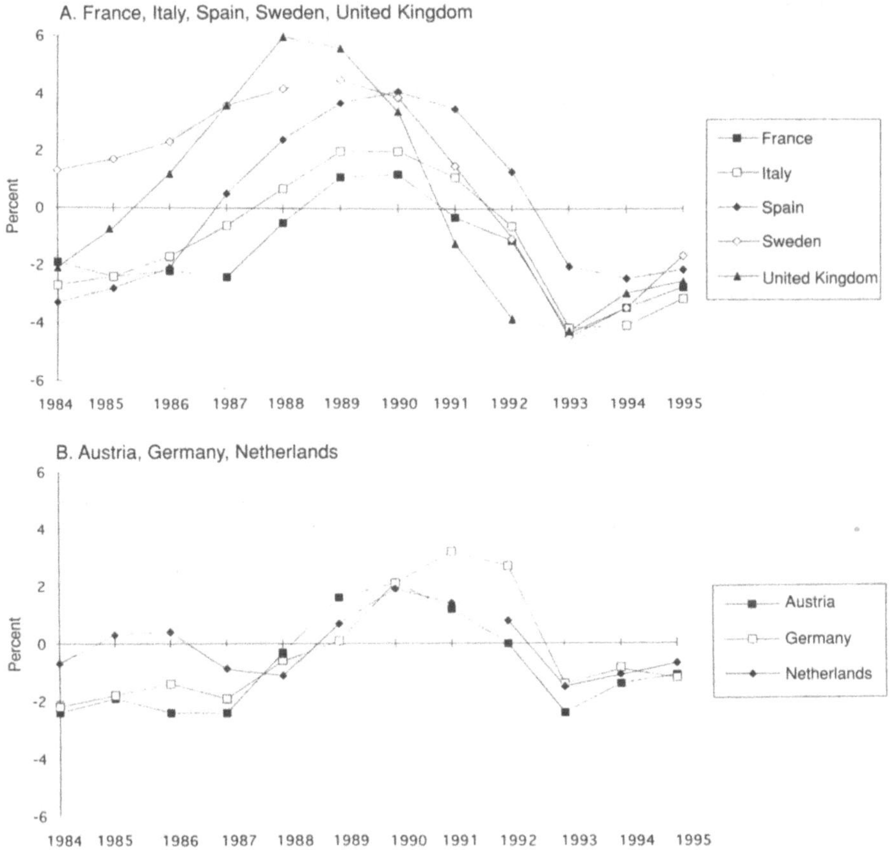

Figure 4.6. Output gap (annual observations)
Source: *OECD Economic Outlook*, 58 (December 1995, annex table 11), 1995 preliminary.

more trouble in the late 1980s and early 1990s after capital controls had been removed.

4.6. The Accession of Central and Eastern European Countries: Are Capital Controls Necessary?

For the CEEC countries, the lessons for joining ERM II are clear. If the inflation rate, and open-market nominal interest rate, in any one CEEC are substantially higher than those of the core countries, then a naked commitment—one without restraints on flows of financial capital—to a fixed band for its exchange rate might be unwise.

Figures 4.7a, 4.7b, and 4.7c show that inflation in the producer (wholesale) price indexes in almost all the CEEC countries since the early 1990s has been—and continues to be—substantially higher than in Germany. The happy exception seems to be Croatia (Figure 4.7c). Following a major stabilization program at the end of 1993 to bring down high inflation, the Croatian price level has been as stable as Germany's. Slovakia also shows (Figure 4.7c) only slightly higher price inflation than in Germany. And both Croatia and Slovakia have had stable exchange rates against the mark since late 1993 (Figure 4.8c). However, both Croatia's and Slovakia's short-term interest rates remain more than 5 percentage points higher than those in Germany (Figure 4.9c).

Contrast this experience with that of the Czech Republic, Hungary, Poland, and Slovenia, which have all had and continue to have substantially higher price inflation than in Germany (Figure 4.7a). All have ongoing exchange depreciation against the DM (Figure 4.8a) except for the Czech republic, which in 1997 underwent a severe exchange-rate crisis that forced it to devalue. And these four countries have been operating with nominal

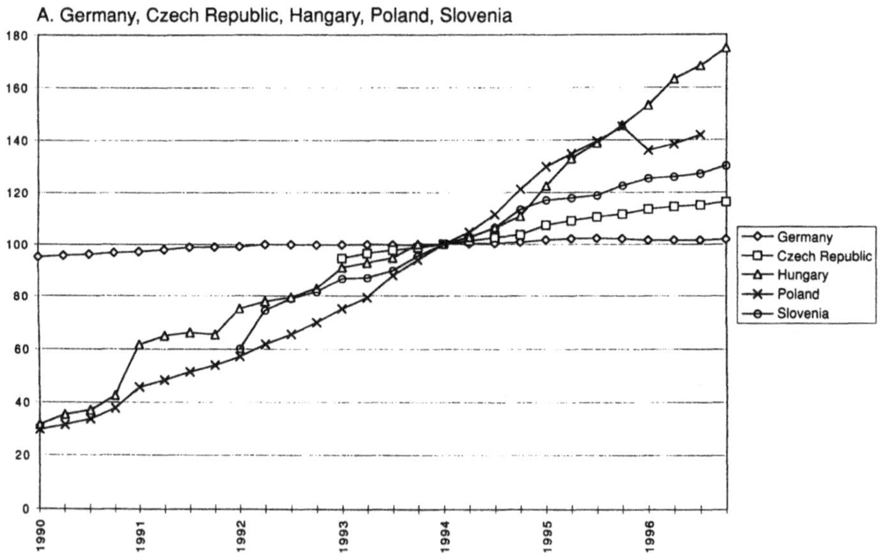

Figure 4.7. Producer Prices (1994 Q1 = 199)
Source: *IMF International Financial Statistics*, line 63.
Note: The Hungarian series has been adjusted for a break in 1994.

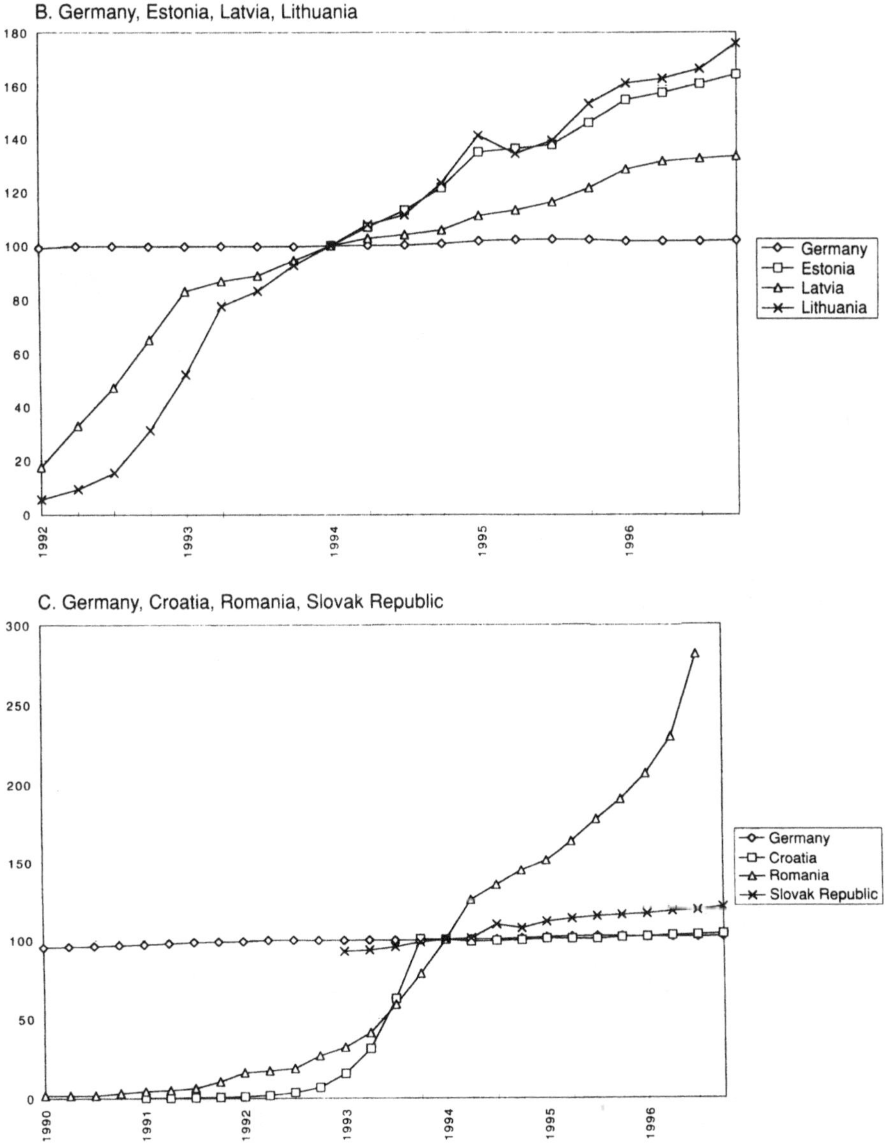

Figure 4.7. (continued)

interest rates more than 10 percentage points higher than those in Germany (Figure 4.9a).

The upshot seems to be that Croatia and Slovakia would be good candidates for accession to ERM II with a fixed parity commitment *provided*

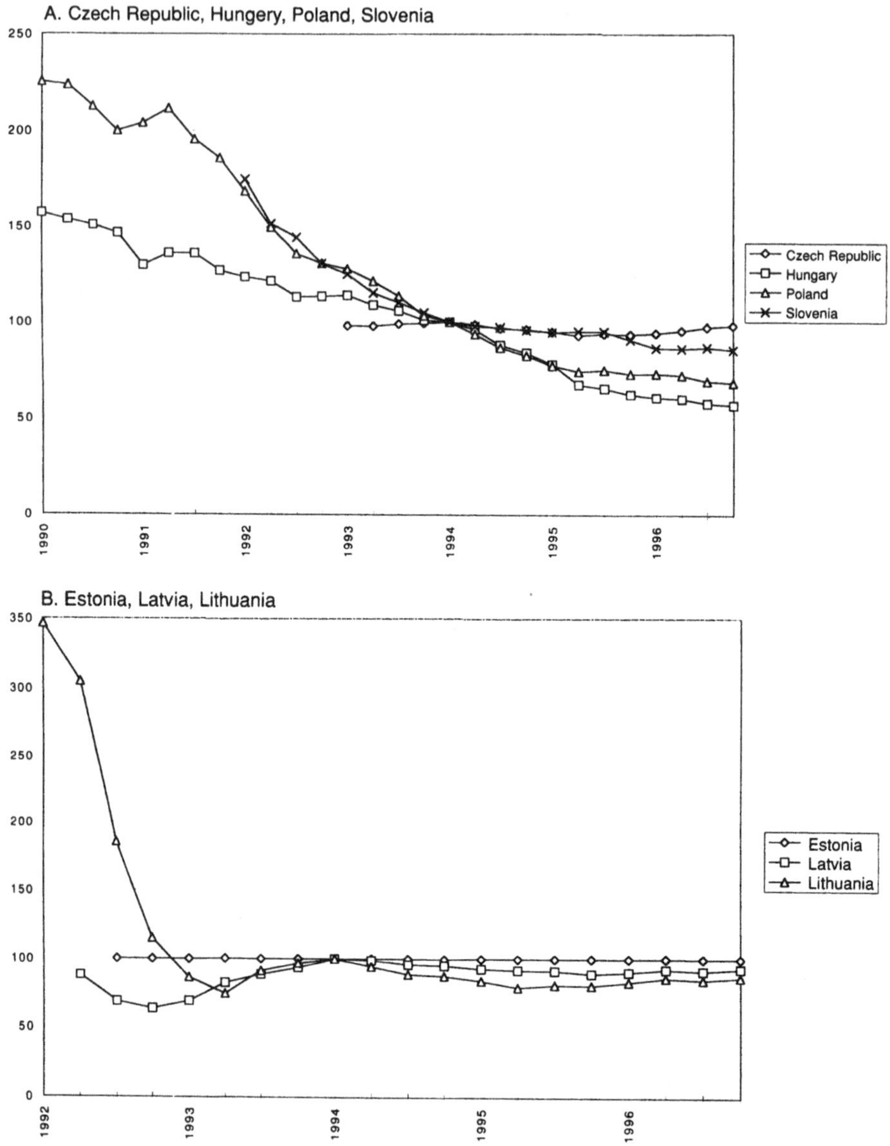

Figure 4.8. Nominal Exchange Rates Verses German Mark (1994 Q1 = 100)
Source: *IMF International Financial Statistics*, line rf.

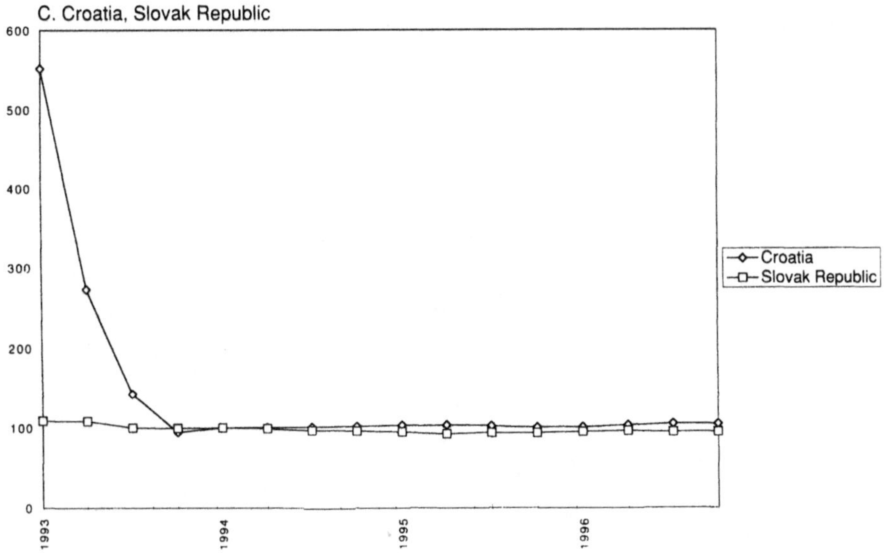

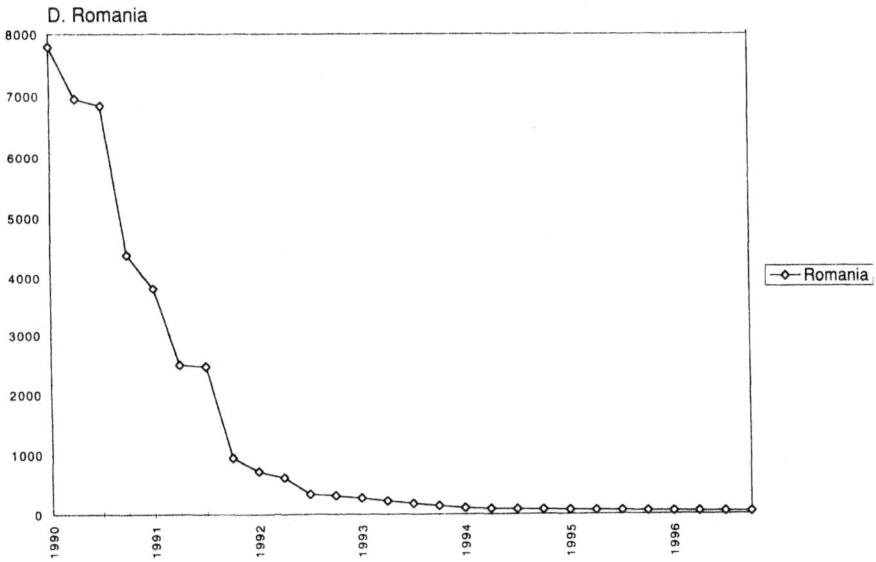

Figure 4.8. (continued)

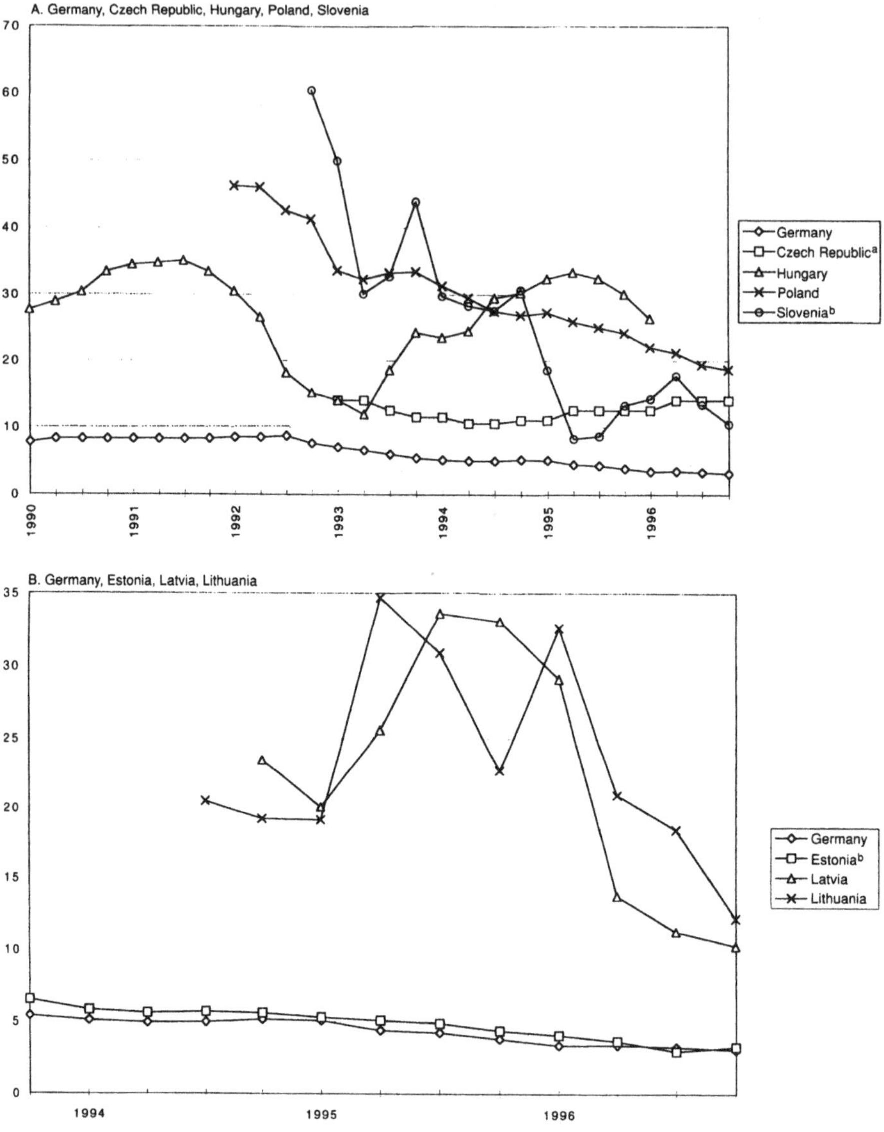

Figure 4.9. Treasury Bill Rates

Source: IMF International Financial Statistics, line 60.

Note: a. Refinancing rate. b. Interbank rate. Before 1994, Croatian rates were extremely high (between 200% and 2,100%) and have been omitted for the sake of clarity. c. Money-market rates. d. Refinancing rates.

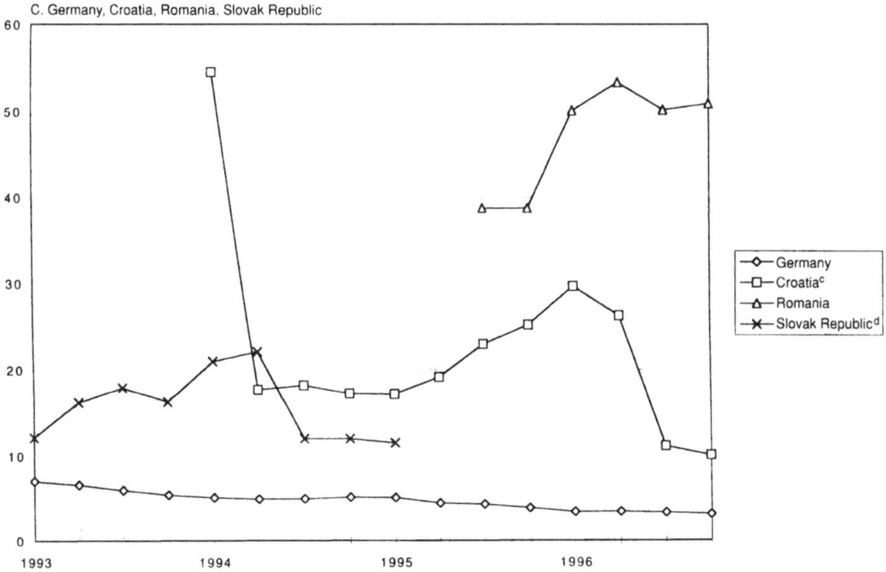

Figure 4.9. (continued)

that they maintain exchange controls on capital flows—particularly on inflows of short-term "hot" money. In contrast, the inflationary momentum in the Czech Republic, Hungary, Poland, and Slovenia suggests that ongoing exchange depreciation (hopefully fairly smooth) is, and will be, necessary. Thus, their accession to a formal exchange-rate obligation under ERM II is probably best deferred. These inflationary CEECs will also likely need restrictions on capital account—probably on *both* inflows and outflows.[2] The terms under which they join the EU must be carefully crafted.

Among CEEC countries, the Baltics—Latvia, Lithuania, and Estonia—have the most puzzling macroeconomic behavior Their nominal exchange rates against the mark have been unchanging since 1993 (Figure 4.8b). Yet, inflation at their wholesale levels has remained very high (Figure 4.7b). In particular, Estonia, with its hard currency-board arrangement with the mark, has seen its price level rise buy more than 15 percent per year since 1993. To a naive outside observer, these three countries' patterns of inflation coupled with fixed exchange rates seem similar to those of Britain, Italy, Sweden, and Spain in the late 1980s. Indeed, Figure 4.10b shows ongoing substantial real exchange appreciation in all three Baltic countries similar to their Western European counterparts a decade earlier (Figure 4.5a)—which, of course, were then followed by the cyclical downturns and forced depreciations in the early 1990s.

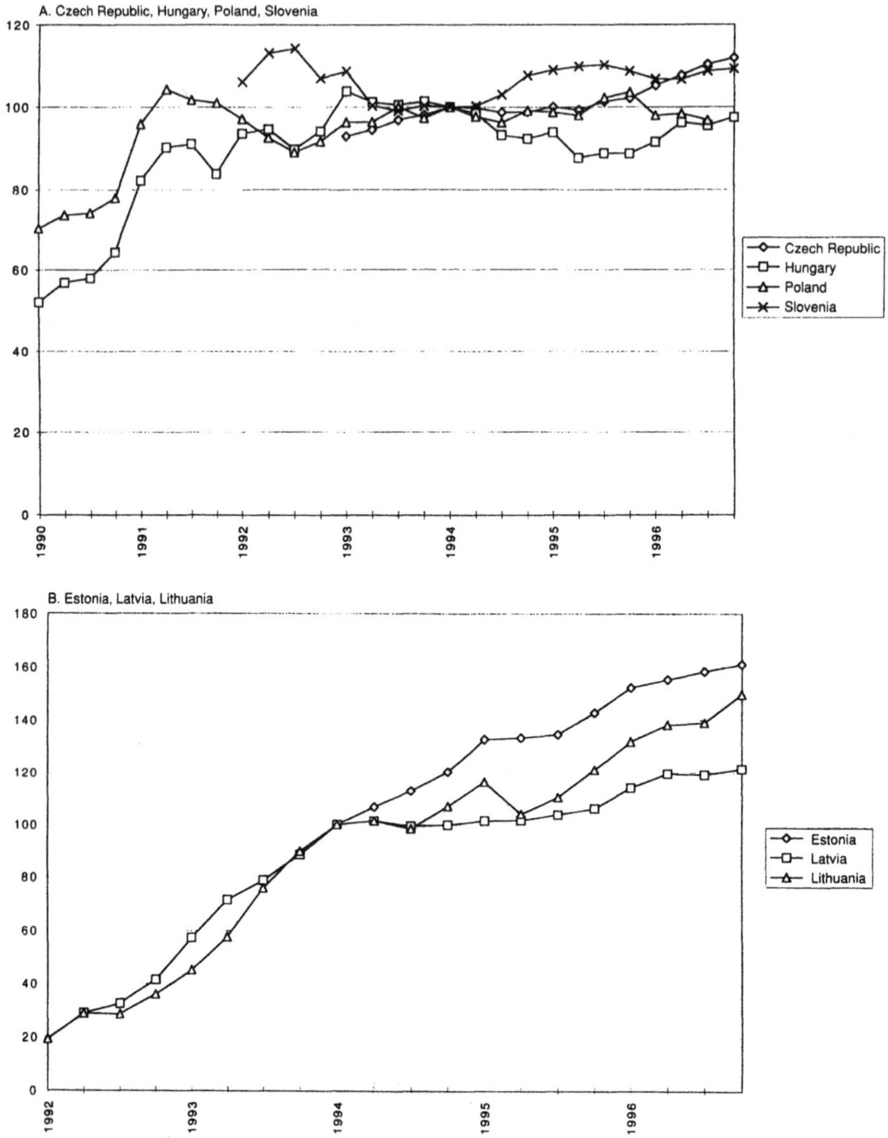

Figure 4.10. Real Exchange Rates Verses German Mark (1994 Q1 = 100)
Source: *IMF International Financial Statistics*, lines rf and 63.
Note: The Hungarian series reflects an adjustment in the producer price series.

Figure 4.10. (continued)

What can we conclude from this mixed pattern? The rules of the game for accession to the EU and to a new exchange agreement should permit transitional peripheral countries to impose capital controls, particularly on flows of "hot" money, when circumstances warrant. Attempted disinflation, using the exchange rate as the nominal anchor, is one of those circumstances. So is concern for weakly regulated banks and other financial institutions, which might otherwise borrow too much at short term in foreign exchange, as happened in East Asia. Moral hazard in banks could bid up interest rates in domestic currency to falsely high levels. In the absence of capital controls, entering into a fixed exchange-rate commitment with large cross-country differences in nominal interest rates between the center and the periphery is perilous—particularly if you are on the periphery. But prudential controls on banks and other domestic financial institutions can restrain unusual short-term flows of hot money without significantly restricting foreign direct investment or normal trade credit.

Once disinflation in any CEEC was successful with interest rates more or less aligned with the EMU countries, it could become a full-fledged member of ERM II by declaring an exchange parity within a narrow band against the euro with a relaxation of exchange controls on capital account. This new parity would then be defended vigorously by bending national monetary policy toward stabilizing a common producer price index with other European countries. As described in our analysis of ERM II, each peripheral country would aim for virtual exchange stability with the center. If a speculative attack forced suspension of its parity commitment, domestic monetary policy would aim to nudge the exchange rate back to its traditional parity with the euro as soon as practicable.

Notes

1. This overborrowing syndrome can well be aggravated if disinflation is part and parcel of a more general program of economic liberalization, as in the British case (McKinnon and Pill, 1996, 1997).

2. Tanzi and Blejer (1982) showed that economies with ongoing depreciations are likely using inflation to tax the domestic banking system so that deposit rates of interest are depressed below (shadow) loan rates. This wedge between deposit and loan rates than could generate simultaneous outflows and inflows of financial capital that are not socially warranted.

References

Baldwin, R., J. Francois, and Richard Portes. (1997). "The Costs and Benfits of Eastern Enlargement: The Impact on the EU and Central Europe." *Economic Policy Review: A European Forum* (April): 125–176.

Bartolini, L., and A. Prati. (1997). "Soft Versus Hard Targets for Exchange Rate Intervention." *Economic Policy Review: A European Forum* (April): 15–52.

Bordo, M.D., and F. Kydland. (1995). "The Gold Standard as a Rule: An Essay in Exploration." *Explorations in Economic History*.

De Grauwe, Paul. (1996). "Reforming the Transition to EMU." In Peter Kenen (ed.), *Making EMU Happen, Problems and Proposals: A Symposium* (pp. 16–29). Princeton Essays in International Finance No. 199. Princeton, NJ: Princeton University Press.

Eichengreen, Barry, Andrew Rose, and Charles Wyplosz. (1995). "Exchange Rate Mayhem: The Antecedents and Aftermath of Speculative Attacks." *Economic Policy*, 21 (October): 249–312.

Krugman, Paul. (1997). "Are Currency Crises Self-Fulfilling?" *NBER Macro Annual Conference 1996*. City: NBER.

McKinnon, Ronald I. (1993). *The Order of Economic Liberalization: Financial Control in the Transition to a Market Economy* (2nd ed.). Baltimore, MD: Johns Hopkins University Press.

McKinnon, Ronald I. (1996a). "Monetary Regimes, Government Borrowing Constraints, and Market-Preserving Federalism: Implications for EMU." In Thomas Courchene (ed.), *The National State in a Global/Information Era: Policy Challenges*. Kingston, Ont.: Queen's University.

McKinnon, Ronald I. (1996b). *The Rules of the Game: International Money and Exchange Rates*. Cambridge, MA: MIT Press.

McKinnon, Ronald I. (1997). "EMU as Device for Collective Fiscal Retrenchment." *American Economic Review* (May).

McKinnon, Ronald I. (1999). "Exchange-Rate Coordination for Surmounting the East Asian Crisis." *Asian Economic Journal* (February).

McKinnon, Ronald I., and Kenichi Ohno. (1997). *Dollar and Yen: Resolving Economic Conflict Between the United States and Japan*. Cambridge, MA: MIT Press.

McKinnon, Ronald I., and Huw Pill. (1996). "Credible Liberalizations and International Capital Flows: The Overborrowing Syndrome." In T. Ito and A. Krueger (eds.), *Financial Deregulation and Integration in East Asia* (pp. 7–48). Chicago: NBER, University of Chicago Press.

McKinnon, Ronald I., and Huw Pill. (1997). "Credible Liberalizations and Overborrowing." *American Economic Review* (May).

McKinnon, Ronald I., and Huw Pill. (1998). "International Overborrowing: A Decomposition of Credit and Currency Risk." *World Development*, 26(7) (July): 1267–1282.

Miller, Marcus, and Alan Sutherland. (1991). "The Walters Critique of the EMS: A Case of Inconsistent Expectations?" *The Manchester School*, 69 (supp.): 23–37.

Obstfeld, Maurice. (1994). "The Logic of Currency Crises." *Cahiers Economique et Monetaires* (Bank of France), 43: 188–213.

Obstfeld, Maurice, and Kenneth Rogoff. (1995). "The Mirage of Fixed Exchange Rates." *Journal of Economic Perspectives*, 9(4) (Fall): 73–96.

Ohno, Kenichi. (1993). "The Purchasing Power Parity Criterion for Stabilizing Exchange Rates." In Dilip Das (ed.), *Foreign Exchange Markets and International Capital Flows* (pp. 394–415).

Pill, Huw. (1995a). "Financial Liberalisation and Financial Management in the Open Economy." Ph.D. dissertation, Stanford University, June.

Pill, Huw. (1995b). "Target Zones and the European Monetary System: A Reconciliation." CREG Memo 313, Stanford University, February.

Tanzi, Vito, and Mario Blejer. (1982). "Inflation, Interest-Rate Policy, and Currency Substitution in Developing Countries." *World Development*, 10(9): 781–789.

Walters, Alan. (1986). *Britain's Economic Renaissance*. Oxford: Oxford University Press.

Walters, Alan. (1990). *Sterling in Danger*. Institute for Economic Affairs. London: Fontana Press.

Williamson, John. (1985). *The Exchange Rate System* (2nd ed.). Washington, DC: Institute for International Economics.

Williamson, John. (1994). "Managing the Monetary System." In P. Kenen (ed.), *Managing the World Economy Fifty Years After Bretton Woods*. Washington, DC: Institute for International Economics.

World Bank. (1993). *The East Asian Miracle: Economic Growth and Public Policy*. Oxford: Oxford University Press.

5 A MODEL OF REAL EXCHANGE-RATE DETERMINATION IN TRANSITION ECONOMIES

Clemens Grafe

London School of Economics and CEP

Charles Wyplosz

Graduate Institute of International Studies, Geneva and CEPR

5.1. Introduction

The role of the exchange rate in the early phase of transition remains a source of debate among analysts and policymakers. At stake are important issues like the need to peg the exchange rate as a nominal anchor to control inflation, the risk of overvaluation, the effect of real appreciation on structural changes, the proper evolution of the current account, the reaction to capital inflows, speculative attacks, and, more generally, the conduct of monetary policy. Most analyses used in these debates are based, explicitly or implicitly, on theories developed for nontransition economies. Some argue that the relevant framework should be based on the experiences of developing countries, which, in common with transition, have fairly underdeveloped financial markets and trade barriers. Others observe that capital mobility is *de facto* quite high and trade barriers quite low, so that the proper reference is theories that fit developed economies. Yet the behavior of the exchange rate in transition economies exhibits some unique features that warrant separate theorizing.

In particular the transition process presents two original characteristics. First, quite independently of the chosen exchange-rate regime the real exchange rate steadily appreciates once the economy is liberalized

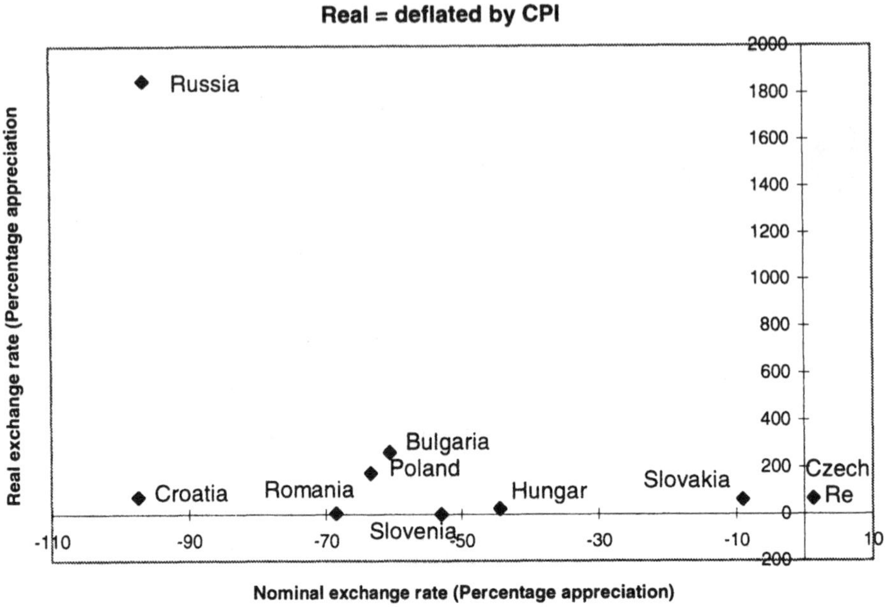

Figure 5.1. The Real and Nominal Appreciation
Source: IMF.
Note: Equally weighted averages of exchange rates against the U.S. dollar and the DM. The real exchange rate is computed using CPI indices. The period of observation is chosen for each country to start at the time of the last large devaluation, and it extends as far as possible:

	Beginning	End		Beginning	End
Bulgaria	Feb. 91	Sep. 94	Romania	Jul. 93	Dec. 95
Croatia	May. 92	Aug. 94	Russia	Jan. 92	Dec. 96
Czechoslovakia	Jan. 91	Dec. 95	Slovakia	Jan. 91	Dec. 95
Hungary	Jan. 91	Apr. 95	Slovenia	Jan. 92	Aug. 94
Poland	Jan. 90	May. 95			

(Halpern and Wyplosz, 1997). Second, there is no apparent link between the evolution of the nominal and real exchange rates. Figure 5.1 shows cumulated nominal and real appreciations for nine countries for which data is available. Russian nominal (3,000 percent) and real appreciation (1,800 percent) dwarfs the other observations, but the conclusion stands: excluding Russia the coefficient of partial correlation between the nominal and real exchange rates depicted on Figure 5.1 is –0.15. This observation is not sensitive to the choice of real exchange rate. When the real exchange rate is defined as the ratio of the CPI to the PPI (meant to be a proxy for the nontraded to traded good price ratio) correlation is also –0.15, and it is 0.03 when we use the average dollar wage. Taken together, these two characteristics make the transition countries stand apart.

Developed countries do not exhibit trend appreciation. Fast-growing developing countries do tend to have an appreciating real exchange rate, which is often seen as a manifestation of the Balassa-Samuelson effect (Balassa, 1964), which occurs in presence of rapid productivity gains. When the gains are higher in the traded-good than in the nontraded-good sector, and if wages are equalized across sectors, the real exchange rate appreciates. Yet if transition, indeed, is largely a story of accelerated productivity gains, the Balassa-Samuelson effect does not look like a promising start. Support for this effect is not readily found in the data for a good reason: productivity gains in the nontraded-good sector must have been very large since services were nonexistent or very underdeveloped under central planning, while the traded-good sector has undergone a collapse in output with only limited labor shedding.

The absence of any link between nominal and real exchange-rate changes stands in sharp contrast with the evolution observed in most non-transition economies. Normal countries typically display very high short-term correlations between the nominal and real exchange rates. This is commonly understood as an indication of price stickiness.[1] In high-inflation countries prices are known to be quite flexible, but the nominal exchange rate depreciates roughly at the speed of inflation so that the real exchange rate changes little. This is not the experience of transition countries, even those that have suffered high inflation.

In transition economies there seems to be enough price flexibility to cut the link between nominal and real changes. Consequently, the real exchange rate can be seen largely as a variable in its own right. Halpern and Wyplosz (1997) show that, to some extent, the real appreciation corresponds to a correction following the initial excessive nominal and real depreciation that accompanied the launch of most price-liberalization programs. This effect is not enough, however, to fully explain the observed behavior. Their results point to the role of various structural factors. What these factors are, and how they operate, remains largely unexplained at this stage.

As far as we know, there is not yet any paper that proposes a theory of the real exchange rate in transition economies. Such a theory must start form the defining characteristics of the transition process. We have already mentioned a high degree of price flexibility—and this concerns wages too—so that we need to focus on real shocks and/or market imperfections to explain movements in the real exchange rate. The persistence of an unproductive state sector is a primary suspect. In addition, much recent evidence shows that the expansion of private activity in Eastern Europe is less impaired by labor-market frictions than by a shortage of capital (OECD, 1995; Konings, Lehmann, and Schaffer, 1996) and that budget constraints remain quite soft (EBRD, 1995; Cornelli, Porks, and Schaffer, 1996). Case studies confirm that investment is almost entirely financed out of retained earnings (Aghion and Blanchard, 1994; Cornelli, Porks, and Schaffer, 1996).

The theory that we propose here must be considered as a first exploratory step. We focus exclusively on the real side of the economy and abstract from any nonneutralities that could contribute to explaining the evolution of the real exchange rate. This may be too strong an assumption, but it allows us to explore the two-way linkages between structural changes and the real exchange rate. Our simple model is designed to capture the transformation process as initially described by Aghion and Blanchard (1994), Blanchard (1997), and Atkinson and Kehoe (1993). It emphasizes the role of the old and inefficient state sector as well as the lack of adequate financing for the emerging modern corporate.

Traded goods are initially produced by a state sector meant to capture the large manufacturing base that most transition countries inherited. This sector is gradually replaced by a new private sector that is slowed down in its emergence by a financing constraint. To keep the model tractable we assume full employment. As the old state sector gradually declines, it relinquishes labor that can flow into new more productive activities. Although the new sector is more productive, it cannot immediately absorb all workers from the old sector because capital accumulation is financially restricted. To that effect, we assume that financial markets are absent so that investment has to be financed by current profits. The real exchange rate is defined as the relative price of nontraded and traded goods. We take the extreme view that the nontraded-good sector only requires labor as factor input. This sector did not exist beforehand; as it does not need to accumulate capital, it can jump into existence at the start of the reform process. The relative price of traded and nontraded goods turns out to be directly related to the real wage. For this reason it controls the speed and the success of the transition process described as the gradual elimination of the state sector and its replacement by the new traded and nontraded good sectors.

The next section presents the model. Section 5.3 looks at the behavior of the real exchange rate at the outset of liberalization, assuming an instantaneous big-bang. Section 5.4 explores the subsequent evolution, from big-bang to the steady-state, which is described in Section 5.5. The last section concludes.

5.2. The Model

We consider an economy with three sectors: the old state sector that produces an internationally tradable good, a modern private sector that also produces an internationally tradable good, and a modern private sector that produces not internationally tradable services.

5.2.1. The State Sector

A common inheritance of all transition countries is a large, often inefficient, industrial sector. The technology used in the sector is mostly outdated and inefficient compared to modern equipment from abroad. The countries were either financially unable enough to import western technology or restricted from doing so because of Cold War politics (restrictions on technology transfer and 5-forth). Furthermore, marginal products of labor and capital vary a lot across and within industries because the market forces that usually equate them under perfect capital and labor mobility were not allowed (Castanheira and Roland, 1996). We model this fact explicitly as follows. The old state sector comprises a continuum of firms that operate under a Leontief technology:

$$y^S(j) = \min(a_1 K^S(j), a_2(j) L^S(j)) \tag{5.1}$$

—that is, capital is specific to each production line j and allows different levels of output per worker. Since competitive forces were not at work prior to transition, there is no reason to believe that even companies that produced identical goods were equally productive. We order the production lines such that labor productivity is rising in j, —that is, we assume

$$j_a > j_b \Rightarrow a_2(j_a) > a_2(j_b).$$

State firms only take the decision to operate a production line, setting $a_2(j)L^S(j) = a_1 K^S(j)$, or to abandon it. The assumption that capital productivity a_1 is the same across firms plays no role in what follows as we will consider that capital is redundant in this sector so that effectively $y^S(j) = a_2(j)L^S(j)$. Employment $L(j)$ is assumed to be uniformly distributed over $[0, a_{2mas}]$—that is, production lines are all of the same size.

We capture the continuing existence of soft budget constraints in the state sector by assuming that profitable firms subsidize those that face losses.[2] As a whole, therefore, the state sector just breaks even. Postredistribution, profit is exactly nil in all state firms, and there is no further investment. Inherited capital is just a sunk cost so that the only cost to the state firms is labor costs. Workers are homogeneous, and wages are taken to be the same throughout the sector. This assumption is natural given the system of cross-subsidies in firms steeped in the equalitarian tradition of the communist regime but is not essential to the analysis. It implies that the wage is equal to average labor productivity in the state sector.

We further assume the existence of nonpecuniary benefits in the state sector (such as low effort) as well as the opportunity costs of leaving the sector (harder effort, relocation, loss of state employment privileges such as tenure, social services, housing, and so on). The resulting fixed cost F of moving out of the state sector drives a wedge between wages there and the modern sector. Such a limit to labor mobility is often blamed for the slow emergence of a private sector (Burda, 1993; Aghion and Blanchard, 1994). This assumption is not essential for the dynamics of the model, but it allows for interesting comparative static results.

5.2.2. The New Sectors

The two other sectors did not exist under central planning. They become latent at the outset of transformation. The traded-good sector produces industrial goods with a Leontief technology as well:[3]

$$y^{\mathrm{T}} = \min(b_1 K^{\mathrm{T}}, b_2 L^{\mathrm{T}}). \tag{5.2}$$

To capture the fact that the new modern sector is more efficient than the state sector, we assume that the most efficient state firm is just as efficient as firms in the new sector:

$$a_{2\max} = b_2. \tag{5.3}$$

The nontraded-good sector uses only labor. The extreme assumption that no capital is needed in the production of nontraded goods could be relaxed, but the model would be much less tractable. The only assumption that is really needed for the effect we want to study is that the production of nontraded goods is less capital intensive than the production of industrial output, which is less controversial:

$$y^{\mathrm{N}} = cL^{\mathrm{N}}. \tag{5.4}$$

All technical coefficients are constant. This assumption permits us to limit the sources of growth to just two factors: (1) the accumulation of capital in the traded-good sector and (2) sectoral adjustment as workers from the nontraded sector into the traded sector. Adding technological progress would certainly improve the realism of the model but is not needed for our purposes. We already know that technological progress affects the real exchange rate if it is biased toward a particular sector along the lines of the Balassa-Samuelson effect. Since such a channel is well known and is not specific to transition economies, we simply acknowledge its existence and look for *other* sources of real exchange-rate changes.

5.2.3. Labor Market

Free entry into the nontraded good sector implies that firms in that sector earn zero profits. Wages are then set to be

$$w^{N} = cp, \tag{5.5}$$

where p is the relative price of nontraded goods in terms of traded goods ($p = p^{N}/P^{T}$) and w^{N} is the real wage in terms of the traded-good price. Throughout the chapter p is our definition of the real exchange rate (and increases when there is real appreciation).

With perfect labor mobility across sectors, wages are equalized up to the fixed cost F of leaving the state sector:

$$w^{T} = w^{N} = w^{S} + F. \tag{5.6}$$

With wages flexible and free entry into the nontraded sector, there is no open unemployment.[4] Therefore, the total labor force is

$$\underline{L} = L^{S} + L^{T} + L^{N}. \tag{5.7}$$

5.2.4. Financial Markets

When transformation starts unexpectedly, all labor is in the state sector. The service sector starts to operate immediately since no prior capital accumulation is required. In contrast, the modern traded-good sector needs first to invest in physical capital, which raises the issue of financial markets.

With very few exceptions, firms have not been able to raise outside money. Banks typically do not lend to firms, and stock markets have yet to provide capital for more than a few blue chips (EBRD, 1995). This motivates our simple assumption that neither firms nor households have access to financial markets. Investment is entirely financed through retained earnings. If w^{T} is the real (in terms of traded goods) wage in the traded good sector, investment is therefore

$$dK^{\mathrm{T}}/\mathrm{d}t = y^{\mathrm{T}} - w^{\mathrm{T}}L^{\mathrm{T}}, \quad \text{if} > 0, \qquad dK^{\mathrm{T}}/\mathrm{d}t = 0 \text{ otherwise.} \tag{5.8}$$

The same could apply to the state sector, but our assumption that it does not operate profitably implies that it will not invest.[5] Note that, for simplicity, there is no depreciation of capital. Capital keeps its value forever unless it is abandoned, as will be the case in the state sector. When capital is abandoned, its value drops immediately to zero. The emerging modern private industrial sector can be seen as growing out of new greenfield investment projects, a feature that does not appear too far from the truth.

5.2.5. Goods Market

Consumers consider the traded good—itself perfectly substitutable with foreign goods—and the state-sector good as perfect substitutes. This assumption is not realistic as state goods are mostly of very low quality, but we keep it because it makes the solution more tractable. None of the substantial results are affected by this assumption even though imperfect substitutability allows for some further results mentioned in the last section.

Consumers have Cobb-Douglas type preferences over the two categories of goods, traded plus state sector goods, and nontraded. Personal disposable income is labor income $w^{\mathrm{T}}y^{\mathrm{T}} + w^{\mathrm{S}}y^{\mathrm{S}} + w^{\mathrm{N}}y^{\mathrm{N}} = cp\underline{L} - FL^{\mathrm{S}}$, plus net transfers from abroad Z:

$$C^{\mathrm{T}} = \alpha(cp\underline{L} - FL^{\mathrm{S}} + Z) \tag{5.9a}$$

$$pC^{\mathrm{N}} = (1-\alpha)(cp\underline{L} - FL^{\mathrm{S}} + Z). \tag{5.9b}$$

Profits are not distributed to shareholders, rather they are entirely used to finance productive investment and therefore do not affect spending. Note that the fixed costs of moving out of the state sector F reduce disposable income. This formulation clearly embodies the efficiency costs of maintaining the state sector, measured by the opportunity cost FL^{S} of moving workers to the modern sector.

With little commercial lending, residents are not able to use the current account to smooth out spending. Furthermore, in the early phase of transition, private capital inflows are predominantly loans and transfers from institutional lenders and direct inflows, most of them associated with privatizations (Calvo, Sahay, ad Vegh, 1995). The proper description of the situation would probably involve credit rationing for households and firms. We take a shortcut: financing is made possible only through foreign transfers. The amount Z of foreign transfers is exogenously set and remains fixed forever. Unless the transfer is a grant, and grants do not last forever, this formulation violates the country's intertemporal budget constraint. This is the price to be paid to avoid a more complex model.

The two good market-equilibrium conditions are

$$Z + y^{\mathrm{T}} = y^{\mathrm{S}} = C^{\mathrm{T}} + dK^{\mathrm{T}}/dt \tag{5.10a}$$

$$pC^{\mathrm{N}} = pY^{\mathrm{N}}, \tag{5.10b}$$

where we assume that investment goods are the same as traded goods. Obviously, one of these two equations is redundant because of Walras's law.

5.2.6. Emergence and Growth of the Modern Sectors

Economic transformation is described as the development of the modern traded- and nontraded-good sectors described by (5.2), (5.4), and (5.8). Given the full-employment assumption (5.7), the other side of the coin is the decline of the state sector. Which production lines are closed first? The new sectors will be drawing workers out of the state sector by offering them continuously growing wages. This will be made possible through capital accumulation in the traded-good sector and by rising relative prices in the nontraded-good sector, which brings us back to the setting of wages in the old state sector. Labor-market equilibrium (5.6) requires that wages also grow in the state sector. For this reason, productivity must also rise in the state sector, and this implies closing down the least efficient production lines first.

We have already made the following assumptions: workers are identical but production lines in the state sector, while of the same size, and heterogeneous and ranked by labor productivity. The state does not claim dividends, and profitable firms subsidize loss-making firms, with the state sector just breaking even as a whole. This set of assumptions determines the size of the state sector since it implies that the wage is equal to average labor productivity. Let $x(t)$ be the productivity of the marginal production line still in operation at time t, as shown in Figure 5.2. Average productivity is $\tilde{a}_2(t) = (b_2 + x(t))/2$ and $w^{\mathrm{S}} = \tilde{a}_2(t)$. By closing down the least productive lines, average productivity increases over time as $x(t)$ rises and more workers switch to the two new sectors.

The labor-market equilibrium condition (5.6) along with (5.5) implies

$$(b_2 + x(t))/2 = cp(t) - F,$$

which gives

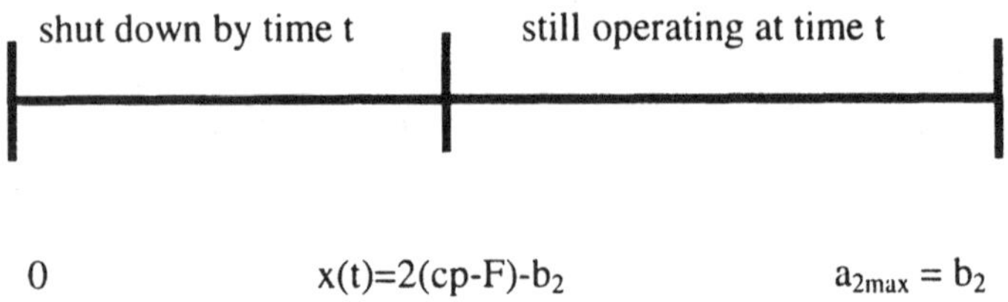

Figure 5.2. Productivities in the State Sector

$$x = 2(cp - F) - b_2, \tag{5.11}$$

where we have dropped the time subscript. The low-productivity state sector shrinks when the real exchange rate, henceforth defined as the ratio of nontraded- to traded-good prices p, appreciates.

This feature can be seen as a Balassa-Samuelson effect in reverse. The standard Balassa-Samuelson effect is driven by the supply side (Obstfeld and Rogoff, 1996). Here it is driven by the demand side. To meet higher demand for its output, the underdeveloped nontraded-good sector must raise its relative price to raise wages and attract workers. The state sector works under an aggregate budget constraint; to maintain its labor force, it must improve its aggregate productivity, which is achieved by closing down the least efficient units. Over time there could be investment in modern equipment. While this is entirely possible, we assume that state firms that invest are reclassified in the new traded-good sector and offer the correspondingly higher wage. Allowing state firms to invest would not change the results. Note that the higher is the wage gap F the larger is the state sector.

Employment and output in the state sector are

$$L^S = \underline{L}(b_2 - x)/b_2 \tag{5.12}$$

$$y^S = \tilde{a}_2 L^S = 2(cp - F)(b_2 - cp + F)\underline{L}/b_2 \tag{5.13}$$

Quite clearly $y^S \geq 0$, since the fixed cost F cannot exceed the real wage in the new sector $w^T = w^N = cp$. Otherwise transition never takes off. As long as $b_2 \geq cp$ equations (5.2), (5.6), and (5.8) along with the assumption that the traded-good sector is run efficiently (no redundant capital or labor) imply that

$$dK^T/dt = (b_2 - cp)L^T. \tag{5.14}$$

As the modern traded good sector accumulates capital, it can expand and hire workers away from the state sector. Since (5.2) implies that $y^T = b_1 K^T = b_2 L^T$, we have

$$dL^{\mathrm{T}}/dt = (b_1/b_2)(b_2 - cp)L^{\mathrm{T}}. \tag{5.15}$$

Hiring in the new sector depends negatively on the real exchange rate. When employment in the new sector is low (at the outset of reform), a successful transition can occur only if the real exchange rate is sufficiently low.

5.3. Big Bang

We now characterize the situation on day one of the transition. We assume a big-bang policy that instantaneously establishes market conditions, frees prices, wages, and trade and allows firms to be created. The only remaining legacy of central planning is an inefficient state sector that continues to operate with soft budget constraints even though there are no net subsidies from the rest of the economy. Initially, there is no capital in the new sectors. The tradable sector first has to invest and cannot immediately produce goods. The nontraded-good sector, which does not need capital, immediately starts to produce. Its size is determined by demand. The initial situation is described as follows:

$$L^{\mathrm{T}} = 0;\ b_2 L^{\mathrm{S}} = 2(b_2 - cp + F)\underline{L};\quad L^{\mathrm{N}} = \underline{L} - L^{\mathrm{S}} \tag{5.16}$$

$$cp = (1-\alpha)(Z - FL^{\mathrm{S}})/(\alpha\underline{L} - L^{\mathrm{S}}). \tag{5.17}$$

The link between employment (or output) in the state sector and the real exchange rate is represented in Figure 5.3 with two possible configurations. In both cases, the LL line that describes the labor market conditions (5.16) is downward sloping. It corresponds to the reverse Balassa-Samuelson effect discussed above: to hire more workers from the state sector the nontraded-good sector must raise the real wage and therefore its relative price p.

The curve NN represents the good market-equilibrium condition (5.17). When $Z > \alpha F\underline{L}$, the NN schedule is upward sloping: the real exchange rate increases with the size of the state sector. Indeed, a large state sector implies that output in the nontraded-good sector is in short supply. For a given level of demand, a reduced supply translates into a higher relative price. The level of demand, however, is also affected by the size of the state sector because of larger efficiency losses that depress disposable income and demand. When the inefficiency associated with the wage gap F is large enough (when $\alpha F\underline{L} > Z$), this second effect dominates and the NN schedule is downward sloping.

The situation at the time of big bang ($t = 0$) is at the intersection of

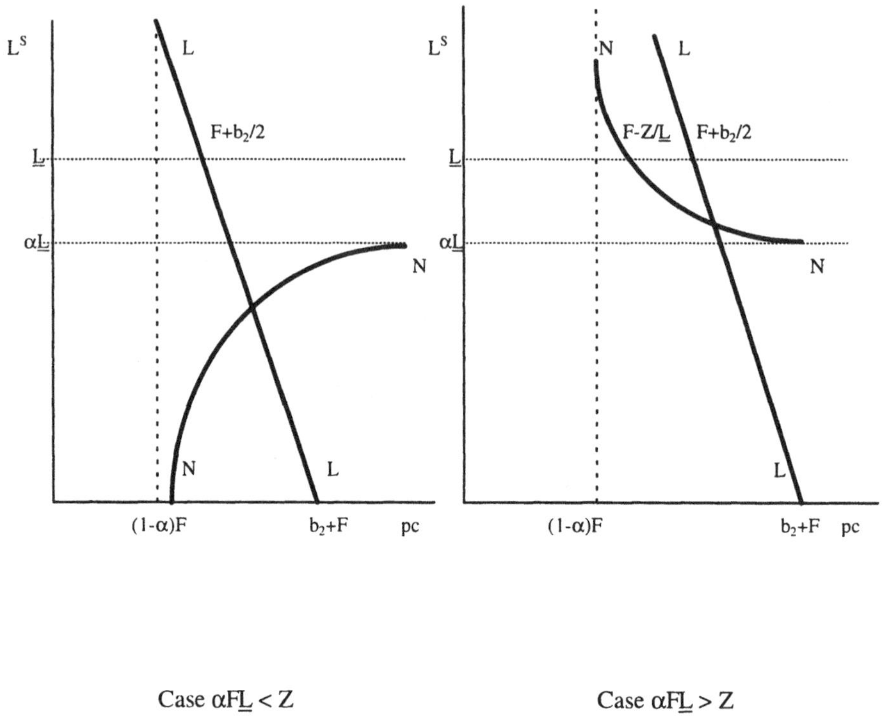

Figure 5.3. The Situation After the Big-Bang

the two schedules.[6] Figure 5.3 shows the instantaneous birth of the non-traded-good sector. Employment in the state sector (L^S) falls below its initial value $\underline{L}$, which makes room for employment in the nontraded-good sector ($L^N > 0$). Pent-up demand for the nontraded goods that were not provided by the old state sector is instantaneously satisfied. This is a standard feature of the early days of transition when kiosks, snack bars, and other trades suddenly appeared along the streets of many Eastern European cities.

Figure 5.3 also helps to understand the role of the economy's structure and of exogenous factors. Only two productivity factors matter. First, the higher is labor productivity in the nontraded-good sector (c) the less the real exchange rate (p) appreciates.[7] This illustrates the main feature of the model embodied in (5.5) and (5.6): the function of the real exchange rate is to determine the real wage and therefore the size of the state sector. The higher the real wage, the more productive the state sector must be in aggregate, and therefore the more it must shrink under the assumption that the least productive product lines are first closed down. To achieve a given size, the nontraded-good sector must offer the corresponding real wage. This wage is equal to the real value marginal (and average) labor productivity, a combination of volume productivity c and relative price p.

The second productivity that matters is b_2 in its role as the highest labor productivity in the state sector ($a_{2\max} = b_2$), which determines the sector's average productivity. A higher b_2 leaves the NN schedule unchanged while the LL schedule shifts to the right. If the state sector is more productive, the nontraded-good sector must offer a higher real wage to displace workers, and this requires a higher relative price.[8]

Quite intuitively, an increase in foreign capital inflows (Z) results in a more appreciated real exchange rate. Foreign financing does not affect the labor market so the schedule LL in Figure 5.3 remains unaffected. As Z rises, the NN schedule shifts down in both panels. The state sector shrinks because the additional flow of foreign currency increases disposable income and raises demand for both goods. The additional demand for traded goods is satisfied through additional imports as the current-account deteriorates. On the other side, the demand for nontraded goods has to be met by domestic production. The relative price of nontraded goods and the real wage in that sector increases as a response. The state sector responds to higher wages abandoning more production lines and freeing labor. The laid-off workers join the nontraded-good sector and increase the supply of nontraded goods.

A higher wage gap F is also accompanied by a more appreciated real exchange rate. Graphically, in Figure 5.3 the LL schedule shifts to the right because labor exit out of the state sector is reduced, forcing the nontraded sector into a higher relative price to offer a higher real wage. The NN schedule shifts to the left because the wage gap inefficiency rises, reducing disposable income and demand for both traded and nontraded goods. The figure, confirmed by Appendix A, shows that the real exchange rate always rises—that is, that the first effect dominates the second. The reason is that a larger wage gap reduces the demand for both goods, while it reduces the supply of nontraded goods (L^N goes down) and increases the supply of traded goods (L^S goes up). Inevitably, therefore, the relative price of nontraded goods has to rise.

The effects of the two exogenous factors F and Z are linked, revealing an interesting complementarity. Starting from a situation where no foreign financing is available ($Z = 0$), and holding F constant, imagine that Z increases. Eventually, when Z/F passes the threshold $\alpha\underline{L}$, we switch from the right-hand side to the left-hand side panel in Figure 5.3. At that stage L^S falls below $\alpha\underline{L}$: the share of labor employed in the nontraded-good sector becomes less than the share of spending on output from that sector. This illustrates the fact that foreign financing allows the inefficiency cost associated with the wage gap to be overcome: by providing them with means to purchase foreign goods international financing reduces the dependence of consumers on the distorted trade sector. This raises an incentive issue not captured in our model: foreign grants that make domestic distortions less crippling may result in less energetic efforts to introduce hard budget constraints in the state sector. This has profound effects on the transition process that follows.[9]

5.4. Transition Dynamics

Once it starts operating, the modern traded-good sector invests its entire profit margin into productive capital.[10] As indicated by (5.15), this happens when the real producer wage is lower than labor productivity ($w^{T} = w^{N} = cp < b_2$). This requires that the relative price of nontraded to traded goods, the real exchange rate p, be sufficiently low. From (5.17), we see that at time $t = 0$ this condition is not necessarily satisfied. If the wage gap F is large relative to foreign financing Z and labor productivity b_2, the modern industrial sector does not take off, a sort of transition trap. Equally well it is possible that foreign-capital inflows increase the demand for goods to the point where the whole labor force is employed in the nontraded-good sector. This effect can be interpreted as a form of Dutch disease. Only when the capital inflows are reduced or labor mobility is increased can the economy transform itself successfully. We further discuss the possibility of such traps in more detail in the appendix.

The evolution of the economy after the big bang is described in Figure 5.4. The path of the economy is found by combining (5.7), (5.12), and (5.10b) to obtain

$$L^{T} = \alpha \underline{L} - (2L/b_2)[-cp + A + B/cp] \tag{5.18}$$

with

$$A = b_2 + F + (1-\alpha)F$$

$$B = (1-\alpha)[Zb_2/(2\underline{L}) - F(b_2 - F)],$$

which is unambiguously upward-sloping for the possible values of the real exchange rate $b_2/2 + F < pc < b_2$ (see Appendix A). The real exchange rate will always exceed $b_2/2 + F$ because $b_2/2$ is the wage level paid to state workers if all production lines in the state sector are still operated. Because the demand for nontradable goods is nonzero by assumption, a nontraded-good sector has to emerge. It can attract workers only by paying more than

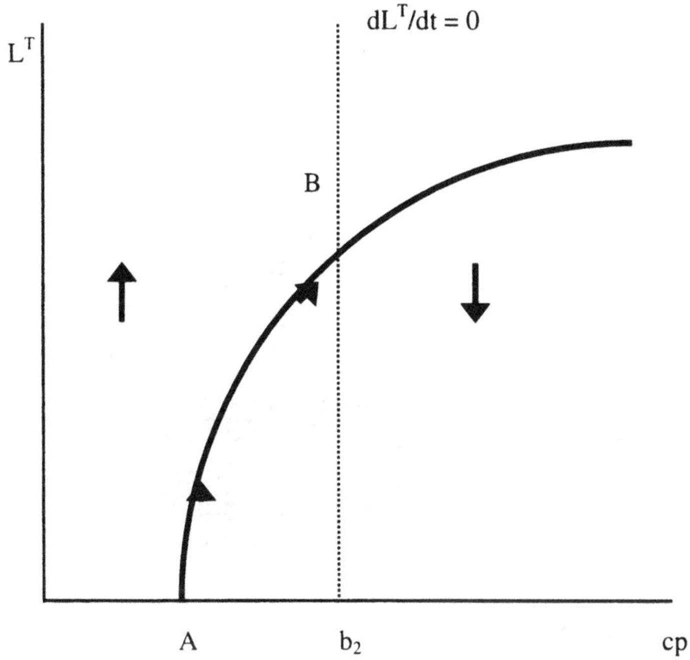

Figure 5.4. Transition Dynamics

$b_2/2 + F$. If the real exchange rate exceeds b_2, transition cannot start either because the modern traded sector does not even begin to accumulate capital as pointed out above. The schedule $dL^T/dt = 0$ corresponds to (5.15) and considers only the case of a successful transition—that is, $cp(0) < b_2$.[11]

Point A in Figure 5.4 represents the initial situation where the modern traded-good sector has not yet started to operate. It is enough that some arbitrarily small amount of financing be made available to that sector for capital accumulation to start and for employment L^T to grow. The figure reveals that, along the way, the real exchange rate appreciates. The reason is not productivity gains or other familiar interpretations from the growth literature. In the zero steady-state growth economy depicted by the model, the absolute amount of capital that needs to be accumulated gradually declines. Consequently, retained earnings progressively decline, and this allows the real wage to rise. It is the real exchange appreciation that allows the real wage to increase (see (5.5) and (5.6)).

Hiring in the traded good sector (measured by changes in employment L^T) initially rises; then it peaks and eventually levels off as productivity in

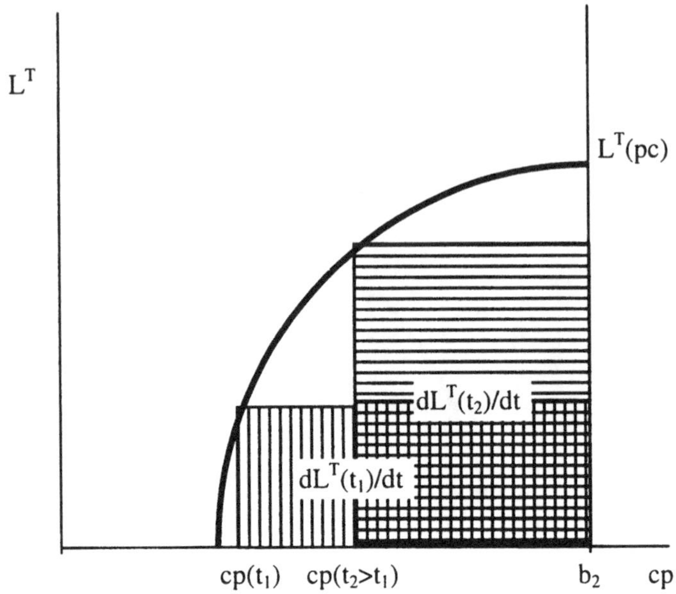

Figure 5.5. Hiring in the New Sector

the state sector converges to productivity in the modern sector. By assumption the production lines that are closed down as the state sector shrinks are the currently least productive ones. The process continues until the last remaining line has the same productivity as the modern state sector less the wage gap ($a_2 = b_2 - F$). Hiring is proportional to the size of the rectangles shown in Figure 5.5.[12] High foreign financing and relative low obstacles to labor mobility help the new traded sector initially to emerge without a strong appreciation.

The evolution of the size of the nontraded-good sector is ambiguous. It depends on the relative size of the wage gap and the amount of foreign financing. The nontraded-good sector tends to decline the more abundant is foreign financing and the lower are the barriers to labor mobility.[13] To understand why, suppose that the wage gap F is zero. The nontraded-good sector is not financially restricted at $t = 0$ and jumps to a point such that a share α of disposable income $Z + \underline{L}pc$ is spent on a supply cL^n of nontraded goods at a relative price p. Goods market equilibrium then implies

$$\alpha(Z + \underline{L}pc) = pcL^n. \tag{5.19}$$

This equilibrium condition implies that employment in the nontraded sector must decline as the real exchange rate p appreciates. Why? Given the technology of the nontraded-good sector as described by (5.4) and the no-profit assumption, the real wage *measured in terms of the nontraded good* remains constant and equal to c. In the absence of a wage gap, by (5.6), the same holds for all real wages. The real exchange-rate appreciation implies that disposable income *measured in terms of the nontraded good* $Z/p + \underline{L}c$ declines because the amount of foreign financing is not adjusted to compensate for the decline of the relative price of traded goods. Thus both substitution and income effects of the change in the relative price p act toward reducing the demand for nontraded goods. This effect can be overcome if labor income in terms of the nontraded goods is increasing during the transition period. The wage gap does just that. Labor income in terms of nontraded goods $c\underline{L} - F\ \underline{L}^{S}/p$ is rising during the transition. The aggregate efficiency loss associated with the wage gap decreases in line with the declining employment in the state sector and the appreciating real exchange rate. This effect raises employment in the nontraded sector because it is proportional to disposable income measured in terms of the price of nontraded goods. In the end, the evolution of the number of workers in the nontraded sector depends on the relative size of these two effects.

5.5. The Steady State

The steady state is characterized as follows:

$$cp = b_2 \tag{5.20a}$$

$$L^{S} - (2F/b_2)\underline{L} \tag{5.20b}$$

$$L^{T} = \alpha\underline{L} - (1-\alpha)(Z/b_2) - [1-(1-\alpha)(F/b_2)]L^{S} \tag{5.20c}$$

$$L^{N} = (1-\alpha)\underline{L} + (1-\alpha)(Z/b_2) - (1-\alpha)(F/b_2)L^{S} \tag{5.20d}$$

Eventually, opportunities to earn nonzero profits in the new traded-good sector disappear, and the economy converges toward its steady state. At that stage the relative price of traded goods is not held up by the finance constraint anymore, and the real exchange rate equals b_2/c, the relative productivities in the traded and nontraded good sectors, as in any normal Leontief economy. It is affected by neither foreign financing nor the wage gap. Yet the presence of the wage gap preserves the state sector from complete extinction and therefore reduces the size of the modern sectors. Finally, external finance Z increases disposable income and the size of the nontraded good sector, while it reduces the size of the traded-good sector as it provides (free) financing for the purchase of foreign goods. This last feature is unrealistic for the long run because it ignores the nation's budget constraint. It may have some relevance in the medium run, as well as for fast-growing transition economies that outgrow their external indebtedness.

5.6. Conclusion

This chapter presents a model of the real exchange rate during the transition process. The model emphasizes the link between productivity, capital accumulation, real wages, and relative prices as the old state sector gradually makes room for the modern sectors to expand.

A key issue is how to model transition to study the behavior of the real exchange rate. We have argued that two features are specific to the transition process: the absence of any correlation between the nominal and the real exchange rate and trend real appreciation. The first characteristic justifies ignoring nominal aspects. The second characteristic points toward the Balassa-Samuelson effect, but closer scrutiny suggests that this effect is unlikely to be more than a small part of the story. Accordingly, we have deliberately shut off the Balassa-Samuelson channel to better analyze alternative sources of real appreciation.

Instead, the model proposes to represent transition with the following five features. First, a weak banking system and a fuzzy transformation of property rights result in the almost complete absence of lending to the new private sector. The model is crude in assuming that investment is solely financed by retained profits, but it is well known that information problems can lead to the breakdown of bank lending (Akerlof, 1970; Stiglitz and Weiss, 1971). Second, parts of the old manufacturing sector continue to operate under soft budget constraints. This has the effect of freezing resources in low productivity production lines, many of which are actually effectively insolvent. The resulting inefficiency affects both the demand and the supply sides. Third, labor mobility away from the old state sector is limited by a variety of factors inherited from the command economy, including access to housing, health, education. This effect is captured through an admittedly ad hoc gap between wages in the modern sectors and wages in the old state sector. Fourth, transition is described as the instantaneous release of pent-up demand for services and for internationally traded goods, along with access to foreign financing that permits a discrete jump in the supply of internationally traded goods. The result is the emergence of a market-determined real exchange rate, the ratio of the price of nontraded goods to the price of traded goods. Finally, the dismantling of

"Berlin walls" is accompanied by the availability of foreign financing. The model, again, is crude in treating this financing as exogenous and constant, but the main conclusions are unlikely to be overturned by a better account of intertemporal budget constraints.

A number of results emerge. First, the real exchange rate is just the other side of the coin of the real wage.[14] Labor costs and the real exchange rate need to be initially low to allow the new traded sector to generate high enough profit margins to be able to expand. At the same time a continuous real appreciation is needed to attract labor away from the state sector, which is then forced to close down inefficient production lines. The link between real appreciation and rising productivity in the traded-good sector can be seen as a Balassa-Samuelson effect in reverse. Productivity increases are a reaction to the real appreciation, not the exogenous driving force behind it.

Second, the proper level of the real exchange rate is a knife edge. Too low real wages do not provide incentives for labor to leave the state sector. Too high real wages reduce retained earnings and accumulation in the modern manufacturing sector. In the latter case, another outcome occurs: there exist only the old manufacturing sector and the low capital-intensive service sector. This knife-edge property gives rise to *transition traps* described below.

Third, frictions in the labor market and subsidies to the state sector (here cross-subsidies inside the state sector) enhance this effect by requiring higher real wages and a more appreciated real exchange rate. The frictions can be so high that a modern manufacturing sector cannot emerge at all. This is a first case of transition trap.

Fourth, foreign finance tends to offset the effects of subsidies and labor-market frictions. Under certain conditions it sustains demand and tends to appreciate the real exchange rate, which, in turn, imposes tougher foreign competition on the old sector. Put differently, limits to foreign borrowing causes the real exchange rate to be undervalued (given the productivity levels) and keeps real wages too low.

Fifth, if too large, foreign finance can lead to another transition trap akin to the Dutch disease. A large supply of foreign funds props up demand, which leads to real appreciation and high real wages. This can wipe up profits in the modern traded sector and, given the financial-market distortion, block investment and the development of state-of-the-art manufacturing.

These results suggest a number of policy implications. These implications are specific to the model, of course, and must be considered with great circumspection until more research determines their robustness. The first implication is that it is futile and possibly counterproductive to resist real appreciation. The real appreciation is the market channel through which labor is attracted out of the inefficient state sector. Yet much as undervaluation blocks transition by preventing labor from migrating in the modern sectors (traded and nontraded goods), overvaluation may wipe out profitability in the new manufacturing sector.

The model also illustrates the crucial role IMF or World Bank money plays in the early days of reform. In the absence of outside sources, such financing allows the debilitating effects of distortions in the labor and financial markets to be overcome. This is true even though we assume that foreign loans finance pure consumption. The popular argument that a current-account financed consumption boom is harmful does not hold in this model. Since we do not impose the long-term budget constraint on the country, this implication may have to be qualified. Nevertheless, it is important to keep in mind that the inflows, although entirely consumed, raise the productivity of the economy and help the country to outgrow its external debt. Still the model should not be taken at face value. To the very least, direct investment is preferable because it accelerates capital accumulation over and above addition to retained earnings and because grants may act as a disincentive to the elimination of soft budget constraints in the state sector.

Other modeling strategies are possible. We have explored a version of the model where the good produced by the state sector is an inferior imperfect substitute to foreign manufactured goods, so that demand declines as income increases. In that setup the role of the real exchange rate is not to crowd out the state sector (which declines because of capital depreciation and obsolescence), and real appreciation is not linked to productivity gains. Instead, because it determines real wages in the traded good sector, the real exchange rate affects the distribution of revenues between labor and firms. In the absence of financial markets, this is what determines the level of investment. Real appreciation sets in as the need for capital accumulation financed by saving declines.

Quite clearly, the model presented here should be seen as a first exploration of complex phenomena. While we believe that the results shed some light on the role of the real exchange rate during the transition process, further research must explore some of its limitations.

First, we have explicitly eliminated sector-level productivity changes that give rise to the Balassa-Samuelson effect. The interplay of this effect with those outlined here may lead to interesting dynamics.

Second, we have assumed that financial markets are missing. Even though financial markets have played a limited role so far, their influence is growing and needs to be acknowledged. This concerns domestic markets that allow both for private savings and intertemporal consumption smoothing as well as outside borrowing. This also concerns foreign borrowing and the link between domestic and foreign interest rates. Our assumption of a constant and permanent flow of income from abroad is quite unrealistic. Our conjecture is that what is important is that the country has only limited access to international capital markets.

Third, labor-market frictions are captured by the existence of an exogenous and constant wage gap. A more explicit modeling of the labor market is obviously needed. An alternative natural extension would be to introduce explicit subsidies to the state sector. In the absence of a proper treatment of government subsidies including the state's budget constraint, Appendix B shows that there exists an equivalence between subsidies and the wage gap.

Fourth, the adoption of Leontief technologies greatly simplifies the analysis. It is unlikely that allowing for substitutability between production factors will change the main results.

Fifth, the assumption of price and wage flexibility leads to full employment. This is obviously unrealistic. What is needed is a model that explains transition unemployment. To be relevant such a model would also need to explore other sources of unemployment factors than Western-style wage rigidities, including mismatch, search costs, and rent seeking.

Finally, to keep the model tractable, we have left out all nominal variable in the model. This rules out the study of nonneutralities that may interfere with the transition process.

Appendix A.

This appendix establishes

1. The statement in Section 5.4 that the real exchange rate is increasing during the transition process,
2. The conditions on the parameter values that have to hold to allow the new traded sector to emerge,
3. The exchange rate at big bang that depends positively on the size of the wage gap F.

1. We know from equation (5.15) that hiring in the new sector is positive as long as the relative price p doesn't exceed the ratio of the productivities in the two new sectors b_2/c. We can use this fact to show that the real exchange rate p monotonically appreciates. The slope of the $L^T(cp)$ curve (5.18) is given by

$$dL^{\mathrm{T}}/dt = 2\underline{L}/b_2(1 + B/pc^2)d(pc)/dt, \tag{5.21}$$

where $B = (1 - \alpha)\ (Z/2\underline{L}\ b_2 - F(b_2 + F))$.

The left-hand side of equation (5.21) is positive as long as $cp < b_2$. Hence the real exchange rate is monotonically increasing for $cp < b_2$ as long as

$$1 + B/c^2 p > 0. \tag{5.22}$$

If condition (5.22) holds at $t = 0$, it also holds for the subsequent higher exchange rates. To show that it holds at $t = 0$, we first solve explicitly for the initial exchange rate. The real exchange rate at $t = 0$ follows from equations (5.16) and (5.17):

$$cp(0) = -Q/2 \pm (Q^2/4 + B)^{1/2}, \tag{5.23}$$

where $Q = (\alpha - 2)\ (F + b_2/2) < 0$.

To make sure that the real exchange rate is well defined for any parameter value, we check that the term under the square root is unambiguously positive:

$$B > -Q^2/4 \Leftrightarrow (1-\alpha)(Zb_2/(2\underline{L}) + b_2^{\,2}/4) > -\alpha^2/4(F + b_2/2)^2, \tag{5.24}$$

which is clearly true for all parameter values.

The initial exchange rate $cp(0)$ has to exceed $F + b_2/2$ to allow the new nontraded sector to draw workers out of the state sector (we exclude a negative employment level in the nontraded-good sector). This condition rules out the lowest of the two solutions in (5.23) (corresponding to the case where the square root is subtracted):

$$cp(0) \geq F + b_2/2 \Leftrightarrow -(Q^2/4 + B)^{1/2} \geq \alpha/2(F + b_2/2). \tag{5.25}$$

Now we can prove that the real exchange rate monotonically appreciates. Given that the initial exchange rate is low enough to permit a successful transition, it appreciates if (see (5.22) and (5.23)):

$$1 + B/c^2 p > 0 \Leftrightarrow Q(Q^2/4 + B)^{1/2} < 2(Q^2/4 + B). \tag{5.26}$$

This inequality holds for all values of F and Z because the left-hand side is negative ($Q < 0$) while the right-hand side is positive (see (5.24)) for all parameter values. □

2. We now derive the conditions that ensure that the new traded sector can develop. For that to happen firms in that sector must make positive profits at $t = 0$:

$$b_2 > cp(0) \Leftrightarrow b_2 + Q/2 > (Q^2/4 + B)^{1/2}. \tag{5.27}$$

A necessary condition is that the left-hand side of (5.27) be positive—that is,

$$b_2 > -Q/2, \quad \text{which is equivalent to } b_2 > 2(2-\alpha)/(\alpha+2)F. \tag{5.28}$$

From (5.26) one concludes that for the transition to be successful it must be that

$$((1-\alpha)F/b_2 - 1)F + \alpha b_2/2 > (1-\alpha)Z/(2\underline{L}). \tag{5.29}$$

As long as (5.28) and (5.29) hold, the initial exchange rate is in the interval

$$b_2 + F/2 < cp(0) < b_2.$$

When either (5.28) or (5.29) does not hold, the transition cannot start. The initial exchange rate is too high to earn positive profits in the traded-good sector. The steady state is instantaneously reached at big bang with the share of labor employed in the state and the nontraded sector being determined by demand, the size of the capital inflows, and the wage gap. This outcome occurs if

- Either the limitations to labor mobility F are so high that the new traded sector cannot compete profitably with the old state sector (5.28),
- Or capital inflows are so large that the real exchange rate appreciates to levels where the domestic new sector cannot compete with imports from abroad (5.29). □

3. In Section 5.3, we saw the wage gap F has two opposite effects on the initial exchange rate. It reduces both the supply of (by increasing the costs) and the demand for (by reducing aggregate income) for the nontraded goods. We now show that the first effect dominates the second so that the initial exchange rate unambiguously rises with the wage gap F. The admissible solution in (5.23) implies that

$$dcp/dF = \frac{1}{2}\left(-dQ/dF + (Q^2/4+B)^{-1/2}\left(\frac{1}{2}Q\, dQ/dF + dB/dF\right)\right).$$

$$dB/dF = -(1-\alpha)(b_2+2F) < 0$$

$$dQ/dF = (\alpha-2) < 0.$$

Some algebra shows that

$$dcp/dF > 0 \Leftrightarrow 1/2Q + (dB/dF)/(dQ/dF) = -\alpha^2/(4-2\alpha)$$
$$(F + b_2/2) < 0 < (Q^2/4+B)^{1/2},$$

which proves that the initial exchange rate depends positively on the wage gap F. □

Appendix B. The Case of Subsidies to the State Sector

So far we have assumed that the state sector as a whole has to break even. This is unrealistic since in most transition countries the state sector as a whole is a net recipient of subsidies through direct transfers, cheap credit, or other means. In this appendix we allow for explicit subsidies. We assume that the state-sector firms receive a fixed amount of subsidies S per worker. These transfers are financed by a flat consumption tax that could also be interpreted as an inflation tax. As before the state sector pays all its revenues out to workers. Average productivity must again be equal to the cost per worker. The productivity of the least efficient firm still operating at time t is now given by

$$(b_2 + x(t))/2 = cp(t) - (F + S), \tag{5.30}$$

which implies

$$x(t) = 2[pc - (F + S)] - b_2. \tag{5.31}$$

Given the exchange rate the productivity of the least efficient state firm still operating is now lower than in the no-subsidy case. The same is necessarily true for the average productivity in the sector, and the number of people employed in the state sector is correspondingly higher as shown by the modified equation (5.12):

$$L^S = 2\underline{L}(b_2 - cp + (F + S))/b_2. \tag{5.12'}$$

Assuming that, like companies and households, the government has no access to financial markets the tax rate s on consumption is determined by the size of the subsidies:

$$s(cp\underline{L} - FL^S + Z) = SL^S. \tag{5.32}$$

The consumers budget constraint can then be written as

$$pC^N + C^T \leq (1 - s)(cp\underline{L} - FL^S + Z) = cp\underline{L} - (F + S) + Z, \tag{5.33}$$

and demand is given by (5.9) changed to

$$C^T = \alpha(cp\underline{L} - (F + S)L^S + Z) \tag{5.9a'}$$

$$pC^N = (1 - \alpha)(cp\underline{L} - (F + S)L^S + Z). \tag{5.9b'}$$

A comparison of equations (5.9a′), (5.9b′), and (5.12′) with equations (5.9a), (5.9b), and (5.12) readily shows that subsidies S affect the economy in the same way as the wage gap F does. Subsidies that are financed by raising a flat consumption tax do not add to the analysis.

Notes

1. This result is standard textbook wisdom (see, e.g., Obstfeld and Rogoff, 1996).
2. We present in the appendix a model with subsidies.
3. Allowing for factor substitutability would not change the results but greatly complicate the formulation.
4. Alternatively, there can be labor hoarding. The model allows for redundant labor in the state sector.
5. Alternatively, one could argue that the corporate governance structure of state firms does not allow for retained earnings. Profits could be accumulated only by adandoning more production lines and laying off more workers than necessary to break even in the short run, a decision that is very difficult to push through under an diffuse ownership structure.
6. The *NN* schedule admits another branch corresponding to $cp < (1 - \alpha) F$, which is not shown in Figure 5.3. Appendix A shows formally that there is no admissible solution on this branch. The appendix also rules out a second solution with lower value of p than the one shown in the case $F\underline{L}\alpha > Z$. Graphically this second solution corresponds to the other intersection (not shown) further up along the *NN* schedule on the right-hand-side panel, where $LS > \underline{L}$, which is impossible, of course.
7. Technically, labor productivity c and the real exchange rate p only appear as cp.
8. The effect on employment depends on the configuration. In the left-hand-side panel of Figure 5.3, L^S increases with b_2 while it decreases on the right-hand-side panel. This is again a manifestation of the inefficiency associated with the wage gap.
9. This observation leads to an alternative interpretation of the beginning of transition, presented so far as an exogenous event which leads to the discrete emergence of demand for nontraded goods. One can see transition starting when the wage gap exogenously declines from a very high level, which so far prevented exit from the state sector. One might even consider that an inefficient state service sector used to exist and disappears at day zero and is replaced by the new sector that does not have to accumulate capital.
10. To start operating the traded-good sector needs capital and to accumulate capital it needs to first generate profit. To break the logjam, it is assumed that at $t = 0$ it receives for free an infinitesimal fraction of transfers Z. This should be regarded as a parable, of course.
11. For the parameter values F and L that induce an initial exchange rate higher that b_2 the economy is stuck on the $L^T = 0$ axis.
12. Hiring is given by $dL^T/d = b_1/b_2(b_2 - pc)L^T$. The $L^T(pc)$ curve in Figure 5.5 can be either convex as depicted ($Z/\underline{L} > 2F(1 + F/b_2)$) or concave ($(Z/ + F/b_2\underline{L} < 2F(1 + F/b_2)$).
13. Employment in the nontraded-good sector is declining for $Z > 2F\underline{L}(1 - F/b_2)$; otherwise, it is increasing.
14. This matches the facts: across transition countries we find a correlation coefficient of 95 percent between dollar wages and the nontraded/traded good price ratio.

References

Aghion, P., and O.J. Blanchard. (1994). "On the Speed of Transition in Central Europe." NBER Working Paper 4736. Cambridge, MA: National Bureau of Economic Research.

Akerlof, G. (1970). "The Market for Lemons: Quality Uncertainty and the Market Mechanism." *Quarterly Journal of Economics*, 89: 488–500.

Atkeson, A., and P. Kehoe. (1993). "Social Insurance and Transition." NBER Working Paper 4411. Cambridge, MA: National Bureau of Economic Research.

Blanchard, O.J. (1997). *The Economics of Post-Communist Transition*. Oxford: Oxford University Press.

Balassa, B. (1964). "The Purchasing Power Parity Doctrine: A Reappraisal." *Journal of Political Economy* 72: 584–596.

Burda, Michael C. (1993). "Unemployment, Labor Market Institutions and Structural Change in Eastern Europe." CEPR Discussion Paper 746. London: Centre for Economic Policy Research.

Calvo, G., R. Sahay, and C. Vegh. (1995). "Capital Flows in Central and Eastern Europe: Evidence and Policy Options." IMF Working Paper 95-57. Washington, DC: International Monetary Fund.

Castanheira, M., and G. Roland. (1996). "Restructuring and Capital Accumulation in Transition Economies: A General Equilibrium Perspective." CEPR Discussion Paper 1372. London: Centre for Economic Policy Research.

Cornelli, F., R. Portes, and M.E. Schaffer. (1996). "The Capital Structure of Firms in Central and Eastern Europe." CEPR Discussion Paper 1392. London: Centre for Economic Policy Research.

Dornbusch, R. (1982). "Stabilization Policies in Developing Countries: What Have We Learned?" *World Development* 10 (September): 701–708.

European Bank for Reconstruction and Development (EBRD). (1995). *Transition Report.* London: EBRD.

Halpern, L., and C. Wyplosz. (1997). "Equilibrium Exchange Rates in Transition Economies." IMF Staff Papers. Washington, DC: International Monetary Fund.

Konings, J., H. Lehmann, and M.E. Schaffer. (1996). "Job Creation and Job Destruction in a Transition Economy: Ownership, Firm Size and Gross Job Flows in Polish Manufacturing 1988–91." CERT Discussion Paper 96–11. Edinburgh: Centre for Economic Reform and Transformation (Heriot-Watt University).

Obstfeld, M., and K. Rogoff. (1996). *Foundations of International Macroeconomics*. Cambridge, MA: MIT Press.

Organization of Economic Cooperation and Development (OECD). (1995). *Short-Term Economic Indicators, Transition Economies 2/1995*. Paris: OECD.

Rebelo, S., and C. Vegh. (1996). "Real Effects of Exchange Rate Based Stabilisations: An Analysis of Competing Theories." CEPR Discussion Paper 1220. London: Centre for Economic Policy Research

Stiglitz, J., and A. Weiss. (1971). "Credit Rationing in Markets with Imperfect Information." *American Economic Review* 71(3) (June): 393–410.

6 FINANCING THE TRANSITION TO A MARKET ECONOMY: EXTERNAL BORROWING IN THE BALTICS AND CIS REGION

John Odling-Smee

International Monetary Fond

Basil Zavoico

International Monetary Fond

6.1. Introduction

The external debt[1] of many countries of the Baltics and Commonwealth of Independent States (CIS) region (hereafter BCIS)[2] has been growing rapidly in recent years. Although not especially high by the standards of most developing countries, the current level of debt is nevertheless remarkable, given that it was zero or close to zero less than six years ago. This statement does not apply to Russia, which began with all the inherited debts of the USSR but subsequently experienced slower growth in debt. Given the different position of Russia, the focus of this chapter is on the other BCIS countries. This chapter discusses the role that external borrowing has played in the transition process and some of the risks it poses. On the one hand, it clearly makes sense to borrow abroad to help finance the difficult transition period. In a formal sense, this is justified by consumption-smoothing considerations and the need to supplement domestic savings to finance essential investments. The fact that most of these countries still have lower levels of debt than many developing countries supports this argument. Moreover, international capital markets are increasingly eager to lend to these and other economies in transition, and their financial terms are improving.

On the other hand, there is a risk that the option of borrowing abroad will weaken efforts to transform the economy and its institutions, including governments. Growing external indebtedness is less readily justified when the country has little to show for it in terms of its progress toward a market economy or improved capacity for growth. This is especially true if governments are the main debtors and their budgetary room for maneuver is reduced by the rise in the associated debt-service payments.

A balance must therefore be struck between taking advantage of growing external borrowing opportunities and not allowing such borrowing to finance wasteful expenditures or delay the transition process. The chapter therefore focuses attention on the supreme importance of maintaining the momentum of structural reforms (including strengthening the intermediation role of the financial system) and fiscal consolidation, while at the same time controlling and containing the growth of external indebtedness. It also draws attention to the characteristics of BCIS countries at this stage of the transition that point to the need for them to be more cautious that other countries in allowing their external debt to rise.

The chapter first summarizes what has been happening and explains the main reasons for the rapid rise in borrowing abroad. It then looks ahead at possible future developments, discusses their sustainability, and reviews the conditions for ensuring that external borrowing makes a positive contribution to the process of transition in the region.

The chapter is concerned with debt-creating capital inflows. Foreign direct investment does not give rise to the same difficulties. Indeed, it is highly desirable in these economies because of its implications for the transfer of technology and management and financial skills and for integration into the world economy. Similarly, the chapter is not concerned with questions about the size and financing of the current account of the balance of payments.

6.2. What has Happened in the BCIS Countries?

Since the dissolution of the Soviet Union in late 1991, virtually all the new independent states on its territory have obtained substantial foreign financing from multilateral, official bilateral, and private creditors. The character and amounts of such financing were determined by the different stages of transition, success in achieving macroeconomic stabilization, medium-term growth prospects, endowments of natural resources, and perception of relative creditworthiness by the international investment community. In general, countries, more advanced in the transition process have been more successful in mobilizing private capital flows, while countries less advanced have relied more on official disbursements.

Total external finance of BCIS countries during 1993 to 1996 from all identified sources (including Russia and including flows between BCIS countries) amounted to about U.S. $160 billion.[3] There were wide differences between countries in their reliance on different sources of external financing (Table 6.1). Some countries were able to mobilize considerable nondebt-creating flows because they were attractive for foreign direct investors (such as Estonia, Latvia, Kazakhstan, Azerbaijan), they were beneficiaries of grant aid (Armenia and Georgia), or for other reasons. Countries also differed in the extent to which they accumulated arrears as a form of financing or were able to reschedule debt.[4] In what follows, the focus is on the external debt totals, without much distinction between the sources of financing.

There are several features of these financial flows and the resulting debt that are worthy of note. At the end of 1996, the debt burden was not very high in most BCIS countries either in absolute terms or if compared with other economies at similar income levels (Table 6.2). This mainly reflected initial conditions as all BCIS countries, with the exception of Russia, started with little or no external debt.[5] However, almost immediately after the breakup of the Soviet Union most BCIS countries resorted to external borrowing to meet their financing needs, and in some cases this led to a rapid increase in external debt.[6] By the end of 1993, the median external debt/export ratio had reached 36 percent, and it continued to rise to 59 percent at the end of 1996. However, not all countries experienced continually rising external debt/export ration: in Latvia, Kazakhstan, Russia, and Belarus the ratio was lower in 1996 than in 1994.[7]

Available evidence suggests that the overwhelming proportion of borrowing during this period was undertaken by public or publicly guaranteed debtors. Accordingly, in most CIS countries—with Russia the main exception—the stock of outstanding external debt is almost entirely owed by governments and therefore constitutes a future budget obligation.[8] Of this amount, a high proportion—including most borrowing from the IMF and the World Bank—represented the accumulation of external debt on market (or near market) terms.[9]

Analysis of the public expenditure record of borrowing countries indicates that most spending, irrespective of how it was financed, was used to support current budget outlays, including the settlement of arrears on wages and pensions, with only relatively small amounts devoted to investment

Table 6.1. Baltic states and commonwealth of independent states, sources of external financing, 1993 to 1996 (in percent of total identified financing)

	Nondebt-Creating Flows[a]	*Official Loan Disbursements*[b]	*Private Loan Disbursements*	*Debt Rescheduling*	*Accumulation of Arrears*	*Use of Fund Credit, Net*
Advanced reformers						
Estonia[c]	63.1	11.2	23.0	0.0	0.0	2.7
Latvia	50.6	23.5	19.1	0.0	0.7	6.1
Lithuania	30.6	39.7	19.2	0.0	0.0	10.4
Intermediate reformers						
Armenia[c]	51.8	28.2	6.6	2.3	3.3	7.9
Georgia[c]	26.6	14.1	4.0	28.1	18.4	8.8
Kazakhstan	50.2	14.5	26.2	3.2	−2.2	8.1
Kyrgyz Republic	24.4	55.3	2.1	7.4	1.6	9.2
Moldova	26.9	28.8	5.4	3.1	19.1	16.7
Russia	6.8	14.9	12.9	50.2	4.4	10.8
Late reformers						
Azerbaijan	54.1	11.1	22.6	5.7	1.1	5.4
Ukraine	12.7	14.6	7.1	30.1	17.8	17.7
Uzbekistan[d]	----------------	90.0	----------------	0.0	0.4	9.6
Others						
Belarus[d]	8.4	-------- 48.3	--------	0.0	32.5	10.8
Tajikistan	12.2	12.2	0.5	47.6	25.8	1.6
Turkmenistan	14.5	43.6	0.0	37.1	4.8	0.0

Source: IMF staff estimates.

a. Nondebt-creating flows consist of grants, foreign direct investment, and private portfolio investment.

b. Official disbursements include bilateral credits and international financial institutional lending (excluding IMF credit).

c. Country has grants in excess of 15 percent of total financing.

d. Data availability limits breakdown by category.

Table 6.2. Baltic states and commonwealth of independent states external debt/exports (in percent)[a]

	1993	1994	1995	1996
Advanced reformers				
Estonia	12.3	9.2	8.8	9.4
Latvia	15.3	23.5	19.6	18.5
Lithuania	18.9	26.9	29.3	34.7
Intermediate reformers				
Armenia	76.3	77.9	121.6	168.0
Georgia	4.4	204.4	258.8	255.5
Kazakhstan	38.7	73.2	59.8	55.8
Kyrgyz Republic	86.6	105.1	135.0	128.0
Moldova	56.7	82.3	90.8	102.5
Russia	181.6	152.6	122.6	126.4
Late reformers				
Azerbaijan	6.0	51.9	69.8	67.1
Ukraine	32.9	59.2	59.6	58.6
Uzbekistan	36.1	37.7	44.1	56.7
Others				
Belarus	36.1	47.4	32.7	16.3
Tajikistan	111.6	136.1	124.4	186.0
Turkmenistan	6.2	12.7	26.4	39.5
Memo item				
Croatia	46.2	53.2	70.8	69.5
Czech Republic	54.2	64.6	61.0	60.3
Hungary	267.2	319.8	206.1	201.4
Poland	276.1	183.8	122.7	111.5
Argentina	442.0	430.1	361.9	357.2
Mexico	341.5	330.0	361.6	402.8
Brazil	308.1	286.8	245.9	194.9

Source: IMF staff estimates.

a. Exports of goods and services except for Latvia, Lithuania, Belarus, Kyrgyz Republic, Tajikistan, and Turkmenistan, which are exports of goods only. External debt includes public- and private-sector borrowing from multilateral and bilateral lenders as well as private sources (mainly commercial banks), except for Estonia and Russia, which is only public and publicly guaranteed debt. Debt also includes rescheduled debt service and arrears accumulations.

expenditures. In only five out of fifteen countries was investment more than 10 percent of total government expenditure in 1996, and in only three was it more than $2^1/_2$ percent of GDP (Table 6.3).[10] Thus, it can be inferred that only a small proportion, if any, of external borrowing by the government in BCIS countries contributed to capital formation.

As overall debt levels increased, the sovereign direct external borrowing of a number of BCIS countries has been characterized recently by a shift toward private-market financing, particularly through Eurobond issues (Russia, Ukraine, Kazakhstan, and Lithuania), private placements (the Baltics and Moldova), and purchases by nonresidents of treasury bills and other short-term government securities (Russia, Ukraine, Kazakhstan, and Moldova).[11] These developments have been facilitated by the fact that a number of BCIS countries, including Kazakhstan, Estonia, Latvia, Lithuania, Moldova, and Russia, have obtained country ratings (as of September 1997).[12]

At the same time as BCIS central governments have been increasing their presence, in international capital markets, market borrowing by regional governments, municipalities, and state and private enterprises has also been increasing at a rapid pace (mainly in Russia and the Baltics). Although data regarding the use of resources borrowed by these entities are sketchy, there is some evidence that a higher proportion has been used for investment purposes, including infrastructure improvements, than in the case of borrowing by central governments.

In almost all cases disbursements by the IMF and the World Bank have represented a significant proportion of total capital flows, the exceptions being Tajikistan and Turkmenistan, where reforms have been slow to take hold (Table 6.4). Agreement with the IMF on financial and structural reform programs has often been an important catalyst in mobilizing both private and public financial flows.

6.3. Motivation for Borrowing Abroad

This buildup of external debt and its concentration in the government sectors of the BCIS countries raises the question of why foreign borrowing has been so attractive. There are several important reasons for these developments.

A key factor was the emergence of large government budget deficits. As a result of the substantial and prolonged contraction of output—in most cases a cumulative decline in the order of 25 to 50 percent of GDP relative to 1990—there was a sharp fall in government revenues, which was

Table 6.3. Baltic states and commonwealth of independent states government investment (in percent)[a]

	Government Investment/Government Spending					*Government Investment/GDP*			
	1993	*1994*	*1995*	*1996*	*1997*	*1993*	*1994*	*1995*	*1996*
Advanced reformers									
Estonia	7.6	10.7	11.4	12.1	10.7	2.0	4.1	4.6	4.9
Latvia	3.3	2.8	2.3	4.6	7.1	1.2	1.1	0.9	1.7
Lithuania	9.7	10.2	10.6	8.0	6.9	3.2	3.0	3.0	2.2
Intermediate reformers									
Armenia	—	21.7	22.7	15.5	15.5	—	9.6	6.8	4.1
Georgia	—	1.2	8.5	8.8	7.8	—	0.3	1.1	1.2
Kazakhstan	4.4	10.2	3.0	3.2	4.8	1.4	2.3	0.8	0.8
Kyrgyz Republic[b]	—	3.4	3.3	2.4	19.2	—	1.0	1.0	0.6
Moldova	8.7	6.5	6.3	5.9	3.9	2.6	2.6	2.5	2.3
Russia	6.7	11.0	6.0	4.8	—	2.9	4.8	2.0	1.5
Late reformers									
Azerbaijan	—	1.7	3.3	2.6	7.2	—	0.6	0.6	0.5
Ukraine	3.8	7.4	6.0	3.2	4.7	2.7	3.8	1.4	1.3
Uzbekistan	4.3	9.0	16.1	17.9	18.7	2.2	3.5	6.1	7.1
Others									
Belarus	0.6	0.5	0.4	0.4	9.6	2.5	1.7	1.3	1.2
Tajikistan	10.4	24.3	8.2	12.0	8.3	6.3	14.9	2.4	3.0
Turkmenistan	18.0	9.5	14.6	15.2	9.9	3.6	1.1	2.1	2.4

Source: IMF staff estimates.

a. Excludes net lending.

b. Excluding public investment program.

c. Identified capital expenditure only.

Table 6.4. Baltic states and commonwealth of independent states outstanding use of IMF and world bank credit/total external debt (in percent)

	1993	*1994*	*1995*	*1996*
Advanced reformers				
Estonia	55.9	51.8	56.4	47.0
Latvia	57.7	56.1	51.2	31.3
Lithuania	54.8	49.0	41.4	30.0
Intermediate reformers				
Armenia	—	15.9	45.4	49.7
Georgia	—	4.2	16.4	26.0
Kazakhstan	4.8	17.3	21.0	27.5
Kyrgyz Republic	—	32.1	44.9	48.1
Moldova	45.6	51.3	56.2	48.3
Russia	2.6	4.0	9.2	12.1
Late reformers				
Azerbaijan	0.0	0.0	31.9	47.1
Ukraine	0.0	6.4	25.5	34.6
Uzbekistan	0.0	0.1	18.0	17.7
Others				
Belarus	9.6	11.0	25.8	40.1
Tajikistan	0.0	0.0	0.0	6.0
Turkmenistan	0.0	0.0	0.2	0.4

Source: IMF staff estimates.

compounded in most cases by a concurrent restructuring of the tax system and tax administration. This was combined with substantial pressures for maintaining spending levels, not least because industrial restructuring was placing strains on social safety net expenditures and prompting budgetary support to large state enterprises in difficulty.

Although the response of governments to large fiscal deficits in the early years was to finance them by central bank credits, experience of hyperinflation soon persuaded them to reduce deficits and to look for external and domestic nonbank financing. Russia legislated against direct central bank financing of the budget in 1995, and many other countries de facto adopted the same policy at around the same time. However, given continued budgetary difficulties, the pressure to tap every potential source of noninflationary finance was intense.

Attitudes to borrowing abroad (and also domestically) by governments may not have been as far sighted as in other countries. The combination of the Soviet experience, when defaults by governments on loans were not uncommon and contracts were not seen as binding, and limited experience of sovereign borrowing may have led to an underestimate of the future burden implied by rising indebtedness. Support for this view comes from the frequency with which BCIS governments incurred arrears in servicing external debts (especially among themselves). The situation was not helped by poor coordination between government agencies responsible for contracting foreign debt, weak monitoring and implementation mechanisms, and the absence of a comprehensive medium-term framework for analyzing and taking decisions about external borrowing and debt.

Borrowing abroad has appeared to be cheaper in the short run than borrowing from domestic financial markets, and longer maturities have been available on foreign loans. Monetary stringency and uncertainties causing residents to hold savings in foreign currency rather than in the banks or in domestic securities tended to keep domestic interest rates high. Moreover, in 1995 to 1996, the trend toward greater stability in exchange rates implied that the advantage of lower nominal interest rates abroad was not offset by exchange rate depreciation. Thus, borrowing abroad, even with spreads over prime borrowers as high as 500 basis points, in many cases represented substantial savings over domestic alternatives (including if allowance was made for any expected depreciation of the domestic currency). For example, when Russia signed its U.S. $1 billion Eurobond issue in November 1996—which was priced to yield 9.3 percent—the average Russian treasury bill yielded about 40 percent on an annual basis. The short-term cost savings to the budget were sizable, even if some devaluation of the ruble was allowed for.[13] Cost considerations were an important motivation not only for central governments but also for municipalities and other local governments in BCIS countries, where the ability to borrow abroad without the explicit approval from their governments (in some cases circumventing domestic legislation limiting access to domestic, but not foreign, capital markets) made such financing especially attractive.

While the need to finance budget deficits was a major cause of the external debt buildup, the proximate cause of many debts was the need to finance imports. This was especially true in the case of financing energy imports, which were mainly oil and gas imported from Russia and Turkmenistan by other BCIS countries. Sometimes, the government or energy producers of Russia extended loans to partner countries to enable them to import energy. More often, the imports took place without payments being made, and the resulting arrears were in many cases subsequently converted into intergovernmental loans.[14] For example, at the end of 1996,

Turkmenistan's external claims for such debt amounted to almost U.S. $1.2 billion, equivalent to about nine months of imports of goods.

The needs of the borrowers has been matched by the growing enthusiasm on the part of the international financial community to lend to BCIS countries. This has reflected a perception that these countries had lower external indebtedness than most developing and transition economies and were therefore worthwhile risks, especially as substantial margins could be picked up relative to traditional sovereign borrowers. At the same time, medium-term bond yields in many traditional markets—though not in other emerging markets, which have also experienced increasing market interest—have either stabilized at relatively low levels or have fallen. This has prompted many international investment managers to try to enhance performance by increasing the weight in their portfolios of higher-yielding sovereign instruments in the BCIS region and elsewhere. Strenuous efforts have been made by investment houses to obtain a foothold in a number of these countries, even if it meant cutting their management fees or otherwise absorbing the costs of placing loans.

6.4. What Lies Ahead for the BCIS Countries?

Compared with developing countries and many other transition countries, the BCIS countries are at an earlier stage of financial development and integration into international capital markets. This early stage is characterized by greater reliance on external borrowing by governments, which are perceived by international lenders to be the least risky debtors among all prospective borrowers in these countries. As reform proceeds, good stabilization track records are established and domestic financial and capital markets developed, it is expected that external borrowing by governments will be supplemented and eventually superseded, first by private borrowing (mainly by banks and larger enterprises) and then by private nondebt-creating flows, in particular portfolio investment and foreign direct investment.[15] Indeed, there are early signs that this process has begun in the Baltic states.

However, at the present time the prognosis for BCIS countries is that external borrowing will continue and that the principal borrowers will remain governments and other governmental entities. This is mainly because, despite considerable progress in macroeconomic stabilization, the fiscal position of many BCIS governments is expected to remain under significant pressure over the mediumterm. For most BCIS governments these pressures will also be exacerbated by rising domestic and external debt-service obligations—especially considering the prospective bunching of maturing debt over the next two to three years.

A greater proportion of borrowing over the next few years will come from private sources, especially international bond issues and commercial bank credits, and a smaller share will come from the international financial institutions (IFIs), reflecting the perception in the international financial community that the creditworthiness of BCIS countries has improved materially. This in turn has been enhanced through progress in macroeconomic stabilization and structural reforms. Access to capital markets is likely to be easiest for those countries with substantial endowments of natural resources, such as Kazakhstan and Russia. At the other extreme are countries such as Armenia, Georgia, Kyrgyz Republic, and Tajikistan, which have been beset by adverse initial conditions or civil conflicts and have the lowest incomes in the region. These are likely to continue to tap official sources for their external borrowing, which will largely be on concessional terms and will be used to support their balance of payments.

At the same time, it is worth noting that some of the domestic factors responsible for the relative attractiveness of external borrowing in 1994 to 1996 may in the future provide less of an impetus to contracting of foreign debt than in the recent past. Most important, domestic interest rates in the main borrowing countries (especially Russia and the Baltics) have trended down sharply over the past year or so at the same time as domestic financial markets have deepened and strengthened; maturities have also been lengthening. The relative advantages of borrowing abroad have thus diminished and may in the future create incentives for the governments of these countries (and other borrowers) to place greater reliance on domestic markets, thereby dampening somewhat their recourse to external sources of finance. There would, of course, also be scope for governments to refinance maturing external debt with new domestic debt, thus giving rise to the possibility of a potentially sharp drop in external debt/GDP ratios over the mediumterm. Moreover, the strengthening of domestic banking systems and rapid development of capital markets (including equity markets) in some BCIS countries will increasingly make the region attractive to mainstream investors and prompt a greater volume of nondebt-creating flows.

6.5. Implications for Sustainability

The growth of external debt in many BCIS countries over the past several years cannot but raise the question of sustainability. What further increase in indebtedness would be in countries' interests?

The case for continuing to contract external debt is clear. It expands a country's opportunity set, thereby enabling it to finance—assuming appropriate macroeconomic policies are implemented—in a noninflationary fashion more consumption, more investment, or both. Given the decline in consumption that has already occurred in most countries and the need to maintain political support for continued reforms, resources that enable consumption to be higher than it would otherwise be are desirable. Moreover, the resumption of growth requires an adequate amount of investment.

As for the relative amounts of additional consumption and investment that more external borrowing permits, what really matters is that any additional consumption now should not be at the expense of a major reduction in future consumption (when the time comes to service the external debt). This does not necessarily mean that additional borrowing should mainly finance investment spending directly. It could finance it indirectly—for example, by reducing pressures on domestic credit markets and thus "crowding in" private investment. The key thing, however, is to ensure that the breathing space afforded by the borrowing is used to press ahead with structural reforms. With greater macroeconomic stability becoming widespread in BCIS countries, the emphasis now must be on speeding up the structural reform program, including liberalization, privatization, legal reform, tax reform, banking-sector reform, loosening trade barriers, and deregulation. The aim must be to create an environment that encourages private economic activity and investment, thereby permitting an early resumption of rapid and sustainable growth, which in turn will enhance the ability to service the external debt.

In some case external borrowing will be directly linked to the implementation of structural reforms, as with the conditional lending of the IMF and the World Bank. It is often believed that there is less conditionality attached to borrowing from markets rather than the IFIs, and a shift in this direction could, in the short run, result in a lessening of the pressure for structural reform. But markets can be unforgiving over the medium run, and the timing of changes in market sentiment is unpredictable.

A second reason for borrowing abroad is that it is cheaper than borrowing domestically. This reflects both the higher domestic real interest rates than those abroad and the tendency for the real exchange rate to appreciate.[16] This advantage can be expected to decline over time. First, the real interest rate differential will narrow as confidence in the domestic currency and domestic financial institutions returns and the financial system becomes more efficient and reduces its bad debts. Second, the real exchange-rate appreciation will not continue indefinitely, although there are few signs in any country that it has reached its limit. In one or two countries (for example, Latvia), the cost advantage of short-term foreign borrowing has already disappeared, although in others it looks as though foreign borrowing will generally remain cheaper than domestic borrowing for the time being. The main threat to the cost of foreign borrowing in these countries may be a sharp depreciation of the currency because of a loosening of monetary and/or budgetary policies or a loss of confidence for other reasons; any such developments must be avoided if foreign borrowing is to remain the cheaper option.

Special mention should be made of two sectors, the government and energy sectors, which have given rise to much of the external borrowing in the past. In addition to structural reforms that benefit the whole economy, it would help to contain the external indebtedness problem if these sectors were reformed so as to reduce their deficits. In the case of the government, tax structures and tax administration in most BCIS countries need to be reformed so as to improve tax compliance, including by encouraging the shadow economy to come out into the open and reduce the tax burden on compliant taxpayers. On the expenditure side there remains much room for rationalizing the structure so as to streamline the administration, reform health and education services, target the social safety net to the most needy, and eliminate subsidies for economic activity. In the energy sector, the key requirement is that domestic energy suppliers should collect payments from consumers that reflect the true costs of energy to the country.

The general warning against slowing the pace of reform when more external borrowing becomes available is especially important in these two sectors. It is true that in some BCIS countries the increased availability of market borrowing has led to a reduction in domestic borrowing or the clearance of payments arrears, the latter being a necessary though not sufficient step toward putting government finances onto a sustainable basis. But in others it has been associated with an increase in the budget deficit and the postponement of necessary fiscal reforms. Short-sighted attitudes to borrowing on the part of governments encourage such a response. Similarly, the availability of external financing of energy imports, usually in the form of payments arrears that subsequently became consolidated into government debt or are paid off through equity transfers, permit the indefinite postponement of fundamental reforms in the energy sector and consumer behavior.

While the risk that the reform effort is undermined by foreign borrowing is the main one, there are others that might be mentioned.

There are risks associated with the short-term maturity of much of the external debt that has already been contracted.[7] In some BCIS countries substantial amounts of such debt will need to be refinanced within the next few years because of the bunching of repayments. Private credit markets abroad or at home (if it is refinanced domestically) may have difficulty in smoothly absorbing relatively large quantities of debt, especially if much new debt is being issued at the same time.

As the stock of external debt grows, countries will be increasingly vulnerable to changes in perceived creditworthiness on the part of the international financial community, especially in settings where data dissemination is poor and shifts in maroeconomic policy, and public policy in general, may not be well articulated by the authorities and thus easily misunderstood abroad. Accordingly, events that in more developed countries would have little or no bearing on sovereign creditworthiness—for example, selected bank failures or contagion effects from other countries, may in BCIS countries undermine international confidence to a sufficient degree that it may curtail further access to external credits, with material consequences for public-sector programs or banking systems that have grown to rely on such financing. Such changes in sentiment can also trigger precipitous outflows of portfolio investment and a withdrawal of overdraft and other short-term interbank credit facilities (as in the case of Mexico in 1994 to 1995), which could have serious implications for the stability of otherwise viable domestic financial institutions.

All of these risks arise in most developing and transition countries to some degree. The main factors that distinguish BCIS countries include the following:

- *The scope and difficulty of the fiscal and structural reforms* that are needed. There is a risk that mistakes will be made or that reform fatigue will set in, especially if money can be borrowed to postpone implementation of essential reforms;
- *The uncertainty* associated with the novelty of the transition from planned economies to market economies, the paucity of information about the economy, the persistence of various forms of nonmarket behavior (such as nonpayments), and the inexperience of economic agents in transition economies with the functioning of market economies;
- *Short-sighted attitudes toward borrowing*; and
- *Weak systems for monitoring and managing government debt and new borrowing.* Government borrowing programs at both central and local government levels are typically not integrated into a medium-term framework that takes explicit account of exchange-rate risk, interest-rate risk, and the overall maturity structure of both domestic and foreign debt.

All of these together point to the need for BCIS countries to be considerably more cautious than many other developing and transition countries in borrowing abroad, at least initially. As uncertainties diminish, debt management improves, and, most important, fiscal and structural reforms take hold, the risks of borrowing abroad will decline. Those countries that have moved furthest in these directions can afford to take more advantage of foreign borrowing opportunities than those that have moved least. The Baltic countries, which are the leaders in these respects, paradoxically have relatively low debt burdens. This reflects their recognition of the risks, as well as relatively sound public finances and a reluctance to borrow in the absence of good investment projects. Some of the other countries, especially those with relatively high debt burdens, should be cautious about increasing their foreign exposure.

Acknowledgments

This chapter draws heavily on the IMF Working paper "External Borrowing by the Baltics, Russia, and Other Countries of the Former Soviet Union: Developments and Policy Issues" by Ishan Kapur and Emmanuel van der Mensbrugghe (WP/97/72, June 1997). We are grateful to the authors of that paper and to Jorge Márquez-Ruarte for many helpful comments. The views expressed are those of the authors and do not necessarily represent those of the International Monetary Fund.

Notes

1. The concept of external debt in this chapter embraces financing from all foreign sources, including from other BCIS countries.

2. The BCIS region includes fifteen countries: Armenia, Azerbaijan, Belarus, Estonia, Georgia, Kazakhstan, the Kyrgyz Republic, Latvia, Lithuania, Moldova, the Russian Federation, Tajikistan, Turkmenistan, Ukraine, and Uzbekistan. The reason for treating them as a group rather than, say, also including transition countries in central Europe or, alternatively, excluding the Baltics is that—apart from Russia—they share the common characteristic of zero or close to zero external debt at the end of 1991.

3. Most of the data cited in this chapter are subject to wide margins of error and can be used only to indicate broad orders of magnitude.

4. Arrears were a larger problem than indicated in the table because those that were subsequently consolidated into intergovernmental loans appear as official loan disbursements rather than accumulation of arrears.

5. During 1992 to 1993 most CIS countries completed a "zero-option" agreement with Russia under which Russia de facto inherited the external debt obligations of the Soviet Union to official and private creditors.

6. From early 1992 most countries also incurred monetary obligations to the Central Bank of Russia through their positions in the correspondent accounts of their central banks, These were converted into government debt to Russia for most countries.

7. The fall in Belarus' external debt/exports ratio in 1996 was largely due to an agreement with Russia in February 1996 under which many mutual bilateral claims were offset.

8. The main exception is borrowing from the IMF, which in most countries is a liability of the central bank and is therefore not directly a budget obligation. It should be noted that central banks' foreign assets rose considerably during recent years, so that the net debt position is generally somewhat better than the gross debt position illustrated in the tables.

9. The main exception was concessional borrowing by IDA-eligible countries, namely Armenia, Azerbaijan, Georgia, Kyrgyz Republic, and Tajikistan.

10. However, in some countries, such as Kyrgyz Republic, an important proportion of the government's external liabilities arose from government guarantees to enterprises for imports of capital goods (which are not included as investment in Table 6.3).

11. Nonresidents' holdings of government paper denominated in local currency are not included in the debt totals in Table 6.2.

12. However, only the Baltic countries have investment-grade ratings.

13. Of course, a comparison of the final cost to the budget of domestic and foreign borrowing will depend on exchange-rate developments during the entire life of the external loan and on future interest-rate developments on domestic markets.

14. Up to mid-1993 a similar mechanism, which also generated external debt, was the debiting of liabilities for imports to the correspondent accounts between central banks.

15. For developing and transition economies combined, capital inflows in recent years have generally been nondebt-creating: they have taken the form of equity investment either directly in the form of portfolio investment or as the counterpart of privatization operations. This has allowed for a general decline in the burden of external debt (expressed as a percentage of GDP) that started in late 1980s and continued through the 1990s. This trend is expected to continue into the next millennium. See *IMF World Economic Outlook*, October 1996 (pp. 35–41).

16. The real appreciation of the exchange rate also dampens the impact of growing external debt on some conventional indicators of indebtedness (in particular the external debt/GDP ratio).

17. Excluding rescheduled debt, much of which has tended to be rather longer term—particularly between Russia and the London and Paris Clubs—with grace periods ranging from seven to ten years and with final maturities of twenty to twenty-five years.

7 CAPITAL FLOWS AND STABILITY OF FINANCIAL SYSTEMS IN EMERGING COUNTRIES

André Icard

Bank for International Settlements

Many developing countries have made enormous progress in the last decade in nurturing more open and more liberal financial markets. A central aspect of this change has been increased openness to international capital markets, perhaps one of the most momentous reforms in the developing world during the last decade or so.

The prevailing sentiment about this change is certainly one of satisfaction. Foreign capital is going to emerging markets on a major scale even though the flows have not been regular over the past two decades. Integration in world capital markets has begun to provide, in many people's eyes, an effective discipline for economic policy, and closer integration has usually been accompanied by better domestic policies, microeconomic as well as macroeconomic.

But some events—notably the Mexican financial crisis three years ago and more recently instability in some other emerging markets—have tempered such satisfaction. As a result of this, investors are, in general, assessing their risks more carefully. In addition, governments in recipient countries have learned about the dangers of excessive reliance on volatile capital flows. And the international community has found itself having to face the consequences of sudden movements of capital of a quite unprecedented magnitude.

In recipient countries, intense capital flows raise delicate issues about monetary policy: What exchange-rate policy should be implemented? How should a rational interest-rate policy be defined when internal needs are in conflict with external influence? Should some elements of exchange control be introduced? How should large-scale sterilization be implemented in the domestic market?

But capital flows also generate concerns about the stability of the financial sector in recipient countries. This is the topic I would like to focus on.

In all countries, the task of those in charge of safeguarding the stability of the financial system has never been an easy one. However, the job is becoming even more demanding as a result of the phenomenal growth of financial markets following the tide of deregulation and globalization of the last twenty years or so. The awareness in official circles, especially in emerging countries, that financial-system fragility poses a serious potential threat to the stability of the real economy, both at the domestic and international levels, has been growing for several years.

In this chapter, I try to draw some general lessons from the experience gained by some emerging countries in this respect. These lessons are, I believe, also valuable to countries in transition.

I start by giving some overview of the integration of emerging markets in the world capital market. I then go on to discuss the policy issues that intense capital flows pose to emerging financial sectors. In a third section. I discuss ways to strengthen the stability of financial systems in this environment.

7.1. Integration of Emerging Economies in the World Capital Market

After the gradual weakening that began with rising U.S. short-term interest rates in 1994 and the interruption occasioned by the Mexican crisis at the beginning of 1995, 1996 marked a period of strong recovery in private capital flows to the emerging-market economies.

Record levels were reached, and total net private flows to Latin America and Asia in 1996 alone exceeded total flows for the entire 1980s. These flows took the form of bank borrowing, securities issuance, and equity investment. By contrast, official flows have remained relatively flat.

Two powerful forces are driving the emerging-market economies toward increased integration with international capital markets. First, the widespread movement toward market-oriented economic reform in developing economies has increased the number of countries that are considered to be creditworthy and has also led to heightened demand by these countries for investment financing. Second, investors in industrial countries are continuing to diversify their financial portfolios, a trend reinforced by the cyclical decline in short-term interest rates in industrial economies in 1990s.

Aggregate flows show clear evidence of integration with the international capital market, and so does the evolution in the cost of funds to developing country borrowers. Indeed, average spreads on new bonds issued by emerging-market countries have declined from their high levels of the early 1990s, in line with a similar decline in spreads on U.S. junk bonds. But closer analysis shows that the spreads on emerging-market debt for given maturity and creditworthiness have declined much more.

The gain for the emerging-market economies from more integration in world capital markets is significant. The first and most obvious benefit is access to foreign savings. International capital markets can allocate the savings of capital-rich countries to capital-scarce but more rapidly growing economies where the returns to investment can be much higher. Developments since the early 1990s illustrate well this allocative function of international capital markets. During the 1980s and especially after the 1982 international debt crisis, much of the developing world (and particularly Latin America) was starved of foreign capital: annual inflows of both private and official capital averaged U.S. $25 billion over the decade. But in the following five years, inflows were in the range U.S. $65 billion to $10 billion each year. Last year, they jumped up to U.S. $150 billion. This helped to sustain high growth rates in emerging countries while inflation was maintained under control.

Yet there are also other important benefits—even if less obvious because they come through indirect channels. These benefits have to do with the effectiveness of domestic financial intermediation—both in mobilizing domestic savings and in ensuring they are efficiently allocated. Paradoxically, the old policies of trying to prevent people from moving their savings abroad often meant that funds were simply kept out of the country altogether. Controls were in any case never very effective, and Latin America in particular suffered from heavy capital flight in the 1980s. Once liberalization had assured domestic investors that money brought in could be taken out again, flight capital returned: liberalization thus contributed also to the mobilization of domestic savings. By compelling policymakers to keep interest rates high enough to keep the bulk of savings onshore, it also contributed to the efficient use of domestic savings. In the past, negative real interest rates meant that savings were often channeled to sectors where returns were very poor. Now investment has to yield returns that are up to international standards.

At the same time, such developments can serve to deepen and to diversify domestic financial markets. An effective financial industry can grow up. New securities markets can emerge and so start to reduce the large reliance on short-term bank finance. All in all, the, a major gain from better capital-market integration is much more effective domestic financial intermediation.

However, greater integration in world capital markets makes the financial environment of emerging markets more complex for policymakers. I highlight two kinds of changes in international financial markets that lead to greater uncertainty in capital flows from financial markets to emerging countries.

The first point to note is increased volume of transactions in today's markets. The implication of this is that the effects of a market disturbance could be considerably greater and affect a wider array of participants than was the case twenty years ago. Since low transaction costs have increased the speed of adjustment in prices to changes in market conditions, positions can be switched almost instantaneously, creating an increased volatility of flows that emerging markets are not in a position to cope with easily.

The second point I want to stress is that domestic systems are increasingly exposed to shocks emanating from abroad, as cross-country capital flows are growing rapidly. The removal of exchange controls has enormously increased the ability of capital to cross borders in search of higher yield or to flow back in quest of higher security. Such flows can now be large enough to pose significant problems for financial and economic stability in the countries most affected. Of particular concern today are the implications of such flows for emerging markets. They are mostly economies that are both growing fast and rapidly liberalizing their economic structure. The pace of economic change stands behind both the demand for and the supply of internationally mobile capital. Emerging markets offer an excellent opportunity for diversification to global investors, but at the same time their rapid growth and vulnerability to swings in sentiment again generates risks of sudden changes in the capital flows directed to them.

7.2. Policy Issues Linked to Capital-Flow Instability

We have just seen that the benefits of capital flows have not come free: they have been accompanied by new problems of economic management. This was dramatically exemplified by the financial crisis that hit Mexico in 1995. The story is by now familiar, and I do not believe it necessary to repeat it. However, this experience and the less serious ones that other developing countries have had can be characterized by four main features that appear to be of rather general interest.

- *Disconnection* from real investment,
- The marked *volatility* of securitized flows,
- The *stock-adjustment* nature of foreign investor interest in a "new" country, and
- The *unpredictability* of the timing of market reaction to "fundamentals."

Let me explain briefly what I mean by these four features.

First, disconnection. In the past, capital flows to the developing countries were often tied to particular investments, to particular users. Direct investment is one well-known form where investment was tied to specific real investments. Official lending was also in many cases geared to a particular investment. Part of the problem with bank lending in the 1970s was that it became disconnected from real investment projects. From the late 1980s, portfolio investment has become much more important. The links with the end-user and with real investment are now quite indirect.

Second, volatility. As we have already seen, portfolio flows are inherently volatile: investors holding marketable papers can sell them instantly. This can lead to huge outward flows and to large changes in domestic-asset prices. This has become a quite general problem in all but the deepest financial markets. The emerging markets are all the more sensitive because their financial markets are small compared with the flows of foreign capital. Nonresident funds are generally more foot-loose and thus tend to initiate price movements in these markets.

Third, the stock-adjustment aspect. Radical economic reform will often lead to a major reassessment of future prospects. If, at the same time, domestic capital markets are opened to foreign investors, these changes may prompt foreign investors to seek a step adjustment in their stake in reforming countries. As the readjust their portfolios to bring this adjustment about, the new flows into the country can be unusually heavy. Likewise, when there is a political or economic setback, investors are likely to seek a step reduction in their exposure.

Finally, the unpredictability of market reactions. Changes in underlying fundamentals do not always trigger an immediate market reaction. Quite often a deteriorating macroeconomic situation will elicit virtually no response from the markets—perhaps because monitoring mechanisms are inadequate or perhaps because each market participant is confident of his ability to "get out" before the crunch comes. Yet when markets do react they often do so very sharply.

These characteristics of capital flows raise a number of policy issues, both for the countries receiving the capital flows and for the international financial community more broadly.

What can recipient countries do to shield themselves from the worst effects of capital-flow instability, while not sacrificing the very real benefits that open capital markets bring? The answer obviously cannot be of a general nature as each country has its own specific situation and there cannot be a set recipe applicable to all. Let me just develop for you three general topics that emerge from experience:

- The role that some controls of capital movement can play,
- The significance of current account deficits for macroeconomic and other policies, and
- The development of domestic financial markets.

Let me start with *capital control*. The importance of keeping capital markets as open as possible needs to be underlined for all the reasons I began this chapter by outlining. Nevertheless, this does not necessarily mean that capital markets should be opened overnight. It may be wiser to phase out restrictions on capital flows in a more planned and gradual way. The liberalization of short-term inflows can come relatively late in the reform process. As such flows can be highly volatile, this measure can be fully justified. Many feel that the temporary retention of certain obstacles to short-term capital inflows can buy time while people learn to live in a new environment and domestic financial markets develop.

But can controls of capital movements be effective in today's world? Some would argue not: they invite evasion and an increasingly successful search for loopholes. And they provide fertile ground for corruption. This view is probably well supported in the case of controls over capital outflows—if only because funds are placed outside the country's jurisdiction. Whether the same objection is justified in the case of capital inflows is, however, more nuanced. Indeed, a close examination of experience of relatively advanced developing countries in Asia, as well as Chile and Colombia, does suggest that obstacles to certain types of inflow can be quite effective, at least in the short run. In designing restrictions, it is probably more effective to rely on "market-friendly" techniques that are easy to phase out gradually. This ease of phaseout is important because controls are not a permanent solution and countries still have to learn to live in a new environment of much more volatile capital flows.

Let me turn now to the second topic, which is the *significance of current account deficits*. In the new world of much increased private capital flows the old view that a country's current-account position should dictate the macroeconomic policy has been thoroughly discredited, and rightly so. It would, however, be equally naive to think that current-account deficits have no bearing at all on the desired stance of macroeconomic policy. This is only partly because the accumulation of large deficits over a number of years affects a country's net foreign-asset position. More important, perhaps, is what lies behind the deficit and how it is financed.

Countries with large current-account deficits that reflect low or declining domestic saving rates or that are financed by "hot" money need to be aware of their vulnerability. They need to promote domestic saving, both through fiscal policy and through structural policies designed to encourage private-sector saving. And they need to move away from reliance on short-term borrowing, particularly short-term borrowing denominated in foreign currencies.

More generally, countries receiving substantial inflows need to be especially prudent in their macroeconomic and other policies, even when the international capital markets seem to be giving them gratifying votes of approval.

I would suggest that economic policy in the capital-importing countries may need to build in an extra "safety margin" in a world of highly volatile capital flows. The reason for this is that an inflow of capital tends to make a country's financial situation look healthier than it really is. It does this by increasing domestic income and lowering interest rates. This affects especially the apparent soundness of the banks: inflows imperfectly sterilized improve banks' liquidity. At the same time, liberalization often encourages more active lending. All this can look fine as long as the boom continues and asset prices are rising. But when a country is faced with a reversal of inflows, interest rates have to rise, often substantially, and this almost inevitably leads to an increase in bad loans. It is very important that the standards imposed on, and supervision of, banks accurately reflect the risks being run. In many emerging-market countries the banking system is rather fragile, particularly in the early stages of the reform process.

The third set of issues for the emerging-market economies concerns what can be done to improve the *functioning of domestic capital markets*. One intrinsic problem is that such markets are very thin. In part, this reflects inadequate infrastructure—ill-defined disclosure rules, loose accounting practices, and other factors that can contribute to unduly opaque financial markets. In part, it reflects inadequately developed financial intermediaries such as pension funds and so on. Putting all this right inevitably takes time. A second problem is that, in the development of debt markets, it is usually the short-term markets that develop first. The development of long-term bond markets follows only after confidence has been built up, sometimes over many years. Hence the proportion of short-term debt instruments is often very high in new or immature financial markets. The relative lack of long-term instruments leaves borrowers in the market very exposed to shifts of sentiment and can exacerbate volatility. As they become deeper and more long-term, domestic capital markets in the emerging economies should become more stable, but this is a process that takes time. In both regards, however, I would again note the achievements of some Asian countries and Chile in developing large domestic pension funds that can help to foster deep long-term financial markets, and this obviously enhances stability.

Finally, it should not be forgotten that the banking systems in many countries have inherited a marked degree of fragility from earlier times when market discipline was lax. Strengthening bank supervision therefore deserves high priority among the policies needed to make financial systems more resilient.

7.3. Strengthening the Stability of Financial Systems in Emerging Countries

A growing body of recent academic research has focused on the interaction between financial and macroeconomic stability. It provides a theoretical confirmation of what has always been the belief of financial authorities—namely, that weak financial systems, and episodes of severe strains or outright failures in financial institutions and markets, can have serious repercussions on overall economic stability.

There are several channels through which such effects can be transmitted. Balance-sheet weakness at financial intermediaries severely affects their ability to channel funds from savers to borrowers with adverse implications for investment.

A further set of channels has to do with contagion effects where the failure of one or a few institutions can lead to strains elsewhere in the financial system because of the interconnectedness of activity and mutual exposure through the payment system.

Finally, financial instability can have a direct impact on the ability of a country to pursue a prudent macroeconomic policy. International experience shows that the fiscal costs of the resolution of widespread financial failures can be high. To avoid the high costs of closure or recapitalization of financial institutions, the authorities may be tempted to maintain a looser policy stance than that warranted by the prevailing macroeconomic conditions hoping that the extra liquidity would help financial institutions out of the straits. In such circumstances financial markets may also sense the unwillingness of the authorities to defend rigorously any existing exchange rate target and a speculative attack may quickly follow.

In such an environment, improving the resilience of financial systems appears essential. How to achieve this objective in emerging countries will be the first point I focus on. But conversely, experience shows, in developed as well as emerging economies, that the general economic environment in which financial institutions operate is a key element for the stability of the financial system. This if the final point I would like to focus on.

In addition to problems that are common to all financial firms and that are also extremely sensitive in developed markets, such as capital adequacy or rish monitoring, *financial institutions in emerging markets* are confronted with an additional set of difficulties that I would label "starting-point problems" and that demand special attention from regulators and supervisors. They relate to the structural characteristics of these markets and the growing pains of financial reform. While there is no doubt of the long-run benefits of financial system liberalization, reforms inevitably create conditions that can lead to severe strains if not managed properly. We have ample experience from both emerging as well as industrial countries of inadequate preparation for financial liberalization being linked to severe banking crises. Second, the greater prevalence of government intrusion in many aspects of financial institutions' operations in emerging countries, coupled with relatively looser controls over connected lending, presents initial conditions that can create serious problems.

The threat to banking system soundness that derives from these structural characteristics can be accentuated by the markedly higher volatility of macroeconomic conditions in emerging markets. The sources of this volatility are both external, in the form of variable terms of trade, foreign interest rates, and real exchange rates, and internal, in the form of higher and more variable inflation and less stable growth rates. Changes in these conditions are very frequently associated with large swings to already sizable capital flows, which if not properly managed can create major disruptions.

In sum, financial institutions in emerging markets not only are subject to more severe shocks but at the same time are often less well equipped to deal with them. These risks and vulnerabilities suggest that supervisory authorities in these countries have an even harder task than their colleagues in industrial countries in ensuring that the appropriate structures are in place to deal with the problems. This is a point that also applies to transition economies in particular. A case can certainly be made for a stronger capital cushion to permit the financial system to absorb these shocks. Perhaps even more important, however, is ensuring that the proper incentives are in place to pursue prudent and diversified lending strategies. This raises the fundamental question of the quality of banks' management in emerging markets, which is of prime interest to local authorities. This also includes the all-important accounting criteria that allow impaired loans to be recognized and dealt with before they threaten the lending institution's survival capacity.

Before leaving this question, it should be underlined that prescribing what needs to be done to foster healthier financial systems is only part of the job. Of crucial importance is generating the "political will" to ensure that effective regulation and supervision does actually take place. This is why the work being undertaken by the Basle Committee on Banking Supervision is so vital. The development of guidelines, established by an international group of supervisors under the auspices of the Basle Committee can develop "peer pressure" that should insulate supervisors, at least to some extent from domestic political pressures.

Having discussed some ways in which the resilience of individual components of the financial system can be strengthened, let us turn now to the all important *interactions between the stability of the financial system and that of the more general economic environment in which financial institutions operate.* In a world where markets are increasingly deeper and stronger, it is neither practical nor desirable for governments to try to counteract underlying market forces. The major effect of official action is essentially indirect through the impact that it has on market participants' expectations. Policymakers, however, still have the responsibility to avoid creating excessive volatility in macroeconomic policies and conditions.

Prudence dictates that economic policy actions should be mutually consistent and sustainable. Sudden shifts of policy, or stubborn insistence on maintaining an unsustainable policy course, can only increase the risks to the financial system.

This is certainly true in the case of advanced economies, but the volatile character of the economic environment in emerging markets provides and additional reason why economic policymakers should be particularly careful in avoiding actions that further aggravate the fragility of their financial system. Financial liberalization seems to have brought with it both higher short-term volatility and a heightened tendency to misalignment.

Relatively large and easily reversible international capital flows have also exacerbated certain inherent problems in their financial structure. The policy response to this challenge has to be one that reduces the components of volatility that are under the control of the domestic authorities, while at the same time leaving a margin of insurance against unavoidable shocks and taking measures that reduce their impact to the financial system.

Disciplined monetary and fiscal policy strategies are the best response to the firs task. Fiscal policy in particular has to make judicious use of capital inflows recognising their volatile nature. Wringing the most out of capital inflows for short-term growth is a very risky strategy as these can be easily reversible with disastrous financial consequences. A more prudent approach should aim for high sustainable rates of development while as a first priority ensuring financial stability. In addition, the management of foreign-exchange reserves should reflect these realities and adopt policies that go beyond the old rules of thumb and toward more sophisticated strategies that provide for a larger cushion of financial resources against volatility-induced losses.

7.4. Conclusion

I started by outlining why the emerging markets have much to gain from greater openness to international capital markets—from improving the intermediation of domestic saving as much as from facilitating the supply of foreign savings. Many have benefited greatly from the decisive steps in that direction taken in recent years. Yet the nature of capital flows has changed. Heavier reliance on portfolio capital—as against direct investment and bank or official lending—means that countries have to set their economic policies in a financial environment that is much more volatile and unpredictable than before. This new situation calls for greater prudence in the setting of macroeconomic and other policies. It also calls for great attention to the stability of financial systems. Over time these systems will become more robust as they become larger, well-capitalised and as they learn from their mistakes. In the meantime there is much that governments and other official bodies can do to strengthen stability in their financial sector. For all these reasons, learning to live with modern international financial markets is both a necessity and a challenge for the emerging market countries.

It is also a challenge for the international financial community. While there is a clear role for official action in certain circumstances, the players in financial markets must know that they have to face all the consequences of their decisions and of their potential mistakes, if effective and stable markets are to develop. The scale of financial flows is nowadays too vast to be offset by any feasible scale of official assistance that is not supported by strong macroeconomic policies designed to ensure the rapid restoration of external equilibrium. For that reason, international markets must be consciously discriminating and look closely at all risks, especially country risk.

The international financial community has a role to play in spotting problems at an early stage and encouraging prompt corrective action. This is much less disruptive than waiting too long until a brutal adjustment occurs. If these lessons are not forgotten, capital inflows can continue to further economic development to the mutual advantage of both the developing and the industrial worlds.

II TRANSITION AND INTERNATIONAL TRADE

8 GEOGRAPHIC DIVERSIFICATION OF TRADE IN TRANSITION ECONOMIES

Oleh Havrylyshyn and Hassan Al-Atrash

8.1. Introduction

The process of transition from a socialist centrally planned economy to a capitalist market economy was recognized early on as a comprehensive one, requiring a long time, even if the beginning needed to be quick or shock-like. If for convenience we mark the beginning as Poland's January 1990 leap toward the market (Sachs, 1993; Blejer and Skreb, 1997, esp. Introduction), nearly a decade has passed, and much has been learned, much has been achieved, and, especially in those countries that started later, much remains to be done. One of the many areas of change in the transition concerns external trading relations—that is, the shift from trading patterns established by central-plan decisions to new patterns (geographical and sectoral), determined by comparative-advantage decisions reacting to market signals. This chapter addresses only this last aspect of transition, but we narrow the issue somewhat, focusing on the degree of openness of trade and the geographic diversification of export patterns since 1990. A full assessment of shifts to comparative-advantage trading patterns remains difficult at this stage because of data quality problems. Despite the data shortcomings, some clear trends are seen already based on an analysis of a number of transition countries and a comparison with nontransition countries.

During the Soviet period, the economies of the region had an export-import pattern that was highly inward-oriented toward trade with each other; this was particularly marked for most of the republics of the USSR but a bit less so for Russia. Independence and transition to market, together, should have resulted in two changes: first, increased external trade relative to GDP as the central-planning restrictions on foreign trade are lifted and, second, strong reorientation of trade to the rest of the world to achieve a more "normal" geographic distribution[1] as central-plan directives are removed. However, political independence alone is not enough to achieve all the expected reorientation. Rather, the extent and speed of such geographic diversification are also affected by the degree of structural reform achieved—that is, the degree to which market signals are allowed by policy to work effectively. As different transition countries have achieved a varying degree of such reforms, one should expect a varying and correlated degree of geographical diversification of trade patterns. The chapter tests both of these hypotheses, subject to the limited time since the transition began and the continued data shortcomings.

The chapter is structured as follows: Section 8.2 briefly outlines the macroeconomic stabilization achieved so far, while Section 8.3 sketches out the evidence that trade of transition economies, which collapsed in the early part of the decade, has recovered to a considerable extent in all countries, even the late starters. In this section we also describe the shortcomings of the trade data. The first hypothesis that transition countries have begun to attain a degree of overall trade openness comparable to other, market-oriented economies of similar size and level of development, is tested in Section 8.4. In Section 8.5 we present the basic data on how much geographical diversification had taken place between 1990 and 1996, and Section 8.6 then goes on to test our second and central hypothesis that diversification is greater for economies that have achieved greater progress in reforms. Finally, Section 8.7 draws some implications for trade and related policy, as well as for the broader strategy of achieving effective integration into the global economy.

8.2. Macroeconomic Stabilization

All transition economies to a varying degree have made strides in macroeconomic stabilization. Table 8.1 provides basic macroeconomic data for a sample of transition countries, including the Baltic, Russia, and other

Table 8.1. Selected economic indicators (in percent)

	Real GDP Growth (annual percentage change)			CPI (period average)		
	1992	*1993*	*1996*	*1992*	*1994*	*1996*
Advanced reformers (average)	–3.5%	4.1%	–4.2%	22.2	19.2	13.6
Czech Republic	–6.6	2.6	4.4	11.1	10.1	8.8
Hungary	–3.1	2.9	0.3	24.7	21.2	19.8
Poland	2.6	6.0	5.5	43.0	32.2	19.9
Slovakia	–7.0	4.9	6.5	10.0	13.4	6.0
High-intermediate reformers (average)[a]	–25.8	1.7	3.3	812.8	73.1	27.6
Bulgaria	–5.6	1.8	–9.0	82.0	121.9	310.7
Estonia	–21.6	–0.1	3.1	1,069.3	47.7	23.1
Latvia	–35.2	2.1	2.5	951.3	35.9	18.7
Lithuania	–37.7	1.0	3.6	1,020.5	72.1	29.7
Romania	–8.8	3.9	4.1	210.0	136.7	38.8
Low-intermediate reformers (average)	–26.3	–14.6	2.0	1,118.6	3,936.4	33.1
Armenia	–52.3	5.4	5.8	824.5	5,273.4	18.6
Georgia	–44.8	–11.4	10.5	887.4	15,604.7	39.4
Russia	–14.5	–12.6	–2.8	1,353.0	302.0	47.8
Kazakstan	–2.9	–17.8	1.1	1,515.7	1,879.9	39.1
Kyrgyz Republic	–13.9	–20.0	5.6	854.6	228.7	30.4
Moldova	–29.1	–31.2	–8.0	1,276.4	329.6	23.5
Late reformers (average)	–16.7	–15.1	–2.0	922.4	1,374.6	51.6
Azerbaijan	–22.1	–18.1	1.3	912.6	1,664.4	19.8
Ukraine	–17.0	–22.9	–9.0	1,210.0	891.2	81.0
Uzbekistan	–11.0	–4.2	1.6	644.7	1,568.3	54.0
Others (average)	–14.8	–17.6	–2.5	873.2	1,440.5	495.8
Belarus	–10.0	–12.2	2.6	969.9	2,222.1	52.6
Turkmenistan	–5.3	–19.0	–3.1	493.0	1,748.9	992.0
Tajikistan	–29.0	–21.5	–7.0	1,156.7	350.4	442.8

Source: Data provided by the authorities and IMF staff estimates.
a. Excluding Bulgaria.

countries of the former Soviet Union (BRO). The countries are classified into five categories—namely, advanced reformers, high-intermediate reformers, low-intermediate reformers, late reformers, and others. The classification follows the liberalization index constructed by de Melo, Denizer, and Gelb,[2] but given the apparent resolution of most conflicts in the region and the record of stabilization achieved in several of these countries since 1995, we have modified the groupings somewhat, as in Odling-Smee and Zavoico (1997).

The general trend is toward much lower inflation and a very gradual resumption of growth. However, performance varies by country and differs more markedly across than within country groups. The advanced and high-intermediate reformers have attained a relatively high degree of price stability and are well on their way to economic recovery, while only some of the low-intermediate reformers have realized the growth that should ensue from price stability. The late reformers have made clear progress in price stability but have not in general seen a turnaround in economic growth. Two outliers on growth are Belarus and Uzbekistan; while they have undertaken only limited reforms, they already show positive growth in 1996. A question remains about the sustainability of this growth that apparently coincides with a rapid credit expansion and a rebound of inflation. This pattern is also very reminiscent of that for Bulgaria and Romania in 1994 to 1996: growth followed by a rebound of inflation generated by credit expansion and then output collapse in 1996 to 1997.

A typical case of a late reformer is Ukraine, which since 1994 made visible progress in stabilizing its economy. Inflation has fallen from over 1,200 percent in 1992 to just over 80 percent in 1996 (and is expected to fall further to about 15 percent in 1997). However, this has not yet translated into an economic recovery. Indeed, in 1991 to 1996, GDP has cumulatively fallen by more than 55 percent and is expected to fall in 1997 albeit at a lower pace.[3] One explanation for the lack of recovery is given by Kaufmann (1997): a continuation of antiprivate-business policies and slow progress in liberalizing the economy at the micro level. That explanation is broadly applicable to other slow reformers, that have not yet seen a significant turn around in growth, a central point of the EBRD's *Transition Report for 1997.*

8.3. Collapse and Recovery of Trade

Foreign-trade statistics in the BRO countries need to be interpreted with great caution. With the economic transformation and the elimination of the large foreign-trade organizations that relied on one currency and an administratively established exchange rate, the methodology of collecting and recording data markedly changed. Even after the dissolution of the USSR, the system of collecting statistics has evolved.[4] Furthermore, trade data for the USSR were generally based on prices that deviated substantially and nonsystematically from world prices. Some partial correction for this pricing problem is provided by the 1989 special study of the USSR Statistics Committee, which recalculates trade using world prices. Nevertheless, analyzing trade behavior of each of the BRO countries and interrepublic trade comparisons before and after the dissolution of the Soviet Union is very difficult, and the data presented in Table 8.2 should be treated with large grains of salt.

Table 8.2. Exports of BRO and other transition countries (in millions of U.S. dollars)

	1990	*1992*	*1994*	*1996*
Armenia	$3,616	$7	$216	$258
BRO	3,508	—	—	—
ROW	108	—	—	—
Azerbaijan	8,936	1,571	637	630
BRO	8,212	796	282	316
ROW	724	775	355	314
Belarus	31,098	3,438	2,459	5,138
BRO	27,646	2,386	1,544	3,838
ROW	3,452	1,052	915	1,300
Estonia	3,487	355	1,305	2,077
BRO	3,288	—	574	810
ROW	199	—	731	1,267
Gerogia	5,683	77	121	322
BRO	5,166	—	76	213
ROW	517	—	45	109
Kazakstan	15,770	244	2,875	6,230
BRO	13,988	—	2,076	3,663
ROW	1,782	—	799	2,567
Kyrgyz Republic	3,339	315	281	494
BRO	3,249	236	166	390
ROW	90	79	115	104
Latvia	6,820	774	990	1,424
BRO	6,513	378	503	676
ROW	307	396	487	748
Lithuania	7,892	689	2,029	3,281
BRO	7,213	—	1,171	1,864
ROW	679	—	858	1,417

Table 8.2. (continued)

	1990	1992	1994	1996
Moldova	5,389	470	565	1,140
BRO	4,985	313	413	848
ROW	404	157	152	292
Russia	227,083	39,742	63,078	81,438
BRO	146,241	—	15,328	18,649
ROW	80,842	—	47,750	62,789
Tajikistan	3,369	29	492	770
BRO	2,759	—	110	347
ROW	610	—	382	423
Turkmenistan	4,798	64	673	1,693
BRO	4,601	—	342	—
ROW	197	—	331	—
Ukraine	$73,738	$11,308	$12,111	$15,547
BRO	60,318	6,000	7,463	8,841
ROW	13,420	5,308	4,648	6,706
Uzbekistan	12,717	162	1,844	2,649
BRO	11,331	—	859	1,099
ROW	1,386	—	985	1,550
Other transition countries				
Poland	13,624	13,186	17,240	24,440
BRO	2,084	1,213	1,603	3,397
ROW	11,540	11,973	15,637	21,043
Hungary	9,593	10,730	10,588	13,145
BRO	1,936	1,404	1,080	1,236
ROW	7,657	9,326	9,508	11,909
Bulgaria	2,075	2,495	3,441	4,543
BRO	976	579	406	913
ROW	1,098	1,916	3,035	3,630
Czech Republic[a]	11,640	12,313	13,998	21,916
BRO	3,016	1,309	798	1,205
ROW	8,624	11,004	13,200	20,711
Slovakia[a]	11,640	12,313	6,691	8,831
BRO	3,016	1,309	468	645
ROW	8,624	11,004	6,223	8,186
Romania	5,867	4,367	6,160	7,645
BRO	1,478	607	407	405
ROW	4,389	3,760	5,753	7,240

Sources: Direction of Trade Database (IMF) for 1992 to 1996 data on BRO countries and all data on other transition economies, and Foreign Trade Statistics in the USSR (World Bank) for 1990 data on the USSR.

a. Prior to 1993, Czechoslovakia.

Despite these caveats about the quality of data, there seems to be little doubt that exports more specifically intraregional exports in BRO countries dramatically declined at the start of the transition.[5] This was due to several factors including the disintegration of interrepublic trade links and of the interrepublic payments system, the fall in incomes and demand throughout the BRO countries, the substantial worsening in the terms of trade, and the acute shortage of foreign exchange. The decline in trade with eastern Europe following the collapse of the CMEA also contributed but to a much smaller degree, as trade in BRO countries was more highly concentrated. As the study of the World Bank (1995) shows, in 1990 the share of interrepublic trade was in excess of 80 percent for BRO countries, except Russia, where it was about 65 percent. (See also Section 8.5.)

Since 1992, there has been a slow recovery in trade in all transition countries, including the slow reformers. In general, the advanced reformers both among the BRO countries and the other transition economies in central and eastern Europe have made significant progress in integrating their economies into the global trading system. Thus, the share of trade of Estonia, Latvia, and Lithuania as well as Hungary, Poland, and the Czech and Slovak Republics with the BRO countries has fallen significantly in recent years. The advanced reformers were also successful in concluding trade agreements with major trading partners, and regions that have opened up their exports to new markets. The slower reformers, on the other hand, have made more modest progress in shifting trade away from the BRO countries and toward the rest of the world.

Finally, it is notable in Table 8.2 that trade in 1996 in all BRO countries remains smaller than in 1990 subject to the caveat of data comparability for these years. This reflects partly the fact that nontradable activities have gained in importance in recent years, the incomplete process of structural reform and resource reallocation, as well as the still lagging recovery of these economies.

8.4. Trade Openness

The most commonly used measure of trade openness is the ratio of exports and imports to GDP (henceforth TOR). Because the Soviet-period data for both trade and GDP are not readily comparable to the measure in a market economy, it is a questionable exercise to analyze changes in this ratio, as not only is the numerator subject to uncertain data problems but so too is the denominator. We, therefore, pose the question differently: how did this ratio in 1995 compare to that in other, more established market economies?

Table 8.3. Regression results of trade openness ratio[a]

Variable	*Coefficient*	*Standard error*	*T-statistic*	*Probability*
C	−1.358524	0.475403	−2.857623	0.0050
GDP	−0.278293	0.028337	−9.820872	0.0000
GDPPC	0.711946	0.062271	11.43295	0.0000

R-squared	0.552455	Mean dependent variable	3.614303
Adjusted R-squared	0.545057	S.D. dependent variable	0.945983
S.E. of regression	0.638060	Akaike info criterion	−0.874749
Sum squared residual	49.26163	Schwartz criterion	−0.806516
Log liklihood	−118.7139	F-statistic	74.68188

a. All variables were logged and adjusted to purchasing-power parity. The number of observations was 124 (countries).

But comparing such a ratio across countries can also be very misleading unless one controls for the effect of an economy's size and its level of development, as it is a well-known "stylized fact" that larger countries generally have lower TOR, and more developed ones generally have a higher TOR. Thus, following a procedure that is not clearly founded in theory but is commonly practiced, we have done a regression analysis for 131 countries with TOR as dependent variable and GDP and GDP per capita (GDPPC) as independent variables to test whether the transition economies are as open as comparable market economies. Given the significant misalignment in the exchange rates, we have adjusted all variables for purchasing-power parity. The results shown in Table 8.3 are fairly similar to other such regressions for the TOR.[6] As expected, TOR is lower the larger the size of the economy (GDP) and higher the greater the level of development (GDPPC), and both variables are statistically significant at the 1 percent level.

There are some necessary qualifications to the above method of comparison. As noted, the regression specification, while often used as a rule of thumb adjustor to the simple TOR measure, has little basis in theory, and therefore it may not be at all superior to a good-judgment qualitative analysis of the TOR itself. Further, as Pritchett (1991) notes, the results of such regressions are not always very robust—that is, changes in time period, definition of independent variables, sample coverage, and so on can lead to significant differences in results, with the same country changing from positive residuals to negative ones in different regressions analyses. For this reason, we have done the regressions with numerous specifications of the model to test for robustness of results.[7] While the results and fit do vary

Table 8.4. Trade openess ratios for selected group of transition countries

	TOR[a]	*TOR*[b]	*Deviation in percent of STD*
Albania	47.75	60.23	0.86%
Armenia	77.58	11.80	–2.76
Azerbaijan	76.31	18.27	–1.47
Bulgaria	100.95	27.62	–1.57
Croatia	91.81	78.28	0.02
Georgia	43.67	14.56	–2.00
Hungary	69.69	47.85	–0.75
Kazakstan	71.15	26.37	–0.90
Lithuania	69.81	48.14	–0.66
Poland	50.79	24.21	–1.27
Romania	57.53	24.73	–1.07
Russia	43.60	27.79	0.15
Slovak Republic	126.08	58.91	–0.76
Slovenia	103.58	89.31	–0.86
Ukraine	94.65	23.42	0.60

Source: World Economic Outlook database.

a. TOR calculated using GDP based on official exchange rate.

b. TOR calculated using GDP based on purchasing-power-parity exchange rate.

marginally, they are surprisingly robust to the different specifications. The results shown in Table 8.3 and used in Table 8.4 are for a specification in logs with PPP adjustment, which gave the best overall fit.

The values in the last column of Table 8.4 suggest that many countries, especially in central Europe and the Baltics, have economies that are as open as similar (in the sense of size and per capita income) market economies—that is, they have positive values of deviation of residual. In this region, only Bulgaria, Romania, and Poland (the last being somewhat surprising) show TOR values far below the cross-country norm (negative residuals beyond one standard deviation). Nevertheless, for the countries that appear more open, none have positive residuals close to or beyond one standard deviation—that is, there are no instances of highly open economies as can be found in East Asia.

The results also suggest that most BRO countries remain relatively closed compared to other economies of similar size and level of development. Indeed, for Armenia, Azerbaijan, Belarus, Georgia, the Kyrgyz Republic, Moldova, and Uzbekistan, the absolute deviation of the residual in percentage of standard deviation exceeds one. The main exceptions are the Baltic countries, Kazakstan, Russia, and Ukraine, which are shown to be relatively open. The results for Russia and Ukraine are somewhat surprising. Their trade openness ratios at 23 to 28 percent are as high or higher than for many transition economies of a much smaller size (Caucasian, Central Asian, and several central European ones like Poland and Romania). Indeed, the ratios are higher than or comparable to those of several medium-sized developing countries (such as Argentina, 20 percent; Brazil, 11 percent; Chile, 27 percent; and Colombia, 13 percent), though much lower than those for more advanced emerging economies or industrial countries (such as Austria, 122 percent; Finland, 94 percent; Hong Kong, 284 percent; Korea, 57 percent).

We do not have a good answer to the surprising results for Russia and Ukraine. One possibility would be that incomplete confidence in a country's macroeconomic stability puts a premium on external trading activities that are a vehicle for capital flight and substitution into hard currencies. But this should also result in much higher trading ratios for other BRO countries. For Russia, the revival of natural resource exports may be part of the explanation, and one possible explanation for Ukraine's high ratio is strong continuation of previous BRO links. Finally, for both countries, it's quite possible that the Soviet period TOR for these two republics was in fact not out of line with that of similar market economies; since Russia and Ukraine were the major exporting republics then, they have reestablished the old trading links earlier than the others.

One final possibility is, of course, that the regression, notwithstanding its robustness, produces some anomalies; this could be the explanation not only for Russia and Ukraine but perhaps also for Poland. As shown in the appendix, there are a handful of individual cases that appear to be far out of line with common perceptions: Australia and the United States are shown to be relatively closed, while India is shown to be relatively open. While outside the transition group only these three cases seem to fit very poorly, this is enough to suggest some caution, and we therefore consider it of value to provide the reader with the unadjusted TOR, which is shown in Table 8.4, and a full set of data for all 131 countries in the appendix, allowing for a more qualitative individual judgment.

8.5. Diversification in Geographic Patterns of Trade, 1990 to 1996

A simple comparison of trade direction shifts is difficult because of the data problems described in Section 8.3. Thus, the evolution since 1990 shown in

Table 8.5. Share of exports to BRO of selected transition countries (in percent)

	1990	*1992*	*1994*	*1996*
Advanced reformers (average)	21.8%	10.9%	8.1%	9.0%
Czech Republic[a]	25.9	10.6	5.7	5.5
Hungary	20.2	13.1	10.2	9.4
Poland	15.3	9.2	9.3	13.9
Slovakia[a]	25.9	10.6	7.0	7.3
High-intermediate reformers (average)	70.7	28.6	34.2	33.7
Bulgaria	47.1	23.2	11.8	20.1
Estonia	94.3	—	44.0	39.0
Latvia	95.5	48.8	50.8	47.5
Lithuania	91.4	—	57.7	56.8
Romania	25.2	13.9	6.6	5.3
Low-intermediate reformers (average)	88.5	70.8	58.3	55.6
Armenia	97.0	—	—	—
Georgia	90.9	—	62.8	66.1
Russia	64.4	—	24.3	22.9
Kazakstan	88.7	—	72.2	58.8
Kyrgyz Republic	97.3	74.9	59.1	—
Moldova	92.5	66.6	73.1	74.4
Late reformers (average)	87.6	51.9	43.1	44.9
Azerbaijan	91.9	50.7	44.3	50.2
Ukraine	81.8	53.1	38.4	43.1
Uzbekistan	89.1	—	46.6	41.5
Others (average)	88.9	69.4	45.3	59.9
Belarus	88.9	69.4	62.8	74.7
Turkmenistan	95.9	—	50.8	—
Tajikistan	81.9	—	22.4	45.1

Source: Table 8.2.
a. Prior to 1993, Czechoslovakia.

Table 8.5 must be highly qualified, as the data for 1990 are not comparable with later years. With this strong proviso, we can nevertheless conclude from the orders of magnitude, that diversification of exports to new markets outside the BRO countries did take place. Indeed, even if we take 1992 as a starting point, this trend is evident. There was a high degree of regional interdependence in the Soviet Union, rooted in the centralized state planning system. In 1990, interrepublic trade accounted for well over 80 percent of all trade of each republic, except for Russia where this was about 65 percent. Central European transition economies generally had a more diversified pattern of trade as they replied less on the trade and payments system of the CMEA and they began diversifying away from the USSR before 1990. Thus, the share of exports with the USSR in 1990 was already as low as 20 percent for Hungary and 15 percent for Poland.[8] Since 1990, there has been a noticeable shift in the geographic pattern of trade, particularly for the BRO countries. By 1996, the share of exports to the states comprising the former USSR had declined to less than 60 percent, except for Belarus (75 percent), Georgia (66 percent), and Moldova (77 percent).

Table 8.5, which groups countries again by degree of progress in reforms, also suggests that the advanced reformers both among the fifteen BRO states and the other transition economies in central Europe have generally made the most progress in diversifying exports. By 1996, the share of exports to the BRO states by most non-BRO advanced reformers was in the single digits. The advanced BRO reformers (Estonia, Latvia, and Lithuania) probably made the most progress in shifting trade away from the BRO states, reducing the share of exports from about 94 percent in 1990 to 48 percent in 1996. Low-intermediate and late reformers made much less progress, with the export share falling from 89 percent and 88 percent in 1990 to 56 percent and 45 percent in 1996, respectively. For the others, the decline is least, from 89 percent to 60 percent.[9]

Clearly, there has been a noticeable shift in the geographic pattern of trade toward the rest of the world. The advanced reforms among the BRO countries have the highest share of trade to the EU, averaging around 45 percent for Estonia, Latvia, and Lithuania in 1996. These reformers as well as other transition countries in central and eastern Europe also concluded trade agreements with major trading partners that have helped open new markets. The share of trade to the EU for the late reformers, on the other hand, was still only about 10 percent in 1996. Some BRO economies have increasingly redirected their trade not to industrial countries but to neighboring developing countries. For example, the share of Azerbaijan's trade with the Middle East and Asia has increased from 15 percent in 1992 to over 30 percent in 1996. Similarly, the share of Turkmenistan's trade with the Middle East and Asia has increased from 1 percent in 1992 to 10 percent in 1996.

Despite its shortcomings, the data suggest two conclusions: first, almost all the transition economies have been redirecting their exports from old markets within the USSR, and second, more advanced reformers have achieved a great degree of such geographic diversification. Section 8.6 attempts to test more precisely the second conclusion.

8.6. Econometrices Analysis of Trade Diversification

In this last section we ask the question: what factors explain the different degree of trade diversification achieved by different transition countries? We use a variant of the gravity model, in effect a *disequilibrium, gravity model* reflecting the assumption that the diversification process is not complete and that the trade with new markets is not yet at the equilibrium level predicted by a gravity model. Consider a standard-gravity model formulation[10] with the dependent variable X^*_{ij} being the equilibrium level of exports of i to j as a share of total exports (this share formulation allows us to drop $GDPi$ from the model and gain a degree of freedom), Y_j is GDP of destination j, D_{ij} is distance from i to j. Thus, we have in loglinear form the equation

$$X^*_{ij} = a_1 + b_1\ Y_j + c_1 D_{ij} \quad (b_1 > 0; c_1 < 0). \tag{8.1}$$

If, further, X^d_{ij} is the actual (still disequilibrium) level of exports, and the extent it approaches equilibrium is positively related to progress in structural transformation ($INDEX_i$) and negatively related to the change in the real effective exchange rate ($REER_i$), we can posit

$$X^*_{ij} - X^d_{ij} = a_2 + b_2\ INDEX_i + c_2 REER_i \quad (b_2 < 0; c_2 > 0). \tag{8.2}$$

We simplify to one major new destination, Europe, so that

$$Y_j = Y_E \tag{8.3}$$

and substitute (8.1) and (8.3) into (8.2) to obtain an equation for the actual or disequlibria export share:

$$X^d_{iE} = 8 + \$_1 INDEX_i + \$_2 DIST_{iE} + \$_3 REER \tag{8.4}$$

where

$$8 = (a_1 - a_2 + b_1 Y_E); \$_1 = -b_2, > 0; \$_2 = C_1, < 0; \$_3 = -c_2, < 0$$

Equation (8.4) is estimated in an OLS regression pooled for the two years 1995 and 1996 using the sample of seventeen countries of Table 8.5 (excluding countries in conflict); the source for the share of exports to the EU in total exports is the same as that for Tables 8.1 and 8.5; INDEX is taken from the EBRD indices on transition progress (EBRD, 1997), DIST is the road distance from each country to the "middle" of Europe (Frankfurt); and REER is for the BRO countries a dollar-based index and for central Europe a trade weighted index with 1994 as the base year.[11] While a 1994-based REER is perhaps too recent to reflect changes in competitiveness, a

Table 8.6. Regression results of the determinants of exports to the EU[a]

Variable	*Coefficient*	*Standard error*	*T-statistic*	*Probability*
C	18.15961	13.26594	1.368889	0.1812
Index	15.82445	3.303587	4.790082	0.0000
Distance	–0.00913	0.002446	–3.73178	0.0008
REER	–0.11888	0.027876	–4.26449	0.0002

R-squared	0.706363	Mean dependent variable	33.69706
Adjusted R-squared	0.677000	S.D. dependent variable	20.63638
S.E. of regression	11.72830	Akaike info criterion	5.034140
Sum squared residual	4126.590	Schwartz criterion	5.213712
Log likelihood	–129.824	F-statistic	24.05570

a. The White procedure was used to correct for the hetroskedacity of the panel data. The number of observations was 34.

longer period is not available, and an absolute level estimate is not easily doable within any degree of accuracy.

The results are shown in Table 8.6. First, we can see that the explanatory power for a cross-country regression is quite high, with $R^2 = 0.706$. Further, the T-statistics show high levels of significance for the coefficient estimates of all three explanatory variables. Finally, and most important, the positive sign of the INDEX coefficient confirms our prior hypothesis: that *transition countries that have made the most progress in structural reforms have also gone furthest in diversifying their exports to new destinations*. The negative sign for the real effective exchange-rate coefficient supports this conclusion, suggesting that the maintenance of a competitive exchange rate also contributed to effective export diversification.

There are some caveats, as always. Our model is incomplete in a number of respects: first, demand-side constraints such as EU import barriers are not included; second, exchange-rate volativity effects, which may be as important as level effects, are not analyzed; and third, diversification outside of the EU is also not analyzed. On the first, any bias comes only from possible differential treatment by the EU of imports from different countries; this is probably relevant for the central European versus other cases and may even be relevant for individual BRO cases. But the extent of such differential treatment is by no means easy to quantify, and for this chapter we have not attempted to obtain such information. On the second, volatility of exchange rates is also not so easy to quantify for transition countries given the very short period of time.

Table 8.7. Regression results of the determinants of exports to non-BBRO countries[a]

Variable	*Coefficient*	*Standard error*	*T-statistic*	*Probability*
C	84.00973	18.29481	4.591999	0.0001
Index	8.880586	4.231688	2.098592	0.0444
Distance	−0.01615	0.003098	−5.212453	0.0000
REER	−0.211353	0.034374	−6.148679	0.0000

R-squared	0.663534	Mean dependent variable	60.09412
Adjusted R-squared	0.629887	S.D. dependent variable	26.42697
S.E. of regression	16.07735	Akaike info criterion	5.664954
Sum squared residual	7754.440	Schwartz criterion	5.844526
Log likelihood	−140.5481	FBstatistic	19.72065

a. The White procedure was used to correct for the hetroskedacity of the panel data. The number of observations was 34.

The last caveat could be dealt with in an expanded analysis using a full-blown gravity model with all destinations for exports. We have not attempted such a large research exercise, but we have undertaken a crude version of this (see Table 8.7), which gives us reason to doubt there would be much more information provided by full-blown gravity regressions. In Table 8.7 we present the result of a regression in which the independent variables are the same, but the dependent variable is exports shown to all non-BRO destinations, rather than the EU. The formulation is, at best, a conceptual short-cut, because the distance variable should reflect distances to all other non-European destinations as well. But the general results of the regression are not dramatically changed—that is, the overall explanatory power, the coefficient signs (but not coefficient values), and statistical significance are similar—which strongly suggests that actual global diversification of transition countries is dominated by diversification toward European markets. Recall further from Section 8.5 the finding that, with the few exceptions of some Central Asian economies' expansion of exports to Asia and Middle East regions, the bulk of new, non-BRO market penetration has been in Europe.

Subject to the incomplete specification and partial global coverage of our disequilibrium gravity model, we extent the analysis in an illustrative way to ask the question: what would be the share of exports to EU if progress in structural reforms was more ambitious? Specifically, what would be the share of exports to EU if the EBRD index showed maximum reform

Table 8.8. Simulated share of exports to the EU for selected transition countries, 1996 (in percent)

	Actual Share	*Fitted Share (actual index)*	*Fitted Share (index = 4.0)*[a]
Advanced reformers			
Czech Republic	58	56	65
Hungary	63	55	65
Poland	66	51	62
Slovakia	41	53	66
High-intermediate reformers			
Bulgaria	40	44	66
Estonia	51	44	57
Latvia	44	44	59
Lithuania	33	40	57
Romania	56	42	64
Low-intermediate reformers			
Russia	33	34	51
Kazakstan	18	14	36
Kyrgyz Republic	3	20	41
Moldova	10	37	58
Late reformers			
Ukraine	10	23	48
Uzbekistan	24	19	45
Others			
Belarus	10	2	37
Turkmenistan	5	0	46

Source: Simulations based on regression coefficients of Table 8.6.
a. Assumes liberalization index equals 4.0.

(index = 4.0)? Table 8.8 summarizes the results of such a simulation for 1996. What is most striking in the results is the magnitude of potential diversification still in the future. Even for countries very advanced in reforms (Poland, the Czech Republic) one might still expect as much as 8 to 10 percentage points increase in the levels of exports to EU to 65 percent or so of total exports. For those least advanced in reforms, generally further east, one might expect more than a doubling, from magnitudes of 10 to 20 percent to 40 to 50 percent. While this simulation exercise is very tentative and for many countries the actual 1996 values are far below the fitted ones, with present levels of the INDEX variable the orders of magnitude of the values in column 3 are not far out of line with other similar analyses.[12] Thus the earlier study cited for Ukraine gave a value of all non-COMECON of 82 percent; it would not be unreasonable to have 48 percent of this go to Europe. Similarly, earlier work by Rosati (1993), Wang and Winters (1992), Collins and Rodrik (1991), and Havrylyshyn and Pritchett (1991) suggests a broad order of magnitude with the share of exports of central European economies to western Europe of one-half to two-thirds.

8.7. Conclusions and Policy Implications

The evidence of trade patterns and changes over the last seven years, despite data shortcomings, clearly shows that many transition countries especially in central Europe and the Baltics, have trade to GDP ratios not dissimilar to those of market economies of comparable size and level of development. But many others, especially in the BRO group, appear to be far less open. Further, all transition economies in the former COMECON bloc have broken out of their intraregional orientation and have began to diversify their exports geographically to western Europe and other regions of the world. But the evidence also shows clearly that the degree of diversification varies considerably and appears in particular to be closely associated with the degree of liberalization and reforms achieved. That is, the more advanced are reforms, the more this geographic diversification. Finally, it appears from analytical studies based on gravity model that many countries are still far from achieving the geographic pattern of trade that might be considered "natural"—that is, the pattern expected when a more fully functioning market economy is in place.

There are several important policy implications from these results. The most direct one is that, to the extent expanding trade in new directions based on comparative advantage is an important element of successful restructuring and resource reallocation, much remains to be done in terms of liberalization and reform in some transition economies. Second, greater access to EU markets via association agreements or other arrangements may give an added boost to reorientation of trade. Third, the model broadly confirms the importance of a competitive exchange rate in achieving diversification of the new markets in Europe. Fourth, our model confirms the simple message of gravity models: for the transition economies of the former-COMECON group relatively close to western Europe the huge size and proximity of these markets implies a dominant share of exports will in the longer term go to those markets. A fifth issue arises that the present chapter does not address: what value is there in the short to medium term of elaborating bilateral or multilateral trade agreements among the transition countries? The tradeoff will already be between the short-term positive effect of reviving lost trade and the medium-term negative effects of trade diversion and possible reinforcing of old efficient trading relations of the central plan period.

Acknowledgments

This chapter was prepared for the Third Dubrovnik Conference on Transition Economies, June 25–27, 1997, Dubrovnik. We are grateful to Mario Blejer, Peter Kunzel, John Odling-Smee, and Gur Ofer for helpful comments. The views expressed in this chapter are those of the authors and do not in any way represent the position or official views of the International Monetary Fund.

Notes

1. *Normal* here is meant *to* convey the notion of a trade pattern that geographically reflects the effects of size and proximity (as in gravity models), and sectorally reflects the comparative advantage of the country.

2. The index is intended to measure the duration as well as depth of reforms in transition countries. Three criteria were used to measure progress: (1) liberalization of internal markets (the degree of liberalization of domestic prices and abolition of state monopolies, (2) liberalization of external markets (the degree of liberalization of the foreign trade regime), and (3) private-sector entry (privatization of small-scale and large-scale enterprises and banking reform) (see Blejer and Skreb, 1997, ch. 1).

3. The only BRO country not affected by conflict and experiencing larger collapse in GDP during the 1991 to 1996 period is Moldova; some of that may be weather related.

4. For a fuller discussion of statistical issues affecting the measurement of trade, see Belkindas and Ivanova (1995).

5. Trade flows, particularly in the early stages of transition, are probably under-reported due to under invoicing, smuggling, the slow processing of trade documentation, and transit trade.

6. See Pritchett (1991), Balassa and Bauwens (1988), and Havrylyshyn and Kunzel (1997) for comparisons.

7. For example, in one specification, official exchange-rate dollar value was used; in another specification, the variables were adjusted for PPP with linear and log formulation; in yet another, population was used instead of GDP as proxy for size; and, finally, dummy variables were used for transition countries. Moreover, the sample of countries used was changed to test for differences in overall fit.

8. Rosati (1993) argues that by the early 1990s the diversification to new markets in Europe and elsewhere had been essentially completed for the central European transition economies.

9. The shares to the BRO countries may in fact be higher for slower reformers because the data source used does not include unrecorded barter trade, which is likely to be mostly

Appendix. Results of Trade Openness Regression

	Pol	*GDI*	*GDPP*	*GDPPC*^{c}	*GDP 3*	*Imports*	*Exports*	*TOR*^{c}	*TOR*	*RESID*	*Dev from*	*IN % STD*
Albania	3.45	2.38	690.76	547.57	1.89	0.86	0.28	60.23	47.75	1.14468	0.53796	0.89
Argentina	34.40	280.00	8,139.44	6,806.52	234.15	23.78	23.85	20.34	17.01	−0.3939	−1.0006	−1.65
Armenia	3.73	1.29	344.91	2,268.46	8.46	0.80	0.20	11.80	77.58	−1.0802	−1.6869	−2.78
Australia	18.20	350.55	19,256.84	19,700.19	358.62	72.92	68.89	39.54	40.45	−0.3672	−0.9739	−1.61
Austria	8.53	233.23	27,349.09	19,074.60	162.67	100.33	98.81	122.42	85.38	0.56595	0.04077	0.07
Azerbaijan	7.43	2.78	373.78	1,560.80	11.60	1.27	0.85	18.27	76.31	−0.289	−0.8957	−1.48
Bangladesh	120.38	32.29	268.21	1,489.65	179.33	7.32	4.52	6.60	36.66	−0.512	1.11869	1.84
Belgium	9.97	269.20	27,011.70	19,678.58	199.09	176.76	188.16	183.30	135.56	1.00365	0.39693	0.65
Belize	0.21	0.59	2,765.75	2,509.51	0.54	0.32	0.29	114.14	104.02	0.35147	0.25525	0.42
Benin	5.45	2.05	376.06	1,750.58	9.54	0.71	0.50	12.65	58.88	−0.7927	−1.3995	−2.31
Bhutan	0.67	0.30	452.48	920.58	0.61	0.18	0.13	49.19	100.07	0.25762	−0.3491	−0.58
Bolivia	6.79	6.02	886.13	2,121.86	17.95	1.63	1.25	16.02	47.77	−0.5176	−1.1243	−1.85
Brazil	164.08	716.98	4,369.81	6,226.68	1,021.64	61.73	52.69	11.20	15.96	−0.5172	−1.1239	−1.85
Bulgaria	9.03	12.97	1,437.38	5,253.05	47.41	6.62	6.48	27.62	100.95	−0.348	−0.9547	−1.57
Burkina Faso	11.00	2.33	211.84	733.52	8.07	0.68	0.34	12.65	43.79	−0.22	−0.8267	−1.36
Canada	29.38	565.63	19,249.47	21,419.32	629.39	197.67	211.54	65.02	72.35	0.22719	0.37953	0.63
Chile	13.83	67.30	4,867.54	9,854.40	139.93	18.41	19.69	27.23	56.61	−0.5089	−1.1156	−1.84
China	1,208.07	697.62	577.47	2,866.36	3,501.04	135.28	147.24	8.07	40.50	0.05012	0.5566	0.92
Colombia	36.29	79.32	2,205.17	6,554.83	235.76	16.43	13.68	12.77	37.96	−0.8307	−1.4374	−2.37
Costa Rica	3.56	8.96	2,516.16	6,752.91	21.21	4.04	3.93	37.56	88.89	−0.4432	−1.05	−1.73
Cote d'Ivoire	14.22	10.08	703.83	1,857.09	26.41	3.59	4.45	30.47	79.82	0.32767	−0.279	−0.46
Croatia	4.80	16.63	3,465.05	4,063.73	19.50	8.61	6.66	78.28	91.81	0.62929	0.02257	0.04
Cyprus	0.62	8.64	14,033.24	15,418.31	9.48	4.47	4.27	92.14	101.20	−0.3578	−0.9645	−1.59
Denmark	5.23	172.73	33,034.06	20,635.31	107.90	57.31	64.73	113.10	70.65	0.31653	0.29019	0.48
Djibouti	0.62	0.50	799.42	988.68	0.61	0.29	0.20	79.63	98.49	0.68851	0.08179	0.13
Domininca	0.07	0.22	2,898.15	2,849.71	0.21	0.15	0.10	119.71	117.70	0.04577	−0.561	−0.92
Dominican Republic	7.92	12.06	1,522.28	3,918.13	31.03	3.27	3.29	21.16	54.45	−0.5236	−1.1304	−1.86
Ecuador	11.76	17.43	1,482.70	4,932.24	56.52	5.34	5.27	18.77	60.85	−0.6405	−1.2472	−2.06
Egypt	58.92	58.94	1,000.45	4,051.04	238.68	18.16	14.93	13.86	56.14	−0.4027	−1.0094	−1.66
El Salvador	5.89	9.30	1,578.86	2,881.55	16.62	3.62	2.05	34.11	60.94	−0.0011	−0.6079	−1.00
Fiji	0.82	1.99	2,422.66	6,322.14	4.95	1.21	1.13	47.29	117.77	−0.5709	−1.1776	−1.94
Finland	5.07	124.98	24,669.71	17,624.44	89.29	36.89	47.46	94.47	67.49	0.19614	0.41058	0.68

Appendix. (continued)

	Pol	*GDI*	*GDPP*	*GDPPC*[c]	*GDP 3*	*Imports*	*Exports*	*TOR*[c]	*TOR*	*RESID*	*Dev from*	*IN % STD*
France	57.36	1,538.80	26,828.50	20,974.27	1,203.02	324.98	360.89	57.01	44.57	0.29096	0.31576	0.52
Gabon	1.06	5.11	4,805.38	4,328.04	4.60	1.85	2.96	104.61	94.21	0.47242	0.1343	0.22
Gambia	1.11	0.36	326.28	977.53	1.09	0.21	0.16	33.69	100.94	–0.0021	–0.6088	–1.00
Georgia	5.41	2.89	533.21	1,598.92	8.65	0.79	0.47	14.56	43.67	–0.6148	–1.2216	–2.01
Germany	81.60	2,412.48	29,565.02	19,587.71	1,598.34	549.96	570.19	70.08	46.43	0.62513	0.01841	0.03
Ghana	17.38	6.32	363.29	2,108.91	36.66	2.12	1.58	10.09	58.57	–0.7768	–1.3835	–2.28
Greece	10.44	114.32	10,947.48	8,931.07	93.27	30.76	18.83	53.17	43.37	0.11743	–0.4893	–0.81
Grenada	0.12	0.30	3,150.48	4,477.51	0.43	0.21	0.17	88.97	126.45	–0.3733	–0.98	–1.62
Guatemala	10.62	14.78	1,392.44	3,781.84	40.16	3.72	2.80	16.24	44.11	–0.6913	–1.298	–2.14
Guinea	6.68	3.67	549.76	702.87	4.70	0.96	0.80	37.44	47.87	0.74501	0.13829	0.23
Guinea-Bissau	1.08	0.25	234.25	759.31	0.82	0.09	0.04	15.71	50.93	–0.6643	–1.271	–2.09
Guyana	0.75	0.63	833.48	2,668.75	2.01	0.44	0.53	47.96	153.55	–0.1936	–0.8003	–1.32
Honduras	5.96	3.71	621.87	2,082.14	12.39	1.58	1.56	25.32	84.63	–0.1495	–0.7563	–1.25
Hungary	10.21	44.44	4,353.58	6,340.67	64.73	16.36	14.61	47.85	69.69	0.15424	–0.4525	–0.75
Iceland	0.28	7.04	25,596.71	18,924.04	5.20	2.24	2.47	90.51	66.92	–0.6886	–1.2953	–2.13
India	934.36	322.44	345.09	1,433.26	1,339.19	45.94	37.92	6.26	26.01	0.02215	0.58457	0.96
Indonesia	194.54	201.18	1,034.16	4,091.61	795.97	56.61	53.27	13.80	54.62	–0.079	0.68569	1.13
Ireland	3.58	61.93	17,284.49	15,897.29	56.91	40.84	48.14	156.34	143.67	0.64797	0.04125	0.07
Italy	56.26	1,087.18	19,324.88	19,948.43	1,122.26	255.09	300.84	49.54	51.13	0.16687	–0.4398	–0.72
Japan	125.14	5,134.30	41,027.43	21,454.70	2,684.91	420.01	494.71	34.07	17.82	–0.0166	–0.6233	–1.03
Jordan	4.58	6.56	1,432.80	4,942.45	22.65	4.81	3.43	36.40	125.56	–0.2341	–0.8408	–1.39
Kazakstan	16.60	16.72	1,007.02	2,717.54	45.11	6.16	5.73	26.37	71.15	0.0611	–0.5456	–0.90
Kenya	30.17	9.10	301.53	1,331.11	40.16	3.54	2.97	16.20	71.52	0.04966	0.55706	0.92
Lao, PDR	4.57	1.52	331.92	2,332.50	11.38	0.66	0.44	9.71	72.90	–1.2125	–1.8192	–3.00
Lebanon	3.13	10.99	3,510.45	3,281.33	9.86	6.35	2.69	91.68	82.21	0.74978	0.14306	0.24
Lesotho	1.99	1.06	532.94	2,493.30	4.95	1.11	0.20	26.38	123.41	–0.4922	–1.0989	–1.81
Liberia	2.76	2.31	836.23	886.72	2.45	0.78	0.81	64.94	68.86	0.94901	0.34229	0.56
Lithuania	3.76	7.77	2,068.24	2,999.21	11.27	2.85	2.58	48.14	69.81	0.20679	–0.3999	–0.66
Luxembourg	0.40	19.29	48,230.03	35,912.25	14.36	13.08	19.15	224.40	167.09	0.04597	0.56075	0.92
Madagascar	13.13	3.20	243.61	750.93	9.86	0.99	0.75	17.58	54.19	0.14814	0.45858	0.76
Malawi	9.79	1.47	149.65	795.42	7.79	0.58	0.42	12.91	68.60	–0.2672	–0.8739	–1.44
Malaysia	20.17	87.33	4,330.55	10,363.12	208.24	86.72	83.43	81.71	194.84	0.66476	0.05804	0.10

Mexico	94.84	286.30	3,164.26	7,732.97	699.68	55.26	67.49	17.54	42.87	−0.3282	−0.9349	−1.54
Morocco	27.14	32.42	1,194.44	3,466.96	93.99	11.33	8.89	21.52	62.38	−0.1113	−0.718	−1.18
Mozambique	17.42	1.48	85.[illegible]7	807.93	14.08	0.96	0.41	9.78	92.73	−0.3912	−0.9979	−1.64
Nepal	23.21	4.79	206.57	1,214.30	26.62	1.74	1.15	10.85	60.25	−0.4003	−1.0071	−1.66
Netherlands	15.46	395.47	25,585.21	19,474.02	300.87	200.17	223.08	140.67	107.02	0.86129	0.25457	0.42
Neth. Antilles	0.23	2.23	9,750.18	2,147.95	0.43	1.29	1.37	612.28	119.00	2.0786	1.47188	2.43
New Zealand	3.52	58.56	16,650.05	16,335.73	57.83	17.18	17.79	60.47	59.72	−0.3168	−0.9235	−1.52
Nicaragua	4.53	1.77	390.90	2,172.63	9.86	0.73	0.33	10.78	60.10	−1.0973	−1.704	−2.81
Niger	8.92	1.89	211.57	788.44	7.03	0.38	0.29	9.54	35.55	−0.592	−1.1987	−1.98
Nigeria	97.22	67.32	692.43	1,540.35	149.76	9.69	10.75	13.64	30.35	0.13999	0.46673	0.77
Norway	4.36	146.15	33,489.85	21,308.96	92.99	47.25	56.04	111.08	70.68	0.23425	0.37247	0.61
Pakistan	127.75	60.38	472.61	2,238.86	291.61	12.74	9.86	7.75	37.44	−0.5061	1.11283	1.83
Panama	2.68	8.23	3,072.86	6,041.21	16.18	2.88	2.83	35.31	69.41	−0.5011	−1.1078	−1.83
Papua New Guinea	4.10	5.48	1,334.04	2,376.97	9.76	1.81	3.08	50.10	89.27	0.37221	−0.2345	−0.39
Paraguay	4.91	9.37	1,908.58	3,879.74	19.05	2.62	2.22	25.38	51.60	−0.4706	−1.0773	−1.78
Peru	24.94	58.94	2,363.42	3,973.38	99.09	12.11	7.38	19.68	33.08	−0.283	−0.8897	−1.47
Philippines	69.14	74.15	1,072.46	2,813.40	194.51	34.06	21.33	28.47	74.70	0.51973	0.08699	0.14
Poland	38.65	118.29	3,060.79	6,429.82	248.13	27.75	32.33	24.21	50.79	−0.1631	−0.7698	−1.27
Portugal	9.38	102.74	10,952.95	11,105.49	109.97	43.33	35.90	72.05	77.11	0.312	0.29472	0.49
Romania	22.71	35.69	1,571.67	3,656.40	83.03	11.20	9.33	24.73	57.53	−0.0446	−0.6513	−1.07
Russia	148.69	408.60	2,748.01	4,311.69	641.10	84.20	93.94	27.79	43.60	0.52352	0.0832	0.14
STP	0.13	0.05	356.79	515.96	0.07	0.05	0.01	83.59	120.88	0.59756	0.00916	0.02
Senegal	8.52	4.87	571.52	1,802.48	15.35	1.80	1.54	21.74	68.55	−0.1397	−0.7464	−1.23
Seychelles	0.08	0.53	6,961.69	5,689.53	0.43	0.29	0.28	132.49	108.28	−0.1456	0.75232	1.24
Slovak Republic	5.35	17.32	3,233.64	6,915.29	37.07	10.63	11.20	58.91	126.08	0.14529	−0.4614	−0.76
Slovenia	2.00	18.91	9,453.66	10,969.26	21.93	9.81	9.78	89.31	103.58	0.08684	−0.5199	−0.86
Solomon Islands	0.38	0.32	831.82	2,289.81	0.88	0.26	0.22	55.19	150.95	−0.174	−0.7808	−1.29
South Africa	42.47	133.93	3,153.45	4,112.22	174.65	32.29	32.01	36.82	48.01	0.47672	0.13	0.21
Spain	38.69	559.62	14,464.98	14,500.15	560.98	132.33	132.45	47.20	47.31	0.15262	−0.4541	−0.75
Sri Lanka	18.61	13.00	698.83	3,479.52	62.93	6.46	4.88	18.02	87.19	−0.403	−1.0097	−1.66
St. Kitts	0.04	0.23	5,308.16	4,821.73	0.21	0.15	0.13	136.35	123.83	−0.1985	−0.8052	−1.33
St. Lucia	0.16	0.56	3,555.99	3,419.27	0.54	0.39	0.38	142.27	136.79	0.35153	0.25519	0.42
St. Vincent	0.11	0.26	2,345.38	2,317.77	0.26	0.18	0.13	118.84	117.42	0.245	0.36172	0.60
Sudan	26.47	5.02	189.66	1,498.64	44.55	0.93	0.68	3.61	32.03	−1.5072	−2.1139	−3.48
Swaziland	0.91	1.15	1,263.38	4,012.44	3.64	1.03	0.90	52.97	168.21	−0.2193	−0.826	−1.36
Sweden	8.85	230.61	26,070.11	19,022.67	168.27	79.79	94.35	103.49	75.51	0.40933	0.19739	0.33

Appendix. (continued)

	Pol	*GDI*	*GDPP*	*GDPPC*[c]	*GDP 3*	*Imports*	*Exports*	*TOR*[c]	*TOR*	*RESID*	*Dev from*	*IN % STD*
Switzerland	7.06	306.14	43,391.25	23,405.53	165.14	97.10	110.53	125.73	67.82	0.45115	0.15557	0.26
Syria	14.36	47.57	3,312.62	5,809.70	83.14	6.61	4.75	13.66	23.88	−0.9674	−1.5742	−2.59
Tanzania	29.20	4.26	145.84	651.16	19.01	2.19	1.10	17.33	77.39	0.418	0.18872	0.31
Thailand	59.67	162.76	2,727.78	7,849.51	468.35	82.67	71.12	32.84	94.49	0.17657	−0.4301	−0.71
Togo	4.12	1.30	314.83	1,236.05	5.09	0.50	0.45	18.70	73.40	−0.3289	−0.9356	−1.54
Tonga	0.10	0.16	1,682.92	1,469.78	0.15	0.11	0.04	105.99	94.71	0.30178	0.30494	0.50
Trinidad	1.35	5.12	3,777.81	8,930.90	12.10	1.90	2.11	33.12	78.29	−0.9243	−1.531	−2.52
Tunisia	8.82	18.13	2,055.56	5,483.56	49.21	8.68	8.04	33.99	92.29	−0.1607	−0.7674	−1.26
Turkey	62.07	167.33	2,696.03	5,614.27	346.06	40.21	34.72	21.65	44.78	−0.0857	−0.6924	−1.14
Uganda	19.90	6.00	301.76	1,398.47	27.83	1.55	0.70	8.11	37.57	−0.7795	−1.3862	−2.28
Ukraine	51.70	36.01	696.41	2,814.49	145.52	17.64	16.44	23.42	94.65	0.24344	0.36328	0.60
United Kingdom	58.21	1,105.12	18,985.92	19,043.37	1,108.46	321.77	314.34	57.39	57.56	0.34358	0.26314	0.43
United States	263.07	7,253.78	27,573.82	26,429.36	6,952.70	902.05	807.35	24.59	23.57	−0.2263	−0.833	−1.37
Uruguay	2.34	17.86	5,598.47	8,533.63	27.22	3.53	3.25	24.92	37.99	−0.9507	−1.5574	−2.57
Vanuatu	0.17	0.23	1,361.63	2,266.20	0.37	0.13	0.10	61.01	99.78	−0.3075	−0.9142	−1.51
Vietnam	74.35	20.19	271.57	186.50	13.82	9.00	6.94	115.31	78.94	3.11462	2.5079	4.13
West Samoa	0.18	0.15	823.49	2,180.58	0.35	0.10	0.06	45.95	106.99	−0.5791	−1.1858	−1.95
Yemen	16.77	10.72	639.31	1,812.35	27.26	2.62	2.21	17.41	45.08	−0.2008	−0.8075	−1.33
Zambia	9.69	4.07	419.70	783.46	7.59	1.60	1.30	38.23	71.37	0.82199	0.21527	0.35
Zimbabwe	11.40	6.17	541.26	1,465.76	16.70	2.88	2.74	33.63	91.07	0.46727	0.13945	0.23
Hong Kong	6	143	23.421	24.500	149.852	214	211	283.73	296.80	1.20546	0.59874	0.99
Korea	45	455	10.146	11.867	532.701	156	150	57.47	67.21	0.47776	0.12896	0.21
Singapore	3	85	28.705	22.714	67.3566	134	149	420.49	332.74	1.43021	0.82349	1.36
Taiwan, Province of	21	258	12.035	15.701	336.11	121	126	73.51	95.90	0.39644	0.21028	0.35

Source: Table 8.3.

a. millions of U.S. dollars.

b. billions of U.S. dollars.

c. Adjusted for purchasing-power parity.

d. Not adjusted for PPP.

within BRO countries and becomes relatively less important as reforms advance. It would have been possible in some cases to search out individual country studies, that give better estimates of trade including barter effects. But to maintain consistency, we have used one source for all countries, the IMF's *Direction of Trade Statistics*. As an example of alternate values, MacArthur (1997) estimates the share of Ukraine's exports to other BRO countries at 58 percent in 1996, compared to our estimates of 43 percent.

10. For a review and a clear theoretical basis of such models, see Asilis and Rivera (1994).

11. An increase in REER reflects an appreciation in the real exchange rate while a decrease means a depreciation in the real rate.

12. The fitted share value for Belarus and Turkmenistan merit some explanation. Technically, this reflects the very sharp appreciation of (REER) in 1996, which the model translated into a strong loss of competitiveness. The values are not very realistic and reflect the model's limitations, especially in cases of little progress in reforms.

References

Asilis, Carlos, M., and Luis Rivera-Batiz. (1994). "Geographic Trade Patterns and Economic Policy." IMF Working Paper 97-16. Washington, DC: IMF.

Balassa, Bela, and Luc Bauwens. (1988). *Changing Trade Patterns in Manufactured Goods: An Econometric Investigation*. Amsterdam: Elsevier.

Belkindas, Misha, and Olga Ivanova (eds.). (1995). *Foreign Trade Statistics in the USSR and Successive States.* Washington, DC: World Bank.

Blejer, Mario, and Marko Skreb (eds.) (1997). *Macroeconomic Stablilization in Transition Economies*. Cambridge: Cambridge University Press.

Collins, Susan, and Dani Rodrik. (1991). *Eastern Europe and the Soviet Union in the World Economy*. Washington, DC: Institute for International Economics.

European Bank for Reconstruction and Development. (1997). *Transition Report 1997*.

Havrylyshyn, Oleh, and Lant Pritchett. (1991). "European Trade Patterns after the Transition." World Bank Working Papers on Trade Policy 748. Washington, DC: World Bank.

Havrylyshyn, Oleh, and Peter Kunzel. (1997). "Intra-Industry Trade of Arab Countries." IMF Working Paper 97-47. Washington, DC: IMF.

Kaufmann, Daniel. (1997). "The Missing Pillar of a Growth Strategy for Ukraine." In Peter K. Cornelius and Patrick Lenain (eds.), *Ukraine: Accelerating the Transition Market* (ch. 15). Washington, DC: International Monetary Fund.

MacArthur, Alan. (1997). "Current Trade Policies and Proposals for Reform." In Cornelius and Lenain (1997, ch. 13).

Odling-Smee, John, and Basil Zavoico. (1997). "External Borrowing in the Baltics and CIS Region Financing the Transition to a Market Economy." Paper delivered at the Dubrovnik Conference on Transition Economies, June 25–27.

Pritchett, Lant. (1991). "Measuring Outward Orientation: Can It Be Done? World Bank Working Paper 566, January. Washington, DC: World Bank.

Rosati, Dariusz. (1993). "Problems of Post CMEA Trade and Payments." In John

Flemming and J. McRollo (eds.), *Trade Payments and Adjustment in Central and Eastern Europe* (ch. 5). London: Royal Institute for International Affairs and European Bank for Reconstruction and Development.

Sachs, Jeffrey. (1993). *Poland's Jump to the Market Economy*. Cambridge, MA: MIT Press.

Ukrainian European Policy and Legal Advice Centre. (1997). *Ukrainian Economic Trends*. Kyiv: Tacis Services.

Wang, Z.K., and Alan Winters. (1992). "The Trading Potential of Eastern Europe." *Journal of Economic Integration*, 7: 133–136.

9 THE FISCAL IMPLICATIONS OF TRADE LIBERALIZATION IN TRANSITION COUNTRIES

Vito Tanzi, Adrienne Cheasty, and Kristina Kostial

Fiscal Affairs Department, International Monetary Fund

9.1. Introduction

Trade liberalization has rightly been a central component in strategies for development. Tanzi (1989, 1991) has highlighted the costs of trade restrictions, whether tariffs or quotas. The rapid push toward trade liberalization in transition countries may nonetheless not have been unambiguously positive because it is likely to have been costly in terms of lost tax revenue. This is especially true of the countries of the former Soviet Union (FSU). The revenue problem, and its policy implications, are the topic of this chapter.

The chapter advances the argument that a more gradual process of trade liberalization might have provided a valuable fiscal cushion, without making the trade regimes of late-transition countries more restrictive than those in other countries at comparable income levels. Specifically, a relatively modest, temporary, across-the-board import surcharge could have made—and could still make—a useful contribution to the fiscal adjustment efforts of these countries, while avoiding undue distortions.[1]

Table 9.1. Post-uruguay round most-favored nation tariffs on nonagricultural products for selected countries (rates in percent)[a]

	Transition Economies	*United States*	*European Union*	*Australia and New Zealand*	*East Asia*	*Africa*	*South Asia*
Forestry products	1	0	0	0	3	16	10
Fishery products	6	1	11	1	7	21	4
Mining	2	1	1	1	5	12	19
Textiles	8	8	7	15	16	35	56
Clothing	11	15	11	35	8	41	64
Lumber, pulp, and paper	4	0	1	4	6	21	19
Petroleum	5	1	1	1	8	13	34
Chemicals	6	3	4	8	10	15	34
Primary steel	6	0	1	2	6	15	35
Primary nonferrous metals	4	3	6	6	9	22	59
Fabricated metals	6	3	3	13	12	26	60
Transport equipment	12	5	6	20	15	20	25
Other machinery	7	2	3	9	11	13	30
Other manufactures	6	2	3	7	10	21	35

Source: Francois, McDonald, and Nondstrom (1995), from the GATT integrated database (IDB).
a. Tariffs are weight-averaged, based on MFN trade as reported in the IDB.

9.2. Low Customs Duties in Transition Economies

It is perhaps not widely recognized that important trade liberalization has already taken place in the economies in transition. Table 9.1 shows that the nominal import duties in transition countries are now significantly below the world norm. Indeed, in a majority of categories, they are lower than everywhere else except the United States and the countries of the European Union. Furthermore, for reasons discussed below, the *effective* tariff is still lower—5 percent on average (6 percent in Eastern Europe and 4 percent in the FSU).[2] There are, of course, many remaining anomalies in the customs duties of transition countries—for instance, high maximum rates on some products—and red tape acts as a significant barrier to trade. But, to a large extent, trade liberalization is a fait accompli, and red tape, while it may impede imports, does not generate fiscal revenue.

The fiscal consequences of this trade liberalization are as one would expect: tax revenues and nontax revenues from trade taxes are now very low in transition countries, thus reducing these countries' ability to finance needed expenditures and generating large fiscal deficits. Table 9.2 shows

Table 9.2. Revenue from trade taxes: a comparison of transition and nontransition countries (in percent of GDP, latest avaliable year)

	Percent
Transition countries	1.5%
Central and Eastern Europe	2.5
Former Soviet Union	0.9
CIS	1
Baltics	0.5
Nontransition countries in same income bracket	4.4
Transition low income	1.3
Nontransition low income	6.5
Transition lower middle income	1.2
Nontransition lower middle income	3.8
Transition upper middle income	2.9
Nontransition upper-middle income	3.3

Sources: World Bank (1996), IMF data.

Notes: All data for transition countries are from 1995, data for other are latest avaliable (1992 to 1995). The income brackets chosen are bounded by transition countries; for instance, low-income nontransition countries do not include poorest African countries because their incomes are below Tajikistan's, the poorest transition country.

Transition low-income countries are Tajikistan, Albania, Azerbaijan, the Kyrgyz Republic, Armenia and Georgia. Upper-middle-income transition countries are the Czech Republic, Hungary, and Slovenia. All others are lower middle income.

revenues from trade taxes in percent of GDP for transition countries and for other groups of countries at similar income levels. Transition countries collect only one-third of the revenues from foreign trade taxes collected by the other countries. The disparity is more pronounced between former Soviet Union countries and the rest of the world (less than a quarter) and is still greater between low-income transition and nontransition countries (one-fifth). In contrast, the three transition countries in the upper middle-income levels collect 88 percent of the trade taxes collected by nontransition comparators.

Both the trade liberalization and the low revenues from trade taxes are easy to explain. First, though planned economies imposed high taxes on most foreign trade (imports but also exports and foreign-exchange transactions), these were mainly part of the administered price system; they automatically disappeared with price and exchange-rate liberalization.

Second, all countries have to a greater or lesser degree followed an orthodox transition model, which strongly discourages the imposition of trade taxation. In other words, these countries have followed the example of the advanced countries rather than that of the developing countries, which often have more similar economic structures. Opening the economies to competition and to technology transfer was implicitly considered more important than generating fiscal revenue and providing temporary protection to the existing industry to limit the output collapse.

A third related reason is that transition countries see WTO membership as a benchmark of successful transition and have been reluctant to create tariff barriers that would give the impression that they are moving away from the goals of WTO.

Fourth, at the outset of their transition, many of the former Soviet countries, and to a lesser extent the Eastern European bloc, having been part of a common economic area, were reluctant, for political reasons, to put barriers between each other; therefore, the share of their trade that is intraregional has been practically excluded from their tariff regimes. Because of these considerations, the tariff systems of transition countries apply to a smaller share of total trade than the tariffs of many nontransition countries at equivalent income levels.

Finally—and again a problem of particular importance in the former Soviet Union—the administrative capacity to collect trade taxes is limited by the absence of well-functioning customs administrations. Many borders are new, and even where controls had previously been in place, the capacity of customs to value goods and administer a tariff on a rapidly expanding menu of imports remains inadequate. Moreover, low salaries have created stronger incentives than elsewhere for turning a blind eye to smuggling. In other words, for a given tariff wall, collection is lower than in nontransition countries. This, of course, implies that trade liberalization is not the only reason for low revenue from foreign trade.

9.3. Fiscal Implications

While there are obvious benefits that derive from a free and open trading system, there are also clear fiscal costs when countries forego badly needed revenues, and these revenues cannot be made up in other ways.

The decline in total tax revenues in transition countries has been sharp, particularly in the FSU countries, where governments' inability to finance basic public expenditures has led in some cases to social unrest and to opposition to the market economy. Revenue in FSU countries fell by an average of 11 percent of GDP between 1991 and 1995; for Eastern European countries, the decline from peak to trough is estimated to have been even higher.[3]

In FSU countries, the drop in foreign trade taxes can explain around 5 percent of GDP out of the 11 percent of GDP overall revenue decline. In the Soviet Union in 1989, 63 percent of GDP was collected from trade taxes, 60 percent of which came from imports (IMF et al., 1991, p. 282). For the successor states, by 1995, trade revenues amounted to less than 1 percent of GDP on average. This does not imply, of course, that if trade liberalization had come more slowly, the revenue decline would have been half as severe. There is no question, however, that the rapid trade liberalization contributed to stabilization difficulties. Besides eliminating trade tax revenues, the liberalization no doubt also contributed to the decline in other taxes—such as those on enterprises—by rendering existing technology, capital, and knowledge obsolete.

In Eastern Europe, the story is somewhat different: particularly during the 1990s—relatively late in their transition—several of the Eastern European countries expanded their reliance on trade taxes to generate more revenue. (This reassessment of the need to use the trade tax instrument is described in more detail below.)

Moreover, while hard to quantify, the fiscal costs of liberalization must have exceeded the losses in tax revenue. They have also included the costs to government that come from the inevitable period of dislocation when an economy is exposed suddenly to a new relative price structure (Blejer and Cheasty, 1990, p. 75). Such costs include unemployment benefits, retraining schemes, foregone income tax revenue from bankrupt enterprises, and so on.

Obviously, adjustment was necessary for transition countries. However, an argument could be made that a more gradual trade liberalization would have been beneficial. It is possible that, if firms had been given more time to restructure and to adapt to new competition, they might have been able to shoulder a higher share of adjustment costs. Bankrupt enterprises pay no taxes and provide no training. Likewise, new enterprises usually pay almost no taxes for several years.[4] It is difficult to prove that the output decline might have been less pronounced if liberalization had come more gradually. However, a strong case can be made that temporary protection through some import duties could have reduced fiscal losses for the FSU countries.

9.4. Fiscal Prospects from Further Trade Liberalization

For policymakers, the relevant question now is the appropriate trade tax strategy for the future. Given that significant liberalization has already taken place, if there were to be further rounds of tariff reduction, the fiscal impact would not be large. If there were indirect fiscal gains, they would not come automatically, and they would be difficult to measure.

The direct fiscal *losses* from further liberalization would be small because of the low current level of customs duties and revenue from them. The indirect losses—the expenses of dislocation—are harder to quantify and are likely to vary from country to country, depending on initial conditions, factor mobility, and other specific features.

It could be argued that important fiscal *gains* could come from liberalization-induced expansion of trade and from faster growth in the domestic market and in the exportable sector. However, for several reasons, second-round gains from liberalization are also unlikely to be sizeable.

First, though obviously there is no direct correlation, the fact that revenues are low suggests that gains within the domestic economy from further liberalization may also be limited. In particular, the price savings from cutting tariffs further, which could be passed on to consumers to raise real incomes and encourage the growth of domestic markets (and their associated tax bases), do not appear large. In this respect, an OECD study (Goldin, Knudsen, and van der Mensbrugghe, p. 95), which simulated the impact of full trade liberalization on regions of the world, found that full *multilateral* liberalization would raise FSU real income by 0.9 percent and lower the income of Eastern Europe by 0.1 percent.[5] The magnitude of these gains suggests that the loss to the budget from lower trade taxes—albeit small—would not be easily offset by higher income tax revenue. And one might expect the gains from unilateral tariff cuts to be even smaller.

Second, as experience since the late 1980s suggests, the expansion of transition countries' exports depends on political decisions by the European Union, the United States, and other trading partners as well as on improved competitiveness from unilateral tariff reductions. Hence, second-round gains from liberalization-induced trade expansion would not come automatically. A number of considerations are relevant. For one, the OECD estimates that, for seven out of twelve CIS countries, more than

25 percent of their exports outside the region are in "sensitive" areas—meaning that their competitiveness and access to foreign markets are reduced by various international arrangements, such as the EU's Common Agricultural Policy and the Multifibre Agreement (OECD, 1994, p. 34). Another constraint is that antidumping actions cover an important number of commodity groups for some countries[6] and are considered a significant deterrent to infiltration of markets in Europe and the United States (see, for example, Mobius, 1996; Prusa, 1996). Finally, the income gains in the study quoted earlier accrue mostly from across-the-board liberalization of agricultural trade; liberalization in manufacturing alone would not benefit either the FSU or Eastern Europe (see Goldin, Knudsen, and van der Mensbrugghe, 1993, tables 3.2, 3.3, 3.5).

Third, because market access is so contentious, much of the projected growth in transition countries is predicated on the reestablishment of intraregional trade links that have lapsed because of the output collapse. But, as mentioned, trade is free or nearly free between some FSU countries and among the Visegrad countries. These existing free-trade areas set a limit to the scope for further taxable gains from liberalization.

Fourth, second-round gains could arise not only from lowering the tariff wall but also from removing nontariff barriers to imports. But formal nontariff barriers (usually quotas), while well publicized and clearly distortionary, apply to limited numbers of specific goods and many of these barriers have already been dismantled; moreover the nontariff barriers that are more pernicious in industrial countries, such as health and standards restrictions, more or less do not apply. The more informal red tape could be more difficult to eliminate through liberalization. Thus, again, the gains from liberalization are likely to be limited by the small size of the prior restrictions.

Finally, if there are gains from liberalization, they may not necessarily be captured by the budget. For that to happen, an economy must be able to tax incomes or domestic consumption as effectively as trade. But transition economies have even more difficulty collecting domestic taxes than trade taxes.

Empirically, it would be difficult to isolate changes in trading patterns inspired by a reduction in protection from trade shifts caused by the other structural changes that have affected comparative advantage and relative prices. Hence, if there were to be gains from dismantling tariffs, it might be difficult to identity them.

All of these considerations, suggest that fiscal gains to countries arising from further trade liberalization may not be very important in the medium term.

9.5. The Revenue Potential from Trade Taxes

Without significant reversal of the liberalization achieved to date, a *moderate and temporary* import surcharge on all imports could provide useful revenue to countries that have not gone too far in completing their transition. The case for a temporary surcharge may be made on several grounds.

9.5.1. Revenue Potential

First, as already mentioned, the potential for revenue from trade taxes is too high to ignore in the face of the difficulties that the countries are having in raising tax revenues. Some simple calculations can provide an impression of the foregone revenue potential. Table 9.3 compares actual 1995 trade tax revenues in transition countries with the theoretical revenue they could have collected if they had taxed their imports *with the average tariff* applied by countries with IMF structural reform programs, the so-called ESAF countries.[7] The ESAF countries have been chosen for comparison, not only because recent data are available but also because the governments of these countries are required to finance significant programs of structural reform. Though the exercise in Table 9.3 differs from Table 9.2 both in method and in source data, the implications of both tables are similar. On average, transition countries collect only one-quarter of the trade revenues they could, in principle, collect without unusually burdensome tariff regimes. Eliminating the Baltic states, which collect only 5 percent of potential revenues, would give a more representative ratio of one-third. In other words, transition countries could triple their revenue from trade taxes while taxing trade at the same rate as countries which are also financing structural reform.

As the table shows, small countries would tend to benefit more than the larger ones; an across-the-board tariff would not be a panacea for Russia's revenue problems, for instance. Such a result is somehow appropriate because the small newly independent states were disproportionately affected by the disruption in trading relations caused by the liberalization in the early 1990s.

Obviously, there are problems with this type of simulation. For example, imports would have been probably lower if the effective tariff had been higher. But the reported results are not meant to be taken literally; rather, the simulation is used to make the point that there is significant scope for revenue enhancement through an *average* taxation of imports. Looking at Table 9.3, it may be noted that sixteen of the twenty-two transition

Table 9.3. Transition countries: potential revenue from trade tariffs in 1995

	In percent of GDP				*In percent*	
	Imports 1995	*Actual Trade tax Revenue 1995*	*Actual Total Revenue 1995*	*Potential Revenue from a Uniform Tax of 19.2% on Imports*	*Actual Relative to Potential Revenue*	Memo: Effective Tariff Rate
Average total	29.8	1.5	28	5.7	0.3	*4.9*
Average Eastern Europe	38.9	2.5	34.4	7.5	0.3	*6.3*
Average FSU (including the Baltics)	23.7	0.9	23.8	4.6	0.2	*3.7*
Average CIS	16.1	1	21.4	3.1	0.3	*6.1*
Average Baltics	54.2	0.5	33.6	10.4	0	*0.9*
Albania	26.6	3.8	17.7	5.1	0.7	*14.3*
Bulgaria	38.9	2.5	36.2	7.5	0.3	*6.1*
Croatia	43.2		32.1	8.3		
Czech Republic	45.7	1.4	44.2	8.8	0.9	*3.1*
Hungary	35.4	3.6	46.6	6.8	0.5	*10.2*
Poland	24.6	2.3	29.2	4.7	0.5	*9.3*
Romania	26.5	1.3	31.9	5.1	0.3	*4.9*
Slovakia	48.7	1.2	30.6	9.4	0.1	*2.3*
Slovenia	51	3.6	46.2	9.8	0.4	*7.1*
FYR Macedonia	48.2		28.8	9.3		

Table 9.3. (continued)

	In percent of GDP				*In percent*	
	Imports 1995	*Actual Trade tax Revenue 1995*	*Actual Total Revenue 1995*	*Potential Revenue from a Uniform Tax of 19.2% on Imports*	*Actual Relative to Potential Revenue*	Memo: Effective Tariff Rate
Armenia	26.4	0.4	14.2	5.1	0.1	*1.5*
Azerbaijan	18.4	2.3	19	3.5	0.7	*12.3*
Belarus	18.3	1.7	43.7	3.5	0.5	*9.3*
Georgia	1.4	0.3	5	0.3	1.1	*21.4*
Kazahstan	7.2	1.2	16	1.4	0.9	*16.7*
Kyrgyz Republic	11.7	0.8	15	2.2	0.4	*6.8*
Moldova	16.1	0.5	17.7	3.1	0.2	*3.1*
Russia	9.3	1.6	27	1.8	0.9	*17.2*
Tadjikistan	53.3	0.3	14	10.2	0	*0.6*
Turkmenistan	3.1	—	9	0.6		
Ukraine	11.8	0.8	41.3	2.3	0.4	*6.8*
Uzbekistan	16.5	0.9	35	3.2	0.3	*5.5*
Estonia	70.1	0.2	41.2	13.5	0	*0.3*
Litva	40.7	0.7	36	7.8	0.1	*1.7*
Lithuania	51.7	0.6	23.5	9.9	0.1	*1.2*

Sources: Economic Commission for Europe (19, p. 37); IMF (1996); IMF data.

Notes: All averages are unweighted. For countries with export taxes, their actual trade tax revenue includes these receipts. The rate chosen to estimate potential revenue is 19.2 percent, which is the average ESAF country tariff.

countries for which data are available collect less than 50 percent of the estimated, potential revenue. In other words, they could collect significantly more revenue even if (1) international-average tariffs were to be levied on only half of their current import levels, (2) their import elasticities were relatively high, (3) they maintained tariffs at a below-average level, or (4) their administrative capacity remained lower than in nontransition countries.

9.5.2. *Administrative Ease*

Second, trade taxes are the traditional fallbacks of countries, such as developing countries, which have difficulties in collecting revenue from domestic tax bases. In the words of Richard Musgrave, they provide important "tax handles" to countries in need of revenue (see Musgrave, 1969). The reason is that it is far easier to administer taxes at a few points of entry to a country than to extend the tax net to domestic tax bases. An across-the-board tariff is easier to administer in part because it minimizes or excludes exceptions from liability. This is not to imply that there are no administrative problems. In fact, problems with customs have been important constraints on revenue collection. The point is merely that, when administrative capacity is limited, the returns to concentrating this capacity in collecting trade taxes might be expected to be higher than in collecting alternative revenue sources.

9.5.3. *Limited Distortions*

Third, the inefficiency cost of an across-the-board tariff is possibly smaller than the costs of many alternative ways of raising the same amount of revenue or, for that matter, the cost of an equivalent fiscal deficit. The reason is that a low across-the-board surcharge often reduces the dispersion in effective protection, which is an important intermediate goal in liberalization. If it is low and broadly based, a uniform tariff on imports does not create strong incentives to evade the levy or to change spending patterns.

9.5.4. *Instrument for Capturing the Private Sector*

Fourth, trade taxes are a good proxy for taxing the incomes of the fast-growing trading sectors in transition countries. In particular, they may be the best way of taxing the informal sector, both by taxing the imported inventory of small traders and the luxury imported goods that are the rewards of those who earn large incomes.

9.5.5. Evidence from Eastern Europe

Finally, several transition countries have introduced import surcharges, without any apparent adverse consequences. Croatia, Poland, Slovenia, and Macedonia have applied different types of surcharge, and in each country, growth resumed while the levies were in place.

The Polish experience may be taken as a representative example. In 1991, to stem a fiscal crisis, the government raised import tariffs to an average of 15 percent. The following year, it introduced an additional turnover tax of around 6 percent on imported goods to allow it to rationalize its overall tariff in line with EU arrangements without losing revenue. This was dismantled gradually and eliminated from the beginning of 1997. Trade revenues rose from 0.7 percent of GDP in 1990 to 3.5 percent of GDP at their 1994 peak. Poland grew at 6 percent in 1994, and investment by 9 percent—an outcome widely attributed to the government's having successfully controlled its finances. Growth since then has averaged around 52 percent p.a.

As regards the other countries mentioned, Croatia introduced a 10 percent import surcharge in 1994. Its budget went into surplus and growth became positive. Growth has continued to accelerate, to 5 percent in 1996. Macedonia introduced a surcharge and cut other import exemptions in 1994, raising trade tax revenues by more than 1 percent of GDP and by a further 1 percent of GDP by 1995—following additional base-broadening. 1995 was the last year of negative growth for Macedonia. Slovenia levies two across-the-board surcharges; they have not prevented it from growing at an average of more than 4 percent of GDP since 1994. In sum, in all of the examples cited, the positive impact of the surcharges in the public finances appears to have outweighed any negative impact from the additional temporary protection.

It is notable that all these examples come from Eastern Europe, where the transition has been underway for longer. The import surcharges were introduced some time after the transition had begun, when the countries had had a chance to assess their fiscal experience and to evaluate their options. It is also important that the adoption of an import surcharge did not rule out for Poland compliance with its commitments to dismantle tariffs under the EU Association Agreement. Finally, it should be noted too that some of these surcharges are now being dismantled as planned, having served their purpose as temporary stopgap measures; it has proven possible to respect the distinction between a necessary short-term stabilization expedient and the reinstallation of permanent protection.

9.6. Concluding Remarks

The conclusions from the chapter are easily summarized. This closing section also addresses the problem of the most tangible constraint seen as limiting possibilities for trade taxation in transition countries.

Import duties are definitely second-best policies. When a country has the option of relying on domestic revenue sources such as general sales taxes, income taxes, excises, and so on, generally these sources are to be preferred to import duties. However, when these domestic sources are not able to provide the needed resources, foreign trade taxes may provide a convenient, even though second-best, source of revenue that allows a country's government to engage in a hopefully productive and needed role. The reliance on import duties must always be limited in time, and these taxes must be phased out as soon as it becomes feasible. At this juncture many of the economies in transition, and especially those of the FSU countries, have a strong need for revenue. Under these circumstances, they could learn from many developing countries and rely for a while on import duties of a general, across-the-board nature. The chapter has argued that the cost of doing so may not be as high as normally assumed.

A major reason for not relying more on trade taxes in FSU countries and not in Eastern European countries was that many of the borders were new and efficient customs administrations did not exist and had to be built from scratch. For this reason, collecting trade taxes was difficult for some of these countries. Some have argued that, because of the insignificance of trade taxes, the use of resources in developing customs administrations would be a waste. Thus, why not bypass the trade-tax stage of development, a stage common in developing countries and use instead the scarce resources for the development of domestic tax administrations? Unfortunately, this argument is not as attractive as it may appear. Modern customs administrations are a crucial input into the control of several taxes and in performing other duties. Even if no tariffs were levied, customs would be important in collecting revenues from VAT and excise taxes, in deterring smuggling, and in compiling statistics. In many countries, as much as 50 percent of revenue from the value-added tax is collected at customs. The IMF is currently cautioning the countries that are considering joining the

Russia-Belarus-Kazakstan customs union that a fully operational customs function will continue to be needed even if all trade barriers are dismantled. In other words, though taxing trade may continue to be more difficult for these new countries that elsewhere, there are few administrative savings from not taxing it. Given the difficulties that FSU countries are having with domestic taxation, foregoing the revenue that could be obtained from some positive level of tariffs may entail significant costs.

Finally, the Soviet Union had a developed customs administration. Thus, trade with the rest of the world could be taxed. After the dismantling of the Soviet Union, a uniform tariff could have been imposed against imports from outside the Soviet Union. Such a tariff would have produced a trading area made up of the countries that were created after the dismantling of the Soviet Union. The revenue from such a tariff could have been shared among the new countries. And the external tariff could have reduced the short run costs of transition associated with the fact that the opening of the borders rendered immediately obsolete much of the existing industry.

Acknowledgments

An earlier version of this chapter was presented at the Third Dubrovnik Conference, June 25–27, 1997. The authors would like to thank the participants at the conference for valuable comments. The views expressed in the chapter are those of the authors, and do not necessarily represent those of the International Monetary Fund.

Notes

1. See, for instance, Tanzi (1991b, p. 27). This and other Tanzi articles argue that the economies in transition, for a while, should base their tax systems on those of the developing countries. The latter often collect about a third of their tax revenues from foreign trade taxes.

2. Measured as tariff revenue over imports; figures are for 1995.

3. See Belanger (1996); the calculation—an average decline of 16.7 percent of GDP—excludes the successors of the former Yugoslavia.

4. Tanzi (1991) warned that in future years the most dynamic part of transition economies would also be the most difficult to tax.

5. Multilateral liberalization is defined by the authors as setting domestic prices to world market prices and eliminating input subsidies, in each of the regions modeled.

6. For instance: for Belarus, 66 percent of commodity groups are subject to antidumping actions; for Georgia, 44 percent; for Lithuania, 30 percent; and for Slovakia, 26 percent.

7. Actual revenues in 1995 include export taxes in some FSU countries; many of these have since been eliminated. Revenue potential is, however, more conservatively estimated,

using only imports as a base, because this chapter does not advocate taxing exports. As of November 1996, there were forty-three ESAF countries, including transition economies: Albania, Armenia, Georgia, Kyrgyz Republic, Bolivia, Guyana, Honduras, Nicaragua, Bangladesh, Cambodia, Lao P.D.R., Mongolia, Nepal, Pakistan, Sri Lanka, Vietnam, Benin, Burkina Faso, Chad, Congo, Cote d'Ivoire, Equatorial Guinea, Mali, Niger, Senegal, Togo, Burundi, Kenya, Madagascar, Malawi, Mauritania, Tanzania, Uganda, Zambia, Zimbabwe, Ethiopia, Gambia, Ghana, Guinea, Guinea-Bissau, Lesotho, Mozambique, and Sierra Leone.

References

Belanger, Gerard. (1996). "The Revenue Decline in Eastern Europe." Mimeo, IMF, December.

Blejer, Mario, and Adrienne Cheasty. (1990). "The Fiscal Implications of Trade Liberalization." In Vito Tanzi (ed.), *Fiscal Policy in Open Developing Economies* (pp. 66–81).

Francois, J.F., B. McDonald, and H. Nordstrom. (1995). "Assessing the Uruguay Round." In W. Martin and L.A. Winters (eds.), *The Uruguay Round and the Developing Economies*. World Bank Discussion Paper.

Goldin, Ian, O. Knudsen, and D. van der Mensbrugghe. (1993). *Trade Liberalization: Global Economic Implications.* OECD.

IMF, World Bank, OECD, EBRD. (1991). *A Study of the Soviet Economy* (Vol. 1).

IMF, (1996). "The Customs Union in the CIS." Mimeo, August.

Mobius, Uta. (1996). "European Union Anti-Dumping Policies." *Economic Bulletin*, 33 (May): 29–36.

Musgrave, Richard. (1969). *Fiscal Systems*. New Haven, CT: Yale University Press.

OECD. (1994). *Barriers to Trade with the Economies in Transition*. Paris: OECD.

Prusa, Thomas, J. (1996). "The Trade Effects of U.S. Anti-Dumping Actions." NBER Working Paper 5440, January.

Tanzi, Vito. (1989). "Impact of Macroeconomic Policies on the Level of Taxation and the Fiscal Balance in Developing Countries." *International Monetary Fund Staff Papers* (pp. 633–656). Washington, DC: IMF.

Tanzi, Vito. (1991a). *Public Finance in Developing Countries*. Aldershot: Edward Elgar.

Tanzi, Vito. (1991b). "Tax Reform and the Move to a Market Economy: Overview of the Issues." *The Role of Tax Reform in Central and Eastern European Economies* (pp. 19–34): OECD.

United Nations Economic Commission for Europe. (1996). *Economic Bulletin for Europe*, 48 (December).

World Bank. (1996). *From Plan to Market.* World Development Report: World Bank.

10 WHAT IS SPECIAL ABOUT ENDOGENOUS INTERNATIONAL TRADE POLICY IN TRANSITION ECONOMIES?

Arye L. Hillman

Department of Economies, Bor: Ilan University, Israel

Heinrich Ursprung

Department of Economies, University of Konstanz, Germany

10.1. Introduction

All countries conduct international trade, their governments choose international trade policies, and general theories explain the sources of comparative advantage that underlie the gains from freer international trade, while theories of endogenous policy explain trade-policy decisions. The theories encompass in their generality those countries that have a socialist past and have only in the 1990s embarked on the path to private-property market economies. Are there, however, required modifications, or special aspects of the general theories that merit stressing in application to the transition economies?

If there were no special aspects associated with transition, a study of the international dimensions of the transition economies could be complete in the recommendation that liberal trade policies be pursued. If we were to observe that this recommendation is not followed, we could call on the established theories of endogenous policy to explain how political-economy considerations lead governments to deviate from efficient policies.[1] We would also have to say something about market access for exports abroad—that is, are governments in export markets inhibiting the realization of the transition economies' comparative advantage?—and we would recommend that market access be provided (as it has been under various agreements, in qualified form).[2] We would also expound on the merits of becoming part of the responsible international community via membership of the World Trade Organization; but again this recommendation would be quite generally applicable to any country one might wish to choose anywhere.

History and the legacy of institutions, which are important in determining feasible economic actions and policy responses (see North, 1990), specify for the transition economies (as for any country) the unique characteristics that can be identified as making the transition a special economic and political environment. The specific feature that we propose to stress as meriting special emphasis in the international trade policies is a technology gap that is the legacy of socialism and, related to this, the prospect for technological and quality advance via privatization that allows for foreign investment.

Not all trade, of course, is equally affected by the technology gap, and some is not at all (agriculture and raw materials). However, for nonmilitary industrial manufactured goods the technology gap has been substantive. Since socialist industry did not place the same stress as competitive Western producers on appealing to consumers' tastes for quality and product diversity, domestic factories were severely disadvantaged if exposed to Western competition, unless the lower price at which goods were offered or protectionist policies could compensate. It is natural enough that domestic consumers should prefer to purchase the more modern sophisticated and fashionable imported foreign goods, if they can afford to do so. The domestic factories, besides coping with adverse domestic conditions of the initial transition, therefore confront the relative dissatisfaction of their own past captive consumers.

Since domestic factories are at the same time often repositories of privilege (see Bogetić and Hillman, 1995; Gelb, Hillman, and Ursprung, 1997), or constitute the primary means of sustenance and economic survival of a region or town, political pressures can readily lead to protectionist policies. Mercantilist perceptions readily take hold; why, for example, waste precious foreign-currency reserves on foreign goods when a domestic factory making a good that can serve the same purpose has excess capacity? If the factory has not been privatized, the de facto residual claimants to the factory's financial surpluses will make this case; and if the factory has been privatized, the case for protection will be made by the new private shareholders, who will often include managers and workers. The workers' committees will make the case independently of any ownership of the factory's stock. Strong political will is required to resist such pressures; and since the pressures are not always resisted in the West, one should not be too surprised if the pressures are not resisted under the more adverse conditions of the transition.

The alternative to protection as a means of improving the competitive position of the domestic factory is to improve the quality or sophistication of the domestic good and to allow a reputation to be developed that the local good is not inferior to foreign imports or at least that the price differential in favor of the local good more than compensates for any quality differences. This in general requires the cooperation of foreign investors who can provide new technologies and management and marketing knowledge. This is particularly so where markets are dominated by multinational firms; if abroad local firms are disadvantaged relative to multinational firms, the same applies *a fortiore* to local factories in the transition economies.

If foreign investment and knowledge bring the domestic factory to Western standards of quality and technology, the consequent new improved domestic good, produced by a foreign investor (perhaps in a joint venture), can more readily confront foreign competition in the home market and abroad. Projectionist pressures are alleviated, and distortionary protectionist policies become unnecessary to sustain the domestic factory.

This outcome of liberal trade policies facilitated by foreign investment is based on a link between endogenous international trade policy and the means chosen by governments to privatize the state factories. Just as is the case with trade policies, privatization decisions are, however, also not necessarily based on efficiency considerations alone.[3] The foreign ownership necessary to place the domestic factory on a competitive footing is at the expense of more popular (or populist), or more directly politically self-serving, privatization policies that transfer ownership of state assets to managers, workers, and the domestic population at large. There is added complexity in that the domestic interests with ownership or claimant stakes in the domestic factory benefit from the technological and managerial inputs of a foreign investor. There is ostensibly an "optimum" privatization policy for domestic interests; they would wish a stake in the domestic factory but would also wish that foreign "strategic" investors have sufficient stake to provide adequate incentives for the foreigners to improve the domestic factory and product.

The ideal outcome that absolves a government of the need to accommodate to protectionist pressures can involve a joint venture to combine foreign and domestic ownership. The foreign investor is, however, necessary to improve the competitiveness of the domestic factory. Improved domestic technology and quality provided by the foreign investor permits the domestic factory to fare better in face of import competition and so permits trade liberalization at lower political cost to the government. Our subsequent model, set out in Section 10.3, demonstrates the potential obstacles that nonetheless arise in seeking to achieve the ideal outcome of liberal trade facilitated by technology and quality-enhancing foreign investment.

An aversion to privatization by sale to foreigners, of course, in itself is sufficient to compromise the ideal outcome. Even if, however, there is no such aversion, or the aversion is limited, there remains the question of whether that the foreign investor can be relied on to cooperate with the policy design. For while a government can choose the form of privatization and the trade policy, a foreign investor's decision to purchase a share of the domestic factory in a privatization program does not ensure the foreign investment required for technological improvement. This is so independently of pronouncements made by the foreign purchaser or contracts signed; because of asymmetric information and moral hazard, contracts can only be incomplete.

The foreign investor may not cooperate in the government's design because of a conflict in the preferred means of confronting import competition. A foreign investor may after privatization well prefer a protectionist policy, thereby avoiding the effort and expense of technologically and managerially upgrading the domestic factory. This conflict of interest introduces strategic aspects to the decisions taken by governments and foreign investors. For the foreign investor—or any investor—a protectionist policy is a less expensive means of confronting higher-quality import competition than making the costly investments necessary to improve the domestic product. Yet the only reason that foreign investment may be part of a government's privatization program is precisely that the foreign participation is anticipated to allow a more open economy because of domestic technological improvement; hence governments may be disappointed with the outcomes of their privatization policies. At the same time a foreign investor who does follow through with a program of technological and quality improvement of the domestic factory may be disappointed to see profits from the investment dissipated by more liberal trade policies, since the investor has not foreseen that his investment reduces the political cost of exposing domestic production to foreign competition. A forward-looking foreign investor will not find himself in this situation; he will have not made the investment in the first place, since he will have realized that trade-liberalization decisions are endogenous to his investment decisions. And if the government has been sufficiently prescient to anticipate this outcome, privatization by sale to the foreign investor will not have occurred in the first place. A game-theoretic framework demonstrates the different outcomes that can be expected to arise—and shows how trade policies, foreign investment, and privation are tied together. Before proceeding with the model, we consider however how the initial conditions arose.

10.2. The Historical and Institutional Background

10.2.1. A Technology Gap as Heritage

Economic organization under communist regimes included planned conduct of international trade, since socialist international trade was simply a continuation of domestic planning. Within the organizational framework provided by the Council for Mutual Economic Assistance (CMEA), the country's trade planners met and planned their international trade, on an annual basis and also on a longer-term basis, just as was required to complement domestic planning (see Schrenk, 1992). The planning was the antithesis not only of markets but also in particular the notion of competition—as had to be the case, since the principles of organization of a socialist economy are inconsistent with import competition.[4] The "untamed" market imported from abroad would threaten the centerpiece of the socialist form of organization, which was the stability and predictability of domestic production and employment; capitalism was judged to place an unfair burden of market adjustment on workers who were displaced from their jobs whenever the whim of market forces introduced changes in demand patterns and competing supply. A primary aim of socialism was to tame these forces and thereby to ensure worker security. The CMEA planners were therefore complemented by the exclusive state-trading companies that were part of the socialist order and that ensured that planned export commitments were met and that imports were distributed in accord with the domestic plan.[5]

There was a perception among those researching socialist trade that the (then) Soviet Union (SU) was being disadvantaged by the CMEA, for two reasons. The SU was exporting at disadvantageous terms of trade relative to Western-market international prices (Marrese and Vanous, 1983). Also, and more important as background for our model, the commodity composition of trade was disadvantageous to the SU, since the SU was providing the Eastern European countries with raw materials and natural resources that were qualitatively on parity with goods traded in world markets (and were readily saleable for hard currency or in exchange for Western goods), while the Eastern European countries were, for their part in CMEA exchange, exporting manufactured goods that were technologically and qualitatively inferior to similar Western goods.

These economic advantages to the Eastern European countries had the effect thereby of locking the Eastern Europeans into the CMEA and of providing a disincentive to look westward for trading partners (see Hillman and Schnytzer, 1992). For the SU the conditions of the CMEA trading arrangement were part of the cost of hegemony.

Although world-market competitiveness or international comparative advantage were not principal determining considerations in assigning goods to be produced in different countries in the CMEA system, the Eastern Europeans' qualitatively inferior goods were readily acceptable in CMEA exchange. The qualitative inferiority had no serious consequence for the factories located in the different countries. When the terms of trade advantages are added to the ready acceptance of the technologically inferior goods, the elements of a dilemma are introduced in Eastern European exit from the CMEA. The immediate economic losses are matched against the political connotations. While the CMEA was a feature of past coercion, it was nonetheless in the end more so the SU (or Russia) that instigated the end of the trading system.[6] The end of CMEA trade placed a substantial economic burden on the East European countries (see Tarr, 1992; on Hungary, see Oblath and Tarr, 1992). In the words of one leading World Bank expert at the time, "the time of breastfeeding was over"—or words to that effect.

The breakup of the Soviet Union also disrupted traditional exchange patterns. Exchange had been part of the internal planning mechanism of the Soviet system. Where there had previously been planned shipments of goods within one national boundary, the interconnected plants and factories found themselves in different national jurisdictions, with new politicians and bureaucrats exercising their new sovereign policy discretion—and what is better as a statement of new sovereignty and international boundaries than *international trade* policies?[7] Another means of proclaiming new sovereignty is to introduce a national currency. And if, for example, the Ukrainians introduce their own national currency, against which the near hyperinflating ruble is strong, there is understandably great reluctance for foreign suppliers to accept this currency as either a means of payment or a determination of value, especially the new banking system takes weeks to transfer funds.

The new national trade policies and national currencies were but one element of the disruption. Additionally, what was now international trade had previously been *intrafirm* vertically integrated national shipments. The interfactory shipments were fundamental for the continuation of past economic relationships. A factory in the Baltics, for example, could be integrated, in the form of both supply of intermediate goods and customers for final finished products, with Russian, Khazak, Ukrainian, and Belarus factories for the same good. Under the circumstances, with new international trade policies, new national currencies, and market transactions when previously there was no need for a means of payment, great ingenuity was required to maintain the vertically integrated economic relationships.

It is moreover of interest in considering the trade policies adopted in the former Soviet Union, outside of the Baltics, that trade restrictions were the precise opposite of the tendencies observed in the west. In the West, departures from free trade generally entail impediments to competitive imports—import duties, import quotas, artificial quality, health constraints, and so on that disadvantage imports or keep foreign goods out of the country. The import restrictions of the West reflect a philosophy that is mercantilist—"it is better to sell than to buy." In the former SU the tendency was to impose policies that restrict exports (see Michaloupolos and Tarr, 1994),—that is, the policies ostensibly were directed at keeping domestic goods at home for domestic consumption. The export taxes and quotas were complementary to domestic price controls that made purchase at domestic prices and sale at world prices profitable. That is, the policies created rents and made export quotas and illegal exports privately valuable. The domestic prices, in particular for natural resources, maintained at below-world-market prices, provided favored conditions for those who did have the right to export. And those who had not been assigned, or had not acquired, the right to export could pay the additional transactions costs and smuggle.[9]

In a consideration of international trade policy, Estonia merits special mention because of a policy of almost complete laissez-faire economic liberalism. Even here, however, one will never know however whether the inept "Russian factories" were exposed to the force of free trade out of a correct perception that free trade was the best international trade policy to follow or because the "Russian" factories were a vestige of Russian colonialism, having been set up by the Russians to employ basically Russians.

10.2.2. Privatization and Foreign Investment Experiences

In the other component of our nexus—privatization policies and foreign investment—we confront a range of experiences. In the Hungarian case, for example, there was extreme reliance on foreign investment. Whatever could be sold to foreign strategic investors was sold, with all the adverse political connotations that such a policy could entail, and—in some of the early "spontaneous" privatization—with perhaps some of the improprieties and/or misjudgments that seem almost unavoidable when managers and politicians are negotiating the sale of state property (which everyone and no one owns) to foreign investors.

The Hungarian model was taken to its logical conclusion in the former German Democratic Republic, where virtually everything was sold to outsiders who could infuse Western technology and management culture. The conditions of privatization process were not public information, but when the Treuhand's task was done and all the sums had been added up, the East German manufacturing sector (the jewel in the crown of CMEA industry) had been sold at a *negative* price. It would, of course, be politically difficult for a national sovereign government to negotiate the sale of its complete manufacturing sector to foreigners at a negative price. Since the German Treuhand's experience may be as close as is possible to objectively honest and fair sale of socialist assets, and since East Germany was the jewel in the crown, we are given a general idea of how the technological and quality deficiencies of socialist industry affected asset worth under market-determined conditions—although the Treuhand did include social clauses in the conditions of sale.

The Czech model gave greater weigh to retained domestic ownership and attempted to follow a path suggesting social justice in dispersing ownership widely over the general population. Here, too, however, where the domestic factories were technologically advantaged, foreign investment displaced or complemented the privatization vouchers issued to the population. Where foreigners did not take control, incumbent managers also managed in many instances to fare quite well from the new assignment of ownership. Nonetheless, in terms of intent and publicity—and comparative outcomes—the Czech model was the most intense in pursuing an objective of distributing state assets to the people, for whom in theory the Party had held the assets in trust.

Another case with distinctive attributes is Bulgaria—although this is a story of economic failure. By 1997 there had been little privatization of state-owned industry[10] (although there had been substantial privatization by restitution of property). The Bulgarian economy had held together precariously, with the benefit of proximity to Yugoslavia during the international embargo, and then collapsed in late 1996. Popular street demonstrations brought down the (new-socialist) government in February 1997 (election in April 1997 confirmed the change). A common answer to whether the economic collapse was due to incorrect government policies, or to opportunism and self-interest, is "each of the above." The use of state enterprises for private profit was a disincentive for the government to privatize. Talk of privatization at the same time also discouraged domestic investment, since the private beneficiaries of profit were not the owners of the factories and could not therefore ensure the property rights to any investments that they might make. And the absence of privatization also ensured the absence of foreign investment, which restricted access to the technologies and knowledge required to transform Bulgarian state enterprises to Western standards of competitiveness.

10.3. A Formal Model

10.3.1. The Domestic Market

We turn to consider a formal model that allows use to investigate with more precision how the postsocialist technology gap affects international trade policies, with links to foreign investment and privatization. We begin with the domestic market and the domestic factory. We consider one factory as the producer of a domestic good. This is consistent with the legacy of planning (and usually market socialism as well). The good produced by the domestic factory provides broadly the same service as an imported good that is competitively supplied to the domestic market. The foreign good is, however, of superior quality. The domestic market is segmented between the domestic good and imports. Some part of the population cannot afford imported Western goods because the goods are too expensive for them and they make do with the local product. Another part of the population that has fared well in the transition has incomes and wealth consistent with purchase of the foreign good. Under these conditions, to portray the domestic market, we require a model of segmented demand.

Let us consider therefore a domestic good that provides more or less the same service or has more or less the same substitutable use as an imported version of the same good. The total quantity consumed by domestic consumers is D units, composed of Q units produced domestically and Q^* units imported. The respective demand functions for the locally produced variant of the good and the imported variant are

$$Q = [a\gamma + (2-\gamma)P^* - 2P]/2b \geq 0$$
$$Q^* = [(a-P^*)(2-\gamma)]/2b \geq 0, \tag{10.1}$$

where (a,b) are positive constants, γ is a constant between zero and unity, and P and P^* are the respective prices in the domestic market of the domestic and foreign goods.

We observe that, in this demand specification, domestic demand Q for the domestically produced good depends on the prices of both the domestic and the foreign good: in particular, as the price of the foreign good decreases, consumers switch from the domestic to the foreign good. However, for those people consuming the foreign good, the price of the domestic good is of no consequence in determining their consumption. That is, once the income level has been reached where the foreign good can be purchased, demand for the foreign good is independent of the price of the domestic good. The well-off part of the population consuming the foreign good does not view price of the domestic good as a consideration in choosing consumption.

Still, if the foreign good is sufficiently expensive (if $P^* > a$), no domestic consumer buys the foreign good (it is too expensive) and only the domestic good is consumed. This opens the avenue for protectionist policies (which increase the price P^*) to support demand for the output of the domestic factory.

Although the well-off consumers who purchase the foreign good (when $P^* < a$) are not responsive in their demand to the *price* of the domestically good, they are responsive to the *quality differential* between the domestic and foreign good. This quality differential is reflected in the value of γ. In the above demand functions, the quality difference is greater, the larger is the value of γ. The minimum domestic quality, for given foreign quality, is when γ equals zero. As γ increases in value (up to a bound of unity), the domestic and foreign goods become closer substitutes in consumption, although (we assume here) even when γ attains its feasible maximum the imported foreign is of superior quality. The gap has however closed. As γ increases, we obtain from the demand functions (1) and (2) the relation

$$\frac{\partial Q}{\partial \gamma} = -\frac{\partial Q^*}{\partial \gamma}. \tag{10.2}$$

That is, the better-off part of the population (who is consuming the imported foreign good) responds to the increase in domestic quality by substituting consumption from imports to the improved domestic product. The demand response to quality change is symmetric: we see that the change in domestic demand for the domestically produced good is precisely offset by the change in domestic demand for the foreign good. Changes in γ therefore leave total demand unchanged and affect only the composition (or segmentation) of domestic demand.

A higher value of γ is beneficial for the economy. That part of the population consuming the domestic good (in general by far the larger part) receives a higher-quality good, while as γ increases, more domestic consumers willingly choose the domestic good over the foreign alternative. At the same time, a fall in the domestic price P^* of the foreign good has a smaller disruptive effect on domestic demand for the output of the domestic factory, since the higher γ, the less sensitive the output of the domestic factory to import competition—that is,

$$\frac{\partial Q}{\partial P^*} = -\frac{(2-\gamma)}{2b}, \tag{10.3}$$

so that

$$\frac{\partial\left[\frac{\partial Q}{\partial P^*}\right]}{\partial \gamma} < 0. \tag{10.4}$$

To describe protectionist policies, let us denote by P^w the given world price (in domestic currency) of the foreign good, and let T represent the protective effect of a protectionist policy, so that

$$P^* = P^w + T \tag{10.5}$$

At a constant level of domestic output, we have

$$dQ = 0 = (a-T)d\gamma + (2-\gamma)dT, \tag{10.6}$$

and hence

$$\frac{dT}{d\gamma} = -\frac{(2-\gamma)}{(a-T)} < 0 \quad \text{for } dQ = 0 \tag{10.7}$$

and

$$\frac{d^2T}{d\gamma^2} = -\frac{2}{(a-T)} > 0 \quad \text{for } dQ - 0. \tag{10.8}$$

Equations, (10.6) to (10.8) describe the tradeoff between technological improvement of the domestic product and the application of protectionist policies. As depicted in Figure 10.1 a given level of domestic output can be preserved by different combinations of γ and T; the higher γ, the smaller the level of T required to sustain a given level of domestic output.

Although the government can choose T, the value of γ is the consequence of an investment in technology improvement of the domestic factory by a foreign investor. The domestic production function is

$$Q = F(\overline{\kappa}, L, K), \tag{10.9}$$

where the arguments in F are respectively the fixed domestic capital stock of the factory, the number of workers employed, and an investment of

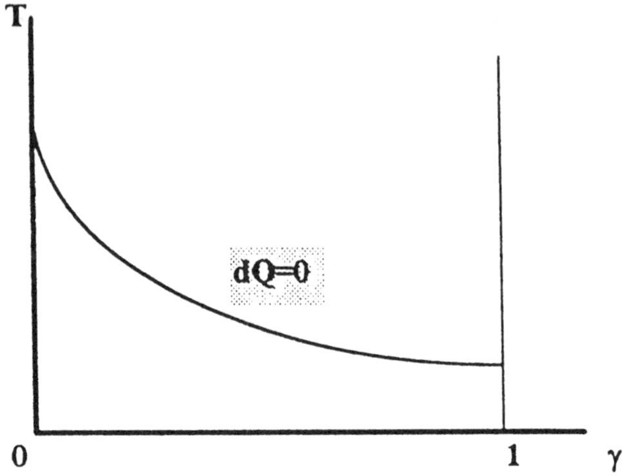

Figure 10.1.

capital by the foreign investor. The larger is this latter investment (which financed by the foreign investor), the larger is γ, where

$$\gamma = f(K), f' > 0, f'' < 0. \tag{10.10}$$

The objective of the foreign investor is to maximize profits. As a preamble to production, the investor makes an outlay to secure a share of ownership s of the factory and incurs an expense rK (in current flow terms) in provision of foreign capital. With the average variable cost of production subsequent to these outlays by the foreign investor given by c, and substituting for total domestic production Q from the demand function, total profits of the domestic factory *from continuing operations* are

$$\prod = (p-c)Q = \frac{(P-c)[af(K)+(2-f(K))(P^w+T)-2P]}{2b} \tag{10.11}$$

and the profit function of the foreign investor *net of the privatization expense and the cost of the new capital K* is

$$\Pi^f = s\Pi - rK. \tag{10.12}$$

The decisions facing the foreign investor and thus (1) the price P at which to sell domestic output and (2) the amount to invest in providing K. The profits in equation (10.12) depend on the international trade policy T chosen by the government and also the share s of the domestic factory that has been sold to the foreign investor. The foreign investor's profits therefore depend on four decision variables, two of which the investor himself chooses (P and K) and two of which the government chooses (T and s), so that

$$\prod^{f} = g(P, K, T, s). \tag{10.13}$$

10.3.2. What Does the Government Want?

We now have to consider what the government wishes to achieve in choosing T and s in (10.13). A government may wish to exercise its policy discretion to secure political objectives such as increasing political support and probability of reelection. These objectives may be furthered by choosing policies that are appealing to voters at large or policies that benefit narrower interest groups whose expression of support may take the form of not only votes but also financial contributions or direct provision of political resources (see Potters, Sloof, and Van Winden, 1997).

We encounter, to begin with, the considerations that enter into the determination of endogenous protectionist policies. Consumers at large lose from protection. Offsetting the broad discontent of consumers is the support for protection from two industry-associated interests, domestic shareholders in the domestic factory whose returns from ownership increase with protection, and workers employed in the domestic factory, whose job security is enhanced by protection against import competition. A politically optimal protectionist policy balances off these countervailing interests.

The foreign investor, of course, also gains from protection. We treat the foreign investor here, however, as politically passive.[11] If foreign investors *do* make contributions to the government, then it is *all* shareholders (domestic and foreign) who appear in the political-support function as seeking to persuade the government to adopt protectionist policies (although domestic shareholders can make their support felt via voting as well as financial contributions and foreign investors do not vote).

We can expect that the broad-based losers from protection will exceed in number the industry interests (shareholders and workers) who gain from protection and also that privatization will have often made workers and domestic shareholders coincident. A positive value of T is therefore inconsistent with fully informed and participating majority voting, and an appropriate model thus appears to be one where relative coalition size and the relative stakes of gainers and losers in policy outcomes have a principal role.

Since we are only looking at one industry (or factory) in the economy, we proceed by supposing that, for narrow interest groups, the effect of protection on incomes dominates changes in utility due to changes in the price of the industry's output or in the price of the competing imported foreign good. More formally, this is also the result in a specific-factors general-equilibrium model for nondiversified industry-specific factor owners. Although the two domestic interest groups benefiting from protectionist polices—domestic shareholders and workers employed in the domestic factory—often overlap, we shall view them separately. In either case we are dealing with rents secured by industry-specific factors of production.

The total income accruing to domestic shareholders is

$$\Pi^S = (1-s)\Pi, \tag{10.14}$$

and since total profits Π are increasing in T, domestic shareholders support protection (for given s).

For workers employed in the factory, denote the wage in employment as w^e and alternative income if a worker leaves employment in the factory as w^u, and let the probability of a worker retaining his or her job be ρ. Via the production function, the number of jobs L is an increasing function of output Q. Hence expected income of a worker who does not know whether his or her job will survive an output contraction is

$$Ew = \rho(T)w^e + [1-\rho(T)]w^u, \tag{10.15}$$

where

$$\frac{\partial Ew}{\partial T} = w^e - w^u > 0 \tag{10.16}$$

and so workers evidently support protection.

Protection is opposed by consumers at large, or more generally by individuals in the economy with incomes specialized to other industries and also individuals with diversified asset portfolios (see Cassing, 1996). The government understands that the greater T, the less the broad support from the public.

Placing domestic shareholders, workers, and the public at large into a political-support function, we have

$$M = M\{\Pi^s, Ew, T\}, \quad M_1 > 0, M_2 > 0, M_3 < 0. \tag{10.17}$$

We shall proceed by adopting a linear functional form, so that $M_i = \alpha_i$ (constant). The level of T chosen is then the solution to

$$\frac{\partial M}{\partial T} = \alpha_1 \frac{\partial \Pi^s}{\partial T} + \alpha_2 \frac{\partial Ew}{\partial T} + \alpha_3 = 0. \tag{10.18}$$

Figure 10.2 assumes an interior solution at T^M.

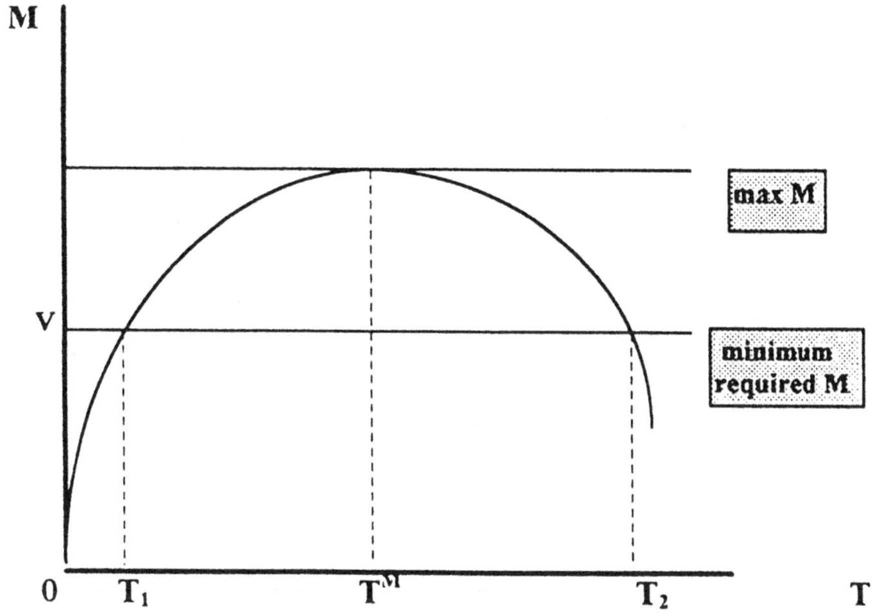

Figure 10.2.

Derivation of an endogenous policy equilibrium such as T^M is a standard exercise (see, for example, Hillman, 1989, ch. 4). Here, however, we have the special characteristic that the government's choice of trade policy as the solution to equation (10.18) depends on privatization via s, the value of which reflects the government's inclination to sell to the foreign investor rather than allocate ownership shares domestically. That is, the solution to (10.18) is subject to the value of s that a government chooses.

Protection T^M and the value of s can be substituted in the profit function of the foreign investor, who then chooses the domestic price P and the foreign-capital investment K in the light of the government's policies. In Figure 10.3 T^M further implies a value γ^M. This, however, assumes that the government chooses its policies first and that the foreign investor reacts to the policies in his own decisions. We shall see that this sequencing need not be the case.

Before considering the nature of equilibrium outcomes, let us consider a different government. Suppose that the new government wishes to liberalize international trade policy or has obligations to liberalize. Liberalization is, however, not unconditional, since the new government must make allowance for the political cost of exposing the domestic factory to foreign competition. The decline in shareholders' stock values and in workers'

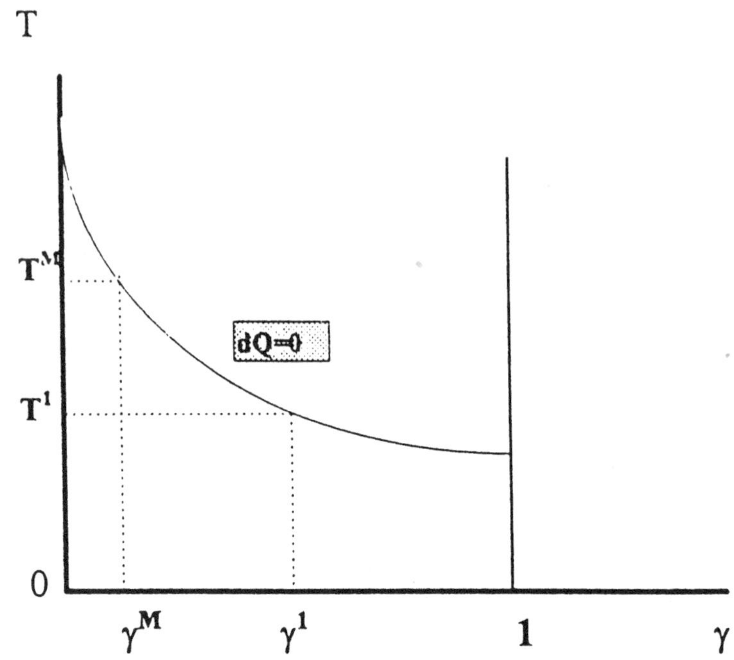

Figure 10.3.

expected incomes impede full liberalization. In Figure 10.2 the government can countenance no political support lower than V (or corresponding political discontent). Political support V is consistent with levels of protection T_1 and T_2. Since the government departs from T^M in quest of a more liberal trade policy, it chooses T_1. At a constant level of domestic output, we observe in Figure 10.3 the higher value γ_1 of domestic technology and quality required to confront import competition under the liberal trade policy.

If the foreign investor were to provide the increased foreign capital for the domestic factory, the government's popularity (with the same maintained level of protection T_1) would rise. An increase in K benefits domestic shareholders and workers, the former by the increased profits of the domestic factory and the latter via the employment consequences of output expansion. From equation (10.17),

$$\frac{\partial M}{\partial K} = \alpha_1(1-s)\frac{\partial \Pi^s}{\partial K} + \alpha_2 \frac{\partial Ew}{\partial K} > 0. \qquad (10.18)$$

And if this is so, the government can maintain its political-support level V at a lower level of protection than T_1.

What sort of equilibria can we expect here? In particular, note that the foreign investor bears the cost of K, which increases γ and which thereby by improving the quality and technology of the domestic factory permits the government to liberalize trade policy at a lower political cost incurred by greater import competition.

10.3.3. Equilibrium Foreign Investment and Endogenous Trade Policy

We can model the government and the foreign investor as involved in a noncooperative game. The government chooses the level of protection for the privatized factory, and the foreign investor chooses the foreign capital that is to provided to enhance the quality of output and technology of the factory. The government wants T low and K high. The foreign investor has precisely the opposite preference.

Figure 10.4 shows the reaction function of the government as AB. The government requires political support at least as high as V. Set $dM = 0$ at $M = V$, and it follows readily from the above that

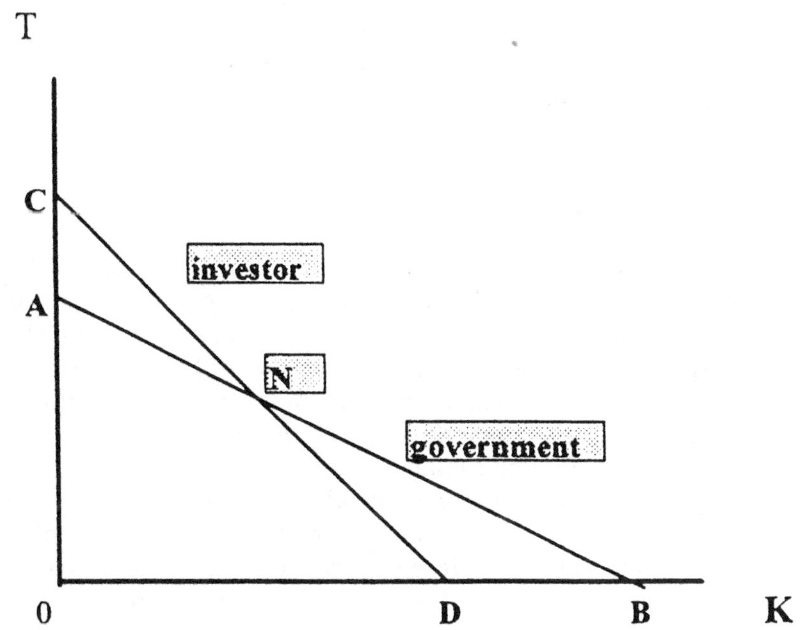

Figure 10.4.

$$\left.\frac{dT}{dK}\right|_{M=V} < 0 \tag{10.19}$$

That is, the government responds to increases in K by liberalizing trade. As in Figure 10.4 the reaction function AB of the government is negatively sloped. For any level of K chosen by the foreign investor, the government requires a sufficiently high T to sustain V; and the smaller is K, the higher the level of T the government is required to choose.

The foreign investor chooses the domestic price P and foreign capital K to maximize profits, with solution being given from

$$\frac{\partial \Pi^f}{\partial K} = s\frac{\partial \Pi}{\partial K} - r = 0 \tag{10.20}$$

$$\frac{\partial \Pi^f}{\partial P} = MR - c = 0.$$

Let the solution be P^0 and K^0.

The solution depends on trade policy. Protection increases the domestic price of the local output—that is,

$$P^0 = P^0(T), \frac{dP^0}{dT} > 0. \tag{10.21}$$

The foreign investor's profit-maximizing response in choice of foreign capital provision is given by[12]

$$K^0 = K^0(T), \quad \frac{dK^0}{dT} \gtrless 0. \tag{10.22}$$

A simple case is the reaction function CD in Figure 10.4, with the foreign investor always responding to trade liberalization by increasing foreign capital. Liberalization then results in dual benefits to domestic consumers of the locally produced good, via a reduced price *and* improved quality.

The Nash equilibrium is at the point N in Figure 10.4. This is the equilibrium in the absence of possibilities of commitment by the government to maintain a particular trade policy and by the foreign investor to provide a particular amount of foreign capital.

N is also the Stackelberg equilibrium when the government can commit to maintain a trade policy. As Stackelberg leader the government can choose any point along the foreign investor's reaction function CD. However, points that lie below the line AB are inconsistent with the level of political support V sought by the government. Hence, the minimum T and the maximum K that the government can achieve is at N.

There is one further possibility of an equilibrium that is of particular interest. Suppose that the government cannot commit to maintain a level of T but the foreign investor can commit to a chosen K. That is, the foreign investor is then the Stackelberg leader and can choose any point along the government's reaction function AB. Then the foreign investor chooses the point A where no costly infusion of foreign capital occurs, and the government satisfies its political popularity constraint by choosing high protection (the maximal protection on the government reaction function). In this latter case the foreign investor as Stackelberg leader has internalized the government's reaction function and thus bases investment decisions on the recognition that any profits due to increased K will be dissipated by the government's using the technological enhancement of domestic production to liberalize trade. There is thus no incentive for the foreign investor to provide foreign capital for the domestic factory.

From the government's perspective, the equilibrium at N is preferable to A. In the equilibrium at A, the government has been unable to liberalize trade, and also the domestic factory has not benefited from foreign investment. Domestic consumers who cannot afford the imported good lose in a move from N to A because at A they consume a low-quality good at the higher price facilitated by protection. Domestic shareholders have benefited from protection but have forgone the increase in the value of their shareholdings from the provision by the foreign investor of the foreign capital. Similarly workers in the factory have gained by the protective effect of the tariff.

If the government is lacking political support, it can always increase T (see Figure 10.2). Thus in the move from N to A, the government compensates for the reduced K by higher protection that benefits domestic shareholders and workers.

A government only responsive to the interests of people for whom the domestic factory is a source of income—that is, a government captured by the factory—but nonetheless sensitive to political support would, of course, itself freely choose the equilibrium at A.

We can distinguish here socially desirable and undesirable equilibria. The investments K by foreign investors are privately profitable and would take place were there not strategic considerations impeding the investment. The investor refrains from investing because of the knowledge that the investment is an invitation for the government to adopt a more liberal trade policy. Because international trade policy is endogenous to the investment and the investor is aware of this, privately profitable and socially desirable investments therefore do not take place.[13]

The investments would, however, take place if the government had a means of credibly committing to a trade policy so that trade policy were not endogenous or discretionary. Thus if the government commits to a policy of bounded tariffs in the context of international or multilateral obligations, the equilibrium at N becomes feasible.

Lower political support requirements move the reaction function AB downward in Figure 10.4 and hence move the equilibrium at N to a more liberal trade policy and higher foreign investment, while also the equilibrium at A becomes a more liberal trade policy. A government not at all concerned with the interests of shareholders and workers in the factory would choose the equilibrium at the point D, with no protection and thereby maximal foreign investment. A government obliged by international agreements to follow an unqualified policy of free trade would do likewise.

10.3.4. Privatization Decisions

The privatization decision is here joint with trade policy. The above equilibria hold for any strictly positive value of the share s of the factory privatized by sale to the foreign investor. However, the decisions of the foreign investor with regard to foreign investment affect the decision that a government might choose to make regarding sale to foreigners and distribution of the shares among the domestic population (that is, regarding the value of s).

There are two reasons why a government might wish to sell to a foreign investor. We have focused on the technology and foreign investment aspect of benefit from sale to foreigners, but also revenue might be a consideration. However, let us suppose that revenue is not a motive. Then the only benefit of sale to a foreigner is the technology and investment that the foreigner with provide.

If the government perceives that the equilibrium will be at the point A, it has no incentive to sell to the foreign investor and will not sell to foreigners if political popularity is adversely affected.

Consider now again the political support function. Suppose that there is popular aversion to sale to foreigners; this aversion can be purely emotional or reflect nationalist sentiment or can be based on perhaps reasonable concerns regarding the implicit terms of personal benefit when state assets are sold by negotiation. We then add a fourth term to the political support function and have

$$M(T,s) = M\{\Pi^s, Ew, T, s\}, \quad M_1 > 0, M_2 > 0, M_3 < 0, M_4 < 0. \quad (10.23)$$

Note that for domestic shareholders there is an interior value of s that is optimal. At $s = 0$ they receive none of the profits of the domestic factory. However, since

$$\frac{dK}{ds} > 0, \qquad (10.24)$$

profits increase with s because of the increased foreign capital provided by the foreign investor. A government that sought to maximize political support would choose less than the value of s optimal for domestic shareholders because of the popular aversion to sale to foreigners. At an interior solution the government's choice of s is the solution to

$$\frac{\partial M}{\partial s} = \alpha_1 \frac{\partial \Pi^s}{\partial s} + \alpha_4 = 0. \qquad (10.25)$$

That is, if $\alpha_4 = 0$, the government maximizes political support by choosing the s, which is optimal for domestic shareholders. The chosen privatization policy trades off larger profits of the factory against the smaller share of profits received by domestic shareholders when s increases. A political-support maximizing equilibrium is depicted in Figure 10.5 at T^a and s^a at the point N^a. This equilibrium requires that the government can commit to the chosen trade policy. The government is again here a Stackelberg leader.

Let us return now to the government that chooses policies subject to a minimum political-support constraint. If the government cannot commit to its trade policies, there is no foreign investment, and in the absence of foreign investment, equation (10.26) is negative. Hence there is also no privatization to foreigners.

If the government can commit in choice of trade policy (so that it is the Stackelberg leader), the choice of policies is subject to an iso-political support contour such as in Figure 10.5. All combinations of T and s along a contour are policies yielding the same political support. With required political support designated as V, the point N^b in Figure 10.5 thus corresponds to the point N in Figure 10.4—where in Figure 10.5 the interdependence between privatization and trade policy is explicit. The policies chosen subject to political support being at least V are then T^b and s^b at the point N^b. Trade policy is more liberal. However s^b can in principle be larger or smaller than s^a.

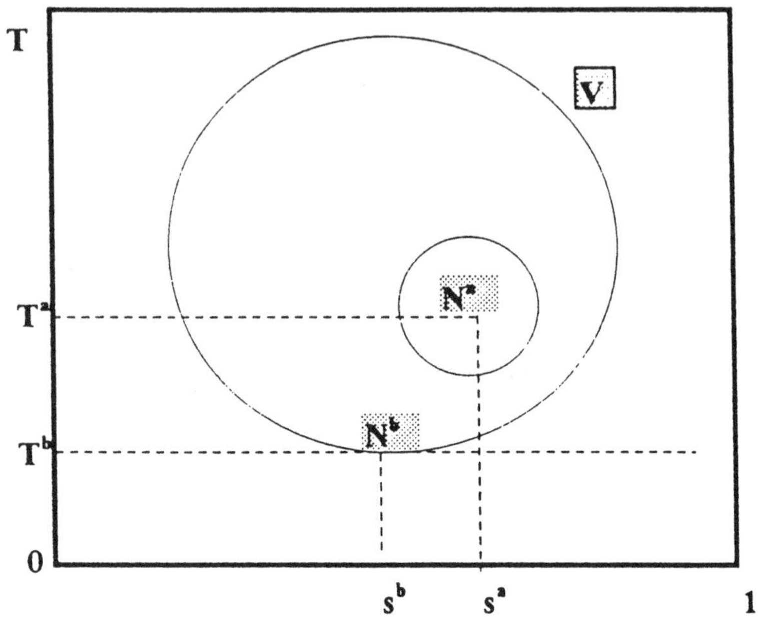

Figure 10.5.

10.4. Concluding Remarks

10.4.1. Mistakes and Misperceptions

Both governments and investors can make mistakes or be subject to misperceptions. Governments can privatize by selling to foreigners whom they anticipate will provide private capital to improve the factory and find that no foreign capital is provided. The equilibrium is then at *A*.

Or a foreign investor may provide capital to improve the factory, only to find that trade policy is endogenous to the investment decision. For example, consider the case where the investor's reaction function has the shape shown in Figure 10.6. If the investor is not aware of the endogeneity of trade policy, when the government announces a level of protection T^1, the investor responds with foreign capital K^1, but then the government liberalizes trade to T^0. Had the investor confronted a level of protection T^0, he would have chosen to make the smaller investment K^0, and so he has over-invested.

But then, if the investor were aware that trade policy is endogenous to the foreign capital he provides for the factory, he would choose the point

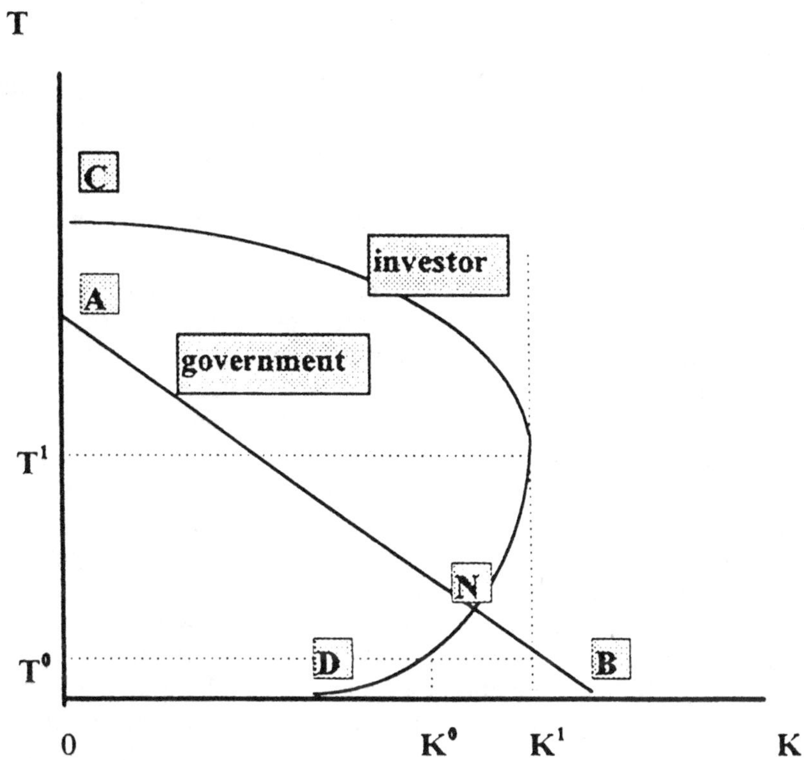

Figure 10.6.

A on the government's reaction function, where he provides no foreign capital subsequent to privatization and enjoys maximal protection (that is, the level of protection is that which the government considers is required for its political support purposes, if no technology or quality improvement takes place). The government is then disappointed with the outcome of its privatization program and has reason to regret the sale to the foreigner.

10.4.2. The Case for the Limited Big Brother

If these anticipations and forethought are excessive requirements of calculations and thinking is sequential, then such regret mistakes will be made as unanticipated responses occur. These "mistakes" become the source of conflict and misunderstanding between foreign investors who are content with the capabilities of the domestic production facilities in which they have acquired a controlling interest, and governments whose expectations for privatized factories are not realized. And also between governments that liberalize trade when foreign investors believe they have bought into a protected market and have perhaps paid the present value of protectionist rents, so that foreign investors insist on continued protection when governments wish to adopt more liberal policies.

Our model suggests that a primary virtue of economic integration is the credibility provided to governments' international trade policy intentions. This facilitates the socially desirable outcome, with accompanying privately profitable foreign investment to complement privatization of the domestic factory. And misunderstandings between governments and investors are avoided.

The privatization of East German industry examples the good outcome of the model. Viewing West Germans as foreign investors, we have virtually $s = 1$. Trade liberalization was *de jure* immediate via reunification. Hence K had to be large to sustain the privatized factories. The privatization contracts included protection of workers and assurances regarding K. Massive direct subsidies were also provided to maintain requisite minimal popularity. Further, in this case, we can infer a zero or low weight on domestic shareholders (that is, $\alpha_1 = 0$), giving the government flexibility in dealing with unproductive noncompetitive socialist capital. There was, however, no government of East Germany that had to face political constraints in implementing privatization and trade policies; privatization by sale to foreigners and free trade were imposed from outside. And the "big brother" took much of the burden. As we have observed, when it was all over, the Treuhand had sold East Germany industry for an aggregate negative price.

The East German case, with the big bother (see Siebert, 1993), illustrates the enormity of the problems of transition. What should countries do that have no big brother, and what should we expect of such countries?[14] Our model has shown how without a big brother, and with a government that requires popular support, protectionist pressures that are invariably present impede the privatization and foreign investment that are part of the solution for an exit from transition. Indeed, there is an evident case for an adoptive or surrogate big brother.

The surrogate big brother is not expected to make massive resource transfers but can simply tie the hands of the little brother (by limiting trade-policy discretion), so that the little brother cannot be induced to do things that he really would prefer not to do (provide high levels of protection to noncompetitive domestic factories) but has to do because of inability to commit to do otherwise. The surrogate big brother would then make foreign technology-improving investment feasible as part of a privatization program and a liberal trade policy. By reciprocity, the surrogate big brother would be expected to provide return market access in response to the little brother's liberal trade policies.

Acknowledgments

This cooperative research was supported by the Max Planck Prize in economics and also draws on previous research supported by the World Bank. The views expressed in this chapter are those of the authors and should not be attributed to any organization that has supported this research.

Notes

1. For a review of these theories, see Hillman (1994a) and Rodrik (1995).

2. On market access issues, see Winters and Wang (1994), who also provide an account of the trade of the central and eastern European economies. On issues concerning the volume of trade and achievement of normalcy in international trade, see also Baldwin (1994), Gros and Gonciarz (1996), and the interchange among the latter (Baldwin, 1997; Gros and Gonciarz, 1996; and also Kellman, 1997).

3. For a broad overview of diverse political-economy dimensions of transition, see Hillman (1994b).

4. "Market-socialist" type economic systems likewise could not countenance import competition (see Hillman, 1991).

5. The international payments system was of little consequence, since trade was basically barter, which absolved countries of the need for foreign exchange. Nor under the CMEA planned barter system were values of traded goods very meaningful. One is reminded of the story of the man with three dogs of no particular breed to sell, for which he requests $100,000. The man plies the streets with his dogs and his offer of sale. One day he is seen without the dogs but has with him two cats. An acquaintance asks him if he managed to sell the dogs for the price he was asking, and the answer is: "Of course. I have exchanged the dogs for these two beautiful cats each valued at $50,000." Because of the conditions of barter, CMEA trade values were just as meaningful.

6. It was Russia insisted in the early 1990s that trade was to be conducted at world prices, with payment for exports in hard currency, thereby ending the EE's advantageous terms of trade and the barter system. One can imagine that the EE might have wished to separate the politics from the economics—that is, to keep the CMEA trading system and to proceed with the dismantling of the empire. For the Russians, the offset to their economic loss was the benefit of political subjugation, and that benefit was no longer present.

7. See, for example, the studies in the volume edited by Michalopoulos and Tarr (1994).

8. Here also issues arose regarding the distribution of the gains from trade among the new independent republics. See Brown and Belkindas (1993) on the internal redistribution implied and Tarr (1994) for calculations of the effects of individual countries' terms of trade.

9. In the early to mid-1990s the Baltic countries, in particular Estonia and Latvia, which have no domestic endowments, became nonetheless leading world exporters of aluminum and copper, transshipped from Russia.

10. Privatization had been limited to small investments in ice cream, chocolates, and petroleum distribution. The national truck transportation company had, however, been privatized by foreign sale.

11. This need not be the case. See our 1988 and 1993 papers.

12. See our 1996 paper for an explicit solution.

13. These investments are therefore to be distinguished from quid pro quo investments which are privately unprofitable but which are made explicitly to influence trade policy decisions. The quid pro quo in these cases is that the foreign investor makes the investment to reduce imports, thereby reducing protectionist pressures and ensuring lower trade barriers (see Bhagwati, Brecher, Dinopoulos, and Srinivasan, 1987). This literature has as its motivation Japanese investment in the United States. In the circumstances that were describing, the foreign investor is not disadvantaged by protection but rather benefits. The investor is not an importer and so is not concerned with ensuring market access but rather with protecting the value of the investment made in the domestic factory in the face of potential import competition.

14. Other countries have big brothers, although not as generous as the German big brother. Estonia has Finland; Latvia has Sweden and also Germany.

References

Baldwin, Richard. (1994). *Towards an Integrated Europe*. London: Centre for Policy Studies.

Baldwin, Richard. (1997). "Comment on Gros and Gonciarz (A note on the trade potential of Central and Eastern Europe)." *European Journal of Political Economy*, 13: 187–188.

Bhagwati, Jagdish N., Richard A. Brecher, Elias Dinopoulo, and T.N. Srinivasan. (1987). "Quid Pro Quo Foreign Investment and Welfare: A Political-Economy-Theoretic Model." *Journal of Development Economics*, 27: 127–138.

Bogetić, Željko, and Arye L. Hillman (eds.). (1995). *Financing Government in Transition, Bulgaria: The Political Economy of Tax Policies, Tax Bases, and Tax Evasion*. Washington, DC: World Bank.

Brown, Stuart, and Misha Belkindas. (1993). "Whose Feeding Whom? An Analysis of Soviet Interrepublic Trade." In *Former Soviet Union in Transition, Joint Economic Committee, U.S. Congress*. Washington, DC: U.S. Government Printing Office.

Cassing, James. (1996). "Protectionist Mutual Funds." *European Journal of Political Economy*, 12: 1–18.

Gelb, Alan, Arye L. Hillman, and Heinrich W. Ursprung. (1997). "Rents as Distractions: Why the Exit from Transition Is Prolonged." In Nicolas Baltas, George Demopoulos, and Joseph Hassid (eds.), *Economic Interdependence and Cooperation in Europe*. Springer Verlag.

Gros, Daniel, and Andrzej Gonciarz. (1996). "A Note on the Trade Potential of Central and Eastern Europe." *European Journal of Political Economy*, 12: 709–721; rejoinder *European Journal of Political Economy* (1997), 13: 195–196.

Hillman, Arye L. (1991). "Liberalization Dilemmas." In Arye L. Hillman (ed.), *Markets and Politicians: Politicized Economic Choice*. Boston: Kluwer.

Hillman, Arye L. (1994a). *The Political Economy of Protection* (2nd ed.). New York: Harwood.

Hillman, Arye L. (1994b). "The Transition from Socialism: An Overview from a Political-Economy Perspective." *European Journal of Political Economy*, 10: 191–225.

Hillman, Arye L., and Adi Schnytzer. (1992). "Creating the Reform-Resistant Dependent Economy: Socialist Comparative Advantage, Enterprise Restructuring, and the CMEA." In Arye L. Hillman and Branko Milanovic (eds.), *The Transition from Socialism in Eastern Europe: Domestic Restructuring and Foreign Trade*. Washington, DC: World Bank.

Hillman, Arye L., and Heinrich Ursprung. (1988). "Domestic Politics, Foreign Interests and International Trade Policy." *American Economic Review*, 78: 729–745. Reprinted in J. Peter Neary (ed.), (1996), *International Library of Critical Writings in Economics: International Trade*. Cheltenham: Edward Elgar.

Hillman, Arye L., and Heinrich Ursprung. (1993). "The Multinational Firm, Political Competition, and International Trade Policy." *International Economic Review*, 34: 347–363.

Hillman, Arye L., and Heinrich Ursprung. (1996). "The Political Economy of Trade Liberalization in the Transition." *European Economic Review, Papers and Proceedings of the Tenth Annual Congress of the European Economic Association*, 40: 783–794.

Kellman, Mitchell. (1997). "Comment on Gros and Gonciarz (A note on the trade potential of Central and Eastern Europe)." *European Journal of Political Economy*, 13: 189–193.

Marrese, Michael, and Jan Vanous. (1983). *Soviet Subsidization of CMEA Trade with Eastern Europe*. Berkeley: University of California Press.

Michalopoulos, Costantine, and David Tarr. (1994). *Trade in the New Independent States*. Washington, DC: World Bank.

North, Douglass. (1990). *Institutions, Institutional Change, and Economic Performance*. Cambridge: Cambridge University Press.

Potters, Jan, Randolh Sloof, and Frans van Winden. (1997). "Campaign Expenditures, Contributions, and Direct Endorsements: The Strategic Use of Information and Money to Influence Voter Behavior." *European Journal of Political Economy*, 13: 1–31.

Rodrik, Dani. (1995). "Political Economy of Trade Policy." In Gene Grossman and Kenneth Rogoff (eds.), *Handbook of International Economics*. Amsterdam: North-Holland.

Schrenk, Martin. (1992). "The CMEA System of Trade and Payments." In Arye L. Hillman and Branko Milanovic (eds.), *The Transition from Socialism in Eastern Europe: Domestic Restructuring and Foreign Trade*. Washington, DC: World Bank.

Siebert, Horst. (1993). "The Big Bang with the Big Brother: German Unification in Its Third Year." Discussion paper 211, Kiel Institute für Weltwirtshaft.

Tarr, David. (1992). "Problems in the Transition from the CMEA: Implications for Eastern Europe." *Communist Economies and Economic Transformation*, 4: 23–43.

Tarr, David. (1994). "The Terms of Trade Effects of Moving to World Prices on Countries of the Former Soviet Union." *Journal of Comparative Economics*, 18: 1–24.

Winters, Alan, and Zhen Kun Wang. (1994). *Eastern Europe's International Trade*. New York: St. Martin's Press.

III SELECTED COUNTRY EXPERIENCES

11 EXTERNAL DEFICIT, EXCHANGE RATE, AND COMPETITIVENESS IN CROATIA: IS THERE A PROBLEM?

Boris Vujčić

Croatian National Bank and Faculty of Economics

Tomislav Presečan

11.1. Introduction

Looking at the performance indicators of the Croatian economy for 1996—its first postwar year—one cannot help but feel quite satisfied: GDP growth rate at 6 percent, inflation rate at 3.5 percent, balanced budget deficit, and unemployment rate at 10 percent. For a country that has gone through the turmoil of war during the critical initial phase of the transition process, these figures look better than one would expect. The same stable and high-growth environment prevailed in the first eight months of 1997. However, one important indicator of economic performance sheds some doubt on the sustainability of the current economic situation. The current-account deficit accounted for 7.3 percent of the GDP in 1996. Although this was down from almost 10 percent a year earlier, the first eight months of the 1997 again indicate a rapidly rising trade and current-account deficit. Recent experience of the Czech and Asian currency crises warrants increased sensitivity to the large external deficit problems. This chapter aims at analyzing the issue and at providing some insights for the economic policy.

11.2. Main Economic Developments

11.2.1. Legacy of the Past

At the beginning of the transition process, Croatia already enjoyed a considerable openness of the economy and a relative independence of enterprises. Contrary to centrally planned economies, markets did have a role to play in ex-Yugoslavia's economic system. Thanks to that, the relative price structure was more realistic, and, what is more important, both enterprises (managers) and households had the opportunity to learn about market behavior. Better human and more efficient material capital than in other CEECs resulted from a higher degree of openness of the country, relatively better education, and the existence of a nonnegligible private sector and an important (and in part temporary) emigration of Croatian workers abroad. The standard of living was substantially higher than in all CEECs, except Slovenia.

On the other hand, the economic system was suffering from chronically soft budget constraints, a common Eastern disease, which was also severe in the Yugoslav system because the latter was less centralized. In a perverse way, banks were owned by their debtor enterprises, which has resulted in an excessive and inefficient credit expansion; self-managed enterprises, on the other hand, were acting generally as wage, instead of profit, maximizers. A culture of wastage of capital was set up; it was heavily financed by easy Western credits. Inflationary roots were, therefore, deep.

In the aftermath of 1989, Croatia was, however, not able to capitalize on its relative advantages. First, Belgrade prevented stabilization; then it was attacked by the Yugoslav army (Vukovar); finally, it was subject to the consequences of the brutal war in the neighboring Bosnia and Herzegovina. These events resulted in human losses and huge material damages in war-affected areas and led to displacement of hundreds of thousands of persons. At moments, the number of displaced persons and refugees in Croatia has been greater than 8 percent of the total population.[1] In spite of the humanitarian help from the international community, this was a heavy burden for the country.

Most important for the economy, however, was the fact that the occupation of strategic parts of Croatian territory cut the main traffic links (sharply raising the transport costs) between the Central, Eastern, and Southern (Adriatic) parts of the country (including the all important oil pipeline from the coast to the Central Europe), held the Adriatic coast in hostage, and thus destroyed the major Croatian export industry (tourism), endangering the Croatian external position. The level of business risk associated with the war in the region was extremely high, and, consequently, the level of FDIs very low. Pressure on budget was also high, due to the war situation, the need to build up army from the scratch, and the arms embargo. During the 1992 to 1994 period, the current account was, nevertheless, running a surplus (see Table 11.1), essentially because the very depressed level of the economic activity and incomes had drastically reduced imports. It was only thanks to the dramatic slump in real demand and to the transfers from abroad (Diaspora) that the external position could be maintained.

All this, coupled with the collapse of the ex-Yugoslav market, resulted in the decline of the GDP to some 65 percent of the 1990 average, with the industrial production almost halved. In 1993, real households' receipts fell to 36.4 percent of the 1990 average. The absolute bottom was reached in the first quarter of 1993 when the real wages bottomed out at 28 percent of the 1990 average. At the time, investments were practically nonexistent. Immediately before the announcement of the stabilization program in October 1993, the monthly rate of inflation had reached 39 percent at the monthly level (or 2.000 percent on an annual basis).

11.2.2. Stabilization

To a large extent, the success of the stabilization program was due to a good preparation before its announcement. During 1992 to 1993 the authorities simultaneously set up a framework of trade liberalization and a reformed tax system[2] and implemented a program of wage restraint and fiscal retrenchment. In addition, they had to accumulate reserves from the scratch. At the beginning of 1992, the National Bank of Croatia (NBC) had no reserves since the Yugoslav National Bank in Belgrade had succeeded in transferring most Yugoslav foreign assets ($6.0 billion) to the Belgrade. To launch a stabilization, foreign reserves had to be acquired at a time when no external financial sources were available. This contrasts sharply with the experience of most other transition economies (for example, Poland received considerable reserve aid—the so-called Stabilization Fund). Reserves rose (see Table 11.1) from zero in January 1992 to a half billion U.S. dollars at the moment of the stabilization announcement in October 1993, a level roughly corresponding to the average forty-five-day value of imports at a time.

Once the necessary foreign reserves had been acquired, the budget

Table 11.1. Croatia: basic economic indicators

	1991	*1992*	*1993*	*1994*	*1995*	*1996*	*1997*
Real economy (in percent change, period average)							
Real GDP	–20.6	–11.7	–0.9	0.6	1.7	4.3	—
Industrial production	–28.5	–14.6	–5.9	–2.7	0.3	3.1	4.8[a]
Industrial employment	–17.7	–14.9	–6.2	–5.6	–6.0	–7.4	–5.7[a]
Productivity in industry	–13.3	0.3	0.3	3.0	6.6	11.3	11.1[a]
Real net wages	–25.0	–43.8	0.5	14.4	40.2	7.2	12.1[b]
Real retail trade turnover	–26.5	–37.5	–28.1	14.5	16.5	3.4	6.2[b]
Unemployment rate			12.7	13.0	13.9	15.0	10.0[c]
Prices (in percent change, period average)							
Retail prices	123.0	665.5	1,517.5	97.6	2.0	3.5	3.7[d]
Cost of living	124.2	634.0	1,486.3	107.2	4.0	4.3	4.0[d]
Producer prices	146.3	825.2	1,512.4	77.6	0.7	1.4	2.3[d]
Public finance (in percent of GDP)[e]							
Revenues	15.6	20.8	20.0	27.1	29.6	30.3	29.6
Expenditures	20.4	21.1	19.9	26.5	30.3	30.4	32.3
Cash balance	–4.8	–0.3	0.2	0.6	–0.8	–0.1	–2.7
Balance of payments (in millions of U.S. dollars)[f]							
Current account balance	–590.0	823.0	104.0	103.4	–1,712.0	–1,452.2	–1,554.7
(in percent of GDP)	–5.0	8.3	0.9	0.7	–9.5	–7.6	—
Trade balance	–536.1	136.8	–762.5	–968.9	–2,877.2	–3,276.0	–2,022.4
Exports	3,292.1	4,597.5	3,903.8	4,260.4	4,632.7	4,511.8	2,211.2
Imports	3,828.3	4,460.7	4,666.4	5,229.3	7,509.9	7,787.9	4,233.7
Services and transfers	–54.0	686.0	866.6	1,072.3	1,165.2	1,823.8	467.8
External debt	—	—	2,638.3	3,066.6	3,660.9	4,847.2	—
Official reserves	0.0	166.8	612.4	1,405.0	1,895.2	2,314.0	2,326.5

— Indicates not available.
a. Data for 1997 are for the first eight months.
b. Data for 1997 are for the first seven months.
c. Data for 1997 are based on ILO methodology.
d. Data for 1997 are for the first nine months.
e. Data for 1997 are budget amounts.
f. Data for 1997 are for the first six months.

nearly balanced, and wages depressed and largely under control (in the state sector), the government announced a stabilization program on October 3, 1993.[3] The program was characterized by a 16 percent devaluation of the domestic currency and the establishment of an asymmetric peg to the DEM; a lower intervention point was set, and the domestic currency was explicitly allowed to appreciate. The aim was to radically break inflationary expectations in a society traditionally used to denominate (index) important transactions in the DM.[4]

Monetary policy was expressed in terms of a monetary base. From the outset, NBC, via restricted purchases of foreign currency, created a controlled liquidity crisis, and nominal interest rates remained sticky. As a result of such policy and credibility of the policymakers, demand for real-money balances sharply increased, which led to the quick appreciation of the domestic currency. Overall, NBC acted almost as a currency board, since practically the entire monetary expansion was reflected by increases in net foreign assets.

The monetary squeeze and the strong appreciation had two immediate consequences. First, the inflationary expectations shock—resulting from the informational value of the DEM exchange rate—has greatly helped in undercutting expectational indexation. Second, the revaluation has worked against inflation through a large share of imported goods in the domestic market. Inflation collapsed almost immediately.

Price stability now lasts for four years. 1994 ended with a 3 percent disinflation, and the 1997 inflation rate will be around 3.5 percent. The subsequent re-kuna-ization of the previously highly DM-ized economy has put the central bank in the pleasant position of conducting restrictive monetary policy while overshooting its monetary targets. Furthermore, even when the reverse currency substitution of transaction balances has run its course, Croatia can still expect a continuous, although slower, reflow of capital, provided it maintains stability, since the vast majority of household money assets are still kept in foreign currency.[5] Incentives for conducting a prudent monetary policy are therefore very high since the continuation of the stability-oriented policy will be awarded not only by foreign direct investments but also by a reflow of the substantial capital kept in foreign currencies at home or abroad, while any "misbehavior" will be met by immediate reactions from both foreign investors and domestic population that has a built-in instinct to run away from a weak currency.[6]

The stabilization was accomplished practically without any external help. The IMF stand-by program was approved in October 1994, exactly one year after Croatia had launched its stabilization program and achieved price stability. The drawings on the Fund were mainly a symbolic demonstration of international support for the stabilization program. The "allocated" part of the external Croatian debt, as of December 31, 1996, stood at about $4.4 billion U.S. (excluding interest on arrears). In March 1995, Croatia reached an agreement with the Paris club on rescheduling its public debt, with a two-year grace period, while in 1996 agreement was reached with London club as well. Finally, at the beginning of 1997, Croatia received investment-grade credit rating from all three major houses for sovereign risk grading. By September 1997 international reserves stood at $2.5 billion U.S.

11.3. External Deficit

11.3.1. Development

For decades Croatia has run a merchandise trade deficit and surplus in services. Almost balanced merchandise trade during 1992 and 1993 (see Table 11.1) was an exception, caused by the severely depressed domestic demand primarily as a consequence of the open war in 1991, and a low-intensity war situation thereafter (as mentioned above, in the first quarter of 1993 Croatian real wages have bottomed out at 28 percent of their prewar level).[7]

It was only in 1994 when the economic activity (for the first time after 1987) and incomes started to pick up. As a consequence, by the end of the year, trade deficit started to widen (see Figure 11.1), but the 1994 current account was still in surplus primarily due to the partial recovery of the tourism (for the first time after 1990). In 1995, however, both trade and current-account deficits rose sharply. Current account deficit amounted to 9.5 percent of the estimated GDP. Such a high deficit was caused by two factors—on the one hand, by a surge in merchandise trade deficit and, on the other, by a lack of receipts from tourism. A huge trade deficit was primarily caused by rapidly rising incomes, which started in 1994 and continued through the first three quarters of 1995. Lack of tourism receipts, on the other hand, was a consequence of the war operations, in which most of the previously occupied territories were recovered.[8] In 1996, the trade balance continued to deteriorate, but recovery of the services in a first postwar year helped to cut the current account deficit to 7.3 percent of the estimated GDP. In 1997, however, external deficit was rapidly rising: the trade deficit for the first eight months was higher than during first ten months of 1996.

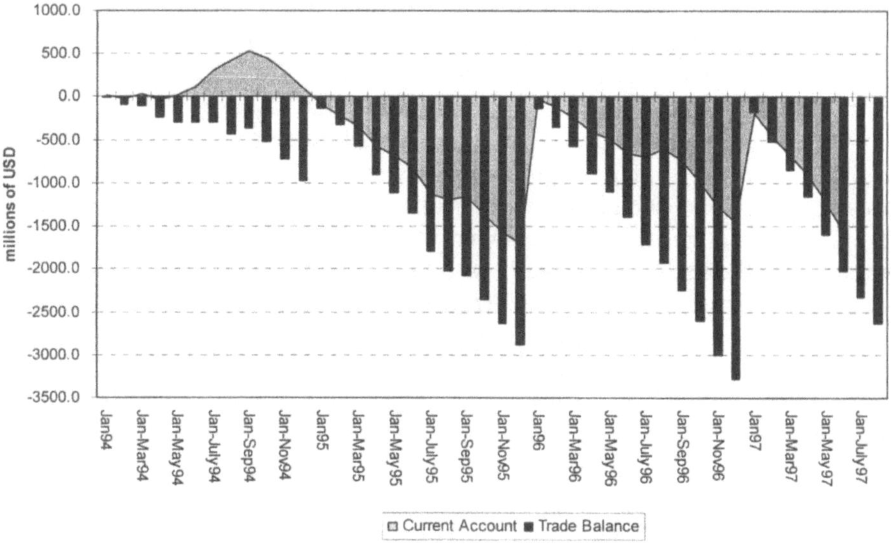

Figure 11.1. Merchandise Trade Balance and Current-Account Balance (cumulative data)

11.3.2. Measurement Problems

Obviously, external deficit seems to be large.[9] The major problem with the analysis of the external position of Croatia, however, is that we are not sure exactly how big it is. We cannot estimate with certainty either the numerator or the denominator of the share of the current-account deficit in the GDP. We believe that the share of the current-account deficit in GDP is in fact lower than it appears from the official data. The main reasons for such a belief are the following ones. First, trade deficit is certainly substantially smaller than it appears in the present statistics because Croatian foreign-trade statistics records exports on the FOB basis while imports are recorded on the CIF basis. Given the high proportion of exports as percentage of GDP (24 percent), that difference alone can account for as much as 2 percent of the GDP. Second, under the item "Other services–Other business services" in the current account, there has been a surge in transactions since July 1996. This surge is unexplainable by anything else but the new payment system instructions that were introduced in the same month. In 1997 deficit under that item rose by approximately three times (amounting to approximately 1.5 percent of GDP for the first eight months), and all indications point to the fact that majority of transactions recorded are, in fact, financial transactions that should be allocated to the capital account of the BOP. Much of the surging deficit under that item, therefore, appears to be the pure consequence of piling up of the accounting errors and omissions under that item (in other words, item "Other services–Other business services" seems to have become a "trash can" to which accountants place all transactions for which they are not sure how to allocate them). Finally, a serious problem, with uncertain sign and magnitude, is the fact that purchases of foreign currency and checks from resident natural persons and cash and checks deposited on their accounts are arbitrarily allocated between the current and capital accounts. This is done in a following way: 25 percent of those transactions are recorded as earnings from tourism (travel), and 75 percent is allocated to the capital account. In reality, it is very difficult to say how exactly this transactions should be allocated between the current and capital accounts of the BOP. However, it is likely that a substantial part of those transactions are in fact current transfers, particularly given the large Croatian diaspora, which personally carries foreign currency over the border when they come to the country. These transfers are not captured under the item of "Other sector transfers" in the current account. Nevertheless, they seem to be (partly?) captured under the item tourism credits (based on the 25 percent rule), and, therefore, tourism earnings are most likely overstated by the current methodology. The net effect of correctly measured transfers (underestimated) and tourism earnings (likely overestimated) is, however, uncertain.

There are more, at this point seemingly less important, flaws in the compilation of the BOP. It would be too cumbersome to drag the reader into these methodological problems, but it must be said that the problem is a serious one and deserves detailed analysis (in another paper). That is necessary not only to assess the real extent of the Croatian external imbalance but also to enable its comparison with other countries. Just as an illustration of how economists might be misled by the existing BOP data, let us point out that Poland, for example, allocates 100 percent of currency bought from resident natural persons or deposited on their accounts as receipts from tourism. Even though different percentages most likely reflect the different real flows in different countries, it seems unlikely that the difference could be so large. Therefore, comparisons of current-account deficits of Croatia and Poland on such grounds could be misleading. If, for example, Croatia would use the same percentage rule as Poland, nobody would be talking about the current-account deficit problem, and vice versa. It would be, therefore, interesting to comparatively analyze the BOP compilation methodologies in various transition countries to see how comparable data on current-account deficits in transition countries really are.

Nevertheless, even after allowing for mismeasurement, the external deficit in Croatia is significant and, more important, rapidly widening, which warrants further analysis of the underlying reasons and possible policy reactions.

11.3.3. Main Determinants of the Widening Deficit

In performing such an analysis one would naturally like to start by looking at savings and investment balance developments, since the current-account balance is determined by the difference between national savings and domestic investment. There is more reason to worry when the widening of the current-account deficit reflects smaller savings and less when it reflects an increase in investment. High savings and investment ratios can signal higher future growth through the present buildup of productive capacities and higher creditworthiness to international investors as they diminish risk of the default in the future. That is true, however, only to the extent that higher investments increase growth and thus strengthen the ability to repay external debt. If investments are allocated in an environment of inefficient financial sector (with weak supervision capacity of the authorities), distorted relative prices, or political influence, then high levels of investments may not enhance sustainability of the current account.

The problem, however, is that we cannot look at the national savings (savings gap) to infer more about Croatian current-account developments. Apart from the budget data, there is no possibility of constructing a reliable savings-investment balance for Croatia. The Croatian Bureau of statistics still has not published GDP information according to SNA methodology, and there are no sufficiently reliable sources of data on either investments or private savings (no household consumption survey has been conducted so far!). Therefore, any attempt to analyze the influence of a savings and investment balance on current account would be subject to too much arbitrariness.

One available part of that balance, however, suggests that opening up of the budget deficit is a part of the explanation for the widening of a current-account deficit. Although at a planned 2.7 percent of the GDP it does not look excessive (and, judged by previous years, realization might well turn out to be lower than plan), such a deficit still reflects expansionary fiscal policy, since the 1996 budget was balanced (see Table 11.1).

On the other hand, a widening external deficit is fueled by strongly

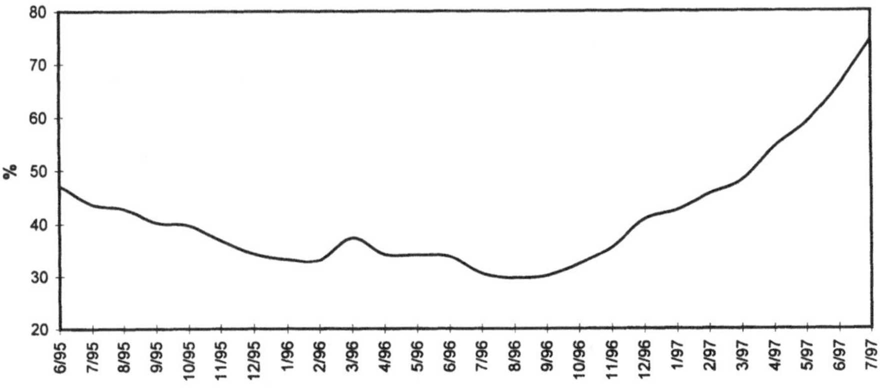

Figure 11.2. Growth Rates of Loans to Households (monthly year-on-year indices)

increased consumer lending. Financial structure in Croatia is dominated by the banks, as in other transition countries and their credit behavior decisively determines both the investment activity of the firms, as well as the intertemporal budget constraint of the consumers. It was only recently that Croatian banks seriously tapped the relatively less risky consumer loan market. Due to the explosion of consumer lending in 1997[10]—lending to households surged by 74.5 percent per year in July (Figure 11.2)—private consumption was set on a steep expansionary path.

Increased household credit activity was coupled by a rise in real net wages of 12 percent in the same period. Although wage growth is just slightly higher than productivity rise in manufacturing sector, it represents a continuance of the four-year trend and, moreover, a new pickup in wage growth after slowing down in 1996 (see Table 11.1). That might well lead to consumer decisions being made on the basis of extrapolation of such a trend into the future, when, in reality, such a trend is unsustainable. This might be particularly dangerous in a situation of underdeveloped financial system, particularly if the banks have inadequate capability to asses credit risks and if central bank still does not have sufficiently developed supervision capabilities.

Finally, a third important determinant of the rapidly widening current-account deficit are one-time tariff exemptions for the war-affected part of the population. These were granted to the broad spectrum of population and, coupled with emergence of cheaper car loans, are mostly used for car imports. Car imports more than doubled in the first eight months of 1997, which, if continued, might alone contribute with close up to 2.5 percent of the GDP to the widening of trade and current-account deficits. Fortunately, since the exemptions are one-time and most of them will be consumed in 1997, the imports on that account should soon be automatically adjusting downward.

11.4. Some Indicators of Competitiveness

11.4.1. Unit Labor Costs

Current-account deficit in Croatia is by and large determined by a large and growing merchandise trade deficit. Labor costs in manufacturing are an useful indicator of the developments in competitiveness of that sector. However, there are many limitations on the informational content of the numbers that we can construct for Croatia. First, it is only since March 1994 that we have available comparable data on gross labor costs. Gross labor costs that we construct for Croatia are a much better indicator than net wage costs, since they also include costs of social security and health insurance, as well as all other payments for labor services within a firm or for work that has been contracted out to other foreign and domestic sectors. As more work is contracted out, this costs become increasingly important (see Feldman, 1994, for Germany). For the period before March 1994, however, only data on net wage costs are available in a meaningful format. Second, there is a serious question about the quality of the manufacturing production indices that are quantitative rather than value-added measures of the output in the manufacturing sector. Most likely the index of manufacturing production understates the real economic activity in that sector. Not only is the index based on a quantitative measure, but it also does not capture enterprises with fewer than twenty employees, which are becoming increasingly important part of the overall economic activity and are likely have above-average productivity gains. Therefore, ULC index most likely somewhat overstates the true rise in unit labor costs.

Looking only at the poststabilization period (Figure 11.3), for which we have better-quality data on gross labor costs, would paint too dramatic a picture. By the end of the period, unit labor costs were up by some 40 percent over beginning 1993. This was on the wings of the rapidly rising total labor costs. Taking a broader perspective (Figure 11.4), however, suggests that the unit labor costs have been only catching up to their prewar level. By mid-1997, unit labor costs were some 10 percent higher than in 1989 but also were lower than in the second half of 1990 or in 1991.

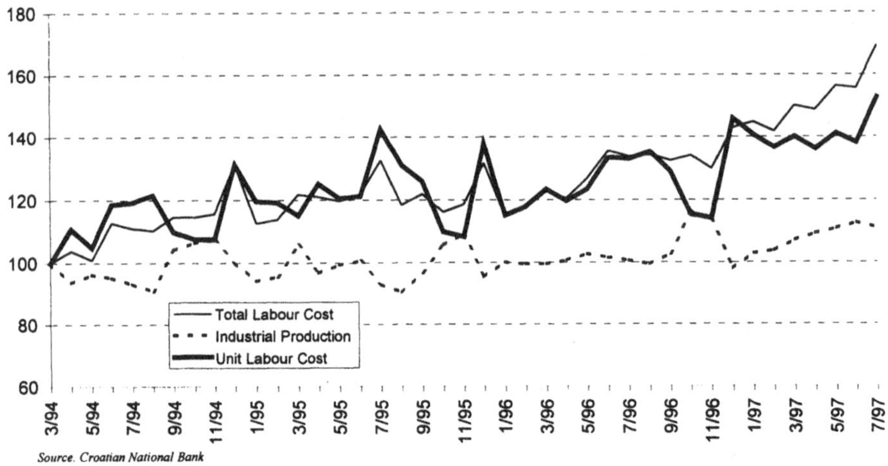

Figure 11.3. Unit Labor Costs: Manufacturing (3/1994 = 100, gross wages)

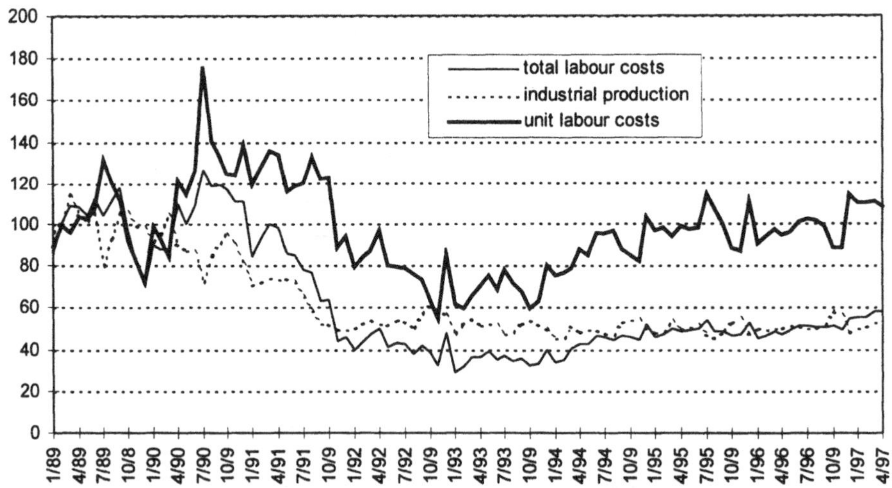

Figure 11.4. Unit Labor Costs (net wages, 1989 = 100)

Two general trends are detectable. Rapid fall in unit labor costs in the midst of the war, caused by a dramatic fall in unit wages that more than offset decline in productivity and, then, a relatively rapid catchup after the stabilization program during which wages clearly outpaced the rise in productivity.

The question is whether the unit labor costs were catching up too fast in the poststabilization period and, therefore, eroded the competitiveness of the domestic industry. Judging from Figure 11.3, that appears to be the case: during the last three years the gross wage bill rose rapidly. That, however, should not be as bad as it looks at first glance. On one hand, it reflects a catchup from the very depressed war level. On the other, that rise might have had a disguised positive effect on the overall economy. Though it might sound somewhat speculative, we are convinced that such a rapid catchup of wages had an efficiency-wage-like effect at the level of the whole economy. A very depressed level of wages, as was the case during the war, is known to hinder the efficient allocation of production factors and, therefore, lowers productivity. One form of this negative effect was the outflow of the best-quality workers from Croatia. Had that trend continued, the long-run costs for the economy would be enormous—particularly because Croatia is a small country that cannot therefore replace such human capital losses.

Of course, that rise in wages might have been good, provided only that it did not overshoot the "equilibrium wage" by much. Where the equilibrium is at this moment, however, is very difficult to say. Nevertheless, the trend of a renewed faster rise of wage bill in 1997, after the more moderate rise since mid-1995, which followed the initial quick catchup, gives reason for concern—especially so since it coincides with the rapid consumer credit expansion, growing fiscal deficit, and first indications of the possibly renewed soft-budget constraint behavior on the side of a small number of large states owned enterprises that have recorded above-average wage growth.

11.4.2. Cost of Capital

It must be noted that, as is well known, measures of competitiveness based on unit labor costs do not capture prices of other inputs. An important one is certainly the cost of capital. To the extent that firms invest on a borrowing basis, this cost is directly represented by the interest rate. If the firm has its own accumulated capital, then the interest rate represents the opportunity cost of investments in new equipment.

The Croatian economy has for long been subjected to crippling interest rates. Next to the war, the exorbitant level of real interest rates (25 percent on short-term credits in 1995) was perhaps the most important factor of choked growth since it made it almost impossible to develop domestic businesses on a borrowing base. On the other hand, it also made it difficult for consumers to purchase big-ticket items.

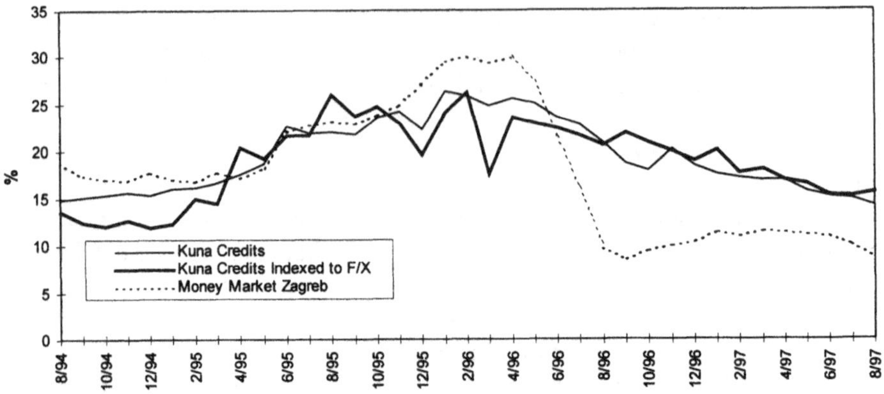

Figure 11.5. Moneys Market Interest Rate and DMBs' Interest Rates on Credits in Kuna

In 1996 interest rates on the money market fell dramatically, from the level of 30 percent at the beginning of 1996 to around 10 percent, where they stand these days (see Figure 11.5). That drop was due primarily to the start of the rehabilitation process in three large state-owned regional banks that were in constant liquidity problems and, therefore, created high and low-risk demand in the money market before the rehabilitation process started.[11]

A downward trend of interest rates on credits in kunas followed the fall in interest rates on the money market, but these interest rates are, nevertheless, still relatively high. Moreover, it is unclear for how long they can continue to fall. Important factors might be working in the opposite direction. First, it is unclear how far and how fast the restructuring of the banking sector will go. It is clearly not enough to financially consolidate problem banks, which has been done so far. It is crucial to quickly find new capable owners that will finish the restructuring process. Second, fiscal policy is set on an expansionary path. If matched with the more restrictive monetary policy to moderate the exploding credit expansion, that will keep interest rates high.

Higher interest rates would be a mixed blessing for the Croatian current-account deficit. On the one hand, and most obvious to the policymakers, they tend to choke real demand, thus taking off the pressure from the growing current-account deficit. On the other, however, they make capital more costly, having a negative effect on productive capacity buildup and, therefore, future competitiveness of the economy. Thus, they also work in the opposite direction. That is particularly true if capital for labor substitution in the tradables sector is (or should be) happening rapidly, as is likely the case in a transition country that is undergoing deep restructuring. The difference between the two effects is that the first one is (choked real demand) usually stronger and works in the shorter run than the other one (choked investments). The net effect on the medium- or long-term current-account developments will be more positive to the extent that domestic companies can borrow abroad (at more favorable terms) while private consumers cannot.

11.4.3. Real Exchange Rates

The most widely used measures of the international competitiveness are PPI- and CPI-based exchange rates. They are also the broadest indices of the overall competitive stance of the economy, since they can directly reflect the position of other, in reality tradable, sectors of the economy (for example, tourism) and indirectly account for various tradable-sector input costs that come from other sectors. Therefore, when the major external imbalance occurs, most of the discussion immediately concentrates on the appropriateness of the exchange-rate parity of the domestic currency.

Figures 11.6 and 11.7 show movement of real effective exchange rates of the Croatian kuna computed on the basis of the PPI and CPI indices. An increase means real depreciation, a decrease real appreciation.

If we want to take a look at the exchange rate before the dissolution of the former state in 1991—that is, for 1989 to 1990 (Figure 11.6) the real effective exchange rate has substantially appreciated in comparison with 1989, but at the same time it is also approximately at the level where it was in 1990. Before deriving any conclusions from such exchange-rate developments, however, we have to face some serious problems. The first is that the official exchange rate for which we have data was almost never used by economic agents. Instead, trade was at the black market rates, for which we have no statistics. Moreover, the economic structure of the ex-Yugoslavia was very different from the Croatian economic structure, and, therefore, the exchange rate, which was administratively set in the National Bank of Yugoslavia, did not reflect well the position of the Croatian economy. One would imagine that the equilibrium exchange rate has always been higher for Croatia than for the former Yugoslavia. Third, we have no balance-of-payments statistics for Croatia from that period, only the merchandise trade statistics, but excluding the republics of the former common state and therefore not comparable with today's statistics. An attempt to look at the trade balance for those years does not reveal anything about the appropriate

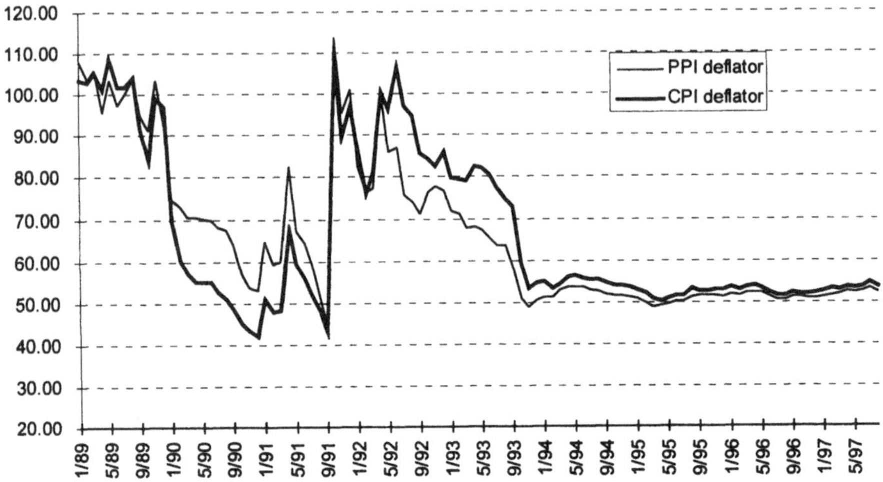

Figure 11.6. Real Effective Exchange Rate (1989 = 100)

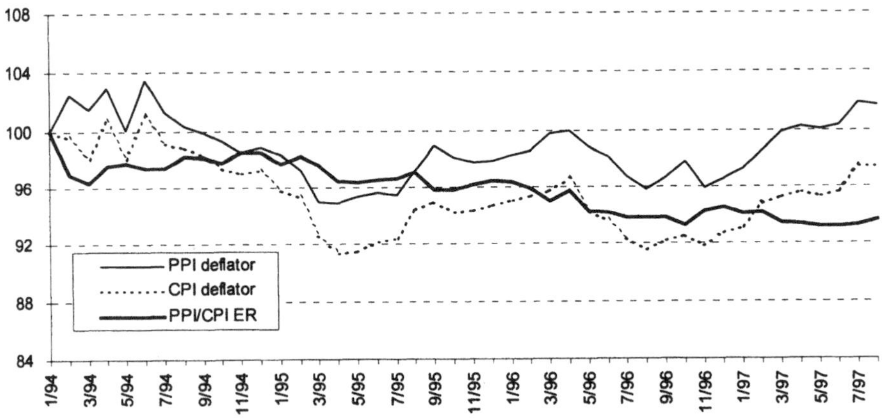

Figure 11.7. Real Effective Exchange Rate, 1994 = 100

exchange rate. Imports covered by exports in 1989 was 79.4 percent, in 1990, 77.4 percent and in 1991, 85.5 percent (normally one would have to allow some time lag for the exchange-rate pass-through on trade volumes, but in 1991 war-related distortions were already present, making the trade data insufficiently reliable). Fourth, the last prewar years were high inflationary years: in 1989 and 1990, for example,[12] inflation rates were 1,200 and 600, respectively. Fifth, from 1991 until 1993 the economic situation was obviously distorted and atypical; this was a period of (semi)war, economic slump, and again hyperinflation. For that whole period, the BOP statistics are relatively unreliable, while merchandise trade statistics are fully comparable only since 1992. That does not allow us to compare the exchange-rate movements with the CA/trade balances. Therefore, we neither have a good base period (which we could take as a benchmark and look at the developments in exchange rate[13] versus developments in the external position of the country) nor any history of comparable (which is necessary if we are to derive any solid conclusions on the appropriateness of the exchange-rate level) (Edwards, 1989).

For one thing, however, these figures demonstrate the role played by the exchange rate in the stabilization program. Although the Croatian exchange-rate regime is officially dubbed managed float, for anyone who takes a closer look at the poststabilization path of the real exchange rate there is little doubt that the exchange rate has actually served as an anchor for the macroeconomic stabilization. That hardly comes as a surprise. Not only is Croatia a very small and open economy, which makes it a natural candidate for an exchange-rate-based stabilization program, but, in addition, Croatian society has long been used to a high or even hyperinflationary environment. During the 1971 to 1991 period, average yearly inflation rate in ex-Yugoslavia was 69 percent, with swings from hyperinflation to temporary price stability. The same situation continued after the independence. Immediately before the announcement of the stabilization program in October 1993, the monthly rate of inflation had reached 39 percent at the monthly level (or 2,000 percent on an annual basis). In such an environment, the exchange rate of the domestic currency against the deutschemark has been universally used for indexation purposes in all sectors of economic activity.

Although from the beginning of the stabilization program the monetary policy has been expressed in terms of the monetary aggregates, what really happened was that at the outset of the stabilization program the nominal exchange rate was almost immediately pushed up by market to its predevaluation level and later sustained as an anchor of the monetary policy. The idea was to set up a stable macroeconomic framework and exert pressure on the real sector to restructure by removing the soft inflationary or fiscal expectations out of the minds of economic agents. The exchange rate was consistent with a balanced current account in 1994, but as the domestic demand recovered, in the next three years the current account started to widen. As is well known, if overvalued, the exchange rate would typically be maintained by high domestic interest rates and by the presence of capital controls (Milesi-Ferreti and Razin, 1996). These are, indeed, characteristics of the Croatian financial market. However, to derive a solid conclusion on exchange-rate overvaluation, one would need a well-established framework of real exchange-rate behavior (Edwards, 1989), which, as demonstrated, we do not have.

Instead, it could be argued that because of a very deep inflationary roots in Croatia, and a fact that trade share amounts to about two-thirds of the GDP, the exchange rate was, and still is, an extremely powerful (signaling) tool of economic policy. Any stronger depreciation is very likely to have a substantial inflationary effect.

Taking a look only at the poststabilization period, the nominal exchange rate against the DEM has been fluctuating within a narrow hand of +/– 2.5 percent (as if it was in "the old ERM"). The real effective exchange rate measured by PPI practically did not appreciate at all as demonstrated by Figure 11.7. That is where the experience of Croatia differs from most other transition countries. Nominal and real exchange-rate stability was achieved thanks to the rapidly converged inflation rate (Table 11.1) toward the average of main trading partners: EU and Slovenia.

Moreover, what is interesting and, also, atypical for a transition economy is that even the internal real exchange rate, measured as a ratio between PPI and CPI indices, did not appreciate by much. Figure 11.7 also depicts a measure that is usually called the internal exchange rate, calculated as a ratio of PPI to CPI indices. This measure is supposed to capture the effect that the nontradables sector has on international performance. The idea is that if the internal real exchange rate appreciates, which means that prices of nontradables rise relative to the tradable, resources will tend to be reallocated away from the tradable-goods sector with the trade balance deteriorating accordingly, and in this sense competitiveness is said to worsen.[14] Its reliability, however, is negatively correlated with the difference between productivity growth across sectors of the economy.

In transition countries, internal exchange rate tends to appreciate much faster than was the case in Croatia as prices of many services are gradually adjusting to the world level from highly distorted situation at the beginning of the transition process when many of them were heavily subsidized. In Croatia, as mentioned at the beginning, the legacy of the past system was also more realistic prices and particularly much higher relative prices of services than in other transition countries. In fact, much of the Ballassa-Samuelson effect has been allowed to run its course in Croatia prior to the de jure start of the transition process.

Finally, if, for the period for which it is possible to construct comparable data, we draw a real effective exchange rate deflated with relative manufacturing labor costs (Figure 11.8), appreciation looks very strong. More-

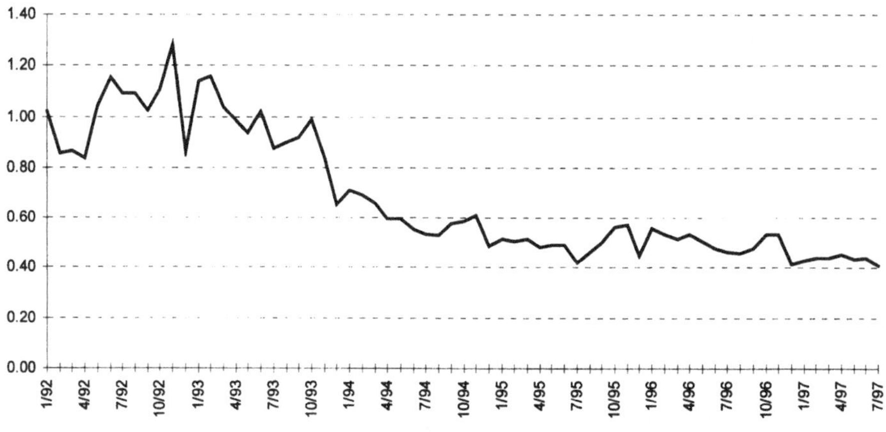

Figure 11.8. Real Effective Exchange Rate (ULC deflated) (1992 = 100)

over, exchange rate constructed in this way demonstrates important real appreciation also in the poststabilization period. Again, however, it must be pointed out that thus constructed measure in fact mostly reflects quick catchup of wages from the war-depressed level mentioned above.

11.4.4. Direction of Trade

Direction of exports and amount of intraindustry trade could also serve as useful indicators of the developments in competitiveness.

Figures 11.9 and 11.10 depict a general picture for 81 percent of Croatian exports (52 percent with the EU and 29 percent with former YU). Croatia has a constant surplus in trade balance with states of the former Yugoslavia. These comprise almost entirely of Slovenia, Bosnia, and Herzegovina, while trade with Macedonia is small and with today's Yugoslavia has only recently been established again. With Slovenia, Croatia constantly runs a deficit, while with other states it more than offsets a surplus.

Recovery of the trade relations with neighbors is, of course, good news. Inability of the merchandise sector to significantly raise exports to the EU, from the level that has been achieved during the war (Figure 11.10), however, is a worrisome fact. It points to several possible problems. Either the slow economic activity in the EU (which coincided with the start of recovery in Croatia) prevented the faster rise in exports to that market, or the export sector hasn't done a sufficiently good job in restructuring to increase exports to the more competitive market of the EU, or lack of the

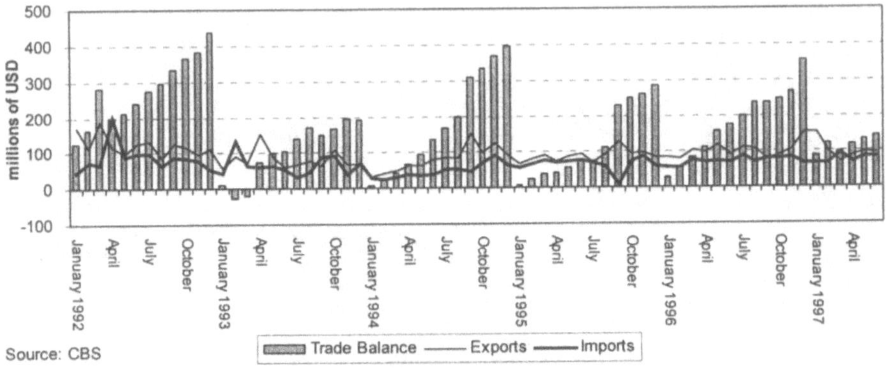

Figure 11.9. Merchandise Trade with Former Yugoslavia

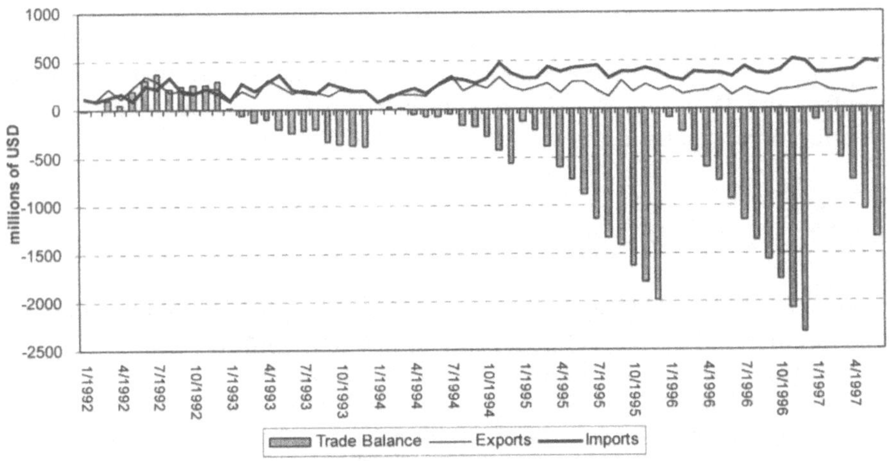

Figure 11.10. Merchandise Trade with EU-15

association agreements with the EU, as opposed to other central and east European transition countries, has resulted in trade diversion. All of these reasons have likely contributed to the relatively slow export growth to the EU[15] in comparison with other transition countries (see Table 11.2). Moreover, the association agreements of CEECs with the EU and the CEFTA agreements of which Croatia is still not an active member certainly had some trade-diversion consequences with respect to Croatia.

Table 11.2. Structure and growth of exports of manufactures for selected transition, SITC product groups 5 to 8, 1993 to 1995

Country/Period	*1993–1995 Exports Share of SITC 5–8 (percent)*	*Base Index 1993 = 100*
Croatia	74.17	124.32
Czech Republic	81.27	141.11
Poland	75.45	169.84
Slovak Republic	84.35	159.47
Slovenia	91.12	143.80
Comparator group	80.95	154.97

Source: Trade Analysis and Reporting System; Croatian Bureau of Statistics.

11.4.5. Intraindustry Trade

It has been argued that the indices of intraindustry trade (IIT) can be used to infer about the competitive position of an economy toward its trade partners (see Havrylyshyn and Kunzel, 1997). The logic behind such an argument is that the higher IIT indices would reflect a more diversified trade within the given trade categories—that is, the trade that is more targeted toward specific market segments. It is therefore assumed that such trade is more competitive than otherwise would be the case.

However, it is necessary to emphasize that the IIT does not represent a factor or a variable that can influence the competitiveness of a given economy in a similar manner such as exchange-rate changes and/or changes in fiscal or monetary or trade policy stance. It merely serves as an additional indicator in assessing what is likely to have been happening with the competitiveness of a given economy in the area of external trade in manufactures.

If the above-mentioned relation between the IIT and competitiveness holds, it should be possible to observe the following linkages:

- A correlation between the changes in the IIT indices and the changes in the exports of manufactures (assuming that growth in exports of manufactures is due to an increase in competitiveness of the given industries) and

- A correlation between the IIT level and the share of exports of a given economy within the world and/or regional exports (assuming that it would indicate more competitive manufacturing relative to the other exporters, which should therefore yield a bigger market share).

We shall try to examine whether the Croatian and the comparator group IIT indices and exports of manufactures fit with the above-mentioned reasoning and what conclusions could be drawn on basis of such evidence.

Following the first published empirical findings (Verdoon, 1960) on the existence of the two-way trade in commodities that are produced using the similar factor mix—the intraindustry trade (IIT)—the literature on the topic has been growing at a fast pace[16]. Product differentiation, imperfect competition, and economies of scale are usually taken as reasons for departure of the observed trade flows from what the standard Heckscher-Ohlin (H-O) trade model based on the concept of comparative advantage would seem to indicate as the expected trade pattern.

Furthermore, numerous empirical studies[17] have shown the various determinants of the IIT level between the trade partners. It has been established, among other things, that the IIT would tend to be higher as the level of economic development between the trade partners was more similar. The countries that have experienced fast GDP growth and are successful exporters have also seen the increase in their IIT levels. The explanation behind such a development seems straightforward: as they strive to compete at the international markets, these countries would need to deepen their specialization in certain market niches to stay in these niches and/or to capture their market shares.

The basic Grubel-Lloyd indicator (GL) will be calculated to assess the levels of IIT, since it represents the most frequently used measure.[18] It is calculated using the following formula:

$$(X_{ij} + M_{ij})$$

where *Glij* is the IIT level of *GL* basic indicator for an industry *i*, *i* = 1, 2, 3, . . . *n*, of an economy *j* for a given time period; *Xij* is exports of an industry *i* of an economy *j* for a given time period, *i* = 1, 2, 3, . . . n; *Mij* is imports of an industry *i* of an economy *j* for a given time period, *I* = 1, 2, 3, . . . n. The indicator assumes values between 0 (no IIT) and 100 (all trade is IIT trade).

We can also use the indicator to calculate the overall IIT in manufactures for a given economy. The weights will be the shares of industries *i* in total manufactures trade of an economy *j*, as can be seen from the formula below. *Glj* will therefore indicate the IIT level in trade of manufactures of an economy *j*, again assuming values between 0 and 100.

$$GL_j = \sum_{i=1}^{n} GL_{ij} \frac{(X_{ij} + M_{ij})}{\sum_{i=1}^{n}(X_{ij} + M_{ij})} = \frac{\sum_{i=1}^{n}(X_{ij} + M_{ij}) - \sum_{i=1}^{n}|X_{ij} - M_{ij}|}{\sum_{i=1}^{n}(X_{ij} + M_{ij})} \cdot 100.$$

GL indices have been calculated using the SITC three-digit data for trade in manufactures[19] for Croatia[20] and for the control group of four countries—the Czech Republic,[21] Poland,[22] the Slovak Republic,[23] and Slovenia[24]—which are European transition economies rather similar to Croatia concerning the recent patterns and levels of their development.

Data consist of values of exports and imports of manufactures denominated in current U.S. dollars with all trade partners. Before turning to the calculation of IIT indices and trade of manufactures, let us briefly look at the surface of broader picture of data on commodity trade of all these countries during the 1993 to 1996 period.

Croatian export performance fares badly if compared to the export performance of the comparator group (Figure 11.11). Indeed, if 1993 is chosen as the base year, Croatian yearly exports have grown only by 15.3 percent over the following three years, while exports of the comparator group have increased by 63.3 percent. Moreover, Croatian exports per capita are substantially smaller than in all comparator country except for Poland (which is not really a small open economy to the extent that other countries are).

In terms of share of manufactures in commodity exports, Croatia is somewhat different from the comparator group. On average, around 74 percent of Croatian commodity exports are classified into SITC product groups 5 to 8 during the 1993 to 1995 period, relative to 81 percent of the comparator group (Table 11.2).

However, the growth of Croatian manufactures exports has a similarity with the growth of comparator countries manufactures exports in a sense that these have grown significantly faster relative to the overall exports during the 1993 to 1995 period. In Croatia, the overall exports had grown by 18.7 percent, while the manufactures had grown by 24.3 percent; export growth of the comparator group manufactures was 55 percent compared to some 50.1 percent growth of overall exports during the 1993 to 1995 period. Nevertheless, the difference in growth rates of exports of manufactures is large, and if it is to persist over the medium term, the Croatian economy would be faced with a significant loss of its export markets share for manufactures.

It can be established that the four countries' manufactures exports

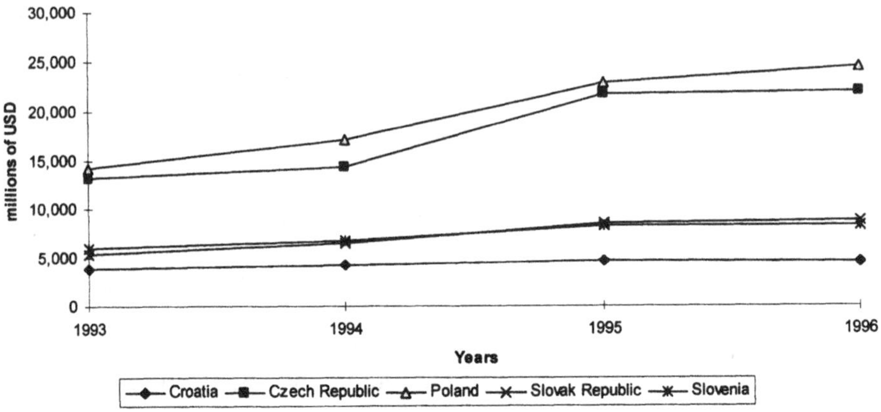

Figure 11.11. Exports of Selected Transition Economies, 1993 to 1996

represent direct competition to Croatian exports in terms of their geographical destination (Table 11.3): the large EU market is by far the most important export destination both for Croatia (on average, 56.8 percent of total 1993 to 1995 exports was directed to the EU15 market) and for the comparator economies (the respective number is 59.3 percent over the same period). However, this share has been on decrease during the same period for Croatian exports: it has declined from 56.2 percent in 1993 to 51 percent in 1996 and increased for the comparator economies manufactures exports from 58.2 percent in 1993 to 59.9 percent in 1996.

Under the assumption of absence of significant differences in terms of access to the EU market during the given period between Croatia and the comparator group economies, it could be inferred that the underlying reasons for the pronounced differences in export performance are to be found at domestic markets. In addition, a difference in terms of a preferential access to the EU market—which is an expected consequence of signing the series of association agreements with the EU by the comparator economies—would only enhance the export prospects of these economies relative to Croatian exports.

Although the availability of data at the SITC three-digit level is limited for the comparator group of countries so that developments could not be traced throughout the whole period, looking at the calculated GL indices for these countries seems to yield somewhat mixed picture of developments in the area of competitiveness.

The IIT indices of the comparator group economies seem to go along with their relatively stronger overall export performance in manufactures:

Table 11.3. Exports of selected transition economics to the EU, 1993 to 1996 (millions of U.S. dollars)

Country/Year	*1993*	*1994*	*1995*	*1996*
Croatia	2.214	2.178	2.523	2.302
Percent share in total exports	56.24%	62.88%	58.43%	51.02%
Czech Republic	6.354	7.480	9.273	12.750
Poland	9.794	11.929	16.039	16.248
Slovak Republic	1.618	2.340	3.208	3.645
Slovenia	3.855	4.473	5.569	5.362
Percent share in total exports	58.20%	58.62%	60.05%	59.86%
Average shares				
Croatia, 1993–1996	56.79%			
Comparator group, 1993–1996	59.34%			

Source: Direction of Trade Statistics Yearbook, 1997.
Note: Values represent the entries under the line DOTS World Total for the respective countries.

for three out of the four economies, there has been an increase in the IIT in manufactures since 1993, while the Croatian IIT has been on decrease since than (Table 11.4). Furthermore, it could be concluded that the comparator group overall IIT in manufactures is on the higher level than the Croatian IIT. However, more data would be required to derive firm linkage between IIT developments and previously mentioned export performance.

Somewhat mixed element in the picture appears when data on the IIT at the SITC product groups level are considered (Table 11.5): these suggest that the comparator group's superior overall performance is not even. Namely, the Croatian IIT is higher than the comparator group's IIT in cases of trade in basic manufactures and miscellaneous manufactured goods.

To draw more specific conclusions about the linkage between the IIT and competitiveness of these economies, we need to perform a statistical analysis of the existing data at the SITC product group level. Two hypothesis could be tested: that the relative changes in IIT indicators at SITC three-digit level[25] were correlated with (1) the respective relative changes of exports and (2) the respective relative changes of share in total exports of manufactures of the four countries.[26] We looked at correlations to asses whether the hypotheses about the link between the IIT and the export performance in trade of manufactures are valid. Due to the availability of data, however, at this stage we were restricted only to 1993 to 1994 changes.

On average, it could be said that the link between the export

Table 11.4. GL indices of IIT in manufactures, 1990 to 1996

Country/Year	*1990*	*1991*	*1992*	*1993*	*1994*	*1995*	*1996*
Croatia	50.40	47.02	53.69	52.65	52.25	52.68	51.57
Czech Republic	n.a	n.a	n.a	65.22	66.04	n.a	n.a
Poland	55.91	48.27	49.59	43.94	45.78	n.a	n.a
Slovak Republic	n.a	n.a	n.a	n.a	62.10	n.a	n.a
Slovenia	n.a	n.a	62.14	63.19	67.14	n.a	n.a

Source: Trade Analysis and Reporting System; Croatian Bureau of Statistics.
Note: Exports under SITC product groups 5 to 8 are considered as exports of manufactures.

Table 11.5. GL indices of IIT in manufactures by SITC product groups, 1994

SITC Product Group/Country	*Croatia*	*Czech Republic*	*Poland*	*Slovak Republic*	*Slovenia*
Chemicals (5)	54.14	70.97	46.59	77.70	61.21
Basic manufactures (6)	68.37	58.97	44.83	48.05	68.28
Machinery and transportation equipment (7)	38.30	67.97	51.87	70.35	72.21
Miscellaneous manufactured goods (8)	63.95	70.60	36.21	62.83	59.14

Source: Trade Analysis and Reporting System; Croatian Bureau of Statistics.

performance and the IIT in manufactures is significant and has an expected sign, both for the comparator group (correlation coefficient of 0.637) as a whole and for Croatia (correlation coefficient of 0.901). Indeed, a growth in exports was accompanied with an increase in IIT in 1993 to 1994 for all four economies. This correlation is the most pronounced for the SITC group 6 (Basic manufactures), while it is very weak—almost nonexistent—for the SITC group 8 (Miscellaneous manufactured goods), again, both for the comparator group countries and for Croatia.

On the other hand, the expected correlation between the shares in total exports of manufactures and the IIT seems to be almost nonexistent in the case of the comparator group countries (correlation coefficient of 0.088), while it is very strong in case of Croatia (correlation coefficient of 0.967).

If we are to draw some more general conclusions from the results, cer-

Table 11.6. Correlation coefficients, 1993 to 1994 changes

SITC Product Group/Country	*Croatia*	*Comparator Group*	*Czech Republic*	*Poland*	*Slovenia*
Correlation between the relative changes in IIT and the relative changes in exports					
Chemicals (5)	0.864	0.555	0.077	0.901	0.549
Basic manufactures (6)	0.994	0.711	0.784	0.715	0.906
Machinery and transportation equipment (7)	0.784	0.562	0.473	0.530	–0.069
Miscellaneous manufactured goods (8)	0.270	0.106	0.168	0.898	0.182
Total manufactures (SITC 5–8)	0.901	0.637	0.642	0.731	0.395
Correlation between the relative changes in IIT and the relative changes in share of exports					
Chemicals (5)	0.972	0.437	0.079	–0.143	0.649
Basic manufactures (6)	0.992	–0.008	0.565	0.071	0.863
Machinery and transportation equipment (7)	0.918	0.618	0.347	0.512	–0.065
Miscellaneous manufactured goods (8)	0.511	0.030	0.213	0.123	–0.010
Total manufactures (SITC 5–8)	0.967	0.088	0.438	0.085	0.415

tainly a study based on the more comprehensive data sample is required—both in terms of the countries involved and in terms of time span that should be analyzed.

11.5. Concluding Remarks

It is clear that present rapid widening of the Croatian current-account deficit (even after allowing for possible mismeasurement) needs to be reversed. That can be achieved through a combination of fiscal, income, and monetary (credit) tightening to control surging real demand that has been fueled primarily by the expansion of these same factors (some of the deficit due to one-time tariff exemptions will be automatically adjusted downward once the exemptions have been consumed). If such a policy mix comes into being, the Central Bank will be able to stick to the nominal exchange rate as an anchor of the poststabilization macroeconomic policy. That certainly looks to be the best option for monetary authorities, given the abovementioned informational role of the exchange rate. Substantial devaluation of the domestic currency would not be a good choice at this time.

Short-run macroeconomic retrenchment, however, might not be enough. Analysis of the competitive position of the Croatian economy, although preliminary, suggests that, compared to other transition economies, competitive stance of Croatian manufacturing sector seems to be worsening. Croatian exports are growing much slower than in comparator countries, and the share of exports to the EU is on a decline. On average, much slower growth of Croatian manufactures exports relative to the comparator group of transition countries is accompanied with slower trade specialization within the product groups; on the other hand, the fast growth of exports of manufactures in the comparator group economies is followed by a higher trade specialization within the product groups; therefore, it could be said that the differences in the level of specialization are capable of indicating the changes in external competitiveness in these product groups; clearly, lower overall level of the Croatian IIT and lower rates of change of the IIT point toward the Croatian lagging behind the fast improvements in competitiveness of the comparator group economies.

A natural consequence of a slower growth of the Croatian exports of manufactures relative to the exports of manufactures of the comparator transition economies is that the share of Croatian exports in total exports of the analyzed group of countries is on a decrease. This decrease is strongly correlated with the lower level of the Croatian IIT relative to the comparator group IIT—suggesting that the losses of the respective market shares have already began to take place due to a slower response in terms of specialization within the product groups of exportables. If we are to draw some stronger conclusions from the results, however, a study based on the more comprehensive data sample is required—both in terms of the countries involved and in terms of time span that should be analyzed.

The competitive stance of the economy might look better if tourism is included. The underlying potential of the tourism is high, especially judged from the present low levels (approximately 50 percent of the prewar level). However, although tourism is a natural candidate to become a Croatian star export industry, our feeling is that it would be dangerous to rely too heavily on the tourism. When compared against the EU countries, the share of receipts from tourism in Croatian BOP is comparable only to the Greece. If judged by Greece, however, which has concentrated too heavily on monoculativating the tourism industry, such a strategy does not appear to be a formula of success. Moreover, due to the high sensitivity of the tourism to the security problems, its potential must always be politically weighted.

These findings suggest that problems of external imbalance are deeper and that export potential, as a crucial determinant of the sustainability of external deficit, and eventually major determinant of growth for a small country, will not improve enough if the structural reforms are quickly not pushed farther.

We mention here only two important elements that were missing from the Croatian transition so far: foreign direct investments and European integrations. Both of them have, to a large extent, been exogenous to the economic policymakers. Had they been present, they might have significantly improved Croatian export performance as they did in most other central and East European transition countries.

Importance of FDIs for exports of transition countries is well documented (see, for example, Corado, Wysokinska, and Witowska, 1996; Stankovsky, 1996), as well as for growth (Borensztein, DeGregorio, and Wha Lee, 1994). FDIs are particularly important for a small country because only a few large investments in a small country can have overwhelming impact on the overall (especially international) economic performance.[27] For an illustration of the potential of FDIs, it suffices to say that 80 percent of all exports in Hungary come from foreign direct investments. And judged by export performance, Hungary, together with the Czech Republic, which has also received large amount of FDIs, is best among transition economies; this year, for the first time, it even runs a surplus in trade with the EU. A West European counterpart—and another example of how a huge current-account deficit in a small economy could be reversed with the help of foreign investors—is Ireland (see, for example, Walsh, 1996). Hoekman and Djankov (1996) have recently shown on a sample of transition countries that FDIs are positively correlated with increased intraindustry trade, while IIT is positively correlated with better export performance.

As opposed to other transition economies, however, in Croatia FDIs were practically nonexistent until 1996—the first postwar year—when they amounted to $0.5 billion. That has put Croatia in third place among transition economies on a basis of FDI per capital for 1996. Most of these investments, however, were rather portfolio investments in two blue-chip companies listed on the London Stock exchange.[28] Foreign greenfield investments are practically nonexistent in Croatia.

Another important missing element in the Croatian story were European integrations, from which Croatia is still excluded. It is not a member of CEFTA, nor has it concluded an accession agreement with the EU.[29] The natural consequence was a trade diversion with other European economies, and a lower degree of trade integration with the EU.

Both of these potentially very positive but missing elements of transition were, up until recently, hostages to the war (as opposed to the experience of other CEE countries). However, provided that the political perspectives will continue to improve, these two important factors, together with faster domestic privatization/restructuring, might soon help the Croatian economy to improve its competitive stance.

What is the outlook for a possible crisis due to the growing external imbalance? A current-account deficit, even a large one, is less worrisome if it can be financed on acceptable terms. Given the present level of debt to GDP and debt service paid to exports of goods and nonfinancial services ratios, which presently stand at 30 and 11 percent, respectively, there does not seem to be, at least not immediately, a threat to the Croatian external liquidity.

Neither does the likelihood of a major currency attack seem to be high at this point. As opposed to the Czech Republic, where foreign investors reacted to the growing trade and payments imbalances by taking short koruna positions, in Croatia they simply do not hold enough kuna-denominated securities to seriously move the markets (or, from their perspective, to profit enough), so the currency is not threatened by a run from that direction. However, a major problem might come from another direction. If there is an instability in the domestic banking sector, for whatever reason, and some people lose deposits, this might give rise to an immediate run on foreign-currency deposits that were lately either redeposited back to the domestic banking sector on a wave of rising confidence or even attracted from abroad by relatively high interest rates. As a large part of the current-account deficit is financed through a rise of foreign-currency deposits in commercial banks, that would then have very serious consequences for the whole economy. Also, if the Croatians become wary about the possible devaluation or, even worse, if they experience substantial and quick depreciation, they will most likely immediately run from the domestic currency, pushing it farther down in a spiral fashion, while igniting high inflation expectations again. Financial markets have a long memory, and Croatians are particularly sensitive to the banking-sector credibility (with their experience of occasional partial expropriations of foreign-exchange deposits) and have a built-in instinct to run away from a weak currency.

The major difference between a currency attack that comes from foreign investors and the domestically induced one is that the later one usually comes later. It is argued (Krugman, 1997) that speculators and investors usually make crises happen before they would otherwise happen. The Croatian financial market is still protected from foreign speculators by capital controls and because it is otherwise still underdeveloped and poorly integrated into the international financial market. That might be a mixed blessing. Whether it is good or bad depends primarily on the policy reaction of the authorities to the growing external imbalance. In a way, being temporarily protected from financial markets allows for some grace period. If the authorities react well to the signs of longer-run unsustainability of the current external position, they might engineer a soft adjustment, avoiding the costs associated with sharp market jitters that are usually associated with speculative attacks. However, if authorities do not react promptly and adequately, being sheltered from international investors and speculators only makes things worse. In such a case, a future crisis imposes higher costs on the economy than if its underlying reasons have been corrected earlier. In other words, in a country like Croatia, good governance can (but only temporarily) make advantage of capital restrictions and still underdeveloped and poorly integrated financial market, while bad governance would be better subjected to the disciplining effect of an open capital account.

Notes

1. Which is, as a matter of comparison, equivalent as if Germany would accept 6.4 million refugees, or, say, Italy, 4 million.
2. One of the key stabilization elements was a successful reorganization of the tax service, which made it possible to reduce the government deficit even though war-related expenditures strongly increased. The fiscal policy measures together with the reorganization of the tax services led to a substantial reduction of the budget deficit from 4.6 percent of GDP in 1991 to 0.8 and 0.6 percent in 1993 and 1994, respectively, in spite of substantial expenditure increases. In the absence of such reforms, the stabilization program would have certainly been short lived.
3. A new foreign-exchange law was passed at the very beginning of the stabilization program; it introduced de facto current-account convertibility. De jure current-account convertibility has been is in place since May 1995 (Article VIII of the IMF Articles of Agreement). Capital-account transactions are still subject to substantial restrictions, but the repatriation of earnings from foreign investment is unrestricted.
4. Because of this tradition, many prices (gas, electricity) mechanically fell as the exchange rate appreciated.

5. These financial streams are generally difficult to asses/predict, which puts monetary authorities in a difficult situation.

6. This has a particularly painful history in Croatia, dating back to ex-Yugoslavia's occasional partial expropriation of foreign-currency savings, with the last episode being frozening of foreign-currency savings by Croatian government after independence. These were transferred into public debt and represent some 60 percent of the outstanding central-government debt.

7. In comparison with 1990, which was the last prewar year. However, 1990 was a year of uncharacteristicaly high wages; therefore, the drop in real wages might be somewhat exaggerated when compared to the last prewar year.

8. War operations took place during May and August of that year and therefore practically wiped out foreign tourists.

9. If they haven't done it before, then the trigger point for economists to start to scratch their heads about the current-account deficit is when it becomes larger than a psychological rule of a thumb—5 percent of the GDP.

10. Loans expanded as interest rates declined (see Figure 11.5).

11. The first rehabilitation process started in 1995 in a regional bank that was most badly hurt by the war. In 1996, rehabilitation was initiated in two other big regional banks. Both of them received liquidity injections and had their bad assets carved out. Finally, at the beginning of 1997, rehabilitation process started in the country's second largest bank, Privredna banka.

12. But also before.

13. It is, also, only since 1992 that NBC has started to publish the exchange rate of the Croatian currency because that was the time when Croatia gained monetary independence and introduced its own currency.

14. This effect may be partly aleviated to the extent that foreign-exchange receipts come from sales of services (tourism) in the domestic economy. In such a case appreciation of the internal exchange rate may, in fact, draw some resources into the tradable sector.

15. Plus, in the case of Figure 11.10 the appreciation of the U.S. dollar in 1996 to 1997.

16. Two books by Helpman and Krugman (1985, 1989) summarized the main features of theory of intraindustry trade in a systematic manner for the first time, as well as the policy implications of these developments.

17. The book by Grubel and Lloyd (1975) represents the first systematic attempt to classify and explain the empirical phenomenon of IIT.

18. Alternative measures could easily be used given the existing data set and calculating speed of a spreadsheet. However, we doubt that the end results would significantly differ from the ones obtained using the basic GL indicator.

19. Here defined as the four SITC product groups: 5, Chemicals; 6, Basic manufactures; 7, Machinery and transportation equipment; and 8, Miscellaneous manufactured goods.

20. SITC three-digit data available for 1990 to 1996 period.

21. SITC three-digit data available for 1993 and 1994.

22. SITC three-digit data available for 1990 to 1994 period.

23. SITC three-digit data available for 1994.

24. SITC three-digit data available for the 1992 to 1994 period.

25. 1994 relative to 1993.

26. Since there were no comparable data for the Slovak trade at the SITC three-digit level, the comparator group consisted of the three economies (the Czech Republic, Poland, and Slovenia).

27. Not least because positive technological spillovers are stronger in a case of FDIs than simple international trade.

28. Classified as FDIs on a basis of international standard 10 percent rule.

29. In fact, it hasn't even god a trade agreement so far.

References

Borensztein Eduardo, Jose DeGregorio, and Jong Wha-Lee. (1994). "How Does Foreign Direct Investment Affect Economic Growth?" IMF Working Paper 110.

Corado C., Z. Wysonkinska, and J. Witowska (eds.). (1996). *Foreign Direct Investment, East and West: The Experiences of the Czech Republic, Hungary, Poland, Spain, and Portugal (early results).*

Edwards, Sebastian. (1989). *Real Exchange Rates, Devaluation and Adjustment.* Cambridge, MA: MIT Press.

Feldman, A. Robert. (1994). "Measure of External Competitiveness for Germany." IMF Working Paper 113.

Grubel, H.G., and P.J. Lloyd. (1975). *Intra-Industry Trade: The Theory and Measurement of International Trade in Differentiated Products.* New York: Wiley.

Havrylyshyn, Oleh, and Peter Kunzel. (1997). "Intra-Industry Trade of Arab Countries: An Indicator of Potential Competitiveness." IMF Working Paper 97-47. Washington, DC.

Helpman, Elhanan, and Paul Krugman. (1985). *Market Structure and Foreign Trade.* Cambridge, MA: MIT Press.

Helpman, Elhanan, and Paul Krugman. (1989). *Trade Policy and Market Structure.* Cambridge, MA: MIT Press.

Hoekman, Bernard, and Simeon Djankov. (1996). "Intra-industry Trade, Foreign Direct Investments and the Reorientation of East European Exports." CEPR Discussion Paper 1377.

Krugman, Paul. (1997). "Currency Crises." The Official Paul Krugman Web Page, http://web.mit.edu/krugman/www.

Milesi-Ferreti, Gian Maria i Razin Assaf. (1996). "Current-Account Sustainability." Princeton Studies in International Finance, No. 81, October.

Stankovski, J. (1996). "The Role of FDI in Eastern Europe." *Austrian Economic Quarterly*, 2.

Verdoorn, P.J. (1960). "The Intra-Bloc Trade of Benelux." In E.A.G. Robinson (ed.), *Economic Consequences of the Size of Nations*, Proceedings of Conference Held by the International Economic Association, London (pp. 291–318).

Walsh, B. (1996). "Stabilization and Adjustment in a Small Open Economy: Ireland, 1979–95." *Oxford Review of Economic Policy*, 12(3): 74–86.

12 EXCHANGE-RATE POLICY IN THE CZECH REPUBLIC: THE PERILS OF STICKING TO FIXED EXCHANGE RATES

Fabrizio Coricelli

University of Siena, CEU Budapest, CEPR

Tosovsky told the Chamber the crown drop followed pressure on the currencies of Thailand, Malaysia, and Philippines. "When a situation like this develops, the market usually looks where are similar problems, and in this case it concerned the Czech Republic," he said.

—Reuter news, May 22, 1997

12.1. Introduction and a Chronicle of the Recent Crisis

The stability of the Czech crown during the period 1991 to 1997 (during 1991 to 1993 the crown of the former Czechoslovakia) was considered an example of success in maintaining macroeconomic stability in a period of radical economic changes. The budget deficit was under control throughout the transition, monetary policy was always prudent, inflation was among the lowest in transition economies, and unemployment remained extremely low (Table 12.1). The stability of the crown coincided as well with political stability: the Czech Republic was the only transition country that did not experience a change in the government since the start of reforms. Most transition economies that adopted the exchange rate as a nominal

Table 12.1. Czech republic: main economic indicators

	1990	*1991*	*1992*	*1993*	*1994*	*1995*	*1996*
GDP growth	−0.4	−14.2	−6.4	−0.9	2.6	4.8	4.4
Inflation (CPI)	10.8	56.6	11.1	20.8	10	9.1	8.8
Unemployment rate	0.8	4.1	2.6	3.5	3.2	2.9	3.5
Budget deficit (−)/GDP	−0.1	−2	−3.3	1.4	0.5	−0.8	−0.5
Current account/GDP	−1.1	0.4	−0.3	0.7	−0.1	−2.9	−8.6
CNB foreign-exchange reserves, billions of U.S. dollars	0.2	0.7	0.7	3.8	6.2	14.0	12.4
Exchange rate, Czech crown to US$	18	29.5	28.3	29.2	28.8	26.6	27.1

anchor during stabilization abandoned it soon after they were out of the stabilization phase.

Against this background, the currency crisis of May 1997 caught by surprise most observers. As stated above by the governor of the Czech National Bank (Mr. Tosovsky), the crisis was induced by factors unrelated to the fundamentals of the Czech Republic—namely, the attack on East Asian currencies that supposedly spread to the Czech Republic.

The crisis of May 1997 was a sobering experience. In the second half of May the Czech crown was under pressure. It was pushed into the depreciation band, falling rapidly toward the lower limit of the band, despite the intervention of the CNB. On May 26 the CNB abandoned the exchange-rate parity, shifting to a free floating. Nevertheless, it seems that the CNB continued to adopt an exchange-rate target, although it did not announce any reference rate.

The May crisis brought to the surface the vulnerability of a country that despite remarkable achievements was still affected by (1) an endemic weakness of its banking system (plagued by bad loans that remain at about 30 percent of total loans, despite a sequence of clearing attempts by the government and (2) a fuzzy structure of property rights and control of firms. As a result of the privatization process, banks and firms are linked through obscure chains of controls, with the likely emergence of insider lending (see Boeri and Perasso, 1997).

Moreover, although a great success, the low rate of unemployment increasingly shows its connection with lack of deep restructuring of the economy. This may in fact be one of the ultimate causes of the macroeconomic difficulties of the Czech Republic. As in Poland and other transition economies, deep restructuring is likely to entail high transitory costs that require some degree of accommodation on both the exchange-rate and inflation sides. The public internalized that the government was averse to accepting significant real costs. As a result, the public rightly assumed that the Czech authorities were not ready to defend the exchange rate if that meant significant output costs. Interestingly, the same contradictory policy of "strong exchange rate" contributed to the slowdown of the economy that paved the way for the May crisis. This process seems consistent with recent theoretical developments that question the benefits of fixed exchange rates in a context in which credibility is endogenous, depending crucially on the state of the economy (Obstfeld and Rogoff, 1995). As stressed by recent extensions of the classical "balance-of-payments crisis" model of Krugman, a country is vulnerable to a currency attack even when fiscal and monetary policy are sustainable. This can happen when the government has an implict threshold in terms of output or unemployment indicators. Beyond that threshold, the authorities are unwilling to defend the currency. If understood by the public, this process can lead to self-fulfilling attacks.[1]

A recent statement by Vaclav Klaus (1997) and other coalition leaders effectively summarizes the above arguments:

> The current economic situation is not only an accidental fluctuation, but it also reflects long-term trends and phenomena inside the Czech economy. Among those belong low efficiency of the banking system, deepened by rescue actions by the state, bailout of ineffective activities from budget funds, extensive secondary payment inability (read interenterprise arrears) caused by low effectiveness of the legal system, which prevents the enforcement of law, opaqueness of ownership rights. . . . Those are the main factors that contributed to the evolution of a soft economic environment, nonexistence of a proper business environment and capital market, and the survival of a large part of an inefficient corporate sphere. The result of that is, apart from others, a faster growth of wages than productivity. That caused extremely high domestic demand originating with personal consumption, which became—along with high and growing investment—the main source of the growing imbalance in external relations. The fact that the extent of openess of our economy is larger than some of our trade partners contributed to that. The declining competitiveness of the economy was manifested by a gradual decline of economic growth and, from that, the resulting tension in the state budget and the trend toward an imbalance in public finances. *Low unemployment in this situation is rather a result of these unfavorable phenomena than an expression of a dynamically developing economy.* The parallel running of an extraordinarily high deficit of the current account of the balance of payments, problems with keeping the budget in balance, and political instability necessarily had to lead to an attack on our currency. . . . We are saying

> openly to the public what these stabilization and recovery steps will mean in the near future. A lowering of public spending, a tightening of the environment in banking and credit area, and a fast and effective recouping of debts in the private sector will lead to a temporary economic inhibition. Instead of growth of the economy we have to expect rather an economic decline, accompanied by a significant growth of unemployment. The changed exchange rate will cause a temporary increase in inflation. All of these phenomena will mean a decline of real wages and other income.

The interpretation contained in this document is rather different from that of Tosovsky, who blamed international speculators that, in a process similar to the so-called Tequila effect encountered after the Mexican crisis of 1994, moved from attacks on East Asian currencies to the Czech crown. However, the contrast is only superficial. We argue in this chapter that the timing and extent of the currency crisis were associated with the behavior of global investors that reacted to news and signals not necessarily linked to fundamentals. This seems to be confirmed by the mild effects of the abandonment of the exchange-rate band in May.

Nevertheless, the crisis brought into the open underlying inconsistencies in economic policies and the fragility of the Czech financial system. This chapter briefly reviews the experience with the exchange-rate policy since 1990, when the Czech Republic was part of the former Czechoslovakia. We find pitfalls in the approach since the start of reforms. Specifically, we question the rationale for the large exchange-rate devaluation in 1990 that likely paved the way for the subsequent difficulties encountered by the Czech Republic. The main thrust of the chapter rests on the difficulties of managing exchange-rate policy in the context of a "structural" change in the equilibrium real exchange rate, compounded by temporary shocks to the real exchange rate arising mainly from capital inflows. Inconsistent macroeconomic policies played as well a key role. A main inconsistency was the attempt to maintain fixed exchange rates while liberalizing capital flows and at the same time adopting money supply targets. More generally, it appears that the Czech authorities tried a shortcut to achieve Western European inflation rates with the wrong set of instruments. In fact, given that the Czech Republic started reforms with a balanced macroeconomic situation, it could have probably achieved soon after reforms Western rates of inflation if it had avoided the sharp depreciation at the outset of reforms. Furthermore, if inflation convergence was the main target of policies, it could have been achieved through an explicit inflation targeting. The Czech Republic had no history of inflation, no currency substitution, and a rather effective system for tax collection. In these circumstances, it could have exploited some independence in monetary policy to achieve its inflation targets. Moreover, within that alternative approach, liberalization of the capital account could have been postponed. However, a government with no track record is tempted to adopt a target that is visible and perhaps linked also to national pride, like the currency. The recent economic literature (Cuckierman, 1995; Leiderman and Bufman, 1995) emphasized the fact that transparency may collide with the buildup of credibility. Indeed, the exchange-rate target may lead to inconsistent policies and weakening credibility. We discuss some simple analytical models tackling various aspects of the phenomenon and then examine the Czech experience in the light of these models.

Our main conclusion is that the exchange rate should not have been devalued at the beginning, allowing for an initial step toward the necessary real appreciation. After the initial stage, the Czech Republic could have shifted to an inflation targeting in the context of a crawling band, consistent with the inflation targets of the government. A more flexible exchange rate could have implied an inflation rate higher than that actually experienced by the Czech Republic and more similar to those of Poland and Hungary.[2] These more realistic inflation targets could have allowed a deeper restructuring of the economy. Furthermore, the adoption of inflation targets should have been accompanied by slower liberalization of controls on capital movements. The CNB could have built its reputation on its ability to meet inflation targets and not on the basis of a stable exchange rate.

Our empirical analysis shows that the pass-through from exchange-rate changes to inflation in the context of the Czech Republic is not very high. Thus, a more flexible exchange-rate policy could be consistent with lower inflation targets achieved through the use of domestic policy instruments.

12.2. Exchange Rate as a Nominal Anchor During Stabilization

When still part of the former Czechoslovakia, the Czech Republic adopted the exchange rate as nominal anchor during the stabilization program in 1991 that accompanied the liberalization of the economy. Among PCPEs, the Czech Republic started reforms from the most favorable macroeconomic conditions. During the previous regime, the country was able to avoid major imbalances, both internal and external. The reform process was launched with an economy with minimal external debt and with a history of lack of significant shortages. Thus, there was no inflationary pressure from bringing into the open hidden inflation. Notwithstanding these favorable initial conditions, during 1991 inflation jumped in the first months of reforms and was on average about 50 percent with respect to the previous year. Rather than a persistent inflation, however, it was largely a price-level jump that took place in 1991. Indeed, by March 1991 monthly inflation had declined to 4 percent for the CPI and zero for the PPI. Although precise analyses are still missing, it can be argued that most of the initial inflation jump was due to the sharp devaluation of the exchange rate that was carried out in several rounds during 1990. The success in achieving rapidly low rates of inflation, together with a remarkable stability in both fiscal and monetary policy, led most observers to neglect the inconsistency of the policy pursued by the Czech authorities. With hindsight, the whole exchange-rate strategy that collapsed during 1997 was faulted since the beginning of reforms. For the focus of this chapter is on the more recent events, we will discuss only briefly the rationale, or lack of it, of the exchange-rate policy followed since 1990.

12.2.1. Excessive Devaluation and Inflation Inertia

In transition economies that adopted the exchange rate as a nominal anchor, the initial step devaluation was rationalized as a cushion in a context of high uncertainty on domestic inflation after liberalization. To avoid an appreciation at the outset of reforms, the exchange rate was devalued well in excess of forecast inflation. In countries with significant monetary overhang, a high degree of dollarization, and very high protection for tradable sectors, the initial large devaluation could be justified. There are, however, important counterarguments, in addition to the objection to the choice of undervalued currency in the case of the former Czechoslovakia.

The first objection regards the combination of a devaluation of the exchange rate of about 100 percent in 1990 and a target of stable money supply. As discussed at length in Calvo and Coricelli (1992), this policy leads to a sharp decline in real credit and real monetary balances, which is likely to have adverse effects on the real side of the economy. Indeed, a step devaluation followed by fixing of the exchange rate implies a jump in the price level of tradables. Furthermore, tradable goods enter as inputs into production of nontradables. Thus, a generalized jump in the price level takes place. As the nominal stock of money is held constant by policy design, the real stock of money falls. Ultimately, M2 increased by 23 percent in 1991 in the face of an increase in prices by more than 50 percent. It is unclear why a country starting with no major imbalances needs to engineer a reduction in the stock of real monetary balances in the context of a structural trasformation that by necessity increases sharply the number of monetary transactions (Janackova, 1994). In fact, as argued in Calvo and Coricelli (1993) and discussed below in connection with the exchange-rate policy, the contraction in real money supply conflicts with the need to move to a low stable rate of inflation and thus rate of growth of money supply (see Sargent, 1982, for a clear exposition of the conflict between the reduction in the *rate of inflation*, and thus rate of growth of money, and the need to increase the initial stock of money, in a situation in which the *price level* is downward rigid). The contraction in the real stock of money causes an unnecessary decline in output in economies already hard hit by other shocks. The initial sharp contraction in real balances may have also contributed to the worsening portfolio of commercial banks, a problem that affected the Czech Republic throughout transition.

The tight financial conditions contributed, together with wage policy, to enforce a large drop in real wages. Thus, the sharp nominal devaluation translated into a sharp real devaluation, validated by a downward flexibility of real wages.[3] As a result, the Czech Republic entered transition with a large cushion from an undervalued exchange rate (see Halpern and Wyplosz, 1995).

This undervaluation raises a second main objection to the strategy outlined above. With a highly undervalued exchange rate, the exchange rate can hardly serve as a nominal anchor. Indeed, assuming some degree of inertia in the price system, prices adjust only slowly to the new conditions. Thus, over time the price level increases to gradually erode the initial (disequilibrium) undervaluation of the real exchange rate. Given the uncertainty on the interpretation of the real appreciation after the initial sharp devaluation, this process poses problems for the conduct of macroeconomic policies. Indeed, the authorities need to establish how much of the postliberalization inflation they have to accommodate.

A third important objection relates to the issue of reputation building. Indeed, governments in transition have to reputation from past actions. This gives them a so-called period of honeymoon at the beginning of reforms. However, governments need to establish their reputation and the credibility of their policy strategies after the initial stage of reform. Specifically, the central bank needs to establish its reputation as an inflation averse institution. The use of fixed exchange rate, coupled with an adjustment of inflation needed for convergence to world prices, deprives the central bank from effectively using monetary instruments and from having a final target (inflation) on which its policies can be evaluated.

All three objections are strengthened by the fact that ultimately transition entails an appreciation of the real exchange rate. This implies that the initial devaluation is an attempt to push the real exchange rate well below its equilibrium level, a policy that inevitably leads to inflationary pressures.

Thus, to sum up, the initial strategy of undervaluation of the exchange rate was ill designed and contributed to the policy inconsistencies that afflicted the Czech Republic in the second stage of transition.

Before discussing more recent developments, we briefly touch on three aspects of exchange-rate policies, trying to provide a framework of reference for the evaluation of the causes of the collapse of the Czech exchange rate policy in May 1997: (1) the issue of real exchange rate in the process of restructuring of the economy (briefly discussed within two simple "real" models), (2) the relation between monetary policy and real exchange dynamics in a model in which the real exchange rate is likely to overshoot (appreciate above) its long-run level, and (3) the management of exchange rates in the context of significant capital flows. This issue concerns both the policy responses to capital flows and the problem of consistency between internal and external objectives.

12.3. Real Exchange Rates and Structural Change During Transition

Transition involves large reallocation of resources across sectors. The artificial compression of the service sectors in the previous regime implies a shift of resources, labor, and capital from the oversized industry to services. This process implies a change in relative price in favor of the service sector. As the two sectors can also be distinguished as nontraded (services) and tradable (manufacturing) sectors, the change in relative prices corresponds to an appreciation of the real exchange rate (price of nontradables in terms of tradables). Figure 12.1 shows a simple two-sector diagram, with labor as the only mobile factor. Tradable goods are assumed as numeraire. On the vertical axis are measured wages in terms of tradable goods and the value of marginal product of labor in the two sectors (nontradables on the left and tradable on the right). The two lines depict the marginal product of labor in the two sectors in relation to levels of employment. First, consider the case of well-functioning labor markets, with a unique wage. *E* denotes the initial equilibrium point, with full employment. Transition can be described as the shift of labor from tradable to nontradable sectors. Thus, the new equilibrium would be at point *E'*. Point *E'* implies an increase in the price of nontradable goods, thus an appreciation of the exchange rate. It also implies an increase in real wages, measured in terms of tradable

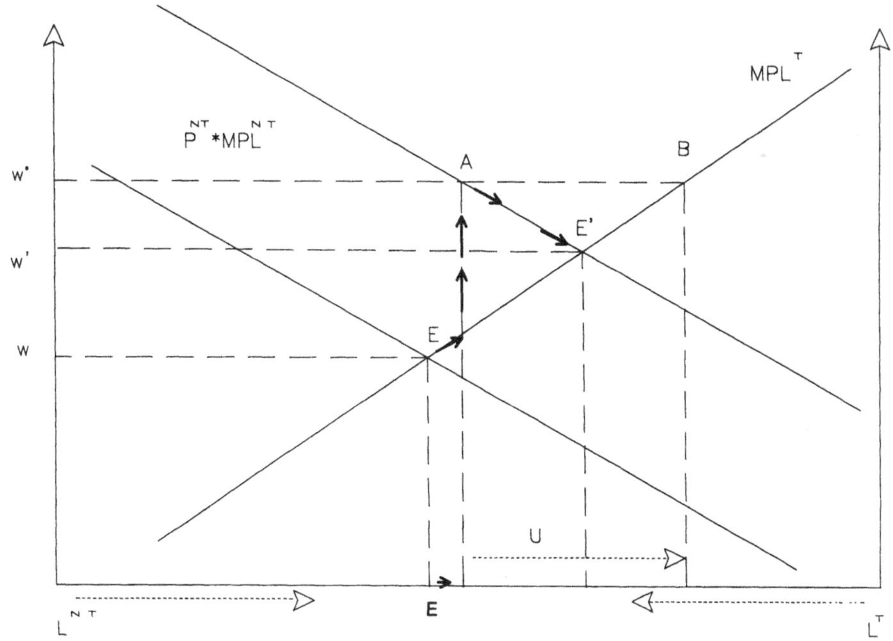

Figure 12.1.

goods. Assume that the reallocation of labor takes place gradually. Thus, if the transition is a smooth process, one should observe a movement along the segment E-E', with a gradual appreciation of the exchange rate and a gradual increase in wages. However, one can conceive a different scenario, possibly more realistic. The value-marginal product of labor in the non-tradable sector jumps to the new steady-state level. Labor, however, does not adjust instantaneously, perhaps because of the need to invest resources to absorb labor (see Chadha and Coricelli, 1997, for a model of labor reallocation during the transition). A possible outcome could be that wages jump to the new value-marginal product, at a level w_o. At that level of wages, demand for labor is given by A for nontradable goods, and B for tradable. Thus, employment in the nontradable good sector remains constant, while employment in the tradable sector declines and unemployment arises. Eventually, real wages decline toward their long-run equilibrium E'. Employment in the tradable-good sector increases, together with the increase of employment in the nontradable-good sector. If one considers the price of tradables as the product of the nominal exchange rate and the foreign price, it is easy to see that the final movement toward equilibrium can be achieved through a devaluation of the nominal exchange rate. However, devaluation implies a reduction in P^{nt} and thus the system converges to a new equilibrium E'', in which real wages are equal to w_o but employment in the tradable good sector is higher than at E'. The behavior of real wages in terms of the consumer basket composed by both tradable and nontradable goods is ambiguous.

This simple framework highlights some interesting points. First, if we measure competitiveness in terms of labor costs, we obtain that in the presence of wage pressure there can be an overshooting of the appreciation of the wage-based real exchange rate. The real exchange rate measured as ratio of tradable to nontradable goods also can display an overshooting when the adjustment takes place via a devaluation of the nominal exchange rate. The key issue is that the dynamics of the exchange rate crucially depends on the behavior of real wages.

Table 12.2 presents some numerical calculations of the process taking place in Figure 12.1. We consider two cases, each corresponding to different size of the reallocation of labor. Initially, most workers are employed in the tradable sector (1.9 out of a total labor force of 2). In the first case, at the end of transition, employment in the tradable sector shrinks to 1.5, while in the second case it drops to 1. The second column of the table displays the behavior of wages, which increase with the shift of labor across sectors. The other columns contain the behavior of the relative prices, total output, and total labor productivity (total output divided by total employment).[4] It is apparent that the larger the reallocation of labor, the larger the productivity gain, the larger the increase in wages, and the larger the real appreciation. Wages (in terms of tradable goods) increase at a rate below the rate of productivity growth. If wages are somehow indexed to the price of nontradable goods, then the process changes, and the outcome with

Table 12.2. Labor reallocation and real appreciation: an illustrative numerical example

	P_{nt}/P_t	*Wages*	L_{nt}	L_t	Q_{total}	*Productivity*
(i)	1.01	0.36	0.10	1.90	1.60	0.80
(ii)	1.94	0.41	0.50	1.50	2.45	1.23
(iii)	3.00	0.50	1.00	1.00	4.00	2.00
Percentage changes						
(ii)/(i)	92	12	400	−21	53	54
(iii)/(ii)	54	23	100	−33	63	63

unemployment, lower increase of employment in the nontradable sector, and ultimately lower increase in productivity will emerge.

Despite its extreme simplicity this example highlights one point that appears relevant in the experience of the Czech Republic—namely, the increase of real wages well beyond the increase in productivity and the consequent adverse effect on overall economic activity.

A second useful "real" model for addressing the rationale of real appreciation, which has been often referred to (Hrncir, 1995, among others), is the Ricardian model of Dornbusch (1980).

12.3.1. Real Appreciation, Restructuring, and Specialization in Higher Value-Added Production

A strong currency is often identified as an important channel for inducing an efficient selection of more productive activities. Indeed, an undervalued exchange rate can be considered as an implicit subsidy to exporters, which can make competitive a larger set of production. Conversely, an appreciating real exchange rate drives out of the market the less productive activities that are not able to compensate the implicit tax with higher productivity (or higher quality etc.). The model of Dornbusch (1980) provides a useful framework to illustrate this mechanism. Consider a continuum of activities, ranked on the basis of unit labor requirements in production, in relation to the requirements abroad. Commodities are ranked on the basis of technical efficiency, with the more efficient commodities near the origin. Relative wages determine the dividing point between home and foreign production. The higher the relative wage in the home country, the smaller the number of commodities produced, and the higher the average efficiency of home production. If we measure real exchange rates on the basis of labor costs, it is apparent that a real appreciation (meaning higher relative wages in the samecurrency) leads to a shift to specialization toward more efficient production.[5] Hrncir (1995) discusses this issue for the case of the Czech Republic, arguing that the initial undervaluation of the currency produced an inefficient specialization, providing implicit subsidies to inefficient firms.

This argument seems to have some value in a static context. However, if one evaluates productivity in a dynamic context, the effectiveness of a policy of strong currency has to be qualified. Singapore, for instance, adopted an explicit policy of high wages to remodel its product specialization toward more efficient production. Chadha (1991) analyzed that experience illustrating the conditions for the success of that strategy. In a dynamic setting the growth of productivity requires investments, either in human or physical capital (or both). If investments are forward looking, expectations about the future performance of the economy, the sustainability of high wages, or strong currency policies become crucial. We take up below this issue, discussing it in relation to foreign investment.

Because of the absence of major macroeconomic imbalances at the beginning of reforms in the Czech Republic, it can be argued that the microeconomic rationale briefly discussed in this section might have been an important element in the choice of a stable currency, in the face of rising inflation. However, if such microeconomic considerations were important, it remains unclear why there was a sharp undervaluation of the currency at the beginning of reforms.

Furthermore, in the context of a transition economy it is of paramount importance to assess whether the institutional framework providing incentives and rewards for restructuring is in place. Indeed, a simple constraint in the form of a strong currency may not be a sufficient stimulus for restructuring in a context in which property rights are ambiguous and the allocation of credit inefficient. Indeed, ambiguous property rights may make uncertain the appropriability of return to restructuring, while inefficient credit allocation may hamper restructuring processes that require external fnancing.

Summing up, looking from a pure "real" side of the issue, a policy of strong currency requires consistent behavior of wages, supportive investments, and efficient credit markets. All these three elements emerged in the experience of the Czech Republic, showing the limits of the policy of a strong currency for an economy in transition when conditions for efficient restructuring are missing or highly imperfect.

The next section discusses the extension to a monetary model, which illustrates the likelihood of an overshooting of the real exchange rate in an economy in which the central bank runs a tight monetary policy, while at the same time intervenes to defend the exchange rate in the context of capital mobility.

12.4. Real Exchange-Rate Overshooting With Exchange-Market Intervention and Tight Monetary Policy

Consider a simple aggregate demand model in which output depends on the real exchange rate (the model is taken from Dornbusch, 1980). Over time, prices change according to a Phillips curve. There is capital mobility, but it is less than perfect. Domestic interest rates are determined by a standard LM relation. Capital movements depend on interest-rate differentials adjusted for expected devaluation. The only twist to the model is the policy intervention of the central bank, which intervenes in the foreign-exchange market when the rate of depreciation of the nominal exchange rate is different from the rate of growth of domestic credit. This intervention determines the dynamics of international reserves, which in equilibrium equals the balance of payments.

Box 1 contains the equations of the model. After substitution, the system can be reduced to two dynamic equations in the dynamics of the real exchange rate ($de/dt - dp/dt$) and real monetary balances ($dM/dt - dp/dt$). Figure 12.2 shows the dynamic path of the real exchange rate and of real monetary balances, following a policy of tightening monetary policy. From this simple model, Dornbusch derives two main conclusions. First, the tightening of monetary policy determines a real appreciation, which in some cases may be due to rising inflation with an appreciation of the nominal exchange rate. Second, the real appreciation is eventually reversed during the path toward long-run equilibrium.

$i=Y-\alpha(M-p)$	LM
$Y=\beta(e-p)$	Aggregate demand
$\dot{P}=\phi Y+\dot{M}$	Phillips curve
$\dot{R}/M=-\theta(\dot{e}-v)$	Intervention rule
v=rate of growth of domestic credit	
$\dot{R}/M=g(e-p)-\delta Y+\xi(i-i^*-\dot{e})$	Balance of Payments
$\dot{M}=v+\dot{R}/M=v-\theta(\dot{e}-v)$	

Box 1. Dornbusch Model

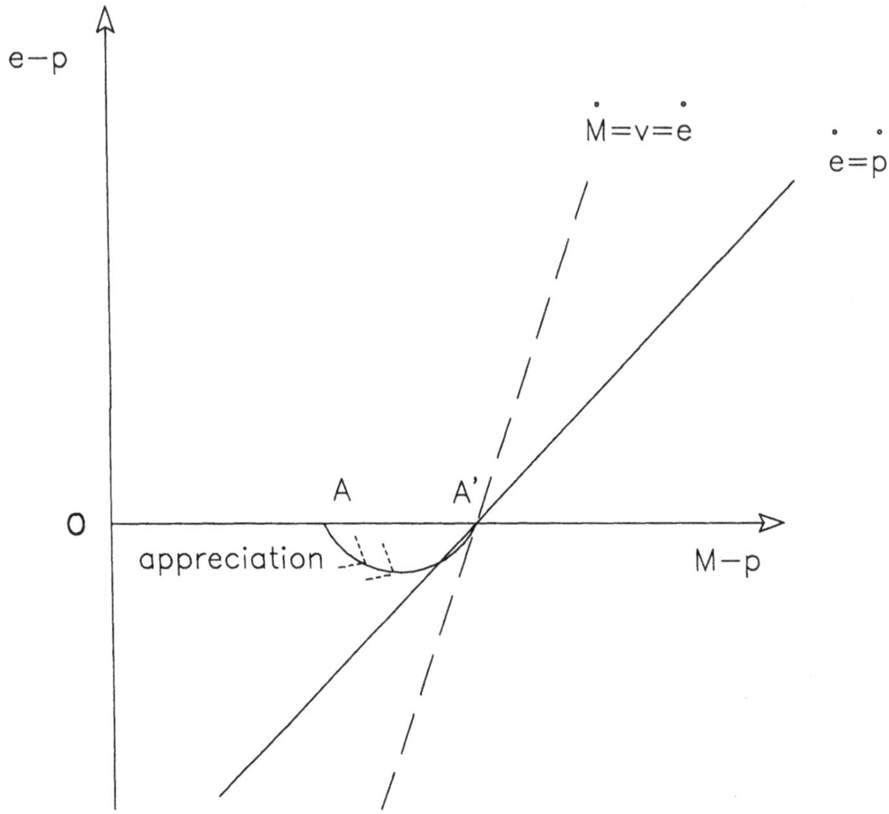

Figure 12.2. Real exchange rate dynamics and monetary policy

Along the transition path, the real appreciation of the exchange rate causes a decline in economic activity.

As in the Sargent example cited in Section 12.1, a solution to the problem is to engineer a one-time increase in the money stock, followed by a reduction in the rate of growth of credit expansion. This would ensure moving instantaneously to a new long-run equilibrium with lower inflation. Again, the main problem with such a solution is the credibility effect of a policy of tightening the rate of growth of money that starts with a jump in the stock of money. It is hard to convince the public that this is only a one-time change in the stock, consistent with a permanent decline in the rate of growth of money, hence of inflation.

If one adds fiscal policy to the model, the results will be strengthened and can be interpreted in terms of the relative stance of fiscal and monetary policy. Indeed, an expansionary fiscal policy would lead to an increase in the domestic interest rate, capital inflows, and a strengthening of the nonlinear path described in Figure 12.2.

Despite its obvious limitations the model underlines the inconsistencies between the use of monetary policy to achieve lower inflation and, simultaneously, the use of an intervention function to stabilize the exchange rate.

Both the real models and the monetary model sketched above, however, neglect key aspects of the problem of exchange-rate management in a world of integrated financial markets and forward-looking actors in the economy. The experience of the Czech Republic, as well as of several episodes of recent currency crises, can hardly be understood without taking into account the behavior of international investors, the response of policymakers to capital inflows, and the assessment of the public of the credibility of the exchange-rate peg. These elements allow a discussion of the vulnerability of a country to a currency run, as well as the interpretation of the dynamics of the current account in relation to the expectations of the public on the behavior of the exchange rate.

The next section briefly reviews some recent contributions to the analysis of currency crises.

12.4.1. Temporary Shocks to the Real Exchange Rate

While the discussion above focused on the adjustment process to long-run levels of the exchange rate, for the analysis of actual experiences it is important to acknowledge that economies are subject to temporary shocks to the real exchange rate. Of particular importance for the case of the Czech Republic and of other transition economies are shocks coming from exogenous changes to international conditions (for instance, changes affecting capital inflows to the country). Calvo, Reinhart, and Vegh (1995) examine the basic theory behind the effects of changes in international interest rates. A reduction of world interest rates implies an appreciation of the domestic real exchange rate. The country can either tolerate this temporary appreciation or can try to avoid it. Calvo, Reinhart, and Vegh (1995) show that a policy oriented to keeping constant the real exchange rate is necessarily inflationary, unless fiscal policy is changed. It is indeed important to remind that fiscal policy can absorb the shock to the real exchange rate. Lacking the fiscal instrument, the only way a temporary shock to the real exchange rate can be neutralized is through tight monetary policy if, and only if, there are effective controls on capital movements.

Thus, even from the perspective of an optimizing intertemporal model it turns out that inflationary pressures are bound to arise if the authorities try to avoid the real appreciation of the exchange rate. Putting together the various elements emphasized so far, it is apparent that in the Czech Republic inflation, even if lower than in other transition economies, has gradually produced an appreciation of the real exchange rate that the authorities have been trying to avoid through a policy of a fixed nominal exchange rate. Once again, policy conduct is bound to be inconsistent with a final target of reduction of inflation to Western European levels. Note, however, that from a welfare point of view, avoiding temporary swings in the real exchange rate is the optimal policy. This policy, however, should be embedded in a consistent exchange-rate rule, such as a crawling band, that explicitly assumes a real exchange-rate target. Inflation would be higher and more persistent than with a fixed exchange rate. Welfare, however, will be higher and policy more transparent.

Once the real appreciation has taken place, the optimal behavior of consumers—consumption smoothing—induces a growing deficit of the current account and growing capital inflows.

12.5. Capital Flows and Currency Crises: Credibility, Portfolio Adjustment, and Vulnerability to Currency Runs

In a series of influential papers Calvo and others have stressed the importance of credibility issues for understanding the effects of programs that rely on the exchange rate as a nominal anchor (Calvo and Vegh, 1989). In its simplest form this view can be summarized as follows: if the exchange-rate anchor is not credible, the public expects a devaluation some time in the future. This leads to an anticipatory demand for imported goods, especially durables. If tradable and nontradable goods are complements, there will be a generalized increase in demand with attendant inflationary pressure. Thus, there is a temporary demand and possibly output boom. The real exchange rate appreciates, and the current account of the balance of payments deteriorates. Eventually, the expectations of devaluation may become self-fulfilling as the deterioration of the current account is interpreted as a sign of weakness of the fundamentals.

These theories, however, have been developed to analyze the puzzling business cycle that characterized several exchange-rate-based stabilization programs. It is nevertheless a useful framework to analyze the dynamics of the real exchange rate and of the current account when the exchange-rate peg is not perceived as credible. The reasons for such lack of credibility are, however, taken as exogenous.

The literature on currency crises deals with the factors that are behind the collapse of an exchange-rate arrangement.

The first-generation theories, based on Krugman's model, identified in the fiscal imbalance the source of the inevitable drying up of reserves and eventually of the collapse of the exchange rate. Fiscal deficit, current-account deficit, and the gradual reduction of reserves should be observed before the attack to the currency. Maintaining the same structure of the model, it was also observed that the attack to the currency could arise because of self-fulfilling prophecies. If the public decides, for reasons that are not necessarily linked to underlying macroeconomic disequilibria, that the current exchange rate is not sustainable, it can then cause the actual collapse of the currency by behaving in a manner consistent with such collapse. In a world of rational expectations, such self-fulfilling prophecies can always arise when the price of an asset, such as the exchange rate, depends on the expectations of the people about the price itself.

The possibility of a crisis in the context of sound fundamentals stimulated new developments both in the theory of currency crises and in the empirical work. Two relevant directions stand out. First, an optimizing government is unlikely to defend the exchange rate irrespective of the social costs of such behavior. It is likely that, even when the central bank could defend the parity, it may decide not to do it because it considers the costs too high. Thus, the commitment of the government to a given exchange rate is never perfect. This implies that the public likely internalizes the possibility of a change in the exchange rate, which always exposes the currency to potential runs, even when they could be unjustified from the point of view of fundamentals. This is the main argument against fixed or semifixed exchange rates put forward recently by Obstfeld and Rogoff (1995), who provide evidence that in several instances currency crises take place even when the central bank has enough reserves to counteract a speculative attack.

The second, possibly complementary, direction relates to behavior of global investors and the possibility of herding behavior.

12.5.1. Portfolio Diversification and herding Behavior

Currency crises are often seen as resulting from irrational behavior of international investors. By contrast, Calvo (1995) showed that some of the key features of a Mexican-type currency crisis can be explained in a simple optimizing portfolio model. The so-called globalization of financial markets led to an increase of possibilities to diversify internationally the portfolios of investors. The emergence of investment funds in search of such diversification provided a large demand for diversification. Portfolios of these investors comprise investments in several areas of the world, from developed to emerging markets. These are, in principle, welcome developments, as they allow for a reduction of risks for the single investor. However, Calvo stresses the fact that the more diversified the portfolios are, the more investments in a given country become sensitive to changes in local returns or news. Sometimes this news is not related to the fundamentals of the country in question. The idea is quite simple. If an investor has investments in a large number of countries in its portfolio, the "loss" in terms of diversification of pulling out investments from one country is minor. Thus, if the investor receives information, more or less founded, that returns in a given country are declining, it has an incentive to withdraw its investment there. In a world of imperfect information, investments can react to arbitrary news, and, furthermore, the behavior of investors tends to be homogeneous as in the case of "herding" behavior. The argument is that the larger the number of countries in which an investor diversifies its portfolio, the lower the incentive to collect information (costly) on a single country. As a result, investors may react to news that is unrelated to the fundamentals of a country. This story holds in the context of homogeneous investors. However, it can be shown that it applies as well in a world of heterogeneous investors, with different, though partially overlapping portfolios. This extension allows to introduce explicitly "herding" behavior in Calvo's model and probably adds some realism to his model.[6]

As in Calvo (1995), investors diversify internationally their portfolio. Investors have to decide whether to collect costly information on the true return in a specific country. We slightly modify Calvo's model, by assuming heterogeneity among investors. We introduce two types of heterogeneity: one relates to the set of countries forming the portfolio of each investor, and the other is given by the fact that some investors purchase information, while others do not. Each investor has a portfolio that partially overlaps with that of other investors.[7] Consider the decision of investors about a specific country. Starting from an initial equilibrium, assume that one investor receives new information about the return in the specific country. Like in Calvo, news about the decline in the return in the country will trigger a fall in investment. The sensitivity to news of the investment is higher, the higher the degree of diversification of the portfolio. What would the other investors do? They update their expectations on the return to their investment by observing the behavior of the other investor. In principle, they should react only if the behavior of the other investor depends on changes in the return in that country. However, the behavior of a single investor could change because of changes in its wealth or because of changes in returns in other countries in which the "neighboring" investor does not invest. Because of uncertainty about the true reason for the changing behavior of the first investor, the others will attribute a positive probability that the change is due to a reduction in the estimate of the return to investment in that country. Thus, other investors as well will reduce their share of investment there. The intensity of the reaction depends on the type of investor. Those who do not collect information will react abruptly, pulling out all their funds. The "informed" ones will adjust their share in a manner similar to the first investor. They could even maintain the same share if they find out that the first investor has reduced its share because of specific factors, unrelated to the return in the country.

Thus, in a world of highly diversified portfolios and consequently uninformed investors, capital flows tend to be very volatile and sensitive to news.

This raises important questions on the appropriate policy response of the host country to capital flows.

12.6. The Policy Response to Capital Inflows

Table 12.3 summarizes the influential view of the International Monetary Fund on the policy responses to capital inflows in a country with "balanced" policies, like the Czech Republic. As expected, the appropriate policy response depends on the causes and nature of the inflow. If the causes of inflows are mainly internal, either an upward shift in money demand or a sustained increase in the marginal product of capital, then fiscal adjustment and sterilization should be used simply to smooth a possibly too rapid inflow. In the case of a shift in money demand, the equilirium real exchange rate does not change: neither nominal rates nor inflation should change. In the case of increasing productivity of capital, the equilibrium real exchange rate appreciates. Hence, policies should accommodate that. When the causes are external, and thus subject to reversal when external conditions change, the policy response is more relevant. As discussed in Section 12.4, the temporary pressure on the real exchange rate can either be accepted or counteracted with policies aimed at keeping the real exchange rate constant. The targeting of the real exchange rate is likely to produce higher inflation. Inflationary pressures can be reduced by adopting sterilization policies or by tightening fiscal policy. Sterilization, however, may be effective in the short run, and it implies fiscal costs. Fiscal adjustment would be

Table 12.3. Macroeconomic policy matrix for a country with a balanced policy experiencing capital inflows

		Other Factors	
	Increase in Domestic Demand for Money[a]	*Sustained Inflows (e.g., increase in productivity of domestic capital)*	*Temporary Inflows (e.g., fall in international interest rates)*
1. Sterilization	Central-bank intervention may be needed to smooth fluctuations in interest rates.	Some sterilization may be necessary to limit the effect on liquidity and to smooth fluctuations in interest rates.	Sterilization is appropriate to contain the impact on liquidity.
2. Exchange-rate appreciation	The equilibrium real effective exchange-rate does not change.	Depending on degree of exchange-rate flexibility, the warranted appreciation of the equilibrium real effective exchange rate can be achieved partly through nominal appreciation and partly through increases in the prices of nontraded goods; for a predetermined exchange rate, a step appreciation or a decrease in the rate of crawl should be considered.	Some temporary nominal appreciation of the exchange rate may be warranted, if there are constraints on sterilization, but the equilibrium real exchange need not change.
3. Fiscal policy	No policy response is required.	Fiscal policy may need to be tightened, especially if the absorptive capacity of the economy is limited relative to the size of the inflows. Experience suggests that a tighter fiscal stance has been necessary in many countries to facilitate the noninflationary absorption of large flows.	If the constraints on sterilization are too severe, and the external competitive position in weak, then some fiscal tightening may have to be considered. However, the time it takes to implement fiscal measures makes fiscal policy an unwieldy instrument in the short term.

a. This applies to an upward shift in the domestic demand for money function.

a more reliable response. However, significant fiscal adjustment has implementation lags that may limit the viability of this instrument in the short run.

If inflows are massive, it is unlikely they can be fully neutralized. Thus, temporary pressure on the real exchange rate is likely to arise. This, in turn, induces a temporary boost in spending, both consumption and investment. Increased demand reinforces the pressure on domestic inflation. If the authorities react by tightening monetary policy, domestic interest rates are likely to increase, thus increasing the incentives for further inflows.

The current account of the balance of payments deteriorates, signaling the likelihood of the unsustainability of the real appreciation.

Whether these tendencies are likely to give rise to a crisis situation depends among other things on two elements. One is the composition of capital inflows; the other is the fragility of the financial sector. We turn to a brief discussion of these two issues.

12.6.1. Composition of Capital Flows and Likelihood of Reversal

The argument reviewed above seems to be highly relevant for portfolio investment and other forms of short-term investment. In contrast, direct investment is generally considered as a less volatile form on capital inflow and thus less likely to be affected by sudden reversal of flows. Although this argument has certainly some value, the mechanisms that induce global investors to pull out their portfolio investments may to some extent apply as well to foreign direct investment. In transition economies it is often difficult to distinguish between direct and portfolio investments. Even neglecting measurement problems, the peculiar conditions of transition economies make the two forms of investment similar. Consider the case of a foreign direct investment consisting in the purchase of the controlling shares of a company. If the cash transfer from abroad is small with respect to the actual market value of the asset, it may happen that the value of the flow of returns on the asset covers very quickly the initial investment. An investor with a long horizon is likely to reinvest its earnings in the country and possibly transfer funds from abroad to develop the company. When expectations about the return of the investment change, the investors will stop the flow and likely will pull its accumulated earnings out of the country. Even if the asset remain in the country, there is an important effect in terms of flows. While these changes are unlikely to cause a sudden currency crisis, they can determine pressure on the currency that is then compounded by the behavior of short-term flows. Given that FDIs are likely to have an important effect on the real side of the economy, their volatility may determine volatility in overall economic activity. The reasons for the small initial capital investment of the foreign investors depend on the way privatization is undertaken and the lack of transparent procedures for asset purchase, in addition to difficulties in finding the "right" price of assets and, in some cases, the pressure to quickly sell assets to improve the government budget in the short run.

More generally, unclear property rights and corruption may lead to transformation of real assets into liquid assets subject to high volatility (both of asset prices and property), as asset transfers will be determined by short-run profit considerations.

12.6.2. Vulnerability of the Financial Sector

The work of Calvo, followed by others (like Sachs, Thornell, and Velasco, 1995), underlined the importance of the fragility of financial markets as a key factor in currency crises. The fragility of the financial sector can arise for two main reasons: (1) capital inflows are intermediated by the banking system, leading to a lending boom that exposes banks to a mismatch between maturity of deposits (short-term) and loans, or between currency denomination of loans (local currency) and deposits (foreign currency); and (2) related to the first element, a lending boom is usually associated with an increase in the riskiness of loans. A significant share of loans becomes nonperforming, and unless banks continue to roll over loans, the quality of their portfolio would be revealed with the risk of the spread of a bank run.

For the Czech Republic the main weakness of the banking sector was linked to two elements. First, the large share of bad loans. According to estimates of the Czech National Bank (CNB) in 1996 the share of doubtful loans in the total loan portfolio of banks was above 30 percent, despite a sequence of intervention of the CNB to clean banks portfolios since the start of reforms. Second, as a result of privatization strategy, the relations between banks and firms became fuzzy. As in other reforming countries, a hydra of nontransparent relations developed, through a chain of control rights that obscure the real position of banks and firms. This likely gave rise to insider lending, with a consequent weakening of banks' portfolios. In addition, insufficient regulation and supervision permitted the growth of weak small banks that failed in several cases, providing an image of weak and unstable banking sector.

12.7. The Experience of the Czech Republic: the Road to the Currency Crisis

During 1990 the crown was devalued three times, moving from 14.29 to 28 crowns per dollar at the end of 1990 (Janackova, 1994). Starting in January 1991, the crown was pegged to a basket of currencies, including the German mark, the U.S. dollar, the Austrian shilling, the Swiss franc, and the British pound. The weights were supposed to remain constant for twelve months. For two years the exchange rate remained fixed. In May 1993 the basket was modified and reduced to only the dollar and the mark counting for 35 percent and 65 percent of the basket, respectively. The exchange rate was allowed to oscillate within a band of ±0.5 percent. In February 1996 the band was widened to ±7.5 percent. The exchange rate remained around the central parity in the first half of 1996, to move afterwards in the appreciation area. In May 1997, following the attack on the koruna the CNB abandoned the band and adopted a managed float system.

In this section we evaluate the Czech experience on the basis of recent experiences in Latin America and on the basis of the discussion of analytical models presented above.

12.7.1. Empirical Evidence on Other Developing Countries

Table 12.4 reports indicators of currency crisis and variables that may be correlated with them. The crisis index is measured in terms of the extent of devaluation of the exchange rate after the attack to the currency. According to the discussion in Section 12.6, indicators of vulnerability to a currency crisis are (1) the magnitude of real exchange-rate appreciation before the crisis, (2) the presence of a lending boom, and (3) the ratio of M2 to gross reserves.

Comparing the Czech Republic with the sample contained in Table 12.4, one obtains the following results (Table 12.5). First, the index crisis is well below the level reached in Mexico and in countries like Argentina affected by the tequila effect of the Mexican crisis. The Czech crown devalued by about 10 percent during the crisis. Second, there was not a lending boom effected by domestic banks. Credit to GDP increased by 14 percent during the period 1992 to 1996. Third, the reserve adequacy indicator was more favorable in the Czech Republic. The ratio of M2 to central bank reserves was 3.3 in 1996 (in Mexico it was 9.1). Finally, the indicator of real exchange-rate appreciation was the only one comparable to the crisis countries. From January 1991 to March 1997, the crown appreciated by 43

Table 12.4. Crisis and financial indicators (percentage change, except where indicated)

Country	*Crisis Index*[a] *(IND)*	*Real Depreciation*[b] *(RER)*	*Lending Boom*[c] *(LB)*	*Reserves Adequacy*[d] *(M2/R)*
Argentina	20.2	48.0	57.1	3.6
Brazil	17.7	−29.6	68.3	3.6
Chile	−5.7	−7.5	13.3	1.4
Colombia	4.2	9.2	20.5	1.5
India	−1.2	43.0	−3.1	6.3
Indonesia	1.3	11.8	0.7	4.6
Jordan	−1.5	35.5	4.2	2.5
Korea	−3.7	−10.3	8.4	6.5
Malaysia	−2.6	9.8	4.0	2.1
Mexico	79.1	−28.5	116.2	9.1
Pakistan	0.7	20.4	−7.7	6.6
Peru	−2.9	−45.4	156.1	1.5
Philippines	7.2	−6.7	50.0	4.1
South Africa	1.1	−6.8	8.1	21.5
Sri Lanka	0.7	1.2	28.9	2.0
Taiwan	4.4	16.2	46.0	4.7
Thailand	−1.8	0.2	39.2	3.7
Turkey	−2.5	−12.1	−32.8	3.2
Venezuela	7.6	16.2	−38.5	1.4
Zimbabwe	1.6	44.2	55.7	2.6

a. The crises index (IND) is a weighted average of the exchange-rate devaluation rate with respect to the U.S. dollar and the percentage change in foreign-exchange reserves between November 1994 and April 1995. Because the two series have different volatilities, the weights applied to each series (for each country) are given by the relative precision (the inverse of the variance) of each series over the past ten years.

b. Real depreciation of the exchange rate (RER) is the percentage point change in the real exchange-rate index between the average of 1986 to 1989 and the everage of 1990 to 1994. The real exchange-rate index is a weighted sum of bilateral exchange rates (using domestic and foreign (CPI) against the dollar, the mark, and the yen). The weights sum to one and are proportional to a country's bilateral trade share with the United States, the European Union, and Japan. Note that a positive (negative) value of RER signifies that the real exchange rate is depreciated (appreciated), relative to the base period.

c. Lending boom (LB) is the percentage change between 1990 and 1994 in the ratio of the size of the claims of banking sector (demand deposit banks and monetary authorities) on the private sector to GDP.

d. Reserve adequacy (M2/R) is the ratio of the broad measure of the money stock, M2, to the stock of foreign-exchange reserves in November 1994.

Table 12.5. Czech republic: indicators of vulnerability to currency crisis

	1992	*1993*	*1994*	*1995*	*1996*
Money and official reserves					
M2/CNB reserves	25.1	6.4	4.8	2.8	3.3
M2/Total reserves	5.9	4.0	3.4	2.3	2.4
Credits to firms and households in real terms (deflated by PPI index)					
Total	100.0	103.4	114.7	120.6	127.3
In crowns	100.0	102.3	111.6	110.9	114.4
In foreign currency	100.0	138.8	221.4	459.2	579.9
Total credit/gdp	100.0	104.3	112.8	113.2	114.4
Credit and deposits by maturity					
Credit	100.0	100.0	100.0	100.0	100.0
Short term	38.3	41.2	40.7	41.9	43.3
Medium term	27.3	28.8	30.1	29.1	25.9
Long term	34.4	30.0	29.2	29.0	30.8
Deposits	100.0	100.0	100.0	100.0	100.0
Short term	71.9	72.1	72.0	72.1	75.8
Medium term	20.5	21.0	22.6	22.3	18.1
Long term	7.6	6.9	5.4	5.6	6.2
Mismatch	1.88	1.75	1.77	1.72	1.75
Commercial bank interest-rate spread					
Difference	7.0	7.1	5.9	5.8	5.8
Ratio	2.1	2.0	1.9	1.8	1.9
Interest rates					
Lending	13.5	14.1	13.1	12.8	12.5
Ppi	9.9	13.1	5.3	7.6	4.8
Real	3.3	0.9	7.4	4.9	7.4
Deposits	7.2	7.0	7.1	7.0	6.8
Cpi	11.1	20.8	10.0	9.1	8.8
Real	−3.5	−11.4	−2.7	−2.0	−1.9
Wages: percentage changes with respect to previous year					
Nominal wages	22.50	25.30	18.50	17.50	18.00
Real consumer wages	10.26	3.73	7.73	7.70	8.46
Real producer wages	11.46	10.79	12.54	9.20	12.60

Source: Author's calculations on CNB, OECD, and IMF data.

percent, a figure similar to Argentina and almost twice as large as that of Mexico.

In sum, the real appreciation of the exchange rate appears the main element of similarity between the Czech Republic and crisis-prone countries. Yet the crisis of May 1997 raises the important question on why did it happen even though—on the surface—most indicators pointed to a stable situation. These indicators would have indeed suggested that the real appreciation was an equilbrium phenomenon, without any need to be reversed. However, if one assumes that there was an overshooting of the real appreciation, due to a sequence of exogenous shocks (capital flows) and endogenous response of the economy, including policy response, then the crisis can be interpreted as an acceleration of the needed adjustment toward an equilibrium—more depreciated—exchange rate.

The simple analysis of macroeconomic flow indicators, however, is not sufficient to provide a convincing answer. Indeed, the current account deteriorated sharply in 1995 to 1996 (Tables 12.6 and 12.7). This deficit was only partially financed by capital inflows; it also caused a gradual decline in

Table 12.6. Czech republic: trade balance and current account, 1993 to 1996 (in percent of GDP)

	1993	*1994*	*1995*	*1996*
Trade balance	1.1	1.2	7.9	11.5
Current account[a]	–0.4	0.1	2.9	8.6

[a] Negative sign indicates a surplus.

Table 12.7. Czech republic: GDP, consumption, and investment (percentage change with respect to previous year)

	1993	*1994*	*1995*	*1996*
GDP	–0.9	2.6	4.8	4.4
Consumption	2.0	3.0	3.4	5.0
Households	2.9	5.3	6.4	6.0
Government	–0.1	–2.3	–4.3	1.9
Investment	–2.2	22.1	36.8	21.2
Fixed	–7.7	17.3	16.1	12.4
Inventories[a]	–11.1	–8.1	16.4	–6.3

[a] In billions of Czech crowns.

official reserves. Thus, there were signs of a trend toward a Krugman's-type balance-of-payments crisis induced by unsustainable fundamentals. However, a widening current account would be predicted by the consumption-smoothing model. Is it the magnitude of the current account deficit that argues against an interpretation based on optimal consumption smoothing? This is hard to say. Additional indicators are needed to establish whether the growing current-account deficit reflected an unsustainable underlying situation that triggered the crisis or whether the latter emerged for reasons largely independent of fundamentals—as stated by Tosovsky in the quotation at the start of this paper.

The more recent literature on currency collapse has emphasized three main aspects, relevant for the Czech experience. First, currency crises tend to be associated with a fragile financial sector. In this respect, currency crises resemble financial crises studied, for instance, by Minsky. The idea is that the crisis is preceded by a weakening of the financial sector. This can take place through a mismatch between the maturity of deposits and loans, a mismatch by currency composition of deposits and loans, or a deterioration of the quality of the loan portfolio not matched by provisions. All three aspects characterized, for instance, the currency crisis in Mexico in 1994, and ultimately the weakening of the financial sector, mainly the banking sector, was affected by a lending boom that represented the intermediation of the funds brought in by the capital inflows.

As noted above, such a lending boom did not occur in the Czech Republic. Nevertheless, the fragility of the banking sector was an important factor in increasing vulnerability to a currency attack. Since the start of reforms, the Czech banking system was plagued with a large share of inherited bad loans. Several measures were taken to isolate the banking system from the influence of such loans. However, bad loans continued to accumulate over time. Estimates are that even in 1995 to 1996 about 30 percent of the loan portfolio was either doubtful or clearly nonperforming.[8]

Another important aspect is that a large component of capital inflows took the form of borrowing by firms and banks (Table 12.8). Thus, capital inflows reflected also the inefficiencies of the domestic financial sector. This can be easily seen from Table 12.5, which displays extremely high and persistent interest-rate spread. Interest-rate differentials with foreign interest rates remained high, above 6 percentage points, and increasing after 1994 in coincidence with the large capital inflows.

As expectations of devaluation increased, debtors in foreign currency tried to extinguish their debts. Simultaneously, demand for foreign currency by households increased in 1996 (CNB, 1997).

In sum, although on the surface the conditions of the Czech Republic

Table 12.8. Branch structure of total tangible investiments (at 1994 prices, according to prevailing activity of firms (NACE), in percent and growth rates)

	1993	*1994*	*1995*	*1996*	*Growth Rate 95/93*	*Growth Rate 96/95*
Total in bilions of Czech crowns	284.5	332.6	380	411.4	33.6	8.3
Total in percent	100	100	100	100		
Agriculture, hunting, and related activities	3	3.7	2.9	2.8	31.5	4.5
Mining of coal and lignite; extraction of peat	2.3	1.8	1.5	2	–13.2	48.7
Manufacturing industry	26.4	25	19.8	21.6	0.0	18.3
Manufacture of food products and beverages	4.4	3.6	2.5	3.1	–23.9	33.6
Manufacture of chemical products[a]	2.8	2.6	1.6	2.2	–22.9	46.4
Manufacture of other nonmetallic-mineral products	3.1	2.4	2.4	2.3	3.2	3.7
Manufacture of basic metals	2.9	2	1.6	2.2	–26.7	47.3
Manufacture of machinery and equipment	1.6	1.7	1.4	1.4	16.7	9.2
Manufacture of motor vehicles, trailers, and semitrailers	2.4	2.8	2	3.1	14.8	64.8
Electricity, gas steam, and hot water supply	8.4	9	15.8	10.2	149.6	–30.1
Construction	2.3	2.4	2.3	1.9	32.8	–9.1
Wholesale trade and commission trade, except of motor vehicles	2.1	4.9	3.9/1.5	1.6	145.3	17.6
Land transport; transport via pipelines	2.8	4.1	3.7	5.1	79.1	50
Post and telecomunications	4	3.4	5.3	7.5	76.5	52.7
Banking[b]	9.3	9.5	10.2/12.6	12	46.4	3.3
Public administration and defense; compulsory social security	11.5	11.7	11.6	11.8	34.4	10.6
Health and veterinary care, social activities	3	3	2.7	2.1	18.9	–13.9

Source: CSO Division of Investment, Construction and Energy Statistics.

a. In 1996 a portion of firms active in coking, oil refining, nuclear flues, and other radioactive elements manufacture was included into the branch “manufacture of chemical products.”

b. Investments of firms providing financial leasing services are in the period 1993 to 1995 partly recorded within wholesale trade and partly within banking. In the following period of 1995 to 1996 they are recorded, in accordance with NACE, only within banking.

prior to the May crisis appeared different from the crisis-prone countries, a closer look at the conditions of the financial sector point to greater similarity.

Nevertheless, we argue in the next section that the Czech crisis fits rather well into the Obstfeld model of endogenous credibility, in which the weakening credibility of the exchange rate parity depended crucially on the combination of deteriorating current account and slowdown of economic activity. Policies adopted likely contributed to the process. It remains unclear whether the real exchange rate overshot its long-run level or the depreciation after the crisis represents an episode along a trend of still appreciating exchange rate.

12.7.2. An Interpretation of the Czech Episode

To evaluate the Czech crisis, its possible causes and consequences, we begin by addressing the issue of the extent of the real appreciation of the exchange rate.

12.7.2.1. Indicators of Real Exchange Rates. Charts 1 and 2 display the behavior of several indicators of exchange rate of the crown in the 1990s. Chart 1 reports the behavior of an effective exchange rate, based on a weighted average of the exchange rate against the dollar and the mark. This basket was relevant from May 1993 to 1997. The nominal rate remained rather stable throughout transition. As the rate of inflation in the Czech

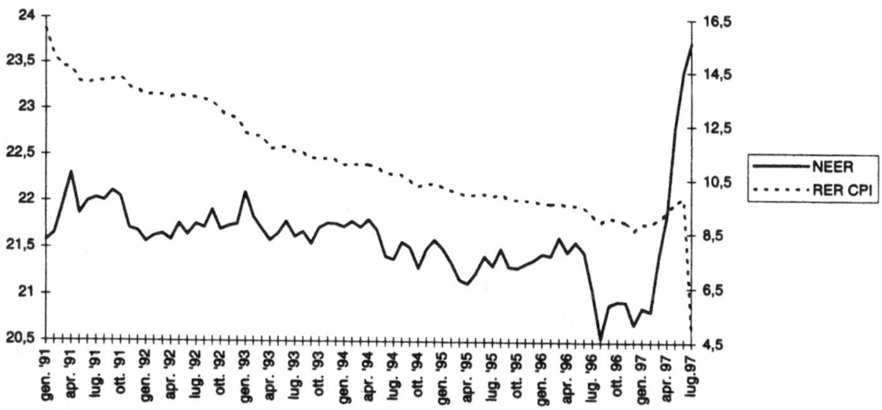

Chart 1. German Mark (65%) and US dollar (35%)

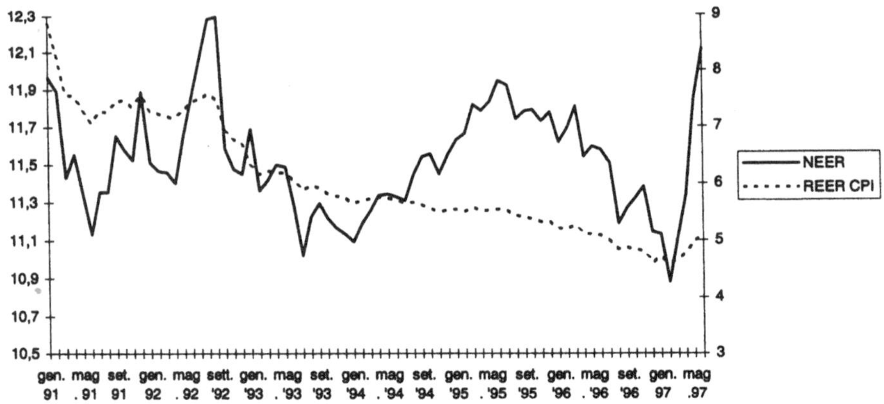

Chart 2. Effective exchange rates (weights based on trade data)

Republic remained well above the rate of inflation in Germany and the United States, the real exchange rate continuously appreciated. The cumulative appreciation, measured in terms of consumer prices, in the period January 1991 to March 1997 was about 46 percent. Because of the sharp depreciation in 1990, it is unclear whether the Czech crown was overvalued. Several observers considered the exchange rate in 1995 as still significantly undervalued, on the basis of purchasing-power-parity (PPP) rates. Hrncir (1995), for instance, estimated for mid-1995 a PPP of 17 crowns per U.S. dollar against an actual rate of 26.1. Halpern and Wyplosz (1995) as well argued in 1995 that the real exchange rate of the Czech Republic had to appreciate.

These views receive some further support from an index of real exchange rates based on trade weights (instead of the simple basket comprising U.S. dollars and deutsch marks). Chart 2 displays the behavior of such index, indicating a smaller appreciation with respect to trade partners. Considering the whole period, it does not make a large difference if one considers the real exchange rate in terms of producer or consumer prices. Concentrating on the period of significant capital inflows (1994 to 1996) yields different results. From January 1994 to September 1996 the trade-weighted PPI-based real exchange rate appreciated by 7 percent, while the CPI-based rate appreciated twice as much, by 14 percent.

As argued in the preceding sections, a definition of the real exchange rate based on indicators of competitiveness or PPP calculations may not be very useful as a guide for short- to medium-term behavior of the exchange rate. Indeed, the trade and current accounts of the balance of payments

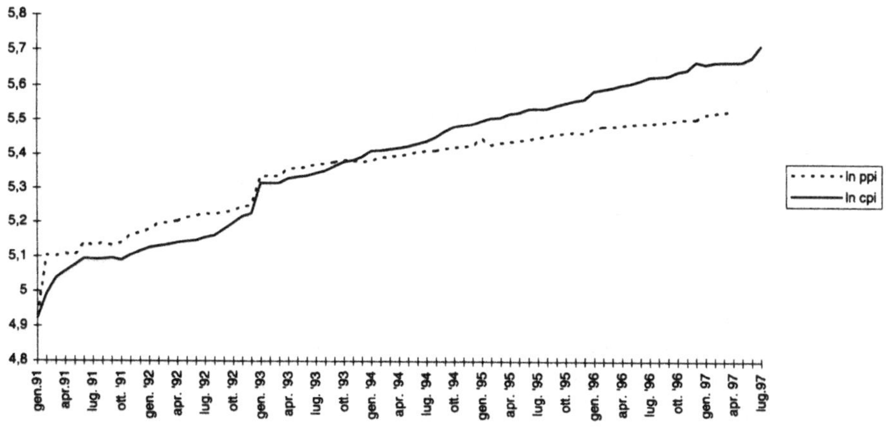

Chart 3. Inflation rate

crucially depends on intertemporal considerations. These considerations give a dominant role to expectations of the public on the future behavior of exchange rates and to policies affecting interest rates. Moreover, in this approach, the capital account of the balance of payments is not simply a financing item of the current account. In fact, the capital account can affect the behavior of the current account, depending on how the public interprets the degree of temporariness of the inflows. Finally, the public anticipates the policy of the authorities. As keeping a certain level of exchange rate may imply significant costs, the public may establish a threshold after which it assumes that sooner or later the authorities will abandon the exchange-rate parity (or the band). The state of the economy plays a key role in this respect. The public is likely to assume that the government will not defend the exchange rate if this implies significant output costs in a context of an economy that is already slowing down. This aspect is usually compounded by political constraints. A weak government is unlikely to sacrifice further its popularity to maintain the exchange rate. These factors played a key role in the Czech experience.

Going back to exchange-rate indicators, if the intertemporal model is relevant, perhaps a more significant indicator of the level of the exchange rate is the relative price of tradable and nontradable goods. This relative price can be approximated by the comparison between the CPI index, which contains a large component of nontradable goods, and the PPI index, mainly affected by tradable goods. Chart 3 displays the behavior of these indices during 1991 to 1997. Interestingly, from 1991 to 1994 producer prices were above the CPI index, while starting in 1994 consumer prices moved well ahead of producer prices. This seems consistent with a view that by 1994 the initial undervaluation of the exchange rate determined by the sharp devaluations of 1990 had been eroded. Interestingly, this approach is confirmed by evaluating the equilibrium exchange rate as the one keeping balanced the current account of the balance of payments, which was indeed balanced in 1994. Since 1994 the increase in capital inflows, combined with the maintenance of a fixed exchange rate system and a policy response leading to high domestic interest rates, caused a temporary and large overvaluation of the real exchange rate. Similar indications come from direct measures of the price of tradable and nontradable goods in the consumer price index. During 1996 the rate of inflation for nontradable goods was almost twice as large as that of tradables (12.5 and 6.7, respectively) (CNB, 1997).

These price trends are also consistent with the dynamics of the trade balance and current account of the balance of payments.

12.7.2.2. The Current Account of the Balance of Payments. The sharp appreciation of the real exchange rate (ratio of tradable over nontradable goods prices) that took place starting in 1994 was associated with a worsening current account of the balance of payments. The deterioration was particularly strong in 1996. The trade account, however, provides a more revealing picture. During 1995 to 1996 the trade account deteriorated by almost twenty percentage points of GDP with respect to 1994. A certain dose of skepticism on the "equlibrium" nature of this trend may be warranted. The changing factors behind the large gap between demand and supply are even more revealing than the pure magnitude of the current account deficit. During 1994 to 1995 the widening current-account deficit was mainly determined by an increase in investment, both fixed and, in 1995, in inventories. In contrast, in 1996, consumption grew faster than GDP, while investments, although still buoyant, decelerated sharply their rate of growth, compared to 1995.

Two facts stand out. First, consumption outpaced GDP growth because of a significant change in government consumption. Government consumption, which declined during 1991 to 1995, marked an increase of 1.9 percent in 1996. The change was particularly large if compared with the fall of 4.3 percent in 1995. Thus, the trend in government expenditure clearly changed. Recall that in the cross-country regression analysis on currency crises by Sachs, Thornell, and Velasco (1996), government expenditure was the only significant fiscal indicator.

Second, inventory behavior changed during 1996. Inventory increased during 1995. They kept increasing during the first three quarters of 1996 but then dropped sharply in the last quarter, in response to the tightening of monetary policy as well as increasing expectations of depreciation of the exchange rate. On the supply side two related facts are worth noting. First, the massive capital investment during 1993 to 1996 did not bring large productivity gains (labor productivity increased by 3.2 percent in 1996). By 1996 economywide labor productivity was still below the level in 1990. The ratio of fixed investments to GDP was above 36 percent in 1995 and 34 percent in 1996, values well above those of advanced market economies, ranging between 15 and 25 percent. Thus the productivity of investments remain low. A main cause of this phenomenon is that investments were concentrated in the nonmanufacturing sector. Table 12.9 shows that during the period 1993 to 1995 the remarkable growth in fixed investments took place exclusively in the nonmanufacturing sectors. Real investments in manufacturing did not increase during that period. Only in 1996 manufacturing investments began to grow as well. Furthermore, a large proportion of investments goods were imported (Table 12.10). This may contribute to a low multiplier effect of investment expenditure.

The second observation relates to the dynamics of exports, which grew only 3.5 percent in 1996, in the face of an increase in imports by 12.7 percent. In real terms, exports of goods remained flat in 1996. While the unsatisfactory performance of exports partly reflected slow growth in export markets, it also raises the question on lack of effects that high investments in productive capacity had on overall exports.

In sum, the behavior of the real economy casts some doubts on a "benevolent" view of the current account as determined by the needed investment and restructuring of the economy. Low efficiency of investment, combined with low unemployment may signal lack of deep restructuring of the economy.

Another factor that may have recently affected negatively the supply response is the sharp increase in real wages. In the period 1994 to 1996 real wages increase by more than 8 percent per year, about three times the increase in productivity in the same period. This increase determined a deterioration of the financial performance of firms. In enterprises with more than twenty-five employees, profit-to-output ratios declined from 7.5 in 1995 to 5.3 in 1996. The number of loss-making firms increased by 12 percent (CNB, 1997).

Growth of output slowed down during 1996. In the latter part of 1996 and first months of 1997, industrial output showed a clear downward tendency.

Table 12.9. Tangible capital investiments of import origin: By branch classification of economic activities (NACE) (current prices, according to prevailing activity of firms, in percent, without households sector)

	1993	1994	1995	1996	*Growth Rate 95/93*	*Growth Rate 96/95*
Total in billions of Czech crowns	46.8	56.6	71.7	90.3	53.0	26.0
Total in percent	100	100	100	100		
Agriculture, hunting, and related activities	2.2	2.1	2.4	3.3	70.7	75.3
Mining of coal and lignite; exstraction of peat	4.1	3.2	2.2	2.0	–19.7	18.5
Manufacturing industry	51.9	45.9	35.6	39.3	5.0	38.9
Manufacture of food products and beverages	6.9	5.8	4.0	5.0	–10.9	56.3
Manufacture of tobacco products	2.5	4.8	2.0	0.9	18.8	–41.8
Manufacture of textiles	3.3	1.9	2.3	2.1	7.0	18.8
Publishing, printing, and reproduction of recorded media	2.2	2.6	1.2	1.1	–15.5	11.7
Manufacture of chemical products[a]	6.0	3.7	2.2	2.5	–45.0	46.1
Manufacture of other non metallic-mineral products	6.5	4.2	3.8	3.8	–11.0	27.1
Manufacture of basic metals	4.0	2.4	1.7	2.7	–34.3	96.1
Manufacture of machinery and equipment	2.2	2.1	2.5	1.8	70.5	–8.4
Manufacture of electrical machinery and apparatus N.E.C.	2.4	1.9	1.5	1.9	–4.0	59.4
Manufacture of motor vehicles, trailers, and semitrailers	6.9	6.4	3.9	9.5	–14.4	210.3
Electricity, gas steam and hot water supply	4.2	8.3	23.8	9.6	760.8	–49.3
Construction	2.2	2.0	1.9	1.4	27.1	–5.6
Wholesale trade and commission trade, except of motor vehicles	2.0	3.3	3.7/2.1	2.5	188.4	49.7
Post and telecomunications	7.8	6.4	7.3	9.1	43.9	56.0
Banking[b]	7.7	8.0	5.7/7.6	12.0	13.5	100.0
Public administration and defense; compulsory social security	2.1	4.3	3.9	7.2	183.1	134.9
Health and veterinary care, social activities	3.6	4.3	3.0	2.5	25.1	5.4

Source: CSO Division of Investment, Construction and Energy Statistics.

a. In 1996 a portion of firms active in coking, oil refining, nuclear fuels, and other radioactive elements manufacture was included into the branch "manufacture of chemical products.

b. Investments of firms providing financial leasing services are in the period 1993 to 1995 partly recorded within wholesale trade and partly within banking. In the following period of 1995 to 1996 they are recorded, in accordance with NACE, only within banking.

Table 12.10. Czech republic: capital account, 1993 to 1996

	1993	*1994*	*1995*	*1996*
(i) In billions of czech crowns				
Direct investments	16.1	21.5	67.0	37.7
Portfolio investments	46.7	24.6	36.1	19.7
Other long-term capital (loans)	23.8	31.9	89.4	73.7
Other short-term capital	1.6	19.0	25.8	–20.6
Total capital account	88.2	97.0	218.3	110.5
(ii) Shares in total				
Direct investments	18.3	22.2	30.7	34.1
Portfolio investments	52.9	25.4	16.5	17.8
Other long-term capital (loans)	27.0	33.0	41.0	67.0
Other short-term capital	1.8	19.4	11.8	–18.9
Total capital account	100	100	100	100

12.7.2.3. Composition of Capital Flows. As noted above, a main difference between the Czech Republic and Latin American countries has been that capital inflows were dominated by loans to banks and firms and by foreign direct investment, rather than by portfolio investments. Table 12.8 displays the flows of capital during the period 1993 to 1996 and the weight of the different items in total flows.

The peak of inflows was reached in 1995. Direct investments and loans, especially long-term, represented the bulk of inflows. Portfolio investments played a minor role. In 1996 inflows slowed down considerable. One element has been the one-time inflow due to foreign participation in Telecom that took place in 1995. This explains the jump in FDIs in 1995 and the consequent reduction in 1996. However, the drop in inflows was not due entirely, and in fact, not even mainly, to the Telecom deal of 1995. Indeed, all forms of inflows declined in 1996. The largest fall was associated with short-term capital, which marked a switch from a positive net inflow to an outflow. Furthermore, although from relatively small flows, portfolio investments fell sharply.

Thus, in 1996 there were signs of reversal of behavior especially in the short-term, likely more speculative, flows. The adoption of the wider band and the anticipation of downward pressures on the Koruna was singled out as the main cause of the fall in inflows. This is rather puzzling, as the wider band was in principle introduced to release some of the pressure that the massive inflows had on the money supply and on the real exchange rate.

Again, it appears that economic policy was based on contradicting targets. The central bank stated that after the initial intervention of about U.S. $700 million in the first quarter of 1996 there was no intervention in the foreign-exchange market. The further decline of reserves U.S. $800 million from March to December 1996 was associated with payments of maturing obligations of the CNB.

12.8. Macroeconomic Policies

In 1995 the CNB tried to counteract the massive inflow of capital-implementing sterilization policies, which implied an estimated fiscal cost of about 1 percent of GDP (OECD, 1996). Despite sterilization, M2 grew above the target. Actual growth was 19.6 percent, and targets were 14 to 17 percent. The central bank was satisfied with developments because inflation was contained to the lower bound of the original target (7.9 percent). The fact that real interest rates increased and the trade account of the balance of payment was deteriorating were not seen as major causes for concern. In fact, the central bank continued to assume that the public expected a continuous appreciation of the Koruna. The following rather confused statement is emblematic (CNB, 1996, pp. 35–36):

> However, on the other side, the fixed exchange-rate regime, which allowed only moderate exchange-rate fluctuation around the monetary index central parity, and in connection with macroeconomic stability and the high interest-rate differential, became a strong stimulus for foreign capital influx followed by money supply growth. . . . The growing inflow of funds to the capital account and a concurrent deepening of the trade-balance deficit *brought about controversial expectations of a Czech crown revaluation or devaluation* (our italics). Due to a growing capital-account surplus (more than quadruple the current-account deficit), expectations of a nominal crown appreciation strengthened.

Thus, the fact that the deepening trade-account deficit and the massive inflow were triggered by the perception of a temporary strength of the Koruna, to be reversed in the future, was not considered a possibility by the CNB. However, if these were the views of the CNB, it is unclear why a tightening of monetary policy was needed. Indeed, expectations of an appreciation should coincide with an expectation of lower inflation. Such contradictory behavior continued in 1996.

We already noted the increase in government consumption in 1996. In the first months of 1997 it appears that loosening of fiscal policy was reflected in deficit data. The combination of looser fiscal policy and tightening of monetary policy created pressure for appreciating the real exchange rate in the second half of 1996.

In February 1996 the band was widened. This had a desired immediate effect of reversing some capital flows. The exchange rate was moving in the depreciating side of the band. However, the CNB intervened to strengthen the currency. The rationale of this policy of inframarginal intervention is unclear, and, in fact, it contributed to the difficulties of 1997. If the objective of the widening of the band was to reduce incentives for short-term speculative capital inflows and to increase the autonomy of monetary policy, the inframarginal intervention that took place in the first half of 1996 appears contradictory. With hindsight, the central bank should have used the increased flexibility to set monetary targets consistent with inflation objectives, rather than artificially strengthen the exchange rate and pave the way for another circle of tightening monetary policy, increasing interest rates, increasing capital inflow, and appreciation of the real exchange rate. This process eventually put strain on the supply response of the economy. The slowdown itself raised the perception of the likelihood of a depreciation of the exchange rate, as criticism mounted toward what was considered too tight monetary policy.

Again, it was not realized that there is a potential conflict between the monetary and inflation targets and the exchange-rate target. Probably, if the central bank had allowed the exchange rate to slide down after the introduction of a larger band, pressure on economic activity would have eased and the expectations of a collapse of the currency contained. A possible argument against this view is that a depreciation of the exchange rate would have had an immediate adverse effect on inflation. As a result, the credibility of the central bank would have been eroded, with the possibility of an attack on the currency earlier than it happened. To assess the relevance of this criticism we analyze the passthrough of exchange-rate changes to inflation.

12.8.1. The Exchange-rate-Inflation Link

Throughout the chapter it has emerged that the objective of reducing the rate of inflation was the main rationale behind the exchange-rate policy followed by the Czech authorities since the start of reforms. We disputed the policy of excessive devaluation carried out in 1990. Nevertheless, a more important issue for the Czech Republic now is whether a more flexible exchange-rate regime could be consistent with the objective of reducing inflation toward Western European levels. In this respect, it is useful to

Table 12.11. Czech republic: correlation coefficients between nominal and real effective exchange rates

	NEER	*REER*
(i) January 1991 to December 1993		
NEER	1	
REER	0.30	1
(ii) January 1994 to March 1997		
NEER	1	
REER	0.80	1

check empirically the so-called passthrough from exchange-rate changes to domestic inflation in the Czech Republic. Since February 1996 the Czech crown has been allowed to fluctuate within a band of ±7.5 percent with respect to a weighted average of dollars and marks. If we consider a trade-weighted exchange rate, we note some variability in the effective exchange rate, albeit small, even in the previous period.

If there is full passthrough from exchange rates to inflation, the movements of nominal and real exchange rates should be totally uncorrelated. Conversely, when nominal and real rates move together, passthrough is absent or only partial. Chart 2 reports the behavior of nominal and real effective exchange rates. Overall, there seems to be little correlation between the movement of the two indices. The real exchange rate moves along an appreciation trend throughout the period, while the nominal rate moves within a narrow band. However, splitting the sample in two subperiods, 1991.01 to 1993.12 and 1994.1 to 1997.03, we find that the correlation is rather high in the second subperiod, which includes the widening of the band. This is summarized in Table 12.11. In the first interval correlation is very low 0.30, while in the second it increases to 0.80. Yet correlation is far from perfect; thus there is a partial passthrough.

We replicated a regression analysis carried out by Leiderman and Bufman (1995) for Israel. The idea is to test the passthrough within a setting in which other factors affecting inflation are taken into account. Specifically, they consider the effects of exchange-rate changes on inflation in a simple monetary model. Furthermore, they evaluate whether the state of the economy has an impact on the extent of passthrough. For instance, one could observe a small response of inflation to a devaluation of the exchange rate when there is substantial slack in the economy. Thus, the coefficient on the exchange rate is a variable that depends on the state of the

Table 12.12. Czech republic: exchange-rate pass-through

Variable	*Coefficient*	*T-stat*	*2-Tail Sign.*
(i) Dependent Variable: Δ%CPI, Sample September 1991 to November 1996, Regression method: OLS			
Constant	0.007	7.40	0.0
Δ%ERATE	0.09	1.20	0.23
Δ%ERATE (–1)	–0.003	–0.04	0.97
Δ%ERATE*Δ%PROD	–1.67	–1.47	0.15
Δ%ERATE*Δ%PROD (–1)	–1.20	–1.05	0.30
Δ%(M1/Y) (–6)	–0.004	–0.51	0.61
Dummy 1993.01 and 1996.01	0.04	7.04	0.0
Adj. R-squared 0.43			
DW 2.06			
(ii) Dependent Variable: Δ%CPI, Sample, February 1994 to November 1996, Regression method: OLS			
Constant	0.006	9.19	0.0
Δ%ERATE	0.02	0.24	0.8
Δ%ERATE (–1)	0.15	2.14	0.04
Δ%ERATE*Δ%PROD	5.83	2.01	0.05
Δ%ERATE*Δ%PROD (–1)	2.83	1.12	0.27
Δ%(M1/Y) (–6)	0.02	1.98	0.058
Dummy 1996.01	0.01	3.16	0.003
Adj. R-squared 0.50			
DW 1.51			

economy. We approximated the latter with a moving average of industrial production.

The following equation was estimated for the period January 1991 to November 1996:

$$\Delta CPI = \alpha + \beta 1 * (\beta 2 + \beta 3 * \Delta PROD) * \Delta ERATE + \beta 4 * \Delta(M1/Y),^{9}$$

where ΔCPI denotes the rate of inflation; $\Delta PROD$ is the three-month moving average of the change in industrial production; $\Delta ERATE$ is the change in nominal effective exchange rate (based on trade weights); $\Delta(M1/Y)$ is change in the inverse of velocity of circulation; with Y proxied by the index of industrial production.

Table 12.12 reports the results of the regression. Since 1994.01 represents a break-point in the regression, we carried the regression also for the subperiod February 1994 to November 1996, which in fact provides more relevant results.[10]

As anticipated, the regression fares very poorly if we include the first period. Both the exchange rate and the monetary variable are insignificant. For the second period, variables are significant. The exchange rate has an effect on inflation with a lag of one month, while monetary changes are transmitted after six months. Interesting, the latter is found as well in econometric analysis of the impact of money supply on inflation by the CNB (CNB, 1997, p. 68). The coefficient of the direct effect of the exchange rate is much smaller than that found by Leiderman and Bufman for Israel (0.91), while it is closer to that found for a low-inflation country like Chile (0.38). Considering the interaction term with the state of the business cycle does not change significantly the result. Of course, this type of regression analysis should be taken as merely illustrative. Nevertheless, it points out to a small passthrough. A 10 percent depreciation of the effective exchange rate would lead to an increase in inflation of 1.5 percent. This indicates that movements in the nominal exchange rate will be absorbed by the real exchange rate and only to a small extent by inflation. While these results cast doubts on the policy pursued by the Czech Republic, they raise optimism on the effects of the depreciation that accompanied the currency crisis in May.

They also suggest that the Czech authorities should base their policy on inflation targets, adopting a more flexible exchange-rate policy—either flexible rates or a wide, possibly crawling band. However, the recent experience of other countries, like Italy, for instance, shows that crucial conditions for the compatibility between a flexible exchange-rate policy and a declining rate of inflation are wage moderation—possibly obtained through an agreement among social partners—and fiscal austerity. These are important challenges for the Czech Republic.

Acknowledgments

I wish to thank, without implicating, Giancarlo Perasso for his suggestions and exchange of views and Lucia Lorenzoni for excellent research assistance.

Notes

1. Coricelli and Milesi-Ferretti (1993) developed a similar model in the context of subsidy policy of the government. Although in a different context, they show the importance of endogenous credibility of policies. Drazen and Masson (1992) developed a model of endogenous credibility, with applications to exchange-rate policy.

2. In Hungary and Poland inflation rates in 1997 were still between 15 and 20 percent.

3. In an optimizing model with traded and nontraded sectors, Calvo, Reinhart, and Vegh (1995) show that in the context of capital controls, a real devaluation can be engineered through a nominal devaluation accompanied by tight monetary policy, as argued in the text.

4. The production function in the tradable sector is $L_t^{(0.5)}$, while that of the nontradable sector is $L_{nt}^{(0.66)}$.

5. See Obstfeld and Rogoff (1996) for an excellent discussion of this model and its extensions.

6. Mutl (1997) contains a simple formalization of what is outlined in the text.

7. One way to rationalize this assumption is that there is a home bias. Thus, residents of different countries will have slightly different portfolios.

8. Furthermore, failure of several banks contributed to give an image of a very fragile banking sector.

9. Note that abstracting from the exchange-rate term, the equation can be obtained from the "quantity" equation: $Mv = PY$, or $P = Mv/Y$; assuming v constant and taking first differences, we get the equation in the text.

10 This is confirmed by a Chow test.

References

Boeri, T., and G. Perasso. (1997). "Privatization and Corporate Governance: Some Lessons from the Experience of Transitional Economies." Mimeo, OECD, Paris.

Calvo, G. (1995). "Varieties of Capital Market Crises." Paper, University of Maryland, April.

Calvo, G., and F. Coricelli. (1992). "Stabilizing a Previously Centrally Planned Economy: Poland 1990." *Economic Policy*, 14 (April): 176–226.

Calvo, G., and C. Vegh. (1994). "Inflation Stabilization and Nominal Anchors." *Contemporary Economic Policy*, 12 (April): 35–45.

Calvo, G., C. Reinhart, and C. Vegh. (1995). "Targeting the Real Exchange Rate: Theory and Evidence." *Journal of Development Economics*, 47(1): 97–133.

Chadha, B. (1991). "Wages, Profitability, and Growth in a Small Open Economy." *International Monetary Fund Staff Papers*, 38(1): 58–82.

Chadha, B., and F. Coricelli. (1997). "Fiscal Constraints and the Speed of Transition." *Journal of Development Economics*, 52: 221–243.

Coricelli, F., and G.M. Milesi-Ferretti. (1993). "On the Credibility of 'Big Bang' Programs." *European Economic Review*, 37: 387–395.

Czech National Bank. (1996). *Annual Report 1995*. Prague: CNB.

Czech National Bank. (1997). *Annual Report 1996*. Prague: CNB.

Cukierman, A. (1995). "Towards a Systematic Comparison Between Inflation Targets and Money Targets." In L. Leiderman and L. Svensson (eds.), *Inflation Targets*. London: Centre for Economic Policy Research.

Dornbusch, R. (1980). "Monetary Stabilization, Intervention, and Real Appreciation." In *Open Economy Macroeconomics*. New York: Basic Books.

Dornbusch, R., S. Fischer, and P. Samuelson. (1997). "Comparative Advantage, Trade and Payments in a Ricardian Model with a Continuum of Goods." *American Economic Review*, 67: 823–839.

Drazen, A., and P. Masson. (1992). "Credibility of Policies and Credibility of Policymakers." Mimeo, IMF.

Halpern, L., and C. Wyplosz. (1995). "Equilibrium Real Exchange Rates in Transition." CEPR Discussion Paper Series 1145.

Hrncir, M. (1995). "Fixed Exchange-Rate Regime in The Stages of Transition: Lessons from the Czech Case." Mimeo.

International Monetary Fund. (1996). *World Economic Outlook*. Washington, DC: IMF.

Janackova, S. (1994). "Transforming the Czech Economy: Role of Convertibility and Exchange-Rate Anchor." Institute for Economics, CNB, Working Paper 24.

Klaus, Vaclav, et al. (1997). *Stabilization and Recovery Program*. May 28.

Leiderman, L., and G. Bufman. (1995). "Searching for Nominal Anchors in Shock-Prone Economies in the 1990s: Inflation Targets and Exchange-Rate Bands." Tel Aviv University, Discussion Paper 4–95.

Mutl, J. (1997). "Capital Flows and Exchange-Rate Policy." M.A. thesis, Central European University, Budapest.

Obstfeld, M., and K. Rogoff. (1996). *Foundations of International Macroeconomics*. Cambridge, MA: MIT Press.

Obstfeld, M., and K. Rogoff. (1995). "The Mirage of Fixed Exchange Rates." NBER Working Paper Series, 5191.

OECD. (1996). *OECD Economic Surveys: The Czech Republic*. Paris: OECD.

Sachs, J., A. Thornell, and A. Velasco. (1996). "Financial Crises in Emerging Markets: The Lessons from 1995." Brookings Papers on Economic Activity 1.

Sargent, T. (1982). "The Ends of Four Big Inflations." In R. Hall (ed.), *Inflation*. Chicago: NBER, University of Chicago Press.

13 TRADE, TRADE POLICY, AND FOREIGN-EXCHANGE REGIMES UNDER TRANSITION: RUSSIA AND THE DUTCH DISEASE

Gur Ofer

Hebrew University, Jerusalem

Vladimir Drebentsov

World Bank, Moscow

13.1. Introduction

Closed economies, especially highly industrialized ones, have much to gain in efficiency, in production, and in welfare from opening themselves up to world markets and free trade. This basic principle has manifested itself in recent decades through the vigorous export-led growth witnessed in a significant number of industrializing countries. It is even more appropriate for economies in transition: in addition to correcting their structural distortions and directing them toward true comparative-advantage trade patterns, opening up also introduces the principles of market economy to their domestic markets. Yet the generally radical liberalization of the trade regime and the almost full convertibility of the local currency in many formerly socialist countries were unable to prevent the initial downward trend in production. This has been partly explained by the large extent and bulkiness of the needed changes, by the high transaction (transition) costs, and by the lack of the time and resources necessary for appropriate restructuring. On the other hand, successful reorientation of trade toward the West was highly correlated with successful internal transition and with resumed economic growth (World Bank, 1996b; EBRD, 1996, 1997, 1998). Among the former socialist countries, Russia stands out as the largest country, the one most in need of restructuring, and the country with the most particular structure of comparative advantage arising from its vast natural resources. The opening of the Russian economy and its interaction with all other aspects of transition constitute the main topic of this chapter. The discussion proceeds on two levels and reflects two sources of tension. On a general level, there is tension between the potential benefits of opening up and the need to prepare the economy appropriately for restructuring, a common problem in all economies in transition (ETs). The second level of analysis deals specifically with the Russian situation and the conflict between the almost immediate ability to export natural resources and keep a positive balance of trade, and the threat this may pose to the overgrown and utterly inefficient manufacturing sector. This is a potentially extreme case of the Dutch disease that may require special policy measures. Overall, Russia's rich supply of energy and other natural resources is a blessing. The Dutch disease is a secondary negative effect that can cause much damage if not appropriately addressed.

The changes in the trade regime and in the trade and balance-of-payment flows constitute major elements in the transitions of former socialist countries. These changes are all closely interwoven and interrelated. On one hand, the changes arising from the heritage of the old system—in the structure of internal demand, the liberalization of domestic prices, the revolution in the supply network, and the internal macroeconomic policies—profoundly affect external financial and trade flows. On the other hand, decisions regarding the trade regime and exchange-rate policies, together with the development of the above-mentioned flows, help shape the nature of the other aspects of the transition process. While each of the twenty-plus countries undergoing transition has made its own decisions on the liberalization of trade and has experienced different results in its balance of payment and trade, there are a number of common policy elements in most countries:

- A far-reaching liberalization of the trade regime and the exchange rate occurred at least up to current-account convertibility and beyond. This liberalization and the simultaneous liberalization of domestic prices brought internal and external prices closer together.
- A gradual process of real appreciation of the exchange rate followed a deep initial devaluation.
- The dollar wage, a rough measure of competitiveness, started out at low levels, reflecting low initial productivity and undervalued domestic currencies. It appreciated gradually and generally resulted in reduced competitiveness and balance-of-payment difficulties. Initial

surpluses turned into deficits, creating pressure for increased protection. (Halpern and Wyplosz, 1996; EBRD, 1998, ch. 3 pp. 32–35).

- The trade structure shifted, both by destinations and by commodity groups. Typically, trade was diverted from former socialist countries toward the West, and as a result the commodity structure became less advanced. There was a modest inflow of capital of all kinds into most of the countries and capital flight from a few (EBRD, 1996, ch. 8; 1998, ch. 4; World Bank, 1996b, chs. 2, 9; Fiani and Portes, 1995).

Within this general trend there were differences among the countries with regard to policy mix and performance indicators of the external sector. These including the inherited external debt variations reflect differences in the economic system of the old regime, the endowment of natural resources, and other exogenous factors. In this respect, the former Soviet Union (FSU) and later Russia (and also Kazakhstan and Kyrgiztan) stand out as exceptions before and during the transition. This is due to the abundance of natural resources in Russia, especially energy resources, that have continually produced a lopsided trade structure and a balance-of-payment advantage. While most former socialist countries have struggled, following the opening, to export manufactured goods that were initially noncompatible with the technology and patterns of demand in the West, Russia could have offered, at least in potential almost unlimited supplies of energy resources and other raw materials to cover its need for imports. Also setting Russia apart are its large size, its pattern of relations with the other states of the FSU, as well as its former status as a world power. Finally, the transition process in Russia has been different and more difficult in a number of respects, including difficulties in achieving macroeconomic stabilization and, despite wide-ranging privatization, in restructuring and upgrading its manufacturing sector. All these manifested themselves in the crisis of August 1998, to which we return later.

This chapter surveys and analyzes the development of the trade regime and of the trade and balance-of-payment flows in Russia during the transition period 1989 to 1997 (and 1998, whenever possible). A general basis for the analysis, for all the former socialist countries, is provided by the common problems inherited from the old regime: distorted prices, a particular structure of demand and its determinants, overindustrialization, isolation from external prices and Western technology, and a different ideology and economic system. The second layer of analysis is provided by the special features of the FSU and Russia before and during the transition, as mentioned above. This a priori analysis (Section 13.2) provides the basis for the description and evaluation of the development of the trade and foreign-exchange regime in Russia (Section 13.3). In Section 13.4 the chapter describes the development of the trade and financial flows. The concluding section evaluates past developments and discusses prospects and policy options.

13.2. The Transition of the Trade Regime: A Priori Considerations

13.2.1. General Considerations

Assume a closed centrally planned economy with its own particular objective function with regard to demand and the composition of production, a unique technology vector and structure of production costs, and, therefore, a distinct set of relative prices, reflecting both supply and demand factors. Further, assume that the planning process is close to optimal and in accordance with the proper relative, shadow prices. Actual prices charged to buyers are different from shadow prices; they reflect social preferences (low rents, free social services), the desire to clear markets in which a quasi-market mechanism of distribution of consumer goods operates, and production incentives (quasi-private collective farmers). The difference between prices paid to producers and market, consumer prices, customarily called *established prices*, was collected as sales taxes or paid as subsidies. From these assumptions, it follows that purchasing prices are in many instances different from the shadow (planning) prices for both consumers and producers. It also follows that in only a few cases do these market prices also have allocative functions.

With the turnaround of the system, three major shifts take place at the same time: planners' preferences are shifted to consumer sovereignty, central planning gives way to an emerging-market mechanism, and the economy opens up to the world market. All radically change the structure of demand and the structure of relative, shadow, and market prices. With the lifting of external barriers and the elimination of internal taxes and subsidies, a uniform set of prices begins to emerge reflecting both shadow and market prices. Ignoring for the time being the resulting shifts in the production-possibility frontier (PPF), these radical changes guide the production structure of the economy in two major directions. First, it moves toward increased preference (at any set of relative prices) for consumption at the expense of military production, investment, and products of heavy industry. These shifts were also caused by the sharp decline in fiscal revenues that limits the spending ability of the governments. Household incomes also declined but to a lesser extent. In addition, there were important shifts in the structure of household consumption demand in reaction to the elimination of past anomalies and in response to changes in relative prices. Second, a diversion of production occurred in accordance with the new potential opportunities of international trade and in accordance with the new relative prices and comparative advantage.

The first change, still assuming a closed economy, is portrayed in Figure 13.1 as a shift along a PPF from Q_1 to Q_2 resulting in more household consumption and less of all other uses. Such a shift occurs even when consumer goods are at higher prices.[1] This shift reflects an increase in the level of welfare from the point of view of the consumers without an accompanying change in total production (or GNP). With the opening up for free trade,

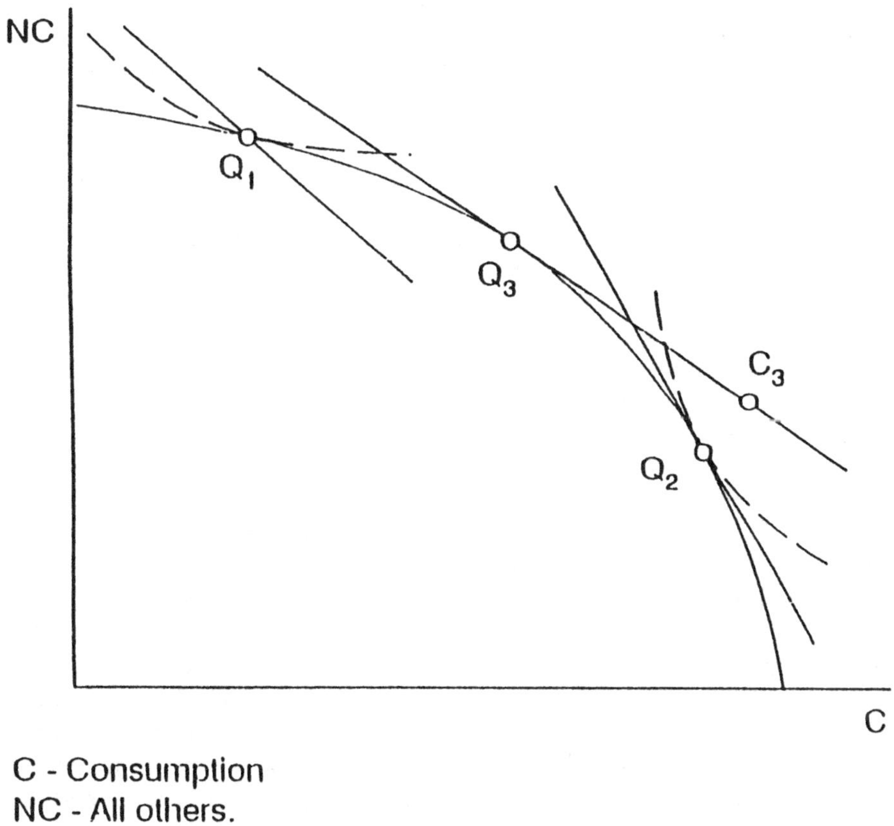

Figure 13.1. Changes in Preferences and Opening for Trade

there will be a further shift of production along the PPF in directions dictated by the differences between (new) domestic costs and world relative prices. At the same time, increased trade will further raise the level of welfare and in this case also increase the value of production and the GNP. Such a move is depicted by the shift from Q_1 to Q_3, under the assumption that consumption goods are cheaper (adjusted for quality or perceived quality) in world markets. In addition to the increase in welfare, one would also expect a resumption of economic growth, while still ignoring transaction barriers and costs and time delays.[2] Given the incompatibility of production technologies between East and West and the minimal experience exporting manufacturing goods, the initial comparative advantage of ETs should have been mostly negatively correlated with the depth of production and of the proportion of added value generated. With few exceptions, the more processing and manipulation applied to basic materials, the lower the level of competitiveness of the product.

There are two objective factors that constrain the immediate reaping of the benefits of the potential gains from trade liberalization. First is the lack of internal and external trade infrastructure, trade support institutions, laws and regulations, know-how and experience, marketing, servicing, transportation, financial and insurance services, and so on to the factors may add the burden of exterval debt inherited from the old regime. It was especially heavy for Poland, Aungary, and to a lesser degree, Russia. A number of "restricting" agreement's partially alleviated this burden (Transition Report, 1998 ch. 3). The second major factor is the need to restructure existing enterprises and production capacity to produce close to the number of potential exportables. Restructuring is a major aspect of the transition process and in some ways one of the most complex. A combination of a number of factors make restructuring especially complex: the former relative functional and technical isolation from the global economy and the overindustrialization of most of these countries. While restructuring in developing countries is related to a small and rather unsophisticated manufacturing sector, in many of the former socialist countries one must deal with manufacturing sectors that include advanced industries and that occupy 40 to 50 percent of their respective national product and a similar proportion of the labor force. A third feature of the nature of restructuring is the relatively high skill level of the labor force in ETs. While the large stock of human capital is a blessing, it imposes a particular burden and a very heavy responsibility on the nature and form of restructuring, due to the incompatibility between the high skill levels of the labor force and the obsolete technological infrastructure of manufacturing. The problem is how to restructure without losing much of the existing human capital and the capacity to continue to properly train the labor force.

The lack of appropriate trade infrastructure has a negative effect on both exports and imports. The slow or delayed restructuring reduces the competitiveness of exportables and the effective protection against importables. Trade infrastructure can be greatly improved by the importation of the relevant services. Foreign-trade companies need to be encouraged to establish offices and to offer trade and related services. Restructuring for competitiveness can also benefit from foreign investment by companies with similar lines of production. The development of both depends on the creation of an appropriate trade regime and trade mechanisms and internal economic environment: institutions and regulations, law enforcement, appropriate economic policies and entrepreneurial incentives. It may depend on prudent industrial restructuring policies on the part of government.

The exchange-rate policy and the behavior of the exchange rate are major determinants of the development of trade. In all transition economies, a number of nontrade-related factors have affected exchange-rate dynamics and thereby the conditions for the development of trade: Under conditions of inflation, economic uncertainty, and political instability, at the outset of the transition, there was an increased speculative or asset demand for foreign currency for both savings and transactions purposes since it was virtually the sole secure assets available, if not the only one. The run on foreign currency took place more commonly before the existence of alternative domestic assets like real estate, government bonds, and other types of financial papers. Capital flight was another possible outlet for such speculative demand. However, large stocks of foreign currency were still held and exchanged domestically. Such nontrade-motivated demand for foreign currency increases its price beyond the hypothetical "normal", trade equilibrium level, thus serving as a de facto additional protection for domestic production and an incentive for exports (Bosworth and Ofer, 1995, Halpern and Wyplosz, 1996; Hare, Estrin, Lugachyov, and Takla, 1996).

The opposite effect on the exchange rate is created by capital inflow, which is attracted by the vast range of investment opportunities, real and financial, in new ventures and/or in the purchase of privatized government enterprises and in government bonds and other financial papers. Such opportunities also reflect the low domestic quality of management and technology, and the great demand for Western technologies, production and market management practices, corporate governance, and other services. These factors, as well as rigid domestic macroeconomic policies, resulted in high rates of interest offered on investments. In addition, capital inflows are supplied through official aid programs of foreign governments and international organizations. All these inflows put a downward pressure on the equilibrium exchange rate and thus discourage exports and reduce the effective protection against imports.

Speculative demand for foreign currency and capital flight are more common during the early stages of the transition, while capital inflow increases during the later stages of stabilization and privatization. The dynamic, joint net effect of these forces gradually brings the exchange rate down (appreciates the value of the domestic currency) to its equilibrium trade level and at a later stage even below it. All other things being equal, this process gradually reduces the level of protection of domestic production, makes exports less profitable and increases the danger of a deficit in the current account. In recent years many ETs have been facing the dilemma of whether or not to limit portfolio capital inflows, due to their negative effect on the current account (Roubini and Wachtel, this volume, ch. 2; EBRD, 1998, ch. 3).

The above analysis assumes a nearly fully liberalized exchange rate and a high level of convertibility of the domestic currency. Nevertheless, a number of transition economies chose a variant of the fixed or pegged exchange-rate policy. In such cases the exchange rate serves also as an instrument of income policy in support of the macroeconomic stabilization effort but tends to stay at an artificially appreciated level. This policy also brings extra pressure on the current account and on export profitability and therefore also causes a policy dilemma between stabilization and competitiveness. In addition, under a fixed or pegged exchange-rate regime with net capital inflow, there is a need to neutralize the resulting monetary expansionary effect (Roubini and Wachtel, this volume, ch. 2; EBRD, 1998, ch. 3).

13.2.2. The Special Case of Russia

Russia appears to be in an inferior position compared to most other East European countries with regard to most of the considerations discussed above that affect the development of trade and competitiveness during the transition and following liberalization. (Most of the other FSU states are in even worse situations.) The reasons are as follows.

First, pretransition Russia was more orthodox in its version of socialism than other countries. The shares of military expenditure and investment were larger than in most other socialist countries, while the share of consumption was smaller. Russia was the most overindustrialized, with a manufacturing sector dominated by heavy industry. Consumption was further biased away from services, private automobiles (and related automotive goods and services), and housing. This was partially due to the planners' objective function—heavily emphasized defense and the arms race. It also resulted from the pattern of Russian trade within the FSU and the socialist bloc, consisting of the importation of food and consumer goods (and machinery) in exchange for energy and raw and basic materials. Thus, following the collapse of intrasocialist bloc trade, Russia was to experience the most extreme structural change in the composition of production. It follows also that it may have the most acute problem of fitting its very highly skilled labor force to the new production structure.

Second, the same is true with respect to the pretransition distortion of relative prices: Russia maintained the lowest prices in the bloc for energy and other raw materials. Beginning a few years after the energy crisis of 1973, Russia began to charge higher prices for energy to its socialist partners without a corresponding rise in domestic prices. While Russia paid low prices to its machinery and heavy industries, it paid higher prices for the same products imported from its neighbors.

Third, Russia was more isolated from the world market. Price differentials between international and domestic prices of traded goods were wider; there was less trade with the West in consumer goods, less use of Western technologies, and less familiarity with Western trade techniques and culture.

In addition to the above, system-driven differences, Russia is also different from almost all the other countries in transition in two other major exogenous aspects: its larger size and its abundance of reserves and production capacity of energy and other natural resources. Russia's natural endowment is a large, potentially compensating advantage, but carries with it the dangers of the Dotch Liscence.

Russia's large size makes it less vulnerable to outside trade competition and less dependent on trade due to its (potentially) large internal and diverse market. Russia's large size also limits the extent and the pace of the penetration of international prices, Western technology, and the institutions and culture of market economy. While foreign investment can become a major factor, both in quantity and content, in the smaller ETs, only an exceptionally large inflow into Russia can have a significant quantitative impact. The large size of Russia is thus a mixed blessing: it creates a breathing spell for restructuring but at the same time diminishes the extent and slows the pace of positive external influences.

The effects of the abundance of energy and other natural resources are somewhat offset by Russia's large size, but they remain dominant, particularly for trade-related issues. This gift of nature was probably instrumental in the shaping of the particular Soviet version of the socialist model. It certainly had a marked impact on the process of Soviet industrialization and on its pretransition trade patterns. The Soviet Union became a major exporter of energy resources, basic metals, and other lightly processed raw materials to the entire Soviet bloc, and energy exports constituted the bulk of exports to the West. The abundance of natural resources, including iron, aluminum, and timber (together with the emphasize on military production), also explains the bias in the industrial structure of Russia toward basic and heavy industry.

Under the old regime there were two highly divergent prices for energy resources. The domestic price was a fraction (1 to 2 percent) of the international price obtained for exports to the West. Recognizing energy as a major source of foreign-currency income, the Soviet planning authorities put a great deal of effort into the development of its production capacity. However, despite these efforts based mostly on domestic technology, during the last decade or so of the Soviet period, the pace of development of new capacity declined, and overpumping was used to keep production up. Even so, the extraction of energy can be considered as a case where pretransition production was planned in accordance with the world market price, the true shadow price. However, most of the energy produced was sold on the domestic market for much lower prices. Despite quantitative planning the low price affected the level of energy consumption and allocation, resulting in a colossal waste of resources.

Under liberalization there is therefore a large potential welfare gain from trade as depicted in Figure 13.2, following Thorenton (1996, fig. 2, p. 210). Q_3 is a production point with no exports, and C_3, with past exports, with an extremely distorted domestic price. C_3 is the postliberalization consumption point, showing lower consumption of energy in response to the higher price and the saved energy resources being exported. Without going into the rationale behind Q_3, the correct posttransition, production point is further out from the present PPF, reflecting the ability of modern Western technologies and managerial methods to increase the production of energy resources (and other raw materials), far beyond the maximum production achieved under the old regime (point Q_4). It is no wonder that the natural-resources sector has attracted the greatest interest among foreign investors, yet without leading to significant outcomes. It is therefore highly plausible that with full liberalization, the comparative advantage of Russia in natural resources is even stronger than was observed before the transition. One has also to take into account the sharp rise in the price of energy resources and other raw materials to the domestic Russian manufacturers, reducing their efficiency and making some of them completely unprofitable or even with negative value added (Thorenton, 1996; McKinnon, 1991, Erickson, 1996; Gaddy and Ickes, 1998). This further increases the comparative advantage of the raw materials sector.

The solid base for large and sustained foreign-currency income stemming from the potential exports of raw materials is in the first place a great economic advantage. It has the potential to support Russian restructuring and

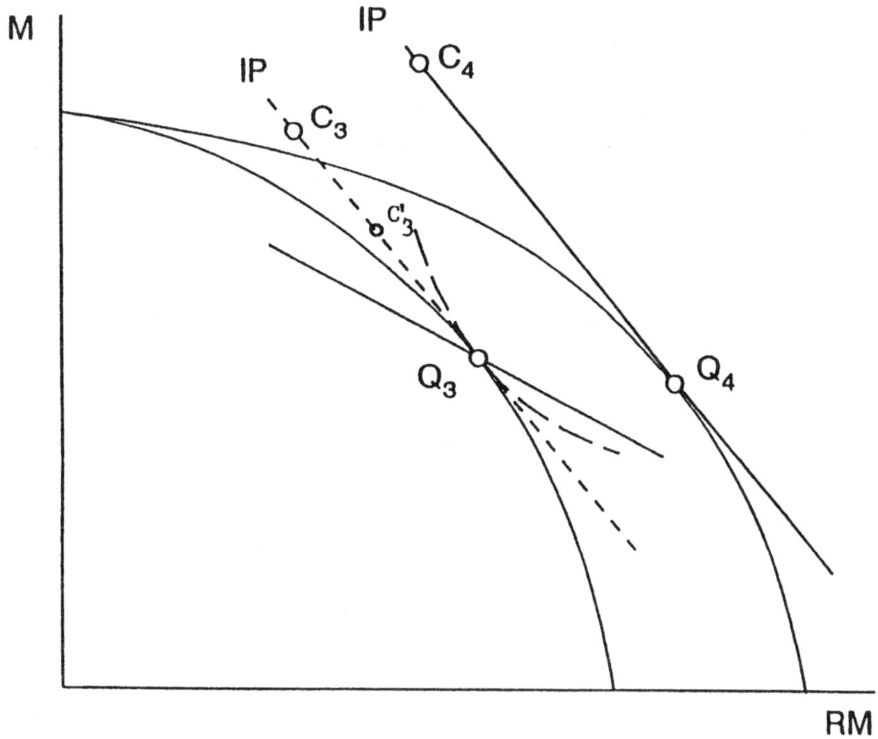

M Manufactures
RM Raw materials
DP Domestic prices
IP International prices

Figure 13.2.

transition and to improve its balance of payments. Indeed, Russia is the only country among the East European ETs that had a consistent positive trade and current-account balance throughout the period (on 1998 see below). This is a major advantage over most other ETs. At the same time it poses a serious potential danger to the overgrown and inefficient manufacturing sector. This is a description of a potentially severe variety of the Dutch disease: the common case of a Dutch disease is the discovery of an abundant raw material resource, while the ex-ante economy is in near equilibrium. Here, in addition to the discovery manifested in the act of opening up, there is also an ex-ante state of extremely distorted domestic prices and of an inappropriate and inefficient manufacturing sector. The latter will also face a steep increase in energy prices, imposing on it further hardship.[3] It is therefore not unreasonable to assume that with the sudden liberalization of the price of energy and full liberalization of trade, there will not be enough time for many potentially sound manufacturing industries to restructure before being drowned by a flood of imports. There will be also a large number of enterprises that will not and should not recover. Russia's large size may provide only a partial shield. This is the main difference between Russia and most other ETs, and it has a very significant impact on trade and the balance of payments, the foreign-exchange regime, and trade policies. While the other ETs must find their comparative advantages somewhere inside their manufacturing sectors, with much efforts and lower wages, Russia may find most of its manufacturing industries to be unprofitable, especially with the appreciated rate of exchange. Such a situation may dictate a particular and different set of policies (Bosworth and Ofer, 1995; Eismont and Kuralbaeva, 1998; and many references on the economics of the Dutch disease, there).

13.3. Trade Regime and Exchange-Rate Policies and Outcomes

13.3.1. Introduction

Russian foreign-exchange regime and trade policies from 1992 to 1998 were basically consistent with its trade position as described above. There were three major trends and some oscillations.

First, the foreign exchange was fully liberalized a few months following the start of the liberalization reforms in early 1992. While there were formal restrictions on capital outflows, foreign currency was de facto legal tender for all kinds of internal transactions and accumulation (saving). Later on, some mildly effective restrictions on transactions in foreign currency were introduced. There was current-account convertibility, subject to limitations discussed below. Until the end of 1995, the rate of exchange responded to the market forces with only relatively minor attempts at intervention by the central bank. During the first three years the nominal rate of exchange depreciated very fast; however, except during the first month of 1992, it occurred at a somewhat lower pace than domestic prices. This resulted in a gradual process of real appreciation (See Table 13.1 and Figure 13.3 below). Since the beginning of 1996, when the rate of inflation also subsided to low two-digit annual rates, the Central Bank of Russia (CBR) shifted to a policy

Table 13.1. Wages, exchange rates, and inflation, 1991 to 1997

	1991	*1992*	*1993*	*1994*	*1995*	*1996*
Monthly wages (rubles)	548	5,995	58,663	220,351	472,392	802,745
Monthly wages (1991 rubles)	548	230	239	281	262	365
Monthly wages (U.S. $)	315	28	63	100	103	157
Monthly wages (PPP $)	227	177	176	167	188	228
Average nominal exchange rate (MICEX) Rb/$	1.74	216	928	2,205	4,566	5,126
Real exchange rate	1.74	8.27	3.78	2.81	2.53	2.33
PPP average exchange rate (RB/$)	2.41	33.8	333	1,318	2,508	3,535
Average nominal exchange rate/PPP average exchange rate	0.72	6.39	2.79	1.67	1.82	1.45
CPI deflator, 1991 = 100	1.00	26.10	245	785	1,806	2,199
Monthly wages (1991 rubles)	1.00	0.42	0.44	0.51	0.48	0.67
Monthly wages (U.S. $)	1.00	0.09	0.20	0.32	0.33	0.50
Monthly wages (PPP $)	1.00	0.78	0.78	0.74	0.83	1.00
Real exchange rate	1.00	4.75	2.17	1.61	1.45	1.34
Average nominal exchang rate/PPP average exchange rate	1.00	8.86	3.87	2.32	2.52	2.01

Source: Goskomstat of RF, CEM, MICEX, SNA, *PlanEcon Report.*

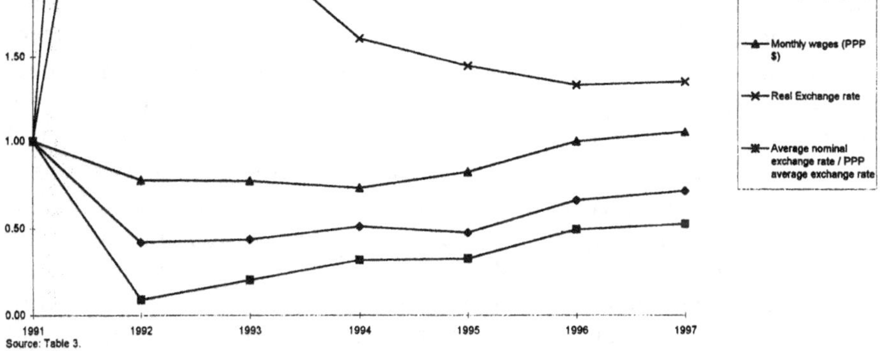

Figure 13.3. Wages and Exchange Rates
Source: Table 13.1.

of a managed or pegged exchange rate, which was officially announced in mid-1996. Initially there was a horizontal band, adjusted every six months, and from 1997 on it turned into an upward sloping one. Practically, the CBR kept the exchange rate almost fixed, except for the periodic adjustments, and then along the center of the corridor, ready to sell and buy foreign exchange to protect the rate. For the first time during the transition there was a period of real depreciation of foreign exchange, by about 6 percent during the third quarter of 1996. Nevertheless, slow appreciation of the ER continued until the devaluation and crisis of August 1998. (On the crisis and its aftermath, see below.)

The second major policy cluster, trade policy, was addressed in general to soften the shock of the initial devaluation and depreciation but specifically, even if not deliberately, it was due to severe shortages, and addressed the problem of the Dutch disease described above. Right from the start, severe administrative restrictions were imposed on exports of energy, metals, and other raw materials. At the same time imports were subsidized. Since then and until August 1998, there has been a consistent trend of gradually reducing the restrictions on exports and of moving from subsidization of imports to (so far) mild protection. Part of this anomaly is a response to the overprotection provided by the initially overdevalued exchange rate. But it has also provided a breathing spell for (mostly) manufacturing to restructure. These policy trends came to at least a temporary halt by the crisis of August 1998, which brought the macroeconomic environment for trade back to the situation of early 1992. The ruble has been devalued steeply to about half of its precrisis value by January 1999, pushing the government to reconsider some previously announced tariff restrictions on imports and at the same time awakening old policies of taxing exports, both by tariff and nontariff instruments.

The third policy cluster is related to the creation of proper institutional infrastructure and mechanisms for the optimal conduct of trade. In addition to the nuts-and-bolts type elements, like border stations, proper forms, and protocols, there are also aspects of uniform processes, such as unified tax rates (whenever applicable)—all arrangements that minimize distortions. Many of these elements are required of members of the WTO, which Russia aspires to join. While new trade mechanisms and routines had to be (re)created with respect to all destinations, there were specific difficulties in the organization of trade with the CIS countries that had to start from scratch and also with former CMEA countries, where trade had to be reorganized on a completely different basis. These requirements and difficulties may have been the main reasons for the slow development of trade with the old and newly created neighbors, trade that picked up steam only very recently (Drebentsov, 1995, 1997; Becker, 1996).

In what follows, we survey the developments of the second and third clusters, with an emphasis on the second (more details can be found in Konovalov, 1994; Drebentsov, 1995; Bosworth and Ofer, 1995, ch. 3).

13.3.2. Trade Policy, 1992 to 1998

As a result of persistent domestic shortages inherited from the Soviet central-planning era, Russian commercial policy, as it emerged in 1992, had been an anomaly. In contrast to the development of trade policy in other countries, Russia's import policy was initially very liberal, while exports were subject to almost every conceivable restriction. In addition to the shortages, the extreme undervaluation of the local currency immediately following the liberalization of the exchange rate just prior to 1992 has contributed to the softness of the government's import policy and the rigidity of export limitations during the early years of reform.

Not surprisingly, the appreciation of the ruble in real terms, the growing import penetration—reaching 60 to 70 percent in some local markets, including Moscow and other major markets (Expert Institute, 1997, ch. 3)—and the narrowing gap between domestic and international prices have caused commercial policy to evolve toward a more familiar international pattern. The government's liberal stance on imports has been steadily evaporating as a result of attacks from outdated Russian industries that are seeking protection against the inflow of foreign goods. Meanwhile, export restrictions had apparently become redundant and had been abolished one after another. As noted above, the 1998 financial crisis stopped these trends, calming down calls for protection and leading to the reintroduction of all kinds of export restrictions.

In addition to macroeconomic changes, Russia's close dialogue with international financial institutions carrying out various assistance programs in the country, in particular the IMF and World Bank, has played an important role in defining Russian trade policy. Russia's entry into the WTO is also influencing trade policy, though this process is currently at a rather early stage. This has become particularly apparent following the crisis, when the government has found it especially difficult to renege on trade policies previously agreed on with the IMF and the World Bank. Even so, by January 1999, a 5 percent export tax on energy and other materials was imposed, with the IMF even pushing for a higher rate, mostly on fiscal grounds.

Finally, Russia's membership in the CIS and, more recently, the formation of the customs union with Belarus, Kazakhstan, and Kyrgyzstan has added to the peculiarity of Russia's commercial policy. Not only has this created three different trade policies—one with customs union members, one with the rest of the CIS (or so-called near abroad), and one with the rest of the world (far abroad)—but it has also affected the choice of specific trade-policy measures implemented in each of the three-trade partner groups. The latter was clearly illustrated in 1996, when Russia resorted for the first time in its history to triggering the Safeguards mechanism envisaged in the GATT/WTO Articles. In this case, trade agreements with the CIS determined the selection of quantitative restrictions over import duties in Russia's attempt to cut imports of ethyl alcohol and vodka (this will be discussed in greater detail). Apparently, there measures would have affected the regime of trade with countries outside the CIS as well, if they had been implemented.

The discussion of Russia's evolving commercial policy during the years of reform is divided into two parts. The first deals with the history of export restrictions, and the second discusses the dynamics of the import regime.

13.3.2.1. Export Control. Government Decree No. 90 (December 31, 1991) laid the basis for extensive export control in the new Russia. First, almost all exports, accounting for over 90 percent of the total value, were subject to licensing. Second, most exports (such as oil and oil products, natural gas, coal, timber, newsprint, pig iron, steel, ferrous metals rolls, all nonferrous metals, fertilizers, fish, and so on) were subject to export quotas as well. Moreover, Decree No. 91 was passed at the same time and established an export tax scheme affecting a broad range of commodities (with the exception of most foodstuffs). All possible impediments were placed in the way of Russian exports. It comes as no surprise, therefore, that the very reasons that made imports desirable at the beginning of the reform made exports equally undesirable in the eyes of the authorities.

Beginning July 1, 1992, two decrees went into effect. Decree No. 349 was passed by the Ministry of Foreign Economic Relations on June 17, 1992, and abolished the mandatory registration of companies involved in foreign trade. Decree No. 434 was passed on June 26, 1992, and shortened the list of goods that exporters were allowed to ship abroad without restrictions. The latter decree introduced a list of over 190 strategic commodity groups (mainly at the four-digit HS level) that were permitted for export only by special exporters as designated and registered by the Ministry of Foreign Economic Relations. Initially, there were about 200 of such companies, and strategic exports accounted for over 75 percent of total exports in 1992.

With the appreciation of the ruble in real terms, particularly after the introduction of the ruble corridor in 1995, and the narrowing gap between domestic and international prices, commodities have gradually been released from export quotas, and export taxes have simultaneously been reduced (see Tables 13.2, 13.3). Of course, this process has been rather disorganized. Some commodities had been excluded from and then returned to the list of products subject to export quotas and finally all export quotas were abolished by January 1995.[4] The same has occurred to strategic exports and goods subject to regular licensing.[5] Licensing and export quotas disappeared simultaneously and were substituted for by registration of export contracts;[6] the list of strategic commodities was shortened and the category of special exporter was abolished in 1994. However, in the winter of 1998 to 1999 the government opted for some indirect restrictions on oil exports, threatening that oil companies that fail to meet their supply commitments to domestic refineries will be banned from access to export pipelines.

Also, five major revisions of the export tax scheme (and numerous ones for individual commodities) were carried out over the five years since the introduction of export duties in January 1992. During 1992 to 1995,[7] the maximum specific rate was reduced gradually from 100,000 ECU per ton to 80,000 and finally to 64,000, and the maximum ad valorem rate from 70 to 40 percent. A complete elimination of export taxes was instituted in 1996, beginning for most products on January 1 and for the rest on July 1 (oil, as usual, was the last commodity to be liberalized). Not surprising, oil happened to be the first commodity for which export tax was reintroduced in the fall of 1998, in the government's attempt to capture part of the exporters' windfall revenues, following the threefold ruble devaluation.

It would be unfair not to mention that export liberalization was not an easy process. It did not go as smoothly as it may appear seem from the above paragraphs. A strong sentiment in favor of either keeping or reintroducing both tariff and quantitative export restrictions has always existed. The Russian government was seriously discussing the return of the export tax on heavy oil and introducing export quotas for scrap ferrous and nonferrous metals as recently as the winter of 1996 to 1997. Requests for such legislation originated from the domestic consumers of these commodities. They were worried by alleged shortages on the domestic market and wanted to reduce exports. Nothing came of their efforts. A strong and firm stand by the international financial institutions in their dialogue with the government has contributed greatly to preventing backsliding in export liberalization. In fact, all the above-mentioned stages in the process of eliminating export restrictions were conditions for the receipt of IMF and World Bank loans. For instance, elimination of export quotas, the category of special exporters, and restrictive clauses of the export contract registration scheme were conditions for the IMF's Stand-by Facility and the World

Table 13.2. Export tax rate before and after changes, 1994 to 1995 (ECU per ton unless otherwise specified)

Code TN VED	*Commodity*	*As of 12/31/91*	*As of 12/11/92*	*As of 11/11/93*	*As of 7/1/94*	*Prior to Changes in 1994–1945*	*Current*	*As of 8/31/95*	*As of 12/26/95*	*4/96–5/96*	*Since 7/1/96*
0305	Frozen fish	20	20	20		10	10	7	7	0	0
2601	Metal ores and concentrates	2	1	0	0	0	0	0	0	0	0
2701	Coal	2	1	0		0	0	0	0	0	0
2709	Crude oil	38	30	30	0	30	23	20	20	10	0
27100D33	Motor gasoline	55	40	40	12	40	12	8 (2 during Nov.–March)	0	0	0
27100D55	Kerosine	52	40	40	12	40	40	10	0	0	0
27100D6	Diesel fuel	52	30	30	10	30	12	8 (3 during Oct.–Feb.)	8 (3 during Oct.–Feb.)	0	0
27100D51	Jet fuel	55	40	40	12	40	20	14	0	0	0
27100D7	Fuel oil	25	15	8	8	8	8	6 (3 during Apr.–Aug.)	6 (3 during Apr.–Aug.)	0	0
271121	Natural gas	31	18	18	5	0.5	2	2	2	0	0
281410	Ammonia	6	4	2	2	2	2	1	1	0	0
290511	Methanol	6	4	3	0	3	0	0	0	0	0
3102	Nitrogen Fertilizers	15	0	5	3	5	3	2	2	0	0
3104	Potash	15	5	3	1	3	1	0.7	0.7	0	0
3105	Mixeo fertilizers	15	6	5	1	5	1	0.7	0.7	0	0
40024	Synthetic rubber	65	65	65	65	65	65	45	45	0	0
4003	Unsaw timber	65	65	65		8	8	4	0	0	0
4407	Sawn timber	50	8	8	8	8	8	6	6	0	0
4702–4703	Cellulose	69	50	30	10	30	10	7	7	0	0
4704	Wood pulp	69	40	15	10	30	10	21	21	0	0
480100	Newsprint	71	80	0	0	0	0	0	0	0	0
7201	Recycled pig Iron	21	15	2	2	2	2	1	1	0	0
7403	Refined copper	500	400	200	100	200	200	0	0	0	0
7601	Unprocessed aluminum	200	130	70	10	70	10	0	0	0	0

Bank's Second Rehabilitation Loan; abolishing export taxes was a condition of the Extended Fund Facility.

There are four additional areas of government export control or direct involvement in exports. These export limitations originated in the government's concerns over capital flight, tax evasion, windfall profits on exports, and, finally, the rapid breakdown of economic ties with the former Soviet countries. The former two concerns prompted the government to introduce certain restrictions on barter exports and to try to implement a system of control over contract price compliance to the "quality" of commodities shipped abroad. The latter two gave rise to the state export of oil and intergovernmental agreements on trade with the CIS.

The compulsory registration of barter export transactions was introduced in 1996 and mandated a waiting period of over 180 days before receiving import shipments. The main objective of this registration was to prevent capital flight in the form of alleged barter exports, which are never matched by equal imports. The government has had the same goal in mind in developing a scheme of control over contract price compliance with the "quality" of exports. When export taxes were in existence, an additional aim of this scheme was to stop export tax evasion through undervaluation of exports. However, these plans were never implemented since the reform-minded members of the government, supported by international financial institutions, rightfully considered such a scheme to be unnecessarily restrictive on exports.

State export of oil was the government's response to the elimination of the export tax on oil in mid-1996. The substance of the scheme was in the government's priority access to export pipelines, which shipments for state orders were privileged for, thus absorbing part of the windfall profits going to exporters due to the remaining gap between domestic and international prices. Such exports accounted for 25 percent of total oil exports in 1996 and were legitimately considered a barrier to free-market competition. Consequently, in the context of negotiating the EFF program for 1997, the government abolished all provisions providing for state exports from its previous resolutions in a special Decree issued in spring 1997.[8]

Exports negotiated within the framework of intergovernmental agreements between Russia and its CIS partners—such agreements were most actively negotiated during the early years of reform—came to a halt due to a mutual inability on the part of participating governments to ensure shipments of specified goods. As a result, compulsory lists of "balanced" shipments, which used to be attached to annual intergovernmental agreements on economic cooperation, were made voluntary as early as in 1994. Moreover, the increased transparency of procurement for state orders (achieved in part by the firm position taken by international financial institutions) eliminated cross-subsidies earlier associated with intergovernmental barter trade. Hence, this area of foreign trade has been liberalized to no less an extent than others.

In summary, it would be fair to say that 1996 was a milestone that marked the end of the first, restrictive phase of the country's export policy, which still constitutes the main thrust of the government efforts, in spite of the partial reversal in the aftermath of the 1998 crisis. Exports were essentially liberalized and the government then moved into the second, promotional phase of export policy. Not surprisingly, import policy was moving in the opposite direction. Incidentally, 1996 turned out to be a turning point for import policy also, as we shall demonstrate below.

13.3.2.2. Import Restrictions. Given the above-mentioned widespread shortages in the Russian consumer and manufacturing markets, it is no wonder that the government did not think twice about liberalizing access to foreign goods when it launched trade policy reform back in 1991. Nontariff barriers were the first to be scrapped. Just prior to 1992, the government adopted Decree No. 90, which eliminated nontariff barriers on imports. Only exceptional items, such as weapons, explosives, nuclear materials, precious metals and gems, and narcotics and poisons were put on the list of goods allowed exclusively for licensed imports by designated companies (special importers). Besides these items licensing was required for the importing of pharmaceuticals, herbicides, insecticides, and industrial waste only.

Tariff constraints were initially liberalized to no lesser extent. On January 15, 1992, the government of Russia issued Decree No. 32 (made effective immediately), which abolished the USSR's import tariff schedule, which had been in effect for almost twelve years. Initially a new Russian import tariff schedule was supposed to be prepared by April 1, 1992. However, it was not until July 1 that it was actually put in effect. The general tariff rate was only 5 percent, with a rate of 15 percent on automobiles and video equipment and 10 to 25 percent on alcoholic beverages. Imports of most foodstuffs and pharmaceutical were not subject to any tariffs. This schedule did not survive for more than two months, and it is noteworthy that during the first eight months of the Russian reform there were practically no tariff or explicit nontariff barriers to imports.

It should also be mentioned that until February 1, 1993, all imports were free from excise and value-added taxes that were applicable to domestically produced goods. Consequently, even the import of luxury goods, which have always been targeted by the government for fiscal purposes, was treated more favorably than local products. Moreover, imported goods were not subject to 28 percent VAT. Hence Russia's policy toward imports could hardly be described as discriminatory in 1992. As a matter of fact, quite the opposite was true prior to February 1993: the tariffs on imported goods were less than the 28 percent VAT, thus favoring imports over domestic goods.

Yet even when excise taxes and VAT were extended to imports in February 1993, this did not totally eliminate the technical discrepancy in applying these taxes to domestic and imported commodities. The customs value was used for calculation of excise taxes on imports, while retail price (excise tax included) was the basis for determining excise tax payment on domestically produced goods (Table 13.3). This effectively meant higher taxation for most domestic products. This situation existed until the Parliament adopted a law unifying the methods of calculation for both imported and domestically produced goods in 1996.

Another important element of trade policy during 1992 to 1993 was the subsidization of imports. Until mid-1992 import subsidies were a component of a system of multiple exchange rates aimed at providing for basic import needs for final consumption. Import subsidies were used to isolate domestic users from differences between domestic and world prices. In mid-July 1992, the transparency of the system was improved by the replacement of multiple exchange rates with a uniform rate (determined by the interbank auction) and direct budgetary subsidies, calculated as import coefficients.

The import subsidies were a major fiscal burden and were estimated to account for almost 25 percent of GDP in early 1992. Subsidy coefficients varied from 61 percent on food products to 90 percent on food-processing equipment. Some 55 percent of subsidies went to industry, and 45 percent to food products (and their inputs). Rapid depreciation of the ruble and the unwillingness of the authorities to pass on the resulting cost increases to the users determined the extent of the subsidies. Over time, however, the import subsidies became insupportable and they were first reduced and then abolished on January 1, 1994.

On September 1, 1992 general tariff rates were raised to 15 percent. For automobiles and video equipment rates increased to 25 percent and for alcohol to 20 to 50 percent (100 percent on plain spirits as of October 15). At the same time children's clothing, printed materials, and some medical equipment were added to the list of goods free of import duties. This regime was in existence until April 1993, when the next across-the-board revision of the import duty schedule was introduced. Tariffs were hiked for vegetables, alcoholic beverages, jewelry, furs, and other leisure goods and reduced for a wide range of imports, ranging from nonferrous metals and chemicals to textiles and railway stock. The most peculiar thing about this revision was that it yielded a reduction in the average import duty as weighted by imports that had never occurred before (Table 13.3). Since that revision it has become routine to introduce significant modifications of the import duty schedule every spring.

The most serious changes occurred in 1994 when the weighted average increased by 5 percentage points. Not only did rates became generally higher, but they also resulted in increased distortions among various commodity groups. In fact, 1994 marked the peak of divergence in import duties

Table 13.3. Effective and nominal rates of excise tax on imported and Russian goods (percent)

	Nominal Rate Prior to Nov. 26, 1993	*Effective Rate*		*Effective Rate as of Nov. 26, 1993*		*Effective Rate as of Feb. 14, 1994*	
Product		*Imports*	*Domestic*	*Imports*	*Domestic*	*Imports*	*Domestic*
1	*2*	*3*	*4*	*5*	*6*	*7*	
Vodka	85	85	567	150	567	250	
Hard liquor	80	80	400	150	400	250	
Cognac	55	55	122	100	122	200	
Champagne wines	47.5	47.5	90	100	90	100	
Port wines	46.5	46.5	87	46.5	87	46.5	
Wine	30	30	43	30	43	30	
Spirits	90	90	900	250	900	400	
Beer	40	40	67	40	67	40	
Tobacco (kg)	37.5	37.5	60	100	60	100	
Cigarettes (per 1,000)	0.0	0.0	0.0	0.0	0.0	0.0	
Cigars (per 1)	0.0	0.0	0.0	0.0	0.0	0.0	
Cigarills (per 1,000)	0.0	0.0	0.0	0.0	0.0	0.0	
Tires	30	30	43	30	43	30	
Passenger cars	35	35	54	42.5	54	42.5	
Trucks	25	25	33	25	33	25	
Oil (t)	0.0	0.0	0.0	0.0	0.0	0.0	
Gasoline (t)	0.0	0.0	0.0	0.0	0.0	0.0	
Gasoline (t)	0.0	0.0	0.0	0.0	0.0	0.0	
Cars	0.0	0.0	0.0	0.0	0.0	0.0	
Jewelry	30	30	43	30	43	30	
Diamonds	10	10	11	10	11	10	
Crystal wear	20	20	25	20	25	20	
Carpets	10	10	11	10	11	10	
Fur clothing	35	35	54	35	54	35	
Leather clothing	35	35	54	35	54	35	

Source: Compiled on basis of governmental resolutions.

* Federal Law 06.12.91 # 1993-1 (as of July 23, 1998).

as measured both by standard deviation and variance coefficient (Table 13.3). Perhaps this trend toward greater differentiation in import tariffs would have continued (Ministry of Foreign Economic Relations experts were seriously involved at that time in what they called development of scientific rates of protection, with the ultimate goal of introducing a distinct rate for each of 9,000 commodity groups) however, it was curbed by Russia's agreement with the IMF on the terms of the stand-by facility. This agreement obligated Russia not only to avoid increases in the weighted average in the course of any further modifications of the import duty schedule but also to reduce ceiling rates from 30 to 20 percent by 1998 and to 15 percent by 2000[9] and to achieve reductions in the weighted average duty of 30 percent and 20 percent by these dates respectively.

Unfortunately, in the spring of 1997 the government informed the IMF that it had decided to cancel plans for maximum rate and weighted average reduction. In fact, by mid-1998, the weighted average for import tariffs rose to 16.5 percent from 13.6 percent in the spring of 1997. Nonetheless, Russia's active attempts to speed up its entry into the WTO, and the most recent collapse of the real value of the ruble, strongly indicate that there will be no negative developments in tariff policy in the near future. An issue of greater concern at the moment is Russia's first experimentation with nontariff restrictions on imports. As stated earlier, Russia had practically no such constraints on imports prior to 1996. However, during 1997 the first technical barriers were put in place, and the first attempts were made to apply the safeguards mechanism for domestic industry protection as elaborated in the WTO Articles. Technical barriers emerged in the form of a ban on imports of chicken drumsticks from the United States and safeguards were triggered to impose quotas on imports of ethyl alcohol/vodka and white sugar.

Luckily, neither of these measures materialized. The ban was never put into effect due to the active opposition of the U.S. government. The Decree introducing import quotas for ethyl alcohol/vodka was revoked two months after publication (again, before quotas were to become effective) in the course of an intensive dialogue with the IMF, while the Decree on sugar quotas was terminated by the President's Office. Cancellation of both the ban and quotas was a positive sign for Russia's commercial policy development. The peculiarity of the ban was not that it was based on health concerns—which are honored by WTO agreements—but that the Russian veterinary service claimed that U.S. exporters were not meeting Russian standards (moreover, this judgment was made on the basis of less than 10 percent of imports). Regarding the first attempts to employ the Safeguards mechanism, the Russian safeguards commission has managed to recommend the introduction of import quotas following an investigation that was consistent with the WTO agreements only in Commission members' imagination.[10]

In conclusion, it may be said that the pattern of Russia's trade policy became more conventional during the years of reform. Exports have become liberalized, while import policy has become more protection oriented. Yet one can be hopeful that Russia will avoid excessive protectionism, particularly of the nontariff kind, even after the current exchange-rate crisis, the most efficient protection against imports, is over.

13.3.3. Foreign-Exchange Outcome

Table 13.1 and Figure 13.3 depict the dynamics of the main exchange-rate-related variables between 1992 and 1997. There are two very clear trends: (1) the appreciation of the real exchange rate and of the (nominal) dollar wage and (2) a marked decline and convergence of the market rate of exchange toward the rate of exchange based on the purchasing power parity (PPP). Both trends follow an initial, 1992, steep depreciation (and devaluation) of both exchange rates and a simultaneous opening up of a very wide gap between the two, when the market exchange rate shot up to a level more than six times higher than the PPP rate. The number one factor that contributed to both trends is the process of relative economic and political stabilization of Russia, up to 1997. During these years, and especially during the second half of the period, the rate of inflation declined substantially: initially negative real interest rates turned positive and high, Ruble-denominated government bonds (treasury bills, GKO) were issued and paid hefty returns, real estate assets became somewhat more accessible and more secure, and even newly issued shares of privatized and nonprivatized enterprises appeared on the market, many of them at very attractive initial prices. On the other side, as mentioned above, the pegging and management of the exchange rate, informally since 1995 and formally since mid-1996 radically reduced the expected profits from transactions in foreign currency. All these reduced the demand for foreign currency and contributed to its depreciation. The pegging of the exchange rate, while helping to reduce the rate of inflation also helped to reinforce the tendency of appreciation: when pressures for devaluation did develop, starting in 1997 (see below), the central bank of Russia (CBR) resisted them and thus contributed to the general appreciation trend.

There was also a trend of increased relative political stabilization, which also contributed to the increased confidence in and therefore demand for the domestic currency at the expense of foreign currency. This process was, however, less smooth, and periods of confidence and fear replaced each other quite frequently, up to the collapse of August 1998. 1995 was a first good year in terms of macroeconomic and political stability. Then came the period of anxiety before the presidential elections in mid-1996, followed by similar scares related to the ups and mostly downs of the state of health of Yeltsin. These merged during the later part of 1997 and then in 1998, with the increased internal political tensions between the government and the parliament, the financial crisis in Asia that finally lead to the crisis in Russia. A major manifestation of these cycles is expressed by the flows of capital in and out of the country, flows initiated by Russians and by the foreign business community, as can be seen in Table 13.4, with data on Russian balance of payment.

Exports of energy and other natural resources helped Russia to keep a large positive trade balance throughout the period, until 1997. Until the end of 1996 this was carried over also to a strong current-account balance. In these two respects Russia was singled out among all ETs of Europe. Starting in 1997, a growing outflow of net factor income, increasing debt service, joined a declining trade surplus, to first drastically reduce the current account surplus (1997) and then to turn it into a negative figure (first half of 1998). The first factor reflected the growing Russian external indebtedness, and the second reflected, among others, the sharply declining prices of energy and commodities starting in mid-1997 and accelerating later, and ever-increasing imports due to the high rate of exchange. As mentioned above, due to the pegging of the exchange rate there was no exchange-rate response to these changes: rather, rates of interests had to be pushed up to sustain the ability to borrow.

The pressures of the capital account to appreciate the exchange rate were never very strong. Assuming that most of what is included under "errors and omissions" reflects another part of the large flow of capital flight out of Russia, then in most years capital outflows almost completely offset, sometimes even more, the official and private inflows put together. It is generally assumed that on average capital flight amounted to about U.S. $20 billion a year, about the size of the trade surplus. 1995 was a below-average year in this respect, when capital flight slowed down considerably for reasons mentioned above. 1996 was an exceptional year on the down side when the capital account was strongly negative and capital flight exceptionally high, reflecting the internal political uncertainty. This explains the slight depreciation of the ER during a few months in 1996. Even the very large portfolio investment, and increasing amount of direct investment into Russia during the "Russian miracle" period since the beginning of 1997, didn't manage to produce a strong capital account surplus. The amount of capital flight in 1997 and 1998, reflects the developing crisis of tax

Table 13.4. Russian federation, balance of payments, 1992 to 1998 (billions of U.S. dollars)

	1992	*1993*	*1994*	*1995*	*1996*	*1997*	*1998 (first half)*
Current account	0.5	12.8	10.5	4.6	12.1	2.9	–6.0
Trade balance	10.5	15.6	21.1	17.5	23.1	17.3	2.2
Exports	53.9	59.7	69.6	81.5	90.5	88.9	36.5
Imports	43.4	–44.1	48.5	64.0	–67.4	–71.7	–34.4
Service balance	–5.5	–1.4	–6.4	–7.9	–5.7	–5.2	–2.5
Exports	0.0	8.2	9.0	12.4	12.9	13.5	6.2
Imports	5.5	–9.5	15.4	20.3	–18.7	–18.7	–8.7
Factor income, net	–4.5	–4.5	–4.1	–5.0	–5.3	–8.5	–5.1
Net current transfers	0.0	0.0	0.0	0.2	0.0	–0.6	–0.5
Capital account	0.3[1]	–2.2	–10.8	10.3	–6.8	6.3	7.0
Transfers	3.0	–0.3	2.1	–0.3	–0.5	–0.8	–0.3
Capital to the public sector	2.6	5.2	2.0	7.7	14.4	21.2	n/a
Assets	—	–3.5	–3.3	–1.3	–0.4	–0.8	n/a
Liabilities	—	8.7	5.2	9.0	14.8	21.9	15.4
Portfolio investment	0.0	0.0	0.0	0.0	7.6	44.1	13.2
Loans, credits, and others	—	8.7	5.3	9.0	7.1	–22.2	0.7
Capital to the private sector (including banks)	—	–7.1	–14.9	2.9	–20.8	–14.1	6.0
Assets	—	–10.9	–16.3	5.2	–31.4	–36.5	–8.2
Liabilities	—	3.8	1.4	–2.3	10.6	22.4	n/a
Direct investment (into Russia)	—	1.2	0.6	2.0	2.4	6.2	n/a
Portfolio investment (into Russia)	—	0.0	0.0	0.0	2.2	1.3	n/a
Errors and omissions	—[a]	–6.3	–0.4	–7.9	–8.1	–7.3	–2.7
Net reserves	–0.8	–4.4	1.9	–10.4	2.8	–1.9	1.7

Source: *Russian Economics Trends*, No. 3, 1998, table 37, pp. 62–63; World Bank Data.
a. Including errors of omissions.

collection (capital flew out to avoid taxes) and then the initial signs of the mounting crisis. Over the covered period, therefore, capital flight from Russia helped to partially offset the potentially unfavorable (from the point of view of trade) appreciation pressure on the ER, suffered by other ETs due to such inflows (Roubini and Wachtel, this volume, ch. 2; EBRD, 1998, ch. 3). It thereby, in an awkward fashion, helped to ameliorate the appreciation pressure of the Dutch disease.

A second factor that ameliorated the appreciation pressures on the Russian exchange rate was debt repayment and servicing of the external debt. In 1992 Russia took responsibility for the portfolio of the external capital account of the Soviet Union, with more than $100 billion of Soviet debt (and nearly $100 billion of debts, which are very difficult to collect, mostly by poor LDCs, and other assets). During the 1990s Russia took new loans, $32 billion by 1997, so that its entire external indebtedness reached $123.5 billion. In 1997 the debt burden amounted to about one quarter of Russia's GDP measured at the official exchange rate, and about 15 percent of the PPP exchange rate, in both cases a rather modest burden. The debt service burden was even lighter, as during the mid-1990s partial rescheduling of this debt was arranged with the Paris and London clubs; and, in any case, Russia paid only part of the theoretical debt service. The actual debt service burden (what Russia actually paid) amounted over the 1990s to 6–7 percent of exports, reaching 10.4 percent during Q1 of 1998, which is not a very heavy burden. (*Russian Economic Trends*, No. 3, 1998, service for this year Tables 38, 40, pp. 64–65). *The difficulties of the Russian government to service the debt up to 1997 were due to the capital flight and to general fiscal difficulties.* The crisis erupted as Russia defaulted on both its debt, and it is now doubtful whether it will be able to meet payments on the debt that has by now reached approximately $140 billion. With the sharp devaluation following the August 1998 crisis, the burden, as percent of GDP (but not of exports), almost doubled (by March, 1999).

We now turn to a discussion of the development of Russian trade and to its contribution to the balance of payment and the equilibrium rate of exchange.

13.4. The Development of Trade and Structural Change

The political and economic transition brought with it a collapse of trade both inside the former Soviet Union and with the former socialist partners. This sharp decline was only partly compensated for by increased trade with the West. CMEA trade declined (by 1992) to less than one-fifth of its pretransition volume and intra-FSU trade to, possibly, a third. Total trade declined by half (Bosworth and Ofer, 1995, pp. 76, 115–116). Since then there is a (more or less) steady trend of increase in the volume of trade to all destinations (Table 13.5). Before touching the data a warning about its quality is in place. The data presented in Table 13.5, records all registered flows (that is, what is covered by the custom administration) plus an adjustment for the so-called shuttle imports (mostly consumer goods brought by people traveling back home from the West) and heavy smuggling. There is a fairly good coverage of exports, which is improving over time. There is extensive misreporting of prices as a means of leaving money abroad. Data in Table 13.5 reflect only registered trade, but data in Table 13.4 on the balance of payments includes adjustments for the above-mentioned biases, made by GosComstat (the Central Statistical Bureau of Russia and for 1998 by the CBR (now accepted also by Goscomstat). Data in Table 13.5 is biased downward mostly in the sphere of imports of consumer goods.

While much of the quantitative expansion of trade took place with the West (both developed and less developed countries, mostly the first group), there is, following a delay of two years, a marked increase in the volume of trade with the two former socialist groups. Trade with former CMEA countries reached bottom in 1994, but since then exports are expanding. Imports are still stagnant, but there may be here a degree of underreporting and of border trade. There are still inherited difficulties to resume trade with these countries (Drebentsov, 1997). Trade inside the CIS has expanded earlier and has continued to grow, where imports are following the expansion of exports with a lag. In 1996 the share of former CMEA and of CIS countries in Russian exports reached 30 percent (Figure 13.4). Following the establishment of the proper institutional channels, the trend seem to be of a total expansion of trade, accompanied by increasing shares of the former socialist partners. In 1997, however, the share of CIS trade declined again, and we don't have data on trade with the former CMEA countries.

So far the structure of trade by commodity groups has not been going through profound changes, and the small changes that have been taking place have more to do with the shifts in the direction of trade rather than with major changes in competitiveness and comparative advantage (Figures 13.5, 13.6). Russian exports, as in the past, are dominated by energy, minerals, other raw materials and metals (some processed), and fertilizers (Table 13.5). Its imports are dominated by food, consumer goods, and machinery. The big changes here are first, the increase in the imports of finished food products and of other consumer goods, of both light industry (textile and shoes) and electronics; and second, the fact that some of these imports are coming from the West. Part of the traditional large imports of

Table 13.5. Russian foreign trade, 1992 to 1997: geographic destination and commodity groups (million of U.S. dollars, percent)—PART I: exports

							Manufactured goods include:			
		Total	All Foods and Agriculture Raw Materials	Mineral Fuels and Electric Energy	Ores, Minerals, and Metals (in Primary Form)	Manufactured Goods	Iron, Steel, Steel Rolls, and Other Metal Products	Chemicals (mostly fertilizers)	Textiles and Clothing	Machinery
Total	1994	63,243.00	2,452.55	25,884.07	7,704.48	26,583.50	6,347.20	4,356.20	1,225.40	3,020.10
		100	100	100	100	100	100	100	100	100
Third countries		69.85	72.7	62.09	89.14	72.54	85.31	75.53	62.83	37.52
CMEA countries		7.89	4.2	11.66	5.51	5.46	2.61	6.66	9.35	10.18
CIS countries		22.27	23.1	26.25	5.35	22	12.08	17.81	27.82	52.3
Total	1995	78,290.20	2,653.35	28,700.69	10,496.39	32,306.31	7,757.90	5,946.20	1,044.30	3,424.20
		100	100	100	100	100	100	100	100	100
Third countries		69.16	80.87	64.92	92.58	76.37	87.34	82.78	66.62	42.56
CMEA countries		10.79	4.31	18.86	5.61	7.28	3.51	6.64	9.47	12.56
CIS countries		18.6	14.82	16.23	1.81	16.35	9.14	10.58	23.91	44.87
Total	1996	84,988.40	2,915.40	36,615.60	11,426.90	29,975.90	8,191.10	5,591.20	822.4	3,410.80
		100	100	100	100	100	100	100	100	100
Third countries		69.63	77.6	64.93	92.87	76.41	88.3	84.08	65.9	42.73
CMEA countries		11.86	4.76	19.72	3.93	6.83	2.37	5.34	7.63	12.54
CIS countries		18.51	17.63	15.35	3.2	16.76	9.33		26.47	44.73
Total	1997	80,363.00	2,451.60	36,661.90	14,570.00	26,679.50	8,037.00	4,755.30	741.2	3,663.40
		100	100	100	100	100	100	100	100	100
Non-CIS countries		85.1	84.5	83.8	94.1	82.2	93	89.4	79.1	58.5
CIS countries		14.9	15.5	16.2	5.9	17.8	7	10.6	20.9	41.5

Table 13.5. (countinued)—PART II: imports

		Total	All Foods and Agriculture Raw Materials	Mineral Fuels and Electric Energy	Ores, Minerals, and Metals (in Primary Form)	Manufactured Goods	*Manufactured goods include:* Iron, Steel, Steel Rolls, and Other Metal Products	Chemicals (mostly fertilizers)	Textiles and Clothing	Machinery
Total	1994	38,649.55	10,757.02	753.32	1,767.80	24,743.77	1,961.00	1,591.00	2,317.70	9,520.10
		100	100	100	100	100	100	100	100	100
Third countries		65.11	68.98	16.29	33.49	68.7	38.98	64.94	61.7	76.38
CMEA countries		8.27	12.6	0.08	2.58	7.27	2.68	6.8	3.7	5.91
CIS countries		26.68	18.41	83.63	63.92	24.03	58.34	28.27	34.6	17.72
Total	1995	46,679.90	12,037.52	966.12	1,348.30	28,022.54	2,616.00	2,515.60	1,877.70	10,658.80
		100	100	100	100	100	100	100	100	100
Third countries		63.47	68.29	27.88	65.42	72.37	30.29	63.06	57.71	82.57
CMEA countries		8.08	12.99	0.18	3.16	7.5	3.1	7.8	3.62	5.69
CIS countries		28.58	18.73	71.94	31.42	20.13	66.61	29.14	38.67	11.74
Total	1996	45,916.90	11,208.40	1,216.50	1,473.20	28,640.95	2,929.20	3,623.30	1,429.60	9,615.80
		100	100	100	100	100	100	100	100	100
Third countries		61.42	60.94	30.16	24.04	72.57	29.53	66.25	60.24	82.82
CMEA countries		7.15	10.79	0.05	7.01	6.73	4.34	5.36	3.44	4.42
CIS countries		31.43		69.79	68.96	20.7	66.12	28.39	36.32	12.76
Total	1997	48,258.30	12,721.70	1,367.30	2,821.50	31,347.80	2,371.20	3,909.00	1,572.90	11,126.60
		100	100	100	100	100	100	100	100	100
Non-CIS countries		80.4	79.4	42.2	65.2	83.8	42.6	81.9	63.3	90.3
CIS countries		19.6	20.6	57.8	34.8	16.2	57.4	18.1	36.7	9.7

Table 13.5. (countinued)—PART III: net exports

Machinery		Total	All Foods and Agriculture Raw Materials	Mineral Fuels and Electric Energy	Ores, Minerals, and Metals (in Primary Form)	Manufactured Goods	Manufactured goods include: Iron, Steel, Steel Rolls, and Other Metal Products	Chemicals (mostly fertilizers)	Textiles and Clothing	Machinery
Total	1994	24,593.45	–8,304.47	25,130.75	5,936.679	1,839.73	4,386.2	2,765.2	–1,092.3	–6,500
		100	100	100	100	100	100	100	100	100
Third countries		77.3	67.89	63.46	105.71	124.15	106.02	81.63	60.42	94.43
CMEA countries		7.27	15.08	12.01	6.38	–18.85	2.58	6.58	–2.64	3.92
CIS countries		15.32	17.03	24.53	–12.09	–5.3	–8.61	11.79	42.21	1.65
Total	1995	31,610.30	–9,384.17	27,734.56	9,148.09	4,283.77	5,141.90	3,430.60	–833.4	–7,234.60
		100	100	100	100	100	100	100	100	100
Third countries		77.56	64.73	66.21	96.58	102.53	116.37	97.24	46.54	101.5
CMEA countries		14.8	15.44	19.51	5.97	5.84	3.72	5.79	–3.71	2.44
CIS countries		3.85	19.83	14.29	–2.55	–8.36	–20.09	–3.03	57.16	–3.94
Total	1996	39,071.50	–8,292.00	35,399.10	9,953.70	1,334.95	5,261.90	1,967.90	–607.2	–6,205.00
		100	100	100	100	100	100	100	100	100
Third countries		79.28	55.07	66.13	103.06	158.97	121.01	116.91	52.56	104.85
CMEA countries		17.38	12.91	20.4	3.47	8.85	1.27	5.32	–2.23	–0.04
CIS countries		3.34	32.02	13.48	–6.53	–67.82	–22.28	–22.22	49.67	–4.82
Total	1997	32,104.70	–10,270.10	35,294.60	11,748.50	–4,668.30	5,665.80	846.30	–831.7	–7,493.20
		100	100	100	100	100	100	100	100	100
Non-CIS countries		92.2	78.2	85.4	101	93.5	114.2	124	49.2	105.7
CIS countries		7.8	21.8	14.6	–1	6.5	–14.2	–24.1	50.8	–5.8

Source: Goskomstat and Customs Committee of Russian Federation.

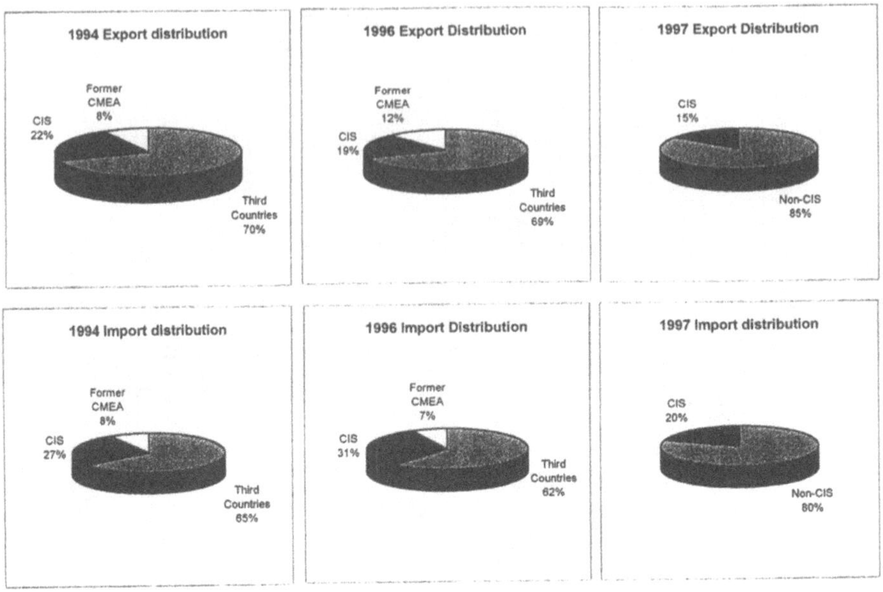

Figure 13.4. Trade by Destination, 1994, 1996, 1997
Source: Table 13.5.

grain under the old regime was replaced by direct importation of meat and other dairy products. The import penetration to consumer markets was very significant: still by the end of 1996 and the beginning of 1997 imports of consumer goods made half of all (retail) trade—nearly 100 percent of all TV sets and tape-recorders, half of the food products, 70 to 80 percent of clothing and shoes (Expert Institute, 1997, pp. 42–27; Eismont and Kuralbaeva, 1998). The Expert Institute paper sites many examples on how local relative production costs became over time higher than world market prices as a result of the appreciation of the ER (pp. 47–51). Trade with the West is even more biased in these directions. (The West is importing less energy and more materials.) Both former CMEA and CIS countries are importing much energy but less of the other basic materials. The two regions, however, are important importers, as well as, exporters of machinery, and exporters to Russia of food and consumer goods.

Most of the expansion of Russian trade had to do with the process of the gradual decline in the restrictions over exports of energy and metals, partly offset, on the one side, by the independent appreciation of the exchange rate and, on the other, the overall decline in the cost of imports

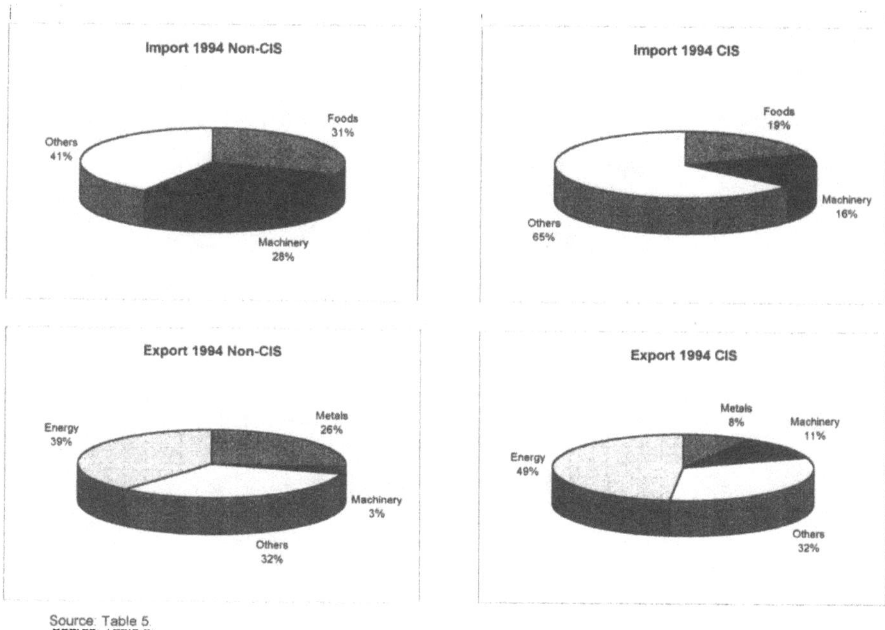

Figure 13.5. Trade by Commodity Groups, 1994
Source: Table 13.5.

and the moderate increase in household incomes. Let's emphasize that almost the entire increase in exports of energy and other materials came from existing production capacity and decline in domestic use, rather than from the expansion of production. In terms of Figure 13.2, the Russian economy is still in point Q_3 rather than Q_4. The new Russian trade is overwhelmingly characterized as the interindustry (Hecksher-Ohlin) type, rather than as the intraindustry type that characterizes developed industrial countries. This is in significant contrast with the pattern of trade of some of the more advanced East European countries, where estimates show that up to half of their trade can be classified as advanced intraindustry trade (Neven, 1996). In particular, we note that there was no increase in the share of Russian exports of machinery in any direction. In general, however, it seems that the breathing period allowed by high exchange rates and restrictions on exports was not used effectively enough by Russian manufacturing to significantly restructure. The crisis of 1998 and much other evidence attest to this (see more below).

Finally, during 1992 to 1997 Russia also experienced constant deficit in trade in nonfactor services ($5 billion in 1996, see Table 13.4). Given the

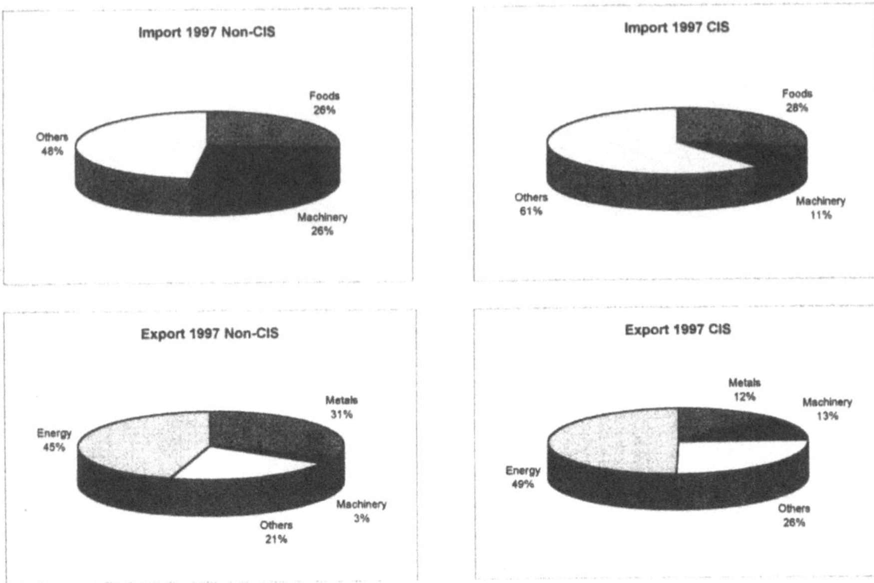

Source: Table 5.

Figure 13.6. Trade by Commodity Groups, 1997
Source: Table 13.5.

little use for business, financial, and market services under the old regime, the great demand for them for during transition and beyond, and the obvious lack of know-how and experience in their provision, one should expect a continued large trade deficit in this area.

13.5. Assessment and Policy Options: Restructuring and the Dutch Disease

The economic and financial crisis that peak red on August 17, 1998, was caused by a number of factors, some exogenous (the Asian financial crisis and its aftermath, the sharp decline in energy and commodity prices on the world market), and some macroeconomic and institutional (large fiscal deficit and very weak tax collection that drove up interest rates on government ruble-denominated bonds (GKOs), the inability of the government to impose the rule of law and to combat corruption and illegal activities). At least part of the crisis was caused by the failure to make adequate progress in the restructuring of the manufacturing sector and other branches of the economy, to increase efficiency and competitiveness. Weak enterprises protected themselves through an elaborate system of barter deals, tax avoidance and evasion, and payment arrears, based on the heritage and practices of the old regime, amounting to a vast network of cross-subsidization of the weak by the less weak. (Gaddy and Ickes, 1998; Expert Institute, 1997). All these put increasing pressure on the rate of exchange and on the small stock of foreign currency reserves of the central bank. Toward the end of the period and continuously through 1998, additional pressures for devaluation were imposed by the declining world-market prices for energy and other basic commodities and the lagging development of their production and export potential and by the increasing outflow of capital. The decline of the real market pressure to appreciate the ER was since 1996 replaced to some extent by the pegging of the exchange rate and the reluctance of the CBR to allow some devaluation (EBRD, 1998, pp. 12–21, 71–76, and passim throughout; *Russian Economic Trends*, No. 3, 1998; Gaddy and Ickes, 1998). In some measure, therefore, the devaluation that erupted to about one-third of the precrisis nominal level (by January 1999) is, among others, also a market reaction to the failure of the manufacturing sector to restructure itself. The sharp decline in the rate of exchange can thus be viewed also as an uprising of this sector against the appreciation of the exchange rate. The ability of Russia during 1992 to 1997 to sustain a positive trade balance, to tolerate the appreciation of its ER, and even to overborrow abroad against this surplus, all based on its (yet underdeveloped) rich natural endowment, must have contributed to an atmosphere of nonurgency for restructuring. It definitely allowed the Russian economy to proceed much longer without it and to postpone the crisis. In these ways the rich resource endowment may have already brought about a number of Dutch disease symptoms that contributed to a slower pace of the transition in Russian. Without this endowment Russia would have been forced to attend to its manufacturing sector much earlier. And, given the slow development of the production and export potential of the resource base and the large outflow of capital, 1992 to 1997 witnessed only a mild dose of the disease. Furthermore, Russia could have used its resource endowment in a more efficient way, through intensive development as a tool to help faster restructuring; but it failed to do so. Whatever the factors that contributed to the crisis, the manufacturing sector is getting now a second chance to restructure, albeit under more difficult conditions.

How to do it better now that an unfortunate "second chance" has presented itself? How to better exploit the rich natural endowment and to avoid the backdrop of the Dutch disease? In the remainder of this section we concentrate on a discussion of the options opened to Russia given its endowment and mention only in passing other elements of a full transition program. The second chance presents itself on the assumption that there is now a period of a few years with a lower real exchange rate, if inflation will be arrested, and that future appreciation will reflect real restructuring and increase in efficiency in manufacturing. The second chance is unfortunate because the first one was missed, and there is a great loss of trust in the government and in the economy and much greater hesitation to invest, on the part of both Russians and foreigners. These probably reduce the ability of Russian to pay its external debt, to attract foreign investment and generate domestic saving and further postpone the day when Russian capital accumulated abroad will start to move back. These may push back to the more distance future the dangers of appreciation due to capital account movements but also will slow down the restructuring process.

There are two main strategic approaches to the development of natural resources, given the dangers of a Dutch disease; first an aggressive development of these resources combined with policies that divert part of the newly created value to an accelerated development of manufacturing. The second is to slow down the potential growth of the natural-resource sector to ameliorate the difficulties faced by the manufacturing sector and avoiding the Dutch disease. In a way Russia was pursuing this second strategy so far, by fefault, invoking the rallying argument of preventing the plunder of Russia's riches by foreigners and in response to pressures from conservative political and economic groups. While until recently there was much interest by foreign investors to develop the energy sector, ownership restrictions and other limitations and barriers prevented this interest from being translated into real results. As mentioned above, while efforts were made to expand exports abroad, much less was accomplished in the expansion of the production of energy, let alone its production capacity. In most sectors, especially oil, production had been dropping. So far there was no serious effort to move from point Q_3 to point Q_4 in Figure 13.2 above. On the basis of this record it may be claimed (as Charles Wyplosz in a comment) that one should not worry about the Dutch disease because wrong government policies will prevent it from occurring.

The first strategic option—fast development of the resource base and the use some of the created income to help restructure the manufacturing sector—is clearly the preferable one. As in other countries suffering from the Dutch disease, active government intervention is needed (Eismont and Kuralbaeva, 1998; Sachs and Warner, 1995, and the many citations thereof). In the case of Russia one could justify a more active restructuring policy even without the complication of the Dutch disease. The enormity of the task of restructuring is far greater than could have been directed by extreme changes in relative prices on short notice. The down side of this strategy is that it requires more active, even direct government intervention in the economy in forms and ways generally included under industrial policy. The problem is to what extent are governments able to conduct such a policy in the right direction and in good faith? Indeed, in many cases highly distorted economies that require radical restructuring also have weak and inexperienced governments to enact the appropriate policies. This is certainly also true about the Russian situation. One point in favor of a proactive government in such situations is that a weak government is forced from below by interest groups to conduct a bad industrial policy. It may be better to have a better one imposed from above, which may be able to drive away some of these pressures. In recommending government interventions in such cases, the choice of means used should take into account the implementation ability and resolve of the government. Given the danger of government failures, any government, and of the weak and inexperienced government of Russia in particular, such interventions should be as general as neutral and as transparent as possible. The following is a list of possible interventions that may have been helpful before the crisis, but that with the appropriate adaptation, when needed, can be implemented also as part of the second chance.

First, most restrictions on the involvement of foreign capital, especially in the resource and the service and financial sectors, should be removed. This will allow a faster and sounder development of the resource base, and the creation of the needed financial resources to bring the manufacturing sector to a level of self-sustained growth. Less restricted foreign entry into the service and especially the financial sector will help to upgrade the functioning of this sector and thereby help improve the performance of the production sector and encourage more external investments.

Second, one should consider a temporary artificial price wedge between natural resources and manufacturing. Such a wedge can take the form of a uniform moderate general tariff on all manufacturing imports with a predetermined and announced timetable of its gradual scaling down and eventual elimination.[11] To guarantee that temporary doesn't become permanent, an agreement with the WHO on such a tax and the commitment to scaling down may be also necessary. Such a tariff fits situations where the rate of exchange is too high due to government pegging. A temporary 20 percent uniform tariff for a country as big a Russia *for the precrisis period* couldn't have created major negative distortions. The level of such a tariff should give manufacturing a breathing spell but at the same time impose enough pressure on enterprises that can recover to restructure. True, it is not easy to calibrate such a tax to create the optimal degree of balance between the carrot and the stick. A tariff on imports is not appropriate right now (early 1999) during the postcrisis period and will have to be considered only if and when the real exchange rate appreciates at a faster pace than productivity in manufacturing. In periods when the ER is too deeply depreciated due to capital account forces, the above-mentioned price wedge can take the form of differentiated rate of exchange, for manufacturing and for natural resources, though appropriate taxes and/or subsidies, along the same principles as the above mentioned tariff—of scaling down over time along a precommitted schedule and, if possible, with WTO approval and sanctions. It is interesting to note that at present the IMF is pushing the Russian government to impose a higher export tax on resource exports than the 5 percent actually imposed.

The precarious state of the manufacturing sector in Russia called in the past and may well call now, for more direct, even though risky interventions. A framework of a national reconstruction and development bank—as independent as possible from the government and as professional as possible, preferably with shared ownership and management of the international institutions—may be considered. It will provide investment loans and extend (by government legislation) tax allowances, in exchange for preapproved radical restructuring programs, including the upgrading of the technological managerial and governance levels and adapting the high level human capital. Joint ventures with foreign companies will receive priority. The subsidy embedded in the credit and the tax allowances will be tied to preset targets of production, exports, import substitution, according to the line of production. They will also be temporary, with a predetermined down scaling schedule. The strict imposition of a hard budget constraint to go along with these program is, of course, an essential element. All sorts of arrears, barter deals, and cross-subsidization should be strictly eliminated. The bank will be initially financed by credits from international institutions and governments, by Russian government funds, and a small share of the revenues of the natural resource sector (if and when world energy and commodity prices allow this). The bank itself will exist for ten years and then will be privatized.

Finally, a concerted effort, but mostly internal, has to be made to upgrade the performance of the government sector, but this is becoming everybody's mantra. Russia is already a highly industrialized economy and there is no way to think of its prospects otherwise. Its exceptional abundance of natural resources will also last for a long time. The literature on the Dutch disease (cited above) emphasizes both the long-term and short-term potential danger of hurting the manufacturing sector by letting the market forces act in complete freedom. Russia will have to face the long-term problem in due time. In the short term there is the problem of radical restructuring of a manufacturing sector that is unfit for an open economy that Russia is aspiring to become and, in a way, must become.

Let's therefore emphasize again in conclusion that the Dutch disease is a side effect of an economic blessing. So far Russia has not taken full advantage of the blessing and therefore has suffered only moderately from the side effect. A much better approach would be to take full advantage of its natural resources as fast as possible, while applying a balanced dose of the medicine to minimize the bite of the disease.

Acknowledgments

Work on this chapter started with the participation of Vladimir Konovalov of the World Bank, Moscow office. Vladimir Drebentsov prepared the section on trade policy. The chapter represents the personal views of the authors. We thank Xenia Krivenko at the Moscow office of the World Bank for extensive work on the data and tables. Zvi Adamovski helped with computations. Sharon Stone and Avital Madeson helped in editing. This version was updated in January 1999 to bring into the picture the devaluation, debt default, and financial crisis of August 1998. Tables were updated through 1997 or mid-1998. We thank Herbert Allen for research assistance.

Notes

1. As can be seen from the diagram, while relative production costs of consumer goods and services must go up, it is not clear whether the new market prices are higher or lower than the former "established" prices. While basic foods and many services were heavily subsidized under the old regime, other consumer goods were quite heavily taxed.

2. "Growth'" can be shown by a shift of the PPF upward or by a move of the production point from a nonefficient point inside the PPF to its surface, which represent an efficient frontier in a market-economy setting.

3. We thank Ronald McKinnon for making this distinction.

4. With the exception of those quotas that were established under Russia's international obligations, such as agreements with the EU on exports of steel, with the United States on exports of aluminum, and so on.

5. That is, licensing not covering specific goods, like weapons, hazardous materials, and so fourth. These exports are typically subject to licensing in all countries.

6. The history of export contract registration is also of interest. Originally, the scheme contained restrictive clauses allowing the Ministry for Foreign Economic Relations to ban exports on the ground of potential damage to Russia's economic or national interests. In the context of IMF-government dialogue on the stand-by agreement these clauses were eliminated in 1994. Eventually, the whole contract registration scheme was proclaimed voluntary in 196 as part of the agreement on the Extended Fund Facility.

7. Put in effect on July 1, 1992, January 1, 1993, and November 1, 1993, and November 1, 1993. This process has also been rather disorganized, with the number of commodity groups subject to export taxation first increasing—from 30 in January to 70 in July 1992—then decreasing to 53 in January 1993, to 29 in November 1993, to 2 in July 1995, and to zero as of January 1995.

8. In fact, eleven decrees and resolutions were amended, leaving five other decrees with similar provisions intact (Presidential decree, July 6, 1997).

9. The maximum import duty rate is still 100 percent according to the Russian law "On the Customs Tariff," yet there had been only a few commodity groups, such as alcohol, weaponry, and so on, which were subject to rates above 30 percent before the Russian government self-imposed a 30 percent ceiling within the framework of the Extended Fund Facility in fall 1996.

10. The Commission failed to demonstrate not only that Russian producers were hurt by rapidly expanding imports, but even that Russian companies were hurt: it turned out, for instance, that both vodka production and manufacturing capacity in the industry continued to grow over the period under investigation.

11. This proposal was made, with respect to developing countries and countries in transition by McKinnon (1991), and is also the main theme of Tanzi's paper in this volume (ch.).

References

Becker, Abrahams. (1996). "Russia and Economic Integration in the CIS." *Survival*, 38(4) (Winter): 117–136.

Bosworth, Barry P., and Gur Ofer. (1995). *Reforming Planned Economies in an Integrating World Economy.* Washington, DC: Brookings Institution.

Dobrinski and Landesmann. 1995. *Transforming Economies and European Integration.* Aldershot, UK: Edward Elgar.

Drebentsov, Vladimir. (1995). "Russia's Commercial Policy from 1992 to 1994: Liberalization Versus Protection." In Janos Gacs and Merton J. Peck (eds.), *International Trade Issues of the Russian Federation.*

Drebentsov, Vladimir. (1997). "Impediments to Recovery of Russia's Trade with East European Small Economies." In Richard N. Cooper and Janos Gacs (eds.), *Trade Growth in Transition Economies. Export Impediments for Central and Eastern Europe* (ch. 8). Cheltenham, UK: Edward Elgar.

Eismont, Oleg, and K. Kuralbaeva. (1998). "Depletion of Natural Resources and Long-Term Perspectives of the Russian Economy." Mimeo, NES, Moscow.

European Bank for Reconstruction and Development. (1996). *Transition Report 1996: Infrastructure and Savings.* London: EBRD.

European Bank for Reconstruction and Development. (1997). *Transition Report 1997: Enterprise Performance and Growth.* London: EBRD.

European Bank for Reconstruction and Development. (1998). *Transition Report 1998: Financial Sector in Transition.* London: EBRD.

Expert institute. (1997). "Russia's Industrial Policy: Principles of Development and Means of Implementation." Mimeo, Moscow.

Fiani, Riccardo, and Richard Portes (eds.). (1995).

Gaddy, C., and B. Ickes. (1998). "Russia's Virtual Economy" *Foreign Affairs*, 77(5) (September–October): 53–67.

Halpern, Laszlo, and Charles Wyplosz. (1996). "Equilibrium Exchange Rates in Transition Economies." IMF Working Paper 96–125. Washington, DC.

Hare, Paul, G. Saul Estrin, Michael Lugachyov, and Lina Takla. (1996). "Russia's Foreign Trade: New Directions and Western Policies." Mimeo, CERT Discussion Paper.

Konovalov, Vladimir. (1994). "Russian Trade Policy." In Constantine Michalopoulos and David G. Tarr (eds.), *Trade in the New Independent States*. Washington, DC: World Bank, Studies in Economies in Transition No. 13.

McKinnon, Ronald I. (1991). *The Order of Economic Liberalization: Financial Control in the Transition to a Market Economy*. Baltimore: John Hopkins University Press.

Neven, Damien. (1996). "Trade Liberalization with Eastern Nations: How Sensitive?" In Riccardo Fiani and Richard Portes (eds.).

Russian Economic Trends. (1998). Moscow: RECEP.

Sachs, J., and A. Warner. (1995). "Natural Resource Abundance and Economic Growth." NBER Working Paper 5398.

Thorenton, Judith. (1996). "Structural Change in the Russian Far East: The Implications for Trade and Factor Markets." *Atlantic Economic Journal*, 24(3): 208–227.

World Bank. (1996a). *Russian Federation: Toward Medium-Term Stability*. Washington, DC: World Bank.

World Bank. (1996b). *World Development Report 1996: From Plane to Market*. Oxford: Oxford University Press.

14 BALANCE OF PAYMENTS, EXCHANGE RATES, AND COMPETITIVENESS: LESSONS FOR TRANSITION ECONOMIES FROM THE ISRAELI EXPERIENCE

Jacob A. Frenkel

Bank of Israel

14.1. Introduction

In this chapter I draw from the Israeli experience in the area of exchange-rate policies, balance of payments, and competitiveness to infer about these issues for transition economies. For this purpose one needs, first, to clarify the definition of transition: Does this concept refer to the lack of markets? Does it mean the lack of institutions? Does transition imply the lack of instruments? Does it indicate a less healthy financial environment? Or does it just mean that the economy is undergoing a process of transformation? And if so, do we need a special theory for each and every one of these cases? I believe not. I believe that one can take into account the special circumstances of a transition economy without having to develop a separate theory. Although it is inappropriate to develop a simplistic blueprint that can be applied rigidly to each and every case, one must recognize that the basic principles of the main corpus of conventional economic theory are much more universal then meets the eye. They are also applicable to the phenomenon called transition economies.

With this perspective, I am going to elaborate on some elements and issues of the Israeli *process* of disinflation, as an example of a small open economy undergoing rapid transformation. My focus is not on stabilization of hyperinflation but rather on the process of continuous reduction of inflation from moderate inflation rates (about 20 percent) toward the long-term goal of price stability. The central question in this content is how to combine exchange-rate and monetary policies with the specific aim of lowering inflation.

14.2. The Israeli Experience: an Overview

Israel experienced a bout of hyperinflation in the mid-1980s. Inflation was running at 400 percent per annum and in 1985, and a major stabilization program was put in place (Figure 14.1). The key element in this stabilization program was a drastic *cut in the budget.* A budget deficit of 15 percent of GDP turned into a small surplus after one year (Figure 14.2). In addition, a new law was enacted forbidding the Bank of Israel to finance budget deficits. As a result, the government had to finance its spending through (current or future) taxes. The second crucial element of the program was designed specifically to *separate the future from the past.* The mechanisms, by which the past gets imbedded into the future, work through long-term

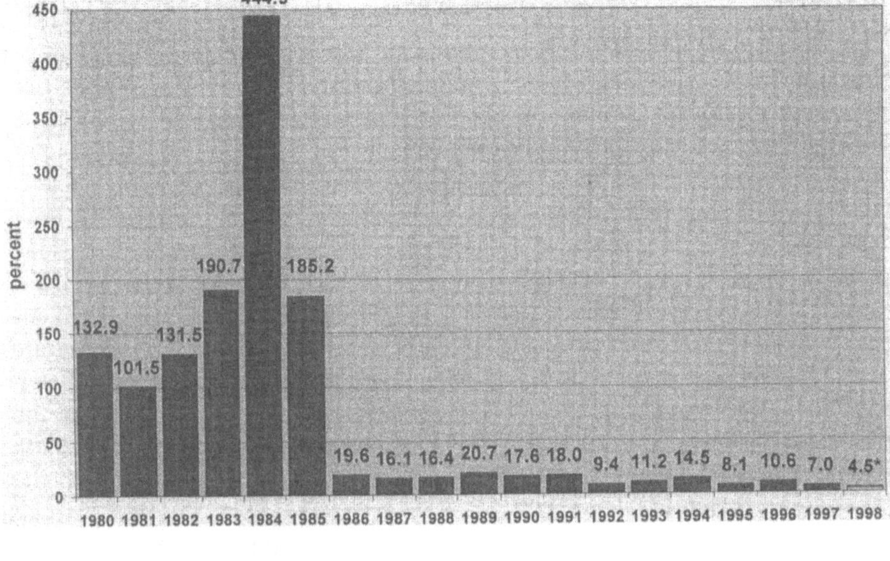

Figure 14.1. The Rate of Inflation

contracts and through expectations. The conception of the stabilization plan was, therefore, that to break the link from the past to the future one must break the inertia that is prevalent in a highly indexed economy. For this purpose, a fixed exchange rate was introduced. Needless to say, this fixing could only be limited in time because, while one can press suddenly on the breaks to break expectations, still, for a considerable period of time, the nontradable-goods sector has life of its own, and inflation continues for a while, thereby eroding competitiveness seriously. Therefore, the question is how to generate an orderly transition from high inflation toward a new growth equilibrium. To attempt to answer this question I analyze a few elements of Israel's exchange-rate system and then connect them to the developments in Israel's inflation.

The stabilization process started in 1985, when inflation reached extremely high levels. Initially, the Israeli currency, the new Israeli sheqel (NIS), was fixed to the U.S. dollar (Figure 14.3). Israel was able to maintain a completely fixed exchange rate to the dollar for a long period, without a significant loss of competitiveness, because during the same period the U.S. dollar depreciated markedly in world markets, and therefore, the exchange rate of the Sheqel against the relevant *basket* of currencies actually depreciated. This mitigated (and for a while offset) the erosion in Israel's effective competitiveness. Still, over time, competitiveness suffered, and as a result occasional devaluations were needed. Following that adjustment, in

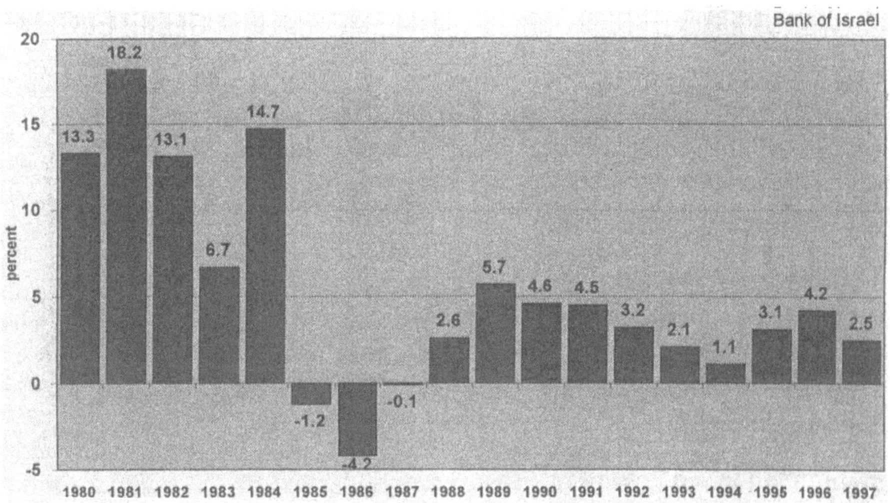

Figure 14.2. Ratio of Public Sector Deficit (+) to GNP 1980–1997

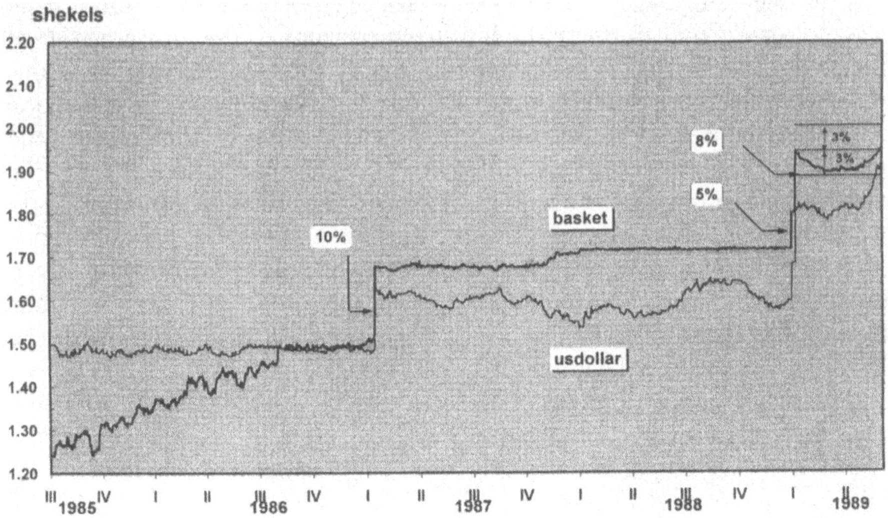

Figure 14.3. The Israeli Shekel Exchange Rate vis-a-vis the Basket and Dollar (July 85–May 89)

1987, the peg changed from the U.S. dollar to a basket of currencies, and thereafter, until 1989, Israel had a trade-weighted basket pegging. There was still a loss of competitiveness because inflation during this period averaged about 18 percent, while the prices of tradable goods, as reflected primarily by the exchange rate, remained relatively fixed.

In 1989, a decision was taken to move to a new exchange-rate system. In the new system the *pagged* exchange rate was replaced by a *band*. The band was set against the basket of currencies with a width of 3 percent on each side. The currency was allowed to fluctuate within the band. As can be seen in Figure 14.4, the band regime did not display a single pattern. During some periods, the exchange rate moved up and down within the band; after an adjustment of the band, the exchange rate moved very closely to the central parity, while after another adjustment the exchange rate moved on the way up within the band, or else it was moving along the bottom of the band. In other words, Israel experienced all patterns of exchange-rate movements within the band.

Several points are noteworthy. First, in an economy that runs at a moderate inflation—say, 20 percent per annum—it became clear that an integral part of the policy package must be occasional once-and-for-all adjustments of the band. This is because it is not possible to sustain con-

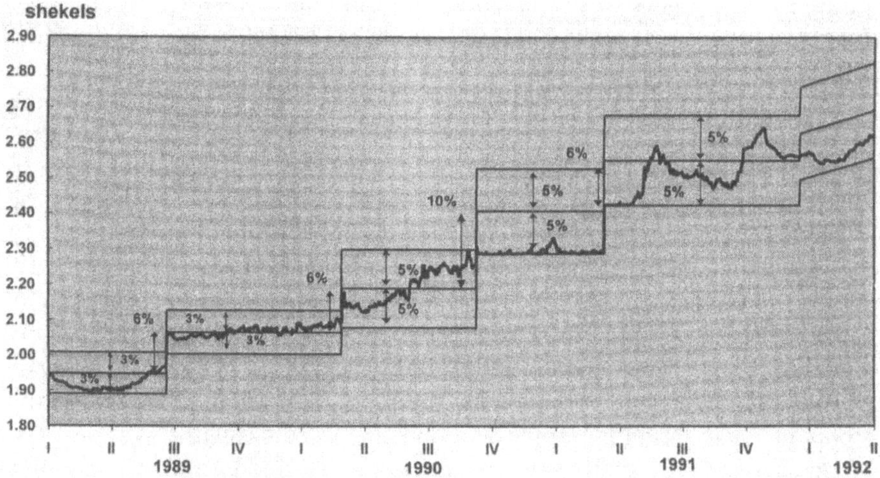

Figure 14.4. The Israeli Exchange Rate vis-a-vis the Basket (January 89–March 92)

tinuous losses of competitiveness. Unless inflation begins to go down at a reasonable pace, which was not the case in Israel, the band must be adjusted. In Israel, during this period, the rate of inflation remained at about 18 percent. The second point relates to the width of the band: as both domestic capital markets, and the capital account of the balance of payments were gradually liberalized, the band was widened to allow for larger variability of the exchange rate in response to large capital flows.

By the end of 1991 it was decided that a significant change in the system was needed. The intrinsic element of instability in the exchange-rate system was the fact that market participants knew in advance that at some stage there will have to be a "once-and-for-all" discrete adjustment of the central parity of the exchange-rate band because inflation continued to run at a pace that was significantly higher than the inflation prevailing in the industrial world. Clearly, as long as inflation is running consistently above the levels prevailing in the countries of the main competitors, a built-in adjustment of the peg is required. But if a built-in adjustment of the peg is required, significant noise is introduced by increasing the uncertainties in the market, since the precise magnitude and timing of the adjustment remains unknown. By 1991 it became evident that this element of instability had been a major source of noise that created, occasionally, a run on the currency with the anticipation that once-and-for-all adjustments are indeed going to take place. This, in turn, required monetary policy to take defensive measures, raising interest rates in abrupt ways and creating further disturbances.

To deal with these problems and to avoid that built-in inconsistency, the crawling band, which is also referred to as the diagonal band, was introduced. This diagonal band was introduced in late 1991 together with an inflation target. The slope of the exchange-rate band was defined as the difference between Israel's *inflation target* and the inflation prevailing in the rest of the world, so that, if one meets the inflation target, one basically avoids the built-in need to change the band again. Therefore, the capacity to meet the inflation target is tied to the capacity to maintain the stability of the exchange-rate regime. Initially, the inflation target was set in a way that resulted in a slope of 9 percent. Then the slope fell to 8 percent and to 6 percent, as inflation fighting obtained some results (Figure 14.5).

Other countries, such as Chile, also have a sloped band, but the key difference between the Chilean and the Israeli experiences was that the Chilean practice was essentially backward looking, with the slope of the band being decided according to past rather than targeted inflation. In other words, past inflation was validated, no matter how it behaved, in setting the exchange-rate path. In Israel's case it was decided to use the band itself as an instrument for fighting inflation through its influence on exchange-rate

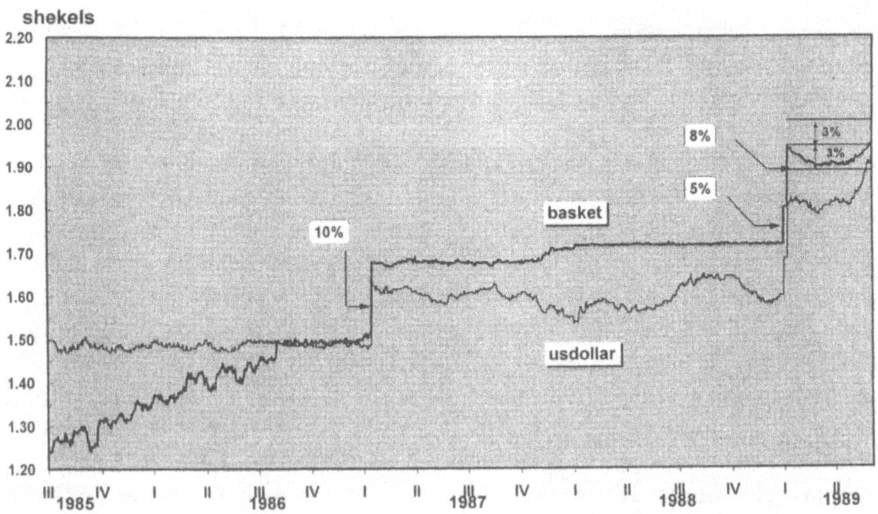

Figure 14.5. The Israeli Shekel Exchange Rate vis-a-vis the Basket and Dollar (July 85–May 89)

expectations and thus on inflation expectations, rather than as a mechanism for accommodating past inflation. The way to obtain this result was to have a forward-looking feature in the determination of the slope.

At the same time, to enhance the depth of the foreign-exchange market, interbank trade in foreign exchange was developed, reducing in this manner the need for the Bank of Israel's presence in the foreign-exchange market. In the past, the only setter of the exchange rate at the end of each trading day was the Central Bank because it was the main actor in the market. Gradually as the foreign-exchange market became deeper and wider, the Bank of Israel could withdraw from it, with fewer and fewer interventions.

The width of the band was also influenced by the degree of capital-account liberalization. When some liberalization of the capital account was allowed, the band was widened. The concept behind the widening of the band is that as more capital movements are allowed, a greater exchange-rate flexibility is needed. Think of the following analogy: if cars are suddenly allowed (and able) to travel at a higher speed than before, a major step in keeping this means of transportation safe is to widen the roads. In late 1995 the exchange-rate band was widened further to ±7 percent, and the exchange rate was allowed to move within the band. Eventually, however, it was realized that the system suffers from a very significant inconsistency. The inflation target was missed in 1994, and as a result interest rates had to be raised significantly to bring inflation back to target. The widened interest-rate differentials attracted foreign capital, and together with the intensification of other financial inflows, associated with the improved prospects for, and image of, the Israeli economy, the capital inflow problem began to emerge. This is a problem that has characterized two types of countries: the emerging economies that become increasingly attractive to foreign investors, and the stabilizing countries that started to attract short-term flows because of the high interest rates involved in the stabilization process.

In the Israeli case a combination of both factors was present. Since late 1993 and especially during 1994, partly due to the geopolitical developments in the Middle East and elsewhere, Israel has become a much more attractive destination for direct foreign investment. This type of long-term foreign investment is a relatively new phenomenon in the Israeli economy. In addition, high interest rates continued to attract significant amounts of capital, and this exerted strong appreciation pressures on the exchange rate. The sheqel indeed appreciated and hit the bottom of the band. At that point the Bank of Israel faced a severe monetary difficulty since, to defend the band, it had to buy foreign exchange, which leads to printing money, which, in turn, may result in the defeat of the inflation target. Therefore, the

Central Bank had to sterilize the unwarranted increase in the money supply. But there is a long list of questions facing a Central Bank in this situation: Can one sterilize, and if so, for how long, and at what cost? Robert Mundell, in his 1960 article, concluded that sterilization policies are not viable in the long run. But in the framework of modern capital markets, often the long run becomes the short run. And the real question, therefore, is how to manage under such circumstances.

In Israel the Central Bank did not give up on the inflation front and ended up accumulating a large amount of international reserves. The cost of sterilization, of course, had quasi-budgetary implications, and some people, not all, started to be concerned about what happens if the inflow process reverses itself. This brings us, then, to the next phase.

14.3. June 1997: The Widening of the Band

The issue of avoiding the high cost of sterilization resulted in a serious debate. There are, indeed, a variety of possibilities to deal with this problem. One is to impose a capital import tax, as was done in Chile. After examining this issue, however, the conclusion we reached is that one can delay liberalization and can slow down the opening of the capital account but that once it is opened, it is very difficult to reverse courses and close it again. Money, as water, finds its way to reach its destination, and it is very difficult to avoid this result. Furthermore, even though the primary purpose of such a tax is not to raise revenue, there is still the danger that what initially is used as a *financial* instrument, intended to differentiate between different types of capital flows, may end up as a temptation for the finance ministry, to use it as another *fiscal* instrument that generates revenue. In any event, in Israel, the decision was, to avoid the imposition of a capital import tax.

There are of course, other possibilities to deal with the capital inflow problem. One of them was to lower the interest rate. Why not? There were many who argued that this is not the time to fight inflation (as if there was a more suitable time to do that). There are many Central Bank governors who share the same experience. In Israel, like elsewhere, many people volunteer advice: chambers of commerce, industrial associations, labor unions, and so on, and that is good because it is free advice. But the fact is that, invariably, the advice is that, "for the good of the country, interest rates should be lowered." We in the Bank of Israel decided that it is a mistake to sacrifice inflation fighting and to lower interest rates to avoid the influx of foreign capital. This would be only a short-term gain because after a while, when inflation rises again, one would need to raise the interest rate anyhow and, therefore, the whole process would start anew.

It has been agreed, however, that what really is hurting is not just the *nominal* appreciation of the exchange rate but the *real* appreciation. This is true but, if that's the case, then it should be evident that monetary policy cannot alter the real exchange rate in a systematic manner, unless one focuses only on the short run. Concerning the determinants of the real exchange rate and competitiveness, it seems that in this matter one really needs to look at the real side of the economy—the fiscal side, the variables that determine relative prices. If anything, theory suggests that nominal policy is relevant for the behavior of nominal variables, and real policy instruments are relevant for the development of real variables. In fact, conventional theory points at budget cuts as the solution to real currency appreciation.

Therefore, instead of levying a foreign-exchange capital-inflow tax, it was decided to advance in the opposite direction: rather than closing the economy toward the world by imposing a capital import tax, we decided to continue with our basic strategy of further opening up the capital account through continued capital-account liberalization. To use another metaphor, the criterion used was the following: if in the long-run one wants to reach a certain place in the north, it makes no sense to pronounce that goal and then to start by going southward, even if it is only said to be for the short-term. And therefore, if in the long run one wants to have an open capital account, then one should use any possible occasion to move in the warranted direction. The Bank of Israel, therefore, decided to open Israel's capital account very significantly in two steps. And to ensure that as the capital account is opened, the pressures for appreciation do not become more severe, the exchange-rate system needed also to be adapted.

In the prevailing system described in the previous section, the government and the central bank have implicitly been providing something like an insurance policy to foreign-exchange traders, though without charging them for an insurance premium. Obviously, this distorted the incentives in the foreign-exchange market toward excessive risk taking. Even if the system is one of an exchange-rate band, the fact of the matter is that once the exchange rate reaches the boundary of that band, this system becomes a different one: it basically becomes a system of a crawling peg. In that sense, traveling along the lower boundary of a sloped band (e.g., during the second quarter of 1997 in Figure 14.5), means getting the worse of both worlds, even though there are some people who argue that crawling pegs give the best of both worlds: some flexibility and some fixity. In my view, which is based on the long experience with crawling pegs, one gets the worse of both worlds. This is so because by defending the peg, the central bank destroys the chances for foreign-exchange markets to develop and to mature. Since in such a system the central bank remains the main player in the market, it delays the development of market instruments for exchange-rate protection such as options, swaps, forwards, and futures. At the same time, not only are the wrong incentives being given to the market, but the central bank is also binding its monetary policy to its exchange-market interventions. Therefore, it was realized that to maintain the interest-rate differential between domestic and foreign currencies and yet not to attract a large foreign-exchange influx, one must allow for the introduction of some additional risk premia in the foreign-exchange markets. It is not necessary to introduce more noise, but one must allow for the "natural" noise to be more fully reflected in the market, rather than suppressing it and letting it be diffused in some other market. And for this purpose one needs to widen the band.

There was a big debate in Israel when the exchange rate was moving along the lower limit of the band. It was argued that if the band is widened, one would get an immediate appreciation. The theory was that the band is akin to a wall, stopping the flow of water, and that if one removes the wall, obviously we know in which direction the water will go. This argument neglected what Malthus had realized long ago: that extrapolations are wrong and that in economics, when we change a regime, the old rules do not apply any more. If you have a little pond next to the wall, and you remove the wall by 10cm, the water is indeed likely to flow and get to the new wall. When you remove it by another 10cm, the water will flow and again get to the new wall. But if you remove it by 15 meters, the water will not necessarily fill up the space; unless there is a slope, the water need not get to the new wall. This is because there is a new regime, a new system. The winds may be different, the actors may be different.

A decision was therefore taken to widen the band. The recommendation of the Bank of Israel was to widen the band in both directions. But the government was very concerned with the possibility of a nominal appreciation, so the band was widened in a somewhat different way (Figure 14.5). First, the upper boundary was shifted upward, and the slope of the lower band was reduced from the previous 6 percent (per year) before to 4 percent. In a forward-looking framework we may say that there is a greater risk of appreciation than before, and, of course, also a greater risk of depreciation than before. The new width of +/–15 percent was again rationalized by a forward-looking argument: if in the longer-term Israel wants to adopt a European-type system, then it should learn what is happening there. The basic principle was, in metaphoric terms, that when there is a wider road, cars would not necessarily skid from one extreme point to the other because actually drivers may drive in a much more steady way just because of the fact that the road is wider.

Let me add the fact that on the day that the band was widened, significant depreciation, not appreciation, took place. This type of depreciation is healthy because it was not administered by the authorities. It rather reflected market forces. As we know, the transmission of a depreciated currency into prices is very different if it has been engineered through (administered) devaluation rather than through a market-determined depreciation. A once-and-for-all devaluation creates a new floor for the exchange rate and provides all the incentives, especially in a small country, for all prices to be marked up in equal proportions. But if the markets require a depreciation of a similar size, the transmission process need not mark up prices equiproportionally, since it is not known whether this depreciation would be permanent. In such a situation the transmission of exchange-rate changes to prices depends very much on the regime, rather than on the actual change in the exchange rate.

In summing up Israel's experience with the exchange-rate system, I want to stress that in this sense Israel is also a transition economy since it underwent monetary transformation. It started with a slope of the exchange-rate band of 9 percent and then it moved to a slope of 8 percent, on to a slope of 6 percent, and then on to 4 percent. Hopefully, as inflation in Israel comes down to levels similar to its trading partners, the slope would become zero (given that the slope of the exchange-rate band is the inflation target minus inflation prevailing abroad) and in the end obsolete. Thus, Israel's inflation story is the mirror image of the story of the exchange-rate band, the dual or the other side of the same coin. What is characterizing the Israeli system now is that the exchange-rate system and anti-inflation strategy are, in fact, married to each other through the setting of inflation targets and of the slope of the exchange-rate band.

14.4. Israel's Monetary Policy

There is a rich discussion in the literature about the transmission of monetary policy and the fact that it takes a long time and affects the economy with long and variable lags. This seems particularly true in transition countries that are experiencing significant structural changes in the financial system and therefore where monetary aggregates lose their meaning. And yet the question is, How can one introduce some elements in the conduct of monetary policy that can shorten the transmission mechanism? This leads into the issue of the indexed and nonindexed government bonds traded in Israel's capital market.

In Israel, during the period of hyperinflation, indexation practices were adopted and became widespread. This became a curse for anybody who wanted to fight inflation. Indexation is a curse because it creates mechanisms and a behavior under the illusion that it is possible to live with inflation. It thus reduces the incentive for fighting it. In addition, it creates a further obstacle in the process of reducing inflation if one has to face the obstacle of inertia because the past of the high inflation is carried directly to the present.

However, one of the positive elements has been that as Israel's government faced increasing difficulties to borrow in the marketplace, it began to issue inflation-indexed bonds. And as inflation came down, the government continued to issue, side by side, indexed and nonindexed bonds. This had the positive side effect of providing the monetary authority with a very useful instrument: it can look every day at the difference in yields between the nonindexed and the indexed bond of the same government, the same maturity, the same risk, except for inflation. The latter is absent in the indexed bonds but present in the nominal bonds. In this manner, one can measure inflationary expectations directly from the capital market according to the difference between the market-determined yields on nominal and issued bonds. There are daily data from which one learns a number of things. First, as it is already known, inflationary expectations are typically highly volatile, depending on the news. But second, we also see (Figure 14.6) the main factors that impact on these expectations. Let's take two episodes: November 1994 and July 1996. Inflationary expectations had reached local peaks—nearly 14 percent in 1994 and a similar level in 1996. At that stage the Bank of Israel decided to raise its lending rate very significantly. Inflationary expectations started falling immediately and dramatically. And when interest rates were lowered too rapidly, inflationary expectations went up again. What we learned from these episodes is that, even if the expectations are very volatile, they do respond rapidly, within a week, sometimes even within a day, to decisive changes in the interest rate. Then the question becomes, How can one use this information for the conduct of policy?

To begin with, one wants to know how the behavior of the expectations is related to actual inflation. Figure 14.7 presents inflationary expectations alongside with actual inflation. Inflationary expectations are measuring, at each point in time, the inflation that is expected in the twelve months ahead—based on the available information until this day—as reflected in the difference between indexed and nonindexed government bonds for

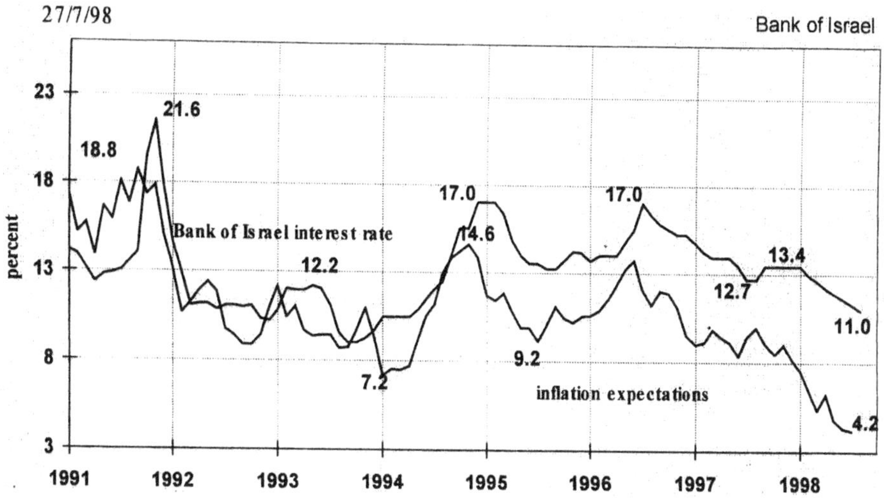

Figure 14.6. Bank of Israel interest rate and Inflation Expectations

twelve months. The schedule of actual inflation describes for each month the price level this month compared with the correspondent price level twelve months ago. We can see that the relation between the two is pretty strong, but there are nevertheless some interesting nuances. In November 1994, when inflationary expectations peaked, the interest rate was raised by 1.5 percentage points, and inflationary expectations reacted by a fall. It took only a very short period of time, less than a month or two, for actual inflation to follow. When interest rates started to come down and inflationary expectations increased, actual inflation was still coming down. At this point the central bank should have raised interest rates promptly. What one needs to do with regard to monetary policy is to look ahead: as inflationary expectations were rising again, the central bank should have raised interest rates more rapidly and in a more significant way. Interest rates were raised, but too slowly. At some stage, in June 1996, inflationary expectations had again reached a peak. The interest-rate response was clear: the interest rate was raised significantly, and it did not take long for actual inflation to follow suit and come down. Right now we are at the lowest level for both inflationary expectations and actual inflation.

So the lesson from all this is: first, if one has an instrument to measure inflationary expectations, one should use it; second, the transmission mechanism has become much quicker; third, it is important to conduct monetary policy within a framework of greater transparency.

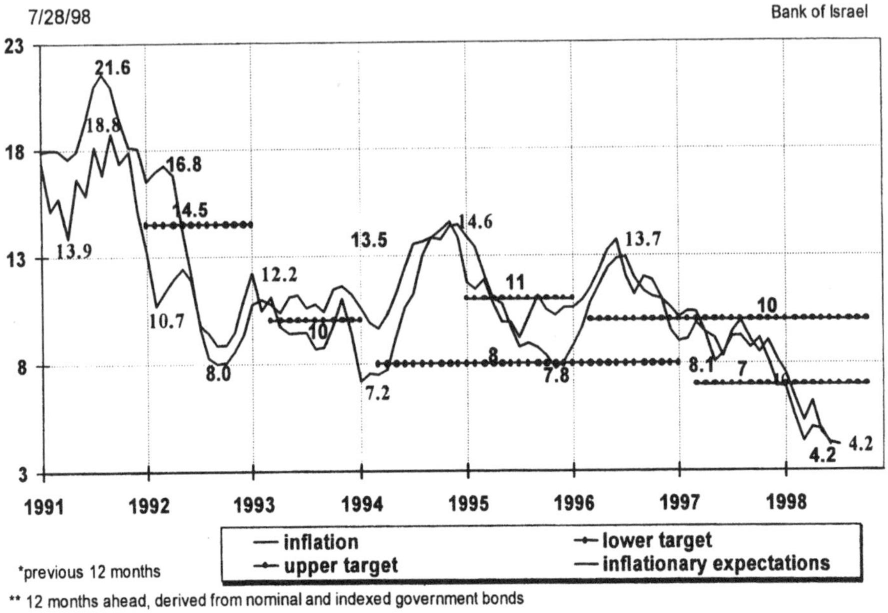

Figure 14.7. Inflation Rate*, Inflation Target and Inflationary Expectations**, 1991–1998

I want to conclude these remarks by noting that in Israel there has been a significant revolution in the conduct of monetary policy in the following sense: in the old days, monetary policy in particular, and economic policy in general, were viewed as antagonistic to the market. The markets were the enemies of policymakers and vice versa. Policymakers had to surprise markets, to announce policies: on Saturday night at midnight, when everything is closed, everyone is surprised, nothing is expected and central-bank policy is done in secrecy. The new approach, which (I believe) is becoming more and more the accepted approach all over the world, views the markets as partners to policymakers rather than as rivals. This does not mean that policymakers have suddenly become nicer people, but it does mean that it has been realized that markets have become stronger and more influential. It has thus become understood that if you cannot beat the markets you should join them.

The Israeli economic experience can be defined as being an economy in transition toward greater openness of the capital account, which at the same time has been in a process of a disinflation, starting from a moderate level. On the question of when to start this transition, the answer is this: do not delay the starting point. There has been a big discussion in Israel about the question of timing: when to do what? I have derived two lessons from the Israeli experience. First, twenty years ago there was a very popular subject of analysis that was called the *order of economic liberalization*. What should you liberalize first? Domestic, external? Trade account first, capital account second? All these concepts are very sensible in a virtual chess game. But in economic policy, there are occasions when one has to *create* opportunities rather than just seize them, and therefore, if one plays the game of the order of economic liberalization and reform according to the book, one is likely to end up by advancing too slowly. My recipe is therefore this: adopt a clear long-run strategy. Once you have adopted it, seize any opportunity that presents itself to advance toward your goals, create irreversible changes in the right direction, and then proceed in a way that creates the next occasion. Second, regarding the question when to start, one should rather start sooner than later. This sounds trivial, but it reminds me of the story of the little boy who was running after the bus, and when he came to the station, the bus had already left the station. And an old man told him; "My little boy, you should have run faster." The boy replied: "No, I ran pretty fast, but I guess I should have started sooner." And I think the little boy was right. When it comes to transition economies we all had a late start, which means that we better start a little sooner, a little faster.

14.5. The Response of an Economy in Transition to a Global Financial Crisis

A final remark on the recent financial crisis that has been unfolding in Southeast Asia and crucially threatening to kindle contagious developments in other parts of the world (as did the Tequila effect in the wake of the 1994 to 1995 Mexican crisis). Like every crisis, the present crisis has its idiosyncrasies. Its timing and vehemence, if not more than that, has certainly taken many observers and policymakers by surprise. However, in a highly globalized financial environment, the effects on worried international investors in emerging markets were rapidly visible. After a prolonged disregard of risk, in favor of an excessive regard for high-yielding investments, worldwide preferences shifted drastically toward risk reduction—now—with an excessive disregard of yields.

Such abrupt shifts in investment and loan portfolios, of course, expose the emerging markets, which are the receivers of these foreign funds, to particular risks. To counterfeit or minimize this vulnerability, policymakers in an emerging transition economy have an important chance—selectivity. In a world of rapidly changing economic circumstances, investors have to become increasingly selective. They have to weigh the factors that drive international investors' funds out of an economy due to a worsening in its fundamentals, against those factors that drive investment funds away from emerging economies in general towards low-risk investments. If a transition economy manages to reduce its vulnerability by improving the economy's fundamentals—mainly through adamant and consistent implementation of a long-run market-oriented strategy of economic reforms—it will gain in the international competition for extra international savings for investment at home. In today's world financial markets, international credit-rating agencies such as Standard & Poor's, Moody's, and others monitor these economies closely and act as an international traffic police for channeling the funds to their most efficient uses. Policymakers in transition economies therefore have to learn to accept the idimension of their political economic decisions.

15 BALANCE OF PAYMENTS, EXCHANGE RATES, AND COMPETITIVENESS IN HUNGARY

László Halpern

Institute of Economics, Hungarian Academy of Sciences

Judit Neményi

National Bank of Hungary

15.1. Introduction

The assessment of Hungary's economic performance has been based on macro dominantly, the major criteria being the rate of growth and inflation. In this respect Hungary was lagging behind not only the fast-reformer transition countries, but behind some slow reformers, as well. The macroeconomic mismanagement in certain periods has been analyzed hundreds of times; the problems related to large-scale corporate restructuring, however, have not been much emphasized. The excessively strict bankruptcy regulations at the outset, the bank and credit consolidation programs, combined with the relatively high inflow of capital ensured the necessary conditions for corporate restructuring, while the weak domestic demand stimulated exports to cover costs in the early phase of transition. Industry-level growth figures reflect great deal of variation; certain manufacturing industries produced a two-digit increase in output and exports in 1995 to 1996, and there are still sectors that have to scale down the activity level.

In 1997 the prospects for growth and containing inflation are better than ever before, but the policy choices are far from clear. In the circumstances of positive trends the challenges are different from those in the pre- and early stabilization phase. It means that reactions will also differ.

The chapter presents the basic elements of development and how the policy can contribute to enhance positive trends when the privatization, the first phase of restructuring—the elimination of nonprofitable businesses—and the major adjustment in fundamentals have been completed.

15.2. Seven Lean Years

The difficulties of the Hungarian economic transition cannot be understood without understanding the most important features of the economic policy of the previous regime. This policy in the 1980s has tried to increase the adaptability of economic agents, while the structure of corporations has been untouched.

The stop-go policy of the 1980s was not successful in preventing the current account from deterioration as restrictive economic policy was always abandoned very quickly when first partial results were achieved. This happened in 1985 as well. Expansion of the domestic demand coupled with increasing exports in nonconvertible currency crowded out convertible currency exports. The growing external deficits forced the government to recall restrictive domestic demand policy in mid-1987. However, the ineffective system of regulation, the badly oriented subsidies, and so on made the adjustment process very slow. Thus, the unfavorable trends continued: the exports to CMEA, for which hard-currency intermediate imports were needed, had been increasing, while convertible exports declined. Consequently, international debt has been growing, the debt service became a real burden. By the end of the 1980s Hungary's creditworthiness had weakened critically, and servicing the huge external debt—the major part of which was accumulated in the second half of the decade—resulted in a serious foreign-exchange liquidity crisis. This was the most important binding condition the Hungarian policymakers had to face with when transition toward market system stared in 1990.

15.2.1. Liberalization and Demand Shocks

In the early 1990s the Hungarian economy was hit by serious shocks. The trade and price liberalization coupled with the dissolution of CMEA accelerated the restructuring and trade reorientation of enterprises. Facing the serious external debt problem and taking into account the weak adjustment capability of corporate sector, the economic policy did not have too much choice how to cope with the combined effects of different shocks in 1990 to 1991. Giving first priority to the improvement in external position a longer-run restructuring program—based on privatization and liberalization—was announced. The weak adjustment capability of the economy on an enterprise level was thought to be improved by diminishing the state's participation in economic activity and by increasing the price and cost sensitivity of enterprises. At the same time it was decided to strengthen financial discipline (bankruptcy law, on act regulating financial institutions, and so on).

The effects of multiple—demand and supply, both external and internal—shocks manifested in the deepening of transformational recession, the GDP fell by close to 20 percent in 1990 to 1992 (see Table 15.1). Shocks

Table 15.1. Main macroeconomic indicators

	1990	*1991*	*1992*	*1993*	*1994*	*1995*	*1996*
Real GDP (%)	−3.5	−11.9	−3.1	−0.6	2.9	1.5	cca. 1
Domestic absorption (%)	−3.1	−9.1	−3.6	9.9	2.2	−3.1	0.0
Private consumption (%)	−2.7	−5.6	0.0	1.9	0.2	−6.1	−2.5
Gross fixed capital formation (%)	−4.2	−10.4	−2.6	2.0	12.5	−4.3	−3.5
Exports (%)		−13.9	2.1	−10.1	13.7	13.4	10.4
Imports (%)		−6.1	0.2	18.6	8.8	−0.7	7.3
CPI	28.9	35.0	23.0	22.5	18.8	28.2	23.6
End-year	33.4	32.2	21.6	21.1	21.2	28.3	19.8
PPI	22.0	32.6	12.3	10.8	11.3	28.9	21.8
End-year	32.1	21.9	13.7	9.5	14.8	30.2	20.1
Nominal effective exchange rate	15.9	14.2	9.6	6.5	16.3	28.8	16.4
Gross wages	28.6	30.0	25.1	21.9	24.9	16.8	20.4
Net real wages	−3.7	−7.0	−1.4	−3.9	7.2	−12.2	−5.2
Unemployment rate	1.9	7.5	12.3	12.1	10.4	10.4	10.4
Savings ratio	6.7	15.1	10.4	4.7	7.7	8.4	10.2
General government balance (%)	−2.9	−2.4	−7.0	−6.7	−9.6	−7.4	−4.8
General government primary balance (%)	−1.0	−0.1	0.3	−2.4	−1.6	1.7	4.5
Current account (%)	0.4	0.8	0.9	−9.0	−9.4	−5.4	−3.8
Gross external debt (%)	64.3	67.8	57.6	63.7	68.4	71.5	62.4
Net external debt (%)	48.2	43.6	35.0	38.7	45.4	38.0	32.2
M3 (annual average) (%)	26.1	27.3	36.4	19.4	14.3	15.3	22.9

Source: National Bank of Hungary.

were absorbed by different factors: the unemployment rate rose to 12 percent by 1992 from nil in 1988, the enterprise profits fell, even turned to negative on average in 1992, and real wages were cut significantly. Assuming downward nominal—wage and price—rigidities, the surge in inflation was unavoidable. The budget balances had been worsening fast, as the drop of revenues was a natural consequence of the fall in output and no major adjustment was decided on the expenditures side, partly because the recession increased social tensions. In addition, the system of budget financing had been untouched until 1992. Prior to 1993 the budget borrowing requirement was covered without upper limit by central bank loans at preferential interest rates, making the government budget constraint soft. The rigidity in the budget structure and the related financing problems contributed, by no means, after 1992 to the persistence of moderate inflation. Only the 1996 amendment of the Act on Central Bank prohibited the direct finance—that is, the purchase of government securities in the primary market.

The microlevel adjustment starting in 1990 to 1991 was leading to the creation of a market-oriented corporate sector. The supply-side reaction, however, was slow—particularly until the bankruptcy law was implemented in 1992—in the sense that the external shocks could achieve only the liquidation of noncompetitive activities in the short run, but the creation of businesses competitive in the long run in the world market could start with a lag. The fall in import demand was not sustainable, and the fragility of the export sector made the first results rather vulnerable.

The period of 1991 to mid-1992 was successful in preventing the external debt from further increase. The current account exhibited a slight surplus, foreign-exchange reserves reached a secure level, and the inflow of foreign direct investment was continuous. By the end of 1992 net debt of Hungary decreased by nearly U.S. $3 billion (see Tables 15.2 and 15.3). The ratio of debt service to exports fell from 49 percent in 1990 to 31 percent in 1992, and Hungary's access to international capital markets improved significantly.

15.2.2. Corporate Restructuring and Macroeconomic Failures

In 1992 signs of inherent equilibrium problems were shadowed by the first partial adjustment in the current account and by the relatively unfavorable external conditions—fall in external demand due to the wars and bad weather hitting agricultural production and exports. The coincidence of deteriorating fundamentals with disadvantageous exogenous conditions made policymakers less attentive to structural problems stemming first of

Table 15.2. Foreign-exchange debt of Hungary (in billions of U.S. dollars)

	1990	1991	1992	1993	1994	1995	1996
I. Gross debt							
1. National Bank of Hungary	17.7	17.9	16.1	18.3	20.2	21.2	16.4
2. Government	0.5	1.5	1.6	2.0	2.3	2.0	2.1
3. Financial institutions	1.8	2.0	1.8	1.8	2.4	2.9	3.1
4. Enterprises	1.2	1.2	1.9	2.0	3.1	4.7	4.7
Total (1 + 2 + 3 + 4)	21.2	22.6	21.4	24.1	28.0	30.8	26.3
II. Net debt							
1. National Bank of Hungary	16.3	13.8	11.7	11.6	13.1	9.1	6.6
2. Government	0.3	1.3	1.5	1.8	2.1	1.5	1.3
3. Financial institutions	0.7	0.6	0.3	0.5	1.4	2.0	1.4
4. Enterprises	–1.3	1.1	0.1	0.7	1.8	2.8	3.5
Total (1 + 2 + 3 + 4)	16.0	16.8	13.6	14.6	18.4	15.4	12.8

Source: National Bank of Hungary.
a. *Excluding interenterprise credits.*

Table 15.3. Foreign-exchange debt of Hungary (in percent)[a]

	1990	1991	1992	1993	1994	1995	1996
I. Gross debt							
1. National Bank of Hungary	83.5	79.2	75.2	75.9	72.1	68.8	62.4
2. Government	2.4	6.6	7.5	8.3	8.2	6.5	8.0
3. Financial institutions	8.5	8.8	8.4	7.5	8.6	9.4	11.8
4. Enterprises	5.7	5.3	8.9	8.3	11.1	15.3	17.9
Total (1 + 2 + 3 + 4)	100.0	100.0	100.0	100.0	100.0	100.0	100.0
II. Net debt							
1. National Bank of Hungary	101.9	82.1	86.0	79.5	71.2	59.1	51.6
2. Government	1.9	7.7	11.0	12.3	11.4	9.7	10.2
3. Financial institutions	4.4	3.6	2.2	3.4	7.6	13.0	10.9
4. Enterprises	–8.1	6.5	0.7	4.8	9.8	18.2	27.3
Total (1 + 2 + 3 + 4)	100.0	100.0	100.0	100.0	100.0	100.0	100.0

Source: National Bank of Hungary.
a. *Excluding interenterprise credits.*

all from the too slow and several times postponed transformation of the budget and public finance. The legal framework of the market economy was completed by new laws and institutional developments (the acts covering financial institutions, the stock exchange, accounting, bankruptcy, and the central bank). At the same time the new regulation triggered a wave of selection among nonviable enterprises by strengthening the fiscal discipline, and the emerging sector was hit by high cost of capital (see Bonin and Schaffer, 1995). Unfavorable signs were manifested in the sluggishness of the modernization and in the increasing size of nonperforming debts. However, the private sector could not escape from the enforcement of fiscal discipline and market competition; thus restructuring was relatively rapid and painful for enterprises, while the growing borrowing requirement had been steadily increasing, which threatened by crowding out private sector in the competition for loanable funds.

From mid-1992 to 1994 there was a shift in the main goals of macroeconomic policy. Taking into account the improving current account in 1992 the target rate of increase of domestic demand was set higher than the target increase in exports to let investments recover, which seemed to be necessary to turn up the trend of falling GDP prevailing since 1990. The first unfavorable signs of export decline were attributed to exogenous factors and were thought temporary. It was expected that increasing domestic demand would contribute to the increase in investments rather than to the increase in imports. According to these objectives the monetary policy aimed at lowering interest rates by not sterilizing excess liquidity stemming from the improving current account and increasing capital inflow.

As the interest rates followed the inflation reduction with a significant lag in 1992 (see Figure 15.1), the monetary policy did not only abstain from sterilizing the excess liquidity but added to it by lowering the rate of mandatory reserves, and the liquidity was further increased by the maturing but not refinanced liquidity treasury bills. This resulted in overshooting the decline of interest rates. The yield on government securities with maturity less than one year and the households' deposit real interest rates became negative in 1993. The household savings had been steadily decreasing (see Table 15.4), and it became unavoidable to halt the trend of falling interest rates.

In 1993 the targets of macroeconomic policy failed completely: the GDP continued to fall, the domestic demand and imports grew strongly by 9.9 and 18.6 percent, respectively, and the exports declined unexpectedly by 10 percent. The wedge between imports and exports growth opened to 30 percentage points, which became the major problem in 1993 to 1994. Closely linked to each other, both domestic and foreign equilibria deteriorated to

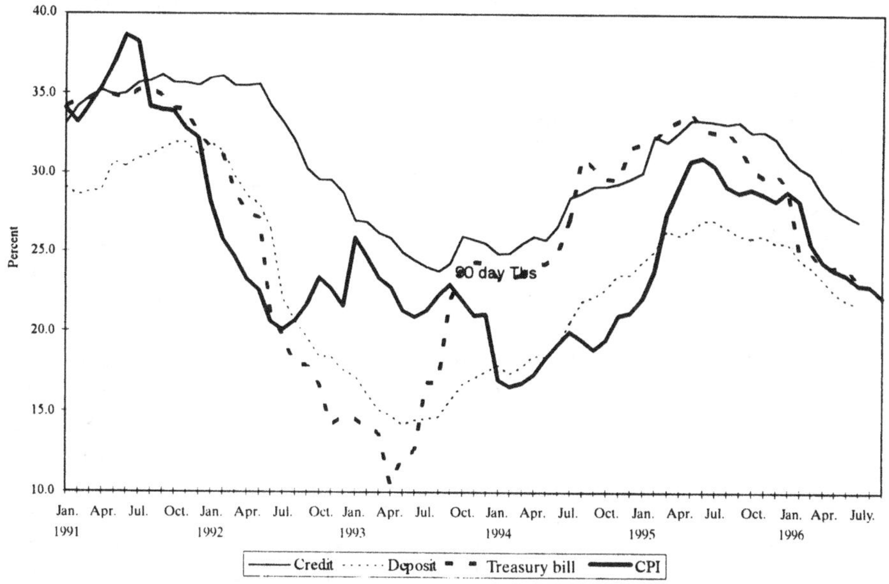

Figure 15.1. Enterprises Credit and Deposit Rates, Treasury Bill-Yield and Inflation (per annum)
Source: National Bank of Hungary.

a dangerous extent. Unfavorable exogenous factors played a nonnegligible role in these failures of the economic performance. The main problem was, however, that measures necessary to make stabilization sustainable had been postponed and that the ad hoc, sometimes contradictory, steps in both fiscal and monetary policy destroyed the public's confidence and fueled inflationary and devaluation expectations. The credibility of the pegged, adjustable exchange-rate system had been completely undermined by mid-1994. The speculations against the forint showed regular volatility as the steadily deteriorating current account increased the probability of a next devaluation (see Figure 15.2).

The current-account deficit in 1993 exceeded U.S. $3.5 billion due primarily to the substantial foreign trade deficit (see Table 15.5). Was it attributable to an appreciating real exchange rate? Indicators of competitiveness reveal that neither PPI nor export-price-based real exchange rates showed a major shift (see Table 15.6). On the other hand, the CPI and GDP deflator, labor cost, and profit-based real exchange rates were increasing. As it was clear that price-based indicators were biased, cost-based indicators had started to increase earlier in 1991 and 1992 so their predictive power was

Table 15.4. The savings-investment balance (percent of GDP)

	1988	*1989*	*1990*	*1991*	*1992*	*1993*	*1994*	*1995*	*1996*
Gross national savings	25.1	25.0	27.3	17.8	15.3	10.6	14.4	20.5	23.2
Households	6.6	7.9	9.1	15.1	12.9	8.2	9.9	10.6	12.7
Government	7.6	5.2	5.1	3.1	0.5	–0.2	–3.2	–2.5	–1.0
Enterprises	10.9	12.0	13.1	–0.4	1.8	2.6	7.7	12.4	11.5
Net asset transfer									
Households				0.9	0.9	0.9	1.0	0.8	0.5
Government	–1.4	–0.6	–1.1	–1.3	–2.2	–1.8	–1.4	–1.6	–1.0
Enterprises				0.4	1.4	1.0	0.4	0.8	0.5
Gross investment	25.3	26.6	25.4	20.4	16.1	20.0	22.2	24.0	25.0
Households	4.9	5.2	3.9	5.4	4.9	5.1	4.6	4.9	5.0
Government	6.2	5.9	3.6	4.3	5.2	4.7	5.0	3.2	2.7
Enterprises	14.3	15.5	18.0	10.7	6.0	10.1	12.6	15.8	17.2
Savings-investment balance	–0.2	–1.5	1.9	–2.7	–0.8	–9.3	–7.8	–3.5	–1.8
Households	1.8	2.7	5.3	9.7	8.9	3.9	6.3	6.5	8.2
Government	1.5	–0.7	1.5	–1.2	–6.9	–6.7	–9.6	–7.3	–4.7
Enterprises	–3.4	–3.6	–4.9	–11.2	–2.8	–6.6	–4.6	–2.7	–5.3
Current-account balance	–0.2	–1.9	1.1	–1.1	–1.0	–9.0	–9.4	–5.4	–3.9

Source: National Bank of Hungary.

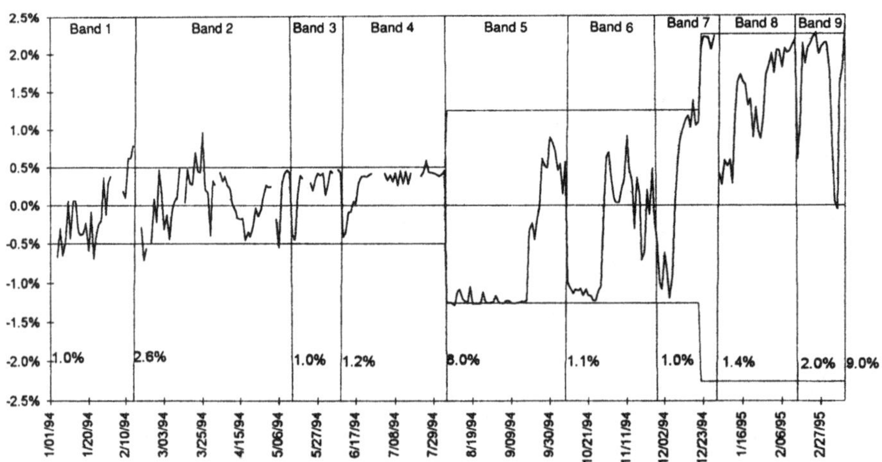

Figure 15.2. Exchange Rate Within the Band in the Adjustable Band Period
Source: National Bank of Hungary.
Note: Vertical lines indicate the dates of devaluation, and the numbers close to the lines show the sizes of devaluation.

Table 15.5. Balance of payments (in millions of U.S. dollars)

	1988	*1989*	*1990*	*1991*	*1992*	*1993*	*1994*	*1995*	*1996*
Exports	5,505	6,446	6,346	9,258	10,028	8,094	7,913	12,810	14,183
Imports	5,016	5,909	5,998	9,069	10,076	11,340	11,248	15,252	16,828
Trade balance	489	537	348	189	–48	–3,247	–3,635	–2,442	–2,645
Tourism net	41	–349	345	560	590	442	503	659	1,288
Investment income net	–1,077	–1,387	–1,414	–1,331	–1,216	–1,130	–1,286	–1,599	–1,454
Unrequited transfer	114	126	727	860	859	732	909	1,127	922
Current-account balance	–807	–1,437	127	267	324	–3,455	–3,911	–2,480	–1,678
Medium-areas long-term capital	555	1,411	204	3,070	432	5,632	2,295	5,601	–2,225
Foreign direct investment	14	187	311	1,459	1,471	2,339	1,146	4,453	1,983
Privatization revenue			8	329	519	1,202	104	3,024	600
Short-term capital	288	–44	–893	–617	5	459	960	1,411	–1,012
Net errors and omissions						778	191	1,224	1,864
Balance of payments	36	–70	–562	2,720	761	2,635	–656	4,532	–1,458

Source: National Bank of Hungary.

Table 15.6. Indicators of competitiveness for manufacturing

Real Effective Exchange Rates (1989 = 100)	*1990*	*1991*	*1992*	*1993*	*1994*	*1995*	*1996*
1. PPI-based real exchange rate	98.0	103.2	102.0	104.4	99.4	94.0	98.0
2. ULC-based real exchange rate	103.1	115.4	139.0	138.8	129.2	107.9	102.7
3. Profit-based real exchange rate (2/1)	105.21 05.2	111.8	136.3	133.0	130.0	114.8	104.8
4. GDP-deflator-based real exchange rate	100.2	104.0	110.1	124.4	125.0	112.7	115.1
5. CPI-based real exchange rate	102.8	114.2	122.2	134.0	131.8	127.1	131.4
6. Export-price-based real exchange rate	96.1	99.2	99.0	100.7	102.6	103.6	105.2

Source: National Bank of Hungary, own computations.
Note: An increase means appreciation.

not credible. Related to the interpretation of indicators of competitiveness, some methodological issues will be treated later. The sharp decline of corporate profitability in 1991 and its rather slow recovery (see Table 15.4) cannot be explained by the exchange rate exclusively, some other factors were already mentioned. Profitability of exports exceeded that of domestic sales, and the investments to increase export capacities were lagging. Corporations have reoriented their sales toward exports in 1991 and 1992 successfully, but it was hampered by new bankruptcy and prudential banking regulations in 1993.

Although the inflow of foreign direct investments was continuous, the current-account deficit had been expanding steadily, and the direct foreign borrowing of enterprises and commercial banks became significant, as well. Hence, the external debt of the country started to rise again.

The year 1994 was the first year of GDP growth after the massive decline between 1989 and 1993. Household consumption was slightly rising, and investments were growing by 12 percent. Since the first signs of recovery in mid-1993 the investment demand had been increasing due to improving financial position of—both domestic and foreign—enterprises and also due to support provided by the government to some large enterprises in the form of state guarantee. The export activity began to recover coupled, however, with high import demand, which reflected the weakness of a domestic supply that was not able to meet increasing demand. The equilibrium targets have been threatened by the expansion of imports. The further deteriorating current account led to accelerating external indebtedness. Since 1992 the general government deficit was continuously increasing, and the twin deficit problem has emerged. In 1994 the medium-term economic program of the new socialist-liberal government aimed at stabilizing and modernizing the economy for the sake of sustainable growth; however, the necessity of major adjustment in the budget was not recognized at once.

The declining trend of inflation was stopped in 1994. The average annual inflation rate was 19 percent, lower than in the preceding year, but the annual indices showed an acceleration again, and the inflationary pressure could have been observed from February. To keep the budget in line with the targets, the government decided to increase the VAT and excise tax rates. The larger—17 percent—devaluation and the significant wage increases contributed to the renewal of inflationary pressure, as well. The deteriorating trade balance resulted in a high—U.S. $3.9 billion—deficit in the current account. Under these circumstances a high level of official reserves—approximately U.S. $7 billion, which was equivalent to seven months of imports—was necessary to maintain the creditworthiness on international capital markets.

15.2.3. Contingency Measures of March 1995

By the end of 1994 it had become evident that macroeconomic adjustment could not be postponed any more. The budget deficit was approaching 9 percent of GDP, and the current-account deficit was about the same size and growing rapidly. The ratios of gross and net foreign debt to GDP increased steadily, and the terms at which Hungary could borrow worsened substantially when the Mexican crisis hit the market. The March 1995 adjustment package was designed to reestablish internal and external equilibrium to fulfill conditions for sustainable growth. The adjustable fixed exchange-rate regime was replaced by a preannounced crawling band aiming at restoring credibility of economic policy and regaining investors' confidence. The fiscal adjustment was thought to be essential from the point of view of longer-term prospects, as the emerging private sector can profit from the continuous decrease of the government sector, while the initial 9 percent devaluation of domestic currency and the temporary import surcharge were to increase competitiveness of the tradable sector. The reduced government-borrowing requirement coupled with improving debt indicators to allow lower tax burdens.

The effect of March 1995 measures was quite rapid and longer lasting than had been expected. The impact of large fiscal adjustment could hardly be foreseen, taking into account that the reduction of government spending was indeed significant in international comparison. Expenditures were reduced by 10 percentage points in real terms within two years; hence it was not surprising that the lagged effect on growth was larger than expected. The results manifested in the improvement of internal and external imbalances. The twin deficits dropped significantly. The ratio of general government deficit to GDP was reduced from the peak 9.6 in 1994 to 4.8 percent in 1996, while the current-account deficit declined by more than 5 percentage points from 9.4 in 1994 to 3.8 percent in 1996.

The trade balance improved by U.S. $1.2 billion in 1995. The improvement was due to two-digit increase of export volume and the stagnation of imports. In 1996 the export dynamism was maintained, while the imports rose by 7.3 percent leading to a slight deterioration of the balance. The other elements of the current account contributed to its larger improvement, too. The net revenue from tourism was growing and almost doubled in 1996. The so-called unrequited transfer fluctuated around U.S. $1 billion with a peak in 1995. The current-account deficit was approximately covered by the foreign direct investment even if the privatization revenues are deducted and we took into account that stock-exchange investments by nonresidents were part of the net errors and omissions through the end of 1996. The privatization revenues were quite sensitive to political influences, and the sell

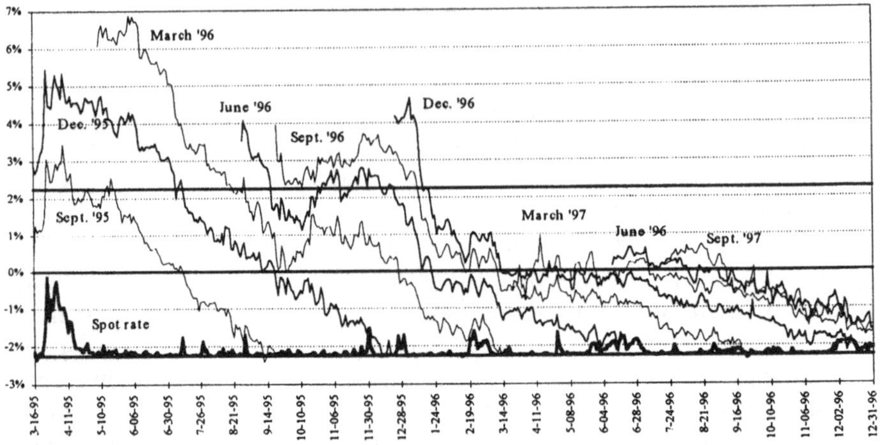

Figure 15.3. Futures Exchange Rates Within the Projected Bands of the NBH and Spot Rate Within the Spot Band, March 1995 to December 1996
Source: National Bank of Hungary.

of telecommunication and public utilities (energy) caused high values in certain years.

All in all, the debt and debt-service indicators have improved significantly. The vicious circle of increasing interest leading to increasing borrowing and debt to GDP ratios turned into a virtuous circle of decreasing interest payments resulting in decreasing borrowing needs and costs, reducing debt to GDP ratios that was enhanced by the prepayment of loans with higher interest rates. The credibility of the exchange-rate policy has been established by the preannounced crawling-band regime, providing better predictability for different economic actors. Expectations remained in the projected exchange-rate band since the end of 1995, and the falling difference between future and spot exchange rates revealed growing credibility (see Figures 15.3 and 15.4). Following the introduction of the new system, the rate of the crawl was reduced gradually from the starting 1.9 percent to 1.1 percent by the second quarter of 1997. The stability of financial markets has increased, and the inflow of FDI has accelerated. The exchange rate has been nearly always on the lower (stronger) edge of the band. The implicit interest rate in forward contracts has been declining, and the risk premia were reduced significantly. Confidence was strengthened by the fact that Hungary reached a stand-by agreement with the IMF and became a member of the OECD in May 1996. Hungarian forint convertibility was declared.

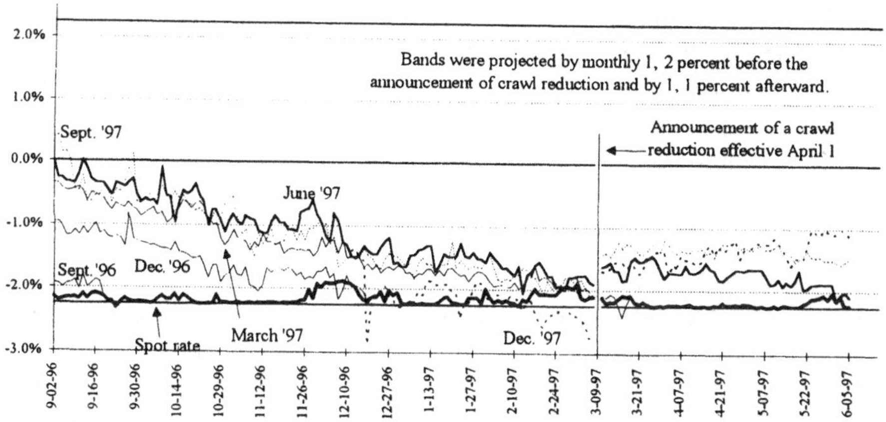

Figure 15.4. Futures Exchange Rates Within the Projected Bands of the NBH and Spot Rate Within the Spot Band, September 1996 to June 6, 1997
Source: National Bank of Hungary.

15.3. Adjustment Problems

Three interrelated issues are selected. First, the disinflation and the exchange rate in its role as nominal anchor will be examined. Second, capital inflow and its sterilization will be presented. Finally, the real exchange rate and competitiveness are analyzed. These three issues are still in the center of economic policy discussions, and they are essential in policy design.

15.3.1. Disinflation and Exchange Rate as a Nominal Anchor

In transition the inflation has other than monetary sources stemming from the catching up of real development of transition countries; thus to achieve it price stability must be probably a longer run project (see Halpern and Wyplosz, 1996). The accommodation of real shocks, the need of once and for all relative price adjustment of the distorted price system—that is, price liberalization—could provide sufficient explanation for the surge in inflation in 1990 to 1991.

The surge in inflation reached a peak in mid-1991—higher than 35 and 38 percent CPI and PPI, respectively (see Table 15.1)—and the main concern of monetary policy shifted to the reduction of inflation while economic policy concentrated on the promotion of growth. However, due to a high level of foreign debt and deteriorating external and internal balances, during the first phase of transition until 1995 changing priorities were attached to the deceleration of inflation and to real targets (growth, foreign equilibrium) as final objectives in monetary targeting. The liberalization of foreign-exchange operations and capital movements resulted in a narrowed scope of monetary policy in controlling money supply. Under these circumstances targeting monetary aggregates was not feasible, and the exchange rate was chosen as intermediate target for monetary policy. The exchange rate was pegged to a basket that was changed several times during 1991 to 1996. The exchange-rate adjustments, however, were directed by considerations of different factors and facing the dilemma how to achieve the double target of containing inflation, on the one hand, and maintaining the—pricel—competitiveness of the tradable sector, on the other hand. The practical realization of PPI-based backward-looking real exchange-rate targeting proved to be a partial anchor to the extent that in this period the PPI reflected inflation incompletely only.

The stubborn 20 percent inflation prevailing in 1992 to 1994 had endogenous sources such like the transition itself and the inertia of expectations. This was a period wen the endogenous relative price changes have been more and more important known as the Balassa-Samuelson effect. While due to the increasing competition the tradable prices have become determined increasingly by the world market prices and the exchange rate, the productivity and wage increase in the tradable sector influenced the non-tradable wages, which, notwithstanding, added some further impetus to inflation. This was one of the factors explaining the widening of the spread between CPI and PPI. These once-and-for-all and permanent relative price changes provide an explanation for the higher inflation in transition (see Figure 15.5).

The energy and public-utility prices were kept practically unchanged between 1992 and 1995, which contributed to the divergence between the CPI and PPI and generated an increasing tension that had to be arranged urgently when a large share of energy sector was privatized in 1995. This is one of the reasons why the spread between CPI and PPI disappeared in 1995 to 1996.

The large gap between consumer and producer real wages increased the conflict between employees and employers; the same nominal wage increase was lower as real consumer wage and higher as real producer wage. The interest rate deflated by CPI was insufficient for households, while the same nominal deposit interest rate plus banking spread as the credit interest rate deflated by PPI reduced the potential of financial interme diation tremendously.

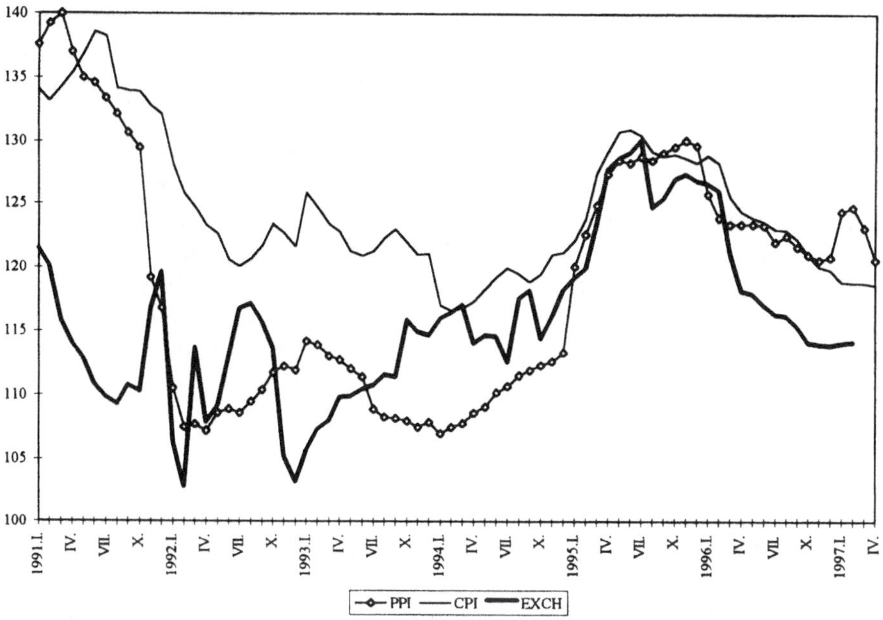

Figure 15.5. Inflation and Exchange Rate (per annum)
Source: National Bank of Hungary.

By 1995 it had been recognized that the practice of dual priorities—reducing inflation and focusing on the current account at the same time—cannot be maintained any more. The inflation was declared to be the only ultimate goal of the monetary policy in the longer run, giving first priority to inflation reduction, and the nominal exchange rate was selected as an intermediate target. However, in this regime the independence of the monetary policy has been reduced. Naturally, with a quasi-fixed exchange rate and liberal capital-market regulation, which Hungary had, there was limited scope for monetary policy in its proper sense.

The operational target of the NBH was the interest-rate differential—that is, to keep domestic interest rates in accordance with the exchange rate and inflation goal. The minimum level of interest rates can be derived from the preannounced band. The interest-rate policy had the task of keeping interest rates as close to the parity rate implied by the rate of crawl as necessary to reduce short-term, speculative international capital movements and as high as necessary to ensure long-run equilibrium between savings and investment. Imperfect capital mobility as a necessary precondition prevailed; otherwise, any departure from parity cannot be sustained. However, in an environment of varying risk, quantitative assessment of the premium may hit the target with limited precision only. Since the exchange rate was almost always on the lower edge of the band, it was the interest rate that absorbed all the positive and negative shocks.

The speed of disinflation is constrained by the relative price changes, by the partly backward-looking expectations, by the fiscal stance, and by the current-account performance. The consistency of all these factors is necessary to ensure the steady path in stabilization and allows the avoidance of backturns. Inflation reduction can only be gradual to avoid loss in growth. It can be efficient only if it is supported by social partners. The sustainability of crawling-band system depends highly on the fiscal stance and on the income policy.

15.3.2. Capital Inflow

When the first results of the 1995 March measures appeared, the credibility of the adjustment strengthened the direction of capital flows reversed, and the excess liquidity stemming from the capital inflow became the major challenge the monetary policy had to face. The surge in capital inflow—if not sterilized—could cause troubles leading to higher inflation and/or current-account deficits; it might entail a systemic risk to the banking sector and therefore to the whole economy when reversed. This is why the NBH followed the policy of sterilized intervention: the central bank intervened on the lower edge of the preannounced band to prevent the exchange rate from further appreciation and sterilized the excess forint liquidity.

In the preannounced crawling-band regime the central bank has an obligation to intervene at the edges of the ± 2.25 percent band width. Since the new regime was introduced, the exchange rate of the Hungarian forint has been practically on the lower (stronger) edge of the band and the NBH foreign-exchange market net intervention amounted to U.S. $3.4 billion in 1995 and U.S. $3.8 billion in 1996, an equivalent of 8 to 9 percent of GDP.

As the NBH followed interest-rate target in its day-to-day operation and as a result the reduction in the net domestic assets counterbalanced the surge in the net foreign assets; thus the increase in the money supply was curbed (see Figure 15.6).

However, the composition of capital inflows has changed a lot. While the annual FDI—privatization revenues excluded—has been around U.S. $1.2 billion to $1.5 billion in the transition period, the privatization receipts varied according to the underlying policy and reached a record $3 billion at the very end of 1995. The current account deficit has been covered by

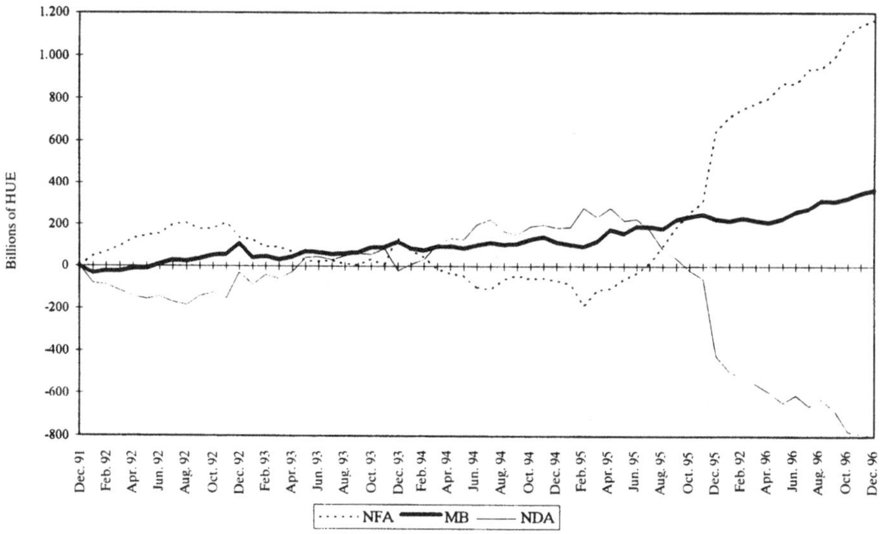

Figure 15.6. Changes in Monetary Base, NDA and NFA (cumulated, December 31, 1991 = 0)
Source: Barabás and Hamecz (1997).

FDI privatization included as a result of the adjustment measures (see Figure 15.7). Growing net errors and omissions are a major concern. Statistical or classification uncertainties are always present; it is not the same from the point of view of sterilization if it were exports, FDI, short-term capital inflow, or anything else.

The interest arbitraging elements started to grow by mid-1994 when the monetary policy was tightened by increasing domestic interest rates. The introduction of the new exchange-rate regime gave a further impetus to these inflows, the amount of which increased due to high spread between the domestic and foreign interest rates taking into account the depreciation of the forint (see Figure 15.8). Until the last quarter of 1995 enterprises and commercial banks—certainly those that had access to foreign source—were seeking foreign loans, as well. When the domestic interest rates started to fall (approaching the parity level in the first quarter of 1996), the interest arbitraging capital inflows disappeared. In 1996 the residents' conversion of foreign-exchange funds to HUF-denominated deposits could be observed, providing an evidence for the growing public confidence. Moreover, as Hungary was upgraded by the most important credit-rating agencies the share of the country in the international investment funds' portfolio was increased, which added to the capital inflow mainly by the end of 1996 and

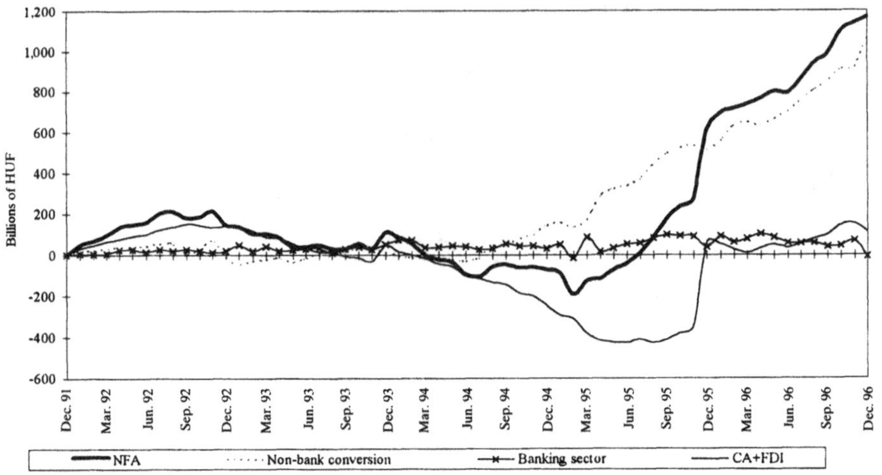

Figure 15.7. Components of the Increase in NFA (cumulated, December 1991 = 0)
Source: Barabás and Hamecz (1997).

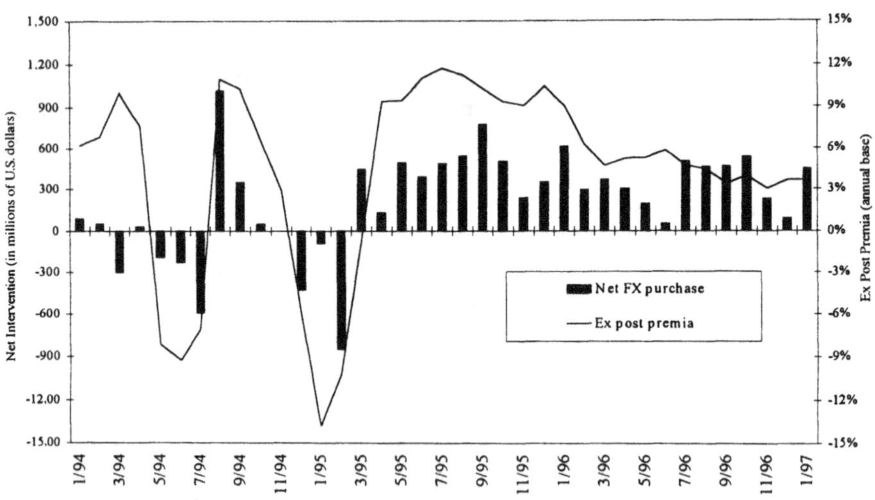

Figure 15.8. NBH Intervention and Forint Premium
Source: National Bank of Hungary.

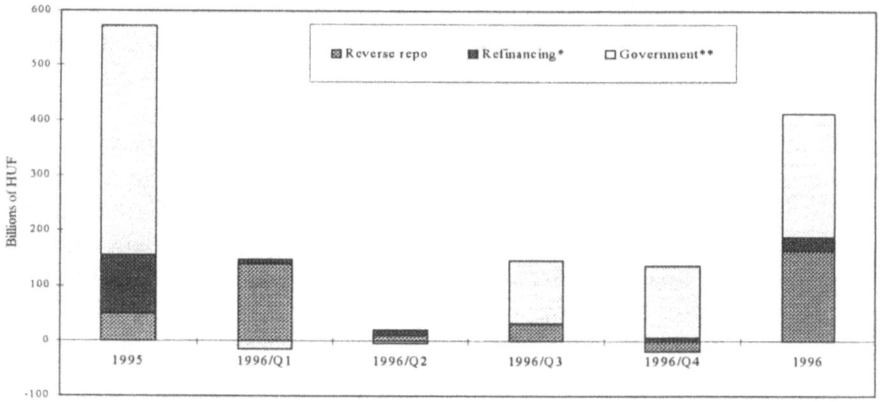

Figure 15.9. Channels of Sterilization
Source: National Bank of Hungary.
*Decrease in refinancing loan.
**Open-market operations of the NBH. Decrease in the stock of government securities plus increase in the single account of the budget.

in early 1997. The Budapest Stock Exchange was booming in 1996, the amount of nonresidents investment in shares could be estimated U.S. $700 million to $900 million. This is included in NEO item of capital account as it has not been identified in the statistics.

The instruments of sterilization differed a lot in 1995 and 1996 (see Figure 15.9). While in 1995 the NBH sold more than HUF 80 billion government securities from its portfolio to sterilize the capital inflows, in 1996 the reverse repos[2] became the main vehicle of sterilization. The government was cautious in using privatization revenues. To smooth monetary aggregates and to keep fiscal stance in line with the stabilization in longer run, the largest part of these nonrecurring incomes has been spent on debt reduction in form of prepayment. The budget borrowing requirement was cut and could be financed from the market. When the capital inflow was the strongest, the government recognized that the most cost-effective way of sterilization was if the budget took part in the sterilization by overfunding.

Due to an active sterilization policy by the NBH, the fall in interest rates was lagged. Ex post we cannot say that a more ambitious interest-rate reduction would have been feasible because the second half of 1995 was the period of regaining investors' confidence, and this always needs some interest sacrifice. Until the interest differential was large, the sterilized intervention was quite expensive, especially in 1995 when the domestic interest rates were high, much over the parity. According to the estimations based on the average interest differential, the excess expenditures spent on sterilization approached 1 percent of GDP in 1995 and fell below 0.5 percent of GDP in 1996. The cost of a sterilized intervention policy appeared in the profit-and-loss account of the NBH, which had already been deteriorating in the second half of 1995 and turned to a significant loss in 1996. The capital inflow allowed the government to swap the forex debt to HUF-denominated securities, and this alleviated the external debt burden, which has to be taken into account in evaluating the cost and benefit of the sterilized intervention policy.

15.4. Real Exchange Rates

Endogeneity and controllability are the major policy dilemmas related to the real exchange rate in Hungary. What is the link between nominal and real exchange rates, and what are the policy variables that will have a lasting impact on the real exchange rate? Is it desirable to have a real exchange rate below or above long-run equilibrium level? Is there a stable relation between the real exchange rate and external performance? In this part we confine ourselves to the interpretation of real exchange rates and examine their development.

Three real exchange rates are used to assess competitiveness.[3] Two of them are widely used—the unit labor cost and the producer-price-index-based real exchange rates—while the third one is the profit-based real exchange rate, which is the ratio of labor cost to price-based real exchange rates and interpreted like the profit margin. It means that the higher the margin, the higher the profitability, hence the better the competitiveness. Here we followed the argument of Lipschitz and McDonald (1992) and Marsh and Tokarick (1994) and claim that in the world of differentiated goods the negative sign of aggregate level price elasticity of demand should not be assumed any more. It should also be added that the same applies to labor costs; higher unit labor costs may reflect the shift in technology and do not necessarily lead to a loss of competitiveness in itself.

The development of real exchange rates for Hungarian manufacturing in the 1990s can be characterized by three different periods (see Figure 15.10). In the first period, which lasted until autumn 1992, there was an important real appreciation; the RERPROFIT increased by 35 percent, RERULC increased fast, while the RERPPI followed a cyclical pattern with decreasing swings. The second period ended in autumn 1994. This was the period during which the three measures moved more or less together.

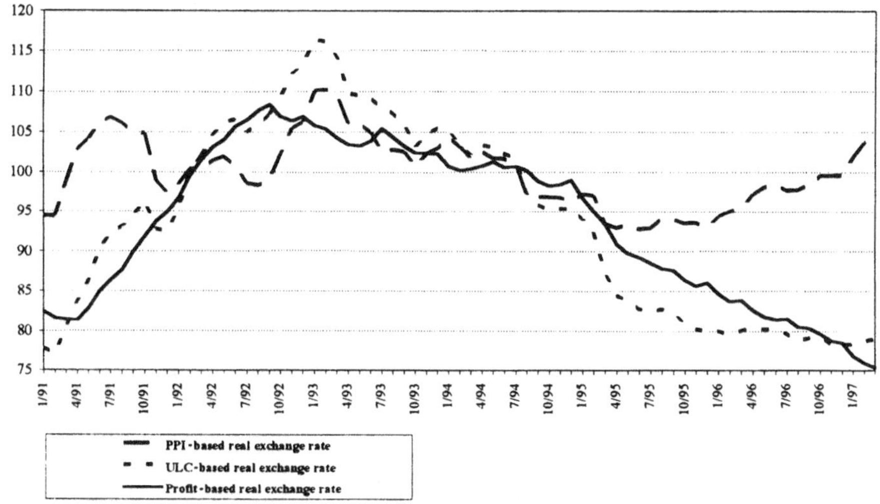

Figure 15.10. Real Exchange Rates (1994 = 100)
Source: National Bank of Hungary, own computations.
Note: An increase means appreciation.

However, the RERULC decreased faster than the RERPPI, which produced 20 percentage points real depreciation. During the third period the RERPROFIT decreased somewhat faster than in the second period, but the most important difference is that the two other real exchange rates are now separated, the RERPPI had changed and started to increase, while the RERULC continued its decline a bit faster in the first half of the period. The overall result is that the level of the RERPROFIT was getting below the early 1991 level by around 10 percent.

The profit-based real exchange rate can be decomposed into two parts: real producer wages and labor productivity. Decreasing real producer wages or increasing labor productivity increases the profit-based real exchange rate, which improves the competitiveness. Increasing real producer wages or decreasing productivity decreases the profit-based real exchange rate, leading to loss of competitiveness.

The three periods assessed for the real exchange rates can easily be interpreted by decomposing the RERPROFIT (see Figure 15.11). The labor productivity declined until early 1992 by 10 percent. Since then it increases continuously by around 10 percent per year. The real producer wages were increasing until the end of 1994; then the trend was modified and fell by more than 15 percent. It is not so easy to separate the first from the second

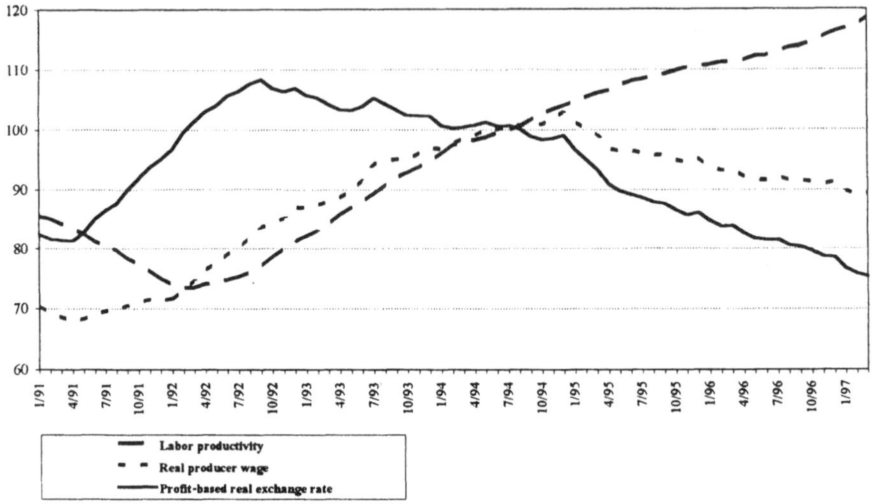

Figure 15.11. Components of Profit-Based Real Exchange Rate (1994 = 100)
Source: National Bank of Hungary, own computations.
Note: An increase means appreciation.

period looking only at the productivity and real wage curves. That is why we would rather base our assessment on the RERPROFIT, which reflects both the acceleration of the labor productivity and the deceleration of real producer wages.

The real exchange-rate indicators did reveal significant appreciation in 1990 to 1992. The trade balance, the major source of external disequilibrium has been worsening only in 1993 to 1994. The exchange rate could have a lagged effect, but the factors presented above had important explanatory power, as well. The developments of the third period raise the issue of competitiveness. Can we rely on wage competitiveness or rather be cautious and not forget about worsening price competitiveness? In a traditional world these two indicators never deviate for long. In the actual Hungarian world two factors can be invoked to assess the external equilibrium. First, the fast increase of machinery output and exports is mainly associated with large-scale investment activity of foreign-owned firms. These increments consist of differentiated goods mainly, which is why the danger of pricing out seems implausible. Second, large real wage cuts in 1995 to 1996 combined with an unchanged increase of labor productivity, which led to a substantial drop in unit labor cost. As the external balance was improving, it is obvious that appreciating PPI-based real exchange rate does not reflect the loss of price competitiveness.

15.5. Policy Challenges, Tradeoffs

The microeconomic transformation proved to be the Achilles' heel of transition. New owners, new entrepreneurs, and new types of production (including technology, employment, and marketing) entered the scene and changed radically the environment for firms. Macroeconomic policy may enhance the process if accompanying measures ensure internal and external equilibria.

Sustainability of transition requires some gradualism in stabilization. Distortions of the CPEs in income redistribution and relative prices—wages, exchange rates, and output prices—explain higher inflation. It is very difficult to choose a single (or multiple) nominal anchor(s) for stabilization, while the well-known methods of shock therapy proved to be other source of distortion. Until the basic relative price distortions are eliminated and the budget reforms are completed, fixing the exchange rate may lead to strong real appreciation of the currency, leading to unsustainable deterioration of the current account.

It may be discussed whether the sterilized intervention policy is sustainable for the longer run or whether the surge of capital inflow should be responded to. It is clearly unsustainable if the high-interest-rate policy is unavoidable. This would be dangerous for Hungary as a new vicious circle might be created, which the government borrowing requirement and public-debt problem. However, the experiences in 1995 and 1996 showed that the market is willing to reduce the required risk premium as the stabilization has been evolving. The views differ concerning the efficiency of a sterilized intervention policy (Calvo, Leiderman, and Reinhart, 1992; Reisen, 1993; Frankel, 1994). In the period 1995 to 1997 Hungary seemed to belong to those countries that applied the sterilized intervention to decreasing costs. This was a combined effect of market-oriented reforms, liberalization of capital markets, and the attractive interest differential. The exchange rate played a special role in the stabilization, which made forint investments more attractive fore residents, as well. Although the sterilization operations added to the HUF-denominated debt, the ratio of debt to GDP improved significantly as the privatization revenues were spent on debt repayments.

The two basic tasks of sterilized intervention are to maintain competitiveness and to prevent the exchange rate from experiencing large fluctuations. The international experiences show, however, that the nature of the disturbances is decisive for policy design. If the country can be supposed to undergo a rapid productivity increase over the longer run, the first priority should be attached to the anchor role of the exchange rate as the

Table 15.7. Industrial output and export in 1996 (annual increase, 1995 = 100)

	Output	*Sales*	*Domestic Sales*	*Export Sales*
Mining	2.4	2.9	0.5	44.6
Manufacturing	2.0	3.0	–3.1	14.1
Food	0.2	0.6	–2.4	14.0
Textile, leather	–3.7	–1.9	–8.5	3.7
Wood, print	–5.6	–4.1	–7.2	14.4
Chemicals	–2.4	–1.0	0.2	–3.0
Nonferrous	1.2	1.6	0.9	11.1
Metallurgy	–2.9	–2.2	–2.9	–1.1
Machinery	16.3	17.7	–6.7	35.6
Other manufacturing	–8.0	–7.9	–6.9	–9.4
Energy	4.8	4.7	2.0	440.7
Industry	2.3	3.1	–1.2	13.5

Source: National Bank of Hungary.

appreciation would not threaten the competitiveness but could help the disinflation. The first signs of dynamic growth in industry can already be observed in Hungary (see Table 15.7). However, it is very difficult to decide the stability of the trends and the outcome of a policy giving a larger role to the exchange rate in the treatment of capital flows.

The system of a crawling band can be well fitted with the final goal of disinflation until the inflation is of two-digit, but even in this period the flexibility of exchange-rate movements can be achieved by widening the band. This might be necessary to cope with the unanticipated shocks of which hopefully the positive ones seem to be more probable at present (see Williamson, 1996). In the light of recent developments, the monetary strategy and exchange-rate policy should be reconsidered, taking into account the changes in the composition of capital inflows, and it is high time to analyze the nature of adverse shocks that the Hungarian economy will have to face in the near future.

Since the introduction of the March 1995 measures, it often has been mentioned that the nominal exchange rate was used as a nominal anchor, while the system was introduced to regain credibility. This latter was more emphasized at the beginning, which explained the relatively narrow band and the cautious policy when changing the rate of crawl. Although it was declared that the ultimate target of the monetary policy was to reduce inflation, before the decisions about the reduction of the crawl the same weights were attached to the competitivity considerations as to the disinflation.

The NBH followed a leaning against the wind monetary policy when it reduced the short-term central-bank interest rates according to the actual inflation decline and tried to achieve moderate positive real yields on the longer end of the yield curve. The annual devaluation of the crawl may be expected around 15 percent in 1997, which is below the inflation forecasts. Taking into account the expected changes in foreign prices the exchange-rate policy will continue to diminish inflationary pressures rather than add to them. The expected real appreciation according to the prices will be counterbalanced by the improving competitiveness on ULC basis.

From time to time there are suggestions that a more ambitious exchange-rate policy would bring lower inflation sooner. While on the face this argument is appealing, this would have led to a hazardous policy when the adjustment program was launched just because of the bad experience of relative price distortions of the preceding years. Ex post it might turn out that the policy was too cautious and a less depreciated exchange rate would have not threatened long-run sustainability of the current account and even would be a significant help in achieving lower inflation. These are relevant considerations, but the relevance concerns more the future than the past. Maintaining a weaker than strictly necessary exchange rate could be thought of as a kind of insurance policy that reduced the probability of speculative attacks in the first period of the new regime. The extensive liberalization of capital movements has very decisive consequences on the monetary policy. Having regained the credibility and taking into account the results in internal and external consolidation, the strategy must be able to treat and profit from the positive shocks (productivity growth in the tradable sector, increasing FDI and so on).

The stabilization practice and theory claim that any form of fix of the nominal exchange rate leads to loss of international competitiveness, since the free float would have led to a more undervalued nominal exchange rate. The nominal exchange rate of the Hungarian currency was almost always on the lower edge of the band; 4.5 percent depreciation was possible at most. The monetary policy may influence the position of the exchange rate within the band, keeping the domestic interest rate above the rate implied by the parity condition risk premium included. As our analysis has pointed out, the interest differential between domestic and foreign interest rates reflecting the risk premium has been falling since the introduction of the crawling-band regime from more than 10 percent in March 1995 to nearly 3 percent in March 1997, and the appreciation pressure still prevails. This combination of fundamentals questions the nominal anchor interpretation of the actual target-zone arrangement. This is why the credibility or insurance arguments seem more convincing. The exchange-rate policy became a symbol or warrant of a commitment and has important role in determining the equilibrium value of other nominal variables. The constant pressure on the exchange rate, however, reveals the presence of disequilibrium. Whether it is an investment for further credibility or simply a welfare loss in higher inflation needs careful examination.

15.6. Conclusions

The further development of the exchange-rate regime in Hungary depends on the role to be played in the formation of macroeconomic policy. In general, the specific form of the exchange-rate regime is of public interest, while for a credible exchange-rate regime the institutional environment and the preferred ways of how to accommodate the expected or unexpected shocks precede its specification. Until recently the role of the exchange rate in strengthening credibility was at the forefront in Hungary, but it becomes more and more important to prepare the switch for a regime with emphasis on flexibility. As has been mentioned, the exchange-rate regime has become the exclusive means—almost a symbol—of credibility, somehow similar to the situation in former Czechoslovakia and Czech Republic. If the role of an anchor—either nominal or credibility—is excessively used, then the unavoidable side-effects become dominant and many have unfriendly consequences.

If there is agreement on the necessity to switch, it is easier to do it during a quiet period rather than being forced to do so by outside impulses. However, decisions are achieved faster in the case of urgency, and the time and situation are advantageous to convince experts and policymakers.

The most important criteria to determine the next exchange regime is its ability to cope with shocks. There is a certain asymmetry in policy formation; a permanent shock of the same magnitude has the tendency to have a larger effect on the negative side in the form of direct devaluation, while on the positive side it is rather thought temporary. In other words, larger magnitude or more time is needed to convince people of the need for a modification in the case of a positive permanent shock. This tendency of asymmetry is general since any international liquidity crisis may have a larger negative impact on the present value of future welfare losses than any form of nonaccommodation of positive shock, which would have required the same magnitude of appreciation as compared to the equilibrium depreciation in case of a negative shock. The welfare loss is due to a higher interest rate, and higher inflation is a result of sterilized interventions in a fixed exchange-rate regime and is weighed less than the same welfare-loss due to exceptional devaluation.

As has been shown, the development of the Hungarian economy during the 1990s did not reveal a clear tradeoff between inflation and competitiveness with respect to the exchange rate. The exchange rate was used for different policy goals according to actual preferences.

The lasting consequences of the contingency measures of March 1995 are positive, although in certain aspects lagged effects are to be expected. Among others, a share of real wage cuts of 1995 to 1996 will be compensated by larger wage increases observed during the early 1997 wage negotiations. The extent of backward-looking wage indexation can be diminished only if the gap between target and actual inflation disappears or at least can be reduced to such a level that can be explained by exogenous shock and is communicated to social partners.

The major problem during this period was that only very noisy information was available on the lag structure and on the shift of structural parameters. The economic policy had to react without knowing them and had to reveal its commitment to some preannounced goals to gain credibility. Meanwhile, the financial intermediation became much more complicated due to the further liberalization of capital accounts, and the private agents and the decisionmakers had to learn the functioning of different instruments by interaction.

Whether the rules of intervention remain or not seems even more important than the specific form of the more flexible exchange-rate regime itself. There are different regimes that are compatible with unchanged intervention rules—that is, that intervene only at the edges or with any other intervention rules. The pros and cons besides the well-known distributional aspects relate to institutional issues. It is very difficult to design communication and decision rules for any randomly generated interventions in a small open country with small number of agents and with a high propensity to leak. Thus, in the case of unchanged intervention rules there is a threat to generate large swings when servicing needs of international debt have a relatively large effect on the foreign-exchange market. This is the case for Hungary; therefore, some procedure is to be applied for smoothing the effect.

Long-run economic policy considerations (EU accession, modernization) urge an ambitious disinflation program. If ambitions are mainly constrained by economic feasibility and no major output loss is to be paid, then disinflation is welcome. However, the equilibrium real appreciation can be achieved easier by higher inflation than by nominal appreciation.

Acknowledgments

This chapter was prepared for the Third Dubrovnik Conference on Transition Economies on Balance of Payments, Exchange Rates, and Competitiveness in Transition Economies June 25–27, 1997, organized by the National Bank of Croatia. Halpern acknowledges the support of PHARE ACE P95-2045-R and Hungarian National Science Fund (OTKA T019698). The views expressed here do not necessarily reflect the official position of the National Bank of Hungary.

Notes

1. The limited validity of price competitiveness will be discussed later.
2. One-week and one-month deposit facilities with the central bank, collateralized by govenment securities.
3. See Lipschitz and McDonald (1992), Marsh and Tokarick (1994), and Halpern (1996) for the interpretation and technical details of different indicators of competitiveness. All the annual indicators are presented in Table 15.5.

References

Barabás, G., and Hamecz, I. (1997). "Tôkebeáramlás, sterilizáció és pénzmennyiség (Capital Inflow, Sterilization, and Money)." MNB Füzetek No. 1997/3. (in Hungarian)

Bonin, J.P., and M.E. Schaffer. (1995). "Banks, Bad Debts and Bankruptcy in Hungary, 1991–94." CEP Working Paper 657.

Calvo, G., and L. Leiderman, and C.M. Reinhart. (1993). "Capital Inflows and Real Exchange Rate Appreciation in Latin America: The Role of External Factors." IMF Staff Papers 40.

Darvas, Z. (1996). "Exchange-Rate Premia and the Credibility of the Crawling Target Zone in Hungary." CEPR DP 1307.

Frankel, J.A. (1994). "Sterilisation of Money Inflows: Difficult (Calvo) or Easy (Reisen)?" IMF Working Paper 159.

Halpern, L. (1996). "Real Exchange Rates and Exchange-Rate Policy in Hungary." *Economics of Transition*, 4: 211–228.

Halpern, L., and C. Wyplosz. (1996). "Equilibrium Exchange Rates in Transition Economies." IMF Working Paper 96-125.

Lipschitz, L., and D. McDonald. (1992). "Real Exchange Rate and Competitiveness: A Clarification of Concepts, and Some Measurements for Europe." *Empirica*, 19: 37–69.

MacDonald, R. (1997). "What Determines Real Exchange Rates? The Long and Short of It." IMF Working Paper 97-21.

Marsh, I.W., and S.P. Tokarick. (1994). "Competitiveness Indicators: A Theoretical and Empirical Assessment." IMF Working Paper 94-29.

Reisen, H. (1993). "The Impossible Trinity in South-East Asia." *International Economic Insights* (March-April).

Williamson, J. (1996). *The Crawling Band as an Exchange-Rate Regime: Lessons from Chile, Colombia, and Israel.* Institute for International Economics.

16 CURRENT-ACCOUNT SURPLUS AND FALLING COMPETITIVENESS IN SLOVENIA

Velimir Bole

16.1. Introduction

High real appreciation of the exchange rate is quite common in the later phases of stabilizing and restructuring economies in transition. A current-account surplus at the beginning also turns into a deficit almost systematically in transitional economies. Among these economies a great variety of exchange-rate regimes were enacted, monetary policy targets used, and fiscal stances achieved. Nevertheless, there was almost no exception in the described time path of current accounts and real exchange rates.

The current-account deficit and real appreciation of the exchange-rate in the later phases of transition were so systematic across economies and time that the corresponding fact could even become a part of a transition economics theory. That undervaluation at a time when markets are liberalized is followed by real appreciation as the exchange rate returns to equilibrium is already stated as a "stylized fact" for economies in transition (see Halpern and Wyplosz, 1996).

It seems that Slovenia, with its managed floating regime, does not fit into such transition stylized fact. Namely, according to the fragmentary empirical evidence, real appreciation was not high until the end of 1996, if measured by retail or producer prices. Besides, the current-account balance didn't drop significantly under zero.

It is documented elsewhere that the permanent efforts of policymakers to contain and neutralize the effects of huge foreign financial inflows prevented considerable real appreciation of the exchange rate, although significant volatility of the real exchange rate takes place during a transition period in Slovenia. However, knowing the permanent pressure of labor costs and corresponding increase of relative prices of nontradables, actual external competitiveness of the economy as well as sustainability of the present satisfactory current-account balance are not clear. The suitability of actual policymakers' sterilization efforts is also, therefore, questionable.

This chapter tries to answer two interrelated questions. First, how sustainable is actual current-account performance, and, therefore, how reasonable are significant policy efforts in promoting exports? Second, has external competitiveness really not changed dramatically so far? The balance of payments, especially some specific current-account items, are analyzed first. Further, external competitiveness of the tradable sector is checked thoroughly. Causes and sustainability of the key item in the actual current account, hiding a rather huge trade deficit, are examined at the end.

The rest of the chapter is structured as follows. In the second section, basic facts about dynamics and the structure of the balance of payments are given. Travel services export, as the crucial item for nonstandard current-account performance, is documented the most. External trade competitiveness is analyzed in the third section. Several overlapping indicators are checked. The appeasing effects of the growing shuttle trade[1] on the current account in the period of transition are analyzed in the fourth section. Causes for a considerable increase of daily tourism and their sustainability are provided. Basic findings of the chapter are presented at its end.

16.2. Balance-of-Payments Dynamics: Basic Facts

16.2.1. Balance of Payments

Basic characteristics of macroeconomic performances in the period of stabilization were given elsewhere (see, for example, Bole, 1997c). Speaking about the balance of payments, a persistent increase of foreign-exchange reserves, a nonnegative current-account balance, and accelerating financial

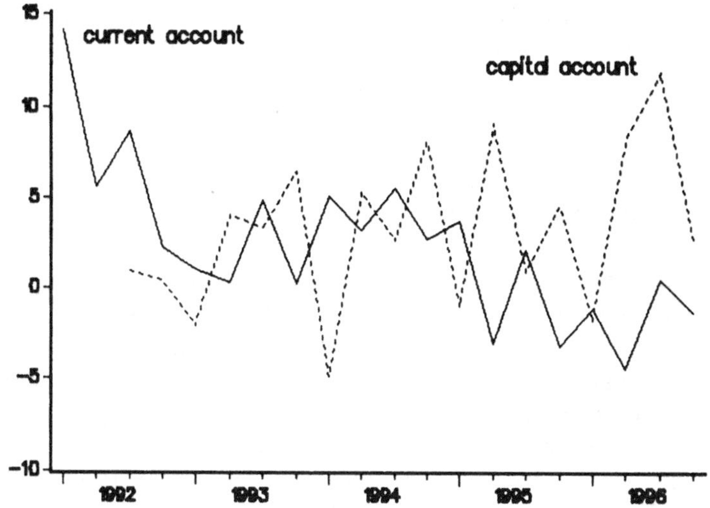

Figure 16.1. Balance of Payments (percent GDP)

inflows have been the most outstanding features of the transition period, so far.

In Figure 16.1, the current-account balance and capital flows are illustrated in terms of GDP. Change in official and commercial bank reserves are not included in the presented capital flows. Apparently the structure of forex flows has changed considerably in the period of transition. A huge current-account surplus (of over 8 percent GDP) in 1992 dropped to around zero after 1994, while financial inflows had increased to over 4 percent of GDP until 1993 and over 5 percent after 1994. Acceleration of financial inflows followed a currency risk premium (and sovereignty risk) drop at the beginning of 1995 and presented an attractive investment grade in 1996 (see Bole, 1997b).

It seems that Slovenia, with a floating exchange regime, does not fit into the standard picture of the more advanced economies in transition, which run significant current-account deficits while absorbing huge foreign-exchange inflows. Because there is also empirical evidence (although only fragmentary) that the Slovenian tolar is the only really overvalued currency among economies in transition (see Halpern and Wyplosz, 1996), a more detailed analysis of current-account dynamics and structure is necessary to make a reasonable "story" on these facts—especially because it is necessary to make an assessment of the sustainability of the present current-account performance of the economy. Namely, facing considerable financial inflows, continuously pushing the real tolar value up, either present (good) current-account performance is only short term or the competitiveness of the economy has increased a lot during the transition period.

16.2.2. Current-Account Balance

The structure of the current-account balance changed considerably after 1991. In the first three quarters of 1992 ("taking-off period") the trade balance was in high surplus. Shrinkage of the internal market after the collapse of the Yugoslav market made many enterprises distress exporters. Exporters severely cut their (tolar) export prices just to keep cash-flow positive and so bought time for restructuring.[2] Actually, enterprises were partly selling assets abroad, so a corresponding portion of the trade surplus was in fact inflow of capital. After this taking-off period, the trade balance dropped considerably. Surplus in services behaved in completely the opposite way; from negligible values in the taking-off period it started to growth in 1992/III (see Figure 16.2).

Increases of the deficit in trade balance and of the surplus in the balance of services were major changes in the current-account structure after 1992. There were two phases in the changing structure of current account after

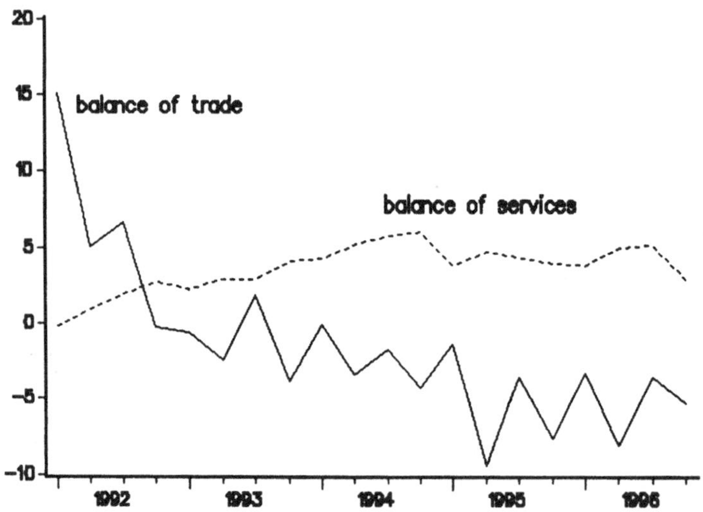

Figure 16.2. Current-Account Balance (percent GDP)

1992. In the period of still manageable financial flows (until the beginning of 1995), the deficit of the trade balance stayed around 2 percent of GDP, while a surplus in services uniformly increased to around 5 percent GDP. After 1994 (in the period of accelerated financial inflows) the deficit of trade balance increased to around 5 percent of GDP, while the surplus of services dropped to 4 percent of GDP.

16.2.3. Balance of Trade

Acceleration of imports was the main reason for the increasing trade deficit after 1992. After 1994 exports and imports per unit of GDP leveled off. Actually both ratios (exports and imports per GDP) started to decline somewhat (see Figure 16.3, imports and exports per GDP).

An investment-driven increase of the foreign-trade deficit would have to be a typical side product of the market restructuring in an economy in transition. Switching from previously internal, almost completely closed markets demands new product niches and a complete technological and technical update of production to increase productivity sufficiently to compete in world markets. So an accelerating of investment goods imports and a widening of the trade deficit could be expected in later phases of the restructuring of transition economies, after basic stability is achieved.

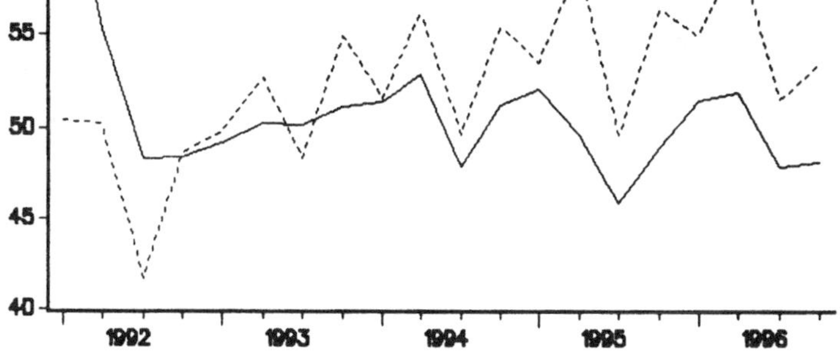

Figure 16.3. Balance of Trade (percent GDP)

Naturally, only investment in the tradable sector driven increase of trade deficit can be reasonable—that is, a sustainable—policy in the long run.

Although Slovenia exported to hard-currency areas a lot, already in the previous Yugoslavia, the collapse of the large and fairly closed internal market pushed the Slovenian economy into a big reshuffling of selling markets and products.[3] To show investment-driven changes of the import structure, the structure of imports is presented in Table 16.1 (in the one-digit standard international trade classification). Figures in the table are given in percentages of GDP.

The changing structure of imports corroborates that significant technological restructuring was under way in the transition period in Slovenia. Imports of investment goods increased the most (in the period 1992 to 1996 from 6.8 to 8.6 percent GDP) and that of raw materials the least (dropped from 32.7 to 30.6 percent). Similar to other more developed countries in transition, catching up to Western levels of private consumption also pushed imports of consumer goods up considerably.

The investment share of GDP increased from 17.3 percent GDP to 22.2 percent GDP in the period 1992 to 1996. However, more than 2.8 percentages points of such an increase of investment share of GDP actually resulted from the expansion of investment in public utilities alone (see, for example, Bole, 1997b).

The path of trade deficit apparently followed a "standard transition" dynamics in Slovenia. That is to say, an increase of trade deficit was implied by the expansion of import of investment goods and consumer goods and steady dynamics of exports (in units of GDP). Therefore, it seems that the

Table 16.1. Imports by sections of SITC (as percentage of GDP)

	1992	*1993*	*1994*	*1995*	*1996*
Food and live animals	3.76	4.00	3.86	3.40	3.44
Beverages and tobacco	0.51	0.37	0.33	0.33	0.33
Crude materials	3.40	2.89	3.29	3.31	2.57
Mineral fuels	5.35	5.85	3.63	3.33	4.02
Oil and fats	0.20	0.20	0.21	0.21	0.21
Chemical products	6.16	6.27	6.20	6.11	6.05
Manufactured materials	9.76	9.58	9.87	10.01	9.99
Machinery and transport equipment	13.13	16.45	16.16	17.10	17.08
Miscellaneous manufactured articles	5.24	6.54	5.56	5.39	6.93
Other	2.27	2.19	1.71	1.48	0.06

Source: *Monthly Bulletin*, Bank of Solvenia.

same "stylized fact" (Halpern and Wyplosz, 1996) story was hidden behind the improving of the balance of services, which almost completely covered the increasing trade deficit.

16.2.4. Balance of Services

Because a balance of services covered a deficit in trade balance, it is important to observe the nature of the balance-of-services surplus to assess sustainability of the present current-account performance of the economy.

Out of items included in the balance of services, transportation and tourism (*travel* according to the IMF definition) have a considerably higher turnover in Slovenia. However, the balance of transportation services was almost negligible (around one-tenth) in comparison with the balance of tourism, in the period of transition. To compare actual dynamics and scale of the balance of tourism versus the balance of services, both balances (per unit of GDP) are presented in Figure 16.4.

Apparently dynamics and scale of the balance of travel had the same characteristics as the balance of total services—that is to say, an increase toward 5 percent of GDP until the end of 1994, a drop to around 4 percent at the beginning of 1995, and steadiness afterward. The only visible difference between the balance of travel and total services is a more pronounced

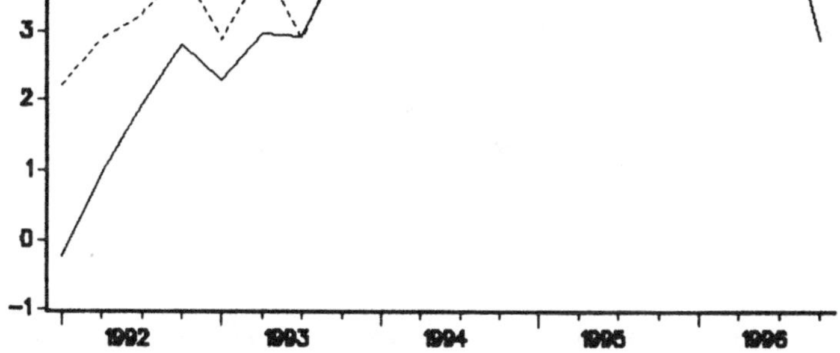

Figure 16.4. Balance of Services (percent GDP)

peak in the second half of 1994, triggered by an acceleration of construction services.

16.2.5. Balance of Travel

Slovenia borders on three much stronger tourist-receptive economies: Italy, Austria, and Croatia. In none of them was the period 1992 to 1996 really successful for tourism. In the same period, the export of travel services almost doubled in Slovenia. Because the number of foreign overnight stays increased by 25 percent[4] and the real appreciation of the tolar was almost negligible (see Figure 16.5) classical tourism (staying in the country at least one night) cannot explain the almost doubling of the export travel services as well as a strong increase of the balance of travel in the same period.

A strong increase in the number of day tourists along the border explains doubling of travel services export, in the period after 1992.

In Figure 16.6, the total export of travel services and daily foreign tourism are illustrated (in terms of BDP). Figures on daily foreign tourism are estimated by an econometric model of shuttle trade (see Bole, 1997a). In Figures 16.7 and 16.8, shares of foreign tourists spending in total spending in retail trade and in hotels and restaurants are given. Corresponding

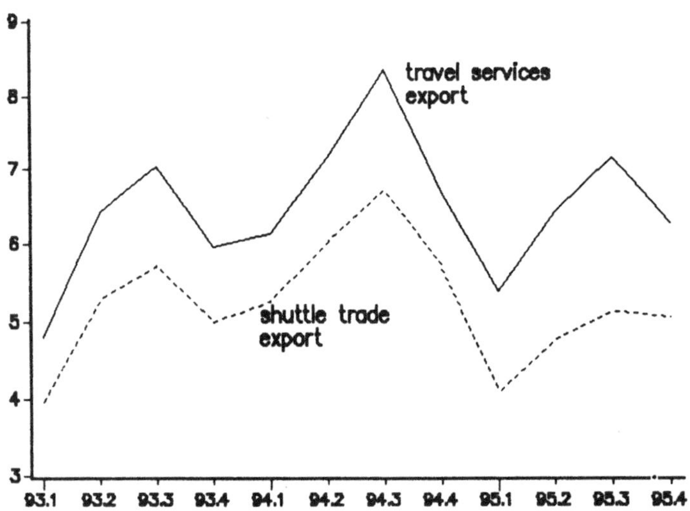

Figure 16.5. Competitiveness Indicators Based on Aggregate Prices

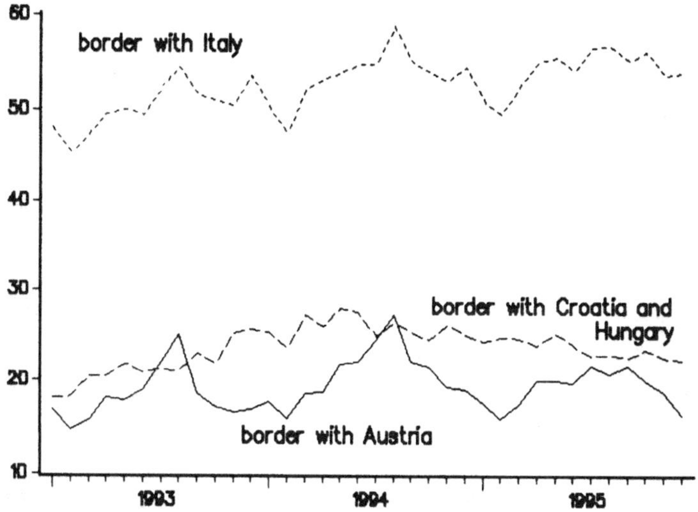

Figure 16.6. Travel Services Export (percent GDP)

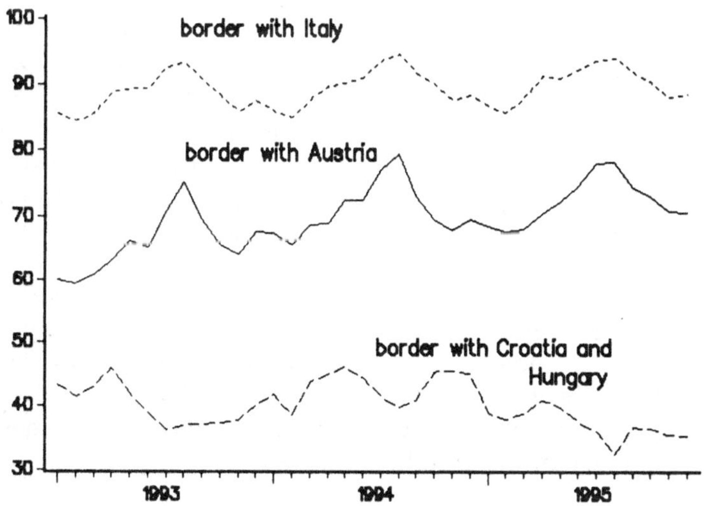

Figure 16.7. Share of Foreign Tourists Spending in Toatal Spending Retail Trade

values are estimated by the regional model of private spending, of which a model of shuttle trade is only a part (Bole, 1997a).

A bulk of the increase in export of travel services until 1995 apparently stemmed from spending by day tourists. Taking into account seasonality, the

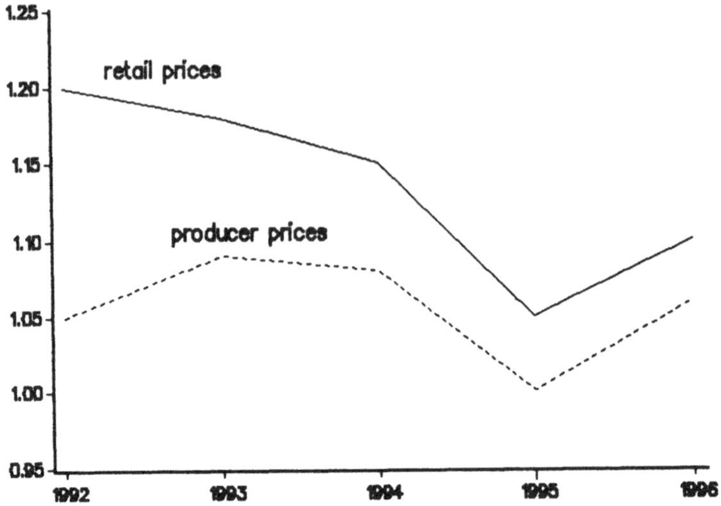

Figure 16.8. Share of Foreign-Tourist Spending in Total Spending in Hotels and Restaurants

share of spendng of day tourists in GDP climbed from less than 4 percent GDP at the end of 1992 to around 6 percent GDP in the second half of 1995. In the same period imports of travel services (from Austria and Italy in winter and Croatia in summer) increased, but only slightly: it still lagged considerably behind the prewar level. So doubling of daily tourism (per unit of GDP) pushed up the balance of travel for almost the whole increase of daily foreign tourism.

In Figure 16.6, a considerable drop in daily tourism at the beginning 1995 illustrated well the sensibility of cross-border trading on real appreciation.

Apparently, a good current-account performance predominantly depends on shuttle trade, so far. Therefore, sustainability and causes of the shuttle trade booming have to be checked, and competitiveness of the rest of tradable sector needs to be evaluated.

16.3. The Competitiveness of the Tradable Sector

16.3.1. Real Appreciation, Wage Costs, and Competitiveness

Independently of foreign-exchange regime, permanent pressure on real, not to mention nominal appreciation, are hardly sustainable in even the medium run if the competitiveness of strategic exporters is endangered. A floating exchange regime is more robust on speculative attacks on the exchange-rate regime in the possible final phase of "financial inflow" episode (see, for example, Blejer). The damaging effects of financial inflows on volatility and appreciation of exchange rate, and therefore on decaying of strategic export sector, could be greater in a floating exchange-rate regime, especially in an economy facing important micro distortions.

In Slovenia, huge financial inflows attained on average 3.5 percent of GDP in the period 1992 to 1996. As we have already shown, appreciation pressure of financial flows was enlarged by a short-term booming of the shuttle trade of almost the same dimension. Although permanent sterilization efforts reduced a real appreciation of tolar (Bole, 1997b), the sustainability of the competitiveness of strategic exporters became highly questionable—especially because income policy had still not been put in place by the end of 1996 (Bole, 1996c).

Significant restructuring on the macro and micro levels took place in transition. An implied increase in productivity could offset a great deal the real appreciation and cost (wage) push pressure on competitiveness. So changes in external competitiveness of the export sector are not necessarily implied by variations of exchange rates and unit labor costs.

Indicators of trends in relative prices, profit margins, and rates of return in the tradable sector have to be studied more thoroughly to evaluate the actual change in export-sector competitiveness.

To reveal trade competitiveness changes of the Slovenian economy, indicators of real exchange rate, unit labor costs, export unit value, profitability of producing traded goods, and constant market share will be presented for the period from 1992 to 1996.

16.3.2. Indicators Based on an Aggregate Price Index

Perhaps the most frequently used indicator of real exchange rate is based on comparison of consumer prices. Its advantage is that it reflects factor-cost dynamics and that corresponding data are published frequently.

However, it is well known that a consumer-price-based real exchange rate may be a poor indicator if the purpose is to measure relative price of tradables (see, for example, Marsh and Tokarick, 1994; Turner and Van't dack, 1993). There are several reasons for that; the most important are that it does include services (nontradables)[5] and does not embrace highly tradable intermediate goods.

To mitigate drawbacks of the consumer-based real exchange-rate indicator while retaining its benefits, the real exchange rate calculated from retail prices and producer prices are presented on Figure 16.5.

When calculating an indicator, five trade partners are taken into account (Germany, Italy, United States, Austria, Great Britain, and France). Exports to these five partners represent around 65 percent of Slovenian exports. Producer prices in manufacturing are used in the corresponding indicator of real exchange rate for Slovenia.[6]

Presented indicators of price competitiveness had some similarities in dynamics in the studied period: modest changes until 1995, a considerable drop in 1995 (by around 9 percent), and a subsequent modest increase in 1996. In the whole period, the real exchange rate based on producer prices indicates a slight increase of price competitiveness, while that based on retail prices shows a considerable drop (by 9.5 percent) in competitiveness because of increased costs of production.

16.3.3. Indicators Based on Costs

An index of relative unit labor costs is often used to evaluate changes in competitiveness originating in domestic costs. The attractiveness of using unit labor costs as an indicator of trade competitiveness is based on interpreting unit labor costs as a measure of profitability of producing tradable goods.

Using labor costs for measuring competitiveness has a number of advantages: among others, it includes information on the major component of production costs, and data are widely available. It is shown elsewhere that, as opposed to the usual (implicit) suppositions, unit labor costs can provide information on the profitability of producing tradable goods only under special conditions (Lipschitz and McDonald, 1992). The unit labor-cost-based indicator of competitiveness had two additional drawbacks. It may give misleading information if significant factor substituting, including intermediate goods, is under way in the traded sector. Besides, it is sensitive to cyclical movements (in labor productivity). To mitigate this last effect, trend values have to be observed.

The relative price index of tradable against nontradable goods could be also interpreted as an indicator of costs. Namely, balance of trade in goods has to be equal to excess demand for nontradable goods (Dornbusch, 1974). So the relative price index of tradables against nontradables can be interpreted as the domestic costs of consuming and producing tradable goods. Because of that, the index of the relative price of tradables against nontradables is sometimes also indicated as the internal real exchange rate.

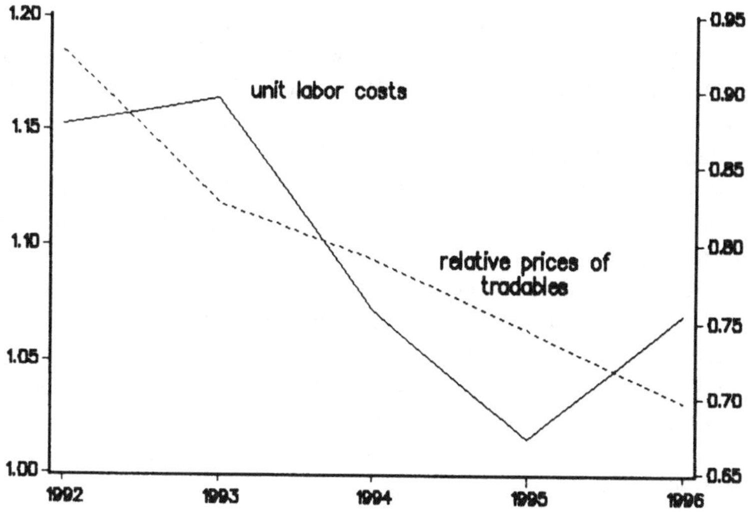

Figure 16.9. Competitiveness Indicators Based on Costs

Analyzing the dynamics of competitiveness by the indicator of internal real exchange has to be used carefully when growth in labor productivity varies across sectors, rigidities in factor markets exist, and real per capital income rises significantly in time (see, for example, Marsh and Tokarick, 1994).

Two important characteristics of transition economies (the faster growth of the service sector and the higher rate of laying off overmanned manufacturing) could cause significant changes of sectoral differences in labor productivity and so damage appropriateness of internal real exchange rate. The second characteristic was especially effective in Slovenia (Bole, 1997c). It pushed labor productivity of manufacturing up. In Slovenia, the net effect of both structural characteristics on sectoral differences in labor productivity is not clear, and neither is the applicability of an internal real exchange rate as an indicator of competitiveness.

In Figure 16.9, indicators based on costs are presented. Relative unit labor costs are calculated for manufacturing; it is compared with the same five trade partners as for real exchange-rate indicators. Labor unit costs for Slovenia are calculated as the total payments to workers per unit of industrial production. Relative prices of tradables against nontradables are approximated with the index of retail prices of goods against prices of services.[7]

Relative unit-labor-cost dynamics was different from that of real exchange-rate indicators. It indicates that reducing hidden employment in manufacturing until 1993 even increased external competitiveness, although real (average) wages also increased considerably. After 1993 unit labor costs show a sharp drop in competitiveness in 1994 and 1995. In 1996 competitiveness improved, according to the unit-labor-costs indicator. In the whole period after stabilization (from 1992 to 1996) external competitiveness dropped by around 8 percent, according to the unit-labor indicator; it actually returned to the same level it had been at in 1990.

Relative prices of tradables were falling continuously in the period 1992 to 1996; till the end of 1996, the real internal exchange rate fell by 21.5 percent. The path of real internal exchange rate was different from other indicators of competitiveness. The most apparent differences of relative prices of tradables comparing with other indicators are uniform decreasing and the absence of any sign of sudden competitiveness increase in 1996 (caused by nominal swing of exchange rate). Obviously, factors affecting competitiveness only through prices of nontradables (wages in nontradable sector) were behind the falling trend of relative prices of tradables—specifically, smaller increases in productivity in the nontradable sector.

16.3.4. Indicators of the Share on Export Markets

When traded goods on a given export market are considered imperfect substitutes across countries of origin, their prices are in principle no longer identical. In a such situation, a comparison of relative export unit values of own (Slovenian) exporters against other suppliers shows the competitiveness position (as a possibility of changing share) on a given foreign market.

There could be some limitations in interpreting values of such a competitiveness indicator. Namely, because the competitive situation could press exporters to "price to market," a comparison of export unit values may not indicate actual relative costs of a country's exporters. Competition between exporters (from different countries) may push some of them to accept prices that do not cover costs in the short run (Turner and Van't dack, 1993). Such pricing to market is especially necessary, if export market sales represent a considerable share of given exporters total sales.

On Figure 16.10, relative export unit values are presented for Slovenia. Export unit values of Slovenian export are compared with import prices on the markets of Germany, the United States, Italy, Great Britain, France, and

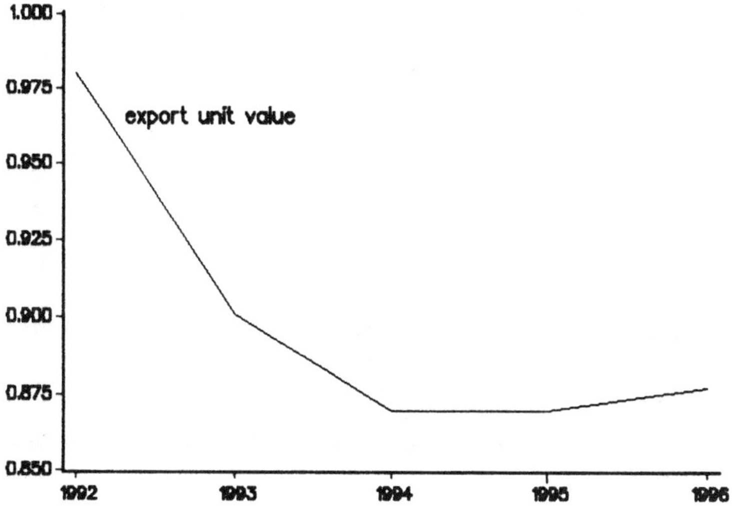

Figure 16.10. Relative Export Unit Values
Source: OECD, *Main Economic Indicators*; OECD, *Economic Outlook*; *Statistical Yearbook*; Statistical Office of the Republic of Slovenia; own calculations.

Austria. In the figure, inverted values of relative export unit values are given to exhibit competitiveness.[8]

Relative export unit values of Slovenian exporters were increasing in the studied period, indicating falling competitiveness. Low relative export unit values from the last quarter of 1991 until the second half of 1992 corroborate already mentioned distress exporting behavior (pricing to market) at the time of the (previously internal) Yugoslav market collapse. After 1992, relative unit export values jumped by 8.5 percent in 1993 and for another 4.5 percent in 1995. In the whole studied period (from 1992 to 1996) the relative export unit value therefore indicates a drop in competitiveness by 11.4 percent. So the indicator based on relative export unit values corroborates a worsening in external competitiveness measured by unit costs of labor, which decreased by almost 8 percent in the same period.

Huge export market switching after 1991 versus detected increase of relative export unit values can be additionally revealed by market-share analysis. Its advantage is that it takes into account both the types of goods and markets to which the analyzed economy exports.

Lack of data limited analysis to only some aggregates of one-digit SIT classification sectors. Structure of market shares of Slovenian exporters is

Table 16.2. Shares on export markets (agregates of SITC sections)

	SITC Sections	*1992*	*1993*	*1994*	*1995*	*1996*
Market share	0 + 1	0.99	0.78	0.82	0.72	0.66
Share in exports		3.11	2.45	2.10	1.54	1.50
Market share	2 + 4	0.99	1.04	1.03	1.08	0.73
Share in exports		2.53	2.14	2.20	2.29	1.85
Market share	3	0.01	0.02	0.02	0.01	0.00
Share in exports		1.84	2.91	0.30	0.15	0.26
Market share	5 + 6 + 8 + 9	7.47	9.71	8.71	8.85	8.12
Share in exports		59.89	62.29	61.36	60.79	57.25
Market share	7	5.01	4.55	6.00	5.91	6.64
Share in exports		32.62	30.21	34.03	35.22	39.14

Source: *OECD—Trade by country (series A); Internal data of the Statistical Office of the Republic of Slovenia; own calculations.*

studied on SITC import sectors of Germany, the United States, France, and Austria. Markets shares for every studied sectoral aggregate are calculated as exports from Slovenia over imports of a given country and the same sector. Calculated ratios are aggregated across included countries. Results are presented in the Table 16.2. For every sector shares in total Slovenian exports of goods are also given.

Slovenian exports in SITC sectors higher than four (chemical products, manufactured goods, and machinery) has a significant share (from 4 to 9 percent) in its export markets.

Apparently there was a considerable restructuring in Slovenian export markets position in the transition period. The economy has been gaining on foreign markets in the sector of machinery and transport equipment. Its share in foreign markets of machinery and transport equipment has been increasing by 0.7 percentage points per year. On the other hand, exporters of chemical products and manufacturing goods have been decreasing their share on their foreign markets by 1.3 percentage points per year, after 1993.

The share of foreign markets of exporters of chemical products and manufacturing goods decreased (in relative terms) more than the share of corresponding exports in total Slovenian exports. On the other hand, the foreign-market share of machinery and transport equipment exporters increased more than the share of corresponding exports in total exports from Slovenia. Compared with other exporters, the external competitiveness of producers of machinery and transport equipment increased in relative terms the most in Slovenia.

16.4. Sustainability of Shuttle-Trade Performance

16.4.1. Sources of Daily Tourism Booming

It is a well-known fact that market-exchange rates are downward biased compared with purchasing-parity values in less developed countries. The main reasons for that bias are differences in the productivity between tradable and nontradable sector; these differences depend on the development of the country.[9] Higher relative prices of services in more developed economies are the most visible effect of this bias.

As developing economies, transition economies would also have to face downward-biased market exchange rates, especially in the first phase. Because of the accelerated growth of the service sector and layoffs in overmanned manufacturing, accelerated decreasing of the downward bias of market-exchange rates could be normally expected in countries in transition.[10] Apparently, that is one source of the story of stylized facts.

However, market-exchange rates may deviate from PPP equivalents for many other reasons, independent of the level of development. Exchange-rate intervention, asymmetric speed of adjustment in goods and asset market, and macroeconomic shocks are only some of them.

Differences between market-exchange rates and PPP values could trigger significant trade along the border, especially for goods with negligible heterogeneity across suppliers. Such trading could be further accelerated, if specific goods (with a significant share in private consumption) have also significantly lower relative prices. In such a case, significant trading across the border can take place even without a big difference between market-exchange rates and PPP values.

In Slovenia after stabilization was launched, relative prices have changed a lot. Probably the most visible characteristics of relative price dynamics was the already mentioned fast increase of service prices and, on the other side, almost constant relative prices of some important public utilities (such as electricity) and lagging of prices of gasoline, other oil products, and gas. Imported raw materials for the last-mentioned products comprises over 95 percent of their producer price. So their regulated (producer) prices were, in principle, updated only for the change of exchange rate in the period after 1992.

Significant changes of relative prices of different products as well as a swinging of market-exchange rate against its PPP value gave a push to cross-border trading in the period of transition.

To illustrate the effects of changing purchasing-power parity of the tolar against its market-exchange rates in Table 16.3, the market-exchange rate

Table 16.3. Market-exchange rates of the tolar as percentage of its purchasing power (along the border)

	1992/II	*1993/III*	*1994/IX*	*1995*	*1996/III*
Austria	70	71	74	76	74
Italy	65	82	84	97	85
Croatia	99	73	106	108	102
Hungary	175	161	166	184	166

Source: *Žižmond (1996a, 1996b, 1996c, 1996d).*

Table 16.4. Market-exchange rates of the tolar as percentage of its purchasing power (along the border) for some items (1996/III)

	Austria	*Italy*	*Croatia*	*Hungary*
Retail products	74	85	102	166
Services	49	70	149	237
Goods	80	89	91	149
Foods	76	88	92	162
Beverages	88	92	77	161
Oil products	57	52	81	68

Source: *Žižmond (1996a, 1996b, 1996c, 1996d).*

in percentages of internal purchasing power is given for all studied years. In Table 16.4, market-exchange rates in percentages of internal purchasing power for specific goods are presented for March 1996.[11]

Figures in Table 16.3 corroborate that the internal purchasing power of the tolar was much higher than that indicated by the market exchange rate against Austria and Italy and that it was almost the same compared with Croatia and much lower against Hungary. However, figures in Table 16.3 indicate also that the internal purchasing power of the tolar (against market exchange rate) decreased in the period 1992 to 1996 compared with Austria, Italy, and Croatia and increased when compared with Hungary.

Because prices of gasoline and other oil products in neighboring countries were increasing according to the changes of the EU average level, cheap gasoline became the most important reason for the proliferation of daily tourism along the Slovenian border with Austria and Italy after 1992. According to the figures in Table 16.4, in 1996 the internal purchasing power of the tolar for oil products was, for example, almost twice as high as the market exchange rate indicated for the Italian lira and Austrian schilling.

Coming to buy gasoline, daily tourists considerably increased spending also on food, beverages, and other products that were cheaper because of the higher internal purchasing power of the tolar, although differences were far smaller than in the case of gasoline or other oil products. Besides, the quantity and quality of the corresponding goods supply increased considerably after private ownership of retail trade enterprises became possible.

Along the border with Italy and partly with Austria a gambling industry (of the American type) operated, which also attracted a lot of daily tourists. It expanded after 1992; however, its contribution to the rocketing of daily tourism after 1993 cannot be identified, as time-series data are not available.[12]

In Croatia a stabilization program was successfully launched in October 1993. Increases of prices were stopped in few months. Aggregate internal purchasing power of the kuna became higher than the market-exchange rate against the tolar.

However, because of changes in relative prices, daily tourism in Slovenia increased. As relative prices of services in Croatia increased much less than in Slovenia (see Table 16.4), the internal purchasing power of the kuna, buying goods was actually much lower than the market-exchange rate (against the tolar) indicated. According to Table 16.4, along the border with Croatia goods were cheaper on the Slovenian side by 9 percent.

Along the border with Hungary, the purchasing power of the tolar was greater comparing with the market-exchange rate only at buying gasoline and oil products.

16.4.2. Volatility

In the period after 1992, the volume of daily travels was much more sensitive to variations of the exchange rate than exports of "standard" travel services. Dynamics of the shuttle trade actually followed even intraquarter volatility of the exchange rate.

To illustrate the sensitivity of daily travel exports it has to be mentioned that the increase of real appreciation at the beginning of 1995 (triggered by acceleration of financial inflows) immediately cut the daily tourist spending share in total travel services export to less that 70 percent. While significant real depreciation in the last quarter of 1995, caused by a powerful central-bank (sterilized) intervention (see, for example, Bole, 1997b) (see Figure 16.8) pushed the spending of daily tourists again to 80 percent of travel-service exports at the beginning of 1996.

Over the longer period, the volume of daily tourism will crucially depend on the difference between the internal purchasing power of the tolar and its market-exchange rate against neighbor currencies, as well as on the sensitivity of shuttle trade on the difference.

Namely, shuttle trade cannot depend on the low prices of only one product such as gasoline for a longer period. The effect of low prices of gasoline will probably disappear in the near future. Slovenia will gradually have to increase prices of gasoline toward the EU average level, at least because of the necessity to increase tax revenue. Besides, neighboring countries will probably also start to defend their tax revenue (Italy already decreased prices of gasoline along the border).

The competitive margin of the new type of gambling industry in Slovenia will also not last for long. It has already triggered changes along the border in neighbor countries.

16.5. Summary

High real appreciation of exchange-rate and current-account deficit is quite common in the later phases of transition. Slovenia didn't face significant real appreciation, and neither did it run a current-account deficit after 1992.

A fast-increasing deficit in goods, which attained around 5 percent of GDP, was hidden by shuttle-trade increases.

The path of trade deficit followed standard-transition dynamics. An increase of trade deficit was implied by the expansion of imports of investment and consumer goods and the steady dynamics of exports (per unit of GDP).

Several indicators of competitiveness show a decrease of 9 to 13 percent after 1992. Because of high increases of wages and social transfers in non-tradable and tradable sectors, instead of the usual real exchange-rate indicator unit labor costs of labor have to be compared when external competitiveness is studied.

There were three causes for the booming of shuttle trade, in the period of transition; cheap gasoline and other oil products, a growing (American-type) gambling industry along the border with Italy and Austria, and a strong currency (kuna) in Croatia after stabilization.

A huge but unsustainable surplus in travel services was of the same dimension as financial inflows. That made policymakers' efforts in sterilized foreign-exchange interventions even less efficient. Implied worsening in external-trade competitiveness could endanger the sustainability of current-account performance.

Notes

1. *Shuttle trade* and *daily tourism* will be used as a synonyams.
2. In 1992 net business surplus was even negative, namely –5 percent of GDP; see, **Statistical Yearbook**, Statistical office of the Republic of Slovenia, 1996.
3. In the previous Yugoslavia up to 36 percent of its sales went to other parts of Yugoslavia.
4. Onernight stays increased from 2 million in 1992 to 2.5 million (see *Monthly Bulletin*, Bank of Slovenia).
5. Under the assumption of homogenous traded goods, the indicator reduces even to relative non-tradables indicator (see, Marsh and Tokarick (1994)).
6. For both indicators falling means decreasing of competitiveness.
7. For both indicators decrease the means of reducing competitiveness.
8. In the figure, increasing indicates improving competitiveness.
9. On the Balassa-Samuelson thesis and its extension, see Bhagwati (1984), Kravis and Lipsey (1983), and Rogoff (1996).
10. Empirical evidence for Slovenia is presented in Bole (1997c).
11. Regular surveys of retail prices were made along the border by EDP, University of Maribor. Results are presented in working papers of the EDP. Months in which surveys were made are indicated in the head of the table (see Žižmond, 1996a, 1996b, 1996c, 1996d).
12. In 1995, 11 percent of travel-service exports stemmed from the gambling industry.

References

Bhagwati, J.N. (1984). "Why Are Services Cheaper in the Poor Countries?" *Economic Journal*, 94: 279–286.

Blejer, M., and G. del Castillo. (1996). "Deja Vu All Over Again: The Mexican Crisis and the Stabilization of Uruguay in the 1970s." IMF Working Papers 96-80, International Monetary Fund.

Bole, V. (1997a). "Data Model for Travel Services Export." Working Papers 97-2, Economic Institute at School of Law, Ljubljana. (in Slovene)

Bole, V. (1997b). "Financial Flows in a Small Open Economy: The Case of Slovenia." Paper presented at the conference. Financial Flows to Transition Economies, Laxenburg, Austria, May. 9–10.

Bole, V. (1997c). "Stabilization in Slovenia: From High Inflation to Excessive Inflow of Foreign Capital." In M.I. Blejer and M. Kreb. (eds.), *Macroeconomic Stabilization in Transition Economies* (pp. 234–255). Cambridge: Cambridge University Press.

Calvo, G.A., L. Leiderman, and C. Reinhart. (1993). "Capital Inflows Problem: Concepts and Issues." IMF Paper on Policy Analysis and Assessment, International Monetary Fund.

Dornbusch, R. (1974). "Tariffs and Nontraded Goods." *Journal of International Economics*, 4: 177–186.

Halpern, L., and C. Wyplosz. (1996). "Equilibrium Exchange Rates in Transition Economies." IMF Working Papers 96-125, International Monetary Fund.

Kravis, I., and R. Lipsey. (1983). "Toward an Explanation of National Price Levels." Princeton Studies in International Finance, No. 52.

Lipschitz, L., and D. McDonald. (1992). "Real Exchange Rates and Competitiveness: A Clarification of Concepts, and Some Measurements for Europe." *Empirica*, 19(1): 37–69.

Marsh, I.W., and P.S. Tokarick. (1994). "Competitiveness Indicators: A Theoretical and Empirical Assessment." IMF Working Papers 94-29, International Monetary Fund.

Rogoff, K. (1996). "The Purchasing Power Parity Puzzle." *Journal of Economic Literature*, 34: 647–668.

Turner, P., and J. Van't dack. (1993). "Measuring International Price and Cost Competitiveness." Bank for International Settlements, No. 39.

Žižmond, E. (1996a). "Prices and Wages in Slovenia and Austria." *Working Papers EDP 2*, vol. 7, University of Maribor.

Žižmond, E. (1996b). "Prices and Wages in Slovenia and Croatia." *Working Papers EDP 4*, vol. 7, University of Maribor.

Žižmond, E. (1996c). "Prices and Wages in Slovenia and Hungary." *Working Papers EDP 5*, vol. 7, University of Maribor.

Žižmond, E. (1996d). "Prices and Wages in Slovenia and Italy." *Working Papers EDP 3*, vol. 7, University of Maribor.

Index

SPRINGER NATURE

GPSR Compliance

The European Union's (EU) General Product Safety Regulation (GPSR) is a set of rules that requires consumer products to be safe and our obligations to ensure this.

If you have any concerns about our products, you can contact us on ProductSafety@springernature.com

In case Publisher is established outside the EU, the EU authorized representative is:

Springer Nature Customer Service Center GmbH
Europaplatz 3
69115 Heidelberg, Germany

FSC
www.fsc.org
MIX
Papier | Fördert
gute Waldnutzung
FSC® C083411

Kolibri 360 GmbH
Ferdinand-Jühlke-Straße 7
99095 Erfurt, Deutschland
produktsicherheit@kolibri360.de